M000119456

CELLINI
FREEDOM FIGHTER

"...Cellini leads readers through the globe-spanning series of adventures that made up his life...well-researched, with plenty of substantiating detail and further information about the many well-known figures he encountered. Cellini tells a fascinating story and keeps the reader enthralled and engaged... "

– *Kirkus Reviews (starred review)*

CELLINI

FREEDOM FIGHTER

VITO "TUTUC" CELLINI
and MICK J. PRODGER

ELM GROVE PUBLISHING
San Antonio, Texas, USA

ISBN: 978-1-943492-38-1 (Hardcover)
ISBN: 978-1-943492-39-8 (Paperback)

The events described in this book are true and factual as recalled and told to the author by Vito Cellini to the best of his recollection. All stories are based on his memories of actual events, locales, people and conversations. In some instances the names of individuals, certain identifying details and locales have been changed to protect the privacy of the people involved, innocent and guilty alike. In some cases events may have been compressed or chronologically rearranged for literary interest. All conversations are based on Mr. Cellini's recollections and are not intended to represent word-for-word transcripts but are presented in a way that evokes the essence of what was being said.

Cover photograph by Francesca Cellini.

All other images contained in this book are the property of the author except as follows: Pages 27, 32, 59 (top), 72 (top left, bottom left), 98, 283 (top), 309 (bottom), 327, 349, 364, 412 (centre & bottom), 424, 451, 453, 493, 528 and back cover, property of Vito Cellini. Page 153, courtesy Pjero Baranović and Gorana Peruzović. Page 192, courtesy Antun Baranović. Page 498, courtesy Pamela Meadows.

Publisher's Cataloging-In-Publication Data

Names: Cellini, Vito, interviewee. | Prodger, Mick J.
Title: Cellini : freedom fighter / Vito "Tutuc" Cellini and Mick J. Prodger.
Description: San Antonio, Texas, USA : Elm Grove Publishing, [2018] | Cover title. | "The events described in this book are true and factual as recalled and told to the author by Vito Cellini to the best of his recollection." | Includes bibliographical references.
Identifiers: ISBN 9781943492381 (hardcover) | ISBN 9781943492398 (paperback)
Subjects: LCSH: Cellini, Vito. | Revolutionaries--Italy--Biography. | Spies--Italy--Biography. | Inventors--Italy--Biography. | World War, 1939-1945--Italy--Personal narratives. | LCGFT: Autobiographies.
Classification: LCC DG556.C4 A3 2018 | DDC 945.091092--dc23

Elm Grove Publishing | San Antonio, Texas | www.elmgrovepublishing.com
Elm Grove Publishing is a legally registered trade name of Panache Communication Arts, Inc.

Contents

For Atticus Sebastian

Foreword

MENTION THE NAME Vito Cellini in the company of anyone with any knowledge of firearms and chances are they will say, "that's the guy who invented the muzzle brake."[1]

Hunters recognize the Cellini name for the system that, since the 1980s, has enabled them to keep their weapon steady and "stabilized" when firing at a prize buck.

To members of the US Special Forces, the Cellini name invokes a special reverence. His "stabilizer" is the stuff of legend. Determined to equip American soldiers with the best weapon accessory available, but unable to cut through the Pentagon's red tape (despite repeated official and unofficial demonstrations of the effectiveness of his system), Cellini privately contracted for the production of 1,000 of his stabilizers for the M-16 rifle (the military version of the AR-15). Production was financed by Texas billionaire businessman and one-time Presidential candidate, H. Ross Perot, who, together with Special Forces legend Major Richard Meadows, subsequently arranged for distribution among members of the US Army's elite Delta Force. These "stabilizers" became cherished possessions and many were passed down to future generations of those serving in the special forces.

Cellini has custom-adapted his "stabilizer" system to fit almost every known handgun, hunting rifle, assault weapon and even shotguns. His products, along with his expertise, have been sought by military and law enforcement personnel, as well as outdoor sportsmen, all over the world.

Since obtaining the original patent for his design, it has been copied, more or less, 135 times (including by the larger manufacturers who subsequently won the government contracts). Yet none comes close

1. *Cellini didn't "invent" the muzzle brake, which was originally developed for heavy artillery weapons. He designed a muzzle brake or "stabilizer" for small arms that could be easily adapted to any calibre and which had the effect of suppressing muzzle flash and noise as well as reducing the recoil of the weapon.*

to the effectiveness of an original Cellini.

In fact, Vito Cellini holds, or has held, 19 different patents for various inventions – not including those he developed for big corporations who paid him a pittance and kept the design. Not all of his designs are weapons related. His wide range of patented inventions includes such things as a scale for measuring plasma, an escape pod for submarines, surgical instruments for critical spinal operations, a chain-less bicycle and a motorized knife for disabled people – to name but a handful. One of his designs – for which he does not own any patent rights – helped put Neil Armstrong and the Apollo 11 crew on the moon in 1969.

But there's a lot more to Vito Cellini's story than his inventions.

His life has been a roller coaster of adventure, danger and intrigue, from gangster to reluctant soldier to freedom fighter to secret agent carrying out "dirty work" for the Allied occupation forces in World War Two. Cellini has never shied away from any challenge. He served with the armies of three different nations during the war – four if you consider he represented both the British SOE and the American OSS while in Bari.

Returning to America with just 12 cents in his pocket, his mechanical ingenuity and silver tongue opened doors that most mortals read about only in fiction. His inventiveness and expertise as a tactical weapons expert have taken him all over the world. He has been an advisor to national leaders and a bodyguard for the infamous. He has been a trusted confidant to members of the New York Mafia and has negotiated with some of the most feared organized crime bosses in Italy. He has never been afraid to take the law into his own hands when he felt it was justified.

Criminals still fear him because they presume he is working with law enforcement. Authorities are still wary of him and assume he must be working with the criminals. In reality, this larger-than-life character acted mostly independently – but always in the belief that he was doing the right thing.

He has been privileged to count some of America's most revered military heroes among his closest friends.

Above all, Vito Cellini is a true patriot and a man who puts truth, honour and justice above everything. And while some of his adventures might make even James Bond blush, unlike the fictional character, Cellini remained faithful to one woman. His beloved Franci.

Now in his 90s, he finally feels comfortable talking about his life, and he isn't pulling any punches.

The good. The bad. The ugly. And the beautiful.

Prologue: Back to America, 1948

FEBRUARY 22ND, 1948. It's a chilly day in New York. Temperatures hover just below freezing, and snow and ice has been reported. New Yorkers huddle together to celebrate George Washington's birthday and curse the cold.

No one pays much attention as yet another ship from the Old World steams up the Hudson River, past the Statue of Liberty, and docks at Ellis Island. Its passengers, dazed and weary but eager to step ashore, pull up their collars and pull down their hats as they get ready to clamber down the gangplank.

The ruins of Europe are still smouldering even though the Second World War ended almost three years earlier. The rebuilding has barely begun in cities devastated by years of constant bombing and street fighting. In Czechoslovakia, the Communist Party, with the backing of the Soviet Union, has just seized power with almost no resistance. Those lucky enough to escape the tyranny of communism have joined other travellers from all over war-torn Europe on ships bound for the promised land of America.

The SS *Saturnia* had left Genoa almost two weeks earlier, stopping just long enough in Naples to take on food and fuel, and pack even more people aboard.

Among the passengers waiting to disembark in New York is a 24 year-old American-born Italian who has survived the horrors of war and is now looking to start a new life in the country of his birth.

On the *Saturnia*'s manifest he is simply passenger number 9011866038892. His name is Vito "Tutuc" Cellini, and he is impatient to be on his way, but he is being detained on board.[1] He is not sure why, but suspects it may have something to do with a heated argument he had with other passengers last night.

He is travelling with his cousin, Francesca, with whom he has been

[1] *"Tutuc" was his formal name in the dialect of Barese, where Cellini grew up.*

madly in love since childhood – although he hadn't realised it until quite recently. They haven't consummated their love, nor even spoken of it (and won't, until much later), but they have often talked of returning to America, and New York City, where they were both born.

In Genoa, Cellini boards the ship alone, but when it docks in Naples, family members come to see him leave. Perhaps even to make sure he really does leave.

Francesca has a surprise in store for both Cellini and her family. She has decided to go with him. She has packed her suitcase and boards the ship to join him. Her father is both shocked and disappointed, not just with her foolish decision to leave Italy, but because Tutuc is regarded by the extended family as a *delinquente.* He begs his daughter not to go, but when she ignores his pleas, his frustration quickly turns to rage. He calls out to a *Carabinieri* and tries to have Cellini arrested for kidnapping, but the *Carabinieri* is powerless and cannot board the ship.

Running alongside the ship, he screams threats at Cellini – reminding him that one of his more violent relatives is currently serving time at Rikers Island and that he will cheerfully join him if that's what it will take to rescue his daughter![2]

*****

FRANCI'S DECISION to join her cousin on board the ship bound for America is impetuous, and surprises even Tutuc, but she is ready to live her dreams. They will travel as close friends, *amore platonico*, looking for a better life and a new beginning.

On board ship, all goes well until the last night of the voyage. Never one to back down from a dispute, Cellini's pride and blunt honesty get the better of him more often than not. He knows perfectly well that it is customary to leave a tip for the waiter on the last evening of the voyage, but with just 12 cents in his pocket and only the clothes he stands

[2] *Family legend tells of a relative of Francesca's father who ruthlessly murdered 22 people in Queens. Being raised as a good Catholic, he went to church and confessed to a priest what he had done, describing in great detail each of his gruesome deeds, one of which involved throwing a man from the roof of a building onto the railings below during a snowstorm. Drifting snow quickly covered up the body and it was several weeks before the snow thawed and the gruesome act was discovered. After receiving absolution, this merciless killer had second thoughts about trusting even a man of God with the details of his sins, so he returned to the church and killed the priest. Fortunately he was eventually caught, but managed to avoid the death penalty and was sentenced to 35 years.*

up in, he asks Franci if she is willing to forgo dinner in order to avoid embarrassment.

To skip dinner is no great hardship to Cellini. He went without food for two days in Genoa before boarding the ship (making up for it by gorging himself at every meal up until now!). He feels bad asking Franci to go without food and even suggests that she should go to the dining room alone – but she insists that they are in this together. They decide, even though it is icy cold outside, to walk the promenade deck of the ship.

By pure misfortune, Cellini bumps into their waiter later that evening. "Thanks for the tip," the waiter mutters sarcastically, wounding Cellini's pride deeply enough for him to grab him by the collar and draw his fist ready to punch him in the face. Another passenger is able to calm him down before the altercation gets out of control. Cellini explains his financial predicament to the waiter and they part on relatively good terms.

Still smarting from his encounter with the waiter, Cellini finds himself in the midst of a heated discussion with some of the other passengers, including a Roman Catholic Priest, on the very sensitive subject of religion. Cellini is never afraid to express his opinion, whether or not it is asked for, and on the subject of religion, his opinions are neither mainstream nor popular with a lot of people. Voices are raised, attracting the attention of the ship's crew who can't help but notice the vociferous and outspoken young Italian.

A stocky and officious man with a heavy moustache and wearing a dark uniform appears and Cellini is asked for his passport and travel papers, which he produces from inside his coat pocket. The passport shows Cellini to be an Italian national, but his papers list his birthplace as New York City. The official takes out a notebook and writes something down. After studying Cellini's face closely he hands the documents back to him, then asks what the argument was all about. Before Cellini can speak, the priest intervenes. Though Cellini doesn't understand everything he says, he senses that the priest is coming to his defence. The priest smiles benevolently at Cellini and the two shake hands. The official bows to the priest and thanks him, then turns to Cellini, scowls and tells him to, "Get out of here, and don't be causing any more trouble."

As Cellini turns and walks away, he hears the uniformed man's parting shot.

"I'm watching you."

He grins at Franci but doesn't turn around.

Next morning, the ship steams into the port of Ellis Island and there is a murmur of excitement among passengers and crew. As Cellini and Franci are about to step onto the gangplank to go ashore, a hand grabs him by the shoulder and he is pulled back onto the deck. It is the moustached official who had interceded during the argument the previous evening.

"I need you to wait here Mr. Cellini," is all he says.

"Not you, Miss," he says to Franci. "You can go ahead."

The two look at each other and Cellini tells Franci to go on ahead. He'll catch up with her later.

He waits with the official while the other passengers make their way off the ship. No words are exchanged, but they take turns trading dirty looks. Cellini waits impatiently.

As the departing crowd begins to thin out, two uniformed officials from Ellis Island make their way up the gangplank and onto the ship. Once on deck, the first official hands them a ticket on which are written four names. Underneath Cellini's name are the letters B.S.I., indicating he will be presented to a Board of Special Inquiry. The two officials introduce themselves as Ellis Island inspectors and immediately start bombarding Cellini with questions, most of which he doesn't comprehend. He is asked several times if he needs to collect his baggage.

"I have no bag," he says, realizing for the first time that he is probably the only passenger on the ship with no suitcase. "I have only what I am standing up in."

A fellow passenger who speaks both English and Italian, and with whom Cellini has become acquainted during the voyage, is one of the last to leave the ship and sees Cellini's predicament. He comes over to see what is going on, but the uniformed officials tell him to keep moving. He has overheard their conversation and warns Cellini that they have guns and have been ordered to shoot him if he gives them any sign of trouble. He also hands Cellini a piece of paper with a phone number on it.

"This is an office in the Empire State Building. Call if you need help and just tell them the Jewish gentleman on the *Saturnia* gave you this number. They'll know who I am."

He winks at Cellini, tips his hat and wishes him luck, then hurries down the ship's gangway for processing. Cellini shoves the piece of paper in his coat pocket and promptly forgets all about it.

After a few minutes, he is escorted down the gangway towards the Ellis Island Immigration Station, an imposing looking brick building that appears all the more severe against the background of a dark grey, wintry sky. In the distance he can see the long line of passengers being processed through immigration and transported to the mainland by ferry. He thinks of Franci and hopes she doesn't have any problems getting through the lines.

Cellini is directed down a staircase known as "The Staircase of

Separation"[3] and told to go straight ahead, where he is shown into a small waiting area and told to have a seat. After what seems like an eternity he is eventually ushered into a cramped room with a wooden table, a chair and a cot along one wall and a very small window high up in the wall.

Though he is at no time placed under arrest or put in handcuffs, he will spend the next three days confined to this room at the immigration station. He is provided with meals and visited by inspectors to make sure he is in good health, but he is given no reason for his detention. And without access to an interpreter, he has little chance of finding out.

Having come to America to enjoy freedom, Cellini finds himself a prisoner on Ellis Island.

*****

FINALLY, AFTER THREE days of staring at the same walls and stilted conversations with his uniformed jailers, two men in dark suits arrive and indicate to Cellini that he is leaving to go to New York City. At first he thinks he is being freed but it soon becomes apparent that his ordeal is not yet over. Their job is to escort him to another facility for further questioning.

Once again he is told to collect his belongings. Once again he declares, to the amazement and amusement of his new companions, that he has no belongings except for what he has on him.

As they depart from the Ellis Island ferry, a big black car is waiting to take them to a large brick building in Columbus Square. Once inside the lobby of the building, Cellini is introduced to an interpreter, a woman with a thin face and pointed features, her jet black hair pulled back into a bun. Though she looks severe, she is pleasant and seems to be genuinely helpful. She pushes the button for the building's elevator, then turns back to Cellini.

The gentlemen in suits, she says, are federal agents. He is to face a Board of Special Inquiry to determine if his United States Citizenship is still valid, so they wish to ask him some questions about his past and the reasons for his visit to New York.

3. *The "Staircase of Separation" was regarded by many immigrants as a very sad place, because families were often divided here if an inspector found something amiss with anyone's papers. Turning right at the end of the staircase led to the railroad ticket station. Turning left led to the ferry across to Manhattan. If directed to go straight ahead it would lead to the detention room. The detention room was a halfway house for people suspected of committing crimes or having medical problems, or those promised a job by a relative who simply hadn't followed through, or those having no money and no way of supporting their families.*

"I was born here in New York! I am American and I am coming home to start a new life!" Though he had been born in New York in 1923, his father had moved the family back to Italy in 1927 and Cellini had grown up on the beautiful Adriatic coast in Bari, later moving to Milan. He had travelled back using an Italian passport.[4]

A bell rings and the elevator door opens. The four enter the car and one of the agents presses the button for the fourth floor. Ever watchful of details, Cellini notices that in America, the ground floor is numbered as floor one. In Italy, the bottom floor is labelled ground, and the next floor up is labelled one, so that if this building were in Milan, their destination would actually be the third floor. This curious cultural difference stands out in his mind and he makes a mental note to remember it.

As the elevator begins its shaky rise, the interpreter explains that anyone who has served in the military of a foreign country may be denied immigration, even if they had were born here. Cellini had worn the uniform of the Italian Army and served with Yugoslavia's Partisans before joining the conquering Allies. Even though his passport and travel papers are in order – and he might have slipped through unnoticed – his altercation on board ship undoubtedly drew attention to him and caused the officers on board to alert the inspectors at Ellis Island.

The elevator bumps to a stop two inches below the level of the floor, then slowly rises and settles into its correct position. The door opens and they step into a corridor with wooden benches placed against the wall. Cellini takes a seat and the interpreter sits next to him. The two agents stand between the bench and the elevator, as if to discourage any thoughts he may have of escaping. They take advantage of the opportunity to smoke and each pulls out a pack of cigarettes and lights up.

After what seems an eternity, they are ushered into a cavernous, dimly lit room that smells of a wood fire and tobacco smoke. He is instructed to take a seat in front of a massive oak table. The interpreter pulls up a small wooden chair and sits beside him. The two agents sit across from them and a third man, older, and carrying a large briefcase joins them. He slams the briefcase down on the table, opens it and pulls out a cardboard file. He looks directly at Cellini and speaks.

4. *In fact, the Italian passport Cellini had used for the voyage was counterfeit, obtained with the help of an American Army intelligence officer in Bari who had connections with a black market forger. The army officer was sympathetic because Cellini had worked with him to track down black market criminals as well as other intelligence work in Italy. Cellini had no way of proving his American birth at that time (his birth records were in New York but no one at the immigration centre was willing to investigate). No record of his birth existed in Italy.*

The interpreter slowly and carefully translates his words. "Do you understand that this is a formal Board of Special Inquiry and that this is a citizenship hearing?"

Cellini nods. The interpreter answers for him.

Without looking up from his desk or displaying any signs of emotion, the older man then asks Cellini if he wants a lawyer.

"No," he replies, indignantly.

The questioning is, at times, conversational and friendly. How was the voyage? What do you notice that's different between Italy and the United States? At others time the questions are more pointed and interrogative. Have you ever been arrested? Have you ever been in jail? Though his interrogators pause occasionally to drink coffee or water, neither he nor his interpreter are offered any food or drink.

Then comes the hammer blow. United States law, it seems, is quite clear. Regardless of birth, serving in the military of a foreign country is considered grounds for revocation of citizenship.[5]

Does he understand what this means? The interpreter clarifies.

He shrugs. "I understand, but I am an American."

He tries to protest that he had no choice in joining the Italian Army. That no one had any choice, and that he did not stay in the Italian Army for very long.

It doesn't seem to matter to his interrogators that he had subsequently deserted the Italian Army and joined the resistance in Yugoslavia. Nor do they seem to have any knowledge of his later work with the US Military Police or his contribution to the Office of Strategic Services (OSS).

His service is never mentioned by the agents questioning him.

"Did you ever join, or have you ever been a member of any political party?"

"No."

"Did you ever join, or have you ever been a member of the Communist Party?"

"No!"

"You are quite sure you have never been a member of the Communist Party?"

"Yes!"

[5] *This was prior to passage of the Displaced Persons Act of June 25th, 1948, which permitted immigration into the US by individuals who were victims of persecution by the Nazi government and its allies, or could not go back to their country because of fear of persecution based on race, religion or political opinions. It applied specifically to people from Germany, Austria and Italy.*

"Yes you were a member of the Communist Party or yes you are quite sure you have never been a member of the Communist Party?"

Realizing they are trying to trick him by catching him out with his poor English, or perhaps to trick the interpreter into phrasing the question incorrectly, Cellini listens carefully to her translation and takes a deep breath before responding.

"I have never been a member of the Communist Party."

The three agents look at each other and shrug.

He is asked repeatedly if he has ever committed a crime, been arrested or been in jail.

He pleads his innocence, explaining that he had been sentenced by the Italian fascist government to 16 years and six months imprisonment for a "misunderstanding" over his leave in World War Two, but that the sentence had been dismissed when he reluctantly agreed to fight at the front. He had spent a few days in the Italian stockade while his case was reviewed before being released to join his unit.

The men look at each other then speak to the interpreter, who phrases the question once again.

The interpreter lays a gentle hand on his arm and whispers softly, "Signor Cellini, it is better if you tell the truth."

"I am telling the truth!"

"Are you quite sure you don't want a lawyer?" The agent's voice reverberates in the room.

Hearing the translation and finding it hard to maintain his composure, Cellini snaps back with the same answer.

"An honest man doesn't need a lawyer, only a crook needs a lawyer," he replies.

He reaches into his coat pocket for a handkerchief and pulls out the piece of paper handed to him by the gentleman on the ship.

"May I use a telephone to call someone?" he asks.

"Who do you want to call?" comes the gruff reply.

"Just a man I met on the ship who said if I ever needed help to call this number. I thought perhaps he might be able to help me explain better... His English was very good and he also spoke Italian."

"Let me see that number," the agent says, and copies it down into his notes.

After a brief huddle the interpreter nods towards Cellini and he is escorted to a small room where he is given the use of the phone. The interpreter stays in the room with him while Cellini dials the number. The phone rings for a long time.

"No reply," Cellini says, neither disappointed nor surprised. He pushes the slip of paper back into his pocket and follows the interpreter back to the interrogation room.

Once again, he is asked if he has ever committed a crime in Italy.

Suddenly, a thought occurs to him and he starts to babble.

"When I was about 9 or 10 years-old I was given a ticket for roller-skating in the street!" he exclaims.

Under fascist laws imposed by Benito Mussolini, roller-skating was considered a decadent American sport and was illegal in Italy at that time.

"It was either pay the fine or spend 24 hours in jail. My father refused to pay the fine, so I went to jail for one day and one night!"

The federal agents stare at Cellini then look at one another. They confer for a few moments, look at some papers, and then motion to the interpreter to come over to the table. The discussion goes on for several minutes, during which time Cellini starts to think he may actually be deported, just for roller-skating.

The interpreter sits back down, glances across at Cellini and smiles. The three officials rise and begin gathering up their papers. One takes out a pocket watch and looks at the time. Replacing it in his pocket, he coughs into his hand to clear his throat and opens his mouth to speak.

"You are free to go Mr. Cellini."

"That's it?" he says. "All you care about is something I did when I was 10 years-old?"

"Good day, Mr. Cellini. You may collect your papers from the clerk's office."

Cellini glares at the interpreter who, for the first time since he met her almost four hours ago, smiles at him.

He is shocked that throughout the proceedings there has been no mention of his service with the Yugoslavian Partisans. He reasons that if these American government authorities are aware of his arrest and detention for roller skating over 15 years ago, they must surely know about his intelligence work with the British and Americans during the war?

He opens his mouth to speak again, but thinks better of it. He thinks of Franci and how worried she must be – and what she would say if she were here, in the room, right now.

"Shut up Ueli," she would say. "Shut up and leave. Now!"[6]

He thanks the interpreter for her kindness and her help, goes to collect his documents from the clerk and walks out of the building. He is free at last.

6. *Ueli, pronounced "Willy," was Cellini's pet name in his local Barese dialect.*

It is a cold, grey winter's day. The wind is whipping up the snow and the sleet and the puddles in the gutter, stinging Cellini's face as he walks down the street. He has no overcoat, no suitcase and no clean clothes, but in spite of the bitter cold he cannot stop smiling, looking forward to a new life in America.

He pulls a piece of crumpled paper from his pocket that he has been carrying since he left Milan. On it is scribbled the name of his great uncle Franco – the brother of his grandmother – and a street address in Brooklyn.

He has no idea which way to go or how far away it is, but his dignity is intact and he still has 12 cents in his pocket.

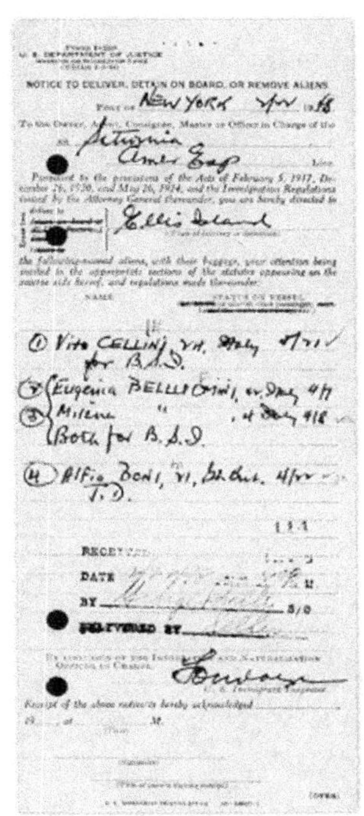

U. S. DEPARTMENT OF JUSTICE

NOTICE TO DELIVER, DETAIN ON BOARD, OR REMOVE ALIENS

Port of New York ... 1948

To the Owner, Agent, Consignee, Master or Officer in Charge of the SS Saturnia, Amer Exp ... Line

Pursuant to the provisions of the Acts of February 5, 1917, December 26, 1920, and May 26, 1924, and the Immigration Regulations issued by the Attorney General thereunder, you are hereby directed to ... Ellis Island

the following-named aliens, with their baggage, your attention being invited to the appropriate sections of the statutes appearing on the reverse side hereof, and regulations made thereunder:

NAME — STATUS ON VESSEL

1. Vito CELLINI ... Italy ... for B.S.I.
2. Eugenia BELLUCCINI ...
3. Milena " ... Both for B.S.I.
4. Alfio BONI ...

RECEIVED

DATE

BY

DELIVERED BY

Manifest listing passengers aboard the SS Saturnia *who were denied entry into the United States at Ellis Island. Vito Cellini's name is top of the list, followed by the letters BSI, which stand for Board of Special Inquiry. (libertyellisfoundation.org)*

Francesca's passport and disembarkation card, which was in good standing. She was allowed to leave the ship and enter New York.

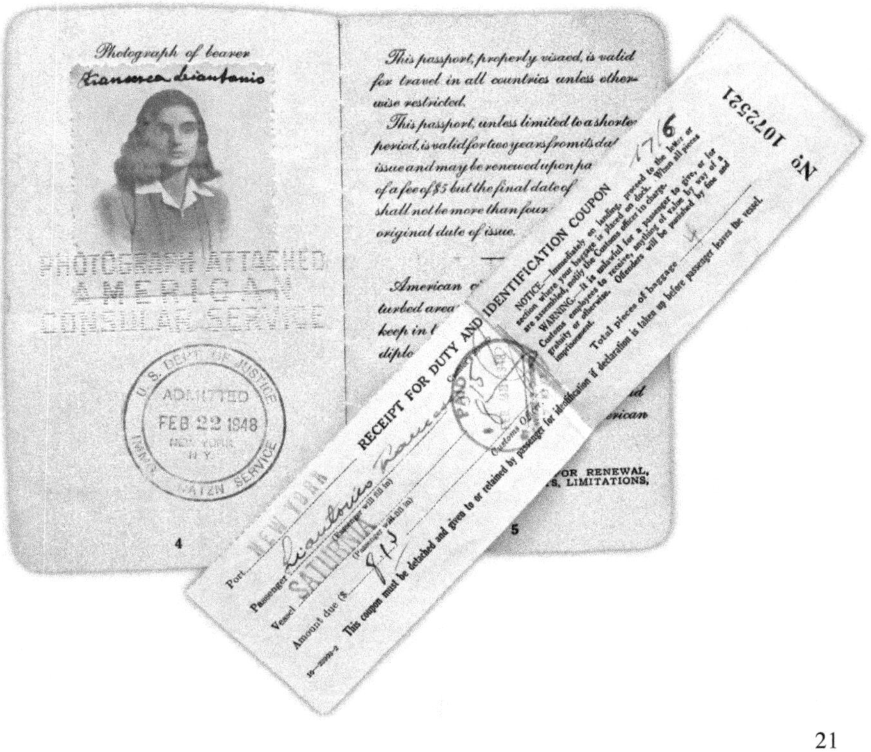

Part I

New York Born. Raised Italian

1. The Acorn Never Falls Far…

Cellini's father Francesco had been born in Bari in 1895, the oldest of seven children. His mother had given birth to fifteen offspring, but only seven survived. Francesco is a loner, and seems to be perpetually in search of a cause, yet destined, almost inevitably, to always choose the wrong one.

When war breaks out in 1914, the Kingdom of Italy claims neutrality, despite having been a member of the Triple Alliance with Austria-Hungary and Germany since 1882. Neutrality is a wise move, if a delaying tactic, since the country is ill-prepared for war.

Italy is courted by both sides and encouraged to join the fighting, each offering a share of the victory spoils. Promised greater territorial gains by the Allies than by their triple Alliance partners, the Italians sign a secret pact with Britain, France and Russia at the Treaty of London in April 1915. Though still under-equipped (1.2 million men – with adequate weapons and uniforms for just over half that number), Italy enters the so-called "Great" War – the "War to End all Wars" – on May 23rd, 1915, opening up a vast new front against Austria-Hungary.

Keen to show his support, twenty-year-old Francesco Cellini signs up immediately as a volunteer "ardito" with the infantry and marches off to win the war.

By late 1917, Italy has fought no fewer than eleven battles against the Austrians along the Isonzo River, with neither side achieving any tactical advantage. In October 1917, reinforced by German troops, Austria-Hungary annihilates the Italian Army at the Battle of Caporetto (the twelfth Battle of the Isonzo). Over 300,000 Italians are killed, wounded or taken prisoner. Among the casualties is Francesco Cellini. Badly wounded in the knee by mortar fire, he develops a serious infection from the unsanitary conditions and loses his left leg from the hip down.

Though Italy does gain control of the Tyrol, as well as a small share of German reparations and a permanent seat on the newly formed League of

Nations, most of the promises made by the Allies at the Treaty of London are unfulfilled. Italy grows resentful of its treatment during the Treaty of Versailles in May 1919, negotiations at one stage becoming so contentious that the Italian delegates leave and refuse to return for eleven days.

Resentment in Italy and distrust of its Allies continues to grow and will become major contributing factors in the rise of Benito Mussolini and his fascist movement.

Meantime, against all the odds, Francesco Cellini recovers from his dreadful injuries, returning home to Bari and marrying his sweetheart, Rosa Terrevoli.

*****

UNABLE TO FIND work because of his disability, as well as the economic climate in southern Italy, and finding it difficult to sustain himself on a pension of just 300 Lire per month, Francesco Cellini, defeated and humiliated but never dejected, decides his future belongs in America. Selling everything they own, the Cellinis – Francesco, his wife Rosa and newborn son Nicola – board the SS *Conte Rosso* and set sail for New York, arriving on August 5th, 1922.

Francesco's sister Gaetana and brother-in-law Nicola Liantonio (after whom the Cellinis' first son is named) are already in New York and will help Francesco and Rosa settle in.

Francesco Cellini enters his occupation on the passenger manifest as shoemaker, even though he has never had any formal training or apprenticeship in the trade. He teaches himself how to cobble, fashions his own tools, and begins making shoes for his fellow immigrant countrymen, known as *paesans,*[1] in the Brooklyn neighbourhood he now calls home. Word spreads of the young Italian shoemaker's skills, and before too long he has built a thriving business.

On August 14th, 1923, Rosa gives birth to her second son, Vito, at their home on Flatbush Avenue, New York.

Vito Cellini's mother is a beautiful woman who turns the head of many men. Eventually Francesco's moody, often abusive, behaviour will drive her into the arms of another *paesan,* with whom she runs away to Chicago. Just two weeks after leaving Francesco, Rosa is taken ill with acute appendicitis

[1] *Paesan is abbreviated from Paesano, which is Italian slang for peasant or countryman. In Italian-American slang it was used to describe a fellow-countryman-immigrant and was used either derogatorily or as a term of endearment, depending on context.*

and dies during surgery to remove her ruptured appendix.[2]

Francesco could certainly be moody and even, at times, quite violent. He has already served six months in prison for stabbing to death a young African-American man with his cobbler's knife because the young black man had the effrontery to call him a *wop.*[3]

Unable to post bond money, he is incarcerated in Sing Sing while awaiting trial. Such are the social conditions in America at that time, the trial is a complete fiasco. His defence is that, being a one-legged man, he could not possibly have carried out an act of such excessive force and violent nature. Witnesses at the trial (no doubt friends from the local Italian neighbourhood) claim that they saw the black man "run at Mr. Cellini and impale himself upon the blade of the knife".

Cellini is acquitted. He often describes his time in Sing Sing as "the best vacation I ever had".

2. *Rumours persisted within the family that Rosa was kidnapped by Chicago gangsters, but this was never substantiated and there is no evidence to support such an outcome. Vito Cellini believes these stories were circulated in order to ease the pain for him and his brother, and perhaps to assuage any guilt that Francesco felt for driving his wife away. He credits the mother he never really knew, and the abuse he believes she suffered, for the tremendous respect and esteem with which he has always regarded women.*

3. *Merriam-Webster states that the first known use of the word "wop" in the United States was in 1908. The dictionary is unambiguous that it originates from a southern Italian dialect term guappo, meaning thug. In those days, the term was considered especially derogatory towards Italian immigrants and it sent Francesco into a rage to be insulted in such a way, especially by a black person.*

Francesco Cellini as a young man in Italy before the Great War (left) and after arriving in America (above right).

A family group, 1927. Clockwise: Francesco, Nicola, Vito and Rosa. This is the only photograph Vito has of his biological mother.

2. Abandoned in Italy

UNABLE TO SETTLE down, or perhaps shamed by the departure and subsequent sudden death of his unfaithful wife, Francesco packs up the two boys and all the family's belongings and heads back to Italy. Although it is a homecoming of sorts for his brother Nicola, for young Vito, the voyage and subsequent arrival in southern Italy is a strange and unsettling experience.

Back in Bari, the recently widowed Francesco Cellini begins seeking female companionship almost immediately. He meets and charms a young woman named Cecigllia who lives in their apartment building. In fact, it is her family who manage the building. He seduces the girl and she becomes pregnant. She gives birth to a son, Angelo, but within a matter of weeks, Francesco becomes unsettled and decides to return to America alone, leaving Ceciglia behind to take care of Nicola and Vito, as well as her newborn son.[1]

Ceciglia is a good-hearted person, if somewhat naive, but her responsibilities as the mother of a new baby, along with her duties as caretaker of the building in which they live, preclude her from taking care of the older Cellini children. Nicola and Vito go to live with their grandparents a few streets away on *Via Pizzoli*, but the boys' grandfather works long hours in a factory producing charcoal for the Italian Railroad company, and their grandmother is occupied with household chores. It is 14 year-old Pasquina, the boys' aunt, who will spend the most time with Vito and have the most influence in raising him.

To all in the family she is simply "Pasqua",[2] but to Vito she will

1. Once back in New York, Francesco Cellini helped to found a branch of the American Fascist Party, which was attempting to promote the virtues of Il Duce in North America. He would return to Italy in 1934 to show his ardent support for the fascist movement and its leader, Benito Mussolini. At that time he resumed his relationship with Ceciglia, who was quick to forgive him for abandoning her. They married and settled down in Milan.

2. Pasqua lived to be 102.

be "Ma" for the rest of her life, and to her he will always be "Ueli".

With eight people in one small room, the accommodation is crowded, but young Vito spends a lot of time outdoors. He and his brother Nicola fight constantly but share a close bond with each other that will only be broken by the tragedy of the war.

*****

YOUNG VITO CELLINI enjoys a wonderful relationship with his grandparents, especially his grandfather with whom he spends almost every Sunday. Vito learns to fish and hunt, and always looks forward to *gelato* on their way home.

It's a simple life in Bari. The family is not wealthy, but they are hard-working people. The living conditions may be crowded, but Vito is well provided for. He is a cunning boy who never misses an opportunity to better himself, often at the expense of others less vigilant, even if they are family members. He is never malicious, but has a highly competitive streak that will always keep him one step ahead of danger.

Later in life, Franci will call him "crazy like a fox".

Christmas in Italy is traditionally celebrated as a religious festival and gift giving does not take place until *La Festa dell'Epifania* – Epiphany (or twelfth night) January 6th.

January 1929, and for his first Epiphany after returning from America, Vito is taken to the best toy shop in Bari by his grandfather and invited to choose any toy he wants. He shows his selection to his grandfather, who asks the shopkeeper for the price of the toy. His grandfather thanks the shopkeeper politely, and they leave the store empty handed. Once outside he takes his wallet out of his pocket, counts out the exact cost of the toy and then hands it over to his grandson.

"The toy is no good and will be broken in a few days or even a few hours," his grandfather says. "Take the money instead and save it, or use it for something practical that will last you a little longer."

Young Cellini is disappointed at first but soon learns his lesson and the value of money. He also learns how to "play the game".

The following year, on *La Festa dell'Epifania*, his grandfather takes him once again to the toy shop and invites him to choose a toy.

"Any toy?" Cellini enquires. His grandfather nods and smiles.

Young Vito scours the store looking at every toy. He picks them up, looks them all over and puts them back down. Convinced that the boy is looking for something with more substance, something that will not break easily or be cast aside after a few hours of play, his grandfather is proud and pleased.

A quarter of an hour goes by. Twenty minutes. The young boy is still searching the toy store.

"He must be looking for something very special," the shopkeeper says.

Almost half an hour after they enter the shop, Vito returns to his grandfather clutching a very large and very colourful box that he has pried from the shop window. He has no idea what it is, but it is without doubt the most expensive toy in the entire shop.

"This is what I want, grandfather," he says, with a broad grin on his face.

It suddenly dawns on Vito's grandfather that the boy has remembered last year's lesson. He doesn't care about this toy, he has been searching for the most expensive toy in the shop knowing he would receive its value in cold hard cash.

Full of admiration for the boy's guile, his grandfather shakes his head and hands over the money.

But he vows he will never take his grandson into the toy shop for *La Festa dell'Epifania* – nor any other occasion again!

*****

IF YOUNG VITO's guile benefits him financially at the expense of his grandfather, so too does his mathematical skill, giving an early indication of his intrinsic engineering skills.

His grandfather has a hiding place, a small hole in the wall of the apartment in which they live, where he keeps his spare pocket change and valuables. While he doesn't particularly keep it a secret, it is cleverly concealed. More importantly, he is always able to tell if anyone else has disturbed the entry hole.

Young Vito would never brazenly open up the entry in the living room. What he does do is size up the position of the hole in relation to the floor, ceiling and walls of the room. Then he steps outside into the courtyard and calculates the exact position of the hiding place from the exterior side of the wall. Allowing for the difference between the level of the floor inside and outside, and the thickness of the walls, Vito takes a pocket knife and begins digging around the stone brick he believes is on the opposite side of his grandfather's hidden stash. Loosening the brick a little bit each time he goes outside, he finally manages to pry it loose and pull it away from the wall.

Sliding his hand inside and reaching around, he finds he has hit the exact spot and pulls out a handful of coins. He shoves the coins into his pocket and carefully replaces the stone in the wall.

He waits to see if his grandfather will notice, or if he does, if he will say anything, but after several days, nothing is said. He uses the money to go to watch a movie.

A few weeks later, young Vito is broke again and wishes he had money to go out with his friends. He removes the stone one more time, puts his hand in and helps himself to another handful of coins. Again, he waits several days before spending any of the money. Again, nothing is said. Young Cellini continues to help himself to his grandfather's funds every few months. He is careful not to take too much and not to do it too often; just a few coins now and then so as not to attract too much attention. His grandfather seems oblivious to the petty larceny going on right under his nose.[3]

If he is aware of it, he keeps it to himself.

3. *Whether his grandfather ever knew or suspected that Cellini was robbing him, will never be known for sure. Cellini believes he probably did notice that money was disappearing, and that he may even have suspected Vito was responsible, but was unable to determine exactly how. He was the kind of man who never accused anyone of anything and would only speak up if he felt he had good reason. Such was the esteem in which Cellini's grandfather was regarded by the local population, when he died, he was given the biggest funeral the town of Bari had ever seen.*

Cellini's beloved "Ma" – Pasqua.

Cellini's grandmother.

Older brother Nicola and Vito.

Cellini's long-suffering grandfather.

3. School Days

At school Cellini is anything but a model student and is, more or less, constantly in trouble. He will joke that the only reason he made it from the third grade to the fourth was because the teacher died of old age.

He is bright and he picks things up quickly. Good at drawing and exceptionally gifted in mathematics, he has no enthusiasm for history or literature and shows little interest in learning to write. The classroom holds very little appeal for a young boy who would rather be outside, gaining practical experience in his own life, instead of locked up in the humid jail-house of a schoolroom listening to stories about someone else's.

Having no interest in book learning, young Cellini's brain is a warehouse waiting to be filled with practical information, and since he isn't gaining anything he considers useful or satisfying from attending school, he will acquire most of his knowledge on the street. He is a patient observer and enjoys studying, copying, practising, perfecting and at times inventing new ways of finding out how things work.

It is through watching the local blacksmith at work in his foundry near the corner of *Via Gioacchino Murat* and *Via Niccolo Pizzoli* that the young boy first develops his love of mechanics and working with metal.

The blacksmith is a figure of fun for most of the schoolboys in Bari. A hefty and rotund man who perpetually seems to have a half-eaten sandwich in his hand, they simply refer to him as *"Fata"* (Fat).

Cellini, however, is fascinated by the techniques employed by the metal worker, and the skills with which he employs them, and asks a lot of questions. He is amused and amazed when the blacksmith tells him that the hot steel used for making horseshoes and horseshoe nails is tempered by dipping it in horse urine to strengthen it. At eight years of age, Cellini has no idea that the ammonia contained in urine provides the necessary strengthening, much less that horse urine obtained from local farmers is a cheap and readily-available source of ammonia. To him it is a magical process, and one that he never forgets.

*****

WALKING TO SCHOOL one day and daydreaming as always, his mind is jerked back to reality by the sound of tuneless whistling somewhere behind him. He turns his head around just in time to avoid getting knocked over by a man on a bicycle. No hands on the handlebars and carrying a shotgun over his shoulder. The man, whom he recognizes as a neighbour, laughs and pedals harder. He is going pigeon hunting. Bari is a small coastal town and though life, for the most part, revolves around the harbour and the fishing port, it is less than a mile to the countryside and woodland areas where *Barises* love to hunt as much as they love to fish in the clear blue Adriatic. Cellini knows that the field the hunter is headed towards is no more than ten minutes away, so he decides to follow along.

Playing truant is not exactly a new experience for him – he has done it before, especially on days when he feels school offers him no reason to want to stay inside. Today, for example is a beautiful day for a walk in the woods or climbing trees. And for watching the pigeon hunter.

Cellini has to run to keep pace with the hunter. Hurrying past the *tufa* quarry,[1] Cellini hopes he won't get seen by his uncle Vito, master stone cutter of the rock used for building the sea wall and many of the old buildings in Bari. After a few more minutes, the hunter gets off his bicycle and turns onto a narrow pathway between trees. Cellini ducks behind a large olive tree and watches. After a few minutes he follows, keeping a safe distance back. Any residual thoughts he may have had about going to school have completely left his head. All he can think of is the adventure ahead.

He keeps the hunter in sight, moving when he moves, so as not to make any noise that will attract his attention. Deeper into the trees and then out into a clearing and a large meadow, the boy never more than 20 metres behind. The hunter carefully lays his bicycle down on the ground, reaches into his coat pocket and pulls out two shotgun shells. He breaks open the weapon, loads, then stands waiting.

To the young boy, it seems like hours before anything happens. From where he is standing among the trees he can't really tell if there are any birds flying. He decides to move closer and maybe climb a tree for a

[1] *Porous sandstone or limestone containing seashells and the remains of small crustaceans. It is used as an inexpensive building material throughout southern Italy.*

better view. As he lifts his foot to step forward the hunter raises the weapon and fires two shots within a second of each other and Cellini jumps. The noise is deafening and echoes around the clearing. Quickly, he reloads and walks at the same time, further into the open field, turns and fires two more shots. Cellini darts forward and takes cover behind a large forked tree. Seeing a knot in the tree at about shoulder height, he pulls himself up, reaches for a hollow to use as a hand-hold and pulls himself up to the gap in the fork. He shimmies up one side of the trunk until he is lying in a prone position between two branches. It's a good hiding place. He's higher up than the hunter and now he can see all the way across the field.

He watches the hunter's every move and copies his actions. He mimics him breaking open the shotgun, reaching into his imaginary coat pocket for two imaginary cartridges and loading them into two imaginary barrels. Then he takes aim with his own imaginary shotgun. As he fires, in perfect time with the hunter, he reacts to the recoil of his imaginary shotgun, loses his balance and almost falls out of the tree. The hunter stops and turns around. Cellini is certain he will get caught but he keeps dead still and doesn't make a sound. The hunter shrugs, loads a couple more shells and walks further into the clearing, turning back every few seconds.

High up in the tree, the boy hears leaves rustling and a pigeon takes flight from somewhere above him. Suddenly, two shots ring out, louder than before, because this time the gun is pointing in his direction and the shots are aimed over his head!

He closes his eyes tightly, puts his hands over his ears and tries to make himself small and safe within his cage of branches. Two more shots. Even louder this time! He feels a shower of dirt landing on him, sprinkling his face and hair, but he daren't move. One more shot and then silence. He waits for the next shot, which he knows must be coming, but it never comes. After what seems an age, he takes his hands away from his ears and slowly opens his eyes. He can see the hunter walking towards the tree, and he knows the game is up.

The hunter stops at the foot of the tree, but instead of looking up, he stoops down to pick something up. First one, then another grey bird that have fallen on the ground almost directly beneath Cellini.

The hunter seems pleased with himself. The tuneless whistling starts up again and he walks back to where he left his bicycle.

Cellini waits until the hunter has gone and makes sure no one is in sight before slowly climbing down the tree. He dusts himself off and wipes his face, Tiny red spots smear across his hand. He rubs his head. More red smears. The hunter must have shot the pigeons directly over his head.

He grins and starts playing with his imaginary shotgun again.

Loading it. Aiming it. Firing it into the sky and the pigeons. Letting the recoil knock him right over this time.

*****

DESPITE SKIPPING SCHOOL often, young Vito Cellini makes friends easily and gets along well with other boys, especially those with a similar predilection for flaunting authority and seeking excitement outside the traditional learning environment.

It is natural therefore, that when Cellini crosses paths with a young boy named Antonio Anibilis – known to all simply as Tonino – they become firm and loyal friends for life.

Tonino is the son of Albanian immigrants who have made their home in Bari. The Anibilis are a very poor family and Tonino spends a great deal of time on the streets, where he soon learns the art of relieving people of their watches, wallets and other belongings that he can sell to make money in order to buy food and anything else he or his family needs.

Tutuc Cellini is both fascinated and enthralled with the skills and motives of his new friend. He admires him and wants to learn how to be like him; to do what he does. He longs to experience things first hand and is open to anything his friend suggests, legal or otherwise. He isn't looking to break the law, nor even for personal gain, so much as he is seeking adventure, excitement and thrills, the same as any youth in every generation.

Cellini will spend a great deal of time with Tonino – and almost get into a great deal of trouble as a result of their friendship.

*****

IT IS AS A RESULT of one of his many adventures with Tonino that, at the tender age of 8 years-old, young Cellini first witnesses tragedy.

It's a horrific accident, but for Cellini it serves as an early lesson not only in dealing with the emotional side of witnessing violent death, but also of the consequences of carelessness and being overeager.

Vito, Tonino and their friends like to ride the tram from one end of town to the other, but of course they have no money for the fare and it is a common practice for them to do so without paying for a ticket. The trolley car runs along the seafront from the old town to San Cataldo and at various points along the journey it slows down enough for them to hop on board, unseen by the driver or conductor.

If they are seen, or if it looks like the conductor is going to come around checking for tickets, the boys will hop straight off and wait for the next trolley.

Soon it becomes a popular game of dare to jump from one moving tram to another, as they pass each other travelling in opposite directions. Even though the boys generally wait until the vehicles slow down to make the jump, it is a dangerous game of chicken that requires perfect timing as well as considerable bravado, of which they have plenty. On one occasion, a kid from Tonino's neighbourhood who Cellini does not know very well has tagged along. Eager to prove himself worthy of his place in the gang, the new kid leaps from one trolley car to another as they pass each other, but mistimes his jump, disappearing between the two vehicles.

Cellini will never forget the tortured scream and his brief glimpse of the boy's body, cut into two by the wheels of the trolley car. The sight of all the blood; the motionless severed legs and the upper body, ripped open and the exposed heart still beating, is burned into his mind. Cellini looks Tonino in the eye, then jumps from the tram and runs home.

The memory of the accident will haunt him for the rest of his life, but it will also serve as a valuable lesson that will help to keep him alive.

*****

ONE DAY, out of the blue, Tonino asks Tutuc if he likes fresh baked bread.

"Yes, of course! Who doesn't?" Cellini replies.

"I know where we can get some. No risk. No danger. And no chance of getting caught, if you're interested?"

"You mean steal it?" says Cellini.

"You can call it that if you want." Tonino shrugs, half expecting his friend to back out.

"It's only Army bread, baked by jailbirds, and I don't see what they do for us, so we may as well help ourselves."

"Anyway," he adds, "we're not stealing the whole shipment. Just a few lousy loaves."

The plan is simple. Tonino, who is a couple of years older then Cellini, has done his homework.

Every morning at exactly the same time, the bread delivery van pulls out of the bakery in the military prison on *Via Travisani* and *Via Carlo Perrone* to deliver the bread, baked by the prisoners and stored in heavy sacks, to the nearby military bases. The van usually drives very slowly up *Via Travisani* and has to slow down or come to a complete stop when it reaches *Via Napoli.* That's when the two young robbers strike. Jumping up into the back of the van, they slice through the bread sacks with a knife, toss the bread out of the back of the vehicle, then before the vehicle gathers speed, jump out, gather up the loaves from off the road and stow them in a sack, then disappear down one of the many alleyways.

It works like a charm, and on their very first attempt, they steal five loaves of bread.

Convinced the van driver will stop and report the theft immediately, the two boys run through alleyways between buildings and hide behind huge rubbish bins while they catch their breath. In fact, the van driver has no idea of the theft until he reaches his destination, so he has no way of knowing when or where along the route the robbery occurred.

The young thieves make their way back to *Piazza Garibaldi,* where they sit on a bench, look at each other and laugh long and loud. Reaching into the sack, Tonino pulls out a loaf, dusts off the road dirt and breaks off a chunk of bread, which he hands to Cellini. Then he breaks another piece off the loaf and shoves it into his own mouth.

"The rest we sell," says Tonino, his mouth full of bread, a blizzard of crumbs spraying all over his friend.

It is the first of many similar bakery heists, and with the extra money they make from selling the bread, they are able to pay for sandwiches, cakes and drinks whenever they go out.

4. *Fil de Zip*

Spring 1934. The evening is cool and humid. A light rain has left behind thin shrouds of mist, creating ghostly shadows on the streets of Bari.

Three small figures emerge from behind a *tufa* stone wall, stealthily passing from shadow to shadow towards the iron gate of the *Liceo Classico.* The gate is locked. The faculty, staff and students, even the janitors, have long since gone home. Nodding to his companions, one of the figures eases between the edge of the iron frame of the gate and the rock wall, squeezing through the gap. They don't call him *"Fil de zip"* for nothing![1] The hinges creak and he pauses, dead still, just for a moment, his heart pounding – not with fear but with excitement.

One more deep breath, one last push, and he is through the gate and into the courtyard of the building.

Once across the courtyard he signals to his friends with a thumbs up. They will walk up and down, lean against the wall, perhaps even kick a rock around in the street, and if someone comes along looking like they are going to open the gate, they will start a mock fight for distraction and make as much noise as they can so their partner can escape.

Liceo Classico is not a grand building, but it is historic. It serves as a preparatory school for Bari's young fascists before going on to complete their education at university.[2] Whether students continue to university or not, they are prepared for military service at the *Liceo*, and the school regularly hosts parades for the *Balilla,* Italy's Fascist Youth organization.[3] As part of their curriculum, *Balilla* members receive weapons training at the school. It is because weapons are stored in the building that Cellini is now attempting to sneak in.

[1] *"Fil de zip" is a Barese slang nickname meaning "thin as a twig".*

[2] *Bari's Università degli Studi Benito Mussolini had recently been renamed in honour of the Italian dictator.*

The small figure strides stealthily across the courtyard to a small window at ground level. Crouching down in the semi-darkness he glances around to make sure no one has seen him, sticks his finger under the edge of the window frame to pry it loose and shakes the frame until it lifts up. Getting down on the ground, he is able to roll inside the building and lower himself into the basement below.

He finds himself in the armoury. The air is thick with dust from the window ledge he has just disturbed, floating in the twilight entering the room through the stained and dirty window panes, reminding him of the dust and smoke in a movie theatre.

He sits down on the floor waiting for his eyes to clear, and smiles to himself.

"Better than my school," he mutters to himself. But then most 10 year-old boys would probably agree that sneaking into a room full of guns is more exciting than reciting passages from Dante. He is not enrolled at the *Liceo Classico*, although he does frequently find himself helping his friends Ricardo and Vito Calabrese, who do attend, with their mathematical homework problems. Now Ricardo and Vito, who told him exactly where to find the guns, are waiting outside, keeping watch to make sure no one interrupts him as he goes about his task.

Looking up he sees row upon row of rifles side by side mounted on a rack on the wall. Just as he is about to stand up and reach for the nearest one he spots a large grey metal cabinet out of the corner of his eye. It's about the size of the dinner table at home, with long thin drawers all the way around.

One of the drawers is open.

It's only a crack, but in the dimness of the room it casts a shadow that looks like a big, open, grinning mouth. He reaches out and grasps the top of the drawer. Stiff at first, it suddenly judders and then shoots forwards towards his face. The sound of metal scraping on metal is deafening, and he thinks it must have alerted every policeman in Bari. Startled by the noise

[3] *The Balilla, or Opera Nazionale Balilla (ONB), was the name of the Italian Fascist youth organization founded in 1926 for boys and girls aged between 8 and 14. At age 14 they became Avanguardisti. A junior association, for 6 to 8 year-olds, was added and the child members were known as Figli della Lupa ("Children of the She-Wolf"), referring to Romulus and Remus of Roman mythology. The organization was originally named after Balilla, the nickname given to Giovan Battista Perasso, a young boy who, according to legend, led the revolt against Habsburg forces occupying Genoa during the War of the Austrian Succession. Figli della Lupa, Balilla and Avanguardisti were all under the auspices of ONB. In 1937 the ONB was absorbed by the Gioventù Italiana del Littorio (GIL), the youth section of the National Fascist Party (equivalent of Germany's Hitler Youth).*

and knocked off balance by the sudden movement of the drawer, the young intruder darts for the cover of darkness under a table below the window ledge and lies still for what seems like hours, listening for any warnings from his friends outside in the street. Hearing nothing except his own heartbeat, he slowly slides across the floor on his knees to the drawer and reaches inside. He feels a heavy piece of cold metal and knows exactly what it is. Picking it up with one hand, he sits back on his haunches to try and take a better look. It's a magazine from one of the rifles, and it's fully loaded. He reaches back into the drawer and pulls out another one, but this one is empty, so he puts it back. Rummaging around for another loaded clip but unable to find one, he decides to settle for just the one, hoping it will fit. The remains of the daylight are almost gone and he can't see too well, so he tucks the magazine into the waist of his trousers, then pulls his shirt down to cover it up.

Standing up, he stretches up to the rack on the wall to lift one of the rifles down. He can't quite reach it, so he looks around for a chair or something on which to stand. In the half light, he stumbles into a box that will do the job nicely, so he pushes it over to the wall and climbs up. Grasping the rifle in both hands, he lifts it upwards and away from the rack, then lowers it to his side as he steps down from the box.

Pausing for a moment to listen for any sound, he climbs onto the table under the window, pushes the window just far enough to look outside and see if there's anyone out there. Seeing nothing and hearing no sound, he pulls himself up onto the ledge, pushes the rifle out as quietly as he can and then rolls through the window onto the clammy stone floor of the courtyard. He carefully pushes the window closed behind him, giving the catch a push to make sure no one will notice that it has been disturbed.

Making his way silently back to the gate, he looks for his friends. He carefully passes the rifle through the gate to one of them and then squeezes his body between the railing and the rock wall, just as he did before. Suddenly he finds himself stuck! Jammed tight, he can't slide through the gap, no matter how hard he wriggles.

For what seems like an age he stands dead still trying to work out why it is that he can get in, but not out, through the gap in the railing. He starts wriggling again, getting nowhere. His friends are beginning to get nervous.

"Come on Tutuc! Quit fooling around!"

"I'm not fooling around you imbecile. I'm stuck! I'm –"

"Shhhh. What's that?"

Footsteps! The sound is off in the distance, but getting louder. Whoever it is must be coming this way. And they are getting closer!

Cellini stops wriggling and keeps perfectly still, deciding that in the semi-darkness being heard is more of a risk than being seen. He doesn't feel fear. Has never known fear. Even when the bigger kids at school try pushing him around he is never afraid of what might happen. He just fights back, punches as hard as he can, and takes all the punishment they can deliver until they are the ones who quit.

This is different.

There is still no fear. Embarrassment perhaps? His family always calls him a *delinquente,* and he always argues that he isn't. If he gets caught red-handed stealing a rifle from the fascist school, that would prove they were right about him all along.

He orders his friends, outside the gate and holding the rifle, to leave him.

"Go!" He says. "I'll meet you by the fountain in half an hour."

"But what about you?"

"Just go. Quickly!"

His friends take off in the opposite direction to where the footsteps are coming from with the rifle in between them.

"At least I won't get caught with the gun," he says to himself – then he remembers the magazine is still tucked in the front of his trousers.

The magazine! Of course! That is why he is stuck!

Now he feels dumb. As dumb as a 10 year-old can feel, that is, caught in an iron gate with a stolen – and loaded – magazine clip in his waistband.

He slides back a little inside the railing, pulls the magazine out of his waistband and holds it tightly by his side, then slips back out through the railing as easily as he had gone in. It seems like an age but the whole time is less than half a minute. The footsteps are louder now. He puts both hands in his pockets, grasping the magazine tightly, and starts to walk towards the seafront to meet his friends.

The footsteps belong to a man walking on the opposite side of the street who doesn't even look up at the kid with his hands in his pockets.

*****

HEADING TOWARDS the seafront he sees a few cars and fewer people. No one pays him any attention. He reaches the corner of *Vittorio Veneto* and *Niccolo Pizzoli* but his friends are nowhere in sight.

He wonders what has happened to his friends. Maybe they got caught. Maybe they got scared and hid the gun somewhere. Maybe they got tired of waiting and went home. He waits a couple of minutes before deciding to cross the road to the waterfront. Just as he gets to the other side, a hand reaches out from behind a clump of trees and grabs him by the arm as a voice shrieks "gotcha!"

It's Calabrese, with a grin on his face as big as a round of pecorino cheese.

Cellini pulls back his fist as if ready to punch him in the face.

"Where's that no good Ricardo?" he says.

"Over here," says a voice from behind an olive tree. The three boys trade mock punches and grin at each other as they sneak behind the sea wall and scramble down to the rocks. They hop over the rocks alongside the jetty, moving as far away as they can from where anyone might hear them. The whole area is deserted. Ricardo hands over the rifle to Cellini as they sit astride massive outlet pipes.

"No bullets," says Ricardo.

"Doesn't even have a clip," adds Calabrese.

They both look slightly crestfallen after the risks they have taken to get this far with their ill-gotten gains, even though it was their small friend who took the biggest risk by breaking into the school to steal the weapon in the first place.

Cellini's grin gets wider as he reaches into his pocket and pulls out the loaded magazine.

Though he is not yet familiar with guns to any great degree, he knows that what he is holding is a Modello-91 also known as the Carcano rifle.[4] He knows because it is the same rifle his father carried in the Great War, and he has studied photos of him holding a similar weapon. He has no idea if the magazine clip he picked up is the right one for the gun, but it looks right, so he tries to slot it in. After a few goes, it slips into the receiver and locks. He pulls back on the bolt and then pushes it forwards. It takes quite an effort but the action is smooth and the bolt locks down.

He points the gun out to sea and, without giving it a second thought, pulls back on the trigger. The sound of the single gunshot echoes around the rocks and off the jetty, deafening his companions. Even through the rifle is modified to fire .22 calibre rounds,[5] the recoil knocks Cellini

4. *The Carcano Modello 91 was produced from 1892 to 1945 and was used in both rifle (fucile) and carbine (moschetto) form by most Italian troops during the First World War and by Italian and some German forces during World War Two. Approximately 60,000 Carcanos were specially produced for Japanese Imperial Naval Forces for use in the war. The rifle identified as being used by Lee Harvey Oswald in the 1963 assassination of John F. Kennedy was a Carcano.*

5. *The Balilla trained with a scaled down version of the Carcano M91 modified to fire .22 calibre ammunition.*

backwards from his precarious perch on the wet pipe. He rolls off still clutching the rifle in his hands and lands on cold, clammy rocks with one foot in a small tide pool. His companions dive off in different directions and all three of them lie perfectly still, face down among the rocks behind the outlet pipe. They listen for the sound of police whistles and sirens that they have seen in movies. They look up to see if they can see the arc of flashlight beams sweeping the waterfront searching for them. They wait for the sound of hobnail boots crunching over the shale, the inevitable hubbub of angry voices and the weight of a heavy hand on their shoulder.

One minute passes. Two minutes. Three. Nothing but the sound of the waves lapping against the rocks.

"Who wants the next shot?" Cellini says.

5. The Key

Liceo Classico is not the only source of illicit weapons for Vito Cellini and his friends.

In their possession is a key, stolen on a dare from behind the counter in the box office of a local movie theatre.

It is another friend, Frank Catacchio, who finally plucks up the courage to accept the dare and steal the key. He has a liking for the girl who works in the ticket office and thinks he can sweet talk his way into her booth and steal it. As it turns out, the girl isn't even there. No one is there, so Frank is able to walk in, lift the key from its hook on the wall and walk out, unnoticed. Frank is a good thief and Vito learns a lot from him.

The boys assume it must be the key for the cinema entrance, which doesn't excite them much. After all, they can sneak in to watch movies without buying a ticket anytime they like. Ricardo says something about being able to break in and help themselves to sweets and candy, but the others aren't impressed. Cellini puts the key in his pocket and forgets about it.

Later that evening, Cellini, Ricardo and Vito Calabrese are standing around outside the tobacco shop owned by Ricardo's parents. Frank Catacchio has made other plans and won't be joining them. The store is closed and shuttered but Cellini starts fooling around with the key in the lock of the shutter. To his amazement, the key turns and the shutter opens.

There and then, the boys decide to go exploring the neighbourhood to see if the key fits anywhere else that may be of interest.

What they discover is that it will open just about every lock in the town of Bari.

Specifically, it unlocks the heavy steel shutters that descend over shop fronts at the close of business each evening. Evidently, the company that installed the shutters must have used the same lock for every shop front, never thinking that anyone would try their key in another lock.

The discovery opens up all kinds of possibilities for Cellini and his fellow *delinquentes*, although they restrict themselves, for the most part, to stealing cigarettes and tobacco, which they give to friends or sell to make extra pocket money. But Cellini also discovers that the key opens the entrance to one of the buildings being used for storage by the Fascist Party. And he knows that they keep guns in the basement of the building.

Cellini is familiar with the building, on *Piazza Giuseppe Massari*, because his father, a devout member of the Fascist Party, works as a custodian for the *Dopolavoro Portuali*, a working men's club for Bari's dock workers, which is housed in the adjacent building. He has been inside the building with his father on many occasions and knows the layout well. When not in use, the building is kept locked and is inaccessible except to local party leaders – or at least to anyone who doesn't possess a key to the building.

Once Cellini discovers that his key will fit, he and his friends waste no time in making plans to break in, especially knowing that the building houses guns. Sneaking out of his grandmother's house one evening, he meets up with Vito Calabrese and Ricardo at the corner of the street and they set off for the fascist administration building, which is just a couple of short blocks away.

As usual, Cellini, *the tree branch,* volunteers to enter the building. The others will wait outside and keep watch. They unlock the entrance using the stolen key and he slips inside, leaving the key with Calabrese, who closes the door and turns the key, locking Cellini inside.

Feeling his way cautiously in the dark, Cellini finds his way to the basement doorway and cautiously makes his way down the steps. The stone is cold and the air feels damp, but the building is quiet and, as he descends the steps, his excitement begins to grow.

He had the foresight to bring a box of matches, and now that he is in the basement, he feels it is safe to strike one. His hands are shaking as the tension begins to mount. He strikes a match but the flash startles him and he drops it on the floor. Unable to see anything for a minute or so, he pulls another match from the box and strikes it. This time he manages to hold on to it. He finds himself in a corridor with an arched ceiling and doors on both sides. He can't tell how long the corridor is but decides to try the first door. It's locked, so he turns to the door opposite and notices that it is slightly ajar. He pushes the door open just as the match starts to burn his finger, so he drops it and reaches into the matchbox for another. As it flares into life, he looks around the small room. He focuses on a large metal cabinet against the wall. The door is not closed all the way, but it is heavy and creaks in protest as he pulls on the edge. Convinced the noise will wake every fascist in Bari, he blows out the match and drops to the floor, huddling against the wall next to the cabinet. After a few minutes of absolute silence he gets up, strikes another match and peers into the cabinet. The cabinet is full of drawers and shelves but right in front of him, at eye level, Cellini spots exactly what he came for. He reaches up, grabs the heavy black pistol and turns to leave the room. Then he stops, and with amazing presence of mind for a 10 year-old, he walks back into the room and pushes the cabinet door almost closed, exactly as he found it. He leaves the door of the room slightly ajar, strikes another match and makes his way back up the basement steps to the foyer of the building.

Now for the tricky bit. He hopes Calabrese or Ricardo are still outside and ready to unlock the door so he can come out. He taps on the door and whispers, "All clear?"

Nothing.

He taps again and calls out a little louder this time, "All clear?"

After what seems like an age, he hears the key turning in the lock. Finally the door opens a few inches and he sees the grinning face of Vito Calabrese bathed in the soft yellow glow of a streetlight.

"Did you get anything?"

"You wait 'til you see what I got!" Cellini replies.

"Now let's get out of here."

*****

THE THREE BOYS head straight to the seafront, across the *Lungomare*, and clamber across rocks to their favourite spot near the water. It's quiet and secluded and well hidden from view. Some of the octopus fishermen might see them from their fishing boats in the morning, but at this time of night, most of them are further out to sea.

Sitting astride a rock, Cellini pulls the gun carefully out of his pocket. It's a Smith & Wesson Top Break revolver. He snaps it open and finds it is loaded.

He thinks about pointing it out to sea and firing a couple of rounds, but instead he tips the cylinder into the palm of his small hand and carefully shakes out all of the bullets. Then he slowly closes the weapon until it snaps shut.

In the distance the three boys hear the sound of a ship's horn and look up but see nothing except the lights of the harbour in the distance.

Cellini straddles a rock and looks around one more time to make sure no one is in sight. The beach is deserted. For a full five minutes he just holds the gun in the palm of his hand, first on one side then the other, studying every detail, every curve, every corner, every edge of the metal. The chequered pattern of the hard rubber grips with the moulded Smith & Wesson factory insignia.

Oblivious to his friends, who are getting impatient, he dry fires the weapon five or six times, pointing it at an imaginary aircraft in the night sky and making noises to cover each click of the trigger.

"Pcheeooo... pcheeooo, pcheeooo..."

In his minds eye, he pictures the movements of the mechanism inside the gun.

What makes the trigger pull back the hammer and strike the bullets?

How does the cylinder turn around like that?

"Let's shoot it!"

The voice of Ricardo penetrates the silent world Cellini has created for himself. He stares at Ricardo and points the gun towards him.

"Or whatever you want to do..." Ricardo's voice tapers off to a whimper as he crouches down behind a rock.

"Don't worry," says Cellini, "I'm not going to shoot you. I already took the bullets out."

"I knew that!" It's Calabrese chiming in this time.

"Are we going to shoot the gun or what?"

Cellini grasps the grip, lifts the barrel catch and tilts the barrel all the way down, then reaches into his pocket and places the bullets back into the cylinder, one at a time. Then he hands the weapon to his friend and tells him to point it at the sea.

Calabrese takes the gun, points it at the sea, just the way he's seen in the movies, and almost in the same movement he pulls back on the trigger. A loud report echoes along the beach as Calibrese's arm jerks upwards almost 90 degrees. He turns and laughs nervously and quickly hands the weapon to Cellini, who offers it to Ricardo.

"Your turn," he says.

Ricardo looks worried but says nothing. He takes the pistol and grasps it firmly with both hands, then points it down at the sea. Ricardo has noticed how the recoil sent Vito Calabrese's arm upwards and, determined not to do the same, he points the gun downwards more. After what seems like an eternity the gun fires for a second time. The bullet hits a rock, causing a loud and resounding ricochet. Ricardo almost topples over from the recoil but manages to steady himself and hands the gun back to Cellini.

Cellini walks over wet rocks to the water's edge and gets down low, so that the muzzle of the weapon is only a few inches above the surface of the sea. Crouching down and grasping the weapon in both hands, he fires into the sea. The noise from the gun is still loud, but nowhere near as loud as the previous two shots. Though he has no idea how or why, he is intrigued by how much quieter the gun is when held close to the water. He repeats the action and fires a second shot into the sea.

"Let's get out of here," says Calabrese. "Someone must have heard this racket."

"You guys can go if you want to," Cellini replies. "I'm not done yet."

They decide to stick around with their friend for a while longer, but Cellini is lost in his own world, and in particular with the weapon in his hand.

He slides the cylinder out and sets it on a rock in front of him. Taking a small pocket knife out of his pocket, he opens the blade. The tip has long since broken off so it makes a perfect screwdriver for the small screws on a revolver. He starts undoing the screws. Fascinated by the mechanics of the weapon, he pauses as each piece is removed to look at it closely. In less than three minutes he has completely dismantled the weapon, taking care to look at each piece as it comes off, then laying it down on a flat rock, making sure he will know how to replace it.

He reaches down to pick up a small spring, but he knocks it with his finger and it rolls off the wet surface. He tries to grab it before it falls but it disappears over the side and lands in a gap between the rocks. Reaching across the rock, he catches the end of his sleeve on the barrel, which wobbles and spins around, knocking several assorted small pieces into the tide pools around the rocks.

Looking around to make sure his sudden clumsy movements didn't attract any unwanted attention, he hands the frame, cylinder, barrel, one grip and other assorted pieces to Ricardo, then gets down on his stomach and tries to see where the missing pieces have fallen. Squeezing his hand between two rocks and stretching down, he comes up with a broken mussel shell between two fingers, which he discards. He manages to find the barrel catch and adds it to the pieces on the rock, but cannot find any of the springs. Those are gone forever. He washes the pieces off in the small pool, where he also finds the other rubber grip, much to the amusement of a nearby hermit crab who might have been thinking about moving in.

He tries to put the pieces back together. Even without the springs and a couple of screws, he still thinks he ought to be able to assemble the gun. However, what had taken less than three minutes to disassemble proves to be too much of a task for the 10 year-old. After patiently struggling to fit the parts together, he finally gives up and shoves the pieces, loose, into his pocket.

Disgruntled, he walks towards the water, and pulls the pieces out of his pocket. One by one, he skims the pieces of metal across the surface of the water and watches them sink.

Turning to his friends he shrugs and says, "We'll go back and get another."

"Only next time, I'll be more careful with the parts."

In the coming months he and his friends will revisit both the *Liceo Classico* and the fascist administrative building several times, each time stealing a weapon of a different type or calibre. Rifles from the *Liceo*, revolvers and semi-automatic pistols from the fascist building. His greatest prize would be an American Colt .45 semi-automatic.

Sometimes, if he feels like it and thinks he can get away with it, he will go to the beach and shoot bullets into the water, but mostly he will take them just for the fun of dismantling the weapons to see how they are put together and learn how they work. Though this young boy has no way of realizing it now, the knowledge he will acquire from these lessons will later save his life, and the lives of those around him.

Something else that he is too young to realise is that he is about to embark upon his first love affair. He is falling in love with guns, and it is a love that will last his entire life. Not as machines of destruction and killing, but as things of great mechanical beauty. His new love will cause him no end of trouble, will get him into a lot of scrapes, and will almost cost him his life on many occasions, but it will provide him with the life full of adventure, risk and challenges that he craves. Along the way, he will meet some of the most influential and dangerous people of the twentieth century.

His new-found love also fosters a contempt for the fascists that will ultimately lead to him despising the entire Italian government as well as their leader, Benito Mussolini, *Il Duce*.

After all, he reasons, how can they be so stupid as to not realise their guns are missing?

And if they do realise, how can they be so stupid as to say and do nothing about it?

And how can his father support such a stupid regime?

6. Pigeons to Roller Skates

IN SEPTEMBER 1934, a magnificent new sports arena opens in Bari, a gift from Mussolini. Funding for the project is a reward for the city producing more male children than any other Italian city of comparable size, in response to appeals by the erstwhile dictator to beef up the manpower of the country for the future.[1]

The official name of the new stadium is *Stadio Della Vittoria* –"Stadium of Victory", but to everyone in Bari, the Coliseum-like arena will simply be known as *Stadio Bambino* – "Stadium of the Baby Boy".[2]

Soon after the new stadium opens, an announcement is made that there is to be a huge shooting competition. The town is abuzz with talk of the event, and Cellini's family, especially his uncles who are all keen hunters and fancy their chances with the best, are hoping to participate. As it turns out, the so-called competition is not open to just anyone and is certainly beyond the means of the majority of the rank and file locals who are blue-collar workers. The event, which is by invitation only, is being staged for

1. *As Hitler did with Germany, Mussolini saw territorial expansionism, if not war, as very much a part of Italy's future. Foreseeing the need for an increase in the general population, he followed the German leader's example in encouraging women to produce multiple children and as frequently as possible. While Mussolini did not share Hitler's obsession with breeding a master race, he did offer rewards recognizing individuals and regions whose contribution was most valuable to the future growth of Italy's youth.*

2. *Stadio Bambino showcased a huge variety of high-profile events, including football matches, motor cycle racing, concerts, theatrical performances, political rallies and athletic tournaments designed to exploit the prowess of Italian youth – and attributable, of course, to the success of the fascist leadership. After the invasion and capitulation of Italy, the stadium was taken over by the Allies and used for baseball games between rival branches of the United States military. It even played host to a game of American football – the first ever played in Italy – in 1944.*

VIPs and special guests from all over Italy, including royalty, military leaders, political dignitaries and wealthy businessmen.

Thousands of caged pigeons are to be released into the stadium and on a given signal participants will open fire and bag as many birds as they can.

Cellini's Godfather Tomasso, himself a keen hunter and sportsman, has ideas of his own. On the day of the tournament, he picks Vito up from his grandmother's house and they set off for *Stadio Della Vittoria.* Tomasso hands Cellini a large burlap sack, folded up. He has his shotgun with him, the breech open and slung over his shoulder.

On the way, they chat about the shooting competition. Tomasso makes his opinion quite clear to his godson.

"It's like shooting ducks in a barrel. Or pigeons, anyway!" says Tomasso. "That's not sport."

He turns to Vito, "You like pigeon, right?" he says.

"You know I like pigeon!" Cellini replies, "And no one fixes pigeon like Pasqua!"

"Well, we're having pigeon for supper tonight," says Tomasso.

"But how? We can't get into Bambino Stadium!"

"We don't have to!" Tomasso replies with a grin from ear to ear, "Because the birds are going to come to us!"

Just beyond the stadium is all open land. There is a block of apartments at one end but, further inland, nothing but pasture and farmland.

The two find a comfortable spot near some trees, about 200 metres past the stadium with a good clear view, and they sit and wait.

"Not long now," says Tomasso, taking two cartridges from his pocket, loading the shotgun and snapping the breech closed.

Within minutes, a loud report echoes around them, coming from the direction of the stadium, followed by volley after volley of gunfire. It sounds as if a firework display is about to begin, except that it's broad daylight. Seconds later, flocks of birds emerge from out of the top of the stadium. The birds seem confused at first, circling in the sky as if uncertain which way to go, then start flying towards where Vito and Tomasso are waiting. Tomasso raises his weapon, waits a few seconds while he draws a bead, and fires once, then aims and shoots again.

"Watch where they land, Vito! It's your job to go and get them!"

He reloads and fires two more shots, bringing down two more birds. Cellini watches intently to see where they land. Two more shots, two more kills.

After about fifteen minutes, Tomasso has just about exhausted his ammunition. Cellini sets off and picks up fifteen birds, which he stuffs into the sack. He counted eighteen falling from the sky so he keeps looking for the remaining three. He finds two more and hopes Tomasso won't be disappointed that he has missed one. Tomasso just smiles.

"We'll get it next time!" he says.

"I think we have enough for dinner!"

Curious as always and meticulous in his attention to detail, Cellini asks his Godfather, "How did you know which way the birds would fly after they escaped from the stadium?"

"Well, to be honest, I couldn't be sure," Tomasso replies, "but pigeons are not sea birds and the stadium is surrounded by water on three sides, so I just thought they would fly south or south-west. I guess I got lucky!"

The shooting competition proves popular with the Italian gentry and becomes a regular event in Bari. Vito and Tomasso will go as often as they can and have their own private tournament, seeing how many of the birds they can bring home for dinner. No one ever bothers them and they always go home with plenty to eat. Tomasso boasts that he is a better shot than all the rich people in Italy because he bags all the ones that they miss!

*****

IT IS ABOUT THIS time Cellini has his first actual brush with the law, and it comes when he least expects it. Borrowing an old pair of roller skates he finds in the house, he decides they would be perfect for making a quick getaway from the scene of his crimes, just in case he ever needs to. But first, he needs to practise, so he heads towards *Corso Vittorio Emanuel* because there is a wide, tree lined avenue he knows he can skate up and down without getting in the way of any motor vehicles. He sits down at the curb, and buckles the skates to his shoes, making sure they are good and tight, and then tries to stand up. Holding onto a tree for support at first, standing with his legs apart, he slowly finds his balance and is able to let go. He moves cautiously at first, legs far apart, short steps, but in no time at all he is propelling himself up and down the street at breakneck speed. He finds that by leaning forward he can go faster, and the faster he goes, the easier it is to stay on his feet. He practises turning, and before too long he's swerving in and out of groups of people, almost knocking them over, and laughing as he goes. He gets to the end of the avenue and grabs a tree, pulling himself around to turn and go back in the direction he came, when he runs full tilt into a police officer deliberately blocking his path.

The policeman takes a dim view of his skating, but Cellini just laughs and tries to take off. The policeman grips him firmly by the arm and does not let go. Unable to gain any traction, Cellini slips and falls to the ground. The policeman bends down, unbuckles the skates and holds them in one hand. With the other hand he takes Cellini by the scruff of the neck, and marches him off to the police station.

Even when he arrives at the police station, Cellini has no idea that he has done anything wrong – except perhaps a little bit of mischief as he swerved around some of the pedestrians on the avenue – but that was just a lark, nothing more. After they fill out a report and write down his name and address, he is led down a set of stone steps and ushered into a cell. The door is shut behind him. It's a very small cell, with nothing but a wooden plank bed and a small barred window that is too high up to see out of, but lets in just enough daylight for him to see his way around.

They're just trying to scare me he thinks to himself. *Well, I'll show them I'm not frightened.* He climbs up onto the flat wooden bed, curls up and goes to sleep. When he wakes up, it's dark in the cell, and he's cold, but he still refuses to be intimidated. He lies in the darkness trying to work out what he's done and what's going to happen next. Eventually the light begins to filter into the cell as the sun comes up the following morning.

The door opens and a different police officer beckons him out.

"OK you can go now. But don't you ever get caught doing that again," he says.

"Doing what?" Cellini says, insolently.

"Doing what *sir*..." the policeman replies.

"Doing what sir," Cellini responds, a little more humbly.

"Roller-skating is illegal in Italy, by order of *Il Duce*. It is an American pastime and very decadent." The policeman is very haughty.

"But I am American, sir!" Cellini says, as if that explains everything.

"Yes, I know you were born there," the policeman replies. "Your father just told me."

"My father is here?" the young boy replies, "Then he will tell you. I had no idea I was breaking the law!"

Francesco Cellini takes his son home. His face is serious and he says nothing, even though young Vito has a million questions.

"Why didn't you come and get me sooner?"

"Why is it against the law to roller-skate in Italy?"

"Why can't we go back to America?"

Francesco maintains his silent, sullen expression until he gets his son home, then he answers his questions.

"I did not come and get you because the police required me to pay a fine to bail you out of jail, and I will not do that. If they had jailed you for a month or a year I would still not have paid. It's time for you to be accountable for your own actions."

"But what is so wrong with roller-skating? Why is it illegal?" His young mind wants to know.

"Because *Il Duce* says so. That is good enough for me and it should be good enough for you."

"I have one more question," Cellini says to his father.

"What?" His father is growing impatient.

"What does decadent mean?"

The courtyard entrance to the old Liceo Classico building is much the same as it was when young "Tutuc" Cellini broke in and stole fascist guns. One notable difference is that the basement level window (centre of picture) now has bars on it!

Lungomare in the early evening. Little has changed since the days when young Cellini and his friends practised shooting over the rocks with a stolen Carcano rifle.

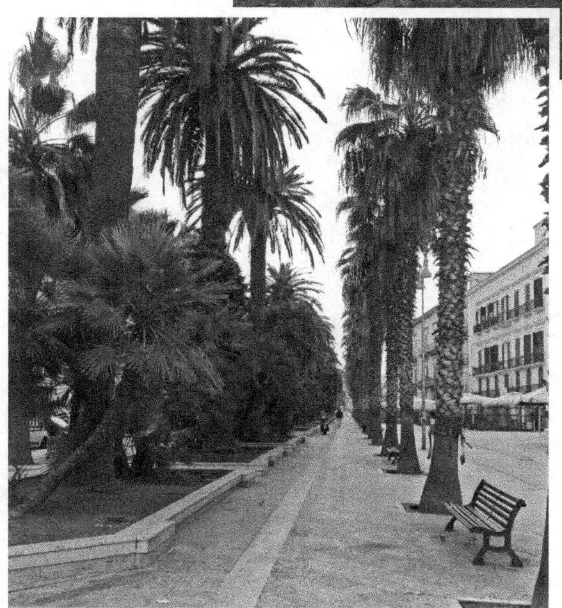

Corso Vittorio Emanuel in Bari's city centre. A beautiful tree-lined pedestrian parkway where, once upon a time, roller-skating was punishable with a jail sentence!

7. First Job

As a result of his inability to concentrate in class and his persistent truancy, coupled with his, at times, wilful disobedience, progress through the formal school system is a slow process for Cellini. By the age of eleven he has finished with school forever.

Fortunately his love for all things mechanical is enough to get him a job almost straight away after leaving school.[1] The father of his best friend Vito Calabrese runs a small machine shop in Bari, working mostly on repairing the boats for local fishermen, though he also takes care of many other local businesses as needs arise, and is willing to give young Cellini a chance to prove himself. Donato Calabrese is also Cellini's Godfather – which undoubtedly helps him to secure the position, even though he begins at the bottom of the totem pole, fetching tools for others and running errands. Donato is impressed with Cellini's amazing ability to learn by watching, as well as the speed with which he is able to solve problems.

While his knowledge of mechanics increases steadily each day, his old habits die hard, and the opportunity to supplement his meagre wages with a few ill-gotten gains often proves to be too much of a temptation. One of his jobs, as errand boy, is to deliver special packages of lead flashing and copper wires to the chief electrical contractor. Gauging the weight and size of the package, it is a simple matter for Cellini to switch it for a similar package full of rocks, having noted that the package remains unattended in the electrician's bag until it is actually needed. He is able to sell the lead

[1.] *As a young boy, Vito Cellini had always been fascinated by mechanical construction and could spend many hours just watching mechanics and engineers while they worked. He once stood close by and watched a welder at work on the local railway track for so long, without eye protection against the bright light of the welding torch, that he suffered partial blindness and extreme pain for almost two weeks. He was never happier than those early years working for Donato Calabrese, who he says was the biggest influence on his career and his inventiveness.*

and copper, and hides the money in a tin, which he buries in a flower bed at the corner of *Via Niccolo Pizzoli* and *Corso Vittorio Veneto* on the seafront at Bari.[2]

He is never suspected of the theft, or if he is, Donato – being a good Godfather – covers for him.

Before too long, Cellini is entrusted with handling the tools of his trade – mostly hand tools, since power tools had yet to come to Bari. At first the work is fun and interesting, and his employer is both kind and understanding. Cellini is a sponge for knowledge and quickly learns how to operate every piece of equipment in his Godfather's tool chest. He even suggests alternative solutions for some of the everyday problems that prove to be more efficient.

But young Cellini needs to be constantly challenged, and after a few months he knows he must move on. Anxious to spare his employer's feelings, he discusses the situation with his father. The simple fact is that Bari, while a major sea port, is essentially a fishing and farming community, lacking any heavy industry. To find more demanding work Vito will need to move to an industrial centre such as Turin or Milan.

Young Cellini feels he has learned all he can from Donato and announces that he is moving on. Donato had been expecting it for some time and wishes his protégé well.

Once the decision is made, it only a matter of time before Cellini moves to Milan. In just a few weeks he will be operating heavy machinery, building parts for aircraft and torpedoes – and contributing to Mussolini's rapidly expanding military machine.

[2] *Cellini used this convenient location as a hiding place for all the cash obtained from his many transgressions, most of which involved petty theft of goods from businesses or lead and copper from local buildings and construction sites, which he later sold. He would use the same location in a few years time to hide the profits from his wartime black market dealings after he returned from Yugoslavia. His hiding place was never discovered, and he was never suspected in any of these crimes, largely, he claims, because he never bragged to anyone about them, nor flaunted the money.*

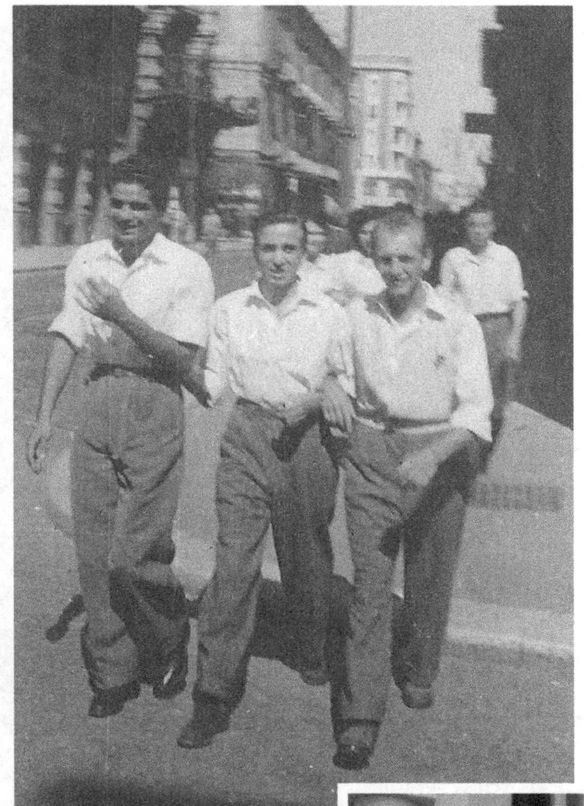

Teenage "Tutuc" Cellini out on the town with his friends Ricardo and Vito Calabrese.

Cellini points to the flower bed at the corner of Vittorio Veneto and Niccolo Pizzoli where he used to bury his ill-gotten gains. Like the Liceo Classico, it too is now surrounded by heavy iron bars!

8. War

Benito Mussolini and Adolf Hitler have become political allies, if not actually friends, as a result of their mutual rise to power and common goal of reparations for the harsh treatment of Germany and Italy at the Treaty of Versailles following the First World War. It proves to be a popular stance, and each is able to take advantage of their electorates.

While both men have improved conditions in their respective countries by creating jobs, modernizing industry and updating transportation systems, much of the investment has been in military technology and inevitably results in territorial expansion, or what Hitler calls "Lebensraum". Hitler's armies invade and occupy Austria and Czechoslovakia, while Mussolini's occupy Abyssinia and annex Albania. Following Hitler's Blitzkrieg in Poland, Britain and France declare war on Germany on September 3rd, 1939. In a show of solidarity, Italy declares war on Britain and France nine months later on June 10th, 1940. Italy's declaration of war comes at the end of the period historians call "the Phoney War", during which the British have been stalling, buying time to rearm and re-equip. They send an Expeditionary Force into France and release several squadrons of aircraft to French bases, but ground troops are beaten back onto the beaches at Dunkirk and forced to evacuate.

Mussolini believes the timing of his declaration of war to be perfect. France is on the brink of collapse (the French government will surrender to Germany less than two weeks later). Assured by Hitler that Britain's surrender will soon follow, Mussolini convinces the Italian people that the war will not last long. Believing the hostilities will be over before Christmas, young Italians flock to join the military. Il Duce is confident that Italy's territorial gains will be considerable, and that his place in history is guaranteed.

Britain does not surrender, and Germany begins making invasion plans (known as Operation Seelöwe, or Sea Lion). For the invasion to succeed, it will need to take place before the winter tides make crossing the English Channel too hazardous for the German troops with all their equipment – but first, the Royal Air Force must be defeated by Göring's Luftwaffe – a task the Reichmarshal promises Hitler will be simple. In what is now known as the Battle of Britain, the RAF prevails. It already has the advantage of radar, and when Hitler makes the tactical error of diverting his bombers towards the British cities instead of its airfields, the RAF has time to regroup. The Luftwaffe is repelled and by September 17th the planned invasion has been postponed indefinitely.

The Regia Aeronautica (Italian Air Force) also participates in the Battle of Britain. In October 1940, approximately 170 Italian aircraft (including 80 Fiat Br.20 bombers and 98 fighters) are transferred to occupied Belgium to form the Corpo Aereo Italiano, but, achieving only limited success, the bombers are withdrawn in January 1941 and the fighters the following April.

*****

ANXIOUS TO DO his part, and keen to make his father proud, Vito's brother Nicola volunteers for the Italian Navy, the *Regia Marina.* 16 year-old Vito is in no hurry to go to war, and begs his brother to reconsider, but Nicola's mind is made up.

"Listen to me, little brother," he says, "You were born in Brooklyn. You are American. This is not your war, and no one expects you to fight for Italy. I was born in Bari. I am Italian. I have to go and fight for my country. Besides which, everyone is saying it will be over by Christmas, and I'll be back before you know it!"

As they say goodbye to Nicola, Francesco Cellini, still loyal in his support of Mussolini and the fascist movement, tells his younger son that he is hopeful the war will be over quickly. It is a rare moment of pragmatism for the elder Cellini.

"If the war is over in six months," he says, "I believe we could win. If it lasts too much longer than that, I am afraid we may lose."

Unfortunately for Mussolini, and for the Cellini family – as well as millions of other Italians – Hitler has greatly underestimated the British resolve. Not only is the war not over by Christmas, but it is not looking like it will over by the following Christmas, either.

Nicola Cellini is posted to serve on the *Trieste*, a heavy battle cruiser in the *Trento* class.[1] Built in 1926, the Trieste is an old but venerable ship. She is fast, but lacks heavy protective armour, making her vulnerable to attack from submarines.

In November, 1940, *Trieste* takes part in the Battle of Cape Spartivento,[2] against Britain's Royal Navy. It is a long-range encounter that lasts under an hour and achieves little for either side, although *Trieste* does manage to score two direct hits on HMS *Berwick.*

At his station as a *fuochista* or stoker in the engine room of the *Trieste*, Nicola sees little daylight while the ship is at sea, and knows little of what is going on above deck. He is grateful that he has the warmth of the engine room and does not have to spend much time in the chilly autumn air. Winter is fast approaching, and for a boy from Bari who is used to the balmy Adriatic coastal climate, up on deck is no place to be.

Still, he looks forward to being able to go home on leave so he can tell his father and younger brother that he and his ship have been involved in combat.

[1.] *The three Trento class cruisers were named after the three unredeemed cities taken from the Austro-Hungarian empire after World War One: Trento, Trieste, and Bolzano. These were the first ships designed to meet the terms of the Washington Naval Treaty, which limited cruisers to 10,000 tons and 8 inch guns. The Regia Marina had to be able to protect the Italian coastline from naval bases, which were widely spread apart. Since speed was a necessity, designers were forced to sacrifice armour and range. It was later concluded that the trade-off in armour put the ships at a considerable disadvantage. Trieste was the first of the three ships to be launched and served as the flagship of the 3rd Division. In 1940, she took part in the battle of Cape Spartivento, scoring two hits on the British heavy cruiser HMS Berwick.*

[2.] *Cape Spartivento, known in Italy as Cape Teulada, is on the southernmost tip of Corsica.*

9. The Cellinis move to Milan, 1937

CECIGLIA IS PREGNANT again, and with winter approaching, she does not want to make the journey into the colder climate of northern Italy, so young Cellini and his father leave her in Bari and head to Milan in search of work.

Having very little money, at least until they are able to find work, they find a place to stay for a pittance in rent; a single attic room in an apartment building on *Viale Monza* managed by Signora Richetta Vigano.[1] Her daughter, a lovely young lady by the name of Giancarla, takes a shine to young Cellini and helps him out with extra food and blankets whenever she is able, as a result of which they become very close friends.[2] The cramped room has a kitchen table and a folding camp bed intended for one person. Father and son take turns sleeping, and on the occasions when both are exhausted and they must share, young Cellini is able to occupy the space left by his father's missing leg.

The owner of the building occupies its finest and largest apartment. Signore Bernini owns one of the best-known toy factories in Milan and is willing to offer young Cellini employment to help offset his rent. The company specializes in tinplate toys, in particular boats, which are painstakingly crafted. Cellini goes to work for Bernini and finds a way to streamline

1. *Signora Vigano was, according to Cellini, quite a characterful woman. Though married, she had not one but two lovers, one of whom was the owner of the building on Viale Monza. She was not particularly discreet about her affairs and Cellini once asked her why she had two boyfriends, to which she replied, "One because he is a great lover and the other because he has lots of money."*

2. *Vito Cellini and Giancarla would remain lifelong friends. Although both were undoubtedly attracted to each other, neither admitted it, and they never had any kind of sexual relationship. They valued each other's insight and sought advice on all aspects of their lives, including their relationships with others. At the time of writing, Cellini still continues to visit Giancarla whenever he is in Milan.*

the manufacturing process, almost doubling production in a matter of weeks. Bernini is pleased, and the Cellinis are often invited to supper in their penthouse, where they meet the rest of the family. The Berninis are rather quiet and reserved except for the youngest daughter, Carla, a cute little 13 year-old who giggles a lot and seems to have a crush on Cellini.

Young Vito Cellini has ambitions beyond the toy trade and hits the streets of Milan looking for employment as a mechanic. He is taken on as an apprentice by VIRTA,[3] a company specializing in the production of cranes and heavy lifting equipment used for loading ships. On the first day he reports for work, brimming with confidence and beaming with delight, he is given a major assignment: clean the toilets!

The toilets are Turkish style – essentially large rectangular porcelain troughs in the ground with no seat and no means of flushing, just a large drain hole over which the occupant must squat, and a plunger. Cleaning them is no simple task – and there are five of them – but Cellini accepts the job with alacrity and, when finished, is praised by the owner of the company.[4]

"This is the cleanest these toilets have ever been since they were installed," he says. "Congratulations – and welcome to VIRTA!"

*****

Cellini and some of his friends manage to acquire a shortwave radio, which they keep carefully hidden for two reasons: firstly, it is now illegal to own such a radio because it can be tuned in to broadcasts transmitted from overseas, including enemy propaganda; and secondly because the radio is stolen property. The boys enjoy listening to popular music on the clandestine radio, but young Vito Cellini is mostly interested in hearing broadcasts about the state of the war, primarily coming from the BBC

[3] *Vericelli Ingranaggi Reattori Trattori Autogru which translates to Vericelli Gears Reactors Cranes and Tractors*

[4] *Cellini later found out that cleaning the Turkish toilets was the initiation for all new employees at the company. Everyone was expected to accept and undertake the worst job in the company if they were to progress to a better position. Anyone who baulked at the task or failed to do a satisfactory job would find himself back on the street looking for work. Cellini passed with flying colours and was never asked to clean the toilets again.*

in England.[5] Though the announcers speak in perfect Italian, the BBC broadcasts are naturally slanted towards the Allied side of the story, which serves to reinforce Cellini's beliefs that Italy cannot win the war. Remembering his father's words about Italian victory only being possible if the fighting is over in six months, Cellini becomes convinced that ultimate defeat is only a matter of time. Of course he has no idea – no one does at this stage – that in another year the United States will enter the war. He fears more than ever for his brother Nicola's life.

Nicola visits his father and brother in Milan when on leave from the navy, and when he does, the siblings sleep in the kitchen of the small apartment, sharing the table as a makeshift bunk bed, with Nicola on top and the younger brother underneath between its legs. It is hard and uncomfortable, but they lie awake talking into the early hours until falling asleep from sheer exhaustion. They also fight a great deal, as brothers do, and though they hit hard and make each other bleed, the bond of love between the two is never in question.[6]

Their conversation often turns to the war, and to Nicola's job as a stoker in the engine room of a warship. He describes the sound of the guns and how the ship shakes and shudders every time they are fired. He makes it sound exciting, but Cellini is not impressed. He fears for his brother's safety in a war he is convinced Italy cannot win.

On his next leave, Nicola returns home to Bari while his ship is docked at Taranto. Vito, who has travelled to Bari with his father to spend time with his brother and the rest of the family, welcomes the opportunity to chat with his brother. Believing that Italy cannot win the war, the younger Cellini naïvely hints that Nicola should seriously consider deserting the navy.

[5] *The BBC Empire Service changed its name to the BBC Overseas Service in November 1939, and by 1941 its programming staff had increased from around 100 people to almost 1,500. They not only brought listeners up to date on the state of the war in multiple languages (from the Allied perspective, of course!), but also broadcast coded messages to members of resistance groups throughout occupied Europe.*

[6] *Young Vito never forgot the time he saw his brother take on – and beat – four bullies several years earlier in Bari, when he was much younger. The four thugs had decided to hassle Vito, who was on his way to watch a movie with one of his cousins. Who should come around the corner but Nicola, who asked the four bullies – all of whom were bigger than he – what they thought they were doing. They told him to mind his own business and tried to shrug him off, but he took all of them on, more or less at the same time. Even though one of them pulled a knife, Nicola used only his fists and left them in a bloody heap on the street.*

"Come to Milan with us," he says. "No one will ever know – and once your ship sails they will not miss you."

His plea falls on deaf ears. Nicola has no intention of deserting.

Before he leaves Bari, Nicola tells his grandmother, with whom he is very close, that he doesn't think he will ever see her again.

*****

CELLINI SERVES his apprenticeship with VIRTA and learns a great deal, but the compensation is poor and father and son are finding it increasingly difficult to make ends meet, even living frugally in the cramped apartment. There are days when it is so cold, his hands stick to the metal tools. He begins to look around for something better and is offered a position at Magneti Marelli. From Marelli, Cellini moves on to work at the Breda plant, where he is involved with building gun turrets for Italian bomber aircraft. Here he operates a powerful belt-driven lathe, for which the heavy leather drive belts require regular maintenance and replacing periodically. His father – who has begun to establish his reputation in the shoe repair business once again, now that they are settled in Milan, is constantly in need of a good source of leather. Young Cellini obliges by bringing home the old, used belts for Francesco, but as time goes by a few of the brand new belts start to disappear from the supply store as well. Though Cellini is never caught, he decides it would be in his best interests to move on and finds employment with the automotive firm Isotta Fraschini. His father is not at all pleased at losing his source of materials, but the extra income from Vito's new job more than appeases him. However, before too long, young Cellini is on the move again, this time to Magnaghi, one of the most important companies in Italy, and vital to the war effort. Headquartered in Naples, Magnaghi has already perfected the use of hydraulics in landing gear for aircraft. Cellini will be making precision parts for the undercarriage retraction mechanism as well as bomb cradles and chassis for torpedoes.

Cellini tries not to think of it as working for the fascist regime. Instead he concentrates on the fact that the increase in pay means the family can move into a bigger apartment, where he will be able to enjoy the luxury of having a bed to himself.

The apartment building on Viale Monza where the Cellini family lived when they first moved to Milan in 1937.

Vito Cellini surprises his old friend Giancarla Vigano while visiting Milan in November 2015.

10. Death of Nicola

It's a cold, clear November night in the Strait of Messina, between the eastern tip of Sicily and the western tip of Calabria in southern Italy – the toe of Italy's boot. Richard Cayley, captain of HMS *Utmost*, a Royal Navy submarine patrolling for Italian ships, has received word that the Italian fleet is on the move. HMS *Utmost* remains silently on the surface, even after its batteries have completed charging in the night air, its crew watching and listening for any signs of activity.

As part of *Operation Crusader*, launched on 18th November 1941 and intended to relieve Tobruk and capture advanced airfields, Royal Navy submarines have been deployed to stalk the Italian fleet. Orders are to intercept and engage any Italian ships attempting to move through the Strait of Messina.

Just after midnight on November 19th, the vibration of propellers in the water is picked up on the submarine's ASDIC,[1] faintly at first, some five miles distant. Shortly afterwards, visual contact is made and the ships are identified as three destroyers and three heavy cruisers of the Italian Navy. Captain Cayley gives the order to fire a salvo of four torpedoes. The first torpedo strikes the trailing vessel – one of the heavy cruisers – amidships, causing a huge explosion and sending flames high into the night sky. It is a direct hit on the engine room of *Trieste*, which seriously damages the ship but is not enough to sink her.[2]

There is pandemonium on board the Italian heavy cruiser, and many casualties, but it will be some time before the full extent of the damage and body count is known. By sunrise, the fires on the *Trieste* are either out or under

1. *ASDIC was a British Admiralty code term for early Sonar.*

2. *Trieste would remain out of action until mid-1942, when she re-joined the fleet. On 10 April, 1943, she sank after being hit by bombs dropped by USAAF B-24s while in port at La Maddalena, Sardinia. After the war, she was salvaged and sold to Spain.*

control. Though badly damaged, the ship remains afloat and begins to make its way to the Port of Messina in Sicily. On board the crew is still struggling to count its dead and wounded.

Nicola Cellini is unaccounted for.

*****

Back in Milan, news from the front is sparse at best and the family is unaware that anything is wrong until one day Cellini is stopped in the street by a neighbour.

"I heard about your brother," he says.

"What?" Cellini replies, as ever expecting a fight.

"You didn't know? He's missing. Missing in action. The mailman just told me. He's got the telegram and he's delivering it to your house."

Vito is struck dumb. His jaw drops and he feels sick.

"Are you sure? Why would the mailman tell you? You're making it up."

He clenches both fists and looks for all the world as though he is about to throw a punch, but the neighbour puts his hands up, palms towards Cellini and says, "Hey, I'm really sorry – I didn't mean to start anything. I mean, I thought you'd know already. I guess you haven't been home? I'm really sorry. I really am, so sorry."

Cellini stares at the ground and shuffles away, his mind in turmoil. Just for a split second it crosses his mind that maybe, just maybe, Nicola has listened to him and deserted. Just as quickly, he dismisses the thought. He knows full well his brother wouldn't do that.

His mind racing, he walks through the town. He thinks about his father and what his reaction will be. He finds himself on *Viale Monza* and staring up at a sign that says *The Merry Widow.* It's one of his favourite movies.

He walks up the cinema steps and goes inside, straight past the ticket booth. He doesn't buy a ticket. Never does, but this time it's not because he's trying to get in without paying. His mind is elsewhere and he doesn't hear the usher ask for his ticket. He walks through the double doors and into the already dark auditorium. He hears Maurice Chevalier singing about Maxim's, so he knows it's still the first act. He slumps into a chair near the back of the half empty theatre and tries to concentrate on the film, but all he can think about is his brother.

At the end of the second act there is an intermission and a newsreel. The war is going well, Italy is winning, beating back the British all over North Africa. Benito Mussolini, over 3 metres tall on the silver screen struts up and down smiling and waving and posturing at the crowds. Now a close up of his classic Roman profile cleverly cut with a close-up of smiling children. Then the screen dissolves into an image of goose-stepping troops. Battleships firing their guns. Fighter aircraft landing and smiling pilots climbing out, gesturing at the camera how many kills they have so far today.

Cellini doesn't remember leaving the cinema but finds himself back on the street and walking towards his home. He pushes open the door and sees his father hunched in a chair at the kitchen table, a piece of cream-coloured paper in his hand.

Francesco Cellini looks up and stares. Not at his younger son but straight through him, as if he doesn't exist. Vito doesn't know how to react. His relationship with his father has never been one where they would embrace. He can see his father's pain, but he doesn't know how to deal with it or what to say.

Within one month, Francesco Cellini's hair will turn snow white from the shock of losing his oldest son.

The Cellini family gathers in Bari to mourn the death of Nicola.[3] It is a sad occasion, but in true Italian style becomes a celebration of Nicola's life and his family. Cellini will get drunk for the very first time in his life playing *Patrone e Sotto Patrene*, a *Barese* drinking game, with his uncles. Drinking with the elders of the family becomes a right of passage as he assumes the mantle of oldest son, but if he is supposed to feel more grown up, it doesn't work. All he feels is a sore head the next day!

*****

CELLINI RETURNS to Milan and goes back to work in the Magnaghi factory. His employers and his workmates are sympathetic, but there is a war on, and almost everyone has by now been touched by loss of a family member. It is commonplace for sons and younger brothers of fallen soldiers to feel anger at their enemies. It is a natural instinct to want to get back at them in any and every way possible, and recruiting offices in every country are full

3. *Some time after Cellini returned to Bari from Yugoslavia, he met a naval officer who had been in Messina at the time the badly damaged Trieste had docked. The officer was able to fill in the details of Nicola's death for Cellini. The engine room of the Trieste, in which Nicola was busy working at the time, had taken a direct hit from one of HMS Utmost's torpedoes, totally destroying that section of the ship and rendering it inaccessible to rescue crews. Nicola's remains were not discovered until workers were finally able to enter the mangled engine room while it was undergoing repairs. His remains were retrieved and transferred for burial at the cemetery close to the naval base at La Spezia. His watch, still on his wrist, was returned to the family along with his other possessions. In 1946, Nicola's remains were reinterred at the newly built Second World War Military Cemetery in Bari.*

of young men and boys seeking vengeance over the loss of older siblings.

Not so for Vito Cellini.

He has always felt that the war was a waste of time. He despises the fascist regime and its hateful leaders. Now he has more reason than ever to detest them; they have taken his only brother, who he loved and worshipped and had begged not to go to war.

His work consumes him as always, but his thoughts are still with Nicola, and his actions are almost mechanical as he continues to grind out precision parts for bomb cradles and torpedo chassis for the aircraft of the *Regia Aeronautica*. It disturbs him that his talent is being employed by the fascist regime, but he counts his blessings that as the sole provider of his family, as well as serving in an occupation vital to the war effort, at least he is exempt from being drafted into the military. That would be something he could not tolerate.

To keep busy and help pass the long nights, he volunteers as a fireman and firewatcher at the factory and takes as many shifts as he can. During air raids, he takes a position on the roof of the factory and watches for fires started by small incendiary bombs dropped by the Royal Air Force on the building. Mostly, these small incendiary bombs land in ones and twos and he is able to extinguish them with a bucket of sand. Any serious fires are to be reported immediately, but in most cases he is able to tackle the small fires on his own. Often, while patrolling on the roof at night during a raid he will hear the tinkling sound of spent cartridge shells – from the gunners in the bombers and the night fighters trying to shoot them down – bouncing on the roof around him.

Though the factories in Milan are important to Italy's war effort, it is the heavily industrial centre in Turin that takes the brunt of the night bombing attacks, and standing on the roof of the Magnaghi building, Cellini can see the fires blazing in Turin, almost 90 miles away.

Besides the excitement of the job, being a volunteer fireman at the factory has another perk; every morning he is given a breakfast of meat and a bottle of wine that he gratefully accepts and enjoys.

Throughout his entire life, Cellini has considered himself an American. Despite having lived in the United States for less than four years and retaining almost no memories of his early childhood in Brooklyn, he never wavers in his loyalty to America, and he never forgets the land of his birth.

He never lets anyone else forget it either.

A born fighter, Cellini is never afraid to raise his fists to anyone who suggests that he is anything other than American. And anyone who disparages America is in for a thrashing!

Studio portrait of Nicola Cellini, pipe in hand, proudly wearing his navy uniform.

Nicola's final resting place at the Second World War Military Cemetery in Bari.

Vito Cellini, all in black, in mourning for his brother, comforted by a family friend.

11. Bicycles, Rabbits and Ducks

SPRING ARRIVES IN Milan and brings milder weather, so Cellini's stepmother Ceciglia decides she will make the journey north to re-join her husband. It is a brave decision because Milan, like all major industrial centres in Europe, has become a target for night-time Royal Air Force bombing raids – but she decides that her place – and her children's place – is with her husband.[1]

Since young Cellini has changed jobs, his pay has increased, and with the extra money he brings in by moonlighting on the black market, Francesco and his son are able to afford better accommodation. A larger apartment in the same building on *Viale Monza* has recently become available and with the help of Giancarla they are able to secure it. The new home will be just perfect for the Cellini family, and Ceciglia arrives from Bari with Angelo, Benita, Antoinetta and the young baby Italia.

The rent is considerably more than they are used to paying, and young Cellini works extra shifts to help make ends meet. He also steps up his black market activities with his friend Negretti.

Negretti has made connections with several farmers just outside of the city. Because of the war, all food is rationed and requires government coupons to obtain legally. Meat is particularly in short supply, but there are plenty of customers for anyone with the guile and fortitude to circumvent the system and evade the *Guardia di Finanza.*[2]

1. *The three cities of Italy's "industrial triangle" – Milan, Turin and Genoa – were subject to area or "carpet" bombing from autumn 1942 until August 1943, with particularly heavy attacks on Milan in mid-February.*

2. *The Guardia di Finanza is a uniformed branch of the Italian government with a military structure. Originally established to combat smuggling, its powers eventually extended to the collection of all taxes and duties (which today also includes retail sales taxes). During the war, the Guardia di Finanza's was responsible for tackling the black market and detaining those responsible.*

Cellini owns a bicycle, and is therefore a welcome addition to Negretti's black market gang, because transportation of the goods is vital to his operation. The boys cycle to neighbouring farms, sometimes as far away as *Lago Como* (Lake Como), where they purchase meat from the farmer, usually horse meat illicitly held back from the authorities, and return to the city where they can make a substantial profit – keeping some for themselves, of course.

In order to avoid getting caught by the *Guardia di Finanza*, who routinely stop travellers to check them for contraband, the boys strap the layers of meat around their bodies, under their clothing. Once sold, the profit is divided up and the principal set aside to reinvest in more meat on the next trip.

The *Guardia di Finanza* do not catch on to the boys' black market activities, but Cellini is almost put out of business when he returns to collect his bicycle one day and finds it has been stolen. Furious, because he and Negretti are about to embark on a lucrative meat buying trip, he does the obvious thing: steals someone else's bicycle and heads over to rendezvous with the gang at their meeting place, a small café in Gorla.

As they are standing outside the café waiting to set off, Negretti sees an older teenaged boy riding along the street on a bicycle and pushing another bicycle alongside. He points and tells Cellini to look around.

"Hey, Tutuc," he says, "That looks like your bicycle!"

"That *is* my bicycle!" Cellini replies. "I'm going to kill that bastard!" He turns and hurls himself at the cyclist, bringing him crashing to the ground and pinning him on top of the two bicycles, their front wheels still turning slowly.

With both fists flailing and a stream of abuse, Cellini turns the perpetrator's face into a bloody pulp. The unfortunate thief is still lying on the ground, screaming, his hands trying desperately to shield his face from any more blows, as Cellini pushes himself up off the ground and begins kicking at him. Suddenly Cellini feels his arms being pulled back and he is dragged away. The thief is lying down, spread across both bicycles like a scene from a mediaeval torture chamber, quivering and moaning and clutching his face. Cellini is being held firmly by an officer of the *Carabinieri,* who is telling him to calm down.

"But that piece of shit stole my bicycle." Cellini is still seething.

"I want to press charges on him for theft."

The *Carabinieri* officer laughs. "You want to press charges? You have to be joking. Listen kid. You've got your bicycle back – consider yourself lucky he doesn't press charges on you for assault! I think he's learned his lesson and it will be a long time before he steals anyone's bicycle again. Now go home and count your blessings!"

Negretti grabs Cellini by the arm and leads him away. One of the others rescues Cellini's bicycle from the heap.

"Now what are you going to do? You've got your own bicycle back and this one that you stole!"

Cellini suddenly sees the funny side.

"Let's sell it. Whatever we get will cover the cost of my troubles."

*****

Occasionally Cellini goes on freelance foraging expeditions, contributing extras to the dinner table by poaching from neighbouring fields, often encroaching on private land and stealing from local businesses. It is not something he is proud of, but feels it is necessary to supplement the family food supply in order to survive.

Things are generally tough all over, and much of Milan's population is doing what they can to supplement their food supplies by raising animals and poultry or growing vegetables. Cellini is already working as many shifts as he can to support his family. He spends much of his free time transporting and selling meat on the black market for extra cash, and continues to volunteer as a firewatcher at night, mostly for the free breakfast – so there is little enough time for him to take on animal husbandry. Besides, stealing is so much easier. Or so he thinks.

A nearby neighbour is raising rabbits, both for his own consumption and to sell to local butchers in order to make a little extra money, and Cellini thinks he wouldn't miss one or two of the creatures.

The bombing has brought curfew to the city, and getting caught outside after dark leads to certain arrest and carries serious penalties. Buildings are locked up at night to prevent anyone leaving, but Cellini is experienced at scaling walls and dodging authority. He decides he can get to the rabbit enclosure by climbing out of his window onto the fire escape, edging his way along the wall and jumping into the adjacent premises. Sneaking out after curfew one night, he makes his way along the top of the wall, lowers himself to the ground and crawls over to the wire enclosure where the rabbits are kept. He is quiet and stealthy. Grabbing first one, then another of the fattest rabbits by the ears, he hurries away.

Now for the tricky bit: he must scale the wall to get back – and for that he will need to use both hands. Having neglected to bring any kind of sack or bag with him, he has to think fast. He clenches the rabbits by the ears between his teeth, one on each side of his mouth, and quickly begins his climb.

Until this moment, he had never realised how much rabbits could wriggle and squeal. He feels sure they will give him away, but right at this moment the fear of losing his supper outweighs the fear of getting caught. Keeping the rabbit ears firmly between his teeth and wrapping one arm around both of them, he works his way back along the wall and hoists himself back into his own apartment. A quick look around. No police? No *Carabinieri*? Not a soul in sight. He breathes a sigh of relief and almost drops the rabbits. Taking one in each hand by the ears, he presents them to Ceciglia.

She is both delighted and disconcerted.

"I don't want to know where you got these from," she says, frowning, then follows that immediately by adding, "Where in the world did you get these from?"

Cellini responds with nothing more than a wide grin.

"Never mind, I really don't want to know."

Francesco Cellini slaughters the rabbits, careful not to waste one drop of blood. They will enjoy the blood, fried for breakfast the following morning. Ceciglia also saves the pelts and begins preparing a stew. Cellini is eager to taste the rabbit, but his stepmother explains that it must cook slowly and that they will eat it the following night at dinner.

Next day, as they are finishing up the meal, Francesco Cellini turns to his son and says, "You need to take the bones back to wherever you got these rabbits and scatter them on the ground. That way, whoever they belong to will think they were eaten by a dog or some kind of wild animal."

Cellini stares at his father in utter disbelief.

"If you think I'm going back there..."

Francesco and Ceciglia look at each other and laugh, but young Cellini takes the instruction seriously, returning the rabbit bones to the neighbouring yard. He finds the task considerably easier with his trouser pockets full of bones than carrying the live, wriggling rabbits in his teeth.

He reports proudly back to his father that he has completed his mission. Francesco just laughs again.

"It was a joke. Why am I cursed with such a strange boy for a son? Do you think the owner won't notice that the bones have been cooked? Would he think some wolf had come down from the mountains, cooked his rabbits before eating them and then left the bones behind?"

Cellini could never tell whether his father was joking or serious. He is disappointed that his efforts in securing the rabbits do not even merit a "thank you", but perhaps his obvious enjoyment of the meal is supposed to suffice.

Cellini also supplements the family dinner table with vegetables from an allotment in the nearby suburb of Gorla. Half swimming and half wading across the nearby *Naviglio Martesana* (Martesana Canal), he carries a small spade, but neglects to take a sack – just as he had with the rabbits – and doesn't realise it until he has dug up several kilos of potatoes. Ever the inventive genius, he removes his wet trousers and ties the bottom of each leg into a knot. Filling the trouser legs with potatoes, he hoists them around his neck and over his shoulders then makes his way back across the canal. Walking home in his sopping wet underwear, he is fortunate once again to attract nothing more than a few strange looks from the neighbours.

*****

FOLLOWING THE DEATH of Nicola, Francesco Cellini desperately wants another son, and he is both proud and happy when Ceciglia announces that she is pregnant once again. Convinced it will be another boy, he is crushed when she gives birth to a beautiful baby girl. They name the child Nicoletta, in memory of Nicola, but Francesco Cellini is distraught. He wanted a son and is unable to conceal his disappointment. Overcome with grief for his dead son and self-pity over having a baby girl, he packs up his belongings and returns to Bari, leaving his wife and family to fend for themselves in Milan.

Putting food on the table continues to be a constant worry for Cellini, but he is grateful to have a good job, and resourceful enough to be able to supplement the food supply with a few ill-gotten gains.

One enterprising neighbour, a few doors away, has acquired several ducklings that he is planning to fatten up so he can offer them to Milan's more well-to-do society. Cellini decides that a duck would make a pleasant change from their regular daily diet. It is a simple matter to find out where the ducks are located from the noise they make, and he starts looking in on the birds. After a couple of weeks he decides the ducks look fat enough to make a good dinner. The only problem is that every time he approaches the birds, they make so much noise he is afraid he would never be able to get away with actually stealing one.

He asks Negretti, the leader of the black market gang, for advice.

"When I get near the ducks, they make as much noise as a dog," Cellini says. "How can I steal one and get it out of there without bringing the owner and the entire *Carabinieri* down on me?"

Negretti laughs. "That's easy! Cellini you just aren't a country boy at all, are you?" He continues, "Take a pocketful of corn with you and throw the corn on the ground, that will keep all the ducks occupied." He pauses, waiting for Cellini to comment, but he is listening intently.

"Grab the one you want by taking hold of the bird by its neck with both hands, then pull on the head and twist at the same time to break its neck." He demonstrates by putting his clenched hands together, one over the other, and twisting, while making the sickly sound of bones crunching out of the corner of his mouth. He grins at Cellini. "It's quick and painless, so the animal won't squawk at all. Then you shove it in a sack, throw it over your shoulder and walk home casually."

Armed with this new-found knowledge as well as a pocketful of dry corn, but still painfully aware of the near disaster when he had stolen two rabbits just a few weeks earlier, Cellini sets off just as the sun begins to go down to snag a duck so he can surprise his stepmother with dinner. He scales the wall then quickly scatters corn on the ground to quieten down the excitable birds before climbing into the enclosure. All goes well at first. He picks out a nice plump bird and lays down a trail of corn to lead it away from the others. Once separated from the pack, Cellini grabs the duck firmly by the neck, as instructed, twists and pulls.

In his youthful exuberance, Cellini pulls too hard and the head detaches itself completely from the body. The duck, mercifully, feels no pain, as blood literally gushes from the open neck all over Cellini's shirt, soaking him. He discards the head and quickly shoves the decapitated bird into his sack, slings it over his shoulder and begins his return journey. Slithering up and over the wall, he leaves a trail of smeared blood on the bricks as he goes.

When he walks in through the door to his own apartment, Ceciglia lets out an almighty scream and rushes over to him.

"*Mama mia!* What happened?" she screams, pulling him to a chair and tearing open his shirt, the blood-stained sack falling to the floor.

"Sit down, let me see. Did you get shot? Stabbed? Does it hurt? How did this happen?"

Cellini is unable to get a word in edgeways but when he finally lifts up his face to look at his stepmother and she sees his trademark ear-to-ear, gap-toothed grin, a different picture starts to form in her mind. She looks at him quizzically.

"What?" She says.

"Mama, look what I've brought you for dinner!" He says, reaching the duck out of the sack.

She frowns, slaps his head in mock disapproval, then takes the duck from him and tells him to go and clean himself up.

Needless to say, the Cellini's eat well that night, and for two more days, on the proceeds of his adventure.

*****

One day Cellini is called into the office by the head of the Magnaghi company.

Whenever he gets called into the office, it's either because he's been fighting or because the engineers need him to produce a new piece of equipment. He knows he hasn't been in any fights lately, so he assumes there is a mechanical problem, which he needs to solve.

Instead, he is handed an envelope, covered in postmarks, which looks like it has been halfway around the world and back. It has already been opened.

"What's this?" Cellini asks.

"Open it."

He starts to open it but before he can pull out the papers inside, the head of the company blurts out, "It's your papers. You've been drafted."

"What?"

"You've been called up into the Army. Congratulations."

"But that's impossible! I'm the sole provider for my family. My father is a disabled veteran of the first war – and my brother just got killed. And what about my job? You told me yourself that what I am doing here is essential war work and that they can't draft me? How can this happen?"

Cellini could go on for hours when he was riled up, as his employer knows only too well.

"I'm not even Italian! I was born in America. I'm an American citizen!"

"Vito, it's no good arguing your case with me. You'll have to take it up with the draft board in Bari. You're to report there straight away."

"Why straight away?"

"Because your father never registered you as a resident in Milan so they sent the paperwork to your home address in Bari. It's taken so long to get here that you're already overdue for your enlistment."

"How did they find me here?" Cellini asks.

"Vito, we have to comply with the law. We are a government contractor. We have to give a list of all employees to the authorities so they can keep track of everyone. When they asked who this Vito Cellini is and why you aren't registered as a Milan resident we had to tell them what we know. These call up papers were sent to you in Bari because that's the last address they have on file. The government had no way of knowing that you are working here in Milan."

"Until you told them!"

Cellini's superior ignores the jibe.

"You need to go to Bari as soon as possible. Take the train first thing tomorrow morning."

"What if I won't do it?"

"Come on Vito, you have no choice. If you refuse to go I'd have no choice but to call the *Carabinieri* and report you. Don't make me do that."

"Bastard," Cellini retorts. "You'd do it, too."

Part II

World War Two.
Soldier, Partisan and Secret Agent

12. Cellini Goes to War

ON THE TRAIN to Bari, Cellini has plenty of time to think about a strategy for dealing with the fascists and getting out of joining the military.

He walks from Bari station to the Army depot to find it absolutely packed with young men reporting for duty, and many more already in uniform and waiting to ship out. He finds a senior NCO and asks where he should report to explain that there has been a mistake with his papers and that he should not have been called up for active service. He tries to explain that he is the sole provider for his family and the NCO is very understanding and directs him towards a long queue of new draftees. He is told to wait in the line, and that once he gets his turn, he'll be able to explain to the officer in charge and that everything would be fine. He would probably be on the next train home.

After waiting about 90 minutes in the slow-moving line of people, Cellini is beckoned to a table stacked with layers of paperwork, behind which is seated a middle-aged, bespectacled sergeant.

"Name," says the sergeant, in a shrill, almost falsetto voice.

"Cellini. Vito Cellini, but there seems to be some mistake —"

"Cellini, Cellini, Cellini…. hmmmm" says the falsetto voice to itself, its owner burrowing behind the paperwork. "Ah yes, here we are."

Papers part and an unhappy face peers at Cellini from between two stacks.

"You are, let me see, one, two, three, four… seven days late for your appointment Mr. Cellini, is there a good reason for that?

"I was in Milan, where I live and work doing vital war work for Magnaghi producing chassis for torpedoes."

"Not according to our records Mr. Cellini. It says here that you are a resident of Bari and that you were notified last week of your call to serve the Kingdom of Italy."

"I can't help it if your records are wrong! I live and work in Milan.

What's more, I'm the sole provider for my family since my brother was killed in 1941 and my father is a disabled veteran!"

He wants to scream, "I'm not even Italian – I'm an American citizen!" but since Italy has been at war with the United States since December 1941, that doesn't seem like a really good idea right at this moment. In any case, he can't prove it. His birth certificate, if his father has even bothered to keep it, will be locked up in a safe in Milan. And he has serious doubts as to whether his father will own up to having a son who is an enemy of his beloved *il Duce.*

His arguments are dismissed with a flick of the hand. It is not only his duty to serve but also an honour and a privilege. Surely his family understands that? He will receive a soldier's pay, a portion of which the paymaster can arrange to send back to his family, so they need not be in any way troubled or inconvenienced. And there are so many wonderful social programmes under *il Duce's* leadership. There are no poor people in Italy!

Cellini need have no worries for his family. They will be well provided for, and proud of his service.

Thus, having travelled 900 kilometres from Milan to Bari (a train journey lasting almost fifteen hours) hopeful of avoiding the draft, Vito Cellini is inducted into the Italian army and instructed to join the 9th *Bersaglieri.*[1]

He is ordered to report for training the following day at the military base in Cremona, just 100 kilometres south-east of Milan.

*****

WITH NO TIME to visit family and friends in Bari, private soldier Cellini, serial number 28230, hurries back to the station in time to board the train for Cremona; a 12- to 13-hour journey back in the direction he has just come from!

He arrives at the military base tired, disgruntled and dishevelled and is ordered to join a perfunctory parade of all the new recruits who, like him, are still wearing their civilian clothes. They are lectured on the great glory that lies ahead for them and for Italy before being dismissed and ushered into the

[1]. *The Bersaglieri (Marksmen) is an elite corps, created in 1836 to serve the King of Sardinia's army, which would later evolve into the Royal Italian Army. Its soldiers wear a distinctive wide-brimmed hat decorated with black capercaillie (wood grouse) feathers. These days the feathered hats are worn only for dress parades, but the feather insignia is imprinted on their combat helmets. Another distinctive trait is the fast jogging pace Bersaglieri use while on parade, instead of marching. Francesco Cellini used to tell his son derogatory stories about the Bersaglieri, no doubt embellished and spread by rival units to mock this elite branch of the Italian army. Mussolini had served with the 11th Bersaglieri in the Great War.*

quartermaster's stores to be issued uniforms.

A cheerfully sarcastic sergeant looks Cellini up and down, guesses his size and hands him a coarse woollen jacket and trousers.

"This is the best suit you will ever own," he says.

Cellini cannot resist a caustic reply.

"Thank you," he says, "but I prefer my own."

For his insolence and insubordination, he is summarily confined to the base for fifteen days. With no way to contact his family to let them know what is going on, nor his girlfriend, Isabella, who expects him back in a couple of days, his anger and disdain towards the fascist government smoulders.

The uniform is ill-fitting and uncomfortable to wear. Worst of all is the footwear. The boots are too big and there are no socks. Instead of socks, Italian soldiers are issued a square of flannel material known as a footwrap for each foot.[2] About the same size as a man's handkerchief, a footwrap is placed diagonally under each foot and folded in from the corners before inserting the foot into the boot. Unless folded perfectly, which is difficult to do in combat situations, they cause terrible blisters. But the worst feature of the footwrap is the dreadful smell that accumulates after a few days. Even if the poor soldier is able to wash and dry the footwrap, which he rarely can, the smell is so bad it can actually betray his presence at the worst possible time.

Training is regarded as something of a joke. There is a lot of marching and physical exercise but little that is of much use in an actual combat situation. Issued with aging Carcano rifles, each recruit is given a total of just five rounds of ammunition throughout the entire training period, with strict instructions that they are to be used wisely. Yet there is no actual marksmanship training to determine what "used wisely" might actually mean. They spend long hours stripping, cleaning and reassembling these well-worn weapons.

Occasionally, recruits get to handle the Beretta and Breda machine guns, but never have an opportunity to fire them.

[2] *It wasn't just the Italians who used footwraps. They have been worn by soldiers of many nations throughout history, and can be traced back at least as far as the 1600s when worn by the Dutch. The Prussian Manual of Military Hygiene of 1869 stated: "Footwraps are appropriate in summer, but they must have no seams and be very carefully put on." Prior to the 20th century, socks or stockings were considered luxury items, which only officers could afford. The German Army used footwraps until the end of World War Two, and they were worn by many Eastern European armies until well into the 21st century. In Russia, footwraps, which had first been worn around 1690, were still being issued in 2013, because they were considered a better fit with the modern boots. Because of their long association with the Russian Army, footwraps are better known by their French name of "chaussettes russes" (Russian stockings).*

They are instructed in the use of the *Bomba a Mano* and given dummy practice grenades. On rare occasions, live grenades are issued for practice, but the Italian Modello 35 is extremely unreliable, and of the two with which Cellini is issued at different times, neither one detonates.[3]

*****

WHILE CONFINED to camp, Cellini has a lot of time to think and stew over his circumstances. The more he thinks about his situation and how unfairly fate has treated him, the more sullen and irritable he becomes.

In the first place, he is the sole breadwinner for the family. His older brother is dead and his younger brother, Angelo, is still in school and too young to work or join the military. His father fought in the first World War and lost his leg. He has a part-time job as custodian of a building but is unable to work long hours or contribute to the war effort. But the biggest chip on young Cellini's shoulder is the fact that he is an American citizen. As of December 1941, America is Italy's enemy so why would it even want him in its Army? True, without any paperwork (his father neglected to register them when they moved back to Bari from New York), that would be difficult to prove.[4]

He is disgusted by the attitude of his fellow recruits, and finds starting arguments a good way to pass the time. Never shy when it comes to expressing himself, Cellini willingly resorts to fists whenever he feels the need to emphasize a point.

Inevitably, his proclivity for fighting gets him thrown into the base prison, though not the private cell he was hoping for. He gets along well with one of his cell mates, a soldier who has returned from the front and

[3] *There were three variants of hand grenade "Bomba a Mano" produced in Italy during World War Two, all with the same designation, Modello 35. Makers were OTO, SRCM (Societe Romano) and Breda. They differed slightly in size and charge, but all used TNT and relied on impact for detonation after the safety pin was pulled. When thrown, a safety bar or cover was designed to fly off in mid-air, however this mechanism frequently failed. Even if the safety cover did come away, the grenade still had to land perfectly on its "striker" in order to detonate. If it didn't land exactly right, it would not explode. Consequently, many of these devices were found lying around unexploded and formed deadly booby traps. The British Army dubbed the grenades "Red Devils" because of their bright paint scheme and unreliability. Source: WWII-Inert-ord.net*

[4] *Had Cellini been able to prove his American citizenship, he might have been interred as a prisoner of war or sent to one of the camps. 72 years later, Italian records still list his birth date, incorrectly, as June 16th (instead of August 14th), although his place of birth has been corrected to Brooklyn, New York.*

is recovering from a bullet wound in his shoulder. The other cell mate is a Sicilian who speaks ill of his wife and brags constantly, in vivid detail, about his extramarital sex life. Cellini does not appreciate this loudmouth and after listening to one story too many about his exploits with young girls, he sets about the Sicilian and beats him severely. Battered, bloodied and bruised, the Sicilian is treated in the infirmary and then relocated to a different cell.

*****

WITH NO IDEA how long he is going to be locked up, especially following this latest altercation with his cell mate, Cellini begins to go stir crazy. He misses his Isabella. He misses his friends.

Not long after being incarcerated, he notices two things about the prison: firstly, that the washhouse and toilet facilities are located alongside an outside wall and that there is a gap between the top of the wall and the roof. He also can't help but notice that by the end of each day, the guards are either too tired or too lazy to walk around the cells and actually do a proper headcount.

He thinks that by hiding in the washhouse at the end of the day and waiting for the right opportunity, it ought to be possible to scale the wall and jump clear.

He decides there and then he is going to leave the prison and visit Milan that night, to see Isabella. He plans to be back by morning, before he is missed.

Once he has made up his mind to do something, there is no stopping Vito Cellini. He makes his way to the washhouse, mingling with a group of other prisoners so as not to attract attention to himself. Once inside he moves to a quiet corner away from the others and looks for a place to hide. Although there are no convenient doors or cupboards to slip inside, one end of the washhouse is in shadow and he makes his way down there, keeping close to the wall to keep a low profile.

He waits for everyone else to leave and waits for the guards to come in one more time. To his surprise, they don't enter the building, and the only sound he hears is the metallic clang of the key turning in the metal door. He's locked in!

After a few minutes, the lights go out and for a while he is left in almost complete darkness, except for the glare of the perimeter lights of the camp shining in through the gap between the wall and the roof. Slowly his vision returns, and in the half light he finds his way to the toilet nearest to the corner and climbs up on the seat. Feeling for the pipe on the wall, he gives it a tug to see how secure it is. It doesn't feel great, and he won't trust it with his full weight, but it will offer some leverage. He grips the cistern for balance, then pushes against the wall with one foot while the other rests against the pipe. With both feet well up off the ground, and his body flat against the wall, his weight is evenly distributed. By straightening his knees he is able to lift his body and feel for the top of the wall, first with a fingertip, then with his whole hand. He pulls with one hand while pushing off the cistern with the other, then pushing off the pipe he swings one leg up onto the top of the wall, hoping that the pipe does not collapse and bring the cistern crashing down. It holds. With one leg over the top of the wall he pulls his body up so that he is lying along the top of the wall. He pauses to catch his breath, looks around to make sure the coast is clear, then drops to the ground on the outside. It's about four metres or so, and he could jump it easily, but he is afraid of turning an ankle or making a lot of noise, so he lowers himself by his hands and then jumps the rest of the way.

Keeping to the shadows and behind trees, he makes his way out of the camp and heads in the direction of the railway station.

He takes the train into Milan to visit his girlfriend. It is the first chance he has had to let her know that he is, unhappily, in the Army.

He doesn't buy a ticket and dodges the ticket collector by moving from carriage to carriage, and, when necessary, hiding in the toilet. He feels like the Tutuc of old and wishes his friends could see him now, in his ridiculous uniform; what fun they would make of him!

He had met Isabella at work and they were immediately attracted to each other. They began going out to movies and dancing but the relationship soon grows much deeper. Now he has been gone for so long with no way of contacting her, he wonders if she is still as keen on him as she used to be. He needn't have worried. Isabella's passion is stronger than ever and he finds no resistance when he leads her to the bedroom.

As they lie in each other's arms, he tries to explain to her about the trouble he is in. He hopes to be free soon, but promises that even if he isn't allowed out officially, he will find a way to visit as often as he can. She asks him about the future, but he has absolutely no idea of where he will be sent, assuming he ever gets out of the military prison.

They spend a few precious hours together before he leaves in time to catch the last train back to Cremona. As he walks out the door, he promises that he will be back very soon. She wants to know how soon.

"I'll surprise you," he says but in truth he has no idea when he will be able to get away, even though Cremona is less than two hours from Milan by train.

Cellini rarely plans ahead, relying on his mettle and his guile to get by. He dozes on the return train journey, keeping half an eye open for the ticket inspector. As the train pulls into the station at Cremona he begins to wonder about getting back into the camp, and into his prison cell, without being noticed.

It is still dark and there are few people about. He is able to sneak into the camp and make his way back to the prison. He scales the stone wall back into the washhouse, lies down in the shadows against the wall where he lay ready to make his escape the night before, and waits for the washhouse to be unlocked and the inmates to start arriving. As they leave, he joins the line and follows them to breakfast. He grabs a tray of food, still thinking it might be his last good meal, and then makes his way back to his cell.

Elated that he has apparently got completely away with his temporary escape, he wonders why he even bothered coming back, but considers it was probably the wise choice.

The jail cell will be his home for just one more week before he is told he can return to his barracks. He is given a very stern warning to keep himself out of trouble and out of fights. Next time the base commander may not be quite so magnanimous.

He resumes his routine of marching, physical exercise and more marching, even though it is enough to drive him half insane. He lives for the weapons training. Stripping and reassembling the Carcano and the Beretta and even the hateful Breda machine gun is better than the endless marching, but there are so few guns available that the trainees have to take turns, and his turn only comes around every few days. Ammunition is in short supply, being needed for the front lines, so each recruit receives just two rounds – reloads with little more than a BB pellet for a projectile – with which to become accustomed to firing the Carcano rifle.

He is told they will soon begin jump training and wonders if this means he is being considered as a paratrooper. Jump training involves leaping from a platform at a height equivalent to three floors, into a disused swimming pool that has been drained and filled with a mountain of sand. Cellini aims for the slope of the sand instead of its peak, but mistimes his jump and lands face first in the sand with his mouth open, biting his tongue quite badly. There are no facilities for stitching him up and it takes several painful days to heal, but he retains his good humour.

"It serves me right," he tells everyone. "If only I would learn to keep my mouth shut!"

He decides he needs to see Isabella again.

Now more than halfway through their basic training, the recruits are allowed to leave the camp for recreation once they have completed their duties for the day. There are a few bars and clubs nearby, but Cellini has a very low regard for the kind of women who frequent them, and an even lower opinion of the soldiers who go looking for them. He considers them prostitutes and has no interest whatsoever in paying for their services either with cash, drinks or just his precious time. He will visit Milan, to fulfil his promise of surprising his girlfriend.

His day's work done, he strides out of the main gate and heads straight to the railway station. He doesn't wait long for the northbound train, jumps aboard, without a ticket, as usual, and settles down for the ride.

The journey soon passes and he hops off the train in Milan and heads straight over to Isabella's apartment. As he walks up the steps it suddenly occurs to him that she is completely unaware of his arrival. He suddenly worries that she may be out.

Or worse, what if she is entertaining another man? Surely not Isabella?

He knocks on her door and is relieved to find that she is home and quite alone. She is absolutely thrilled to see him and practically squeals with delight as she grabs him around the neck and pulls him inside.

"I told you I would surprise you!"

The evening turns into night and finally, after many hours of passion, Vito pulls himself away from the half awake Isabella and tells her he has to go.

"Go where?" she says.

"Back to Cremona. Remember?"

In the semi-darkness, he gathers together various items of his uniform that had been left scattered around the apartment and gets dressed. He tells her he will come back soon, but can't tell her exactly when, so he hopes she will always be home, just in case. Isabella smiles as he gently kisses her on the forehead and tiptoes away, closing the door behind him and pulling his collar up in the cold, crisp early morning air.

His plan is predicated on the idea that discipline seems lax these days, and that as long as he arrives back at the camp in time for his first assignment, which today is further study of the Breda sub-machine gun, he will be fine. He doesn't want to attract the attention of the guards at the main entrance to the camp, but he knows of a gap in the fence to the rear of the guardhouse, which is regularly used by other soldiers who get back to camp after hours.

So far, so good. He crouches behind the bushes and waits for the all clear before stepping out and heading back towards his barracks.

"You there. Halt!"

The voice booms out from somewhere behind him. He stops,

turns and finds himself staring into the face of a *maresciallo* who he doesn't recognize.[5]

The voice booms out again. "Are you a *Bersaglieri*?"

"Yes sir."

"You can't be a *Bersaglieri*."

"Yes sir, I am a *Bersaglieri*."

"Do *Bersaglieri* feel the cold? A draught perhaps?"

"No sir!" Cellini replies.

"Then turn down your collar and don't you EVER let me see you disgrace the *Bersaglieri* uniform again. Do you understand?"

"YES SIR!" Cellini practically screams with relief. He had forgotten he turned his collar up against the cold before he boarded the train. He pulls his collar down and stands to attention for a full minute after the *maresciallo* walks away, beads of sweat forming on his forehead in spite of the crisp morning air.

*****

Having managed to slip away from the camp unnoticed on two previous occasions, once while a prisoner in the military jail, his confidence grows and he sees no reason why he shouldn't to do it again. He decides it's time to make one more clandestine visit to Isabella in Milan. He reasons that as long as he makes it back to the camp in time to fulfil his duties, he isn't doing anything wrong.

At no time will he discuss his plan nor his unauthorized absence with anyone so there is no one who can betray his secret.

He follows the exact same course of action as before: leaving camp and heading to the station, jumping aboard the train without buying a ticket and taking evasive action against the inspector. The journey is uneventful and the passion of Isabella is well worth the risk, which Cellini considers minimal anyway.

He knows he can make it back in time, sneaking in through a gap in the fence behind the guard house and keeping a special look out for the *maresciallo*.

Until one day the return train is delayed. All he and the other passengers are able to find out is that there is some kind of blockage on the track that must be cleared before they can proceed.

Whether it's the result of an air raid during the night – the RAF is

[5] *Maresciallo – warrant officer*

beginning to pepper the industry in northern Italy – or a rare breakdown in the rail system – the train does not arrive back in Cremona until mid-morning, and when Cellini arrives back at the base he finds a larger than usual crowd of armed soldiers waiting at the entrance. The guardhouse is teeming with officers as well as military police. One of them looks up and spots him near the fence and all-hell breaks out. In less then a second, whistles are blowing, soldiers are running, dogs are barking and suddenly Cellini is surrounded, half a dozen rifles pointed straight at him.

He is escorted to the guardhouse and pushed unceremoniously into a cell. He is not sure what is going on until his old nemesis the *maresciallo* enters and tells him to stand to attention.

"Does the prisoner understand that he is under arrest for desertion?"

He tries to speak but is told to shut up except to answer "Yes" or "No".

He answers "No," and is told that it will be explained to him later.

"Does the prisoner understand the severity of the crime with which he is charged?"

Again, Cellini answers "No," and is told it will be explained to him.

"Does the prisoner understand that, in time of war, the penalty for desertion, if found guilty, is death by firing squad?"

13. Court Martial

THE JAIL CELL in which he spends the time awaiting his court martial is quite different from the one he spent his previous incarceration. He is alone this time. The cell is small, cramped and cold. The bed comprises two pieces of wood, both 50 centimetres wide, joined end to end. The base is approximately one-and-a-half metres long and tilted at an angle of five degrees. The headrest is no more than 30 centimetres long and tilted at 30 degrees. There is no bedding, not even a blanket, and no pillow. He will spend three weeks in these uncomfortable and stuffy surroundings until sent for to appear before the tribunal.

On the second day, a young junior officer visits Cellini in his cell. He informs the prisoner that he is to act as counsellor on his behalf at the court martial. The one positive piece of news the counsellor brings is that he doesn't think they will execute him.

"Most likely they'll send you to Gaeta.[1] That's mostly what happens to deserters."

"I am not a deserter!" Cellini insists.

He explains over and over again to his counsellor that he had often visited his girlfriend in Milan but that he had always returned to camp and always would. He had never deserted.

Cellini is as unimpressed with his counsellor as the counsellor is with Cellini's story. He is still fighting mad about having been drafted into what he considers a foreign army. He is mad that he has lost his job – a good job – at Magnaghi. And he is mad that no matter what the outcome

[1] *Gaeta is located on a promontory stretching towards the Gulf of Gaeta, 120 kilometres from Rome and 80 kilometres from Naples. The fortifications date back to Roman times, and have been strengthened and expanded at various times. Today Gaeta is a seaport and tourist resort. NATO maintains a naval base of operations at Gaeta. The castle has been used as a prison throughout its history, and housed many Nazi war criminals at the end of World War Two.*

of his court martial will be, he is unlikely to see Isabella again.

Over the next few days he has several meetings with his counsellor although he doesn't really see the point, because the counsellor doesn't have the answer to any of his questions. He hopes the court martial will provide the answers.

Finally, the big day arrives and he is summoned early in the morning, placed in handcuffs and escorted by two guards along a long stone passageway into a cavernous room with a large wooden desk, behind which are seated three uniformed officers wearing a lot of gold on their tunics and large, square, red hats. He is ordered to stand across the desk from them, where he is joined by his counsellor.

Any hopes of finding answers to his questions or any information about his arrest are soon crushed. This is to be an expedited trial with no time for niceties.

Cellini is asked only for his name and rank. He replies "Vito Cellini, Private," and that concludes his participation in the court martial.

His counsellor steps over to the table and confers with the officers of the tribunal but they speak very softly and Cellini is able to hear very little of their conversation.

After deliberating for a while, the counsellor takes his place alongside the accused and one of the officers stands to deliver the verdict.

"Vito Cellini. You are accused of deserting your post while undergoing training with the 9th *Bersaglieri* Regiment of the Royal Italian Army in Cremona. It is the verdict of this court martial that you are guilty as charged. The punishment for your crime has been set at sixteen years and sixty days imprisonment, to be served at Gaeta Prison."

Cellini is stunned. Sex with Isabella was good, but it wasn't *that* good.

*****

CELLINI OPENS his mouth to try and speak but his counsellor turns to him with a finger to his lips and whispers, "Don't say a word. There is more to come."

The most senior looking member of the tribunal stands and looks directly over Vito's head, rather than into his eyes, and informs him that the tribunal is willing to suggest an alternative to the sixteen years and sixty days sentence. They recognize his keen fighting spirit and exemplary record in training, in particular his knowledge and ability with small arms. Italy needs soldiers like him. If he accepts a posting to the front line, the charges will be dismissed and expunged from his record.

He has 48 hours to decide.

With that, the guards return and escort Cellini back to his cell. The court martial is over.

Still stunned at the events of the past few minutes, Cellini is joined by his counsellor. Now he has even more questions. What front line? Which unit? His fear is that he will be sent to fight against America and her Allies. As an American citizen he cannot accept the idea of taking up arms against his own countrymen, but he doesn't want to say anything out of fear that the counsellor may return to the tribunal with the suggestion that he be interned as a prisoner of war.

His counsellor advises Cellini to accept the offer.

"I'll be back in two days for your answer. If you make a decision in the meantime, let the guards know and they'll send for me." Then he adds, almost casually, "Oh, and by the way, you have a visitor."

Cellini looks towards the cell door and hears the sound of footsteps. They are the footsteps of a man with an uneven gait and they are very familiar to Cellini. He rolls his eyes and shakes his head as the door swings open on rusty hinges and his father enters.

Francesco Cellini is just about the last person Vito wants to see right now. He had been completely unsympathetic to his son's disappointment at being drafted into the Army and now thinks his court martial was probably well deserved. Notified of the outcome of the court martial, Francesco has made the trip to Cremona to implore his son to accept the option of being sent to the front line. Even though he knows it will put Vito in harm's way, and that he may lose a second son, Francesco is more concerned about the public disgrace of a conviction and prison sentence.

Cellini is already 99 percent certain that being sent to the front lines is a better option than 16-plus years in the military prison at Gaeta. Looking into his father's eyes and seeing how much shame it will bring upon him to have a son convicted of desertion by a military tribunal is enough to convince him of the remaining one percent. Though he has never respected his father's politics, and does not think highly of him as a man, he still loves his father. He agrees to the tribunal's terms for having the charges dismissed.

He is ordered to report to the Army headquarters in Fiume, and from there he will be sent to join the 4th *Bersaglieri* in Yugoslavia, where the Italian Army is taking heavy casualties.[2]

[2] *Fiume (now Rijeka, Croatia) has had a divisive history, with its governance often in dispute. Ruled by various neighbouring states at different times, it has been an independent free state on just two occasions, the latest being from 1921 until annexed by Italy in 1924. It became part of Yugoslavia in 1947.*

Relieved that he is not being asked to kill Americans, but still uncomfortable with taking up arms for a cause in which he has no belief, in an army in which he has little confidence, and for a country he doesn't consider his own, Vito Cellini has very mixed emotions and does not sleep well.

*****

CELLINI IS RELEASED into the custody of a sergeant, who is sympathetic to his situation. The sergeant will escort him to Fiume, where he will await instructions on where and when to join the 4th *Bersaglieri.* Fiume is a distribution and transition centre for soldiers.

"When do we leave?" Cellini asks.

"The day after tomorrow," the sergeant replies.

"Is there any way I can visit my family in Milan before we leave?"

The sergeant gives it some thought. He is unable to accompany Cellini because he is still technically on duty, but Vito is somehow able to talk him into letting him go alone. He reasons that since he is being sent to the front lines in Yugoslavia it is highly unlikely he will ever see his family again.

He gives his word that he will return the following day, reiterating that he is not, and never has been, a deserter. The sergeant senses a certain sincerity in Cellini's words and agrees.

"I hope I don't regret this. You will get me into terrible trouble if you go AWOL on me," he says. "I don't want to threaten you but I will hunt you down and kill you myself if you don't show up when you are supposed to."

Cellini sets off for Cremona station once again, this time with an officially issued railway pass in his uniform pocket. He is able to sleep a little on the train and arrives refreshed.

Francesco Cellini, who in the past had been so derisive of the *Bersaglieri,* beams with pride at seeing Vito wearing the uniform. It is especially gratifying, he tells his son, because Benito Mussolini himself served with the *Bersaglieri* in World War One. As in the past, Vito is confused by the changing attitude of his father and their conversation quickly becomes stilted. Vito promises Francesco that he will visit when he is next on leave, but they both know that he is speaking more out of hope than expectation. His father also knows that Vito is much more interested in seeing his girlfriend than his family. Even now he is anxious to leave, intent on stopping at Isabella's home before returning to Cremona.

He has arranged to meet the sergeant who will escort him to Fiume at the station in Milan, and he notices the relief on the sergeant's face as he walks up to him.

"You didn't think I'd come back?" Cellini says.

The sergeant gives him a wry smile.

"Most of the lowlifes in this so-called man's army wouldn't, but somehow you're different Cellini. Now let's get going. We have a long journey ahead of us."

The military camp at Fiume is a transition camp full of individual soldiers who have been on leave, have recovered from prior wounds, or are transferring to another unit and awaiting orders. Cellini is shown to his quarters, a large barrack block that he shares with several other soldiers. He is told if he wants to eat he has to work.

The work is cutting wood, and as long as he is willing to chop, it seems the supply of wood is endless. It's hard labour but Cellini enjoys it after languishing in a jail cell for the past few weeks. He is well fed, with as much macaroni and chicken as he can eat, together with a large chunk of *pane rustico*, the local crusty bread. The chicken is full of bugs, but better than the food he was given in prison and he is happy to eat it all. Along with most of his fellow soldiers, he finds the pasta and chicken satisfying enough and the bread becomes currency for trading with local civilians. Many of the soldiers use it to barter for sex with local women who are willing to prostitute themselves in order to feed their families. Such are the hardships they are suffering as a result of a war that, in spite of Mussolini's continued posturing, is not going well for the Italian people.

Cellini is disgusted with his fellow soldiers for taking advantage of these poor women. He willingly gives his bread to one of the women and wants no sexual favours in return, but she expects to perform for him and is offended by his attitude.

"You don't think I am attractive?" She says. "You don't think I can give you a good time? Just tell me what you want…" She is clearly upset. Most of the women have their "regulars" on whom they rely as providers for them and their families, even though most of the soldiers are not at the camp for very long, and this woman does not want Cellini to get away.

"No. I don't want that," he says. "Please just take the bread and feed your family."

"Perhaps you think I am too old? I have a young daughter who is very beautiful. Perhaps you would like me to bring her for you?"

Sickened by the thought, he tells the woman to take the bread and turns his back.

Not for the first time, Cellini is outraged by what he sees. Not with these poor women, but with the regime that forces them into these circumstances and with the soldiers who take advantage of their situation.

He cannot believe what is going on in Italy. Never a supporter of fascism or of *Il Duce*, now he finds himself despising the dictator and everything he stands for.

Each day he looks for the woman so he can give her his bread. He knows she is allowing others to use and abuse her body, and probably her daughter, but at least he feels that he is doing the right thing, and he senses that she appreciates his intent – which is what matters most to him. After five days of chopping wood, gorging himself on pasta and lice-infested chicken, handing out bread and refusing sexual favours from local peasant women, Cellini receives his orders to join the 4th *Bersaglieri*.[3]

Along with several dozen other recruits, he is to depart for the Port of Fiume at 0600 hours the following morning and be ready to board a boat that will take him to Yugoslavia and the front lines of the fighting.[4]

[3.] *According to Cellini, the 4th Bersaglieri was comprised largely of misfits and troublemakers from other regiments, some in circumstances similar to his own (something along the lines of "The Dirty Dozen" by E. M. Nathanson which was made into a hugely successful movie). Spared from military prison after being charged and found guilty of desertion, the court martial was expunged from his military record, a fact Cellini was unable to confirm until 2018 when the author was finally able to obtain a copy. This was probably due more to chaos within the administration of the Italian Army rather than judicial integrity or compassion on the part of his superiors, since nothing further was added to his service record after March 1943, though he is shown to have been granted "provisional unlimited leave" on July 27, 1944.*

[4.] *From Fiume, the journey to the Dalmatian Coast of Yugoslavia (known as the Governorship of Dalmatia but officially Italian territory after the Rome Treaties of 1941) would ordinarily have been quicker by road, but even though the Independent State of Croatia was under Axis control, communist-backed Partisans were active in the region, especially since many of the German occupation forces had pulled out leaving the Governorship of Dalmatia in mostly Italian hands. To avoid damaged roads and the possibility of running into an ambush, the Italians conducted a lot of their movement of troops and supplies by boat.*

MATRICOLA
N. 28230

Cellini Vito

(cognome e nome)

Residenza all'atto dell'arrolamento Bari

del Distretto di Bari (3) Via Pietro Ravenna 3 - 125

DATI E CONTRASSEGNI PERSONALI	ARRUOLAMENTO, SERVIZI, PROMOZIONI	DATA
Figlio di Francesco e fu Terrevoli Rosa di religione: cattolica nato il 16 - 6 - 1923 a N.W. York Provincia di america Statura m. 1,72 Torace m. 0,88 Capelli: colore neri forma ond. Viso oval Naso retto Mento reg Occhi cast Sopracciglia neri Fronte reg Colorito bruno Bocca reg Dentatura sana Segni particolari Arte o professione meccanico Sa se leggere si scrivere si Titoli di studio Cognizioni extra professionali Inscritto di leva nel Comune di Bari Provincia di Bari Ammogliato con il con autorizzazione Rimasto vedovo il	Soldato di leva classe 1923 Distretto Bari e lasciato in congedo illimitato provvisorio Rinviato ad altra chiamata ai sensi della lettera D) del n. 8 del manifesto di chiamata allegato alla circ. 7... [illegible] 1942 Cessa dal beneficio concessogli ad altra chiamata come da foglio n. 232348 [illegible] della Produzione Bellica [illegible] Chiamato alle armi e giunto [illegible] Reggimento Bersaglieri [illegible]	li 27 Luglio 1944 li 11 gennaio 1943 li 20 febbraio 1943 li 20 marzo 1943

RESIDENZA FISSATA ALL'ATTO DELL'INVIO IN CONGEDO E SUCCESSIVI CAMBIAMENTI

DISTINZIONI E SERVIZI SPECIALI (specchio C del foglio matricolare)

ANNOTAZIONI

CORPO O SERVIZIO	DATA ASCRIZIONE	DATA CESSAZIONE

N. 195 (37) del Catal.

Cellini's military record with the Italian Army. The court martial was expunged and nothing further was added to his service record after March 1943, though he is shown to have been granted "provisional unlimited leave" on July 27, 1944.

14. Yugoslavia, Summer 1943

The complex political structure within Yugoslavia during World War Two is outside the scope of this book but a brief (and somewhat simplistic) overview helps to understand the situation from Cellini's point of view.

The Kingdom of Yugoslavia, as it officially became known in 1929, is divided culturally, religiously and ethnically.

Although Croatia had declared itself an independent state "Nezavisna Država Hrvatska" in April, 1941, it is a puppet state of Nazi Germany under fascist leadership known as the Ustase (Croatian Revolutionary Movement). Led by "Poglavnik" Ante Pavelić, the Ustase operates under the authority and approval of Adolf Hitler. The declaration of independence is therefore not recognized by the Allies, as a result of which, after the war, Croatia will be regarded as an occupied territory of Yugoslavia – thus avoiding sanctions.

While most of Croatia is occupied by the German military or German-equipped Croatian forces, an area of coastline from Zara (Zadar) to Spalato (Split) known as the Governorship of Dalmatia is largely under Italian occupation, having been annexed by the Kingdom of Italy in the Rome treaties. This territory is far from secure, and there is considerable Partisan activity against the occupying forces.

By dividing the country geographically, the Germans had thought it would be easier to control. In fact, they have created more opportunities for the various separatist groups to pursue their own agenda. The German-backed Ustase are right-wing Catholic extremists who had functioned largely as a terrorist organization before the war. Their plans include ridding the country of Serbs, Jews and Romany people.

Serbian Chetniks, led by Draza Mihailovic, are bitter enemies of the Ustase. Their primary goal has always been to eliminate Muslims in Bosnia and Herzegovina and restore the Yugoslavian monarchy. The Chetniks are ostensibly anti-fascist, but Mihailovic discourages resistance against the Germans for fear of reprisals, so they have become reluctant collaborators with German forces fighting against Tito's Partisans.

The National Liberation Army (better known simply as The Partisans) are led by Josip Broz Tito. The Partisans fight against the German and Italian invaders as well as the Chetniks and Ustase (until Italy agrees to an armistice with the Allies in September, 1943, at which time many Italians join the Partisans). The Partisans are fervently anti-fascist and pro-socialist. They fight for Yugoslavian independence and believe that communism offers the best hope for the future. Tito's Partisans are considered the best trained and organized of all resistance groups in Europe, and are embraced as Allies by the British and Americans, who provide them with supplies and assistance.

*****

It is a calm day and the boat journey is smooth, but Cellini is not a good sailor, despite years of bobbing around in small boats as a child and fishing for octopus and other seafood in the Adriatic. He vomits constantly for the first hour of the voyage. At first this amuses his fellow passengers and the crew, until the sight and smell of his unrestrained regurgitation begins to affect those nearest to him, and seasickness starts to spread.

Once emptied of all its contents, his stomach settles down and he starts to enjoy the smell of the sea and the feel of the wind in his face, realizing how much he has missed it since leaving Bari.

It is one of those magnificent early summer days when the sea and the sky are such pure azure blue that, looking towards the horizon, it is difficult to tell where the water ends and the sky begins. On the left-hand side of the boat, land is never far away, as it sails past and between several of the many islands that line the Yugoslavian coastline.

Rounding a rocky outcrop, the boat slows and begins a gentle turn towards the mainland. Most of the soldiers on board have never been outside of Italy and are anxious to see where they are landing – and what kind of reception they might get. Some are expecting to be shot at the minute they leave the safety of the boat. Many are laughing and joking nervously while others light up one cigarette after another. The engines are quiet now, and Cellini feels a bump as the boat nudges up against a wooden pier and comes to a complete stop. Grabbing his gear, he is hustled quickly off the boat along with the other troops. Standing at the gangplank, a sergeant is screaming at the men to board one of the open lorries that are parked on the roadway at the top of the steps leading up from the pier.

Cellini heads for the first lorry and tries to clamber aboard but it is already full and he is pushed back from the tailgate by those already aboard. He almost falls over backwards, tipped by the weight of his knapsack, and rocks backwards and forwards until able to steady himself. Somehow he manages to stay on his feet. The soldiers who had pushed him off are highly entertained by his performance and show their appreciation with rude hand gestures and mock applause accompanied by laughter and whistles. Once steadied, Cellini turns and walks over to the second lorry. He climbs into the back and finds a space to sit on a plain wooden plank close to the cab. The engine is running and the fumes from the exhaust are coming up through the floorboards of the lorry. The smell of the fuel is sickening and he thinks he may throw up again, but having nothing on his stomach, he wretches and heaves but nothing comes up.

A cheer goes up as the first lorry departs, and Cellini looks up in time to see a cloud of sand and road dust churned up by its wheels as it pulls away. His lorry is still not full so will not be leaving for a few more minutes. Soldiers are pushing and shoving, stepping on his toes, and bashing him with knapsacks and rifles as they fight for a few square inches of plank on which to perch. A rifle butt strikes him in the back of the head and he turns around, his fists clenched, ready to punch whoever is responsible, but it is such a mêlée that he has no way of knowing who bashed him. He pays more attention to those around him in case it happens again.

Eventually his lorry sets off. He has no idea where he is or where he will be going and is not interested in making small talk with his new companions, none of whom seem to have a clue where they are anyway. Keeping very much to himself, he is grateful at least to be able to breathe now that the lorry is on the move and the fumes have abated.

*****

THE JOURNEY is bumpy, the road full of dips and potholes and occasionally the driver swerves to avoid rocks that have fallen or been placed by enemy resistance fighters.

Arriving at the camp, Cellini and the other new recruits to the 4th *Bersaglieri* jump, stagger or crawl down from their transport. Covered in road dust and stinking from the heat, their limbs are stiff and cramped. All they want to do is stretch their legs and get out of the hot sun. Instead they are told to line up ready to march to the camp parade ground for inspection by the commander of the regiment. They are told they will jog, double-time, in the traditional manner of *Bersaglieri*.

Forming quickly into ranks, the men are given the order to march.

They pick up their pace and jog towards the makeshift parade ground where the NCO in charge barks orders to "halt" and then "right turn". Facing into the sun, they do their best to stand to attention and wait for the commander to appear.

Five minutes go by. Ten.

After almost 20 minutes, the commanding officer struts out from his tent, his cap in hand and adjutant by his side, and walks towards the rows of soldiers he has left baking in the sun after their harrowing journey.

The first time he sets eyes on his new C.O., Cellini gets the distinct feeling he is going to be in for a tough time. Short and slight, what he lacks in stature, he more than makes up for in pomp and arrogance. Meticulously placing his cap on his head, the officer juts out his jaw in an exaggerated style, reminiscent of the Italian dictator, and begins pacing up and down. He begins delivering a diatribe of invective about their attitude and appearance. It is true that the majority of these newcomers are misfits. Some, like him, may be avoiding prison sentences. Others have been sent to this unit because they are known troublemakers. Right now they are nothing more than a bunch of tired and irritable men who have spent the last few hours of their lives cooped up in a boat and a truck with little food and water and no idea of what to expect. Turning to face them, the officer places his fists on his hips and launches into a well-rehearsed speech about what a devoted fascist he is, and an ardent supporter of Benito Mussolini; that King Vittorio Emanuel is a genius; and that the Kingdom of Italy has already accomplished so much by rightfully claiming Abyssinia and Albania. Strutting once again and gesticulating wildly, he expounds on exactly how, with the help of *Il Duce's* great ally Adolf Hitler, they will accomplish so much more.

He smiles and softens his demeanour towards the men and starts to talk about what a proud and distinguished history the *Bersaglieri* has, noting its origins on the island of Sardinia. He finishes up punching the air dramatically and saying how confident he is that his new men will keep up the regiment's grand tradition by protecting the Kingdom's new lands in Dalmatia.

Hearing the reference to the great history of the *Bersaglieri*, Cellini stifles a laugh, but makes little attempt to control the smirk that breaks across his face. One of the many stories his father used to tell him as a child, with great gusto, was the one about a *Bersaglieri* unit – his father could never remember which unit – suffering the loss of their regimental colours in battle – his father could never remember which battle – but he knew it was the greatest ignominy a military unit can suffer. The story had left a lasting impression. Cellini turns to his right to see if anyone else has seen the humour. Turning back to face the front, he notices the commander glaring in his direction. The officer says nothing and continues with his pep talk, but after the parade is over, when all the others are dismissed to find their accommodation, one of the adjutants informs Cellini that the commander wishes to see him in his quarters immediately.

*****

STANDING TO ATTENTION in the commander's tent, his kitbag by his side and his rifle in hand, Cellini awaits the arrival of the diminutive leader. He doesn't have to wait long.

"Cellini," The officer says. The voice is softer than it had been a few moments ago, outside on the parade ground. Then again the object of his attention is standing directly in front of him and there is no need to shout. He tries to look Cellini in the eye but being shorter, that requires him looking upwards, so instead he backs away, pulls a small sheaf of papers from behind his back and pretends to look at them.

"You find me amusing?" he continues.

"No sir," says Cellini.

"Then what is it that amuses you?"

"Nothing, sir." Cellini lies rather than get himself into more trouble by trying to explain.

"I don't like you, Cellini. I've read your file. I know who you are and why you are here. If you don't like it here, I would be happy to send you back to the prison at Gaeta." He pauses and flips over a sheet of paper as if to emphasize the official nature of what he is saying.

"Sixteen years and sixty days, I believe, is what you were sentenced to?"

"Yes sir."

"This is your chance to make something of yourself. To redeem yourself for the glory of Italy and for *Il Duce*." He smiles a sickly smile, which slowly dissolves into a scowl.

"Never. Do you hear me? Never smile whilst you are on parade unless I tell a joke and give you permission. Do you understand?"

"Yes sir!" Cellini replies.

"Now get out of my sight. Go and make Italy proud of you!"

Cellini salutes crisply. Without waiting for the salute to be returned he turns 180 degrees on his heels. He remembers to jog out of the officer's administration quarters and finds an NCO with a clipboard who helps him to locate his own tent, where he drops his kit and hurls himself onto his cot. He's ready to punch someone. Anyone will do. But he's also smart enough to know where that would lead, so he takes a deep breath and tells himself this hell won't last forever.

*****

No one among the rank and file seems to have any idea exactly where they are, except that they are somewhere near a railway line, because every now and then the sound of a train can be heard quite close by. Rumours are circulating that they are somewhere near the town of Sebenico.[1] They are a way out of the town, the terrain is rocky and hilly, and there are mountains in the distance. They see very few civilians, but are warned to constantly be on guard and watch for saboteurs and infiltrators, and to shoot first, ask questions afterwards.

At first the so-called war doesn't seem a whole lot different to training. There's the same daily routine of getting up, eating lice-ridden, starchy food, marching, cleaning weapons, marching, eating, marching more, eating again before lights out. It becomes easy to lose track of the days.

At first, Cellini gets along fine with the other men in his unit but doesn't form any deep, bonding friendships. Most of them are either Sicilian or Sardinian, and he doesn't particularly trust them. Making small talk isn't his way, although he can get along with anyone who isn't a bully, a womanizer, a liar or an authority figure – which to his way of thinking rules out a large part of the Italian Army. He misses his friends. He especially misses the simple *Barese* food he had grown up with and would give anything for a handful of foccacia stuffed with tomatoes and a thick slice of mortadella.

Hunger is a constant enemy. The food is of poor quality. The only protein in the cabbage water, masquerading as chicken soup, is from the lice floating in it. Even when the food is edible, the officers are always served first and there seems to be little left by the time the men line up for theirs. A sergeant, who seems to be sympathetic towards Cellini, probably because they are both from Apulia, offers him a piece of sound advice.

"Eat slowly," he says. "Chew every bite for as long as you can before you swallow. At the end of the meal you will feel more full, more satisfied."

1. Sebenico (Italian), Sibenika, now Sibenik, Croatia. The camp was at a small nearby town called Perković, close to a railways station. On a visit in 2016, Cellini and the author had a chance meeting with a local olive farmer, Radoslau Perković, who was able to take us to the ruin of the old camp.

The sergeant's advice will stand Cellini in good stead during the months ahead.[2]

He and the sergeant occasionally have conversations about the state of Italy and the war in general. The sergeant doesn't have a lot of time for the officers, and although he won't come right out and say he thinks the war will soon be lost, Cellini suspects he may be thinking that way. In his conversations with the sergeant, Cellini learns a great deal from him about the major forces operating in Yugoslavia: the *Ustase, Chetniks* and Partisans.

Patrols are sent out more or less around the clock, supposedly looking for signs of enemy activity. Cellini likes to volunteer for "point" – the lead position of a patrol group everyone else tries to avoid. He soon gains a reputation for being crazy, but his rationale is simple: if he sees the enemy before they see him he can react quicker; if he gets seen by the enemy before he sees them, at least he may catch them off guard and possibly unprepared for action. In his view, that gives him the best chance of getting away unscathed.

Being point man also means he gets given the biggest gun: the Breda Modello 30. It's a heavy and unwieldy weapon with a side entry clip that he finds tricky to operate. It also has a tendency to jam and Cellini will later come to despise the weapon. His experience with firing weapons up to this time being limited to those he had stolen as a child and his rare and infrequent Army training sessions, he is largely ignorant of combat requirements and he knows it.

All he knows is that he has the biggest gun in the squad and he is out front, leading this ragtag bunch of would-be soldiers.

2. *Cellini met the sergeant in Bari after the war. He thanked him for his advice and they chatted for a while about how the war had gone for each of them. At the end of the conversation Cellini asked if he knew what had happened to the C.O. of the battalion. "That bastard?" the sergeant replied. "Who knows? When the whole thing collapsed he was the first one to flee the sinking ship. I have no idea where or what happened, but I hope the Partisans got hold of him. He deserved it."*

The ruins of the military camp occupied by the Italian 4th Bersaglieri in Perković, a short distance from Sibenik, Croatia.

Perković Railway Station, less than a kilometre from the old Italian Army camp.

Left to right, Pjero Baranović, Radoslav Perković, Vito Cellini and Antun "Tonći" Baranović at the site of the Italian Army camp. Radoslav was kind enough to guide Cellini and the author to the site, which was exactly as Cellini describes it.

15. First Shot Fired!

So far Cellini hasn't had any cause to fire his weapon. It is weeks since his basic training ended, and he longs for a chance to show his prowess, or at least to prove to himself that he can actually still shoot straight. When an opportunity finally presents itself, it is hardly in the manner he expects, but it has its own rewards.

It is early in the morning, and the platoon is out marching. As usual Cellini is about 75 metres ahead of the rest of the pack and off to one side of the dirt road when he hears a commotion behind him. It appears that a donkey has wandered out ahead of the group and they have stopped. The donkey shows no interest in moving and the Italians decide to take advantage of the opportunity to stop for a smoke.

Cellini chambers a round into the breech of the Breda, takes aim and fires at the donkey, hitting it in the neck and killing it instantly. It is probably not the wisest thing he could have done, and the rest of the soldiers scatter and hit the ground, expecting an enemy attack. Cellini races back, waving his arms to let them know it was just him.

"We need to get the carcass back to camp," he says, "donkey steaks are on me for dinner!"

*****

One evening while out on patrol, well ahead of the rest of his squad as always, and heading towards the railways tracks, Cellini feels sure he hears something ahead. He stops, drops on one knee and peers into the blackness. He cannot see anything and has no idea what might be waiting in the darkness. By now all he can hear is the sound of his own heart beating. He keeps perfectly still. The rest of the squad will catch up with him soon. Then he hears it again; the distinct sound of something moving in the bushes ahead of him.

He stands up, cocks his weapon and sprays a short burst, from the hip, in the direction of the train tracks. Sparks fly everywhere and the clatter of bullets hitting the steel rails is deafening. One ricochets off a rail back in his direction and he will swear it goes past his ear with a ringing, buzzing sound. The tracks must be closer than he thinks! He dives to the ground and spreads himself as flat as he can, waiting for something to happen, although he's not exactly sure what. Maybe the sound of someone screaming or moaning in pain? A hail of lead coming back at him? Grenades? Mortars?

Nothing but silence. He lies there for a full two minutes. Slowly he gets up, first on one knee, then back on his feet, the Breda trained in the direction of the train tracks, just in case. He steps backwards, slowly, carefully, one foot behind the other, still staring ahead, squinting to try and see if there is anything or anyone out there.

Stopping every now and again to listen for any sound, or catch any movement, he makes his way back to the perimeter of the camp. He doesn't see the rest of his group until he gets back to the canteen.

"We heard the shots and we came looking for you, but we couldn't find you," is all they have to say. "We thought maybe you were dead."

Bastards, he thinks to himself. He reports his version of the events to the sergeant but leaves out the part about the rest of the patrol abandoning him, deciding he will watch his back more carefully from now on, but he won't turn them in.

The following morning Cellini and his squad are detailed to go back and investigate the incident of the previous night. They are told not to come back until they find some good reason for shooting up the railway lines. Once again, he is happy to be point man – approximately 200 metres in front and to the right of the rest of the group. Unsure of exactly what his position was when he had reacted and fired the shots, he leads off in the direction of the tracks, hoping to find some clues as to what caused it.

He finds the tracks, but can see no sign of any damage to the steel rails, either by saboteurs or from his brief rampage with the Breda 30 last night. Walking along the tracks, looking first one way and then the other, he decides he is offering too high of a profile if there were enemy soldiers in the vicinity, so he drops down the shallow embankment and continues following the path alongside the tracks, among the trees and shrubs. Scanning the terrain from side to side he glances down only occasionally to see where he is stepping. He feels something give under his foot and looks down to see what looks for a split second like a length of partially coiled cable, until he stoops to take a closer look and realises he has stepped on a snake!

Instinctively, in one movement, he steps backwards and swings the barrel of the Breda 30 downwards to point at the snake. He squeezes the trigger but nothing happens. In his haste to dispatch the reptile he has forgotten to cock the weapon! He stands absolutely still, staring at the creature, which miraculously has not moved since being trodden on.

He admires the creature. Its thick, grey body has a distinctive black zigzag pattern along its entire length. He takes a step closer then notices the gaping hole in the creature's body, about 30 centimetres behind its head. The snake is quite dead – and appears to have been shot with a fairly high-calibre weapon. Cellini chuckles to himself. Is this what he heard last night? A snake slithering through the brush in search of its prey? Did he shoot and kill a snake in the darkness? He would love to find out what kind of snake it is. Looking again he makes a mental note of its appearance. The black and grey zigzag is distinctive, but even more noticeable is the small horn on its snout.

Sitting down by the side of the tracks, he waits for the rest of the squad to arrive and proudly shows off the snake. He asks if anyone can identify it, but none can. However, not one of them believes for a minute that he shot it in the dark the previous night. Even Cellini has his doubts, but it makes a good story! The corporal in charge of the squad insists that the snake must have been killed at some other time, possibly by an enemy saboteur. He decides that they need to keep searching for evidence of Partisan activity in the area before they can return to the camp.

Cellini picks the dead creature up by its tail, swings it around and hurls it off into the distance.

They scour the area around the tracks for the rest of the day, killing time, but find nothing that suggests any enemy activity. Staying close to the railway line, they cover several miles, pausing occasionally for water breaks and once for a meal of cold rations. On two occasions, they hear trains coming and scamper down the embankment to hide in the thicket until the they pass. One is a freight train and the other a troop train full of German soldiers, probably on their way out of the Dalmatia area as more Italian reinforcements arrive to take their place. Just before nightfall, the corporal decides they will call off the search and head back to camp. He gathers everyone together.

"I'm not willing to go with Cellini's story about shooting a snake in the dark," he says. "The C.O. would never believe it for a minute, anyway." There are smirks and laughter among the troops, who look condescendingly at Cellini.

For once, Cellini is grateful for the contempt. The last thing he needs is more scrutiny from his C.O.. They form up, Cellini once again ahead and to the right of the rest of the squad, and begin the long walk back to camp. Darkness is beginning to envelop the landscape, and there is a chill in the air, but the only sound he can hear is that of his own footfalls on the rocky ground. As the lights of the camp come into view, he turns away from the rail tracks and heads over the rocky ground towards them. Suddenly, a shrill scream pierces the silence and Cellini stops dead in his tracks. It is coming from around 50 metres behind him, where the squad is following his lead. Did he miss something? A booby-trap? A sniper? Slowly he makes his way back to where the scream came from and finds everyone smiling.

One of his comrades holds up something. "Well done, Cellini," he says, finding it difficult to suppress his laughter. "You scared the hell out of the corporal!"

It's the snake. The same snake that Cellini had purportedly "shot" the night before. The same snake he had found earlier in the day and tossed away into the brush. The corporal had unwittingly stepped on it and scared himself to death!

"It's not the same snake. It can't be," the corporal argued, but the gaping hole in the creature's neck told a different story.

"What are the odds?" says a voice from the ranks "Wait 'til we tell the com—" his sentence is cut short by the corporal, who is not amused. "No one is to talk about this, understand? Not ever!"

Everyone turns and stares at Cellini.

"Don't look at me!" he says, "I'm not going to say a word!"[1]

*****

A FEW DAYS LATER, an order filters through to pack up everything and get ready to move out. The battalion is to relocate further down the coast. They pile into open trucks and begin the slow drive, stopping every now and then to sweep the road for mines or possible attack. Cellini takes his turn on point, walking ahead of the vehicle convoy and checking for likely spots from which to launch an ambush. It is a steaming hot day and he is relieved to get out of the truck and away from the stench of sweat and diesel fumes, if only for a short while.

The journey is tedious but uneventful. Someone jokes about the condition of the roads being so bad that detonating a few mines might even be an improvement. Travelling takes the better part of a day, and they set up camp between the towns of Trau and Spalato.[2] After setting up tents the

[1.] *Several years after the war, Cellini discovered that the snake was a nose-horned viper or "postok", one of the most venomous snakes in Europe.*

[2.] *Trau – Italian name for Trogir, Croatia. Spalato – Italian for Split, Croatia* men are served a meagre meal of Pasta Agiutta.[3] As usual, the officers are served first, and by the time the men line up for their rations there is little left but lukewarm, mushy macaroni. They settle down for the first night in their new digs. Cellini takes first watch so he can sleep uninterrupted for the rest of the night. In spite of the stillness of the night and the sticky heat, he sleeps well.

When not out and about on patrol with his squad, or standing guard at the camp, Cellini takes advantage of every available moment to practise stripping his weapon and reassembling it. Remembering his childhood and the guns he took from the *Liceo Classico*, he takes great care to note every part so as not to lose any screws, nor to have any parts left over. In time, he becomes an expert at handling the Breda.

Mail delivery is usually once a week, but Cellini pays no attention, preferring to get on with his work while others chase down the man with the postal sack. He neither writes nor expects to receive letters and has deliberately not told anyone at home where he is, nor given them any military address to which they can write and have letters forwarded.[4]

He prefers not to expect mail because he sees the negative impact felt by those in the battalion who do not receive it. Their disappointment can seriously impact their ability to function. He finds it difficult to stomach the sight of grown men crying, especially soldiers in uniform who spend as much time bragging about their sexual conquests as they do about their own bravery in combat. It is the biggest bullies, braggers and womanizers who cry the most if they do not receive letters from their girlfriends back home. Cellini has no sympathy. He considers this a weakness as well as a distraction, and it feeds his growing contempt for the men with whom he serves.

3. *Pasta Agiutta is a mix of boiled macaroni and meatballs of unknown origin.*

4. *This would later cause some friction with his cousin Francesca, who was keen to keep in touch and was actually quite concerned for his safety. At the time, Cellini knew he had feelings for his cousin, but didn't realise that she had a crush on him.*

16. Rewarded for Murder

MORALE ISN'T AS high as it could be in the *Bersaglieri* and it isn't all because of the mailman. Rumours are starting to spread about the imminent collapse of the homeland. There is also a lot of talk about the Yugoslav Partisans and what vicious fighters they are – which is very unsettling to those soldiers who are about to enter combat for the first time. So far the *Bersaglieri* hasn't had to face any serious resistance.

Things start to go downhill quite soon after they arrive in Trau. There is one member of Cellini's platoon, a Sicilian, who talks a lot about how much he looks forward to the killing and what he is going to do to these Yugoslav Partisans when he gets his hands on them. Cellini takes little notice. He knows from his experience on the street that there are those who talk and those who do, and that talkers are rarely doers, but he also knows that many of the others in the battalion are very impressionable.

Cellini is no angel. He has done things he knows were wrong and is not afraid of getting into fights. He has always been good at fighting because he has never been afraid of pain and can dish it out as well as take it. But he does not consider this war to be his fight. He cannot bring himself to support, nor agree with, the fascist government, and in particular Mussolini, whom he believes to be a complete buffoon. Yet here he is, wearing the uniform of the *Bersaglieri,* complete with its fake "chicken feathers", living day to day among people he considers lowlifes, fools and, in many cases, cowards. Despite having grown up in southern Italy, being totally immersed in its culture and unable to speak or understand more than a few scant words of the English language, he still considers himself American. He believes Italy was wrong to have sided with the Germans and that it is only a matter of time before the Allies will crush them all.

One morning he and his squad are sent to patrol the outskirts of the nearby town. There are a few people going about their daily routines, walking or riding bicycles on the street. These are simple people; country folk. They might even be called peasants. They are minding their own business, and while they may resent the presence of the Italian soldiers, they don't show it.

The soldiers are not exactly keeping a tight formation, but they are marching with purpose. The Sicilian soldier whom Cellini has already taken a dislike to suddenly breaks ranks and swaggers over to an elderly local man who is seated outside a café with his morning coffee. He speaks but the old man just stares ahead and says nothing.

"Hey, I'm talking to you!" The Italian snaps his fingers in front of the old man's face, then grabs his chin and turns it to face him.

"That's better. You need to look at me when I'm talking to you." He lets go of the man's chin and his face turns slowly away, staring once again into oblivion. It's obvious to Cellini that the man is in some way mentally deficient. Perhaps he was born with a handicap or has suffered a stroke. For whatever reason, he seems unaware of his surroundings, but his unfortunate condition serves only to antagonize the Sicilian.

Grabbing him by the collar, the soldier hauls the old man to his feet and starts screaming and yelling in his face. He pushes him forward and orders him to put up his hands. The old man is slow to react and so the Sicilian gives him a kick in the backside as if to propel him forward. The man stumbles forward, almost loses his balance but stays on his feet, his hands raised above his head, and moves off as ordered.

The rest of the squad takes the opportunity to stop for a smoke and watches as the Sicilian and the old man head towards a cornfield. In the middle of the cornfield, they stop. The Italian soldier, still staring at the back of the civilian, raises his rifle and points it directly at the back of the man's head. Point-blank range. Before he even hears the sound of the rifle shot Cellini sees a puff of smoke from the barrel of the weapon and a jet of dark mist spurting from the front of the old man's head followed by a large chunk of skull lifting up and flying forwards. After what seems like an age, the man falls forward into the green corn. Cellini cannot believe what he has just seen. It is an image that will haunt him for the rest of his life. The Sicilian doesn't even look down at the body. He just turns and walks over to the group of Italian soldiers with a big grin on his face.

"That's another five hundred Lira for me," he says.

Cellini turns to the corporal, who takes a last, long draw on his cigarette before flicking it on the ground.

"What's that about 500 Lira?" Cellini asks.

"I know! Can you believe the Sicilian had the balls to do that?" The corporal seems full of admiration for the cold-blooded murder he and the rest of the squad have just witnessed. He goes on to explain that the commander – the man whom Cellini wished to avoid more than anyone – has offered a reward of 500 Lira for every Yugoslav shot by his brave *Bersaglieri* boys. Not just Partisans and saboteurs, but anyone. Age and gender are not even a consideration.

Cellini has heard stories about such things, but this is the first time he has actually seen it happen with his own eyes.

After the incident with the old man in the cornfield, these needless killings of the local populace seem to escalate, or at least there is less effort to hide them or pretend they are anything other than cold-blooded murder for money. In some cases, soldiers line up and wait their turn to shoot a round into a corpse that is already dead – killed by the first bullet – just so they can claim their 500 Lira. No one even thinks to contradict their claim or suggest that they are cheating. After all, the reward has been promised for shooting any Yugoslavian. There is no condition about whether or not they are already dead. It's easy money.

Sickened by what he sees, Cellini does not participate. He is mocked by many of the others and gets into numerous fights when accused of being a coward. His tenacity in a fight soon establishes that he is no coward, and after a while they leave him alone. He has never lost a fair fight and even takes on two or more at a time. Perhaps by showing them that he is not afraid, he can make some of them think twice about participating in these atrocities against civilians. Regardless, he will not betray his fellow soldiers. It just isn't in his genes to rat them out.

"Besides," he thinks to himself, "they'll all get what's coming to them one day."

*****

SCHEDULED TO MARCH through the town in a demonstration of power and military assertiveness, the C.O. makes a rare appearance and decides to go along.

Before they leave the camp, the platoon is lined up in ranks and the C.O. makes a grand entrance in order to give one of his pep talks. He lectures the men about the importance of showing these people who's boss, emphasizing that the 4th *Bersaglieri* are there to protect them from the evil Partisans. Cellini is utterly astounded by the hypocrisy of a man who is offering a reward of 500 Lira for any Yugoslavian killed by his troops but still has the audacity to talk about protecting the people. He just wants this war – or at least his part in it – to be over.

In the tradition of the *Bersaglieri,* they will jog, or march "double time" carrying their rifles and full equipment. Except the C.O. of course, who actually has a junior officer carry his rifle for him and run alongside – much to Cellini's amusement – although this time he is smart enough not to show an indication of humour. He imagines the C.O., in the heat of battle, talking to his junior officer.

"Lieutenant, load my rifle."
"Yes sir," the lieutenant replies, sliding a clip into the Carcano.
"Now, lieutenant, I want you to cock the rifle, ready to fire."
"Yes, sir," once again he replies. "Cocked and ready to fire sir!"
"Now, lieutenant, pass me the rifle. Quickly! Hold it up to my shoulder."
"Yes sir," the lieutenant replies, in Cellini's imaginary conversation. "Would you like me to fire it for you, sir?"
"Don't be impertinent, lieutenant, or I'll have you court martialled!"

The platoon is called to attention and Cellini returns to the real world. The sergeant gives the order to march, and they set off towards the town. The C.O. won't be marching with them. Instead he will travel in his staff car, a weary-looking Fiat Topolino, commandeered by previous occupation forces and then left behind, driven by his faithful, ever-present, rifle-bearing lieutenant.

Most of the townsfolk stay well out of the way and try to take as little notice as possible of the Italian invaders. Some, especially the children, are fascinated and cannot take their eyes off them as they jog through the streets.

Cellini actually enjoys the double time marching. He likes the rhythm and it helps him think. Though just twenty years of age, he has seen more in his life than most of the other men in his battalion. He has been involved in some hair-raising adventures, broken the law on more than one occasion, been accused of being a *delinquente* by his own family, got into some serious fights and seen quite a bit of bloodshed – but nothing like this. In the short time he spends with the *Bersaglieri* in the Governorship of Dalmatia, he feels he is seeing the very worst of mankind.

He is still shocked over the "500 Lira per head" reward scheme offered by his commanding officer and the way these soldiers have cheated to extort even more money out of it. When the war is over, their deeds will perhaps be deemed "war crimes", and those responsible, if caught and convicted, will be severely punished, but that doesn't help these people right here and now. There is nothing Cellini or anyone else with a conscience can do about it. There are no police to enforce the Geneva Convention or even common decency. The soldiers are the police – or at least they have seniority over local law enforcement officers. Not knowing whom he can trust,

Cellini keeps his thoughts to himself but cannot help wondering if this is typical, and whether the entire Italian Army is like this?

The sergeant barks out the order to halt. They are in the old part of Trau, waiting for the C.O. and his lieutenant to arrive in the battered *Topolino*.

Cellini looks around at the faces of the others in his motley platoon. Stuck in Yugoslavia with this band of misfits and a commanding officer who is handing out rewards for cold-blooded murder, he thinks things are just about as bad as they can be. He is wrong. The worst is yet to come.

*****

THE MARCH INTO town was nothing more than a token show of force. If the locals are impressed, they don't show it. After a mercifully brief talk about the mission of the *Bersaglieri* in Yugoslavia, "To protect the people of the Governorship of Dalmatia by Royal Command of His Majesty the King of Italy and his Excellency the Prime Minister Benito Mussolini," the C.O. checks his wristwatch and abruptly turns and walks back to his vehicle, his lieutenant in tow. Before leaving, the lieutenant tells the sergeant to carry on and make sure the men are back at camp by 2100 hours.

That leaves almost two hours in town. Some of the men decide to make their way back to camp, but most of Cellini's squad decides to stay in town and find a place to have a drink. Cellini decides to stick around. Maybe if he gets to know these people better he can understand them. Besides, the thought of a beer or a grappa is very appealing.

The town has pretty much cleared out. Most of the people have shut themselves indoors to avoid the soldiers. Many of the cafés and inns have closed their doors and shutters, but the men find a quiet, dark bar tucked away in an alley, go in and order beer, local wine and grappa.

After a few drinks they become lewd, loud and horny. Most of these men have not enjoyed the pleasure of a woman's company for quite a while. They ask the innkeeper if there are any good prostitutes to be found locally, but he smiles and shakes his head. After a while, the men, bored and slightly the worse for wear, leave the bar and decide to go looking for women. Walking down the street they hear a commotion coming from inside the courtyard of a deserted building. Edging their way inside they see another group of soldiers standing huddled together in the far corner, up against the building. It's the other half of their platoon – the ones who had left to go back to camp. The huddle goes quiet when they see the squad approaching. There is the distinct sound of a scream, it sounds like a girl, which only lasts a second before it's muffled.

Crowding around to see what's going on, Cellini's drinking companions start laughing, cheering and clapping. A voice in the crowd tells them to shut up if they want to take a turn.

If shooting an old man for money is not considered a crime, then who's to say a little fun with one of the local girls isn't perfectly acceptable too? That's the attitude of the soldiers. They take turns with the girl, those that want to. Some are turned off by the idea of following another man, others have drunk too much and are unable to perform. A few, like Cellini, are just sickened by the whole thing. He leans against the wall and slides his back down until he is in a seated position, his head resting on his knees. The crowd begins to thin out and Cellini cannot help but glance at the girl through the legs of the soldiers still standing around her.

She's young, maybe 20 years-old. Not beautiful in the classic sense perhaps, but pretty and slender, with shoulder-length black hair. She's on her back, her head to one side, her eyes staring straight at Cellini. Her dress is torn and he can see bruises on her arms and legs. There is no anguish on her face. No fear. Just a look of sadness and surrender, as if she had just lost someone or something very close.

He tries to look away but can't. That's someone's daughter. Someone's sister. Someone's cousin. He cannot begin to imagine how he would feel if something like this happened to one of his own sisters or girl cousins. His thoughts turn to his cousin, Francesca. Her sweet, innocent face. Anger wells up in him but he knows that he is virtually powerless and that anything he does will only make the situation worse.

The sound of footsteps running across the courtyard finally breaks Cellini's hypnotic gaze. Screaming – this time it's a man's voice. He stops when he sees the girl on the ground, then starts yelling at the soldiers left standing around her, raising his fists and pounding at the chest of first one soldier, then another. Arms reach out and grab him from behind. He struggles to get free, screaming at the top of his lungs that he is going to get the police. A shot rings out and echoes around the courtyard. The young man falls to the ground in a crumpled heap. The girl, now sitting up, opens her mouth to scream, but a second shot stops the sound from leaving her throat and she falls back onto the stone floor, a puddle of blood forming around her head.

For ten full seconds there is absolute silence, then a voice says, "Let's get out of here!"

Scrambling to get out of the narrow courtyard entrance, the soldiers bump into each other clumsily, reminding Cellini of an old silent comedy film. They run down the street for a couple of blocks before getting into loose formation for the walk back. Cellini, realizing he can do nothing for the poor girl, nor her boyfriend, and not wishing to be caught with two dead bodies, follows a short distance behind.

He overhears one of the soldiers saying "Do you think we'll get our 500 Lira for each of them?" Followed by a few muffled chuckles.

He stops in a doorway and vomits until there is nothing left in his stomach, then dry heaves for a solid five minutes before making his way back to the camp.

By the time he gets back to the camp, his feet are blistered and sore and he decides he needs to bathe them and wash his footwraps. The stench of the cloth, worn thin in some places, is unbelievable and the soles and heels of his feet are raw. While he is waiting for the wraps to dry he reflects on what he has just seen. It seems strangely surreal, as if he is seeing it through someone else's eyes, intruding on someone else's memory. Yet the vision is permanently branded on his own soul and he will bear the scars for the rest of his life. He simply cannot understand the mentality of his fellow soldiers. Even taking into account that there is a war on, he cannot find a way to justify their behaviour. He feels no personal guilt – only shame and disgust for those responsible. He knows he could have done nothing to prevent it happening. It crosses his mind that he might chat to the sergeant about it, but he dismisses the thought quickly. He believes if anyone in the battalion found out he would be disposed of without a second thought. Even if the sergeant supported him and there were someone in higher authority they could report the incident to – which there isn't – it would neither stop it from happening again, nor bring the two young lovers back to life.

If nothing else, his experience with the *Bersaglieri* teaches Cellini that sometimes it pays to act like a coward and play dumb. It's a lesson that will serve him well in the future, but for right now he has to focus on staying alive – and getting as far away from this crucible of hate and greed as possible.

*****

THE OPPORTUNITY PRESENTS itself sooner than he is expecting. A *Ustase* unit that has been patrolling the mountains to the north makes contact with the *Bersaglieri*. They are looking to strengthen their numbers and keen to recruit anyone capable of handling a gun willing to join their ranks. The lieutenant in charge of the *Ustase* unit is Italian and assures the men of the *Bersaglieri* that it is perfectly alright for them to accept this new mission, and that it is with the full support and consent of the Royal Italian Army.

He adds that he, himself, transferred to the *Ustase* only recently and that their impact on the war effort was going to be considerable.

Although he is only a lieutenant, Cellini thinks he must be quite a big shot, because he is well-dressed and has a personal servant to carry his gun for him. Taking the *Ustase* lieutenant's word that the Italian Army has consented to this informal transfer, since neither his own commanding officer nor his platoon sergeant are anywhere to be found, Cellini is one of the first to volunteer, and is joined by a handful of others from his unit. He is neither knowledgeable nor overly concerned with the political situation in Yugoslavia at this point, nor even aware that the *Ustase* is so closely affiliated with the Nazis. His primary motivation is to get away from the *Bersaglieri.*

It may not be the perfect escape, but it is a way out of the Italian Army – and an opportunity for a brand new adventure.

A poignant and disquieting reminder of the war in Sibenik. The concrete posts (above) were used for executing anyone suspected of collaborating with the Partisans by the Italian occupation forces. Today they stand as a memorial to the victims who died here.

Left: Cellini joins fellow Partisan veterans in a wreath-laying ceremony at the memorial, November 2016.

Stone sculpture at the entrance to the memorial site.

17. A Brief Tour of Duty with the *Ustase*

PERCEIVING A LACK of effort on the part of Italian troops in Yugoslavia, Hitler is increasing the number of troops mobilized to the north, including his elite SS mountain troops, intent on wiping out all the Partisan resistance in Serbia and Montenegro. While the area of Dalmatia is still technically under Italian jurisdiction, news of the Italians' failure to control the region has almost certainly reached the German high command by now. What no one on the ground here in Dalmatia knows is that the Italian government is in the process of negotiating an armistice with the allies, even though fierce fighting continues on all fronts.

No doubt aware of the lukewarm Italian presence and perhaps suspecting that it will not be long before the Germans move in and take over the region, the local Ustase is most probably scouting for anyone loyal to the fascist cause and willing to join its forces against the Chetniks, their personal enemy. It would look good for the commander of the unit as well as increasing their firepower.

*****

CELLINI QUICKLY establishes himself as a knowledgeable mechanic and demonstrates that he is more than capable of handling a gun – even though he hasn't yet fired his weapon in anger at any enemy. He confidently strips down and reassembles every weapon he is shown and is given charge of a Breda M30, a light machine gun which was standard issue to the Italian Army. Though classified as a light machine gun, it was common practice to issue one between two soldiers, with one firing and the other reloading the special fixed magazine. He is paired with another volunteer and recent transferee from the Italian Army, who is content for Cellini to do all the firing of the weapon – as long as he also agrees to carry it.

They find the best way of handling the gun is for Cellini to stand behind his partner, resting the barrel over his shoulder with the legs of the bipod grasped in his hands. Keen to test their technique in action, they go out on patrol looking for targets of opportunity.

Making their way up a mountain path, they hear the sound of an aircraft in the distance. It sounds low, so they turn around and, squinting into the sun, see the silhouette of a light aircraft flying slow and low. Very low. Neither has any idea if the aircraft is hostile or friendly, and they are unable to make out any markings, but Cellini recognizes it as a Fieseler Storch reconnaissance aircraft.[1] Based on its extremely low altitude and the fact that it seems to be stalking them, the pair conclude the aircraft must be hostile and decide to take matters into their own hands. Loading a magazine into the Breda, Cellini hoists the barrel up over his comrade's shoulder and crouches low, pointing the weapon up into the air. As the aircraft passes over them, no more than 30 metres in the air, Cellini fires a short burst at the belly of the Storch. The aircraft begins to buck and roll, which Cellini takes to mean he must have hit it, and he cheers. His *Ustase* partner is less optimistic.

"You missed by a mile," he says. "All your bullets were too low."

"Then how come he's flapping his wings all over the place?" Cellini is disappointed with his partner's reaction.

"I think he's trying to tell us something. I think perhaps he's not hostile at all. Maybe he's actually on our side and looking out for us?"

"Oh shit!" Cellini says. He hadn't understood why the pilot put the machine into such convulsions, but his partner's explanation makes sense. He knows full well his bullets fell well short of the target and makes a mental note to correct next time – if there is a next time – by shooting ahead and in the path of the target. His sharp mind has already worked out that to hit a moving aircraft he would need to fire quite a bit ahead of the target.[2]

"Let's get the hell out of here before it comes back around!"

They agree never to discuss the Fieseler Storch episode with anyone, and Cellini decides to be more careful about selecting targets of opportunity in the future. He also decides that he did not leave the *Bersaglieri* in order to

1. The Fieseler Fi 156 Storch (Stork), so named because of its long legs, was a reconnaissance aircraft designed and built for the German Luftwaffe but sold to several other countries, including the Soviet Union, Romania and Czechoslovakia. Since the Ustase were collaborating with the Nazis, it is likely this aircraft was scouting for the Germans and must have been quite surprised when fired upon!

2. Aiming at a spot ahead of a moving target, or "deflection shooting", is a difficult skill to master. It is taught to and practised at great length by fighter pilots and air gunners as well as anti-aircraft gunners. The fact that Cellini was able to work this out for himself was yet another indication of his innate weapons skills.

team up with a group of Nazi sympathizers. Up until the incident with the Fieseler Storch, joining the *Ustase* had been just another adventure in his life, but the realization that he is still on the same side as the fascist Germans causes him to reconsider. He decides that when the time is right, he will move on again.

A few days later, he is entrusted with a motorcycle – a motor tricycle in fact, the Benelli M36, complete with its built-in wooden cargo bed. The Benelli is running rough and no one else seems willing to give it a try but he is happy for the chance to put his dormant mechanical skills to work. While some of his new comrades in arms watch him with interest while he works, they do not approach him. Most leave him alone and he is happy in his solitude. It gives him time to think and plan his next move. After a few days, the Benelli's 500cc engine is running perfectly and he sets off across the mountain trails.

It will be the last the *Ustase* sees of Cellini or their Benelli M36, as well as the Breda M30 and several clips of 9mm ammunition.

Cellini has no idea where he is headed, he is just happy to be on the road. He estimates the Benelli's tank to be about half full, which ought to get him a fair distance. He doubts the *Ustase* group he left behind will bother to come looking for him. They will assume he took a left turn off a right-hand bend and that his broken body is lying in a ravine somewhere, or that he was ambushed by *Chetniks* or Partisans and gunned down. The thought makes him smile, because it occurs to him that one of those scenarios is still highly likely to be his actual fate. He starts making bets with himself which it is to be, then decides to rig the bet by riding the machine more cautiously.

"Hell, Cellini," he says to himself out loud, "if you get yourself shot that's one thing, but riding a tricycle off a cliff would be just plain dumb."

He decides that if the *Ustase* do come after him, he is going to play dumb and say he got lost after taking the Benelli out for a road test.

He rides for what seems like hours up into the mountains, mostly on dirt roads with a lot of sharp, hairpin bends. His speed isn't great because of the steep incline and the poor road surface. The view over the sea is breathtaking, but he cannot afford to spend too much time sightseeing.

Coming out of a tight left turn, his left rear wheel lifts off the ground then slams back down as he oversteers to make another equally tight turn to the right. At that precise moment his worst fears are realised. Ahead of him, crouching down on top of a massive boulder at the side of the road are two very fierce and very angry looking men in a semblance of uniform, but not one with which Cellini is familiar. One has a pistol and the other has a heavy machine gun, which he is holding at the hip and pointing right at Cellini.

*****

SLOWING DOWN to a crawl, Cellini waits for the armed men to make a move. He knows if he tries to reach for his own machine gun they will cut him down before he can lift his hand from the throttle. He wonders why they are not already shooting at him. Without his headgear, his uniform looks similar to what they are wearing, and the thought occurs to him that they think he is one of them. Not only are they not shooting at him, they seem to be waving, as if signalling him to turn around and go back.

As he draws closer, he can see that they are frantically gesticulating at him to turn around and go. He looks up the road past them but can see nothing. Squinting, he scans the horizon, from side to side and then up and down. He catches a slight movement in the corner of his eye, perhaps 200 metres ahead in the two o'clock position. Either his imagination is working overtime or that's the barrel of a very large gun traversing. A tank!

The only people who have tanks up here are Germans! He must have strayed further north than he planned![3]

Cellini doesn't need a second warning. The dirt road he is on is too narrow to turn in a circle, so he pulls in the clutch, puts both feet on the ground and backs up towards the edge of the ravine until he can swing the front end of the Benelli round and head off back in the direction he came from.

He daren't look around for fear of running over the edge of the mountain road, but he braces himself for the attack from behind he knows must be coming. He opens the throttle as much as he dares, and as he slows for a tight bend he risks a quick glance over his shoulder. He sees no sign of anyone or anything chasing him, so he slows down and starts to look for alternate routes across the foot of the mountains.

Finding a route that doesn't look familiar, he decides to take it. He knows the road is heading east, because the sun is behind and to the right

[3] *It is likely Cellini had crossed into Bosnia, although Bosnia had, by this time been ceded to the Independent State of Croatia and was under Nazi dominance. Bosnia is considered to be the geographical home of the Partisans, its mountainous territory offering the perfect hiding place for training and development as well as hiding. In February 1943, a quisling Waffen SS unit: 13th Waffen Mountain Division of the SS Handschar (1st Croatian) was formed in Bosnia, but it proved to be of little value, and many of its troops deserted to join the Partisans.*

of him. It winds gently back and forth but nothing like the treacherous hairpin turns of the higher terrain.

Cellini has been riding since early morning without stopping for food. He is tired and hungry, and it is already beginning to get dark. He knows he cannot get far at night and starts looking for a place to pull off the road to rest. Finding a pasture strewn with rocks but studded with trees that looks to be perfect, he pulls off the roads and kills the 500cc engine on the Benelli. He manhandles the machine into a stand of trees about 100 metres from the road, hiding it as best he can from every angle but giving himself an excellent view of the road. He lays his Breda machine gun across his lap, puts his hands on the handlebars and leans forward across the fuel tank with his pack under his head. In a matter of seconds he is fast asleep from exhaustion.

*****

HE WAKES AS the sun comes up, stretches and yawns and wishes he had a cup of coffee. His water canteen is half empty, its contents warm and slimy on his throat, but it is better than nothing. He decides finding water will be the next priority, but for right now he will hit the road.

Checking the fuel tank, he is confident he can still go some distance before abandoning the motor tricycle and continuing on foot.

Before too long he comes to a bridge over a gently flowing mountain stream. He pulls the Benelli off to the side and pushes it behind the stone wall of the bridge so that it won't be seen from the road. He luxuriates in the cold, clear water, drinking and filling his canteen. Next he washes his hands, face and feet, taking care to keep his foot-wraps and boots dry. After drying himself thoroughly in the morning air, he makes the decision to head back up into the mountains. He'd rather take his chances with the Partisans than run into more Italian troops. He knows the Italians have stayed mostly in the coastal towns, preferring the comfort and relative safety to the rugged mountains.

Besides the occasional goat, there are almost no signs of life on the deserted mountain roads, yet Cellini cannot shake the feeling that he is being watched. Soon enough, the road starts to get steeper and rougher and he finds himself once again struggling to keep the machine under control around the tight bends. He is also starting to be concerned about his fuel situation, realizing he is going to run out fairly soon and be forced to abandon the Benelli and continue on foot.

Pulling out of a bend, the road ahead seems straight and clear for several hundred metres, and in the distance Cellini sees what appears to be some kind of encampment, complete with people – soldiers – and a checkpoint.

It's too late to stop and turn around, and by their movement and activity the soldiers have obviously seen him. He decides to press on and, if necessary, try to bluff his way through. As he gets nearer he realises that at least they are not Germans. A rag-tag mob wearing a mixture of uniforms, though all appear to be wearing a small red star on their headgear. They carry an assortment of different weapons, though he is relieved to notice that none are pointed directly at him. He is not sure whether these men are Partisans, *Chetniks* or some other resistance group of which he hasn't yet heard. They are not hostile, but wary of the stranger.

He stops at the checkpoint, shuts off the Benelli's engine but remains seated on it, in silence, waiting for one of the soldiers to speak. No one speaks for several minutes, then it seems everyone tries to speak at once – but he is unable to understand what they are saying. Though born in Brooklyn, New York, Cellini was raised speaking Italian, in particular the *Barese* dialect.[4] He speaks none of the languages used in Yugoslavia[5] and understands very little English, but recognizes a few words and hears the word "gasoline" to which he reacts by pointing vigorously at the fuel tank of the Benelli.

Smiles break out among the soldiers and moments later a couple of younger members of the group arrive with a large metal container. One of them removes the cap from the Benelli's fuel tank and between them they hoist the heavy can over the machine and begin pouring the precious liquid into the tank. Cellini is amazed at the strength and dexterity of the two young boys who manage to completely fill the tank without spilling a single drop.

The excited conversation continues and he is able to glean that he is not far from the border between Croatia and Bosnia – so he has strayed further north than he realised. He knows that the *Chetniks* – with plenty of German soldiers and weapons to support them – have a stronghold in Bosnia, so he's more grateful than ever to the group of Partisans who waved

[4] *Bari dialect (dialetto Barese) is spoken in the Apulia region of southern Italy, although as southerners moved north in search of work in the twentieth century, they took parts of their speech with them. While it is one of the most distinctive Italian dialects, many variations exist, and it is continually evolving. Even within the province of Bari there are many variations.*

[5] *Yugoslavia was host to numerous languages and dialects at this time. Though similar, each had its own distinct nuances, which would be difficult for a foreigner like Vito Cellini to understand or identify by region.*

him away a few miles back. Once again, his luck has had held out.

With the fuel tank now full, Cellini replaces the cap on the tank and is keen to be on his way, but before he can start the motorcycle, one of the soldiers, whom he presumes to be older and senior in rank, steps up to him and thrusts a clipboard in his chest. Cellini looks at the clipboard and the sheet of paper attached to it, but it makes little sense to him. The senior soldier hands him a pencil and points at the clipboard, then starts tapping it with his index finger.

"Oh, you want me to sign for the gas?" Cellini says, taking the pencil and pointing to a space on the document. The soldier nods and continues tapping the clipboard excitedly.

Cellini signs his name in the space and hands the pencil back to the soldier, who studies the signature for a few seconds then steps back, smiling. He waves Cellini on – pointing back in the direction he has come from. Pointing up the mountain, the direction Cellini was originally heading, the soldier shakes his head and draws his hand across his throat, then spits on the floor.

"Germans?" Cellini says, pointing up the road.

The soldier nods animatedly and indicates for Cellini to turn around. Cellini turns the motorcycle around, waves to the crowd of soldiers and sets off back the way he came. As he rides away, he glances over at the two young boys who are saluting him with a clenched fist. He wonders why these men were so helpful and friendly towards him and can only assume that they took him to be one of them, perhaps a messenger. He is grateful to have a fast-growing beard, which already shows several days growth. For a man who is normally meticulous about his appearance, his dirty and dishevelled appearance may have just saved him.

18. Stukas… And an Unscheduled Flight

MAKING HIS WAY across country on the Benelli M36, now fully tanked up, Cellini heads towards the coast, hopeful of contacting friendly or sympathetic locals who can at least tell him where he is and which way he should go in order to avoid running into German troops who are in the process of occupying much of the area.

He sees very little traffic on the roads, and as he's motoring along he starts to think about where his life has led him so far. He smiles to himself. At least he's away from the Italian Army. It's a beautiful day, the sun is shining and he is enjoying the cool breeze on his face. The Benelli is running well and the throaty roar of its 500cc engine is soothing. Without realizing it, he is starting to relax and enjoy the ride when he becomes aware of a whining noise. Faint at first but getting louder. His first thought is that there is something wrong with the engine and he throttles back, slows down and leans forward over the fuel tank to listen. The high-pitched noise is coming from behind. Cellini looks around over his shoulder. Squinting into the sun he can make out the silhouette of two aircraft diving towards the ground.

He recognizes the distinctive gull-winged silhouette of Junkers Ju 87 dive-bombers.

"Stukas!"[1]

Caught out in the open, he must present a wonderful target of opportunity for the dreaded aircraft. Opening up the throttle, he starts to zigzag down the road to try and make himself as difficult as possible to hit.

[1] *The Junkers Ju 87 Stuka had been very effective in the early German Blitzkrieg "Lightning War" across Europe. Though slow and ineffective against Britain's Royal Air Force in the Battle of Britain, it still had its use against unprotected soft targets such as civilians. The Stuka's reputation as a terror weapon was largely due to the sound of its high-pitched siren mounted to the side of the aircraft, which gave a shrill wail as it entered its dive. The noise struck fear into people on the ground and its effectiveness as a weapon was probably more psychological than destructive.*

Ahead, maybe 500 metres, he sees a stone bridge over a river. Can he make it to the bridge and try to get under it? Only one way to find out. Without a second thought, Cellini opens the throttle wide, puts his head down and races down the road. Fortunately the noise of the Benelli's engine drowns out the fearful whine of the Stukas' sirens as they enter their final dive. He's still 50 metres shy of the bridge when he hears the first explosion. It feels as though the Benelli is going to lift off the ground but somehow he holds it steady. As he gets to the bridge he veers off to the right hand side, into the gully, screams to a halt and dives off the machine and under the stone bridge.

The second dive-bomber overshoots the bridge by several hundred metres, but the sound of the bomb blasts is still deafening and the ground underneath him still shakes from the shockwave. Cellini counts nine separate explosions altogether. If each aircraft carried the usual complement of five bombs, that means one was a dud.

He reflects, once again, on his good fortune. If he hadn't been able to make it as far as the bridge… If the bridge hadn't been there…

He makes the decision that it's time to stop joyriding around Yugoslavia and look for others so he can re-join the fight. He is more determined than ever to fight against the tyranny of fascism.

Once the danger has passed and the dust has settled, an eerie silence follows, broken only by the soft gentle trickle of water over the rocks under the bridge. Slowly getting to his knees, he listens intently for the sound of aircraft engines in case there are any more dive-bombers, but everything is quiet. Stepping out from under the shelter of the bridge, Cellini retrieves his canteen from the Benelli and refills it with fresh water from the river. Climbing back onto the Benelli he takes a good look around in every direction, and starts up the engine before guiding the machine back up the slope he had come down so hurriedly just a few minutes before.

Sitting astride the Benelli at the edge of the road, he pauses just long enough to catch his breath. Once satisfied there is no one else in sight, and no more aircraft in the sky, he sets off along the road – more alert and conscious of his surroundings than before and determined not to get caught out again. He begins to wonder why the Stukas were even attacking, and what their actual target might have been. Surely they weren't just using him, a lone motorcyclist, for bombing practice? It occurs to him that perhaps there are pockets of Partisans in the nearby hills, and they might well be the intended targets. If there are Partisans, perhaps he should try to make contact with them?

Perhaps not. If the Germans are aware of their location, then joining up with a group that it is being hunted from the sky probably isn't the best idea.

He decides to press on alone.

That night as the sun starts to go down, Cellini sees that there are rain clouds gathering to the south and moving quickly towards him. He pulls off the road and into a field, hiding the Benelli in a grove of olive trees. Before long the rain starts, and he shelters under a tree with his legs between the back wheels of the tricycle, protected by the wooden carrying bed. It isn't a comfortable position, but he hopes to remain dry until the rain stops, then he can lie on the dry patch of ground under the motorcycle.

But first he needs to find something to eat.

The olive trees look neglected. The farm – like so many farms and vineyards in Dalmatia – long abandoned by its owners fleeing the Italian occupiers or gone to join one of the resistance groups.

The rain has eased a little to a slow drizzle but Cellini decides this is a good time to go and search for food. It isn't quite dark, but he can see lights far off in the distance. Leaving the Benelli under the trees, he sets off towards the lights.

As a young child, he remembers his grandfather telling him how, if he ever finds himself in need of food and forced to steal it, the best time is at night during a rainstorm. Partly because the sound of the rain covers up a lot of noise and visibility through rain is very difficult; but mostly because no one wants to go outside in the rain to chase a thief, so it's much easier to get away! It seems even the weather is on Cellini's side!

Despite his confidence, he treads softly and stealthily as he gets closer to the lights. As stealthily as possible, that is, wearing boots caked in glutinous mud, slipping on large wet rocks and landing face down on the ground more than once.

Closer to the source of the light he can make out the shape of a building about 50 metres away. It looks like a small cottage, and in the near darkness he can just about make out small plants neatly arranged in rows. He is in a vegetable garden. Not wasting any time, he crouches and starts digging with his hands.

Potatoes!

Shaking off the dirt, he stuffs his pockets with the small round vegetables and looks around to see if can find anything else. A few rows over are some leafy plants, which he presumes are cabbages, and breaking off a leaf, tastes it. It's bitter but he knows it's loaded with nutrition and vitamins and he pulls more leaves, which he stuffs inside his tunic. He's about to turn around and head back when he hears scratching a little way off to his right, and catches a throaty trilling sound. Could it be a chicken? Making his way in the direction of the sound, he finds a hen house, and now that he has disturbed the animals, they start making various clucking sounds and are clearly excited by Cellini's presence. He sneaks around to the back of the coop and locates a small door at the bottom of the structure. Unable to see anything, he opens the door and slips his hand in, hoping to find an egg. At that moment, all hell breaks loose in the coop as chickens start squawking and fluttering as they run around. He feels around, finds two eggs and grabs one, but then can't find the other, which has rolled away.

He withdraws his hand, closes the small hatch and backs away. The chickens are still making quite a racket, and he looks towards the house to see if the noise has attracted any attention, but there are no signs of any activity, so he backs gently away and heads back across the garden to the fields.

By now it is completely dark, so following his tracks back to where he left the Benelli proves to be quite a task, and the return journey takes him twice as long. In spite of this, he still has a smile on his face. The rain has stopped and the sky is clear. The stars are shining and Cellini has food. His pockets are bulging with potatoes and his tunic is stuffed with cabbage – and he is clutching a precious egg in his hand.

Once back under the cover of the trees he knows he is not far from where he left the Benelli and it doesn't take him long to locate it.

He eats well, sips on water from his canteen and settles down for the night on the dry patch of ground he'd saved for himself under the motorcycle.

Back on the road the next morning, he decides he needs to find a city or town and reconnect with humanity in whatever capacity he finds it.

He sets off on the Benelli, but before too long hears the ominous sound of aero-engines overhead once again, and looking over his shoulder he sees a mass of aircraft, high in the sky and trailing white vapour from their wing tips. This time they are not German but American bombers. Big, four-engined silver warbirds – and coming in droves. He pulls off the road so he can get a good look. Jumping off the Benelli, he lies down on his back and cradles the back of his head in his hands. His entire field of vision from left to right is one mass of aircraft glinting against the azure sky.

Are they B-17s or B-24s? He can't be sure – but he is sure of one thing: Now that America is sending over these bombers by day it can only be a matter of time before the Allies win the war.

Once the bombers have flown by and are out of sight, he gets back on his machine, ready to continue on his way. On the horizon, towards the sea, he can see a cluster of small buildings, a thin wisp of smoke coming from one, suggesting signs of life. He will make for that.

*****

ARRIVING AT the seafront in Spalato, Cellini finds the small port is a hive of activity, with boats unloading and trucks departing. Cellini even spots a small seaplane in the harbour.

Not wanting to attract attention to himself until he can find out who is in charge, and whether the city is friendly or not, he drives the motorcycle as close as he dares and finds a place to park it, concealed among trees, then makes his way on foot towards the waterfront. He leaves his hat, jacket and rifle hidden in the wooden bed of the Benelli in order to try and blend with the crowd – but everyone seems far too busy to take any notice of one scruffy, grimy individual who, for all intents and purposes, might have just got off a tramp steamer. Cellini is fascinated by the seaplane. Though familiar with aircraft from his days working on the undercarriage and bomb release mechanisms in Milan, he has never seen an aircraft on floats before. The idea of a vessel that is essentially a boat on the water yet capable of taking to the air appeals greatly to his sense of wonderment when it comes to mechanical devices.

He does not recognize the type. It is a single-engined, high-winged monoplane with room for two people.[2] *Probably a reconnaissance plane*, he thinks to himself. It is moored alongside a pier, and as there is no one nearby, he casually strolls down to the pier to take a closer look.

He does not recognize the markings but it relieved to find that it does not have black crosses on the wings, nor a swastika on the tail – nor does it display Italian markings. Cellini studies the struts and wires holding the machine together, and is surprised by the apparent fragility of its construction. He is so focused on the machine that he doesn't notice the two men approaching from the shore, which is perhaps as well, since his only option is to act as naturally as possible. As they walk past him, both dressed in heavy, oil-stained overalls, one turns and says something to him. It seems like a friendly greeting so he just nods and smiles, pretending to understand, and they continue past. One carries a large satchel over his shoulder and both have leather flying helmets and goggles in their hands. Stepping onto the float nearest the pier, the one carrying the satchel heaves it into the cockpit then climbs up after it. The other, presumably the pilot, walks the length of the aircraft, checking the moving surfaces before climbing onto the float and then up on top of the

[2] *Most likely an old Rogozarski left over from the days when the Royal Yugoslavian Navy had a seaplane base nearby at Divulje. Though long obsolete, Yugoslavian Partisans made use of any and all vehicles they could lay their hands on for transport and reconnaissance.*

wing as if preparing for a flight. He signals to Cellini and points to a rope tied to a bollard on the pier, indicating for Cellini to untie the rope.

"He must think I'm part of his ground crew!" Cellini mutters to himself. "Fair enough! This ought to be fun!"

Cellini grabs the rope and holds on to it while the pilot gets in and starts the engine. After a few minutes of revving the engine and testing all the moving parts, the pilot waves Cellini off and starts to taxi. Instead of letting go of the rope, Cellini deftly steps onto the float of the seaplane, unseen by either crewmember, and wraps the rope tightly around his arm. Still holding the rope in one hand, he grabs for the rear strut as the aircraft picks up speed. He is able to hold onto the strut as long as the aircraft is skimming the water's surface, but as soon as it begins to lift off, he loses his footing and finds himself dangling beneath the float, still clutching the rope tightly in both hands, with it wrapped around his arm. The aircraft is bucking and jerking, its stability compromised by Cellini's weight swinging underneath. Watching the water move away, then come back again, his feet alternately scything the surface and then flying free and clear, Cellini decides this might be an appropriate time to curtail his flying activities. He releases the rope, giving himself a nasty burn on his forearm as it uncoils itself.

He lands with an almighty splash, feet first, and disappears under water for a few seconds. Regaining the surface, he looks around him. He estimates he is less than a kilometre from the shore. Treading water for a few minutes while watching the seaplane circle before heading out towards the islands, he begins the swim back. In spite of his sore arm, he sets a good rhythm, even though he swallows more seawater than he should because of the huge grin on his face and an occasional burst of laughter.[3]

Coming ashore a good distance away from the pier where he had grabbed the floatplane – and therefore quite a way from where he had parked the Benelli – Cellini makes his way back to the pier. He is hopeful his clothes will dry in the breeze as he walks along the seafront, but knows it's going to take a while for his boots to dry, his feet squelching with each step as a reminder. His shirt is almost dry when he reaches the Benelli, which has remained undiscovered, so he removes his still damp shirt, ties it to the back of the motorcycle and puts on the dry jacket. He climbs aboard and sets off once again towards the town.

[3.] *Cellini has no idea to this day why he did this. Like many things in his life, it was an unexpected opportunity to experience something different and exciting. The modern, more controlled version might be a new thrill ride in an amusement park. He had no particular purpose in mind, it was just a spontaneous reaction to his immediate circumstances. Fortune once again smiled upon him and he survived.*

Pulling over to the side of the road to try and work out exactly where he is, he realises how tired the swim has made him and thinks about finding a place to hide the vehicle and sleep, if only a short catnap.

Glancing around, looking around for a possible refuge, Cellini becomes aware of a familiar sound – the wailing, grating klaxon of Stukas again and he knows they are close and getting closer. That sound indicated they are entering their initial shallow dive, and the port city must be their target. Should he stay put? If he happens to be in their line of fire he would be a sitting duck!

He scans the sky trying to find the aircraft. The sound is deceiving and they could be anywhere, but he spots them, tiny specks in the distance over the mountains immediately north-east of Split. Ahead of him, back towards the sea, is a large building, partly on pillars, which Cellini presumes is in case of a high tide. He jumps the kerb on the Benelli and skids down an embankment, hanging on to the handlebars for dear life.

Reaching the building, he cuts the engine then leaps from the still-moving motorcycle and dives under the building, finds a pillar in the centre and sits with his back pressed up against it. The bombs begin raining down – some closer than others. The ground shakes with each explosion and the noise is deafening, but it is the wail of the dive-bombers' sirens followed by the whistle of the bombs on their descent that cause the most terror for Cellini. Not accustomed to experiencing any sense of fear, he rationalizes that what he feels now is the utter hopelessness of having literally no control over his own destiny. All he can do is sit and wait and hope that none of the Stukas' bombs strike the building under which he is sheltered, nor fall close enough to send shards of deadly shrapnel in his direction. He hadn't noticed how many aircraft were in the formation, but he counts 15 blasts. The direct hit never comes and the attack is over as quickly as it began. Silence. He makes his way over to the motorcycle, which he is relieved to discover has also survived the attack, and makes his way slowly towards the harbour.

19. The Prayer

SMOKE HANGS in the air, and in the distance Cellini can see dust and rubble and broken walls where buildings once stood, although the damage seems relatively superficial. Except for a few fishing boats and one or two people wandering aimlessly, probably shell-shocked from the air raid, the harbour is quiet. Crates and pallets lie unguarded, some with goods spilling out of them, but unmolested by the dazed passers by. No one even seems to notice the damp and dishevelled stranger on his three-wheeled motorcycle. Cellini thinks about loading up with food for the coming few days but then refocuses on his original plan to find someone in authority who might help him to connect with a local Partisan group. Seeing an official-looking stone building with the door open, he stops the Benelli outside and cautiously enters. Inside he calls out, "Hallo!" No reply. He doesn't venture too far inside because it is unlit, but the building seems to be completely deserted.

Just inside the door of the building, another doorway leads to a small office and Cellini enters. On a desk he finds papers scattered about and an old pistol. In the subdued light he can just about make out some of the words on the papers – Italian! This place must be some kind of warehouse or storage facility, no doubt recently abandoned by the Italians. The pistol is a type he's never seen before, and he studies it carefully. He is reminded of the days when he used to break into the *Liceo Classico* to steal weapons and he smiles to himself. The engraving on the gun identifies it as an Iver Johnson and he can see straight away that it's a top-break revolver. He wonders how a somewhat obscure American handgun came to be in an Italian warehouse in Yugoslavia. He cracks it open, sees that it is fully loaded, closes it and tucks it inside his coat.

Stepping out of the office, Cellini checks outside the door to see if anyone is around before turning back into the building. Following his nose, he is sure he can detect the unmistakable aroma of aging cheese – a wonderful smell, the like of which he hasn't enjoyed since leaving Italy. Ahead of him is a small stack of cheeses, whole wheels of parmesan, each at least 30 centimetres in diameter, just sitting there, almost begging for him to pick one up.

Cellini grabs the top cheese and drops it on the floor to break the crust. Breaking a small piece off, he tastes it. Wonderful! At that moment it's probably the best cheese he has ever eaten. Swallowing another big mouthful he bends down and picks up a whole, unbroken wheel and carries it outside.

Loading the cheese into the bed of the three-wheeler, he thinks about going back for another but decides against it. Since there is no sign of life down at the harbour, he starts up the motorcycle and heads away from the seafront.

He decides he might have better luck if he leaves the centre of Split and sets off for the outskirts of town.

Once out of Split, Cellini makes up his mind to stop and ask for help at the first place he comes to that shows any sign of life, as long as it isn't obviously a German or Italian stronghold. He is not exactly sure where he is relative to the rest of Dalmatia. He would prefer not to run into any Italians, but if that happens he knows he can bluff his way through. He is hopeful of locating a farm or a church, a school perhaps, where he can stop for a while, maybe even clean up and, if he's really lucky, get in touch with a Partisan group. His beard is long and matted and he thinks he could probably pass himself off as a Partisan just long enough to save his life, even though he doesn't speak any of the Yugoslavian dialects, but he would prefer to meet someone to whom he could explain his circumstances, who might then trust him enough to give him an introduction. The only people he is desperate to avoid are Germans, and he is certain they have not yet occupied the coast, because if they had, he wouldn't have seen so many dive-bombers – their trademark prelude to invasion.

On the outskirts of town, he comes upon a healthy-looking farm surrounded by fields of corn. The farmhouse is obviously occupied, a thin wisp of smoke coming from its chimney and animals gathered around the adjoining barn. In the middle of the cornfield he sees a middle-aged woman picking ears of corn and gathering them in a basket. Pulling the Benelli over to the side of the road, he shuts off the engine and jumps off.

Climbing over a stone wall, he starts to call out to the woman, to let her know he is coming and not to be afraid, that he is not going to hurt her.

Almost at the same instant that he opens his mouth to call out, he hears a familiar wailing, screeching sound coming from above him. Faint at first but getting louder. *Stukas!* He calls out as loudly as he can to the woman, running towards her, yelling and gesticulating for her to run away or at least to get down on the ground. She turns her head and stares at Cellini before looking straight up in the direction of the German bomber. Dropping the basket of corn, she raises her arms into the air and clasps her hands, first in defiance and then in prayer, as the siren wails louder and the leading *Stuka* gets closer to the ground. Three bombs leave the aircraft and the ungainly machine skips, relieved of its load, before beginning its climb away. This time Cellini is so close he can clearly see the black crosses on the side of the aircraft and the swastika on its tail fin. The tone of the siren changes to a lower pitch and then fades away altogether, replaced by the whistling of the falling bombs. Cellini is rooted to the spot.

The bombs hit the ground, the nearest one perhaps 50 or 60 metres in front of him, in the exact spot where the woman is standing. There is a massive, momentary flash of bright light and an eruption of smoke, soil, corn and other debris, followed by a series of earsplitting explosions, one on top the other, as the three bombs hit the ground. The earth shakes and Cellini loses his balance. Instinctively he dives headlong into the corn – far too late to protect himself from any shrapnel coming his way from the blasts – but amazingly, it misses him completely.

*****

As THE SMOKE begins to clear, Cellini runs over to where the woman had been standing. Everything is strangely silent. Pushing his way through the waist high corn, he comes to the edge of a huge crater, which he estimates to be about 15 metres across and almost as deep in its centre. He wades into the soft earth, which turns to mud after a few steps and sucks him down to his ankles. He can hear nothing – not even the sound of his own voice calling out – and realises he has probably been deafened by the blasts. The air is clearing but the smell of earth and gunpowder is still nauseating. There is no sign of the woman. No body parts, no corn basket. Not a shred of clothing. Nothing to suggest she was ever even there. It's as if she never existed.

Cellini sinks to his knees in the mire and stares across the crater in despair. He has never been a religious man. Though raised to some extent to be a Catholic, he had only ever paid lip service to the faith. Now he despises the very notion of any Deity that would allow this war to happen and disavows himself of any such belief. It is not just the death, but the complete obliteration of this woman, gathering corn to feed her family – on top of everything else he has witnessed in this terrible war – that pushes him over the edge of reason. He cannot understand why German dive-bombers would be attacking a farm. Could it be that there are Partisans nearby? Has

Hitler given orders to bomb any target in Yugoslavia, including farms?

His hearing begins to return, but his own voice is still muffled and there is a ringing noise inside his head, as though he is listening through a pillow stuffed inside an oil drum. He turns his face skywards and screams at the top of his lungs.

"Let me live to see all the leaders of this war dead!"[1]

[1]. *To this very day, Cellini has no idea why this thought crossed his mind, nor even if his outburst was a prayer, a demand or just a means of expressing his anger towards a God he didn't believe in anyway. "If it was a prayer," he says, dubiously, "then all I can say is it has been answered. I have outlived all the leaders, the good and the bad, of the Second World War."*

20. Four Beautiful Women to the Rescue

GETTING UP OFF his knees, Cellini staggers back to the Benelli in a daze. He has been close to the receiving end of three dive-bombing attacks in the past 24 hours and survived them all.[1] He has always considered himself to be fortunate and treated life as if it were an adventure. He has taken many risks and seen death "up close and personal" on numerous occasions, witnessed horrible war crimes – but somehow never stopped believing that those who committed them would get payback down the road.

Seeing this poor woman totally obliterated in front of his eyes makes him realise that payback is only possible when enough people get together and decide to make a difference. If he ever had any doubts about his beliefs, he now knows that he has to find a resistance group and join the fight against this tyranny. Sitting astride the Benelli, he sets off on the road, more determined than ever to get back into the war and to do whatever he can to help wipe out this fascist menace. He heads away from the farm, choosing a dirt road that takes him further away from Split. Seeing an old farmhouse in the distance with smoke coming from the chimney, he turns towards it and decides to chance his luck. He can always offer the cheese as a goodwill gift.

*****

TWILIGHT IS BEGINNING to fall, but it is still light enough that he thinks he can knock on the door of the farmhouse without appearing too menacing. As he walks up to the door it suddenly occurs to him that he

[1] *Between September 10th and September 18th 1943, following the Italian surrender, squadrons from Sturzkampfgeschwader 151 (Dive-bomber Group 151) of the Luftwaffe, flying the Ju 87D, completed 206 sorties against the Dalmatian Coast. Zadar, Senj, Split and Dubrovnik were all targeted. It was most likely during these raids that Cellini had his three encounters with the Stukas.*

hasn't rehearsed this scene at all. What should he say? Would they even understand him? What if they really think he's an enemy soldier?

While he is still thinking about this, and before he even reaches the door, it opens and a tall dark-haired woman steps outside, grabs Cellini by the arm and hurries him inside, glancing furtively around as she does so. She closes the door behind him and locks it, then backs away from him and ushers him to a chair by a table on which are set four plates and cups, with a bowl of what looks like hot stew or soup in the middle.

He turns the chair around to face the door – if anyone is going to come in after him he wants to make sure he sees them first. As he soaks in the warmth of the room and the pleasant smell of the stew, he begins to feel himself relax for the first time in days, or is it weeks? Then he becomes aware of another smell. An unpleasant odour that makes him think something must have crawled into the house and died. He realises the smell is emanating from him – his clothes, his boots – his very being – reeks.

His appetite can wait, in spite of the wonderful-smelling food on the table. Right now, what's more important than eating is the need to clean himself up. He implores his hostess to let him wash, using Italian words while rubbing his hands together and then rubbing his palms on his face. To his surprise he is able to make himself understood. He just wants a place to clean himself up. His hostess smiles and nods her head, then raises a finger as if saying, *wait, just one minute.*

She calls out and is joined by three more young women. They are younger than she is, but obviously related. Two are identical – Cellini is certain they must be twins – who look to be about sixteen or seventeen. The third bears a striking resemblance but is younger, perhaps twelve or thirteen. They stare at the grizzly, bearded stranger until admonished by their mother who claps her hands and issues instructions. They jump to action and help Cellini off with his coat and boots, which are still wet from his earlier dunking in the Adriatic. He takes the Iver Johnson pistol from his pocket, careful to pick it up by the butt so as not to appear threatening, and places it inside one of the boots. The girls lead him to a separate area of the house and point to a large tin bathtub.

They indicate that they will fetch hot water and for him to get into the tub, but he waits for them to leave before taking off the rest of his clothes. After a while they return with pans of hot water, soap, a razor and towels, and discreetly leave him to clean himself up.

His first task is to remove the beard. He finds a mirror on the wall and is shocked at what he sees. The beard is thick and matted and takes a while to cut through. Once gone he feels considerably better. The bath is now the perfect temperature and he lowers himself into the tub and luxuriates in the water. It is weeks since he had the opportunity to wash properly, let alone enjoy a hot bath, and he unashamedly lies back and lets the water envelop his body. When the water gets too cold as to be enjoyable, he steps out and wraps himself in a towel and contemplates his good fortune, once again. He looks around for his uniform to put it back on but cannot find it. Drying his thick black hair, he suddenly feels as though he is being watched.

The four women are standing, side by side, a look of amazement on their faces. The mother opens her mouth to speak, her broken Italian is not too bad, and he understands.

"Please excuse us. We do not mean to be rude by staring at you, but when you arrived we thought you were an old man. Your beard, your hair – and – excuse me for saying so – the awful smell…" Her words trail off and she looks down at the ground, embarrassed.

Cellini laughs. "When I looked into the mirror, I thought I was an old man too!" He says, "and I can only apologize for the smell!"

They laugh together and she offers him a course sweater and a worn pair of wool trousers to put on. "I am cleaning your clothes," she says, "but they will not be ready until morning."

He accepts the loan of the clothes, which are ill-fitting but warm, and after putting them on, sits down at the table to join them for their modest supper of stewed mutton, which is mostly bones in water and has obviously already made several trips to the table. After a while he rises from the table and goes to the door, much to the surprise of the women who try to stop him leaving. He raises a finger in the air and smiles.

"It's alright," he says, "Just one minute. I'll be right back."

He opens the door and looks around to make sure it's clear outside, then steps over to the Benelli and picks up the cheese from the back. Returning to the door he hands the large parmesan cheese to the women. The women are overjoyed at the gift and immediately cut into the cheese, sampling small mouthfuls and offering it to Cellini, who is happy to share it. The mother then stops, a look of concern on her face.

"We have very little money," she says, "but we must pay you for the cheese. Such a luxury is rare since the war started and…" Cellini interrupts her, holding up his hand.

"It is a gift from the Italian Army," he says, a big grin on his face, "They won't be needing it any more!"

After enjoying a few bites of the cheese, the woman's daughters say good night and leave to go their room. The woman approaches Cellini, takes his face in her hands and looks him in the eyes. Then she looks down at the floor, takes his hand and leads him towards her bed.

"No, no!" he says, shaking his head. "You do not need to do this.

You should not do this!"

"But the food?" she replies, pointing towards the table and indicating the large round cheese by drawing her hands in a circle.

"I told you, that is a gift. I am so grateful for your help, for providing shelter," Cellini replies.

The woman looks at him, a tear forming in her eyes. "Perhaps, I am too old for you? Perhaps you would prefer… one of my daughters?"

"No!" Cellini replies vehemently. "Please my dear. A woman is not for barter or trade nor for taking advantage of. I have seen many terrible things in this war and I will not be like the pigs in the Italian Army. Please go to sleep in your bed and let me rest here. I will be comfortable with a blanket on the floor."

He knows that she doesn't necessarily understand all the words, but he hopes she catches the meaning and accepts his sincerity.

*****

AFTER A GOOD night's sleep, Cellini is awakened by the sunlight coming through the farmhouse windows, illuminating and warming the spot where he chose to lie down the night before.

He gets up, washes his hands and face in a bowl of water left for him on the table, then opens the door and steps outside. To his surprise, the woman is already up and outside in the yard cleaning up and getting ready for the day. She looks over at him, but before he can speak, she stops working, wipes her hands on her apron and runs off to towards the back of the house, returning a moment later with his uniform, clean and dry and fresh smelling. Cellini takes the uniform, thanks her with a smile and a disbelieving shake of his head, and goes back inside to change.

A few minutes later she follows him inside, goes to the kitchen, pours a large cup of steaming liquid from a pot she has left on the stove and hands it to Cellini. He hopes it might be coffee, but it is just watery broth left from the meal the previous evening. He tries not to look disappointed but the woman can read it on his face and reaches out to take the cup back. Cellini saves face by thanking her profusely, once again, for her shelter and hospitality, and drinks down the liquid, grateful for its warmth.

He indicates for her to sit with him at the table. She hesitates, keen to get back to her chores, but acquiesces. There is an awkward silence as he tries to find the right words to ask her for one more favour. It's a big one that for all he knows might put her and her daughters at considerable risk.

Using a combination of broken Italian and highly expressive mime,

Cellini attempts to ask if she can help to put him in contact with a military organization or group where he can continue his fight against the evil fascists who have overrun Yugoslavia. She looks at him inquisitively, but after a while he senses that she understands.

"Partizani?" she says.

"Yes! Partisans!" Cellini is overjoyed. "I want to join the Partisans!"

She thinks about it for a while. Sitting across the table, a worried look comes over her face and Cellini wonders if perhaps he may have pushed his luck a little too far by asking.

She conveys to him that she needs to go out and that he must wait until she returns. She takes off her apron, hangs it up near the door and wraps a threadbare looking cloak around here shoulders. She points at Cellini and then to the table as if to reaffirm that he is to wait for her to get back. He nods in agreement and she slips out of the door.

*****

FOR WHAT SEEMS likes an age he sits at the table. Then he stands and begins to pace up and down. What if she has gone to fetch the *Ustase*? Or the *Chetniks*? Or worse still the Germans? He dismisses the idea. The kindness she and her daughters have shown him suggests they would never do such a thing.

Even so, when the door opens he is startled and almost jumps out of his skin. It's just the twin sisters coming back after getting an early start and working hard on the farm. Less than a minute later the door opens again and it's the younger daughter. The three of them stare and giggle at the man they first thought must be at least 100 years-old but turned out, after a shave and a wash, to be not much older than they are. Conversation is difficult but everyone smiles a lot.

Cellini is more relaxed and comfortable than he has been for some time, but even so he keeps his right hand on the revolver in his pocket. The girls get on with their chores, in and out of the house, leaving Cellini to fend for himself. Each time the door opens and one or the other of them comes in he feels his hand gripping the revolver tightly. His emotions are mixed. He's embarrassed by his action, but at the same time he knows it is an instinct that could save his life.

After about an hour, the door opens and the mother walks in. She is alone and sits down at the table.

She clearly has something very important to say and pauses, thinking about how best to get her message across. After several false starts, she manages to spit out some words and, along with gesticulations, is able to make herself understood. Cellini is to go with her this evening to meet a man called Nikolas, who is a Partisan. Nikolas speaks Italian as well as the local dialect so they will be able to communicate much better. Then she indicates to Cellini that if he would like to do some work while he is waiting, there is plenty of wood that needs to be chopped. He agrees, happy to help this wonderful family in any way he can. He follows her outside, where she points to a pile of logs with a large axe resting on top.

He realises now how absurd he was to be suspicious and feels guilty for having done so; a woman living alone with her three daughters is highly unlikely to give an axe to a man she doesn't trust and believe in, and Cellini is humbled by the faith shown in him.

After dark, the woman leads Cellini out of the house. He says goodbye to the three daughters and follows her. He wants to say something about the Benelli. Should he attempt to take it with him? He is sure it is almost out of gasoline again and therefore not much use – but hates to let it go. He retrieves his rifle from the back of the motorcycle and hands the Iver Johnson pistol to the woman. She takes it willingly and stuffs it inside her coat pocket as she hurries him along. He tries to keep track of the direction she takes, but there are a lot of twists and turns and soon he realises he could not find his way back, even if he wanted to.

After about twenty minutes, she signals him to stop by touching his arm. She pulls a torch from her coat pocket and flicks it on and off a couple of times into the darkness. Immediately, another torch flashes back in response and she moves forward, pulling Cellini behind.

A large, burly man with a wide smile and a grey, grizzled beard steps out from behind a tree. He has a rifle slung over his shoulder but he makes no attempt to utilize it even though he greets Cellini cautiously. He introduces himself as Nikolas. There is no handshake or contact, just a shrug. He hugs the woman, kissing her on both cheeks, and thanks her for delivering the Italian before waving her away. Cellini takes her hand and thanks her for bringing him this far. He asks if he will see her again, but before she can respond, Nikolas cuts in.

"No," he says, "You will not see each other again." Then adds, "It is better this way."

His Italian is good, though he has a strange accent.

"Come," he says to Cellini. "We must go."

Cellini turns to wish the woman good luck, and to give his best wishes to her daughters. He also wants to tell her to hide the Benelli somewhere or at least find a good use for it, but she has already disappeared into the darkness, silently and stealthily. Her face, and those of her daughters, will always remain with him, for their kindness and gentle, innocent beauty. He turns back to Nikolas.

"Don't you want to know anything about me? How I came to be here in Spalato?"

"What makes you think you are in Spalato?" Nikolas replies, catching Cellini slightly off guard, and it shows. Nikolas laughs.

"Yes, my friend, we are in Spalato – only we call it Split."

"As for learning about you," Nikolas continues, "that is not my job. My job is only to fetch you. The Commander will question you and decide what to do with you."

"What to do with me?" Cellini is taken aback.

"Oh don't worry. If they believe you are telling the truth and they like you, you'll be recruited."

"And if not?" Cellini tries not to sound worried but is beginning to have second thoughts about Nikolas.

"Then you will be shot!" Nikolas says, a toothy grin spreading across his face.

21. Welcome to the Partisans

THEY WALK FOR what seems like at least an hour or more over dirt roads, through woodlands and up some fairly steep terrain. All of a sudden, out of nowhere, they are surrounded by a group of other men, all armed and dressed in similar fashion to Nikolas. Neither hearing nor seeing anything or anyone approaching, Cellini is taken by complete surprise at the stealth of these men. He counts about seven or eight. They seem friendly enough; some pat him on the back and others grab him by the hand. He is led up a fairly steep hill and behind some rocks where he sees quite a few more of these Partisans gathered around a fire. Cellini is ushered to the front of the group, near to the fire, where a tall, distinguished-looking man, clean-shaven except for a thin moustache, turns to greet him.

He introduces himself simply as Poldo.[1]

Discreetly leading him away from the others, Poldo engages Cellini in casual conversation. Cellini finds himself answering a lot of questions and telling Poldo about his background and how he came to be in Yugoslavia. Comfortable in Poldo's company, Cellini opens up, sharing much of his life story from his birth in the United States to his unwilling recruitment into the Italian Army. He leaves out the part about his brief time with the *Ustase*, since that was a mistake he feels is best forgotten. Poldo's comprehension of Italian is good, even though he struggles to understand some of Cellini's *Barese* dialect. He listens intently, and satisfied that Cellini is telling the truth, Poldo nods acceptance and welcomes him to the 4th Battalion of the 9th Brigade, 20th Division of the National Liberation Army and Partisan Detachments of Yugoslavia, as the Partisans were formally known at that time. They walk back to where the rest of the group is waiting.

Cellini takes an immediate liking to the man called Poldo. He comes across as honest and decisive yet very down to earth: a good leader. Many of the soldiers in the battalion are Italian speakers; some have defected from the Italian army and Cellini is not at all sure they are completely loyal or trustworthy. His experiences with the Italian military are still fresh in his memory and he makes up his mind to keep an eye on one or two of these individuals.

*****

LIFE WITH the Partisans is tough. Discipline is strict and there is zero tolerance for anyone who breaks the rules. Respect for women in particular is very high on the list – and there are many women among the Partisans. Recruited initially to serve as cooks and nurses, they soon found themselves toting weapons and in the line of fire, where they have given an excellent account of themselves.

Partisan warfare is guerilla warfare. The Partisans do not wait for the enemy to come to them. They are not defending land or property or possessions and they are not limited by territorial boundaries. They fight to destroy and disrupt a foreign invader who would harm them or take over their lives and the lives of their families. Partisans strike fast and hard, then retreat and regroup ready for their next assault.

[1.] *Leopold "Poldo" Mikulić became the commander of the 4th Battalion, 9th Brigade, 20th Division, on October 5th, 1943 and thus was Cellini's commander for most of the time he spent with the Partisans in Yugoslavia.*

Born to a working class family in Makarska, Poldo grew up to become a master tailor and a member of the then illegal Communist Party, for which he was imprisoned early in 1941. He was released when the Independent State of Croatia was established in April of that year and subsequently instrumental in organizing an uprising in Makarska. Poldo joined the People's Liberation Struggle and went on to serve heroically with the Partisans. He commanded the 4th platoon of South Dalmatian troops "Turudija", and then the 4th Battalion troops "Josip Jerčević", before leading the 2nd Battalion of the 4th Dalmatian Brigade in the Battle on the Neretva River. In late April 1943 his battalion joined the 3rd Dalmatian Brigade in continued fighting around Jubušnja and Vučevo. At the beginning of June 1943 he fought with the 6th Belgrade Battalion of the 1st Proletarian Brigade of People's Liberation Army of Yugoslavia. He participated in the Battle on the Sutjeska River, and then in August 1943, under direct orders from Marshal Tito, was sent to Dalmatia, where he became commander of the 4th Battalion of the 9th Dalmatian Brigade. He was later appointed deputy commander of sthe southern Dalmatia region and commander for the entire Biokovo Mountain and River Neretva area. He retired with the rank of colonel in the Yugoslavian Army.

The author was able to contact a journalist in Split who, during a visit in November, 2015, arranged a meeting with other surviving Partisans, as well as a newspaper interview with Cellini. On recognizing his description of her father in the subsequent newspaper article, Poldo's daughter Gorana contacted the newspaper and a meeting was arranged. Sadly, Colonel Leopold Mikulić had died in 1998 but Cellini was able to meet with his widow as well as his daughter and son in 2016.

This is the first of many lessons that Vito Cellini will learn about armed combat over the next few weeks. Although he doesn't realise it at the time, these lessons will have a lasting impact on him and he will share them with many people, including world leaders and top military personnel.

Cellini forms a comradeship, if not a close friendship, with Nikolas and they invariably find themselves side by side in the food line, or while hiking into the mountains, and eventually in combat. Not long after Cellini joins the battalion he is told that they will be moving up into the mountains to disrupt the Germans making their way across from Bosnia.

After hiking and camping out for several days and nights, they reach a position fairly high up in the mountains and word filters down that the Germans may be nearby, so tonight there will no fires and they must keep as quiet as they can. It is bitterly cold and Cellini dozes fitfully but anticipation of the combat he knows is coming keeps him awake for most of the night. He is one of the first to stir, and after his customary visit to the nearby bushes, he notices his commander, Poldo, perched behind a rock looking towards the adjacent mountain through binoculars. It is barely light as Cellini approaches him and cheerfully wishes him good morning. Poldo looks at him and smiles.

"It will be a very good morning indeed if I can catch one of those bastards by surprise," he says, pointing towards a cliff, 800 or 900 metres in the distance across a rock-strewn valley.

Letting the binoculars hang from a strap around his neck, Poldo pulls his sub-machine gun from behind his back, holds it waist high and takes aim towards the cliff. Even without the aid of binoculars, Cellini had seen the movement over on the cliff and is astounded that his commander would attempt a shot from such range. Poldo lowers his weapon without firing.

"We wait until everyone is ready so that we maintain the element of surprise," he says, taking the gun in one hand and letting the barrel point towards the ground.

In the short time that Cellini has been speaking with Poldo, everyone in the battalion has woken, gathered their belongings and taken up position along the ridge overlooking the cliff, their weapons at the ready. The mules are packed with all the equipment and supplies and tethered out of sight. There will be no breakfast this morning until the fight is done. Cellini is amazed at how quickly these Partisans ready themselves for combat. He recalls how long it took his *Bersaglieri* to form up for a routine patrol.

Although Cellini has witnessed a great deal of violence and death in his twenty years, he is yet to engage in actual combat. He feels no fear because he has no concept of what it is like to be fired at or to have grenades and mortars raining down on him, other than what he gleans from his conversations with Nikolas.

Poldo checks the view through his binoculars once again and raises his hand, indicating for everyone to hold their fire until he gives the signal. Releasing his hold on the binoculars, he raises his weapon to his hip and shoots. Three single shots in less than three seconds. His shots hit the rock harmlessly, well below his intended target. He prepares to shoot again but the gun appears to jam. He tries once more to pull back the bolt and fire the weapon but all he gets is a metallic click.

The rest of the battalion opens fire, peppering the rocks below the German stronghold, but without hitting anything or anyone on the other side. The Germans return fire with slightly more accuracy, but the range is too distant to be effective and the Partisans jeer loudly above the noise of the gunfire.

Poldo looks over towards Cellini and calls out to him, "Hey you! Italian! Come over here!"

Cellini crawls over to where his commander is sitting, holding out the jammed sub-machine gun at him.

"You're Italian, right? Well so is this damn weapon. Can you fix it?"

Cellini looks first at his commander and then at the weapon, a Beretta M38. He has no experience with the weapon, but is intrigued by its twin triggers and would love the chance to take it apart to see how it works. Without any hesitation he replies, "Sure, I'll fix it."

Meanwhile, Poldo pulls a pistol from his holster around his waist, checks that it is loaded and starts firing across the ravine at the Germans again.

He looks at Cellini and says, "What are you waiting for? I gave you a job to do – so go and do it!"

Cellini ducks and slithers away from the ridge and takes shelter behind a stone wall where he sees Nikolas in a crouched position, firing up at the Germans. Nikolas beckons frantically for Cellini to join him, which he does, by crawling on his belly behind the wall.

"They've pinned me down!" Nikolas yells excitedly. "Those Nazi bastards are focusing all their fire on me!" Cellini hadn't noticed and thinks this is a bit of an overreaction from Nikolas.

"They're firing randomly in our general direction," Cellini says, "at everyone… and at the same time at no one. We're too far away!"

Suddenly Nikolas screams out in agony. Collapsing from the crouching position he falls on his back.

"I'm hit!" he says, then screams again, even more loudly. Cellini calms his screams down to a whimper and checks him all over, starting with his head, his chest, torso and legs, for any sign of trauma, bleeding or a wound of some kind, but can find nothing. Then he touches Nikolas on the arm and the screaming starts again, louder than ever. Cellini cautiously takes his arm and runs his fingers along it, expecting to find shattered bone and shards of wet flesh. Instead his fingers locate a small hole in the sleeve of Nikolas's coat, just above the elbow. Pulling the hole open Cellini picks out a small misshapen ball of lead between his forefinger and thumb. It is still hot. A bullet has evidently gone through a gap between the stones in the wall and, using up the last of its kinetic energy, burned through his clothing and lodged against the skin on his arm. He has a minor burn, but the skin isn't even broken.

Cellini gets a lot of fun out of teasing Nikolas about how he screamed like a baby when he was "shot" by the Germans!

*****

THE LONG-DISTANCE skirmish is over as quickly as it began. The shooting slows down and eventually stops, and both sides withdraw to safe ground. There are no serious casualties among the Partisans and presumably the same is true for the Germans. Nikolas is finally convinced that his wound is not mortal, and as the Partisans hike onwards to spend the night in a new location, Cellini's mind switches to other things.

First and foremost he needs to work on Poldo's sub-machine gun. He has no idea what might have caused the gun to jam, and while he is thinking about it, his thoughts drift back to the morning's firefight, and in particular to Poldo's shooting.

He had never stopped to consider it before today, but after watching every one of Poldo's shots going low on the mountain this morning, he has thought about little else all day. It seems obvious that a bullet travelling such a long distance would tend to drop, and that in order to hit your target you would need to aim much higher. But how high? The Italians had never taught him this, and he curses his own ignorance for not being able to work it out for himself. He decides he will talk to his commander as soon as he has a chance. But in order to do that without looking like a conceited idiot, first he needs to show Poldo what a great gunsmith he is by unjamming his weapon and getting it back into working order!

It's the first time he's even handled the M38, so he begins carefully stripping the weapon. He realises he really doesn't know what he's doing but manages to undo a few screws and release the bolt and the receiver. As he does so, the small return spring inside a tube in the bolt shoots out and lands somewhere in the loose dirt, some distance away. Combing through the dirt and stones on his hands and knees, with the light beginning to fade, finding the spring seems like a hopeless task, but one thing Cellini has in abundance is patience. It takes almost two hours to locate the spring, which he puts in his pocket. After a couple of hours wrestling with the weapon, he has a very good understanding of how it works, and can put it back together quite easily, but absolutely no clue as to why it stopped working. In fact it takes him all night, by the light of a glowing fire, to discover that the problem is a spent cartridge that has somehow rotated 180-degrees and become lodged backwards in the breech. Disassembling the gun one more time, he is able to dislodge the offending shell and put it back together in working order, returning it to his commander just as the sun is coming up the following morning. He wishes he could have test fired it before handing it over to Poldo, just to make sure it is fully operative, but of course to do so would attract a great deal of unwanted attention, even if he happened to have any 9mm ammunition.

Acting as though the task was nothing at all, he shrugs off the gratitude of his commander and instead turns the conversation to the topic he had been anxious to discuss; the longer-range shooting on the mountain – being very careful not to criticize the shooting prowess of his commanding officer!

Poldo explains that any rifle can have its sights adjusted for longer distance – that is how snipers set their weapons. He goes on to emphasize that Partisans usually fight at very close range and rarely even use the gun sight. Poldo demonstrates the technique used so successfully by the Yugoslavian guerillas in their fight against the fascists.

"By holding the gun at the hip and using the tip of the barrel to point directly towards the enemy, as though it were an extension of the finger," he says, "it is possible to fire three rounds in the time it would take a marksman to fire one."

"How quickly can you point your finger at three targets?" Poldo asks, raising his arm from the elbow and pointing two fingers first in one direction, then another. He points the Beretta, still level at his hip, at three nearby rocks, each several metres apart, one after the other. The gun is not loaded so Poldo mouths the sound, *"poom, poom, poom!"* and laughs.

"If there are three enemy soldiers shooting at you, you can shoot all of them before any of them can get off a single shot," the commander adds. "Whereas if you take the time to aim carefully by holding the gun up to your cheek and squinting through one eye, you'll be cut down before you can fire a single round."

Though he had never been good when it came to paying attention at school, Cellini is spellbound by Poldo's words. What he says seems so logical and obvious.

It's another lesson Cellini will take with him and pass on to future generations of fighting men.

They talk for a while about guns. Sensing Cellini's genuine interest and love for weapons, the commander asks him a lot of questions and learns a little about his past. He also gleans from their conversation that while Cellini still has much to learn about using guns in combat, he does have a comprehensive understanding of the mechanics of guns; how they work and how sometimes they don't work.

He senses that Cellini may be quite a valuable asset to the 9th Brigade and decides to appoint him as gunsmith and repairman for the battalion. It's an honour the young Italian-American is proud to accept.

"One more thing," Poldo says, as Cellini is about to walk away. "Since you don't mind staying up all night to keep a gun working..." he pauses just long enough to allow the words to sink in and for Cellini to realise he wasn't fooling him pretending it was a piece of cake, before finishing his sentence, "... I'm putting you in charge of the heavy machine gun."

"Which one?" Cellini asks, with some impertinence.

"All of them!" Poldo snaps straight back at him.

While he is to be responsible for the maintenance and smooth operation of all weapons in the battalion, Cellini will personally carry the Breda M37.[2] It's a cumbersome weapon and takes a long time to set up for use, added to which each clip must have the empty cartridges removed before fresh rounds can be installed.

Cellini finds space on a pack mule to stow the gun, its tripod and ammunition, and spends a considerable amount of time, under pressure from Poldo, practising unloading, assembling and preparing the weapon for combat use. Poldo wants it ready to fire in less than five minutes. Cellini can do it in slightly under four.

[2] *In service, the Italian Breda M37 was considered fairly reliable and its powerful, heavy-bullet cartridge had excellent range and penetration. Still, it was the heaviest World War Two 'light' machine gun, and quite complex to use and deploy. It was almost twice as heavy as any of the German machine guns, and the tripod added around 20 kilograms, putting its total weight at around 40 kilograms. Captured examples were used in combat not only by Partisans, but also by British and Commonwealth forces, including units of the Special Air Service (SAS).*

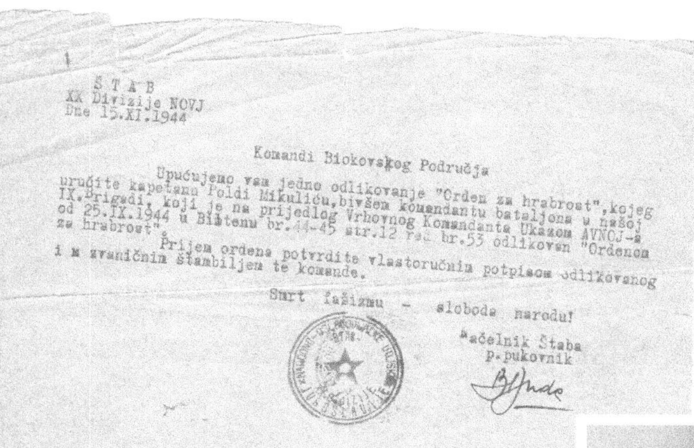

ŠTAB
XX Divizije NOVJ
Dne 15.XI.1944

Komandi Biokovskog Područja

Upućujemo vam jedno odlikovanje "Orden za hrabrost", kojeg uručite kapetanu Poldi Mikuliću, bivšem komandantu bataljona u našoj IX. Brigadi, koji je na prijedlog Vrhovnog Komandanta Ukazom AVNOJ-a od 25.IX.1944 u Biltenu br.44-45 str.12 red br.53 odlikovan "Ordenom za hrabrost".

Prijem ordena potvrdite vlastoručnim potpisom odlikovanog i m zvaničnim štambiljem te komande.

Smrt fašizmu - sloboda narodu!

Načelnik Štaba
P.pukovnik

Original typed order appointing Leopold "Poldo" Mikulić commander of the 4th Battalion, 9th Brigade, 20th Division of the Partisans.

A rare wartime photo of Poldo.

Poldo's widow, Divna Mikulić, shares photo albums and memories of her late husband with Vito Cellini, June 2016.

Cellini meets Poldo's daughter and son, Gorana Peruzović and Božidar Mikulić, June 2016, as the result of a newspaper article about his experience with the Partisans.

22. First Time Under Fire

IT IS NOT long before the 9th Brigade is back in the thick of it. A surprise attack on a German gun emplacement is mounted and Cellini is to take point with the Breda. The plan, as always, is to sneak up as close as possible on the Germans, attack with mortars, grenades and gunfire, then turn and run, everyone going in different directions. It is imperative to have a good rendezvous location after the firefight so that everyone can assemble later.

For whatever reason, the Germans seem to be aware of the impending attack and the shooting starts before the Partisans are in position. It's a rare occurrence but when it happens, the Partisan soldiers break immediately, scatter and regroup as planned.

Being at the spearhead of the attack, Cellini is one of the first to hear the sound of enemy gunfire and, since he is nowhere near ready – nor close to a suitable position – to set up his machine gun, he follows the routine order to break off the attack and make his way to the rendezvous. Hearing bullets going past and imagining himself the target of every German on the mountain, he picks up the pace and his stealthy escape quickly becomes a near sprint down the mountain pathway. He pauses to look back but sees nothing. Gunfire erupts from behind once more and as he begins to run, he instinctively hoists the heavy gun over his shoulder so that the wooden butt is pressed against the side of his face, nearest to the enemy, believing it will shield his face from the hail of bullets he expects to receive at any moment!

Once he feels safely out of range, Cellini ducks behind some shrubs and into the trees. Covering himself with branches and leaves, he makes sure he has a good view of the path behind him in case any of the German soldiers have followed. After about half an hour, he decides to make a move. Keeping to the side of the path, he makes his way to the agreed rendezvous, where he is greeted with howls of laughter and a few whistles from his fellow Partisans.

While making his escape, he had been observed by several of his comrades trying to protect his face with the butt of the machine gun, and they in turn had shared the story with the entire battalion. It would take him a long time to get over the jibes and the sight of them holding their hands up to their faces, while others cupped their hands around their crotch, suggesting that other body parts are more valuable and therefore should take priority behind the gun butt.

*****

IT IS THOSE very delicate body parts that become the first casualty of Cellini's war, though not in the way he might expect or anticipate – and fortunately without permanent damage. A sudden and unexpected mortar attack from the Germans begins while Cellini is relieving himself behind a tree. Buttoning himself up and hitting the ground in an instant, it is one of the few times in his life he can ever remember feeling fear. Never one to shy away from a fight, be it with fists, knives or even firearms – because he always feels he can control the situation and turn it in his favour – this is a whole new experience for him. He cannot see his enemy and has no idea where the hot, explosive metal is coming from, nor where or when the next salvo will land.

The effect of the mortar attack and the fear it brings is profound upon Cellini, and he finds himself unable to urinate for a week following the attack. The discomfort of a full bladder adds to his hatred for an enemy he has yet to come face to face with – but the wait is almost over, he knows.

Later, he will ask why the Partisans did not retaliate and is told that it was a chance hit by the Germans. Every once in a while, the enemy would launch a mortar attack in the general direction of where they thought Partisans might be hiding out. If the Partisans return fire, they give away their position and the Germans send in an infantry battalion to clean up. By keeping quiet and taking cover, they convince the Germans they are off target – and remain safe – for a while longer.

The cool autumn nights and warm sultry days are filled with the stench of body odour, rotten feet and festering wounds, occasionally masked by a nearby Partisan lighting up a cigarette and exhaling the first lungful of sulphur-infused tobacco smoke. The sound of gunfire or grenades can be heard in the distance and sometimes close by. Every so often, the warm sickly smell of cordite wafts by in clouds, briefly masking the more odious aromas.

The Partisans are constantly on the move. Sometimes their hikes take them close to humanity, but more often than not, deeper into the mountains.

When combat comes, it will come quickly and without warning. Patrolling the mountains that shelter Split from the sea, the nomadic warriors are reminded that they must remain alert, twenty-four hours each day, taking turns to rest or to eat and always with someone on guard.

Word spreads that the battalion is planning an assault on the nearby Germans and that everyone is to get ready. It will be a hit and run attack requiring timing, stealth and, above all, silence as they approach. The men divide into groups. Cellini will take point and carry the Breda, without the tripod. He has been practising taking it down and readying it for action for the past few days. He has also been practising shooting from the hip, and though not firing any live rounds, has become used to the notion of using the muzzle as an extension of his finger, pointing towards a target and then immediately switching to fire in a different direction.

Before they leave, Poldo has a few words to share with each man and when he speaks to Cellini it is to reaffirm his confidence and make sure he remembers the lesson from a few days earlier.

To Cellini's surprise, the women also take up arms and join the men to enter the fray. It was always his impression that the role of the women in the Partisans was to act more as camp followers: preparing food and tending the wounded, and he has mixed feelings about women being part of the front line.[1] It is yet another lesson about the Yugoslavian people and their fierce determination to rid themselves of the fascist enemy.

[1] *Feelings he holds to this day. While Cellini does not consider himself in any way a misogynist, he believes that women should be protected from front-line combat situations. Though he greatly admired the Partisan women, he found the sight of wounded and dying females in battle to be very disturbing.*

23. First Blood

THEY'VE HIKED, camped and walked patrols for several days, now they are out on yet another patrol but this time it feels different; more real, or maybe more surreal. Cellini is on point, weapon held at the hip in readiness. Suddenly the sound of gunfire echoes around. Single shots and short, staccato bursts. Not immediately close by but within a few hundred metres. The battalion is well spread out, so it is almost certainly involved somewhere. More shots, closer this time. Instinctively he looks around for cover and sees a rock that will be perfect. As he moves towards it he catches a glimpse of movement in the trees ahead, maybe 30 metres. Germans! Keeping the weapon by his side, he points with the barrel, an extension of his hand – just the way Poldo had shown him – fires a short burst and sees his target go down. Another shadow, 10 metres to the left of the first. This time he can see a rifle being raised and aimed in his direction. Another quick burst. And another. Now he's behind the rock and the only sound he can hear is the beating of his own heart.

More gunfire in the distance. He cannot see any more movement in the direction he was shooting so he crawls out from the rock and, scanning the trees ahead for any signs of life, works his way in the direction of the Germans. He finds three bodies. One he hit square between the eyes, one in the throat and one in the back, with a huge exit wound in the chest.

"This piece of shit must have turned and run away!" he says out loud to no one but himself.

The bodies are still warm but the blood is already starting to congeal, seeping slowly from the wounds like thick dark syrup. The worst part is the smell. Cellini has never been afraid or squeamish at the sight of blood and guts, but the warm sickly smell of death is something he will never get used to.

No time to dwell on the sight or smell now, he needs to find the rest of the battalion.

It seems the firefight is over as quickly as it began. In fact, it lasted over an hour. The Partisans have withdrawn to lower ground and the Germans have retreated to their camp, somewhere across the next ridge. Some good men were lost today but no one will dwell on that. There is no place for sentiment in guerilla warfare. Others are wounded. Those who will survive to fight again are treated and carried on improvised stretchers; those who won't are made comfortable, given a shot of grappa or brandy and left behind.[1]

Tonight they will double the guard at the camp.

It's time for rations to be handed out. Hot food mostly comprises boiled flour water stirred into a thick, tasteless paste with no seasoning, not even salt or pepper.[2] It offers little nourishment and no flavour but it's filling and forms the basis of the Partisan diet, supplemented occasionally by a little meat, if they are fortunate enough to snare a goat or rabbit. Shooting animals is not an option, since it would attract the attention of the enemy and easily give away the location of the brigade.

Once a day, each soldier also receives a handful of dried figs crawling with maggots, along with five cigarettes and a shot of grappa. Cellini had tried smoking once when he was much younger. He didn't care for the taste or the feeling of inhaling tobacco smoke and has never touched it again since. He is grateful that so many Yugoslavians seem addicted to the habit and gladly swaps his five cigarettes for an extra shot of grappa. The harsh liquid burns his throat but soothes his heart and soul. He volunteers to take first watch and takes up a good position, concealed by trees but offering a clear view of the mountain ridge above and the valley below, illuminated by the almost full moon.

His watch goes by quickly as he replays the events of the day on the moving picture screen in his mind, and when Nikolas comes to relieve him a couple of hours later, he settles down at the foot of a nearby tree, his Breda machine gun by his side and a carpet of dry leaves for a blanket.

He sleeps only fitfully but wakes to a commotion, and thinking an attack is imminent, he grabs the Breda. A crowd of Partisans is gathered in the centre of the camp in a circle. In the middle of the circle are two of the younger members of the brigade. They are being pushed and shoved along. Cellini makes his way over to the circle and asks what is going on.

1. *Grappa is a form of brandy that originated in Italy but is popular throughout Eastern Europe, distilled from the skins, pulp, stems and seeds of the grapes discarded after pressing the grapes during wine production. It is still referred to as "grappa" in much of the Dalmatian region of Croatia, although European legislation now forbids the use of the name unless it is produced in Italy.*

2. *Cellini still finds food served with roux sauce, or what Americans call "white gravy", unpalatable.*

It turns out these two young boys – one is eighteen and the other just seventeen – had taken it into their heads to go searching for extra food to supplement their rations at a nearby farmstead. They were both supposed to be on guard duty at the time, but decided it would be okay if one of them slipped away as long as he could get back before their watch was up. He went in search of eggs, potatoes, cabbages or whatever he could find. One of the battalion leaders happened to check up on his partner and found out.

Now justice will be administered. Justice is swift and severe in the National Liberation Army, by order of Marshal Tito and his doctrine: that only by maintaining the strictest discipline within their own organization can they hope to overcome the fascist aggressors. The two boys have no defence and no excuses. Even though only one of them had actually left the camp, both are deemed responsible and found guilty of desertion. The penalty is death by firing squad. The decision is irrevocable and will be carried out immediately.

Partisan soldiers are selected randomly to carry out the punishment by being tapped on the shoulder by a commissar. They quickly form up in the shape of a horseshoe with the two boys standing side by side at the open end. A voice barks out the order to take aim, and the younger of the two boys looks up and stares into the eyes of the commissar, then spits on the ground in a futile act of defiance – or is it bravado?

"Fire!"

A volley of shots rings out in the cold morning air. Two bodies crumple to the ground in a bloody heap, to be quickly carried away and hastily buried.

The interlude serves as a warning to others that the Partisan code of discipline is strict and unforgiving. Cellini is shocked at the severity of the punishment, and it must show on his face, because another Partisan, a seasoned veteran – who Cellini recognizes as one of those with whom he has traded cigarettes for grappa – puts his arm around him and, speaking to him in Italian, begins explaining the rationale.

"There is only one punishment in the Partisans," he says. "We have no prisons, no jails, and barely enough food to stay alive. Partisans do not take enemy prisoners and we do not tolerate any indiscretion among our own people."

It makes sense to Cellini, who, while shocked and saddened by the execution of the two young boys, cannot help but be impressed by the speed and efficiency with which the sentence had been carried out. It was quick and caused the minimum amount of suffering. He looks his new comrade in the eye and asks, "What sort of indiscretions might result in the need for such punishment?"

"A good question, my friend," the veteran replies, and begins listing capital offences, counting them off on his fingers as he does so. "Anything, which, in the opinion of the commissar, compromises the safety and security of the brigade. Any hint of cowardice, insubordination, deserting your post – as you have just witnessed – stealing from your fellow soldiers, being suspected of supporting the fascists…" he spits on the ground to emphasize his disdain, "…oh, and whatever you do, don't touch the women." [3]

"The women?" Cellini is puzzled.

"Molesting a Partisan woman will get you a bullet quicker than anything. That's a directive from Tito himself. The women soldiers are very highly thought of. If you're caught… and make no mistake, you will be caught… " He finishes the description by drawing his hand across his throat from ear to ear and laughs. "But I doubt you have any trouble with the ladies, my friend? A man with your looks?"

Cellini ignores the comment. Some of the Yugoslavian women are very attractive, but with his natural reserve and innate respect for the feminine gender, he would never try to take advantage. He has also seen the courage of the women in battle and believes they know how to take care of themselves.

There are plenty of opportunities for the men to take advantage of the women. The nights are cold up in the mountains and often the only way to stay warm is by huddling together and sharing body heat. Men and women wrap themselves up together in blankets and, even fully clothed, bodies pressed tightly up against each other can stir even the most stoic and resistant of people. Cellini finds many of the female Partisans attractive but fear of punishment and his innate respect for women precludes any attempt on his part to engage in sexual activity.

Cellini thanks his new friend for the warning and turns to walk away.

"One more thing, my friend," the man reaches out and touches Cellini's shoulder as he turns. "If a commissar taps you on the shoulder some time, it means you have been selected for the firing squad. Do not hesitate,

[3] *Any man found guilty of molesting a woman was dealt with severely – with no second chances. Cellini didn't personally witness any situations of sexual harassment – certainly nothing to compare with the atrocities he saw while he was with the Bersaglieri. News of such indiscretions and the resulting punishment came via the Partisan grapevine and served to keep the majority in line. Marriage between Partisans, while not encouraged, was permitted, but married couples were not allowed to fight together in the same unit, so after a short "honeymoon" of two days and nights together, they had to separate and go to different battalions, often losing contact for weeks or months at a time with no news of their spouse.*

no matter what your personal thoughts are and no matter who it is."

Cellini starts to ask the obvious question, "Have you ever –?" but the veteran cuts him short. "More times than I care to think about, my friend."

*****

AFTER BURYING the bodies of the two boys, the brigade packs up and moves on. Cellini has been with the Partisans for a couple of weeks and is beginning to become acquainted with several of the others. Apart from Nikolas, who he still sees from time to time, but is evidently still embarrassed by the incident with the burning bullet, he doesn't make friendships or even get to know anyone by name. The Partisans are a close brotherhood, where each is looking out for all of the others, but to develop friendships is to risk grief and loss of morale when a comrade is lost in combat, and as Cellini has already discovered, there is no room for sentiment in this type of warfare.

There are a few members of the battalion, however, of whom Cellini is not at all sure. Italians who, like him, abandoned their fascist employers at the first sign of defeat, but he is not completely convinced of their loyalty to the Partisans.

While he is not a communist and can never accept communism as a working ideology, he is an ardent "anti-fascist" and willing to fight alongside these Partisans, whose conviction, courage and resourcefulness he admires and respects, if not their politics. He considers himself an American and longs for the day when the Allies from Britain and the United States will knock out the Nazi aggressors and their Italian puppets so that he can join them.

Meanwhile, he will be keeping an eye on some of the Italians in the battalion.

Things are quiet for a couple of days, and Cellini takes advantage of the time to acquaint himself with different weapons – many of which are new or at least unfamiliar to him.

Like so many of the weapons adopted by resistance groups – who were essentially beggars in no position to be choosers – the French made St. Etienne M-1907 machine gun is a dinosaur left over from World War One. It is a beast with a reputation for overheating and jamming. The gun has an adjustable rate of fire from 80 to 650 rounds per minute but overheats and jams regardless of which rate is selected. Cellini learns to strip it down and reassemble it in minutes, and studies it carefully to try and determine how and why it jams so that he can try to prevent it happening in a combat situation. The gun uses a very contrived and, in Cellini's opinion, unnecessarily complicated mechanism, which seems to cause the overheating, and he realises he is just going to have to live with the fact that the gun will jam every now and again.[4]

Another weapon in the Partisan arsenal that Cellini has never fired is an anti-tank rifle, recently acquired by the Brigade. It is heavy and unwieldy, and he knows it will be a difficult weapon to master. What he isn't sure of is its origin. No one seems to know if it is Russian or Polish.[5] He has no experience with tank warfare and has never handled such a massive gun before, but there are rumours that German tanks have been seen in the mountains and the 9th Partisan Brigade knows it is only a matter of time until they must confront German armoured divisions.

While working with the St. Etienne and the anti-tank rifle, Cellini keeps a watchful eye on a couple of the Italians who joined the Partisans at about the same time he did, and who he does not trust fully. He senses that they miss the "old days" of the Italian occupation and still have some admiration for Mussolini, but as yet he has not been able to find any evidence to back up his suspicions. If they are sympathetic to the Axis, they could pose a serious threat to the brigade. Cellini has to be sure. He thinks about discussing it with Nikolas or even Poldo, but dismisses the idea immediately. He has never been a snitch and has no intentions of becoming one now. Instead, he decides to think of a way to trap them into giving themselves away.

Partisans are tough, vigilant and resilient, but they love to sing, when it's safe to do so –not at night around a campfire, but occasionally after eating and collecting their grappa ration. It usually starts with one member who will begin a song. Others join in and in a short time they are embracing and singing traditional Yugoslavian folk songs.

[4.] *The gas piston and operating rod on the St. Etienne M1907 travelled forward instead of rearward, requiring a special system of gears to move the bolt rearwards. The need for such a contrived design arose in order to avoid any patent infringements with the more successful and straightforward Hotchkiss and Browning guns – all because the French government insisted that French troops be equipped with French weapons!*

[5.] *Yugoslavian Partisans used a broad range of weapons, many left over from World War One, and others that were in use before the war and by now quite obsolescent. Supplies from the Allies were still sporadic at this time, although air drops from England were becoming more frequent. Captured weapons also formed a large part of their arsenal, when enough ammunition could be found to make it worthwhile. Anti-tank weapons were very scarce and highly prized and it is likely that what Cellini had was one of the two Russian models (either a Degtyarev PTRD-41 or a Simonov PTRS-41) or a Polish Marosczek 35. Though fairly effective against the early tanks the weapons were less useful against the armour of the new Tiger tanks. Based on Cellini's memory, his weapon was most probably a Russian Degtyarev PTRD. A single shot, bolt-action rifle, 200cm (6' 6") long and weighing almost 18kg (40lb), the gun fired a 14.5 x 114mm (0.57") armour piercing round.*

Cellini decides this would be a good time to catch the one or two of the Italians off guard. He grabs his friend Nikolas by the arm and tells him to keep watching, he may find the next few minutes interesting.

Taking a seat among a group of Italians, he offers to share a little extra grappa he has been stockpiling from his cigarette trades. He waits for a lull in the singing then begins singing a song of his own – having first signaled to Nikolas. Quietly at first, humming the tune before launching into the chorus. It's a marching song very much favoured by Mussolini. Two of the Italians jump up and begin singing loudly, embracing each other and dancing – before suddenly becoming aware that they are the only ones singing and that the entire camp is standing, silently staring at them.

"Goddamn fascists!" Cellini says, getting to his feet and spitting on the ground in front of the two Italians. "I knew you two were not to be trusted." He turns and walks away. The two are quickly surrounded by Partisans.

It is the last Cellini sees of either of them.

From this moment on, Cellini knows he must be on his guard. He has now made himself the centre of attention and brought about, he assumes, the demise of two of their number. Others – especially those who have defected from the Italian Army – will be watching him carefully.

24. Tank!

Across the mountains where Eastern Croatia borders Bosnia, the German 5th Mountain Corps of the Waffen SS is preparing an assault. It is amassing troops ready for what will become the Sixth Enemy Offensive – an all-out assault intended to wipe out Tito's Partisan army once and for all. The 5th Mountain Corps is part of the 2nd Panzer Army, although the number of armoured vehicles in its arsenal has been seriously depleted over the past few months as more and more tanks are needed on the Eastern Front. The SS unit deploys what few tanks it still has sparingly, in an attempt to convince the Partisans that it is stronger than it actually is.

*****

Waking in the dark, shivering with the cold and his clothes damp from the overnight dew, Cellini has no idea how long he has been asleep, but there is plenty of activity going on. The battalion, if not the whole 9th Brigade, is on the move again, higher up into the mountains. News has filtered through that the Germans are about to launch an offensive against all Partisans holding out in the Dalmatian region, and before much longer they will be coming up against seasoned German troops and possibly an armoured division.

The 4th Battalion spends the day picking its way slowly back up the mountains to prepare for the onslaught.

Once they are encamped for the night, Poldo summons Cellini and asks him for his thoughts on the anti-tank rifle. The entire brigade has only four of the weapons between them, and he has managed to obtain one for the 4th Battalion, but he is not entirely convinced of their efficacy against German tanks. He wants Cellini to make sure it is fully operable and, if possible, to test fire it.

Until two days ago, Cellini had never seen such a rifle. It seems to weigh a ton and fires only one shot at a time, manually loaded. The bolt-action is still stiff despite his spending the better part of a day cleaning and massaging the weapon. With patience and copious amounts of grease he is able to get it operating at least to dry fire. He will take charge of the gun, in addition to his Breda. One of the mule drivers is assigned to carry the weapon and keep it close at hand in the event of any combat. Like his commander, Cellini is sceptical about the weapon but eager to test fire it.

From their mountain vantage point, the Partisans have a great view in every direction, provided the weather co-operates, which it rarely does. At this time of year, low cloud is a persistent hazard, so they have to keep their ears, as well as their eyes, tuned in to the surroundings. Scouting parties hike the rocky terrain daily to look for any signs of Germans but find nothing. Then one day there is a report that a tank engine has been heard starting up. Cellini and his partner unload the anti-tank rifle from the mule and follow the Partisans who had reported the sound. The cloud is thick and navigating the rocky track is difficult, especially carrying the unwieldy 40lb PTRD. Keeping a safe distance behind the lead scouts is also a challenge in the conditions, and Cellini finds himself having to jog to catch up as the leaders disappear into the white abyss.

Tired from his exertions, his breathing is heavy as the lead scout signals to him to be quiet and listen by putting his forefinger to his lips. Cellini stops dead and crouches. In the distance – a long way off – he hears an engine. A smile sneaks across his face. He points upwards and towards where the sound is coming from, indicating his intention to climb up and try to get close enough to see the vehicle. The lead scout nods his approval but puts his hand up to stop Cellini. He points to himself as if to say *I go first!*

Sunbeams filter through the thin spots in the clouds and they find themselves at the top of a mountain ridge looking across and slightly down a gentle slope. The distinct deep, throaty rumble of a large petrol engine can be heard in the distance from across the slope. It's faint, but in mountainous terrain sound carries. The engine noise is accompanied by the irregular metallic clunk of iron tracks on the rocky road.

Tank!

Cellini lies down on the ground at the edge of a ravine waiting for the vehicle to come into view on the other side of the valley. Pulling back the bolt on the PTRD anti-tank rifle, he takes one of the large armour-piercing rounds from his pocket and chambers it, all the while scanning the terrain ahead of him for any sign of movement. The cloud nearby is dissolving into thin wisps and he knows it is only a matter of time until the mist begins to lift. When it does, he will be ready to fire.

After what seems like an eternity, but in fact is no more than thirty seconds, the veil dissolves and there, perhaps 100 metres away, a large, heavy-looking vehicle lumbers along slowly, leaving a thin trail of dust in its wake. Staring through binoculars, Cellini can just make out the black crosses on its side.[1]

Without looking away, Cellini hands the binoculars to his partner, the lead scout now lying alongside him. Adjusting the simple iron sight, he takes aim at the tank and squeezes the trigger.

It makes a strange and unique double sound, *ta-poum,* when fired, but that is all Cellini remembers. The recoil of the gun knocks him backwards and off the ground like a rag doll. His ears are ringing from the noise and his shoulder aches from the stock hitting him. As the ringing noise fades he can still hear the sound of the tank engine rumbling along, then it stops.

Did he hit it? He has no idea. He scrambles back to the edge of the ravine, where he is quickly joined by two of his Partisan comrades, all crawling on their bellies. They peer out across the chasm trying to focus on the tank. It has stopped, but the turret has started slowly turning and stops, its gun barrel pointing straight in their direction.

"Run!" he says.

Picking up the PTRD where it had fallen to the ground, he sets off back in the direction from which they had come just a few minutes before, the rest of the group alongside. Suddenly, the weapon seems much lighter than it was before!

They hear the thud of a round being launched from the tank, followed by the whistling sound of the heavy shell making its way through the air. The Partisans dive to the ground, hugging the mountainside as closely as they can. They hear and feel the explosion as the shell strikes the rocks, but it's well behind them and poses no threat. The tank gunner is nowhere close to finding their range and evidently decides not to waste any more rounds.

Cellini and his group decide to make their way back to the camp and report to Poldo. The commander decides it would be a good idea to relocate, since the Germans are now aware of their presence and may send a reconnaissance team out to search for them. The mules are packed up and the 4th Battalion moves out.

Now that he has discovered its whereabouts, Poldo is determined

[1.] *Probably a Panzer II or III light tank. By late 1943, most of the heavy armour had been withdrawn from Yugoslavia to reinforce the war against the Soviet Union. SS divisions that remained behind with orders to wipe out the Partisans still had light tanks available.*

to flush out and destroy the enemy tank and sets about formulating a plan to trap it.

Poldo gathers the senior members of the battalion together. As carrier of the anti-tank rifle, Cellini is included in the group.

"Disabling the tank is the easy part," he says, a smile forming at each corner of his mouth. "The first thing we need to do is find the best place to do it, then get the Germans to put it there for us. That's the hard part!"

"Once we figure out the best place to get them to put the tank, we are going to make a lot of noise and make them think there are a hell of a lot more of us than there actually are so they'll come after us."

Pausing to take a breath and look around the group to make sure everyone is paying attention, Poldo continues, "We'll do that by lighting fires at multiple locations along the road and in the hills, firing a few shots from each location, then moving on, firing a few more shots, and rotating back around. If they think we're a big enough and important enough target, they'll come looking for us with that tank."

"But before we do any of that, we're going to set an ambush for the tank by putting explosives in the road about 100 metres apart. When we've got the tank lined up between the explosives, we detonate them and trap the tank. Then, we attack the infantry."

One of the Partisans interrupts with a question: "Why can't we use the anti-tank mines?"

"It's a good question," Poldo nods, "but the answer is we can't be sure we'd take out the tank. The anti-tank mines we've got are old and obsolete British types and they're not always reliable. In any case, we'd have to be absolutely sure of getting it directly under the vehicle's track to be sure of immobilizing it even partially. By blowing up the road, we trap the tank so they can't move it."

Each squad leader is given an assigned area that he will be in charge of when the time comes to draw attention, and told to delegate firestarters and shooters among his Partisan group. In the meantime, everyone is to keep a low profile, and be as quiet as possible. There will be no singing, no shooting of weapons and no hot food or drinks. No noise of any kind until everything is ready for the ambush. Poldo will go to scout the best spot to trap the tank, and he chooses four men who will go with him; an explosives expert and two strong partisans to help him carry the equipment. The other one is Cellini.

"And bring that anti-tank rifle with you, just in case," Poldo says to Cellini.

They wait until a couple of hours before sunset to begin their reconnaissance for building a tank trap, heading down the ravine and up the other side towards the road where they had last seen the tank and the German mountain troops. Staying well away from the road but always keeping it in view, they stop every few minutes to take a good look at the landscape and make sure there is no sign of activity further ahead.

Poldo finds a spot close to a bend in the road for the ambush. The road is passable but strewn with rocks and boulders, which will be useful to the Partisans in setting their ambush. He signals for the others to wait and quietly asks his demolitions man if he thinks this is a good location.

It's not ideal. The perfect location would be a bridge or a tunnel, but there are none this far up the mountain, and they don't want to go too far out of their way and risk straying into German-held territory. There is a steep rock wall on one side of the bend and a ravine on the other, which means if they are successful the tank will not be able to navigate around the damaged part of the road. It offers great visibility all around so the Partisans can escape quickly after the ambush, but by the same token, the Germans will feel confident they can overcome even a moderately large Partisan force. There is enough cover at the side of the road where the ground levels out that the Partisans will be able to maintain the element of surprise until the last minute.

They wait until it's almost dark, then creep forward towards the road, staying in the shadows. Poldo and Cellini take up position at the edge of the road, about 20 metres apart, while the third Partisan climbs the last few metres onto the road and waits, then crawls across the road and up towards the bend. He starts by carefully digging a hole to plant the explosives. Cellini has the anti-tank rifle loaded, cocked and ready to fire, and positions himself with his back to a sturdy tree offering a clear line of sight up the road.

The demolition man has a large canvas sack with tools and explosives. His helpers are manhandling a reel of cable that will be used to connect to the charges. He lays the sack down and reaches inside for a folding shovel to dig a suitable hole for planting the charges. The hole needs to be deep and wide enough to fill with rocks and boulders to cause maximum damage to the road, as well as any nearby personnel. Digging takes a while. After planting the first charge and partially filling in the hole with dirt, he makes his way over to the far side of the road, the other two men pulling the cable reel and covering the wiring with loose dirt. Pressing his body up against the rock wall, the demolition man sidesteps his way stealthily along the road, continuing to unreel the wire, then back across the road to plant a second charge. Their job complete, they signal to Poldo and Cellini. Uncocking the anti-tank rifle, Cellini props it up against the tree and joins the men in the middle of the road. They fill the holes with smaller rocks, then roll larger boulders across to jam into the holes under which the charges are buried.

All is still silent as they lay the remaining cable across the road, carefully covering it with more dirt dug from the holes.

The trap is set!

*****

CELLINI RETRIEVES the anti-tank weapon and the three men return down the ravine and back to the camp, across the valley about 100 meters away from where the charges are set. Poldo is pleased to find the camp in a state of complete blackout. The men and women of the 4th Battalion have done well. It is as silent as the grave. Everyone has dined on tinned rations and grappa. There is no smell of smoke from tobacco, no smell of cooking or latrines. From more than five metres away, no one would know this was a well-organized Partisan camp.

They will wait until just before dawn to put the next phase of their plan into action. For now they will take turns to grab a couple of hours' sleep, though very few of them manage more than a few minutes doze.

As the sun rises, all hell appears to break loose in the mountains. The smoke from a dozen fires rises into the early morning sky and gunfire erupts all around. Cellini has taken up a prone position with a clear view across the valley to the road where they anticipate the tank will appear, the PTRD anti-tank rifle loaded and ready to fire. He can see the demolition man 20 metres away, crouched down behind a boulder and ready to ignite the charges that will – if he did his job properly – blow out two large chunks of road and leave the German tank stranded and vulnerable. Other Partisans, a small detachment armed with mortars and grenades, have spread out and are hidden behind rocks further down the ravine, ready to move in quickly when the action starts.

The rest of the 4th Battalion – those not immediately engaged in moving around, starting fires and making as much noise as possible – are positioned above and behind Cellini's position, overlooking the road, with orders to hold their fire until the Germans come into view.

The guns fall silent. Poldo must have called a ceasefire. Has the plan worked? Have the Partisans got the attention of the Germans?

The shooting starts again, but this time it's even more intense than before. In no time at all it's a full-blown firefight, with bullets flying in all directions. Nothing is coming Cellini's way because the German fire is concentrated further up the mountain on the Partisans behind him. It looks as though they have fallen for the decoy!

In a brief lull between shots, Cellini thinks he hears the rumble of the tank engine but he can't be sure. Seconds later, his thoughts are confirmed by the unmistakable sound of the metallic clunk of the tracks on the road. He grins and looks across at the demolition man, who grins right back at him. Cellini tightens his grip on the anti-tank rifle, and checks for the eighth or ninth time that the gun is cocked and has a round in the chamber.

It seems like an age before the tank comes into view but soon enough it crawls around the bend. Armed troops in dirty green smocks crouch and make their way along the road between the tank and the rock wall within clear view of Cellini and the others closer to the road. He's itching to open fire but knows the first objective is to destroy – or at least immobilize – the tank. The grey green paint is covered with dried mud and dust that almost obscures the black cross painted on the side of the turret. Blue smoke spews out of the exhausts at the back of the machine as it trundles along the mountain road, its unsilenced engine getting louder. Closer now to the point where the charges are placed, Cellini can feel the ground vibrate as each section of steel track clanks against the rocky surface. The demolition man is still waiting for the exact moment to push the plunger and leave the vehicle stranded. Just a few more metres...

The turret slowly swings around and the gun begins to elevate. The tank is almost past the first set of explosives! *Blow it up!* Cellini thinks and looks across at the demolition man. *Blow it up NOW!* The tank slows and comes to a complete stop. Cellini looks at the demolition man again. He just shrugs. He wants it all the way past the first set of explosives so there is no chance of it escaping. All they can do now is wait and keep dead still and quiet. Cellini keeps the rifle trained on the tracks at the front of the tank so that if they have to make a run for it, at least the vehicle will be disabled.

A deafening thud sends a shockwave across the road and echoes in the mountains as the tank fires its big gun. There is no whistle as the shell leaves the muzzle, just a muffled thud as it strikes the ground somewhere in the distance. The turret swivels a few degrees and the gun fires again. Seconds later a third shot rings out into the hills, above and behind Cellini's position. The explosion of the shell hitting the ground is louder this time and he fears that his battalion has probably taken some casualties, but before he can dwell too much on the potential damage, the engine revs, throws out another cloud of blue smoke, and the tank starts rolling forward again.

Cellini breathes out for the first time since the tank started firing its gun. He wills the tank to move forwards… just a couple more metres… and glances over at the demolition man in time to see him push the plunger on the detonator. *No more waiting!*

*****

THE TIMING OF THE two sets of charges is perfect. The road ahead of the tank explodes and collapses just seconds before a second explosion rips up the road immediately behind the vehicle, causing it to cave in, leaving the tank nowhere to manoeuvre. The accompanying infantrymen are caught totally off guard. Some are killed instantly while others are left wounded and dying. The blasts are massive and what seems like an age after the blast, Cellini and everyone else in the advance Partisan party are showered with small rocks and debris. A huge cloud of dust and dirt enshrouds the mountainside. Hearing the screams of wounded German soldiers, Cellini looks over at where the demolition man had been crouched behind the edge of the road a few seconds earlier in time to see him heading for the lower ground and signalling for Cellini to follow. Cellini concurs. Downhill seems to be the safer route, because it is highly likely that once the dust settles, the tank crew, assuming they have survived, will start firing again upwards. That is also the most likely place for German reinforcements to search. Once they realise that the road was booby-trapped they will almost certainly come looking for the demolition party in the lower ground, but by that time, Cellini intends to be far away.

He can't resist turning around for one last look at the stricken tank before he retreats. Now that the air has begun to clear of dust and debris, he can get a clear picture of the havoc he and his fellow Partisans have caused for the Germans.

The tank is skewed at 45 degrees across the mountain road, precariously positioned with its rear end very close to the edge. Cellini's guess is that it would be risky to use the big gun from this position because rotating the turret and shifting its weight might easily tip it over; so would the recoil of the gun if it were fired. The road is too narrow for it to turn around easily, and it cannot move forwards or backwards because there is a large piece of the road missing at either end.

The demolition man knew what he was doing.

There is shooting but it seems to be sporadic. It seems to be coming mostly from the Germans, and mostly aimed at the top of the mountain ridges where the Partisans had set decoy fires earlier. Putting as much distance between himself and the tank as he can, Cellini scrambles down the side of the mountain. The terrain quickly changes to a gentle escarpment strewn with large boulders, which he uses for cover, darting from one to the next. He picks up a trail he recognizes from the previous day and heads along it, sure he'll run into some of his comrades.

The unmistakable metallic click of a bolt being drawn back, very close behind, startles him but he knows it must be his own unit. Had it been Germans, or even another group of Partisans, there would have been no sound; no warning of any kind. Only a bullet. He turns around to find none other than his old friend Nikolas, who greets him with a huge smile full of crooked teeth, then shoulders his rifle and gives him a huge bear hug.

They join the rest of the battalion. There have been some casualties, but the mission to disable the enemy tank was successful.

25. A Change of Clothes

FOLLOWING ITS ENGAGEMENT with the tank, the 4th Battalion regroups in the foothills and looks for shelter. Tonight they will camp at a ruined Italian Army camp near an old church.

To their delight, the Partisans discover a treasure trove hidden in the ruins; old Italian Army uniforms, including shirts and underwear. This must have been some kind of supply depot for the region, such is the range of clothing available.

It is common in any army for officers to have the privilege of first choice of war booty such as this, but Poldo is different and allows the men to select what they need, provided they maintain order and discipline. Cellini secures a much needed pair of trousers to replace the pair he is wearing, which are truly on their last legs, and a wool shirt. Poldo finds a very high-quality Italian officer's tunic, which he tries on and, to his absolute delight, fits him perfectly. He strides up and down in the tunic as if he were on parade, beaming with pride – then convulses into a twisted heap, reaching around his back and over his shoulders to scratch. The tunic is full of lice!

Unwilling to give up the coat, the commander takes it off and turns it inside out, holding it up to the light to see if he can find the offending creatures. Taking a seat on the ground, he leans up against the stone wall of the church and proceeds to pick the lice from the seams, pinching each one between his fingers to assure himself of its demise. Only when he is fully satisfied that he has removed and killed every last one of the offending parasites does he put the tunic back on.[1]

[1] *Vito Cellini often wondered why his commander was willing to go to such lengths to keep the tunic. Watching Poldo sitting in front of the wall for literally hours on end, picking lice from the coat, was one of his most vivid recollections of his time spent with the Partisans. While researching this book, it was discovered that Poldo was, by profession, a master tailor. The quality of the cloth and the craftsmanship of the Italian uniform would not have been lost on such a man, and that is no doubt why he was willing to go to so much trouble to wear it.*

Opportunities to acquire new clothing are few and far between and by the time the Partisans have finished, the entire inventory of Italian uniforms is exhausted. The old clothes are kept for use as bandages, blankets and rags, or if completely useless for anything else, can be burnt as fuel.

Cellini's boots are also just about worn out. The one good piece of clothing he had been issued by the Italian Army and had guarded with his life is finally exhausted. Now the boots are held together with string. The leather is full of holes and the soles are so badly worn through that there is more string than boot. Worse, they are starting to give him blisters and calluses. He is directed to the shoemaker for the brigade, a sullen but incredibly talented craftsman who will carve Cellini a practical and hard-wearing – if not actually stylish – pair of sandals from old rubber tyres that can no longer be used on the vehicles. He cuts the rubber with a sharp fighting knife, slips it onto Cellini's foot, then carves a little more, until the improvised shoe is a perfect fit. Twine is threaded through holes cut on each side to secure and tighten the shoes. Cellini struts up and down. He couldn't be any happier if he had just bought a brand new pair of wing tips from Macy's. He carefully replaces the canvas puttees, winding the green fabric around his feet and lower legs, then thanks the cobbler and hands him a cigarette. The shoemaker nods and takes the cigarette without saying a word. Cellini walks away with a smile on his face. The blisters are already a distant memory.

*****

After the fierce fighting against a German armoured division, Poldo receives orders that the 9th Brigade, along with the entire 20th Division, is to move out of the mountains and head to the islands where the leaders will confer on future strategy. If they are to survive and carry on their struggle, the Partisans must pull back, regroup and be ready to fight again.

They begin the long journey down the mountains to Rogoznica and from there by boat to the island of Brac, where they will await further orders.

The 9th Brigade still has its mules. The horses are long gone. Most have died in battle or from starvation, or been killed for their meat. Most of the carts are now pulled along by the men and women on foot. The Partisans have acquired additional vehicles, though finding fuel for them is getting more and more difficult. Places on the trucks are reserved for the front-line fighters and saboteurs; machine gunners, mortar crews, explosives experts and weapons specialists.

They will move at night, under cover of darkness, and rest during the day. By late afternoon, everything is packed and they are ready to make a move. Everyone has had a chance to eat far better than usual and rations for the trek have been handed out. As the sun begins to sink below the horizon they set off in small groups led by a small convoy of old Fiat 124 trucks abandoned by the Italians and gratefully liberated by the Partisans. The trucks carry both personnel and supplies. Cellini is keen to get going and is about to climb into the first vehicle when a voice calls out to him.

"Hey, Cellini, where are my cigarettes? Or is my grappa no good anymore."

It is a fellow Partisan with whom Cellini regularly trades cigarettes for his shot of grappa. He is holding a small tin cup and has a big smile on his face. In his eagerness to claim his seat on the truck, Cellini has completely forgotten his regular arrangement. He reaches into his top pocket for the five small, crumpled cigarettes and hands them over in exchange for the grappa, which he downs in one gulp. Turning back to get on the truck, Cellini is pushed away and told that the fare to ride on the lead vehicle is one cigarette – and he has just swapped all of his. His trading partner pushes past, hands over one of the cigarettes and climbs aboard, just as the driver guns the engine and the truck pulls away. There is a glint in the eye of the Partisans chiding him and he takes the rebuke in good spirits, securing a place – free of charge – on the third vehicle.

The lorries are followed by other men and women on foot, horse-drawn carts, and mules loaded down with supplies and ammunition.

The journey is uncomfortable but uneventful. Progress is slow and the convoys stop periodically for rest and food breaks and to allow the Partisans to get off the vehicles, empty their bladders if need be, and stretch their legs.

Almost at journey's end, the truck suddenly brakes and skids, sliding to an abrupt halt. Some of the unwary passengers are caught off guard and fall off the wooden benches, landing on each other in a heap.

Ambush?

Before anyone can react, someone outside the vehicle yells at everyone to shut up and sit back down. Cursing and laughing, the men return to their seats. The explanation, when it comes, is chilling, even to the more hardened soldiers.

The leading Fiat lorry full of soldiers has veered off the road and rolled into the deep water of the Adriatic. Cellini is a strong swimmer and wants to see if he can help, so without a second thought he jumps over the side of the truck, drops his weapon and his kitbag to the ground and runs over to the scene of the carnage. Bodies are bobbing around like grotesque mannequins and men who were on the second truck are scrambling, trying to reach them and pull them ashore. The water is crystal clear, and looking down, Cellini can see the first truck lying on its side, perhaps 10 or 12 metres down. He can see bodies that are obviously beyond help, some trapped in the wreckage and others weighed down by equipment. Almost instinctively, he dives into the deep water – a shockwave running through his body from the intense cold – and swims towards the cab of the vehicle in the hope of finding survivors who might be caught in an air bubble. He reaches for the handle and wrestles with the door. Inside he can see a lifeless body, but no air bubble. There is no glass in the window so with a little tugging the door opens. Grabbing the driver by the collar he pulls the limp body towards him, but the poor fellow is beyond help. He pulls him clear of the vehicle and shoves his body towards the surface.

Cellini has been under the water for almost a minute and his lungs are beginning to burn. Desperate for oxygen, he heads for the surface, exhaling a steady stream of small bubbles as he goes. Replenishing the air in his lungs, he looks around and sees other Partisans still pulling the floating corpses of their comrades towards the shore. He decides to go down one more time but can find no sign of life.

Making his way back to land, another Partisan offers him a hand and pulls him out of the water. As he gets to his feet, one of the senior members of the brigade reprimands him for diving into the water and putting his own life at risk, then more sympathetically pats him on the shoulder and tells him to go back to his transport.

"There's nothing more you can do here," he says.

Deflated, Cellini makes his way back up the road, retrieves his machine gun and kitbag and takes his place aboard his own lorry.

The lorry is full and unable to help carry either the dead or the injured, so the engine is started and the vehicle continues on its way. There are two more trucks in the convoy following behind, both of which have plenty of space for the dead who will be buried once they reach the island.

Soaking wet and shivering as the truck moves away, Cellini counts his blessings. Once again, his luck has held.

If it weren't for his liking of grappa, or the fact that he is one of few Partisans who doesn't smoke, he would almost certainly have been on that first lorry.

26. Makarska

Once they arrive in Rogoznica, the Partisans board boats that will take them to the island of Brac, where there will be a meeting of the battalion leaders.[1]

After the traumatic and wearying journey, the battalion is glad for the opportunity to relax for a few days and get some proper sleep before moving back to the mainland and up into the mountains once more.

*****

Hiking up the Biokovo Mountains in the last of the daylight, Poldo gives the order for the battalion to camp for the night. There will be no campfires for fear of giving away their position to the Germans, so they huddle together in small groups, wrap themselves in blankets and shelter from the winter wind by keeping down low behind the rocks.

Cellini sleeps fitfully, dozing for what seems like only moments at a time. At the very first sign of light, being on the edge of the huddle, he rolls out from under the blanket to find the entire mountain shrouded in a thick, light grey fog. Unsure of which way anything is, he moves quietly and stealthily. Reaching out his hand, he follows the contour of the rock wall behind which they had taken shelter.

In the eerie silence of the morning mist, unable to see and with no sound, the other senses seem to work harder, and Cellini is suddenly aware of an unfamiliar yet quite odious smell, wafting towards him. Faint but pungent, it is a rancid smell, a cross between onions, rotting vegetation and

[1] *Poldo attended the 4th Battalion Party Conference on the island of Brac on November 3rd. The battalion then continued by boat from Brac, landing at Baska Voda, 10 kilometers west of Makarska, on November 5th before heading up into the Biokovo Mountains (Poldo's Diary).*

body odour. Personal hygiene is not easy to maintain when living nomadically in mountainous terrain from day to day, and Cellini would be the first to admit that he and his Partisan comrades probably stink to high heaven – but the foul odour now assaulting his nostrils is quite different – more intense and offensive. Edging his way around the rock towards the source of the stench he reaches a shallow ridge and begins to slowly climb up it. He is unable to see the top of the ridge but notices the smell stronger than ever. After a few steps he hears a sound. Voices!

He stops to listen more intently.

Germans!

So that's what's causing the stink!

He scurries down the ridge and, as quietly as he can, heads back to the Partisan camp. Finding Poldo awake and about to instruct the cooking detail to brew up another batch of flour paste. He tells him of the Germans.

"How far away?" Poldo asks.

Cellini points through the fog to where he has just come from.

"The other side of that rock formation," he says. "Maybe 100 metres at most," he says.

Poldo issues instructions to the men and women with whom he had been talking. In a matter of seconds, they have silently spread the word, from one Partisan to the next. Gathering up their weapons and equipment and packing the mules takes a few minutes at most, and is done with almost no noise. The entire brigade retreats, rapidly but orderly, some down the mountain path they had taken the previous day and others scrambling across the path and down the slope, ready to regroup. One battalion always faces the rear in case the Germans should follow.

It is another lesson in Partisan warfare for Cellini. Never engage the enemy unless you can see them – and only when you have the advantage.

*****

A FEW DAYS LATER, Cellini has another narrow escape.

It is early in the morning and he is looking for a place with some privacy and shelter to use as a toilet (Cellini's favourite euphemism for the act is "writing a letter to the Pope".).

Since they rarely stay more than one night in any given location, Partisans don't set up formal latrines the way a military force usually would; instead, each person is responsible for finding a quiet area, behind a tree or a rock and preferably where no one else has gone before, in which to squat, clean themselves and then discreetly cover up the evidence. It isn't always easy, especially in a large group consisting of both men and women.

On this occasion, Cellini has to walk quite a distance from the camp to find a convenient tree. He pulls his pants down and has just manoeuvred himself into a squatting position when he hears a sudden rapid movement through the trees above him. A small, round, dark grey object lands close by with a thud and rolls to a halt a few metres in front of him.

Grenade!

In one motion he grabs his trousers with one hand, pulling them up just far enough to be able to mobilize his legs. Taking three or four long strides away from the grenade, he dives headlong to the ground and wraps his arms over the back of his head. The momentum with which he hits the ground leaves his trousers around his ankles and his rear end exposed. He waits, it seems like an eternity, for the explosion he knows will rip him apart. Instead, he hears the same familiar thud as another grenade hits the ground some distance behind him.

"Stop!" he yells at the top of his lungs.

Rolling over onto his back, his dignity by now thoroughly compromised, Cellini finds two young Partisan women standing over him laughing. He pulls up his pants and tries very hard to look angry but already he can see the funny side. Though they try to explain, in between giggles, he doesn't understand until others arrive on the scene to find out what the commotion is about. One of the Italian speakers is able to stop laughing long enough to explain that the women were taking the opportunity to practise their grenade-throwing techniques. They had no idea that anyone was in the vicinity and are very sorry – but not to worry, the grenades were only dummies!

*****

LESS THAN A WEEK after his encounter with the grenades, Cellini is once again almost hit by friendly fire – in very similar circumstances. Having decided to *write a letter to the Pope,* he is squatting behind a tree when bullets suddenly begin whistling past his ears and ricocheting off nearby rocks. He has strayed a little too far away from the camp and two young Partisan soldiers have mistaken him for a German. Fortunately, in their youthful inexperience, they open fire from too great a distance, missing their target completely. Cellini literally dodges the bullet yet again! Later, tracking down the culprits, he offers them lessons on how getting closer to an intended target will not only give them a better chance of hitting it, but also enable them to identify in order it to make sure it really is the enemy!

*****

THE 9TH BRIGADE, of which the 4th Battalion is a key part, has spent what seems like weeks in the mountains, moving across country, engaging in skirmishes and firefights almost every day. Cellini has been actively involved in several gun battles. His personal kill tally increases but it doesn't make him feel good. While not actually fighting or running for his life, he spends a lot of time reflecting on the war. He sees others around him boasting about their kills and looting the dead bodies of German soldiers for weapons and other souvenirs but he has no interest in participating. He tries not to judge them for who they are or what they do; their circumstances are different and perhaps they have reason to hate their enemy; a need to take something back. Taking lives is not something he is proud of. He feels no hatred for the German soldiers, only for the leaders who started this war and the bullies who give orders they would never take. He recognizes in the Partisans an honesty and determination – a belief in the cause for which they are fighting – that he has not seen before. But for himself, he understands only one thing – survival. Kill or be killed.

He feels no excitement, nor even fear. His actions become almost automatic and as a result he becomes a successful soldier, well thought of by his Partisan comrades.

He helps bury the dead during any lull after pitched battles. He helps tend the wounded and pack the mules with equipment before moving on to new ground. The days are long, the nights are growing colder and he is grateful for the group huddle for sleeping, even though sleeping for any length of time is almost impossible.

Word filters through the troops that the division has now reached the mountains high above Makarska. The terrain is steeper, more rocky and harder to traverse. Their progress is slower.

To cap it all, Cellini is getting sick.

It begins with a dull headache that over time escalates into severe, migraine-like symptoms. There are no painkillers available, and even if there were, they could not be spared for any but the most seriously wounded. As the headaches get worse, Cellini has dizzy spells, shortness of breath and is nauseous almost to the point of vomiting, even though he has eaten very little in the past few days. Although he tries to ignore the symptoms, he feels he is unable to carry or operate his machine gun without losing his balance. He decides to talk to the medic, an Italian doctor whom he feels he can trust.

The doctor suggests that he may have a fever or picked up an infection and recommends complete rest for twenty-four hours. Bundled in blankets, Cellini takes up residence at the rear of the brigade and, sheltering behind rocks, is able to sleep for several hours. He wakes feeling refreshed and starts to make his way back towards the front, but quickly becomes breathless and weak, losing his balance several times. He decides once again to retreat and rest more.

After several days – he loses track of the exact time – he still doesn't feel any stronger and once again he makes the trek to see the Italian medic. The doctor, usually of a kindly disposition, has a deep frown on his face, and pulls Cellini on one side, leading him away from the crowd.

"Listen, Cellini," he begins. "I don't know what the problem is but I do know that some of the other Partisans are beginning to talk about you. There is even a suggestion that you are avoiding the fight –"

"What?" Cellini interrupts, furious. "Who dares to accuse me, I'll –"

"Calm down! No one is actually accusing you of anything... and we all know that you have contributed a lot to the brigade. All I'm saying is that I can't keep extending your rest period indefinitely." The doctor pauses for a moment to let the words sink in.

"I cannot find anything medically wrong with you," he continues. "You don't have a fever. You're suffering from exhaustion, but so is everyone else. That's just not a good enough reason to keep you out of the fighting, and if there is the slightest suspicion that you are avoiding the enemy…" He doesn't need to finish the sentence. Cellini has witnessed first hand, on more than occasion, the penalty for being suspected of cowardice.

He makes up his mind, right there and then, to re-join the fight, regardless of his physical condition. He also realises he has put the Italian doctor in a difficult position, and that there could be recriminations for him if Cellini is found guilty. He thanks the doctor and tells him he won't be seeing him again unless it's with a German bullet in his head.[2]

2. It wasn't until much later, in 1954, that Cellini discovered the cause of his illness when he suffered similar symptoms after spending an extended period of time in the Sierra Madre Mountains in California. Doctors told him he was suffering from a form of altitude sickness or Chronic Mountain Sickness (also called Monge Disease after the Peruvian doctor who discovered and documented it). It is a loss of tolerance to high altitude after prolonged exposure, resulting in an abnormally low level of oxygen in the blood. Its most frequent symptoms are headache, dizziness, tinnitus, breathlessness, sleep disturbance, fatigue and loss of appetite. The disease can be fatal if the subject does not return to lower altitude. Fortunately for Cellini, the very next day his brigade moved down the mountain, and as a result he recovered. Once again, luck and timing played a part in his survival.

*****

ORDERED DOWN the mountain in anticipation of an aerial supply drop by the Royal Air Force, Cellini gathers his kit together, loads the machine guns onto a mule and begins to make his way down. No one mentions his illness, and mercifully, he is feeling much better anyway.

The sky is overcast and rain looks imminent; there will be no supply drop today. The Partisans hunker down and decide to hold their ground until the following day. While staying in one place longer than twenty-four hours is considered risky, their current location is well protected and offers shelter, as well as good visibility – and the entire 9th Brigade is in desperate need of the supplies.

Next morning, the weather still looks dull, but clear skies have been forecast for later in the day and the supply drop will take place regardless of the conditions. The RAF aircraft has already left its base in England.

Around mid-morning, the Partisans begin gathering wood ready to build a line of bonfires through the pasture along the foothills of the mountains. The bonfires are kindled and lit, then heaps of leaves are thrown on top to create smoke that the RAF pilot will be able to see as the aircraft approaches. Everyone has a job to do – and it has to be done quickly so that the Partisans can vacate the area before the smoke attracts enemy troops as well. Cellini is detailed to grab one of the canisters after it lands on the ground, empty it and load the contents onto the mules, then head back towards the mountains.

The drop goes more or less without a hitch. A huge, black-painted, four-engined bomber, complete with its red, white and blue roundels (referred to by Cellini as "targets") swoops in low, no more than 100 metres above the ground and almost directly over the line of bonfires. As is flies over the waiting Partisans, dozens of cylindrical canisters drop from its bomb bay on small parachutes. Falling from such low altitude, they take only a few seconds to reach the ground, but Cellini and his team must wait until all have landed before moving out to gather the contents, for fear of being struck by a stray canister. Some of the parachutes fail to open, and the canisters burst on the ground like small bombs, hurling their contents and fragments of the casing in all directions, as dangerous as the shrapnel from any grenade or mortar.

Once the aircraft has passed over and the canisters have all landed, Cellini and the other Partisans race over to retrieve them. The battered and broken contents of those that burst open on impact lie spilled all around, but the men focus on the unopened containers first.

The canisters are easily opened and the contents, including food, medical supplies, warm clothing, weapons and ammunition, are loaded into trucks or onto carts and the backs of mules. Once all the intact containers have been unpacked, the troops comb the terrain for loose items that may have survived the impact. In less than half an hour, the brigade has picked up everything of any use and moved on to higher ground, leaving nothing but empty and broken containers.

After reassembling in the hills, distribution of the much-needed supplies takes place. Cellini is given two large, flat cans of rations, which he puts into his trouser pockets to enjoy later, and a wool blanket, which he treasures above everything because of the cold nights.

Before long, the sky clouds over and a torrential rain sets in. The battalion is forced to move on to higher ground to avoid flooding, so loading up once again with their gear, they move on, wading through ankle-deep mud and fording rivers and streams. In one crossing, through fast-moving almost waist-deep water, some of the fastenings break loose and valuable supplies are lost. The move is exhausting, and by the time the rain finally eases off, everyone is soaked to the skin and all their gear is waterlogged.

Cellini leans back against a tree and sinks to the ground on his haunches. He reaches into his pocket for one of the ration tins. He has been looking forward to this meal ever since starting out on the cross-country trek.

Nothing. He slips his other hand into the other pocket. Again, his hand comes out empty. He starts patting his clothes all over, checking every pocket and searching through his belongings, but the ration tins are missing. Slowly the realization dawns on him that they must have come out while he was crossing the river in the tumultuous rain. By now he is used to going hungry, but the disappointment of losing his precious food is almost too much. For a split second he thinks about retracing his steps to look for the ration tins, but he knows it would be a tremendous risk and ultimately a waste of time. He decides to sleep instead and tries to squeeze the water out of his new blanket. Frustrated at the loss of his food and unable to dry the blanket, he balls it up and throws it as far as he can down the hillside before slumping at the base of the tree and falling into a fitful sleep.

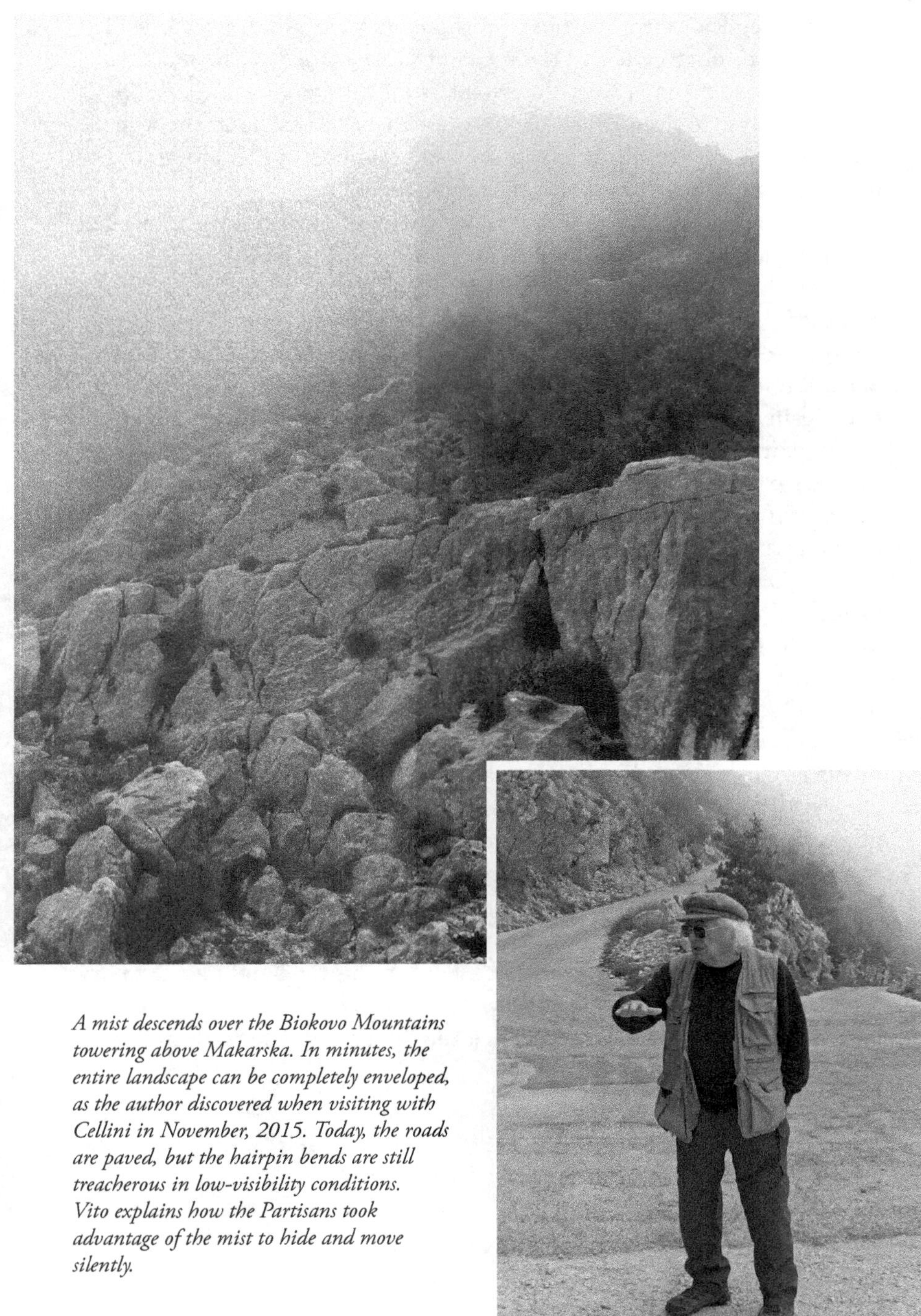

A mist descends over the Biokovo Mountains towering above Makarska. In minutes, the entire landscape can be completely enveloped, as the author discovered when visiting with Cellini in November, 2015. Today, the roads are paved, but the hairpin bends are still treacherous in low-visibility conditions. Vito explains how the Partisans took advantage of the mist to hide and move silently.

27. The Shortest Way Down...

Days of being cold, wet and hungry take their toll on everyone and the battalion is beginning to get irritable. For Cellini, the air drop had brought a welcome interlude from altitude sickness but disappointment at the loss of his rations had made him irritable. The battalion needs to get back into action.

News filters through that the entire brigade will be on the move as soon as darkness falls. That makes everyone feel better. The mules are repacked and they set off back up the mountain road.

Halfway up the mountain, they decide to bed down for the night. After a supper of boiled rice with the usual infusion of maggots, followed by his customary shot of grappa, a tall, dark-haired woman invites Cellini to join her and two other Partisans so they can huddle together and share body heat. He has seen her around the camp on several occasions and was struck by her height as well as her good looks. He is able to discover that she is from Montenegro, though further conversation is somewhat stilted because of the language barrier. He is not sure if she understands, or believes him, when he tells her that he is from New York. Her smile suggests she is dubious, but he is not chased away, which he takes as a good sign.

Sitting down with their backs against a large rock with the two men on the outside, they shuffle as close as together as they can and wrap their arms around each other. The men turn inwards and all draw their legs up, then stretch their blankets across themselves, layering the edges and tucking them underneath their feet and bodies forming a kind of cocoon. Cellini curses himself for having thrown away his own blanket in frustration. As sodden as it was, it would have eventually dried out and he could have at least offered it as a contribution to keeping the foursome warm.

There is no question of any kind of sexual contact, and Cellini feels no sense of arousal, despite the fact that his body is pressed tightly against the Montenegrin woman. They are just four human beings trying to keep warm.

It is another defining moment for Cellini.

He has slept huddled together with other male Partisans before; sometimes with one other, sometimes as many as five or six in a group. The smell of an unwashed male body in such close proximity takes some getting used to and Cellini is amazed at how many different odours it is possible to recognize besides damp wool and gunpowder. He has identified different types of food, tobacco, alcohol, dried urine, blood and remnants of other bodily functions, in addition to ordinary body odours. Thankfully, they almost never remove their footwear or he believes the stench would be unbearable. Cellini finds that as long as he keeps telling himself it will save his life and enable him to keep fighting, he is able to tolerate it. Unless, of course, someone in the close-knit group is unable to suppress a fart, in which case the group generally breaks into muffled giggles, with blankets and caution thrown to the wind.

He is grateful at least that his fellow Partisans do not smell anywhere near as bad as the German soldiers he encountered a while back.

Sleeping with women in the group is somehow different. Though the smell is every bit as pungent as that of the men, Cellini doesn't find it as offensive.

Surprisingly, everyone in the group is able to sleep at least part of the time. When he wakes, his muscles are stiff and he is chilled, but he feels rested and at least he has survived another night.

Poldo calls the battalion together. They will be moving up the mountain again to reinforce other battalions in a surprise assault on a suspected German stronghold. Scouts have reported no sign of enemy tanks but even so, Poldo wants Cellini to pack the anti-tank rifle and have it ready, just in case. They will be moving out in one hour, which gives everyone chance to eat and pack before beginning the day-long hike.

The first wave of Partisans has the element of surprise, but enemy resistance is intense and the Germans do not yield a metre. Partisan warfare relies on quick hit and run raids rather than sustained fighting, but the one thing they have in their favour is mobility and knowledge of the terrain, and the battalion withdraws to a more favourable position from which to attack again.

Cellini is isolated briefly from his immediate group and finds himself in sight of a German mortar crew behind a rocky outcrop who haven't seen him. Remembering the lessons Poldo taught him when he first joined the battalion, he approaches with his Breda machine gun at the hip, an extension of his arms. He fires a short burst at the first soldier as he walks towards the group, then without missing a step, fires a second burst into the second man. The third member of the mortar crew, still in shock at losing his comrades, raises his weapon but before he can find the trigger, Cellini has cut him down as well.

Three short bursts in less than three seconds.

Not bad, he thinks to himself, but before he has a chance to be too self-congratulatory, a bullet cracks somewhere near his head, and another whistles past, far too close. He turns, crouches and runs towards the mountain pathway, back the way he came. The bullets stop but he keeps going. Once clear of the rocky outcrop, he sees several of his battalion making their way up the mountain slope to take higher ground. His instinct is to go down, but seeing them makes him pause, just for a moment. In the split second he has to process the information, he decides that his way is best; down is a better option than up, preferring to give away some ground and fight another day. Should he call out to his comrades? No point. They've made their decision and he has made his. There's no time for a debate. He heads towards the downward slope and scrambles over the edge of the road.[1]

*****

EXPECTING TO FIND his feet on solid ground, he quickly realises, to his horror, that there is nothing but air beneath him. He has misjudged his position and is going over a sheer drop. When his feet do touch the ground, a few metres below, it is at a very steep angle and he is in grave danger of falling forwards onto his head. Leaning back and putting his hands out for stability, he hits the ground hard on his tailbone and half slides, half tumbles down the rocky slope for several seconds, eventually coming to a stop, resting against a large boulder.

The wind completely knocked out of him, he lies perfectly still, struggling for breath. His head is pounding and he can feel his heart thumping against his ribcage. He tries to get up but his back is hurting badly. He reaches up to touch the side of his head and finds it bleeding.

Oh great!

He closes his eyes. He can hear gun and mortar fire in the distance but nothing close to him, so he feels pretty sure he has escaped from the Germans. He strains his neck to look up the slope he has just unceremoniously descended and is amazed to see he must have fallen and slid at least 20 metres. Once more he tries to get up, and this time manages to get

[1] *Cellini made the right decision. He would later find out that the battalion took heavy casualties in the attack and lost several good men among those who chose to go up the mountain. Once again, his luck held and his instincts were proven right.*

as far as a kneeling position. Leaning against the boulder that arrested his rapid descent, he pauses for a moment before pushing himself to his feet. He succeeds in making his way carefully down the rest of the slope, a distance of just a few metres, using his machine gun as a crutch. He is about to set off up the hill when he hears muffled laughter coming from behind. He turns around to find several members of his battalion who had seen his ungracious descent down the mountainside, or at least his landing.

From the distance, they were unable to tell who it was, but once he had made it to the road they recognized him. They are glad to see him. Much joking and embracing takes place before two of the party take his arms over their shoulders and lead him back to the camp. One of the women bathes his head wound and shows him a fragment of bullet she finds. It must have ricocheted off the rock and hit him on the side of the head. But it is his back that is giving him the most grief. He rests, fitfully, but is able to move when the order comes, although the pain is excruciating.

"Here, take this." One of the men who helped him back to camp offers him a small folded piece of paper. Cellini unfolds the paper it and looks at the white powder inside.

"What is it?" he says.

"Don't worry," the soldier smiles. "It will ease the pain and make you feel great."

"What do I do with it?" says Cellini.

"You can either sniff it or put it under your tongue."

Cellini opts for putting it under his tongue and tips the contents of the paper packet into his mouth. The white powder feels like cold velvet and quickly numbs his tongue, but it does ease his pain and after a few minutes he is feeling a lot more mobile.[2]

The battalion must move camp before nightfall, so there is no chance of rest for Cellini – although due to the stimulating effects of the drug he has taken, he doesn't feel like resting. Despite the pain, he is impatient to get going. There is no shortage of volunteers to help carry his equipment and lend him a shoulder to lean on – such is the camaraderie in Tito's Partisan army. Once relocated to a safer area, easier for sentries to protect, they are able to rest up for a few days, allowing time for Cellini's wounds to heal enough to move on his own feet.

[2] *The white powder was almost certainly cocaine, which individual Partisan fighters might have had access to through contact with the black market, a flourishing business in Yugoslavia just as in other countries during the war. At the time, many drugs now considered illicit were legal and had legitimate medical uses, making them more valuable to black marketers. Cellini tried cocaine on one other occasion, after the war, to verify that was what he had been given, but did not enjoy the experience and has not repeated it since.*

28. Farewell to the Partisans

The Brigade is getting ready to move south again. The plan is that they will be heading to the islands and back across to Rogoznica by boat. The few days' rest has done wonders for Cellini and he is keen to get back to the fighting. While they are gathering their equipment together for the move Cellini gets into a conversation with a couple of his fellow Partisans about the general state of the war.

Though rumours have been circulating for some time that the Allies have made advances through Europe, no one is sure of anything. Cellini, however, is sure of one thing: it will only be a matter of time until the Americans arrive and destroy the Nazi menace once and for all. He is not shy of sharing his opinion with others around him, although it doesn't always go over too well.

The Partisans, by and large, had been formed from political activists who resisted the dominance of the Italian fascists and of the internal fascist factions within their own country. Tito's Liberation Army was founded on the principles of communism, and the majority saw their salvation coming not from the Western Allies of Britain and America, but from the Soviet Union.

Now that Poldo was able to confirm that the Western Allies had established a firm foothold in southern Italy, Cellini was even more vocal than usual.

"The Americans will soon be here to help us wipe out these Nazi bastards!" he announces to anyone who is paying attention.

Some around him start cheering, but the cheers are weak and fade as his words are translated into different dialects so that everyone gets the message. Now they glare at Cellini in silence. Some spit on the ground.

Poldo overhears the outburst and shakes his head, smiling at Cellini.

"Don't get too carried away with that idea!" he says.

"While we are indebted to the British and Americans for their support – this is Yugoslavia's war. We are fighting not only against the Nazi invaders, but also internally against many factions of fascism. You see the way we live? We are a social people. Our future is as an independent communist nation, and to achieve that it is to the east that Marshal Tito will look for military support."

The crowd nods and murmurs. One or two of them salute, fists clenched against the side of the head in the Partisan way.

Cellini makes his way over to Poldo.

"You know that I am an American?" Cellini says.

"Yes. You told me when we first met," Poldo replies. Cellini is surprised that he remembers that first conversation. It shows what a great leader his commander is.

Poldo continues, "I never cared where you were from or what you believed as long as you were ready to fight for the Partisans and willing to kill fascists. You have always fought hard and never questioned orders. You are a quick learner and you have become a good resistance fighter, but I know your heart is with the Americans."

"Now that the Allies are in control of the Adriatic ports, many of the trade routes are once again open between Dalmatia and southern Italy. If you want to return to Italy and join the Allies, no one here will stand in your way."

Cellini doesn't even have to think about it. He smiles and thanks his commander, then turns to his fellow Partisans and offers the clenched fist salute as a show of both respect and friendship. Poldo tells Cellini that once they reach Makarska he will make arrangements for him to take a fishing boat across the Adriatic to the port of Bari, where he can find the Allied headquarters and offer his services.

*****

CELLINI SAYS HIS goodbyes to the Partisans.

Some are sorry to see him go, others are still somewhat indifferent, partly from being war weary and partly because they are still not sure about this tough and enigmatic Italian speaker who maintains that he is an American citizen. He steps towards a young boy, no more than 12 or 13 years-old, tousles his hair and hugs him. Cellini has seen him from time to time, and others just like him. He has tremendous admiration for the kids caught up in this adult war, doing their part. The boy is a messenger. He carries no weapon because he is too small, but he runs between groups of Partisans carrying written and sometimes spoken messages.[1] If he is caught he will very likely be tortured and shot for the information he carries, yet he is not afraid and accepts the risks willingly. Cellini wonders if the boy's parents are alive or dead. Are they out there in the mountains fighting, too? Do they know what their child is doing? It brings home yet again the horror of this war and reinforces Cellini's determination to join the Allies and help to free these courageous people.

There is no ceremony for his departure from Makarska, save for the usual daily round of grappa. Poldo hands him a folded piece of paper.

"This letter of safe passage will get you across the Adriatic. Show it to the officials when you stop on the island of Vis and keep it with you.[2] It may even help you when you get to Italy. If you can, show it to the British officials – we have worked longer and more closely with them. Good luck my friend."

Cellini places the piece of paper in his top pocket without even looking at it. He thanks Poldo, shakes his hand and promises that he will return, one day, to Yugoslavia, when the war is over and the fascists are all dead and buried.

Grabbing his kitbag, he walks up the short gangplank onto a small fishing boat. The gunwales are painted bright blue and it stinks to high heaven of fish, but it is the most beautiful sight his eyes have seen in a long time.[3]

He wonders what awaits him back in Bari.

[1] *On a trip to Croatia in 2015, Vito Cellini would meet and become friends with one of these Partisan messengers, Antun "Tonći" Baranović. As a young boy Tonci learned to speak Italian so he could deliver messages to Italian Partisans and the two men enjoyed spending time reminiscing. Tonći would go on to become a national hero playing professional football for Hajduk Split after the war.*

[2] *The island of Vis, just off the Dalmatian coast, was used as Marshal Tito's headquarters and, after the capitulation, as a checkpoint for vessels leaving Yugoslavia bound for Italy. The island was also occupied by British forces who provided supplies and training to the Partisans, and used as a strategic base for RAF fighter-bombers.*

[3] *As Cellini departs on a fishing boat for Bari, the 9th Brigade leaves Makarska at the same time on Partisan boats bound for Rogoznica, arriving on the night of the 2nd and 3rd of December. They reach the Vrdovo Bitelic region on December 6th and attack Vaganj on December 16th. (Poldo's diary)*

At a meeting of the Antifascist Association in Split, Croatia, Cellini was welcomed by veteran Yugoslavian Partisans Ante Adorić, Ante Jelaska, Palmina Piplović and Božidar Papić. Palmina Piplović had served on Tito's staff on the island of Vis and may even have checked Cellini's papers on his journey back to Bari.

Cellini visits the home of former Partisan Lovre Reić, together with Tonći Baranović, November 2015. At the end of his visit, Lovre Reić presented Cellini with a bronze plaque of Tito.

Tonći Baranović with Josip Broz Tito, 1951.

29. Bari, December 1943

By the end of August 1943, the invasion of Sicily – what Churchill describes as the "soft underbelly of Europe" – is complete, and the Allies turn their attention to mainland Italy. During secret surrender negotiations with the Italian government in early September, it is agreed to open the ports of Taranto and Brindisi in preparation for an Allied invasion. A landing in Taranto is quickly planned, code-named Operation Slapstick, utilizing the British 1st Airborne Division. Slapstick is also intended to divert German forces away from the main Allied landings taking place on the same day at Salerno. If both operations are successful, the Allies will gain major supply ports on both Italian coasts (Naples and Taranto). There are no transport aircraft or gliders available for the 1st Airborne Division so they are transported on Royal Navy ships. The landing is unopposed and the airborne division successfully captures the port of Taranto. (In fact, as Royal Navy ships carrying the invasion troops approach Taranto, Italian battleships Andrea Doria and Caio Duilio, along with three cruisers, steam out of the port and sail past the Royal Navy ships on their way to surrender in Malta). Within 48 hours, the ports of Brindisi and Bari, on the Adriatic Coast, are seized without resistance.

As a diversion from the invasion at Salerno, Operation Slapstick is less successful; the only German forces encountered by the British 1st Airborne Division are remnants of the 1st Parachute Division, which engage the advancing force in occasional skirmishes as they withdraw northwards. By the end of September, British troops advance 125 miles (201 kilometres) to Foggia. By the end of November, fishing boats and merchant ships, as well as military supply vessels, are once again sailing across the Adriatic from the Dalmatian Coast to Bari and Brindisi.

Bari and Foggia are of immense strategic importance. Foggia and its twelve satellite air bases become headquarters of the US Fifteenth Air Force, from which they will launch crippling attacks on the oil fields at Ploesti in Romania, among other targets. The port of Bari becomes the chief supply line, not only for the Fifteenth Air Force, but for the allied offensive north and west through Italy.

Bari also becomes the command centre of the Fifteenth Air Force and the 15th Army Group, comprising five divisions of the U.S. 5th Army under General Mark Clark and three divisions of the British Eighth Army under Montgomery, all under the leadership of distinguished and much decorated General (later Field-Marshal) Sir Harold Alexander.

*****

THE COLD AIR is thick and moist as the small fishing boat cuts a path through the smooth Adriatic waters towards the Italian coast. There is not far to go now. Cellini has not slept, but at least for once he hasn't been sick, in spite of the heavy stench of fish that has accompanied him since leaving Makarska the previous day. He won't be sorry to get off this stinking tub and on dry land again.

Even when they stop briefly at Vis, where everyone aboard has their papers checked and Partisan soldiers carry out a rigorous search of the boat, he isn't able to step ashore.

They sail on through the night, and in the early hours, the boat makes one more stop, mooring in the Gulf of Manfredonia, just off the Gargano Peninsula, the "hook" of Italy.[1]

Surrounded by other fishing boats casting their nets ready for the day's haul, Cellini seriously considers jumping off the boat, swimming ashore or boarding another vessel, and then hitching a ride to Bari. He is anxious to meet up with the Americans – his fellow countrymen – who he knows have now occupied his old hometown. He thinks better of the idea and decides to stay on the boat.

A few more hours won't make any difference, he thinks to himself, figuring it would probably take him longer, once he made it to the shore, to try and get to Bari over land anyway. At least if he stays on board he knows he will get to Bari sometime today, or tomorrow, at the latest. He sits down on the deck and folds his arms around his legs, his back resting against the wheelhouse. Careful to keep out of the way of the crew as they go about the business of getting the boat under way, he waits for the boat to set sail on its last leg of this tedious crossing. He is anxious to get back to Italy and join the American forces so he can help finish this war and go

[1] *The Gargano Peninsula is famous for its rocky mountains, white sandy beaches and ancient forest. It is also the site of the oldest shrine in Western Europe, dedicated to the archangel Michael. Gargano was made a national park in 1977.*

home to New York.

The voyage is almost over. Cellini stands and stretches his stiff and aching back, still sore from his tumble down the mountain in Yugoslavia, then crouches and leans over the gunwale, hoping for a taste of fresh air. The sky ahead is dark and there is a heavy grey mist beginning to form on the surface of the water, unusual for early afternoon, even in December. He sits back down and closes his eyes. He is about to cave in to his sheer exhaustion and drift into semi-consciousness when he is prematurely jarred awake by the babbling voices of the fishermen. They are pointing and waving towards the horizon. In the distance, ahead and to the right of the boat, a thick pall of smoke hangs suspended over the land.

He checks his watch. It's almost three-thirty in the afternoon.

There's something else besides the smoke in the sky over Bari; hundreds of small, silver-grey blobs bobbing around just above the skyline. After staring at them for a few minutes he realises they are balloons. For an instant he imagines them to be enemy airships, like Zeppelins, and that the Germans have somehow resurrected these strange craft to bomb his hometown.[2]

As the boat gets closer to its destination, Cellini catches a whiff of sickly sweet diesel oil tinged with sulfur and cordite, faint at first, but getting gradually stronger as they sail towards the port of Bari. There is another smell, something like garlic, which seems to waft across the water. The mixture of smells is pungent and nauseating, even though most of the smoke cloud appears to be blowing inland, away from the fishing boat.

Peering through the haze towards the harbour, he notices something else. Except for the steady throbbing of the engine on the boat beneath him, everything is deathly quiet. There are no fishing boats, no sea birds, no signs of life at all.

What on earth is going on in Bari? he thinks to himself.

*****

It seems like a lifetime ago since he was here, and he wonders about the family and friends he left behind. How has this war affected them? Up until now, he has been wrapped up in thoughts of his own escapades, and about moving on to his next adventure. Now, seeing Bari under a blanket of smoke, he realises that the war is touching everyone, including his family.

2. *They were barrage balloons, rushed into place by the British Army, tethered to the ground and hanging over the city to prevent bombers from finding a way through to their target.*

The musky odour of diesel becomes increasingly pungent and makes breathing unpleasant. The boat lurches first to one side and then the other, turning sharply away from the harbour wall and the obvious carnage beyond. A sudden blast of warm air carries the strong metallic smell across the fishing boat, then it's gone, replaced once again by the cold, damp air, the sickly diesel fumes, and once again that unmistakable hint of garlic.

The silence is broken by the fishermen on board his boat, babbling and gesturing towards the shore, but Cellini understands very little of what is said because they are speaking in the dialects of Yugoslavia, none of which he has ever learned. It suddenly strikes him how much he has missed hearing the *Barese* dialect while he has been away, and how he looks forward to hearing it again from his friends and family.

Closer still, he shades his eyes and peers through the haze once again. He looks for ships, moored in and around the port, but all he can see are masts and cables and strange, deformed shapes protruding from the surface of the water like trees in winter. A smouldering grey hull that used to be a merchant ship looms out of the haze and the small fishing boat has to turn to avoid it, then come around again to slip inside the harbour wall, keeping well away from other burned out hulks and floating debris. Ships of all sizes lie on their sides, smoke seeping from gaping wounds.

The cranes used for lifting cargo from the holds of ships are still and silent. Lit up but locked down and unmanned. The port, usually thriving and bustling, is deserted.

The few crew members not engaged in guiding the fishing boat into port, along with half a dozen other passengers who, like Vito, had bartered for their passage to Bari, scramble from one side of the boat to the other, straining their eyes to get a better look at whatever is going on – or has been going on. The boat lurches and turns, brushing aside floating debris and gliding through almost motionless oily water. In the smoke and haze, which seems denser now that they are inside the harbour wall, it is harder to get a clear view of anything further than a few yards away. The engine noise drops an octave until the throbbing vibration becomes a steady hum.

The fishing boat turns again, moving slowly through the haze, coming back around and leaving the debris field behind before turning once again towards the shore. The silence seems unnatural. It is late afternoon and there should be all kinds of activity. Instead, Cellini feels as if he has sailed into a ghost port. Finally, the boat bumps up alongside a concrete dock, a couple of crewmen jump out and secure the hawser lines, and the passengers, fishermen and crew grab their duffle bags and huddle at the ramp, ready to get off the boat.

Cellini waits for the others to leave, then slowly makes his way over to the opening in the boat and steps onto dry land.

He looks around to get his bearings and recognizes the landing area between *Molo Pizzoli* and *Molo San Vito* from the days when he used to swim in the harbour as young boy. As he steps off the boat, he stumbles, just for an instant. "Damn sea legs," he mutters under his breath. He looks towards the town. The castle walls are almost directly ahead of him and beyond them, to the left, Bari Vecchio, the old town. He wonders what his old friends are up to, or if they are even still here. The old town seems strangely quiet and deserted. Apart from the dozen or so men who have just departed the fishing boat and are now shuffling their way towards the exit, the only signs of life are the barrage balloons, bobbing around in the darkening sky, nudging each other first one way and then the other. There are almost no lights on in the streets or buildings. No cars. No people as far as Cellini can see. Not even a dog or a cat.

This is a very strange homecoming.

*****

THE HARBOUR IS STILL shrouded in dark grey smoke from the smouldering ships. From way off in the distance behind him comes the haunting sound of steel groaning under stress, like some behemoth creature in its death throes. Now that he is away from the water, the abstract and disjointed sound takes on a surreal dimension.

Tired, hungry and confused, Cellini staggers towards the gate at the entrance to the port. A lone British soldier, a corporal standing with a Lee Enfield rifle by his side, comes to attention and gabbles at him in a language that sounds familiar, but one he doesn't understand and cannot reply to. He has heard this language over the past few months and presumes it is Serbian or Croatian or some Yugoslavian dialect. He wonders why the soldier is talking to him in this strange tongue, then remembers he is still dressed in his Partisan uniform – if it could be called a uniform.

He replies in Italian.

"Sir, I do not understand Yugoslavian. I am an American and I have been fighting in Yugoslavia with the Partisan army. When I found out that the Allies had taken Italy I came back as soon as I could to join the American Army."

The corporal raises a finger as a signal for Cellini to wait while he fetches someone else. He returns after a minute or two with another soldier who speaks Italian.

Cellini asks what has happened here and gets exactly the answer he expected.

"Bloody Jerries. An air raid. Only lasted half an hour. But don't worry, everything is under control, or soon will be. Do you have your papers with you?" the Englishman replies.

"I have a letter here from my brigade commander in the Partisan army," Cellini responds, taking a folded and crumpled piece of paper from his pocket. As he hands it over he looks across at the harbour one more time and shakes his head in disbelief.

Why Bari? He thinks to himself. The British corporal studies the piece of paper for a minute and hands it back to Cellini.

"I need to find the American military headquarters, can you help me?" Cellini says.

Always happy to make conversation, Cellini explains that when word filtered through to his brigade about the Allied invasion of Italy, he expressed his joy that the Americans would now be able to liberate Yugoslavia. His enthusiasm was not, however shared by his fellow Partisans who, being communists, were more hopeful of being liberated by the Soviet Army. They had parted as good friends, and the brigade commander did suggest that, if he wanted to rejoin his American comrades, the grateful Partisans would do everything in their power to help him get safely back to Italy.

The British soldier translates for the corporal, who smiles rather sardonically as he replies.

"It depends on which branch you are looking for. They are all over the place." With typical British understatement he adds, "I believe they have their hands full at the moment, with all this mess," pointing towards the docks. "Do you have family in Bari?"

Cellini nods.

"You should go home and spend some time with them. If I were you I would wait a couple of days before you start looking for any of the military authorities. From what I hear, the Yanks have set up supply dumps, sentry posts and road blocks with Military Police all over town, so they're not exactly hard to find."

After thanking the two soldiers and walking away, Cellini sets off along the seafront, still shrouded in smoke. In the distance he hears the ghostly sound of tortured metal as a wrecked merchant ship strains against its mooring, and he turns around for one last look over the harbour.

The evening sky is beginning to settle over the town, but even in the fading light he can see the carnage that, until just a couple of hours ago, he was blissfully unaware of. The port is littered with broken ships, some lying on their sides, many with smoke rising from them. He can just make out masts rising from the water at odd angles and floating debris. The still surface, covered in slimy fuel oil reflected in rainbow patches, shimmers in the lights from a crane. Taking in the damage, he looks around and notices that in addition to the destruction around the port area, several buildings have been hit as well.

Diesel fumes linger, along with the smell of hot metal and burnt gunpowder, punctuated every now and then by the same distinct odour of garlic wafting in the evening breeze.

As he walks along he wonders over and over to himself, *What the hell happened?*

He hopes he might run into someone who can tell him more about the raid. He has seen air raids before; he's been attacked by bombers and strafed from the air with machine guns, but never has he seen such devastation on such a large scale as this. The town appears all but deserted, apart from the occasional passer-by, staring straight ahead with glazed eyes and a stunned look as they hurry somewhere.

Turning from the seafront onto *Via Niccolo Pizzoli,* he has to stop and think for a moment. His grandmother's home – the house he grew up in – used to be on *Via Niccolo Pizzoli*, close to *Piazza Garibaldi.* She since moved a couple of blocks to *Via Pietro Ravanas* so he needs to head over to *Via Trevisani.* As he pauses, he catches the faint strains of music coming from nearby.

Hearing the sound of music brings back all kinds of childhood memories, some good and some not so good, but he finds himself drawn towards the sound. Out of habit he looks around to check for cars or horses before he crosses *Via Napoli,* normally a busy street, but there is nothing in sight and he picks up his pace to see where the music is coming from.

The music is louder now and seems to be coming from a building near the corner of *Via Carlo Perrone*. As he draws closer, a group of people spills out onto the street, laughing and dancing. Most have a glass of wine or beer in hand. It seems strangely incongruous to Cellini, after seeing so much death and destruction, to suddenly find himself in the midst of a wedding party!

The smell of smoke is still very much in evidence, but the guests at the wedding party seem oblivious to it all.

"This is Bari," he thinks to himself. "Life goes on."

A voice calls out, "Tutuc? Tutuc Cellini? Is that you?"

He looks up at the face behind the voice of the young man walking towards him, smiling, arms open wide. The face is familiar but he can't put a name to it. Bari is small town and everyone knows everyone, and with his reputation he isn't surprised to be recognized.

"Come on in, my friend! Come in!"

It's the son of a neighbourhood butcher, Michael. He hasn't seen the family for years, and today is his wedding day! He is happy to see Cellini.

"We thought you were dead! Or in jail perhaps?" He laughs and ushers Cellini through a doorway.

"Please come inside and have something to eat and drink," he says, gesturing towards a table covered with food and wine and beer. "My father will be delighted to see you!"

"Of course," Cellini replies, "And then maybe someone can tell me what the hell is going on down at the port?"

He still cannot remember the bridegroom's name, but names never were his strong suit. In all his time in the army and with the Partisans, he never remembered the names of any of his comrades. But he never forgot a face. The bridegroom beckons his father over to Cellini and they begin to talk about the neighbourhood, old times, Vito's father and a host of other subjects. Cellini steers them back around to the events of the previous night.

"It started at about 7:30 yesterday evening," the butcher begins. "The sirens went off as they often do and no one took much notice. Usually the bombers pass over us or never come near. A couple of minutes later, we heard the engines of the bombers and we knew this time they were coming for us. We couldn't see anything because it was dark, but we all ran inside and hid under the furniture. I dived under the bed. It sounded like there were hundreds of bombers swarming around. It has to be because of all the ships in the harbour. American supply ships started arriving about a week ago and they are stacked up waiting to be unloaded. Everyone has been talking about it." He looks at Cellini, expecting some kind of agreement.

"I just got here. Been in Yugoslavia and got in today." Cellini shrugs as he replies without elaborating.

"How did you get in to Bari? says the butcher. "I thought the port was closed?"

"I was in a small fishing boat with maybe ten or twelve other people. We could see how bad things were when we got close to the harbour entrance. The whole place was completely deserted, but we picked our way through the wrecks and found a place to dock between *Molo Pizzoli* and *Molo San Vito*."

Cellini continues, "But tell me what happened during the air raid?"

"Bombs started raining down," Michael continues. "Even inside the house, under the bed we could hear the whistle as they fell. It sounded like they were mostly in and around the dock area, but I'm pretty sure a few hit the town. Then there was this one massive explosion, ten times bigger than the rest of them. It felt like an earthquake and I thought at first maybe they'd scored a direct hit on the house. The whole town was shaking and the rumble seemed to go on for an age. Next thing we knew, it was all over. We hid under the furniture until we couldn't hear the drone of the engines any more, then went out into the street to see the damage. We could still hear explosions coming from down by the water, but at least the bombers had left. There was this thick cloud of smoke everywhere and everything was covered in dust."

"We stayed indoors until this morning, but I had to go to work because even though the shop is closed, I had to prepare the meat for this wedding. I did see ambulances and military vehicles everywhere, and a lot of people packing up their belongings and heading out of town by bus, car, on horses, bicycles and even push carts." He stops and sips from his wine glass.

"People are afraid of the Germans coming back, but why would they bother? Judging by the way things look, they did a pretty good job of smashing up the port and all the ships in it."

Cellini stares in silence. After a moment lost in thought, he pours himself a large glass of wine and raises it to the groom and his father.

"Salut!" he says, "Now tell me, when do I get to meet the bride?"[3]

*****

He stays at the wedding for a while and chats to a few of the other guests, but no one seems able to tell him anything that he hasn't already learned about the air raid. Everyone refers to the one huge explosion that rocked the whole town, which arouses his curiosity, but he's tired, and the sandwich of prosciutto and provolone cheese has satisfied his hunger, so his curiosity can wait. He excuses himself and continues on his way to his

[3] *Vito Cellini recalls a neighbourhood story about Michael, the local butcher, and his wife Michaelina. Like many Italians, Michael had an eye for the ladies and enjoyed the company of several girlfriends throughout their marriage. One day, so the story goes, Michaelina – who was not known for her culinary abilities – prepared a dish of spaghetti and mussels for her errant husband that he absolutely loved. So much so that he asked her to prepare it again the following day, which she did. When he asked for the same meal again three days in a row, she asked, "What is the matter with you, eating the same food every day?" He replied, "You think it strange that I should want to eat the same food every day?"*

"Of course!" she said, "What kind of man wants to eat the same food every day?" To which he is supposed to have replied, "And yet you think I should want to sleep with the same woman every night!"

Whether true or not, the story typifies Barese humour!

grandmother's house.[4]

He arrives at the house dishevelled and slightly the worse for wear, having drunk several glasses of wine and grappa at the wedding after going almost 48 hours without any sleep. His grandmother and grandfather are absolutely thrilled to see him. She holds him and weeps for joy, apologizes for the state of the house and chides him for not warning her that he was coming.

Too tired to argue, and just pleased to be among family, he falls into a chair, pulls off his boots and is fast asleep within minutes.

*****

WAKING EARLY THE following morning, Cellini sneaks out of the house quietly, so as not to disturb his grandparents, and sets off walking around the town, checking out his old haunts and hoping to run into his old friends.

The town is deserted and strangely quiet except for the occasional military vehicle and a British or American soldier here and there. They all seem to be hurrying to get somewhere else. There is still a smoky haze hanging over the town. The streets are empty and none of the shops are open.

He finds an American soldier standing in the doorway of a building, which he presumes houses supplies. The soldier looks bored and tired. Cellini tries to look inside but cannot see anything or anyone, so he approaches the American and tries to strike up a conversation, hoping to find out something or at least where he could go to talk to someone about joining the US Army. He asks the soldier if he speaks any Italian.

"A little," the soldier replies, "I'm from Brooklyn."

"Me too!" Cellini is delighted to find someone from his own part of the world, even though he remembers next to nothing about his time there. He gabbles excitedly and GI Brooklyn has to ask him to slow down

[4] *Cellini has many fond memories of his grandmother's house on Via Pietro Ravanas, not least of which was the fact that she had a plumbed toilet – a modern feature of which she was immensely proud and one of very few in Bari. The home was on the first floor (second floor in the US) and the toilet was located on an outside balcony overlooking the inner courtyard of the building. It had a roof for protection from the rain and a curtain for privacy, but could, nonetheless, be very cold in winter. The plumbing was quite basic: there was no flushing mechanism. Instead, water had to be poured from a jug down the bowl of the toilet to carry the contents away and into Bari's main sewerage system. Grandma Cellini didn't allow just anyone to use this marvel of modern technology, but Vito was one of the privileged few. One fact that particularly amuses him, looking back, is the lack of paper in those days. Instead, a cloth made from an old potato sack hung on the wall for communal use. The cloth was washed just once a week, along with all the other laundry, so in order to find a clean area on the cloth, it was necessary to hold it up to the light and, being coarsely woven, find a spot that the light would shine through!*

because his Italian isn't that good. Cellini speaks slowly.

"That must have been some air raid?" he says. "Do you know what happened?"

"All I know is there was a bombing attack a couple nights ago, maybe three, I really don't remember because I ain't had much sleep since. Been on guard because they declared an emergency, cancelled all leave and won't even let us go back to base."

Cellini is more than happy to stop a while and chat with him, especially now that he's found out the guy is from Brooklyn. Italians have a way of finding each other. This guy has even learned a little of the *Barese* dialect since he's been here.

The GI continues, "Some of the guys are saying it was *Eyetie* frogmen planting mines on the ships. They say it couldn't have been the air raid that did all this damage, because even the Luftwaffe couldn't sink every ship in the harbour – which is exactly what happened!"

Cellini has been thinking the exact same thing. *How could one air raid sink so many ships and cause so much damage?* He believes that the destruction of the ships in Bari Harbour must have been caused by something more sinister and will hold that belief for many years. Does the idea of divers planting mines on the American ships really sound so farfetched? He doesn't think so, but he keeps this information to himself, because he's pretty sure no one would believe him anyway. Cellini learned at a very young age when to keep quiet and when to speak up. Since no one else has mentioned it, he decides it is probably being kept secret for a reason.

The truth behind this tragic event is far more sinister then Cellini or his new American GI friend could dream, and wouldn't become general knowledge until more than twenty years after the end of the war.

*****

CELLINI HAS ARRIVED back in Bari just hours after one of the deadliest bombing raids of the European war, culminating in one of the largest explosive chain reactions, and the only instance of exposure to chemical warfare in any European city during the entire Second World War.

At 7:25 pm on the evening of December 2nd, 1943, 105 German Junkers Ju 88 dive bombers – all the Luftwaffe could muster at that time – begin attacking shipping in the port of Bari, acting on recently gathered intelligence that American Liberty ships carrying vital supplies for the Allied troops have recently docked. Their arrival follows the capture of Bari by the British 1st Airborne Division almost three months earlier, establishing the port city as a key command and logistics centre.

The bombers attack the ships in waves, each choosing its own target of opportunity; but such is the overcrowding in the harbour that the ships are sitting ducks. Added to which, the port is fully lit to expedite the unloading of the supplies. When a ship is hit, the resulting explosion and fire quickly spreads to adjacent ships and soon it seems as though the whole port is on fire. Twenty-eight ships are sunk in the raid and another twelve damaged. The attack will become known as "Little Pearl Harbor".

The worst is still to come. By pure chance, one of the German bombs strikes the SS John Harvey, a US Merchant vessel, directly in its hold. Unbeknownst to anyone, the John Harvey is carrying a deadly cargo of M-47A1 sulfur-mustard gas bombs. Though chemical weapons are banned by the Geneva Protocol of 1925, and generally regarded as "off limits" by both sides, American leaders want to "be prepared" in case the Germans use them and a retaliatory attack is deemed warranted. Shipment of 2,000 of the gas bombs for storage by the Army Air Forces in Italy has been approved.

The resulting explosion and release of mustard gas is catastrophic. In addition to the immediate casualties caused by the air raid and destruction of ships, the poisonous cloud of gas spreads over the port and across the city, killing and injuring hundreds if not thousands more, both military personnel and civilians. Exact casualty figures may never be known, partly because many citizens leave the city following the attack, possibly developing symptoms later; and partly because the incident is quickly covered up to prevent the Germans from suspecting that the Allies are stockpiling chemical weapons. No one, not even medical staff at nearby hospitals and first aid posts, is told of the mustard gas, so those affected will not receive appropriate treatment in a timely manner. Making it even worse, the liquid mustard mixes with the oil from damaged and destroyed ships in the harbour, soaking into the clothing of those who survive the initial blast, delaying and exacerbating the effects.

Following the immediate raid, rumours are rife that the Germans have dropped poison gas or that the Luftwaffe will be back the following day in even greater numbers. One popular story is that mines have been attached to each of the liberty ships by Italian frogmen who are still on the side of the Nazis. Allied leaders do little to quell the rumours because they do not want word leaking out about the real cause of the devastation and huge loss of life.

On the orders of Allied leaders Franklin D. Roosevelt and Winston Churchill, all records of the incident, including medical reports, are destroyed, making it even more difficult to determine the exact number of casualties. It will be kept secret for many years after the war.[5]

The initial symptoms of the sulfur-mustard gas poisoning mimick those of burns and exposure, and undoubtedly cause many misdiagnoses and consequently incorrect treatment. Rather than removing oil-drenched clothing and having their skin washed, patients are wrapped in towels and blankets that keep the mustard pressed against their bodies. Advanced symptoms include severe blistering of the skin, watery eyes (in severe cases, blindness) and respiratory problems. Worse still, the effects can be spread through contact with the blisters of others, or clothing contaminated by the liquid gas residue, causing even more casualties.

Dr. Stewart F. Alexander, a member of General Dwight D. Eisenhower's medical staff, is dispatched to Bari to study victims and survivors of the air raid, but even he is not told about the release of the gas. Having studied experiments on the effects of various chemical weapons at Aberdeen Proving Ground in Maryland, he observes what he believes to be symptoms of mustard gas exposure in Bari. Even though no one in the chain of command will confirm his suspicions, he convinces medical staff to treat patients accordingly. His action undoubtedly saves many lives.

Dr. Alexander also notices that exposure to the mustard gas seems to suppresses the growth of certain cancer cells, and carefully preserves tissue samples from the autopsies of victims in Bari. His meticulous record keeping and detailed case notes are invaluable in the post-war development of mechlorethamine, a derivative of mustard gas and the first chemotherapy drug.[6]

Instrumental in suppressing the facts of the attack and the use of mustard gas, British Prime Minister Winston Churchill refuses to acknowledge the disaster, believing it will undermine the Allies' ability to launch a successful invasion through Italy. Churchill has always envisioned the primary invasion of Europe being focused through Italy rather than across the English Channel – a major bone of contention between the Allied leaders.[7]

With the Port of Bari closed until February, the main supply route of personnel and equipment to southern Italy is substantially constricted. Ground troops are spread thin and the Fifteenth Air Force, though highly effective against the oil refineries in Eastern Europe, are never able to deliver the same punch against German industry as their counterparts in the Eighth Air Force based in England.

[5.] *Vito Cellini's cousin Frank, a retired heart surgeon born shortly after the war, recalls that his parents often spoke of the air raid. Hearing the deafening explosion and feeling the ground shaking, they fled, terrified, to improvised underground shelters outside of the city. Returning several days later, they found the port littered with mangled and partially submerged ships, many of which were still smouldering. The port was closed for three weeks and was not able to operate at full capacity until February, 1944.*

[6.] *In 1988, Dr. Alexander finally received recognition from the United States Army for his work in the aftermath of the Bari air raid, and for his immense contribution to research for cancer treatments. Ironically, Dr. Alexander died in 1991 from skin cancer.*

7. It could be argued that the attack on Bari had far-reaching effects on the course of the war, forcing the issue in terms of both where and when the planned invasion would take place.

Approaching the old port of Bari from the sea, November 2015. This is the exact same view Cellini had when he returned from Yugoslavia in 1943.

A memorial to those who lost their lives in the air raid of December 2, 1943.

30. The *Delinquente* Returns

CELLINI MAKES HIS way back to his grandmother's house too late for the midday meal, but his grandmother has saved him some meat and bread and will cook him some pasta. His grandfather still works for the railway company, and in spite of the bombing there is a lot of work to be done, so he has returned to work and will not be home until late.

Cellini thinks about his friends and his family, and for some reason he thinks about his cousin Francesca, whom he has hasn't seen in ages. He has no idea what suddenly brought her to mind after all this time, but the thought of her sweet face makes him smile.

He shares with his grandmother his plan to visit the American military base so he can enlist with the army of his birth country. She knows it is futile to argue with him. Once his mind is made up, there is nothing she, or anyone else, can do to unmake it.

"You should talk to your Uncle Nicola," she says.

He looks at her quizzically. He had expected an argument.

"You want to join the Americans? So talk to Nicola. He knows all those guys. He can vouch for you."

How strange that he should have just been thinking about his cousin Francesca just a short while ago and now his grandmother is telling him to go and talk to Franci's father.

"Good old Uncle Nicola," he says, "Do you really think he would help me?"

He thinks to himself, "That side of the family always thought they were better than the Cellinis because they live in Palo del Colle… But if he could help me get in touch with the Americans..."

"Of course he will," says his grandmother.

"Where can I find him?" he says out loud.

"Ha! He'll find you, Ueli. He works for the British military as an interpreter here in Bari and he comes here to the house to eat every day. You just missed him. In fact you missed the whole family – they all come to Bari every day to work."

"Is he going to be surprised to see you when they all come over tomorrow!"

*****

NICOLA IS PLEASED, if surprised, to see his nephew.

"The crazy *delinquente* returns! I never thought you'd come back," he says, cheerfully. "But it's good to see you Ueli. Tell me what I can do for you."

Cellini explains that he needs to go and see the American military and plans to volunteer for service in the US Army. He tells Nicola the story of how he came to join the Partisans in Yugoslavia and shows him the safe conduct pass that was stamped while he was on Vis.

"Come with me to *Corso Cavour* this afternoon and I'll introduce you to my commander. I work for the British Army, but the British and the Americans work together a lot and I'm sure they can help you."

Just then, the door opens and in walks his cousin, Francesca, and her mother.

"Ueli!," she exclaims, what are you doing here?"

"Hi Franci," Cellini replies, her cheerful face making him smile as it always did. She had been 15 years-old the last time he saw her. Now she is seventeen and he can't believe what a beautiful young woman she has grown up to become. They embrace, and for a short time, all thoughts of the war, the air raid and Cellini's plans are pushed aside while the family sit down to eat together.

After the meal, Franci and her mother excuse themselves to get back to work.

"What is that you do?" asks Cellini.

"We work at the laundry on the American base," says Franci.

"We wash and iron the clothes for the soldiers, make sure they are always smart."

"Well, when I join the American Army you can wash and iron my uniform!" Cellini replies.

Just for an instant, the smile escapes from his cousin's face.

"Are you going to join the American Army, Ueli?"

"With your father's help, I certainly hope so," he says, "If they'll have me!"

He goes on to tell his cousin all about his plans for helping America to win the war so he can go home to New York.

"Oh, that's nice," says Franci wistfully, "I'd like to go home to New York, too."

Cellini had forgotten Francesca was an American citizen, also born in Brooklyn and brought back to Italy as a child, just as he had been. There was an awkward silence, then Cellini says, "Fine. You can come with me! But first I have to win the war!"

Grabbing his hat, Cellini turns to his uncle Nicola and says, "Uncle, shall we go?"

31. Meeting the Allied Occupation Forces

Following the capitulation and capture of southern Italy in 1943, the British Special Operations Executive (SOE) establishes a base in Bari code-named "Force 133" (later changed to "Force 266", reserving 133 for operations still being run from Cairo). Flights from Brindisi are run to the Balkans and Poland. The SOE and the American Office of Strategic Services (OSS) share office space in Bari as well as other facilities in the region, including a new packing station for parachute supply containers near Brindisi air base. This is known as ME 54 and employs hundreds of people. The OSS side of the station is known as "Paradise Camp".

One of the biggest problems an occupation army faces is how to house, equip, feed, clothe, maintain and care for the sudden and massive influx of people. Aside from obvious cultural differences between the young Allied soldiers, many of whom had never before been more than a few miles from their homes, and the native Italians, the occupation forces face a logistical nightmare.

The population of Bari more than doubles with incoming Allied military personnel. Traffic through the port increases manifestly, and with it criminal activity soars as the black market kicks into high gear.

The US Army has supply depots throughout the town and though they are supposed to be guarded around the clock, manpower is short – and corruptible. A great deal of material, equipment and commodities is going missing. Weapons, munitions, oil, gasoline and medicine are all vital for the war effort. Others, such as flour and other foodstuffs, are crucial to the well-being of the troops as well as for the local populace, but the increase in materials coming into the port attracts black market criminals from all over the country.

It is difficult enough to get merchant ships across the Atlantic. U-boats are a constant threat to Allied shipping; in 1943, German U-boats would account for the loss of 583 allied ships in total, and though that is fewer than half the number sunk in 1942 (1,322), it still puts a huge dent in the war effort. Added to this, the Luftwaffe employs squadrons of long-range reconnaissance aircraft to keep a watchful eye for the convoys as tired merchant marine crews near the end of their journeys.

Once across the Atlantic, the last thing the Allies need is to have materials and supplies disappearing from the depot, right under their noses. Whether it is to petty thieves hoping to make a few extra Lire or organized crime syndicates – still rampant in southern Italy – the loss of vital materials must be stopped.[1]

The Army turns to the intelligence branches of the occupying forces for help. The British SOE is headquartered in Bari and works closely with the newly-organized American OSS. Both are willing to recruit locals as volunteers who know the neighbourhoods and can move easily among the criminal classes. Though they won't admit it, they are also willing to overlook the activities of small time crooks and local black market traders in order to focus on the big crime syndicates. More importantly, they want to take whatever steps may be necessary to stop Allied soldiers at the port participating in, and profiting from, the theft of these vital supplies – and they are prepared to look the other way if drastic action is required.

Black marketers are highly creative. Besides food, tobacco and other consumable items that can be quickly disposed of, uniforms are disassembled, dyed and converted into civilian outfits; wool blankets made into overcoats. British Army issue long underwear is dyed red and turned into running suits. Vehicles and vehicle parts are especially in demand. Other loot includes weapons and cameras and which are sold "under the counter" in popular shops.

In the early days, the Military Police from the 5th US Army, stationed in Bari, had carried out raids on these daring entrepreneurs, only to discover that many of the items were destined for friends of high-ranking Allied officers. Even a car belonging to a cardinal from the Vatican that was stopped at a routine roadside checkpoint was found to have a complete set of stolen tyres! To avoid embarrassment and fearing repercussions, the MPs were obliged to turn a blind eye.

Perhaps most serious of all is the loss of vital medical supplies, in particular penicillin, causing severe shortages in military hospitals close to the fighting where it was badly needed.

William Donovan, founder and head of the OSS, called Italy "the cesspool of intelligence" and determined to clean it up, whatever it took. A huge part of the problem is the fact that organized crime syndicates continue to operate

[1]. *Allied losses through the black market were far more damaging to the war effort than first thought. It is estimated that between December 1943 and May 1944, the entire contents of one Allied ship out of every three unloaded in the port of Naples was stolen and sold on the black market. Bari wasn't much better.*

throughout Italy, in spite of the occupation. These syndicates control the flow of black market products into most major cities, and there is little the Allied occupation forces can do to stop them. However, organized crime bosses rely heavily on the co-operation of personnel within the Allied military bases and supply depots, whom they coerce by bullying, bribery, blackmail and threats.

To combat this, the SOE and the OSS recruit people with local knowledge, including known hoodlums, in the hope of tracing the supply chain in order to reduce, if not eliminate, their losses.

*****

NICOLA LIANTONIO and Cellini enter an imposing building on *Corso Cavour* and after walking up two flights of stairs, enter a narrow, dark corridor. Nicola opens the first door and ushers Cellini into a small, dimly lit waiting area. There is no sign on the main entrance to the building and there is no sign on the door they have just walked through to indicate where they are going. The empty waiting area has folding wooden chairs but no other furniture. The bleak walls are painted a nondescript dark colour to match the nondescript, dark linoleum floor. The only light comes from an unshaded light bulb suspended from a cord in the centre of the ceiling that sways as the door is closed, causing the occupants' shadows to swing hesitatingly back and forth. In the corner is a door behind which Cellini can make out the sound of voices and typewriters indicating considerable activity. Nicola tells Cellini to take a seat and wait for him while he goes to talk to his employer. He opens the door and the volume of activity instantly increases. As the door closes behind Nicola, Cellini catches a glimpse of a very young man wearing a British uniform seated at a desk.

The young officer looks up at Nicola then back down at his cluttered desk. It is one of about twelve desks, neatly set in rows, each stacked with document folders, typewriters and trays full of loose papers. The walls are lined with black metal filing cabinets, many with drawers open or half open, and uniformed personnel buzzing around.

Moving aside a teacup, the young officer picks up a fairly thick sheaf of papers that are paper-clipped together, and, without looking up from his desk, hands the document to Nicola. He says he needs it back by the end of the day.

"Yes sir," Nicola says, almost coming to attention.

His job is to interpret and translate Italian documents into English for the British military, who are now essentially in charge of all administrative responsibilities for the city of Bari. Most of the documents are old Italian military records and of little consequence, but the new administrators will not know that until they have been translated.

"Is there anything else?" the young soldier asks, this time he looks up at Nicola.

"Yes, there is," Nicola answers, "I was wondering if the captain is in his office this morning?"

"He's in, but he's rather busy, what with this air raid and the clean up and all."

Nicola continues, "My nephew, who is American-born, has just arrived back from Yugoslavia where he was fighting with the Partisans. He wants very much to see if he can join the Americans, and I know you have contacts with the American military."

"Is he here with you?" the Englishman asks.

"He's waiting outside."

"Let me see if the captain is available."

The young officer gets up from his desk and weaves his way in between furniture and people towards the back of the room. After a few minutes, a British Army captain appears, followed by the officer, who squeezes past and reclaims his seat behind the desk.

"Good morning Mr. Liantonio," the captain says, shaking Nicola's hand. "How can I help you?"

*****

LATER, OVER A cup of coffee at a nearby bakery, Nicola tells his nephew that the English captain has given him the name and address of an American officer that they should contact. He could not make any promises, but added that as far as he is concerned, the Allies now occupying Bari could use all the help they can get.

Nicola asks Cellini if he wants to go straight away or wait until tomorrow.

"Let's go now!"

Cellini is on his feet and practically out the door before Nicola has finished the last sip of his coffee.

The building is on *Corso Vittorio Emanuel II,* not far from where, as a young boy, Vito had been arrested and given a ticket for participating in the illegal "American" activity of roller-skating. He smiles to himself at the thought of returning to the scene of his so-called "crime" to participate once again in an "American" activity – ridding his adopted country of the fascist menace.

Entering the building, the two are stopped by a soldier who politely asks them if he can help. Nicola asks for the American officer who's name the English captain had given him. The soldier tells them to follow him and they proceed along a maze of corridors to a large, smoke-filled office full of people, rushing around, yelling and apparently tripping over each other. Cellini is struck by the contrast between this cacophony and the relative calm of the British Army building they had been in just half an hour earlier.

"Wait here while I fetch the major," says the soldier, shouting to make himself heard above the din, then turns and walks away before either of the two can say a word.

After a few minutes, an American officer approaches and introduces himself to each in turn. Friendly and gregarious, he smiles and leads them through the door and along the corridor to another room.

The room, dark and hazy with cigarette smoke, has a brown linoleum floor and the furniture is old and shabby, but mercifully unoccupied and therefore quiet. Apart from the smoke, it reminds Cellini of his old schoolroom, right down to the large chalkboard on the furthest wall. Memories of being slapped across the hand with a wooden ruler and being summoned to the headmaster's office flood his mind.

Although there are windows along one wall, they are covered with makeshift blackout curtains following the recent air raid. The only light in the room comes from bare light bulbs hanging from cords in the ceiling.

Reaching into the pocket of his battledress blouse, Cellini pulls out the folded piece of paper given to him by the Partisans and hands it over to the American major, who unfolds it and studies it carefully before handing it back.

"I was born in Brooklyn, New York, sir. My father brought me to Italy when I was a small boy, so I grew up here in Bari. After the war broke out, I was forced to enlist in the Italian fascist army, but I left the first chance I got and joined the Partisans in Yugoslavia."

Cellini finds himself more at ease as he tells the rest of his story, although he is careful to leave out the part about his court martial. He finishes by saying, "I got back to Bari a few days ago and would like the chance to fight for my own country for a change."

"After what you've been through already," the major says, "you still want to continue the fight?"

Cellini nods.

The major continues. "Well, we can certainly use people with your experience and enthusiasm, but I have to ask you, do you have any documents that would prove your American citizenship? A birth certificate would obviously be ideal, but can you think of anything at all?"

Cellini thinks for a moment before replying. "My father would have all that sir, and he is currently living in Milan."

Nicola has said little except for interpreting the conversation, but feels it is his turn to speak.

"Sir, if I may, I might be able to help. I can vouch for my nephew. I was in New York when he was born and have watched him grow up. My wife's brother – young Vito's father – and I moved to New York in 1923, with our wives, but we came back to Italy a few years after our children were born. My brother-in-law lives in Milan right now and obviously it is difficult for us to contact him and get young Ueli's birth certificate, but I promise he is telling the truth."[2]

The American major listens intently and seems satisfied.

"I don't personally doubt you or your nephew for a minute," he says, "but if young Cellini here is to serve with the US Army, he will need some documentation. Is there anything you can think of that would substantiate his claim to being an American citizen?"

Nicola thinks hard but can come up with nothing.

After a lengthy silence, the major speaks.

"I have an idea," he says, "but I need to make some enquiries and it may take a couple of days."

He takes out a notebook and a pencil and writes something down. Tearing out the page, he hands it to Cellini.

"Go to this place at zero-eight-hundred hours the day after tomorrow," he pauses to point at the piece of paper. "Ask for this officer by name. I can't make any promises, but he may be able to help you."

Cellini glances at the paper. The address is the office on *Corso Cavour* where he had met the British officer a few days earlier.[3]

"I'll be there!" Cellini says, finding it hard to conceal his excitement.

*****

THOUGH EAGER to get back into the fighting before the war is over and still confident of being recruited into the US Army, Cellini is a master at hiding

[2] *Northern Italy, including Milan, was at that time still under the control of the German military and the reorganized Italian fascist forces.*

[3] *The American OSS and British SOE collaborated and co-operated with each other to a very great extent, including sharing facilities. Cellini recalls that while the OSS headquarters was located in the small fishing community of San Vito, about 35km east of Bari, they shared space with the British agency in the city, which is where Cellini mostly reported. The office on Corso Vittorio Emanuel II was the headquarters of the US 5th Army.*

his impatience. Maintaining a nonchalant swagger as he walks around the town, he enjoys catching up and reminiscing with old friends he hasn't seen in years. He always makes sure he is back at his grandmother's house in time for dinner.

Over a bowl of his favourite pasta with rapini, Cellini thanks his uncle for the introduction and for speaking up on his behalf in front of the American officer. His gratitude is sincere, but his manner is patronizing, because he knows his uncle will enjoy the attention.

Cellini glances across the dining table at his cousin Franci, who rolls her eyes and giggles. She seems to see straight through his act. Cellini grins at her, breaks off a piece of bread and uses it to soak up the oily sauce in his bowl.

32. A Volunteer for the OSS

TWO DAYS LATER, at 7:45 am, Cellini is pacing up and down outside the building, the piece of paper with the officer's name written on clutched tightly in his hand as he rehearses exactly what he will say to this officer, assuming he is able to meet with him. Nicola can only watch and roll his eyes at the energy and impatience of his nephew.

At 7:53 am they enter the building and are greeted by the same soldier who welcomed him at the other building when he was with his uncle two days earlier.

Just as cheerful as before, the young soldier once again asks how he can be of help. Cellini hands him the piece of paper with the officer's name written on and Nicola asks if he is available. The soldier reads the name then looks up at Cellini and puffs his cheeks as if to say *he's here but I doubt he'll see you.* Instead he turns and walks over to a desk, picks up the receiver from a black telephone and taps the cradle several times. After a few seconds he asks for the officer by name. There is a short conversation, then he replaces the telephone receiver and walks back over to Cellini.

"Apparently he's expecting you," the soldier says, rather surprised. "Would you follow me please?" Nicola follows Cellini but the soldier stops him. "I'm sorry, sir," he says. "Just Mr. Cellini. Don't worry – many of the senior personnel here speak fluent Italian."

Up three flights of stairs and along several maze-like corridors, Cellini is shown into a small, dark office. All around the room, the floor is piled high with files and documents and in the centre is a desk and two folding chairs. The only source of light is the ubiquitous bare light bulb, swinging from a cord not quite in the centre of the ceiling.

"Come in and shut the door," says a voice from behind several stacks of light brown file folders sitting on the desk, in passable Italian.

Cellini enters and closes the door as instructed. A figure rises from behind the folders wearing a shirt of indeterminate colour and loose-fitting grey flannel trousers. The shirt is sweat-stained at the armpits and the top button is undone. What really stands out is the loosened garish plaid tie, skewed to one side, and the black leather shoulder holster, complete with pistol.

"Mr. Cellini, I presume?" says the man, extending his hand. Cellini nods but looks puzzled. He was expecting to meet military personnel, but this man is clearly a civilian, even though he is carrying a gun.

He wants to ask if he is in the right place, but before he can open his mouth to speak, the American asks if he has his documentation from Yugoslavia with him. He produces the paper and hands it to the officer, who studies it carefully.

Finally, he looks up and says, "So Cellini, did you join the Communist Party?"

"No sir," Cellini replies.

"Did these Partisans make you sign any papers when you joined them?"

Cellini thinks for a moment before replying.

"I had to sign for gasoline one time, up in the mountains."

"But you didn't sign up to join the communists?" the American seems very concerned about Vito's time with the Partisans.

"No sir I did not!" Cellini says once again, emphatically and then continues, "I am an American citizen, I was born in Brooklyn, New York and I — "

The American cuts him off, "Yeah, Yeah, I heard about it. The trouble is you don't have any way to prove that you are an American."

Cellini is asked a lot more questions about his family, which he answers as truthfully and fully as he can. He talks about his older brother Nicola, who had been killed, and how he had tried to talk him into jumping ship. He talks of being drafted, against his will, into the Italian Army but decides to omit the part about the court martial. He speaks of the horrors he has witnessed, the discipline of the Partisans and the inadequate rations.

The American sits in silence for several minutes, looking at his scribbled notes and rubbing his chin between his thumb and forefinger. Finally he speaks.

"I have to tell you straight off the bat that there is no way to get you into the US Army," he says.

Cellini looks disappointed but says nothing.

The officer continues, "If it were up to me," he continues, "I'd sign you up today and send you to the front tomorrow."

"Your uncle, who is very highly respected around here, has vouched for you. That's good enough for me."

"So what's the problem?" says Cellini.

"The problem is *my* uncle!" replies the American with a sardonic smile.

Cellini looks puzzled. The American laughs, "My Uncle Sam!"

"He needs to see birth records. He needs to have documents and paperwork in triplicate that says where and when you were born and pretty much every other detail about your life."

"Is there any way you could contact the people in New York and find the records of my birth?" says Cellini.

"No," the officer says, shaking his head. "There is just so much red tape to cut through. I don't have any power outside of this office. Hell, for that matter I don't even have any power inside this office!"

"Any request I put in for documents from New York will get lost in the paper shuffle before it even leaves my desk." He points towards his cluttered desk as if backed up paperwork was responsible for everything that could possibly go wrong with the war effort.

"Is there anything else I can do? says Cellini, his brow furrowed with frustration.

The American looks straight at Cellini for several seconds as if trying to decide whether he should say what is on his mind. In the end he decides to speak.

"Well, the branch of the United States Military I work for here in Bari can always use help, if you're willing to contribute to the war effort in a slightly different way."

"You are military?" Cellini asks.

"Don't let the fancy uniform fool you," says the American, adjusting his tie and stroking the shoulder holster. Almost as an afterthought he adds, "We don't all wear pinks and greens in this army."

"I'm interested," Cellini says.

The American continues, "It wouldn't be in an official capacity, and I'm afraid there's no way to pay you, because officially you can't be on the US government payroll, but it is important work and with your experience and background, I think you'd be perfectly suited for it."

He pauses before continuing, as if trying to find the right words.

"There is some danger. You'd be helping us fight this war in a big way but on a very different level and you'd basically be on your own."

Always up for adventure, Cellini shrugs and asks what he has to do next.

"We want you to give this some careful thought before you jump in with both feet," the American says. "You'll be working with this office, so you'll report here at least once a week, starting next Monday... if you decide to join us."

Eager to start as soon as possible, Cellini opens his mouth to speak, but the American holds up his hand and interjects before he can form the first word.

"Next Monday, Mr. Cellini."

Cellini leaves the office, his spirits lifted. He has already made up his mind that if he cannot join the front-line soldiers in the US Army, he will do whatever war work he can to help the Allies. He tries to remember the American's name, then realises he never gave it to him.

*****

MONDAY ROLLS AROUND and Cellini returns to the building on *Corso Cavour,* where he is ushered into the same office as before. The American he met before is not there and the man in his place, who seems to know all about Cellini, has worse dress sense and possibly even less charisma than his predecessor. He outlines what is expected of Cellini.

He will spend the next year and a half doing what he later finds out is referred to as "dirty work" for the Allied occupation forces. His orders will come from both the British SOE and from the American OSS. His mission will be to track down those responsible for running the black market – or any other criminal enterprises – from within the occupying military forces.

Vito Cellini is no stranger to the black market, nor to the people who are actively involved in its dealings in Bari and across the Apulia region. His childhood friend Tonino Anibilis is the "go to" person for anything from hand grenades to gasoline to flour, and since Cellini has been away, Tonino has established powerful connections all over Italy. Several of his other friends are scraping together a living in the depressed and war-torn environment by selling whatever they can lay their hands on to anyone who will buy.

Cellini keeps to himself the knowledge that many of his friends are working the black market, though he suspects the Americans probably already know this, and that is why they have engaged his services. They will be aware that he has no intention of betraying his friends, and that having good contacts on the "inside" will be useful to him. In any event, his new employers make it clear to him that they are only interested in catching the military personnel on the bases and within the ports who are supplying the goods and equipment. If the steady supply of goods leaving the military supply depots can be eliminated, the war may even be shortened.

It is a role almost custom-made for Vito Cellini; born in New York, raised in Bari and well-known around town for being streetwise, as well as being toughened up after having spent several months at the front lines in Yugoslavia. Convinced that he will be providing an invaluable service to his country of birth, he eagerly accepts the task.

"What do I do when I find these people?" Cellini enquires of the man.

"Ideally, you will report back to us with all the details and we will inform the MPs, who will arrest them," his superior replies.

"What if the circumstances are not ideal?" Cellini tries not to sound like a smart ass, but fails. The American rolls his eyes and looks at him.

"In that case I would expect you to improvise, Mr. Cellini."

33. Trouble with the Allies

At first Cellini finds himself getting into all kinds of trouble – especially with British and Australian soldiers – because of his lack of understanding of the finer points of the English language. He tries to start up conversations in order to get to know people, but invariably says the wrong thing, which inevitably ends in a fist fight.

Once challenged, he doesn't like to back down, and rarely owns up to a mistake or misunderstanding. Once committed to a fight, nothing will make him quit. Even when the odds are stacked against him, he takes a beating and keeps coming back for more.

A few days after accepting his new position with the OSS, Cellini approaches a group of Australian soldiers near the entrance to the port. They are carrying full kitbags, so he assumes they have just arrived in Bari and enquires about the voyage. Though he is only making polite conversation, his questions arouse their suspicion; prior to disembarking, these rookie troops have been lectured on the importance of not giving away information about any comings and goings at the port, especially since the bombing raid of the previous December. Sensing their hostility towards him, and thinking they are asking him if he is looking for a fight, Cellini tries practising his newly learned American-English to indicate that is not his intention at all. He means to say *get outta here!* – a colloquial way of saying *no, not at all!* In his confused state, what he actually says is, "Come on then!" which translates to *yes, let's fight!* The Aussies need no further bidding and lay into Cellini, leaving him battered, bruised and bloody.

Cellini spends a lot of time following GIs from the port, watching who they make contact with, sitting around in coffee bars listening to conversations, often wasting his time but occasionally learning something of value. He soon discovers that the life of a spy – for that is what he has become – requires an inordinate amount of patience as well as careful concealment.

His endeavours are clumsy at first. He loses track of those he pursues far too easily. Worse, he gets too close and gives himself away. On more than one occasion, his quarry disappears into a doorway or down an alley only to spring out at him and ask him why he is following. Some of his early encounters end in brawls – just like his encounter with the Australians – but he quickly realises that this achieves nothing, and that there are times when it is more advantageous to act dumb, or even play the coward. Finding himself facing an enraged American soldier wielding a commando-style knife, he cowers and begs for his life, claiming that it is all a misunderstanding – even though he has a pistol in his pocket with which he could dispatch the angry man in an instant. For the man to react the way he does, Cellini knows he must be up to no good. By playing the coward, he is able to talk his way out of a tricky situation and walk away unscathed. Picking up the man's trail later, and keeping a safer distance, Cellini discovers that the man's only clandestine activity is a rendezvous with the wife of a local black market seller. Cellini is acquainted with the cuckolded husband and considers letting him know of the affair, but decides against it, because he is a known bully and womanizer himself and by no means a close friend.

Cellini develops an almost intuitive sense of who the so-called "bad guys" are just by watching their mannerisms. Many are novices looking to make a few extra bucks and they can't help but look furtive. Even the experienced crooks have a certain look about them that Cellini recognizes, having spent a good part of his formative years hanging around with crooks and hoodlums. He still feels his successes in actually catching them in the act are few, and even though his commanding officers assure him that he is doing a valuable job, he feels he wants to do more.

*****

THOUGH HIS ORDERS are always verbal and usually delivered with an ambiguity that will enable his superiors to deny any culpability should be caught red-handed by the local authorities, Cellini is under no illusion as to what his task is. Those within the occupation forces – uniformed personnel – are profiting from black market dealings, often at the cost of the fighting men in the front lines who are going short on supplies.

They know what is being shipped and when it will arrive – and they have buyers ready.

He is relieved to learn that his new job will not involve ratting on his *Barese* friends, who are also making a living out of distributing illicit black market products. In fact, it is often through his close ties to local dealers and gangsters that he is able to access the source. It is the source that he is tasked with shutting down, by whatever means necessary.

The knowledge that these criminals in uniform are profiteering at the expense of their own countrymen is incentive enough for Cellini to want to do the job to the best of his ability. He will not be paid officially for his services, but given plenty of latitude so that he is able to make enough to live on from his own private black market sales, mainly cigarettes and tobacco.

Cellini learns quickly that the life of an agent can be solitary – which suits him just fine. He spends a great many nights sleeping on a bench in *Piazza Garibaldi*, using newspapers as a blanket, pretending to be drunk or homeless or just asleep, because he knows this is where a lot of meetings and exchanges take place between the local black marketeers and their military suppliers.

He reports to the office on *Corso Cavour* every week to keep his commander informed of his activities: what he has seen, who he has tracked and any rumours he has heard on the street. Often, he meets with British intelligence officers who are working with the American OSS.

On his first weekly check in, the British issue him with a uniform of sorts to replace his worn and ragged clothing: a khaki battledress blouse and matching trousers and a good pair of marching boots. The uniform has no rank insignia or badges to identify him, but at least he looks smart and official, and since the locals are growing accustomed to seeing the majority of men in similar military attire, he blends well. He is also issued a weapon; a 7.65mm Browning M22 semi-automatic pistol, which he carries not in a shoulder holster, but in his pocket.[1]

There is little to report at first; a few overheard fragments of conversations about incoming shipments, but Cellini is unable to provide names or details. His superiors would like him to penetrate deeper, perhaps get to know some of these individuals and show interest in doing business with them. It entails more risk but he knows how to take care of himself, and is reminded, more than once, that he has the means of doing so. He takes the hint and presumes that he is being given licence to take whatever measures he deems necessary to stop those responsible for blocking supplies to the soldiers in the front lines – or indeed perpetrating any criminal activities.

The British officer, with whom Cellini gets along very well, because he speaks excellent Italian and is of Italian descent, hands Cellini a folded piece of paper and tells him to put it in his pocket. Cellini takes the

[1.] *A trick he learned early from other agents. Shoulder holsters were for desk jockeys who liked to pose. Experienced field agents preferred to carry their weapons in a trouser pocket. That way they could approach any situation with hands in pockets without drawing any suspicion, gun firmly in hand, safety off and finger on trigger. The pockets of the baggy battledress trousers were so roomy that even if there wasn't time to draw the weapon, it could be pointed and fired from inside the pocket.*

paper and without unfolding it puts it in his wallet. The officer tells him that on the piece of paper is written a name – the name of one of the key people that his superiors would like to see eliminated.

*****

After leaving the building, Cellini turns and walks towards to the seafront. Sitting on a rock where he used to hang out with his friends, he takes the piece of paper from his wallet. Holding the still folded paper in his hand, afraid to open it in case the name written on it is that of a friend, or acquaintance, he considers his options.

He could throw it into the sea and claim he has lost it or that his wallet has been stolen.

He could look at the name and if it is someone he knows personally, claim he is unable to find them.

He unfolds the piece of paper and written in pencil is the name "Tedeski". He has never heard of him. He has no idea if Tedeski is Italian, American, British or where he is from.

But he knows he will find him.

*****

He begins searching local haunts, hanging around the rougher parts of town and near the port where he knows some of the dealers hang out. He asks among his friends and contacts, but no one seems to know of any "Tedeski".

He spends a lot of time at *Piazza Garibaldi,* where he knows a lot of the black market buyers hang out together. Most of them are already known to him, if not personally, then at least by sight or reputation, but as the market grows, new buyers are coming onto the scene. He is hopeful of latching onto some of the sellers from the military bases, or their go-betweens. Taking with him a newspaper and a sandwich of mortadella and provolone, he settles down on one of the park benches ready to spend the evening.

He finds as long as he sits on the bench reading the newspaper, no one stops nearby to hold any conversations. He lies down on the bench, folds the newspaper into a makeshift pillow and closes his eyes. For a short time he actually nods off into a doze but is startled by the sound of voices nearby raised in anger. Half opening his eyes, he sees two strangers discussing arrangements regarding a shipment. He has no idea what the "shipment" they are talking about refers to, but senses that legitimate traders would not need to meet in the piazza in order to plan a routine delivery.

The two men leave, each going in a different direction out of the piazza. He has to decide quickly whether to follow one of them – and if so, which one – or stay where he is and try to find other leads. He opts to follow the man who is heading back towards the seafront and therefore the port of Bari.

It is beginning to get dark but Cellini follows the man along *Via Niccolo Pizzoli* towards the harbour. Keeping a safe distance behind, and ducking into doorways and alleys every once in a while, he keeps the man in sight. Instead of turning right towards the port, the man heads off in the opposite direction away from the old town. Thinking he may have given himself away, Cellini drops back even further, leaving at least 100 metres between himself and his quarry. He risks losing sight of him, especially in the twilight shadows, but it's better than getting caught. The man turns off at some point and Cellini loses sight of him and is left guessing as to where he might be. He thinks perhaps he may try to double back and go towards the harbour.

As he tries to make up his mind which way to go, he is distracted by the sound of a street fight that sounds like it is coming from a block or so away. Having lost his quarry, at least for the time being, Cellini hurries towards the sound of the fight to find a soldier on the ground surrounded by thugs who are laying into him with boots and fists, laughing and shouting in *Barese*. Cellini realises these are local hoodlums, although he doesn't recognize any of them. He yells at them to stop and grabs the nearest from behind, swinging him around and hurling him to the ground. He yells at the soldier to get up. Dazed, but conscious, the man rolls away from the mêlée and slowly gets to his knees. One of the thugs steps towards him as if to lash out again but Cellini is quicker and springs forward, landing a sideways blow to his head followed by a full fist to the stomach, knocking the wind out of him. He turns back in time to see a glint of metal. One of the kids comes at him with a knife straight towards his face.

"Stupid move, kid!" Cellini says, grinning at the kid to distract him before grabbing his arm and twisting it hard. He feels something snap and the kid squeals like a pig before the knife hits the ground with a clatter. Cellini kicks the knife away and takes a step towards the other two thugs, who turn and run. The kid who had been thrown to the ground scrambles to his feet and slithers off to join his friends, and the one who was winded helps his friend with the now limp arm, whimpering, to back away slowly before turning tail and staggering off into the shadows.

Cellini turns to help the soldier, who is on his knees and throwing up at the side of the road. He recognizes the British uniform, but speaking very little English, attempts to communicate.

"OK?" Cellini enquires.

The soldier looks at him with a blank expression. His face is puffy from being hit and his uniform is dirty and bloodstained. He just stares at Cellini, blinks a couple of times, and starts to grin.

"Oh Jesus, you're drunk!" Cellini says out loud, even though he knows the soldier probably isn't capable of hearing him, much less understanding his Barese dialect.

"Let's find out where you're from and get you home."

*****

IN BETWEEN HEAVING and spewing what little remains in his stomach, the soldier manages to get across the point that he is with one of the anti-aircraft batteries, installed to protect the city, primarily the port, following the deadly attack on December 2nd. Cellini knows exactly where he is stationed and escorts the soldier back to his billet, where he is greeted at the gate by two Redcaps.[2] Seeing the condition of the soldier's face and clothing, and noticing Cellini's bruised and bleeding knuckles, the MPs naturally assume that he is responsible for beating up their comrade. The drunk soldier is in no fit state, physically or mentally, to refute their assertion and come to Cellini's aid. They start firing questions at him. What branch is he with? Why does his uniform have no badges or rank insignia? Not speaking English, he is unable to explain himself and raises his voice in frustration. One of the MPs draws a pistol on him while the other takes out his whistle and gives it a loud "pheep!" which brings four more Redcaps running quickly to the scene.

"This is not the time to be a hero," Cellini thinks to himself, taking a deep breath to calm down and raising his arms in the air to show he has no weapon. They turn their attention to asking him for his identification. It takes a while to get the message across, but after a while he reaches into his pocket and pulls out his wallet, carefully leaving his Browning pistol behind in the hope that he isn't searched. One of the men, a sergeant, snatches the wallet from out of his hand and starts looking through it.

He finds some paper money, a photograph of Isabella and another

2. *British Military Police. Distinctive because their caps have red covers, hence their nickname, "Redcaps".*

of Cellini's dead brother Nicola in his *Regia Marina* uniform. Then he pulls a piece of paper and opens it up. All it says on it is "Tedeski".

The British police get genuinely excited at the sight of the handwritten name. They begin firing more questions at Cellini that he doesn't understand. One of the Redcaps leaves to find a senior officer, indicating that Cellini is to stay put, and while he is gone, the other holds a pistol trained on Cellini's chest while he continues to question him. He simply doesn't understand, but he senses hostility, and all he can do is shrug. He looks towards the drunken soldier he has recently helped but he is some distance away and still seemingly incoherent. He tries to point towards him and say, "Ask him. Ask your drunken friend!" but it is pointless.

After a few minutes, the other Redcap returns with an officer who speaks reasonable Italian. Cellini is relieved.

"Sir –," he begins, but is interrupted by the officer.

"What the bloody hell are you playing at, you filthy eye-tie?" The Redcap officer obviously thinks the worst.

"Sir, I found this man being beaten up and robbed by a gang of hoodlums, so I chased off his attackers and helped him back here. Why don't you ask him?"

"Don't worry, I will!" the officer replies, "as soon as he is in a fit state to be questioned."

"And what happens to me in the meantime?" Cellini says.

"I'll tell you what happens to you in the meantime," the officer points his finger in Cellini's face. "You're going to tell me everything you know about this... " and he waves the piece of paper with the word "Tedeski" directly under Cellini's nose.

Cellini knows he can't say too much, because his job is specifically to look for military personnel involved with the black market – and he doesn't yet know who he can trust. He hedges.

"It's just a name I was given. Someone who can maybe help me," he says.

"Help you with what?" the Redcap snaps back at him.

"I don't know. Find work, maybe food for my family. I don't know!"

"Who gave you this name?" The officer was not finished.

"A soldier." Cellini is starting to realise that these British MPs must know who Tedeski is and might even be able to help in his quest to find him.

"Which soldier? Who?"

"I don't know his name. I met him at *Piazza Garibaldi.*"

The British officer isn't satisfied, but seems to have run out of questions. He hands Cellini's wallet back, then says, "Wait here." Cellini gets the impression it is not a request, so he waits. The two armed MPs are still standing with him. The officer turns and walks over to the drunk, who is now on his feet, though wobbly, standing in the middle of a small group and being supported by two of his fellow soldiers. The exchange is quick and animated, and after a few minutes the officer returns to Cellini, flanked by two of the soldiers.

"It appears you are telling the truth, at least about rescuing that wretched idiot from being robbed. He's going to spend the night in a cell, and when he wakes up he'll have one hell of a headache, but that's all.

"However, as far as this Tedeski business is concerned, I'm not so sure. I don't have a good reason to arrest you, and I can't be bothered to fill out all the paperwork in triplicate anyway, but I don't trust you."

Pointing towards the two soldiers, he adds, "These gentlemen will escort you to wherever you need to go. I don't want to see you around here again."

With that, the officer turns his back and walks away. The two soldiers lead Cellini away from the seafront and towards an area of open land, skirted by a few abandoned buildings. It's a part of the city he knows well and would prefer to avoid with the two soldiers. He notices they are both wearing holsters with pistols, which is unusual for enlisted men.

"I don't wish to go that way," Cellini says, almost flippantly. "I need to go this way," indicating the road back towards the old town, but without saying a word, one of the soldiers grabs him by the arm and they lead him towards the darkness.

"This doesn't look good," he thinks to himself, but allows himself to be manhandled without any further resistance. Sometimes it's just smart to play dumb. Once they are well away from the lights of the port and shrouded in darkness, the soldier relaxes his grip on Cellini's arm slightly. The other soldier steps in front of him. Cellini hears the unmistakable sound of a pistol being cocked and looks down to see a Webley and Scott revolver pointing straight at his midriff, at point-blank range. He notices the other soldier does not have his pistol drawn and realises this is probably his only saving grace. In one movement he pulls his left arm back just far enough to get some momentum, folds his fingers to make a chisel-shaped fist and brings the blade of the chisel-fist hard into the back of the hand holding the gun. The intense pain causes the soldier to release his grip on the weapon, but by the time it hits the ground, Cellini already has at least a 10 metre start.

Without looking back, he sprints into the darkness, zigzagging left and right as gunshots fill the air around him. He counts six shots, guessing the other soldier must have drawn his weapon and has begun firing, but his aim is well off. Ahead of him is the broken wall of a derelict building. The roof is long gone and the ragged wall, he knows, is made of old and decaying *tufa*. As he leaps upwards, the soft and uneven rock gives under the force of his boot, giving him a toehold while he grasps with his hands for the top. In one movement he clears the top of the wall and lands on hard cement the other side. He continues his dash across the structure, emerging through the remnants of a doorway and back into the soft sandy grass.

Now for the first time he is aware of his own heavy breathing. He realises that the only sound he can hear is his heart thumping in his chest. No more gunfire. He is tempted to slow down and catch his breath but he knows he needs to keep going. He is well aware that each of his pursuers has only six rounds in his pistol, and that he has only heard six shots. Could they have stopped to reload? Have they lost him? It's possible they might have given up the chase completely. It's also possible they're waiting for him to slow down and perhaps give himself away.

When they searched him, they didn't take away his pistol, which was odd – but he has no intention of using it anyway unless things get really desperate. The last thing he needs right now is to be charged with the murder of two British soldiers.

He keeps running until he gets back to the street, then turns and heads back towards the old part of the town, keeping himself in the shadows. He knows the maze of alleyways in *Bari Vecchio* as well as anyone, and there will be people there so he can blend. Occasionally ducking into doorways and lying low for a few minutes to make sure he is not being followed, he starts to think about what has just happened – and why? He wants answers. Tomorrow morning, he will go to the office and demand to know more about Tedeski – and why the British soldiers tried to kill him.

*****

"THE PROBLEM IS we have no idea who this Tedeski is."

Cellini's British commander is completely at a loss to explain the events of the previous evening. He continues, "Why do you think we gave his name to you?"

Cellini is not happy, but says nothing. The expression on his face makes his feelings quite clear.

"Here's the thing," the officer continues. "Word on the street is that Tedeski is a major figure in the black market. We don't know in what capacity. We don't even know who's side he's on. We have checked all our records and there are no military personnel, either British or American, registered with that name. We also have the full co-operation of the local authorities and they couldn't find anyone with that name, either. To be perfectly honest, we're not even sure that's his real name, nor of the spelling – it could be a code name or an alias and it could be T-e-d-e-s-k-i or T-e-d-e-s-c-h-i. He could even be a German spy for all we know."[3]

He pauses to catch his breath and let it sink in, before adding, with typical British understatement, "We were hoping you might be able to turn something up – and it appears you have."

Up to now, Cellini has managed to curb his urge to interrupt, but can do so no longer.

"And you almost got me killed! What good would it do you if I were lying dead in a field or dumped in the sea? How much would you have learned about Tedeski then?"

"Yes, I realise that. But you didn't get shot or, um, dumped – and that's why we trusted you with such an important job, Mr. Cellini. We knew from your experience that you could take care of yourself, and in any event, we warned you that there were serious risks when you volunteered for this assignment. I can only reiterate what a vitally important job it is that you – that the entire intelligence organization of our joint forces – are doing."

Cellini takes a deep breath. He accepts the compliment gracefully, then puzzles over one of the British officer's comments.

"And what do you mean when you say 'and it appears you have'?" What did I find out that is so important?"

The officer smiles as he replies.

"Simply that the soldiers you encountered obviously know who this Tedeski is or they wouldn't have reacted the way they did towards you. We don't know whether they are working with him or against him – but we do know that they know something. We'll follow up with them, in the meantime keep your eyes and ears open."

"One more thing," he says, as Cellini is getting ready to leave. "Let me give you a chit so this doesn't happen again – or if it does we'll know for sure who's side everyone is on."

"A chit?" Cellini replies. "Is that like 'who gives a chit?' " His *Barese* sense of humour gets the better of him.

"Not a 'shit' – a 'chit'." It's a letter of safe passage. If you get held up by any of the Allied forces – and that includes the Italians; police, *carabinieri*, anyone – just show it to them and you'll be fine. Wait here for a moment, I'll be right back."

The officer pulls a sheet of blank notepaper from inside his desk

[3] *Tedeschi, in Italian, can be translated to mean "German".*

drawer and steps out of the office to find a secretary. He returns a few minutes later and hands Cellini the chit, nicely typed and signed at the bottom. Cellini looks at the chit. It will save him from getting beaten up by Allied soldiers, but it won't help him if he comes into contact with the real criminals.

"I know the ideal situation is for me to report everything back to you, but what if the situation isn't ideal? There are some pretty bad people out there. What if I find myself caught up in a bad situation and I can't get word to you in a hurry?"

The British officer thinks about it for a moment before replying.

"Improvise."

It's the second time Cellini has asked the question and received the same ambiguous answer. It's exactly what he was hoping to hear. Now he feels like an agent. He folds the chit carefully and places it in his wallet, at the same time removing the piece of paper with "Tedeski" written on it.

"Here, you can have this back," he says to the officer. "I don't need it. I'll never forget this name."

*****

CELLINI OFTEN ASKS what happens to the people he reports.

The OSS commander has a pat answer, as if he is reading it straight from some manual on policing black market criminals in wartime. "We put tails on them, watch to see what they do, and if we find them doing something, we notify the MPs, who arrest them."

Cellini is not impressed. "What if you don't catch them?" he replies.

"Then we keep watching them for as long as we can, or until we need to reassign the men tailing them."

"So if you don't catch them in the act, they will keep getting away with it?"

The commander looks straight into Cellini's eyes and smiles. His silence is worth a thousand words. Cellini continues.

"I'm sorry sir, I don't mean any disrespect. I just want to know that what I am doing is effective and meaningful."

The commander's reply is cryptic. "It's as effective and meaningful as you make it."

Corso Cavour, where Cellini reported regularly to his British and American commanders.

A bench on Piazza Garibaldi, where he spent many hours pretending to be asleep or drunk in order to gather information on local black market activity.

34. A New Lead?

Vito Cellini's exposure to the full-scale black market being run within the US Military opens up a world of corruption and criminal activity in war-torn Italy, the like of which he never imagined. Though he has his own small dealings with local profiteers, it is nothing compared to what he is now witnessing. Hiding in the shadows brings him into contact with smugglers and thieves as well as violent and desperate men who will stop at nothing to achieve their ends.

Though he is no angel, he has always embarked on his own misdeeds with a sense of glorified adventure, usually managing to escape capture and punishment through his guile and wits. He has never considered himself a criminal or a bad person and seeks to profit mainly from the thrill of his actions. When forced to join the Italian military, he had taken the same philosophical view, looking upon it as a learning opportunity, always pushing the limits of authority to see what he could get away with, yet always staying within the bounds of his own quite lofty moral standards.

This is different.

What began naively as "just another adventure"– albeit fueled by a genuine desire to help the Allied war effort – has introduced him to a world of serious crime: illicit drugs, prostitution and the murder of innocent people, all of which goes against his personal ethics. Cellini is appalled by what he sees but even more disgusted with how little is being done to prevent such crimes. He suspects that someone in authority is turning a blind eye and begins to fear for his life. He has already tracked down and reported several criminals for their offences only to see them back on the street, in the piazza or at local hangouts a few days later. If they find out he is the one responsible for attempting to bring them to justice, who or what will stop them from exacting retribution?

While his assignment is primarily to help stop the theft of vital supplies to the military such as food, fuel and medical supplies, he can't just stand by and watch while rapists, drug dealers and killers not only go unpunished, but remain at liberty to continue their twisted practices.

He needs to be on his guard. More importantly, he starts to think about taking matters into his own hands. What was it that both his American superior and English commander had said when he asked what he was to do "if the circumstances were not ideal" for reporting his findings and having the perpetrators arrested by the MPs?

"Improvise."

In Cellini's eyes that means he is free to take whatever measures he feels necessary, both to protect himself and to ensure that justice prevails. He is not paid for his services by the US government, other than being permitted to keep some of the less crucial spoils such as tobacco, alcohol and occasionally gasoline by the MPs. These he can sell to local businessmen in order to make enough money to live.

For the first time, Cellini begins to see the direction his new occupation is taking him.

Though he has no way of knowing how much it will eventually impact the course of his life, this is the shaping of Vito Cellini: spy, informant, OSS agent – and, above all – survivor.

*****

WHEN IT IS your job to stalk criminals – even when your specific assignment is to hunt down thieves and traffickers of stolen military goods – you enter a dark, netherworld inhabited largely by the very worst of humanity; rapists, murderers, prostitutes and pimps, as well as thieves who would kill you for the coat on your back or the shoes on your feet if there is any profit to be made.

Cellini rapidly comes to understand why the movies he had watched as a teenager referred to the "underworld". He also learns how to tell the difference between the real criminal lowlifes and the ones who are just struggling to survive.

Waiting and watching for activity gives him plenty of time to reflect.

As a youngster, he had indulged in petty crimes, more to prove his ability as a thief or pickpocket or to show how fast he could run away from the scene of a crime than for personal profit. The only real gain was status among his friends, and it had earned him the nickname of *delinquente* from his family. He took no pride in the title.

He recalls one of his many misdemeanours. Being "accidentally" tripped and pushed by Vito Calabrese into the lap of a wealthy young woman on a date in a fancy restaurant; making a grab for her purse while the hapless young lady had been far more concerned with protecting her virtue and dignity.

The memory brings mixed emotions: a smile for the sense of adventure; a shudder at his own naïveté; relief that he didn't get caught and locked up, and possibly funneled into a life of crime, as so many of his contemporaries had done. The knowledge that the very people he is now mixing with would have been not only his accomplices, but probably his only companions.

This war has brought out the worst in everyone, he thinks to himself. Italy is full of real lowlifes. Sexual predators and criminals of every kind and in every class.

The presence of the occupying troops doesn't seem to help – in some ways it makes it worse. Soldiers en route to battle know they may or may not survive the days and months ahead and have little to lose. The MPs do whatever they can, but even though Cellini reports most of what he sees, and is able to give good descriptions of the perpetrators, they say their hands are tied. Even when they do get involved, those they arrest are invariably released due to the lack of evidence, or because someone higher up in command intervenes.

Cellini is once again reminded of the order given to him when he first volunteered for this job.

Improvise.

*****

HE CATCHES A BREAK from one of his small-time black market friends, who tells him there is a big shipment expected into port in the next forty-eight hours. He doesn't know exactly what it is, but thinks it might be medical supplies. He says it's causing a lot of buzz but it isn't anything he has any interest in.

It's not the first time Cellini has been given a lead like this, and most of them amount to nothing, but he has to follow up. He asks his friend if he can give him a name.

"No."

"Well can you point out the dealer to me?"

His friend hesitates to reply and tries to make a joke out of not giving Cellini the information.

"It's some coloured guy who works in the supply depot. I don't know which one. They all look the same to me…"

Cellini isn't smiling. Most of the American GIs who work in the supply depot are black.

He spends the next couple of days hanging around at the dock, watching for any kind of activity that might suggest anything out of the ordinary. A Jeep being driven by a black GI is not that unusual, but when he sees the same Jeep with the same black driver make the same trip for the third time he starts to wonder what it is that is so interesting. He follows the Jeep back to the depot, making a note of its number. He's on foot so the Jeep leaves him behind, but he knows where to go and soon finds and identifies the vehicle.

He climbs into the Jeep and waits for the driver to come back.

He doesn't have to wait long. The GI asks him what the hell he I thinks he is doing and orders him to get out of the Jeep. Cellini doesn't move, nor does he reply, for the simple reason he doesn't understand a single word the soldier has said to him.

The black soldier repeats his order for Cellini to get out, gesticulating with body language. He doesn't touch Cellini. For a black soldier to be seen to make physical contact with a white man, even in Italy, would be to invite the MPs to come down on him hard. Cellini knows exactly what he is being told to do but refuses to move or speak. Once he realises that Cellini has no intention of leaving the Jeep, the soldier eventually calms down and begins to speak in a normal tone of voice. His guard is down.

Cellini reaches across the driver and grabs him hard by the crotch, squeezing until he sees tears start to well up in the black man's eyes. He leans over until his face is inches away from the driver's and he can smell his sour breath. He mouths just one word.

"Tedeski."

He says it without giving away whether he is working for Tedeski or looking for him. He is looking for the slightest hint of recognition, and he sees it in the black man's eyes.

He squeezes harder and the black man almost squeals, raising both hands in submission.

"OK!... OK!"

"Italiano?" Cellini asks if he speaks Italian.

The black GI shakes his head but indicates he has a buddy at the depot who speaks some.

"Andiamo!" Cellini says, resisting the urge to try his English because the beating he received from the Australians is still fresh in his mind. He still isn't confident enough to choose between *come on* and *get outta here*!

At first he has a difficult time understanding the black soldier's friend, who turns out to be another black GI, a corporal, who speaks a strange dialect of Italian with a heavy American drawl. Cellini understands more than he lets on, however, playing dumb and letting these guys think they have the upper hand. They are suspicious. He wants to know about their connection to Tedeski, but they deny any knowledge of anyone by that name. At the same time, he senses that they would like to know more about his own connection with Tedeski. Stalemate.

Cellini lets them know that the people he works for are fully aware of their involvement in black market sales of military property, and that from now on, they will be participating. He makes it clear this is not optional.

The corporal denies all knowledge and tells Cellini to get lost. He exchanges words with the other black GI that Cellini doesn't understand, before telling him, "Get outta here!" Cellini smiles as the first black soldier gets into the Jeep and drives away, leaving the corporal and Cellini in a large warehouse.

"What do you know about Tedeski?" the corporal asks. Cellini says nothing. The corporal smiles and tries to get friendly.

"Look man," he says, "I can't say much in front of the other guy. He's just a junior around here and he don't know nothing about what's really going on. He's just a messenger."

Again, Cellini says nothing. His expression doesn't change at all.

"Are you a cop?" The black man says. As if the thought had just dawned on him, when in fact he'd been waiting for a chance to try and catch Cellini off guard.

"No, I'm a Partisan," is Cellini's reply.

"They pay you well for that?"

"Mostly grappa and cigarettes," Cellini answers, being completely truthful but knowing this will intrigue the other man.

"You mean that moonshine stuff?" He says and starts cackling with laughter. After a while the laughter subsides, leaving behind a wide grin.

"Man oh man. You need to do business with me. You like fine Scotch? I can get you some great Scotch. Bourbon. Gin. Whatever you want."

"What about medical supplies?" Cellini decides he's wasted enough time on small talk and jumps straight in.

The leftover grin disappears from the corporal's face in an instant. He glares at Cellini and says, "What do you know about medical supplies?"

"Not much…"

Cellini knows now that he's got the black corporal right where he wants him. He has no idea what sort of supplies are expected, nor what quantity, much less what their black market value might be, but he isn't going to back down now.

He continues, "…but I know you've got a boatload of them coming in tonight and you're going to need some help getting them out of the depot. I also know you're going to need some help counting all the money.

So I'm here to offer my services."

*****

Just past midnight. It's a moonless night and the area around the port is as dark as it can be, given that it's a busy sea port with container ships and military troopships arriving and departing more or less around the clock. Before December 2nd, 1943, Bari was lit up like a Christmas tree every night, but that was before the bombers came. Since then, everyone has been a little more careful. Current air raid precautions wouldn't stop the German Luftwaffe from attacking, if they were able to spare either the manpower or the resources, but it is just dark and dingy enough to make it a haven for crime. Especially the black market.

Cellini and his new best friend and partner in crime, a black corporal he has known for less than a day, are sitting in a Jeep on a deserted section of *Lungomare* waiting to take delivery of supplies. Supplies of what, Cellini doesn't even know. He's thinking it could be medical supplies but that's all he has been able to find out. Cellini doesn't even know the name of his companion. All he knows about him is that he is employed by the United States 5th Army, which he can tell by the patch on his sleeve, above his corporal's stripes.[1]

When things start to happen, they happen quickly. A large, covered US Army truck, its lights switched off, pulls up 5 or 6 metres ahead of the Jeep. Three GIs jump out of the back, lower the tail board and start unloading small wooden boxes, leaving them directly in front of the Jeep, before reboarding the lorry and departing. No words are spoken, and the men work in such unison and with such rhythm that they have obviously done this many times before. From what Cellini is able to see, the six wooden crates left behind constitute a very small portion of the contents of the lorry, which is fully loaded. They will probably not be missed unless a full inventory is taken.

Less than a minute later, as if timed to perfection, a smaller vehicle pulls up into the spot where the lorry had been. It's a dark van, its badges and number plate smeared with mud and generally tired looking. Two men

[1] *The US 5th Army, under Lieutenant General Mark Clark, replaced the US 7th Army as part of the 15th Army Group, a combined Allied force then under the command of British General Sir Harold Alexander. The 15th Army group had been responsible for the invasion of mainland Italy and controlled the ports of Bari and Brindisi. In January 1944 the army group was redesignated Allied Forces in Italy and then Allied Central Mediterranean Force. In March, 1944, the army group was renamed Allied Armies in Italy.*

step out of the vehicle. They are not wearing military uniforms, but plain, nondescript clothing. With dark knitted hats pulled down low over their foreheads and roll-necked sweaters pulled up over their chins, they open the back doors of the van and begin loading the boxes inside. The corporal signals to Cellini to remain where he is, then jumps out of the Jeep. Cellini looks relaxed, leaning back in his seat with both hands in his pockets, but his right hand is firmly nestled around the butt of his trusted Browning M23 and the safety is off.

The corporal holds out his hand in front of one of the men, who reaches into his jacket, pulls out an envelope and hands it over. The corporal turns to walk back to the Jeep then stops and turns back. Cellini's grip tightens on the pistol in his pocket. The van driver is about to lift the last box when the corporal stops him and says, "Not that one, brother. That one's mine!"

The two men stare at each other for a few seconds, then count the five crates already loaded into the van. They nod and the driver and passenger climb back into the van and drive away. The whole operation, from start to finish, has taken less than ninety seconds. The corporal saunters over to Cellini's side of the Jeep and tells him to pick up the last crate.

"Pick it up yourself," Cellini replies, in no mood to take orders from anyone, least of all a black corporal.

"Suit yourself," the black man replies. "I got my pay right here," he says, patting his bulging uniform pocket with the envelope inside. "That's your share right there in the road. If I pick it up, I get to keep it. Or I guess we can just leave it where it is and let the cops find it in the morning?"

Cellini finds himself disliking this arrogant junior NCO more and more, as much for his irritating cackle as anything. He starts to look forward to the day he can have him arrested and put into a military prison. But for now he will go along.

Cellini asks him what is in the box as he steps out of the Jeep to pick it up.

"Search me, brother," The corporal says, still cackling to himself.

Cellini bends down to pick up the crate as the Jeep engine suddenly bursts into life and shoots off in reverse before turning and speeding away. Temporarily dazzled by the headlights, Cellini almost drops the wooden crate in the road. Laying it down carefully he pulls his pistol from his pocket and points it down the road in the direction of the speeding Jeep, but by the time he has blinked a couple of times to try and regain his night vision, the vehicle is well out of sight.

"Summonabitch," he yells through clenched teeth. He pockets the pistol and sits at the side of the road looking at the wooden crate for a few minutes. *Shooting him wouldn't do me any good anyway,* he thinks to himself. Deciding he probably should get going before he attracts the attention of patrolling MPs or local police, he hoists the wooden box onto his shoulder and starts walking back towards *Bari Vecchio*. He is not far from where he used to hide guns when he was a kid, and decides it would be a good place to hide the crate until he can come back in daylight and open it.

He thinks this would be a good time to call on his old friend Tonino Anibilis.

35. Dirty Work

NEXT MORNING he returns to the hiding place with Tonino. They uncover the box and carry it down to the edge of the water. In the daylight they can see that the crate has some numbers stenciled on it, but no clue as to what the contents are.

They pry the lid off the box, and inside are several dozen small glass vials wrapped in paper. Each contains a small amount of yellow powder and has a paper label attached printed with the words *Sodium Salt of Penicillin.*[1] Neither have ever heard of it and have no idea what it is, except that it is obviously drugs and highly likely to cause a storm when the loss is discovered.

Anibilis doesn't want anything to do with drugs. He has built a very successful black market empire out of dealing meat, flour, tobacco, clothing and even alcohol, but has so far avoided dealing dope. He has found that the police and local authorities will usually overlook a little profiteering on food and clothing, which are in short supply and much needed by the public. For civilians to be able to enjoy the occasional luxury is good for morale. Drugs are in a whole different league, mostly handled by the large organized crime syndicates – and he doesn't want to jeopardize his business – or his life – by stepping on the toes of those higher up the food chain.[2]

1. *Penicillin was the new miracle drug of World War Two and probably saved thousands of lives. This shipment had been intended for a detachment of the 4th Medical Depot Company established at Bari in October, 1943. Soon after this incident, control of the medical depot was handed over to the Medical Section of the Army Air Forces Service Command.*

2. *Tonino Anibilis established a crime network throughout Italy that continued to grow after the war, primarily dealing in stolen goods. Though he would spend almost one-third of his adult life in jail, his family never wanted for anything and he had a solid reputation for never ratting out any of his associates, preferring to "do his time" rather than betray anyone, and there were certain criminal elements he would not deal with, certain products he would not trade in. Though they seldom saw each other after the war, he and Vito Cellini remained friends for life.*

Tonino suggests Cellini might earn some kudos if he were to take it and hand it in to his commanding officer, but he is afraid that he has already waited too long, and that his commander might suspect he has already tried to sell it to his friends first, which could be more trouble than it's worth.

"I'll just tell them the truth about how the deal happened and leave out the part about the extra crate."

Tonino nods in agreement. He picks up one of the vials and skips it across the surface of the sea. The vial spins and skips across the surface as well as any flat stone.

"30 metres at least!" Anibilis exclaims.

"More like 20!" Cellini replies, taking one of the vials and skimming it in the same manner.

"Now that one was 30 metres," he says.

The two of them grab handfuls of the vials out of the crate and start skimming them one after the other, competing with each other, arguing over whose went further. With all the vials gone, they sit back on the beach and laugh, still arguing in fun about which of them is the better skimmer.

Cellini kicks in the sides of the empty crate and tosses it into the water. The two of them walk back to the road and part ways. Cellini now has to go and explain the events of the previous day and night to his commanding officer.

*****

CELLINI REPORTS to the office on *Corso Cavour* within half an hour of leaving Tonino Anibilis. His commander is annoyed at being interrupted and pulled out of a meeting, especially when he discovers that Cellini has actually participated in a theft of government property from the depot. When he finds out that Cellini isn't even able to provide the name of the black corporal who organized the disappearance of the penicillin, he becomes practically apoplectic, despite the fact that Cellini is able to give a perfect description of the black corporal, where he works, even the number of the Jeep he was driving – which his commander points out is no help at all, because the Jeeps are part of the motor pool, and personnel authorized to drive will draw a different one each time.

The commander tells him in no uncertain terms not to get directly involved again. He warns him that if the MPs or the local police happened to bust open the operation and Cellini was caught working with them, there would be nothing he could personally do to prevent him being arrested and suffering the consequences. Which, he points out, doesn't always mean going to trial.

"Sometimes these guys never see the inside of a courtroom," he says. "The Army takes a dim view of black market profiteers within the service, especially when they take something as precious as penicillin."

"What is that stuff anyway?" Cellini asks.

"It's a new miracle drug that cures infections and stops soldiers from dying and losing limbs," the commander replies. "That's all I know, except that it's in real short supply and the Army needs every last drop they can get their hands on."

Determined to help bring the corporal to justice, and regretful of squandering the crate of penicillin with Tonino, Cellini volunteers to go with the MPs to identify the corporal but the commander tells him firmly that would not be a good idea, because it would severely compromise his cover.

"Leave this one to us, Cellini – that's an order," he says and dismisses Cellini.

Later, Cellini will tell Tonino about the penicillin, and to leave it – and anyone dealing in it – alone. Right now, he is anxious to get back to the depot and hook up with the black corporal. He is more than ever convinced that these people can help him get back on the trail of Tedeski. He waits until the end of the day and starts back over to the supply depot and finds the corporal at the motor pool, returning a Jeep.

"Let's walk," Cellini says, grabbing the wiry NCO by the arm and leading him out towards the dock.

"You don't leave me in the middle of nowhere with a box of contraband, do you understand?"

That cackle again. Cellini clenches his teeth and swears one day he will kill this arrogant negro.

"Hey man, I'm sorry. It was just… I was kidding around with you. We're partners now, buddies, so it won't happen again, OK?" He spits on the palm of his hand and offers it to Cellini to shake, but Cellini keeps his hands firmly in his pockets.

"I don't trust you enough to call you 'partner' and I don't like you enough to call you 'friend'. I don't even know your name, or who pulls your strings."

"Ain't nobody pulls my strings," he replies. "I'm a free agent. All these guys around here work for me and I take care of them."

Cellini releases his hold on the corporal's arm. He still hasn't given him his name, but then again Cellini hasn't introduced himself either.

"Hey man. No hard feelings, OK?" The corporal continues, "Look,

I've got a hot date tonight, why don't you come along with me and who knows, maybe we'll both get lucky?"

Cellini doesn't answer. The two of them walk side by side into *Bari Vecchio.*

The corporal steers Cellini down a series of dark alleyways to a bar Cellini knows by reputation but would never frequent. It's a regular pick-up joint for prostitutes. They order a couple of beers and sit down at a table. There are a few other GIs in the bar, but Cellini notices all of them are negroes. He has heard stories about how the American Army doesn't like white and black soldiers to mix but this is the first time he has actually witnessed it. Italian girls with too much make-up and too little clothing are hanging around some of the negro soldiers. The only white people in the bar are Italians, and most of them are pimps or black market dealers, though Cellini doesn't recognize any of them.

Before long one of the pimps approaches the table and Cellini is about to tell him to get lost, but before he can say anything, the corporal greets him and invites him to sit down with them. He ignores the invitation and stands by the table instead. The soldier introduces Cellini as his new business partner and cackles again. The pimp eyes Cellini up and down but doesn't say a word. He turns back to the corporal.

"I got something for you," the pimp says. "But it's gonna cost."

He points towards a dark doorway and beckons towards a small, slight figure standing in the shadow. A young girl steps hesitantly forwards. Cellini reckons she is about fourteen or fifteen at the most.

"I didn't know you were bringing a friend," the pimp says, looking back at the corporal and pointing at Cellini with his thumb. "I only brought one. I guess you guys will have to share."

Cellini feels physically sick. He has to think quickly. His instinct is to deck the pimp, grab the girl and make a run for it, but he knows he would risk getting them both killed. He tries to play along. The corporal thrusts a wad of cash into the pimp's hand, downs the rest of his beer and stands up, taking the girl by the hand. He smiles at Cellini.

"You want to go first or second?" he says, cackling as he turns and walks away. Cellini's patience is wearing thin.

The girl tries to pull her hand away, but the GI pulls her closer to him, roughly.

"Hey little lady, we are going to have some fun," he says.

Cellini gets up and starts to walk after the soldier and the girl. A large Italian steps in front of Cellini, blocking his exit. Cellini is trying to watch where the corporal goes and deal with the belligerent bar employee at the same time.

"You need to pay for the beers," he says.

Cellini reaches into his pocket. As tempting as it is to pull out the pistol, instead he grabs a handful of loose change and throws it in the burly Italian's face. Sidestepping him as he bends to retrieve the coins, Cellini runs off in the direction the corporal and the girl went just seconds before.

Checking dead-end alleys and darkened doorways as he races through the narrow maze-like streets of Bari Vecchio, he interrupts another black soldier with his pants down and a girl's legs wrapped around his waist. Pushing the two of them apart to get a look at the girl, he sees the heavy make-up of a seasoned prostitute, not a young girl.

He finds the corporal in a narrow alley, close to the *Basilica di San Nicola*. He has his back to Cellini and is struggling to pin the girl against a *tufa* wall. She is resisting his attempts to grab at her clothing and he is grinning and cackling as she writhes and flails with her free arm.

"Let her go," Cellini commands.

"So you do want to go first?" the corporal replies, the grin widening.

"I won't tell you again," Cellini repeats the command. "Let her go. Now!"

The corporal takes no notice but continues to grab at the girl with first one hand, then the other, forcing his body weight against her to stop her from moving.

"Are you crazy? I paid good money for this sweet piece of Italian ass and I even offered to share – "

Cellini grabs the corporal from behind, his arm in a vice-like grip around his neck, pressing against his throat, pulling him away from the girl. Now free, she stops writhing but instead of running, stands as still a statue, rooted to the spot, wide-eyed with fear.

"Get away from here," Cellini says to her. "Go home. If you see that man who sold you… sold your…" he cannot finish the sentence, "… just tell him you did what he asked and then went home."

Still in shock, she continues to stand like a statue, frozen in the moment, her mouth open but no sound coming out.

"Go!" Cellini shouts, taking a sudden step towards her and pushing the captive corporal in her general direction. She blinks and the catatonic spell is broken. Edging slowly past Cellini she runs, never once turning to look back.

Releasing his hold on the negro soldier and pushing him away, Cellini isn't sure what his next move should be. The corporal makes the decision easier for him. Turning to face Cellini he draws his pistol from its holster and points it at Cellini's face. He begins swearing and cursing at Cellini, then cocks the weapon. A grin spreads across his face and that irritating cackle starts to dribble out of the corners of his mouth. Staring straight into the gunman's eyes, Cellini lashes out with his fist, striking the hand holding the gun before spinning around and launching his elbow into the chest of his assailant. Grabbing the arm still holding the gun, he backs him hard into the wall, knocking the wind out of him and smashing his hand against a wall to try and get him to release the weapon.

His right hand momentarily free, Cellini reaches into his pocket and draws the Browning M22. Holding it against the corporal's head, he pulls back on the hammer to cock the weapon. The corporal has still not let go of his gun and starts to raise it. A shot echoes around the limestone and *tufa* walls. The cackle is gone forever.

Pinned up against the wall by Cellini's left arm, the body gives the impression of standing upright. There is little blood on the body, most of it was forced out with the point-blank shot and now decorates the walls of *Bari Vecchio*. Pulling the dead man's overseas cap from under his shoulder strap, Cellini covers up the gaping exit wound on the side of his head as best he can, then pulls his arm up around his neck and shoulders. By supporting the dead man's weight on his own shoulders and alternately swinging and kicking at the legs, he is able to propel the body forwards.

By sticking to the shadows and avoiding the more crowded areas, the few people he runs into assume he is carrying a drunk friend – not an uncommon sight in the old part of town. Cellini somehow manages to manoeuvre the body out of the old city and back to the Jeep without drawing any unwanted attention. The exercise is tiring, but it gives him time to formulate the next part of his plan. The easiest and quickest solution would be to dump the body at sea, but if it were to wash up later he knows he would be certain to be questioned. Too many people saw him with the corporal in the bar and, in a crowd of negroes, he will have stood out as one of few natives. He cannot afford for the body to be found.

He props the corpse up in the passenger seat of the Jeep and heads south, taking side streets and lesser known unpaved roads to avoid patrolling MPs. Twenty minutes or so later, well out of the town, he turns onto a dirt road and crawls along slowly for about five minutes, looking around him.

Cellini sits quietly for five minutes or so, with the engine off and the lights out, just to make sure there is no one about. Satisfied he is completely alone, he reaches down for the shovel, stowed on the sill of the Jeep. He grabs it, then walks around to the other side of the vehicle to lift the body out.

It seems heavier than when he put it in the Jeep. Hoisting the body over his shoulder leaving one hand free, he grasps the shaft of the shovel and sets off. His eyes are beginning to adjust to the darkness and he sees a clearing between some trees, at least 50 metres away from the dirt road. He starts to dig and is relieved to find the ground is not hard, despite the lack of any recent rain. In less than an hour, he has dug a hole roughly one and a half metres long, half a metre wide and a metre deep.

"That ought to do," he says softly to himself.

He rolls the body into the grave, straightens it out to lie face up, then reaches in and removes the dog-tags from around the neck. He doesn't even think about looking at them.

"You never bothered to introduce yourself to me when you were alive," he says to the corpse, "so why should I give a shit who you are now you're dead?"

He pockets the dog-tags and feels in the dead man's pockets for any other form of ID. All he finds is a wallet and an opened packet of gum, which he puts in his pocket. He begins to fill in the hole. Flattening out the dirt on top of the makeshift grave, he distributes the leftover soil over a wide area nearby. The whole process takes a little more than an hour, then he makes his way back along the dirt road and returns to the old city, leaving the Jeep in the exact same place it was parked before.

Walking home, he empties his pockets of the dead man's dog tags and possessions and discards them into a street drain.

"Thank you *Il Duce*," he says, smiling at the thought that the new city drainage systems implemented by Mussolini has just helped him to bury the evidence of his action.

He feels no remorse for what he has done. This was a man who stole vital medical supplies from his fellow countrymen for profit, yet instead of being arrested and in jail, he is back on the street, attempting to rape a child. Cellini has seen it before, but at the time he had been helpless and unable to do anything about it. Now he is in a position where he can do a lot.

Once again he remembers his orders.

Improvise.

Cellini is beginning to understand what his commander meant. He is also beginning to understand what being an agent is all about.

36. More Dirty Work

BACK IN THE *Piazza Garibaldi*, Cellini overhears conversations about other criminal activities among the occupying forces that incenses him even more. He listens to men discuss the best places to pick up women, and boast of their sexual conquests, even joking about how sometimes the younger girls are often unwilling, at first, and have to be held down. Cellini is still haunted by the rape and murder of the young girl and her boyfriend in Yugoslavia and these conversations sicken him.

What sickens him even more is the overt homosexuality he witnesses almost daily on the streets; men, often in uniform, approaching other men hoping to engage in homosexual acts. He reports his observations to his superiors but is told repeatedly that there is nothing they can do, and to focus on his job of looking for the black market ringleaders. [1]

Then one day Cellini is resting – or pretending to rest – on a bench in *Piazza Garibaldi*, when he is approached by a soldier wearing a British uniform. The man has a dark skin and shiny black hair, and Cellini notices he has very dark red lips, as if he is wearing lipstick. The man has a strange accent but speaks passable Italian. He asks if he can join him. Cellini sits up and shrugs, swinging his legs down from the bench to allow the soldier to sit. The soldier sits down and slides across the bench, very close to Cellini, their thighs almost touching.

"I have seen you here quite often," he says.

Cellini just grunts. He is keen to see what, if anything, he may be able to learn from this interloper, so he lets the stranger do all the talking.

[1] *Though homosexuality had been technically legal in Italy since 1899, Benito Mussolini's fascist government instituted the Rocco Code, which implied that homosexuality was unpatriotic and politically deviant. Homosexual behaviour was punished with public humiliation and confinement. Once the Allies established command of the region it seemed to become more open, even though it was illegal in all the Allied mililtary forces. The Rocco Code survivd the demise of the Mussolini government and was finally overturned in the 1980s.*

"I know what you are and what you are doing," the soldier speaks again, a hint of a smile on his face. Cellini doesn't know what to think, but he cannot take his eyes off the man's mouth. He wants to ask if he is wearing lipstick or if that is the natural colour of his lips but refrains from making small talk. The man tells him he is from India.[2] He smiles a lot. Far too much, in Cellini's opinion. He leans over towards Cellini, his face now much too close for comfort. Cellini feels the man's hand on his thigh, rubbing his leg and sliding towards his crotch.

"That's enough!" Cellini exclaims in his *Barese* dialect. The Indian soldier has no idea what Cellini has just said and just looks startled, but doesn't move his hand.

In one swift movement, Cellini brings his right elbow sharply up into the man's throat and pushes him against the back of the bench with his left hand. The Indian makes no sound, his larynx most probably shattered. His eyes start to tear up and he stares at Cellini in shock and disbelief.

Cellini helps him to his feet and half carrying, half pushing him, leaves the piazza and leads him to the seafront, looking for a quiet place to finish the job. The Indian is in bad shape, spluttering and gasping, and Cellini struggles to keep him upright.

They stumble along in silence. Thoughts are racing through Cellini's mind. What did he mean when he said *I know what you are and what you are doing*? Does he suspect that I am working with the American military police or does he just think I am hanging around the piazza looking to pick up other men?

The few people about assume they are just two drunk soldiers and no one pays any attention. Drunk soldiers are not an uncommon sight around the port of Bari. Cellini drags the Indian onto the beach. The local fishermen have given up for the day. Glancing around to make sure there are no witnesses, Cellini punches him in the face, hard. The Indian falls to the ground easily and Cellini kicks him in the groin. The Indian doubles up in pain, gasping for breath and barely conscious. Cellini thinks about finishing him off and pulls his Browning pistol out of his pocket. He points it towards the ground, levelling it at the Indian's head. He is about to cock the weapon when he decides this piece of dirt isn't even worth a bullet. He puts the weapon back in his pocket, looks around one more time to make sure there is no one about, then heaves the Indian's body to its knees, drags him towards the water's edge and drops him, half in and half out of the

2. *The 4th Indian Division fought with great distinction at Monte Casino in 1944 and comprised Indian Sikh, Gurkha, Australian, Maori and British nationals. Like many other troops, they were stationed temporarily in Bari.*

sea. The cold water does nothing to revive the injured man lying face up in the water. Still transfixed by the ruby red lips, Cellini turns and walks away.

"Goddamn *finocchio!*" he says.

He has no regrets and cares nothing about whether the man lives or dies. He is nothing more than a pervert looking for a good time. He probably assumed that having seen Cellini hanging around at the piazza, he was fair game. The thought makes Cellini sick.

Later that night, he lies awake worrying that there might be a different meaning to the Indian's words. *What if this queer has figured out my cover? Could he be a potential threat? Should I go back to the beach and finish the job?* He decides he is overreacting but makes up his mind to be more careful in future. Maybe change his habits, just in case. After all, if one person can identify him that easily, maybe others could too? Cellini shrugs. Dead men tell no tales, but he will think about other ways to make sure this never happens again.

37. Fishing with Tonino

CELLINI STILL ENJOYS getting together with his old friends when they are all able to take time away from earning a living. Though most of Cellini's limited social life is centred around his family and his black market associates, he still finds time to get together with his old friends once in a while, usually for a night on the town.

One night after a few beers with his old friend Tonino Anibilis, they decide it would be a good idea to get together and go fishing the following week, something they haven't done since before the war, a lifetime ago.

Tonino and Cellini have always been close, ever since Cellini befriended him when others treated him as an outsider. Immigrants from Albania, Anibilis's family worked hard to raise him and his sister once they arrived in Bari. Anibilis, like Cellini, did not do well in school, but his entrepreneurial talents quickly elevated him to the point that he was now one of the most highly respected black marketers in the Apulia region, with connections all over the country. Tonino was a hard businessman but generous to his friends. He had recently given Cellini a Leica camera that he had acquired but personally had no interest in, and Cellini was becoming a keen photographer.

They arrange to meet outside the old town at dusk the following Saturday evening for some night fishing. Cellini arrives early, his old and warped fishing rod in hand. After a few minutes Tonino arrives accompanied by three of his cohorts, who Cellini knows well. They are carrying large baskets and nets, but no rods or poles. He takes one look at Cellini's old and dilapidated fishing rod and laughs.

"You're not going to catch much with that!"

Fishing with Tonino Anibilis is not the same peaceful pastime Cellini grew up learning from his grandfather. Tonino has decided that fishing should be a profitable pursuit or it is simply not worthwhile.

"Where's your pole?" Cellini asks. Tonino laughs and puts his hand in his pocket. "In here!" he says.

They find a small boat on the beach, pile the nets and baskets inside and push it out into the water. Two of Tonino's friends each take an oar and slowly row out into the night. The sea is calm and the sun is beginning to set behind them, leaving the city silhouetted against the purple night sky. Once clear of the land and the ships, Tonino tells them to stop rowing.

"Now we fish!" he says, a smirk on his face. "Hey Tutuc, you want to see my pole?" He stands up in the boat, legs apart for balance, and reaches into his pocket. After making an obscene gesture at Cellini with his fingers through his pants, he pulls his hand out holding a small rounded object.

"A hand grenade!" Cellini exclaims.

Anibilis laughs, plucks the pin from the grenade, counts to five and tosses it over the side of the boat. It makes a dull but loud thud and rocks the small boat.

Stunned and dead fish float to the surface. Tonino's friends unroll the nets and throw them over the side of the small boat and begin pulling them in, emptying them into the bottom of the boat and then casting them back out for more. Cellini and Anibilis start scooping up fish straight from the surface of the water with their bare hands and loading them into the baskets. There are literally dozens of fish and before long the baskets are full and the bottom of the boat is covered.

They row back to the shore, where Tonino has more friends waiting with vehicles to take the fish.

"What are you going to do with all these fish?" Cellini asks.

"Don't worry my friend! They'll all be taken good care of and you'll get your share later. Now, let's go into town and celebrate!"

*****

CELLINI AND Anibilis leave the rest of Tonino's team to clean up the rowing boat, pack away the fishing equipment and transport the fish. Cellini hands his fishing rod over to one of them and asks him to take care of it. He'll pick it up later when he collects his share of the fish. The two old friends head into *Bari Vecchio*. It's Saturday night so the clubs, bars and trattorias are open. Most are full of Allied soldiers: American, British, Australian, Canadian, Indian together with a smattering of locals. Most of the soldiers have girls hanging on their arms and other women are congregating, hopeful of attracting someone in uniform with spending money.

Even though years may pass between the times they spend together, Cellini and Anibilis trust each other like brothers. They openly discuss their day-to-day activities, each safe in the knowledge that the other will never betray a confidence. Anibilis has been helpful in pointing Cellini in the direction of some of the worst offenders in the black market chain, while Cellini has been careful to protect Tonino and his associates from prosecution.

One of the reasons they get along so well is that, unlike many of their male friends, they share the same sense of moral values when it comes to the treatment of women. They have nothing but contempt for men who try to take advantage of women, and utter disgust for women who allow themselves to be taken advantage of, particularly for money or other personal gain. After a few beers, Tonino looks across at Cellini.

"I'm sick of this place," he says, looking around at the surroundings and frowning. It seems to be full of local women chasing after the uniformed occupation forces. Breaking into a crooked smile, he finishes the thought.

"Let's go fishing again!"

He kicks Cellini on the shin to get his attention, and as Cellini looks down under the table, Tonino opens his cupped hand to show him another hand grenade.

They get up from the table leaving their glasses still half full, walk out of the bar and head into the middle of the town to a nightclub Tonino knows well.

"This place is full of whores and soldiers who don't want to fight," he says. "Time to fish them out I think!"

The entrance to the nightclub is at street level, but down a flight of steps is the club, a sort of speakeasy, dark and dirty, with a reputation for drunkenness and debauchery. These days, the club is frequented mostly by the occupation troops, especially the Australians, who use it to hook up with local girls.

As they get close to the building, Tonino pulls the grenade out of his pocket. Cellini recognizes it as an American Mk II grenade, commonly referred to as a "pineapple" – exactly the same as the one they had used for fishing earlier that evening. He removes the pin as he walks towards the club entrance but keeps the handle firmly in his grip. Then he grins at Cellini, runs over to the doorway and tosses the grenade down the steps into the club.

Sprinting back out and past Cellini, Tonino calls out to his friend, "Let's get the hell out of here!" Cellini takes off as the explosion rocks the street behind him. For a split second Cellini thinks about stopping and going back to help, but he knows it would be pointless. In any event, there are witnesses who will have seen him running away with the man who threw the grenade, so he quickly abandons the idea and focuses on catching up with Tonino.[1]

When he catches up with him, they are several streets away and they are both completely out of breath. Sinking to the ground, they sit with their backs against a low brick wall.

"What the hell was that all about?" Cellini says in between gasps.

"I'm sick of these damn foreign soldiers taking advantage of our women – and the damn women for behaving like whores," Tonino replies.

"Aren't you forgetting that I'm one of those foreign soldiers?" Cellini says, grinning.

Anibilis stares at him. "And if I thought you were like those womanizing summonerbitches I'd shove a grenade up your ass too!"

The pair laugh nervously and slap each other on the back. Cellini knows that Tonino's sister has been harassed by Allied soldiers on more than one occasion. He realises this was Tonino's way of hitting out at those soldiers but also of warning local girls that they are putting all young girls at risk with their promiscuous behaviour.

"Let's get another beer."

[1.] *Cellini was able to check into the incident at his headquarters when he reported in the following week. The disturbance had been reported to MPs, who went to the scene to investigate. Fortunately it was early enough in the evening that few people were there at the time, so the nightclub was nowhere near full. There were some minor injuries, but no fatalities or serious injuries.*

38. Working Both Sides of the Fence

CELLINI NEVER receives, nor expects, any remuneration or compensation for his work with the OSS and SOE. It is made clear from the beginning of his engagement that his services are voluntary.[1]

For Cellini, it is satisfaction enough that he is contributing to the Allied liberation of Italy and helping to defeat the enemy, whether that enemy is in the form of the fascist regime overrunning Europe or serious criminals undermining the war effort. What is even more rewarding is that he is living a life full of adventure; a free agent with authority to do what he thinks best and to "improvise" as and when he thinks fit. He is a self-appointed judge and jury, licensed – when all else fails – to eliminate those he sees as a threat to a decent way of life.

But he has to live and eat, and even though he has a large and generous extended family in Bari who will make sure he always has shelter and never goes hungry, his resources are not infinite. The US 5th Army has tasked him with tracking down the ringleaders of the black market within the military. Small-time black marketers – Cellini's friends – are not being sought out, so he feels able to help them and at the same time help himself.

Several of the MPs at the quartermaster's depot speak passable Italian and allow Cellini to help himself to some of the impounded spoils,

[1]. *The OSS engaged over 24,000 people in various roles between 1943 and 1945. Personnel were drawn from all branches of the military, as well as experts from the civilian world, but a high percentage were locally recruited volunteers. How far the authority of these volunteers extended is not documented and while many worked in offices as clerks, janitors and so forth, there is no doubt that many were sent out into the field, like Cellini, and given assignments that may have been distasteful, or even illegal, for regular paid soldiers to carry out. These tasks were known throughout the organization as "dirty work".*

Cellini has often mused over the fact that while engaged – as a volunteer – in the business of tracking down the more sinister and dangerous black market criminals, he was in fact earning a living, and thus financing his volunteer work, by committing the same crimes, albeit on a much smaller scale.

mostly cigarettes and tobacco. It is just a favour, intended only for his personal use – they have no idea that Cellini doesn't even smoke – but after a while he starts helping himself to several hundred cigarettes at a time, packing them into two suitcases that he then carries across town to a tobacco shop owned by the mother of an old schoolfriend of his who pays him well. The business becomes quite lucrative as word gets around and he expands to other tobacconist shops in Bari.

Far from being seen as a competitor by his friends, they are grateful to him for helping to fulfil the demands of their customers, leaving them better able to concentrate on other much-needed materials and products, such as flour, meat and clothing. In any case, Tonino Anibilis is now recognized as the Godfather of black market operations in the region, and as his close friend and confidant, Cellini is virtually untouchable.

*****

ONE OF THE FIRST tasks Cellini had set for himself, after volunteering his services for the OSS, was to make friends with the men in the Military Police. He needs to find out whom he could trust and ask for favours, but perhaps more importantly, to see who he could do favours for, because he learned early on that having an MP who owes him a favour is a very valuable commodity. As a result of the debacle with the penicillin, he now makes it his business to find out what is coming into the port, and which commodities are selling for the highest prices, so that he can make sure he has a ready outlet for it.

Word on the street is that a shipment of truck tyres is due in at the port. There is a tremendous shortage of rubber in Europe, particularly vehicle tyres, so when available, they sell quickly and fetch premium prices. Cellini strikes up a conversation with one of the MPs, an Italian-speaking sergeant with whom he has become good friends, and asks him to let him know when the tyres arrive. The American is nervous and sceptical.

"I don't mind a few cigarettes or even some whiskey," he says, "but if you're planning to steal Uncle Sam's tyres, you're not getting any help from me."

"I don't need any help from you," Cellini says, affably. "All you have to do is tell me when and where the ship unloads, then go take a leak when I ask you to."

The American isn't convinced, but before he can offer any resistance, Cellini clinches it by saying, "Besides, you owe me."

Everyone owes Cellini. Half of them can't even remember why or what for exactly, but he has them all convinced. Either he set them up with a date or fixed their poker debts. The sergeant agrees reluctantly, but just to keep him honest, Cellini checks in with him every day, until he admits that a shipment has just arrived.

"I want to know where they're going to be stored, and for how long – and I want you to make sure you are on duty so you can look the other way," Cellini says to him.

Cellini makes arrangements to deliver the tyres to Tonino, but he knows he's going to need help with loading and transportation of such heavy and cumbersome merchandise. He calls on his old friend Vito Calabrese and asks him to round up a couple of the gang to help with the heavy lifting.

With everything in place, Cellini sits and waits with the Military Police sergeant until after dark for Calabrese to arrive. He doesn't have long to wait before a large truck, its lights off, slows down and pulls up beside them.

"Time for you to go take a leak," Cellini says to the sergeant. "Take your time, write a letter to the Pope while you're at it, if you like."

Once he is out of sight, two men jump out of the cab of the truck wearing dark woollen hats pulled down over their heads, Cellini recognizes one of them as Vito Calabrese's uncle – brother of Cellini's Godfather Donato – the other man is not familiar to him at all. Cellini is about to speak when Vito Calabrese appears from around the back of the truck. He grabs Cellini's arm and points to the other two.

"Ueli, you know my uncle, and this is a friend of his. I couldn't get anyone else to come at such short notice."

Cellini is not happy with the choice of hired hands, but he will deal with Calabrese later. Right now, they need to load the tyres onto the truck and get the hell out of there. Calabrese's uncle climbs up over the tailgate and starts hoisting the tyres aboard while the other three form a relay team, pushing and rolling the massive tyres from the stack to the back of the truck. With almost all of the contraband aboard, the mystery man climbs into the cab and starts the engine. He waves at Cellini to go and get the last of the tyres on board, but as he and Calabrese are pushing the last two alongside the truck, he guns the vehicle and takes off, leaving them both behind.

"Summonabitch," Cellini says. It's one of the few American-English expressions he's managed to pick up and he uses it frequently.

Cellini and Calabrese are left stranded. They need to make themselves scarce and don't wait around for the sergeant to come back. They start walking quickly back towards the city.

"Now would be a good time for you to tell me why the fuck you brought your uncle and his no-good friend in on this job. Do you have any idea what Tonino is going to do to you… to both of us?" Cellini says.

Calabrese is silent and sullen. Cellini knows his friend had no idea that this would happen, but he makes up his mind that someone is going to pay. He talks to Tonino, who is displeased at the loss of revenue from the tyres, but also sees the funny side of Cellini being sucker punched. Tonino's amusement makes Cellini even more angry, and he decides right there and then to kill Calabrese's uncle, since at this time he has no idea who the mystery man is. Cellini's personal quest for vengeance coincides with his duty, as he understands it, as an agent of the OSS in dealing with the theft of United States government property. He has no compunction about carrying it out.

Somehow, Donato Calabrese finds out about Cellini's plan to assassinate his brother. Whether his son Vito Calabrese tells him of his intent Cellini will never find out, but Donato begs Cellini not to do it.

Out of love and respect for his Godfather, the father of his close friend and the man who had given him his first honest employment, Cellini agrees to call off the killing.[1]

1. *Cellini would later find out that the uncle's mysterious partner was a man called Aldo Moro, a student in Bari before the war who went on to become a professor of law and showed a keen interest in politics. After the war, he helped Vito Calabrese's uncle establish a successful chain of machine shops – and Cellini often wondered if the profits from the theft of his tyres helped to finance their enterprise. Moro became a career politician and served as Prime Minister of Italy from 1963 to 1968 and from 1974 to 1976. In 1978, he was kidnapped and murdered in Rome. The uncle died in an institution for the criminally insane.*

39. Death in the Water

When he was growing up in Bari, Cellini boasted that he had probably spent more time in the sea than on land. He became a very strong swimmer, and it was nothing for he and his friends to swim across the harbour from the beach near *Molo Pizzoli* to the lighthouse on the promontory of *Lungomare Starita* and back again, often several times a day. The exercise helped him develop powerful arm muscles and a strong physique that stood him in good stead for the physical demands of his job as well as his future career as a soldier.

Now that spring is here and the weather is warmer, Cellini decides that he is going to start swimming again. He has missed the opportunity while away from Bari. Even though he had spent some months on the Dalmatian coast while he was with the Partisans, there was never any opportunity to relax or let down his guard.

Swimming across the harbour is out of the question these days. For one thing there is far too much shipping traffic, as more merchant ships seem to arrive every day bringing supplies. The area is extremely well guarded since the disastrous air raid of last December, with anti-aircraft guns and patrols of soldiers. There are even rumours that the harbour is mined to stop torpedoes and enemy submarines. The Allies aren't taking any chances. Cellini confines his swimming to the area west of the harbour on *Via Paolo Pinto* near the rotunda.

He tries to swim for at least an hour every morning. It helps to wake him up, especially if he has spent much of the night dozing fitfully outdoors.

It is a beautiful morning in late April. The sky is the kind of intense blue that seems to be reserved exclusively for the Adriatic. The war is a million miles away as Cellini strips off his uniform and leaves it on the beach, weighed down with a few rocks and in full view of the early-morning octopus catchers who are standing, thigh deep in the shallows, thumping the water and snatching the creatures in their wooden buckets.

He sets off with a slow and steady pace, planning to take his time and enjoy this morning's exercise. The water isn't too deep here; perhaps 10 metres, but it is incredibly clear and Cellini can see all the way to the bottom. As he swims he glances left and right, both above and below the surface, checking for boats and wildlife as well as other swimmers. In the corner of his eye something glints as it catches the sunlight filtering through the water. *Probably a big fish*, he thinks to himself but judges it to be quite a distance away. *Too big to be a fish!* He swims over in the direction he saw the reflection, hoping to catch it again. He isn't disappointed. This time he focuses on the spot and dives down towards it. A sunken boat? An old bathtub someone has discarded?

When the realization of what it actually is hits him he doesn't quite believe it. He gasps involuntarily, simultaneously inhaling and swallowing seawater. Instinctively breaking the surface, he clears his lungs and his throat before diving straight back down onto the wreck of an aircraft.

From directly above he can see the outline perfectly, but without goggles he cannot keep his eyes open constantly. He blinks as he dives deeper, taking in new details each time he opens his eyes. The silver wings and odd-looking double fuselage, each with an engine mounted at the front.[1] Even though he is unable to see any markings on the wings, Cellini knows it's an American plane; the Germans and the British paint their aircraft dull greys and greens. The Americans leave them with a shiny metal finish.

The aircraft looks to be in excellent condition, intact, as though it simply landed on the seabed. As he dives closer to the aircraft he can see the cockpit. Magnified and enhanced by the crystal clear water, every detail comes to life. The cockpit canopy is missing and there is no sign of the pilot, so Cellini assumes he got out OK.

Unable to hold his breath any longer, Cellini hurtles towards the surface, slowly releasing the air trapped in his lungs as he goes. Bursting out of the water and into the warm dry air he takes in a series of long, deep breaths while he thinks about his discovery.

*****

[1] *At the time, Cellini's knowledge of aircraft recognition was somewhat limited. He later identified it as most likely being a Lockheed P-38 Lightning. Three fighter groups operating P-38 Lightnings were based at the nearby Foggia airfield complex at this time (the 1st FG at Salsola, the 14th FG at Triolo and the 82nd FG at Vincenzo).*

SHOULD HE REPORT the crashed aircraft to the local *carabinieri?* He would prefer to avoid communication with the police for fear of drawing attention to his activities. Instead, he will say something to one of his commanders next time he checks in at headquarters, and he takes note of his position from the beach and the rocks so he can find the wreck again.

He wants to continue his swim, but finds he has an irresistible urge to keep scanning the seabed around the crashed aircraft. Swimming in ever increasing circles around the aircraft, he spots a few small pieces of debris, from small fragments of silver metal that probably tore off when the plane hit the sea, to larger pieces including a wheel, its tyre still in place. After he gets about 50 metres away, he finds little or no evidence of the aircraft and is about to resume his swim across the bay, when he spots something yellow in the distance. A speck at first, but its bright colour doesn't quite fit with the surroundings.

Taking a deep breath and blinking several times to clear the salt water from his eyes, he swims along the surface towards the yellow object, checking with each stroke so as not to lose sight of it. He guesses he has covered about 100 metres from where the aircraft wreck is lying. Checking one more time to make sure the little patch of yellow is still in view, he spots it directly beneath him. Closing his eyes and taking a deep breath, he kicks his feet and dives down vertically.

He recognizes the yellow object is a life vest; the type worn by flyers.

Cellini blinks again. The bright yellow life vest stands out from the green and black rocks and the sandy bottom of the seabed. He blinks one more time. Now he can clearly see the silhouette of a human figure. Is this the pilot? The body is lying on the bottom of the sea as if in gentle repose, still and relaxed, an eerie sight. The pilot – if it is the pilot of the crashed aircraft – seems so calm and natural, as though all Cellini has to do is gently shake him and he will wake up.

Except for one detail. The pilot has no head.

Shock more than fear causes Cellini to gasp and he quickly surfaces, spluttering and coughing. A few deep breaths and he turns around and swims back to the body. *If he's wearing a life vest, why isn't he floating?* He thinks to himself on his way down. Heavy straps cover the life vest. *He's still wearing his parachute. That would explain why he never inflated the life vest. Maybe he lost his head in the crash and couldn't release the parachute?*

Other than the life vest and the parachute, Cellini can't really tell what the pilot is wearing. All he can tell is that the poor man's clothing is brown and waterlogged. If it weren't for the yellow life vest, he would never have been seen.

Cellini returns to the surface once again for air. What should he do now? Report the body? Try to look through pockets to see if he can find clues to the pilot's identity?

He dives down one more time. He feels the body and tugs at the clothing but cannot reach any pockets. The body seems to be intact and fairly well preserved – except for the lack of a head. Cellini surmises that it hasn't been there long. *I thought drowned bodies were supposed to float after a few hours or days from the gases inside? Maybe the weight of the waterlogged parachute anchored it down and prevented it from floating to the surface?*

He starts to wonder how the pilot may have been decapitated, then wonders if there is any point in him spending any more time searching for the poor man's head. He scans the seabed immediately around the body but quickly abandons the idea. Finding a little humour, even in such macabre circumstances, Cellini smiles to himself with the realization that searching for a human head on a sandy seabed strewn with hundreds of rocks, most of which are approximately the same size and shape as a human head, seems like a pointless exercise.

With more questions than answers, Cellini reluctantly decides to leave the body alone and report both it and the crashed aircraft to his commander back at the headquarters building on *Corso Cavour.*

Cellini asks to talk to the Italian-speaking English commander who normally briefs him. Explaining the story of the aircraft and the headless pilot in as much detail as he can recall, he asks if he did the right thing to leave it alone and report directly to headquarters. The Englishman assures Cellini that he did exactly the right thing.

"Best not to involve the local authorities," he says. "If we think they need to know, we'll get in touch with them. Best to just bring it to us."

He takes copious notes, repeatedly confirming the exact location and time of Cellini's grizzly discovery. He promises to pass the information along to the US Army Air Force base commanders at Foggia and Brindisi so they can check for missing aircraft and pilots.[2]

Less than a week after the incident of the crashed warplane and its

[2] *A great number of Allied aircraft were lost in the Adriatic and unaccounted for. The resources simply didn't exist to search properly for all those who were reported as Missing in Action (MIA). While fairly good records of MIAs were kept by all sides, there was scant knowledge as to when and where most of them were last seen. During the course of his activities, Vito Cellini visited the Bari seafront area almost every day and at no time saw any salvage boats in the area. He presumed that no search ever took place, or that if it did, it was unsuccessful in raising the crashed P-38 or the remains of its pilot. The aircraft may still be there, but it is unlikely. Shifting sands, tides and the erosion of aluminium by the salt water has probably long since removed any evidence of the crash. In 2016, Cellini, accompanied by the author, rented a small boat equipped with sonar to search the area, but nothing was revealed.*

headless pilot, Cellini is once again making his way along the *Lungomare Starita*. It is the middle of the day and there are people enjoying the glorious early summer weather. He sees a group of people gathered near one of the spots where he used to enjoy diving for mussels when he was a boy and it brings back memories for him. He makes his way towards them, intending to stop and chat, and notices a young man coming to the surface with what looks like a handful of seaweed and realises he is diving for the succulent molluscs just as he used to do. The young diver hands over his catch before diving again into the depths.

Almost a minute goes by and the young man does not return. *This guy must be good*, Cellini thinks to himself, admiring the young man's ability to stay submerged for so long. Another minute goes by and still he doesn't return. Those waiting on the surface start to show concern; their laughter turns to panic and they start peering down into the water. Cellini senses there is something very wrong and calls out to them. They look up but take little notice and resume beating the water in the hope of attracting the attention of their intrepid mussel catcher. Cellini removes his boots as he gets to where a crowd is beginning to form. People are screaming with panic now.

Without uttering a word, Cellini dives into the water and swims down. The sea is no more than 3 or 4 metres deep and quite clear. He can see the young man, lying perfectly still at the bottom. He dives into the water and swims down to the unfortunate diver, who doesn't seem to be trapped or snagged on anything and there are no signs of any wounds. Cellini reaches down to him and tries to grab him by the hair, but his hair is too close cropped and the would-be rescuer is unable to get a grip. Instead he grasps an arm and pulls him directly upwards, breaking the surface perhaps 20 metres from the rocks. Swimming over to the shallows at the shore, dragging the limp and lifeless body with him, he pulls the young man onto the shore and lays him down on his back. There is no sign of life and the others in his group race over to him, some screaming, others just with a look of consternation. Cellini sits astride the body, slapping his face first with one hand then the other, looking for any sign of life. There is no response. He reaches into his mouth to see if he has choked on something but there is nothing there but seawater. The young man is dead. Cellini gets up and tries to explain that he did everything he could, but no explanation is necessary and no one is taking any notice. The group, whether part of the young man's family or just friends, who just a few minutes earlier had been looking forward to their fresh seafood lunch are now standing around in shock, staring at their dead companion. Some are weeping, others are just looking straight ahead in utter disbelief. None are paying attention to Cellini, who walks slowly back to where he left his boots, picks them up and walks home.

He never speaks to anyone of the incident. Disappointed that he was unable to help the young man, he tries to put it out of his mind. He has dealt with death on many occasions and in many ways, but has a difficult time reconciling this because he is unable to come up with a rational explanation for the young man's death.[3]

[3] *This particular event has haunted Cellini for as long and as deeply as any of the deaths he has witnessed, because he felt so utterly helpless. Many years later he discovered mouth-to-mouth resuscitation and cardiopulmonary resuscitation (CPR) but neither had existed in 1944.*

40. An Accidental Suicide

ONE EVENING while having drinks with a few friends, Cellini is introduced to a gentleman named Donald Koch. Donald is an American of Italian descent, serving with the US military in Bari, and he is dating the sister of one of Cellini's friends. It would be more accurate to say the sister of a friend of a friend; one of the crowd that likes to hang around together on a Saturday night. Cellini is certain he has met Koch somewhere before but can't quite place exactly where. Halfway through the evening it dawns on him. He has seen Koch in the building on *Corso Cavour* on more than one occasion.

He would never dream of asking anything about his work, but he is pretty sure Donald must be a field agent with the OSS. Why else would he be here, in Italy? Particularly in Bari?

Some of Cellini's friends are jealous of Donald and aren't shy about making their feelings known. They don't like this American who has swept the young lady, Maria, off her feet, but Cellini takes a liking to him and thinks of him as a kindred spirit, partly because he is an American and partly because he believes him to be an OSS agent. He doesn't discuss any of this with his friends, but encourages them to get to know Koch, and eventually the American is accepted into the fold.

Within a very short time, Donald and Maria are married. Soon afterwards, the couple announces that they are expecting a baby. Koch is a devoted husband and eagerly looks forward to becoming a father. The couple are making plans to move to his home in Michigan after the war.

Koch is a complex individual. He has a wonderful sense of humour which is slightly warped and appeals to Maria. He's smart, but highly-strung and prone to emotional outbursts that everyone, especially Maria, notices are becoming more and more frequent. She decides to talk to Cellini about it. He tells Maria it's the stress of the war and wanting to go home and that she should not worry, but he knows his words offer very little comfort. Cellini understands that Koch's work brings him a great deal of anguish and decides that if he sees him in the office again he will talk to him, if only to let him know he has a friend – and a fellow agent – who understands and sympathizes.

Weeks turn into months and the situation doesn't get any better. Cellini hasn't had a chance to talk to Koch yet, but an opportunity presents itself one weekend. A big party has been organized by the Calabrese family and Cellini arranges to go to Donald and Maria's apartment to pick them up in a Jeep he has borrowed from the Army. Maybe he'll be able to talk to Donald on the way. Maybe he'll talk to him at the party.

He walks in to find Donald and Maria have been arguing. Her six-year-old brother is crying because he doesn't want her to go. Maria is trying to calm everybody down. Donald is pacing up and down dramatically, his hands over his ears and yelling at both of them.

"I can't take any more of this. I just can't. You want me to kill my-self? You want me to just end it all right here, right now?" He says, looking straight at Maria's younger brother as he pulls his .45 semi-automatic out of its holster and points it towards his own head. It's a highly melodramatic act and he knows it. He's done it before. It's a trick he used to play on his own younger brother back home in Michigan whenever he cried incessantly. Donald would point the gun at his own head, and when everyone went quiet, he would grin at his shocked and horrified audience, then put the gun away and take a bow.

This time something goes wrong. Almost at the instant he levels the pistol to his head it goes off. If it had happened a split second sooner the bullet would have hit the ceiling, but instead it goes straight through his temple in front of his right ear and out the top of his head in a shower of blood and brain particles.

Cellini leaps across the room and catches the lifeless body as it sinks slowly down to the ground. Maria is screaming hysterically and he tells her to get the baby out of the room. The gunshot has brought the attention of others in the building. Cradling what is left of Donald Koch's head in his arms, Cellini tells someone to fetch medical help, even though he knows it is too late to save his friend.

The police arrive and the body is removed and taken to hospital. Maria and the baby leave to go and stay with her family but Cellini is detained and questioned for what seems like an eternity at the scene. He feels as though he is a suspect in his friend's death, even though Maria – once she has calmed down – tells them exactly how it happened and that it was a tragic accident. By the time Cellini is eventually released he is exhausted and quite probably in shock. Without even thinking about what he is doing, he heads over to the party, his clothes still soaked in Koch's blood. He explains the story to anyone and everyone who wants to know and gets thoroughly drunk until he passes out.[1]

[1] *After the war, Maria followed up with the plan to move to Michigan with her baby, where they were welcomed and taken care of by Donald Koch's family. Cellini and Maria kept in touch for many years.*

41. The Return of Tedeski

Weeks go by with nothing but dead ends. If it weren't for the excitement of running the gauntlet of the *carabinieri* with suitcases full of cigarettes, Cellini is convinced he would have died of boredom.

He varies the time as well as the locations where he spends his time, in order to avoid becoming too familiar and predictable. This one particular day he has chosen the early morning shift at *Piazza Garibaldi*. Entering the piazza about an hour before dawn, he finds a vacant bench, lies down and covers himself with some pages from an old newspaper pulled from the waste bin. Though primarily a disguise, the newspaper also serves to help keep him warm in the early morning chill. If anyone disturbs him, he will put on an act of being drunk. There are a few people about in spite of the hour, but the park is mainly quiet and no one bothers him.

He is almost dozing off when he is stirred by the sound of raised voices. He thinks at first there is some kind of a dispute and that a fight may break out. Locals who gather on the piazza to play chess frequently get into arguments over their games, but this is different – and these two are not playing chess. They are speaking partly in English and one of them is distinctly American. Cellini struggles to listen in to the conversation. His grasp of English is not good, but he is certain he hears the name Tedeski.

Shuffling his position and rearranging the newspaper gives him an excuse to look around so he can get a good look at the men engaged in this heated discussion. In the grey half-light, he can just about see that the American accent belongs to a heavyset soldier with a ruddy complexion. The other man is Italian but not a local. His accent and dialect suggest Naples but Cellini cannot be sure. Shuffling the newspapers around once again, Cellini slumps back into a position where he can see both of them, even with his eyes partly closed. He listens intently to their dialogue. They are calmer now – their difference of opinion seems to have subsided and their voices are at a more normal level. They are also speaking Italian now, which makes it much easier for him to understand. The name Tedeski is not mentioned again but from the gist of the conversation Cellini is able to understand that someone of some importance will be arriving in Bari later that morning.

Could this be Tedeski? Is this the break he has been waiting for?

Sensing the conversation is coming to an end, Cellini stands, stretching as though he has just woken up from a long nap and is ready to move along. He plans to leave ahead of the two men so that they are less likely to suspect he is following them, then double back and catch them up.

He walks slowly, feigning a drunken gait, towards the west end of *Piazza Garibaldi.* If they leave in his direction, they will pass him in a moment and he can follow. If they don't pass him, he can pretend to stumble, turn around and with any luck get a good look at whichever way they do go. It seems like a foolproof plan.

Neither of the men pass him, so he turns around expecting to see them still engaged in conversation. There is no sign of them.

He makes his way back to the bench and gathers up the newspaper he left behind, all the while glancing around for the two men. He catches a glimpse of the American ambling south and out of the piazza in no particular hurry. He has lost sight of the Italian.

Maintaining his drunken act, he follows the American out of the piazza, lurching from side to side on the footpath. He is almost knocked over as someone ploughs into the back of him, running full tilt. It is the Italian, who evidently stopped to buy cigarettes, judging from the way he is holding the half-unwrapped pack in his hand and gesticulating as he apologizes to Cellini for the collision. If Cellini was trying to stay incognito and unseen, that idea is now history, as the Italian stops and offers him a cigarette to go along with the apology. Cellini thanks him and stoops to help himself to a cigarette, faking a cough so he can cover up his face, but he knows the Italian has already had a good look at him. The Italian excuses himself and joins his American friend. Picking up the pace, they head south, away from the port and in the direction of the railway station.

Keeping a safe distance behind, Cellini walks slowly after them, staying in the shadows. The drunken stagger has gone.

When they get to *Corso Italia*, the pair turns left, heading towards the railway station.

Startled by the sound of a car horn behind him, Cellini ducks into a doorway. A Jeep passes him, its two occupants laughing and waving their arms, causing it to wander all over the road, and stops by the pair. They chat for a few minutes but Cellini cannot hear any of the conversation from inside a doorway some 50 metres away. The American climbs into the back of the

Jeep and it leaves, another fanfare blaring on its horn as it turns off. Cellini stays with the Italian, who walks across the road and enters the station.

Following more closely now, hoping the man he is stalking won't turn around suddenly. He wants to find out where he is going. The man walks into the station building but goes straight past the ticket office and onto the nearest platform.

He's meeting someone off the train, Cellini thinks to himself. He stays inside the building where he can watch without being seen. After about twenty minutes a train arrives at the station. A handful of passengers get off, and Cellini watches intently for a look of recognition on the Italian's face. Either he doesn't recognize anyone, or he's very good at disguising it. Cellini finds himself playing a game of guessing which one of the disembarking train passengers it might be. Clearly not the elderly couple struggling with two rather large battered suitcases and sniping at each other. It's probably not the young woman marching purposefully out of the station, either. That just leaves the short, untidy man with the pronounced limp and the knapsack on one shoulder or the woman with the shiny black hair and the raincoat.

It had never occurred to Cellini that Tedeski might be a woman. The thought intrigues him for a few minutes, but he dismisses it. Instead, he focuses on replaying, in his head, the conversation he had overheard in the piazza. He is certain he had heard someone mention the name "Tedeski". Could he have got it wrong?

No. It's too much of a coincidence. He must be on to something. And if it proves to be otherwise, he'll just go back to square one and start over.

Cellini's money is on the man with the limp.

The departing passengers all walk past the man without the slightest glimmer of recognition. He stays where he is and the train pulls out of the station.

Maybe he's waiting for the next train?

Cellini waits with him, still watching from inside the station building. Ten minutes go by. Twenty. After almost half an hour, another train pulls into the station, but this time almost every door on the train opens and dozens of passengers spill out onto the platform. There are far too many for Cellini to keep track of, so he keeps his eye on the Italian. As the milling horde pushes its way through the building and onto the street, Cellini is jostled and loses his view of the platform momentarily. By the time he looks back, the Italian is gone. It can only have been two or three seconds, but he must have made his contact.

Cellini is optimistic. *There's no way you can get past me in here without me seeing you,* he thinks to himself. Making his way to the exit and back onto the street, he steps behind a pillar and watches as the crowd thins out. He spots the Italian crossing the road, but he is alone.

Following him across *Piazza Aldo Moro*, Cellini is able to keep him in view while staying well out of sight. The Italian walks past the fountain and continues to the hotel *Leon D'Oro*. He turns, glances around over his shoulder then steps through the hotel entrance.

Just a few seconds behind him, Cellini enters the hotel lobby and sees the Italian standing at the desk talking to the concierge. Stepping into the lounge area, he picks up a recently abandoned newspaper from a table and takes a seat where he can see the desk. The concierge indicates for the Italian to take a seat and picks up the phone. The Italian turns and walks towards Cellini. More of the crowd from the station are entering the hotel and form a line to check in.

The Italian chooses a seat directly across from Cellini. Sitting up straight, crossing one leg over the other and holding the newspaper up, he hopes he won't be recognized. All he can do now is use his body language to try to look as poised and sober as he can, in the hope that if the Italian does recognize him, he won't make the connection with the drunk in *Piazza Garibaldi.*

Studying the newspaper intently, Cellini no longer needs a clear view of the Italian to know he is there. He can almost hear him breathing and will certainly be aware if he gets up, which he does, just a few minutes later. Glancing from behind the newspaper, Cellini looks up in time to see the Italian greet someone who has just emerged from across the lobby.

Cellini recognizes him at once. It is the man with the pronounced limp from the railway station.

He watches intently but is unable to discern any of their conversation due to the hubbub in the hotel. The Italian hands the other man a small brown package or envelope, which he puts into his pocket. They stand and talk for a few minutes, then embrace and the Italian leaves. The man with the limp turns and makes his way back across the lobby and waits for the lift.

Cellini has a decision to make. Should he follow the Italian, or stay where he is? It's really not a hard choice. He opts to stay and wait in the hotel. Eventually the man with the limp will come back down and Cellini will find a way to engage him in conversation.

He doesn't have to wait long. He moves to a seat where he can keep one eye on the lobby and the lift for the man with the limp, and the other on the main entrance for the return of the Italian – or anyone else who just takes a seat and waits. There is only one new arrival checking in, complete with luggage. Several people, presumably returning guests, walk up to the concierge desk and ask for their keys. One of the returning guests presses the button and as the lift doors open, the man with the limp strides out. He stops to hand in his room key, turns and moves straight towards the door.

Confident that no one is waiting to meet him, at least not inside the hotel, Cellini discards the newspaper, which up until now, has provided him with his only measure of disguise, and intercepts the limping man before he can even get halfway to the door.

"Tedeski," he says. It is framed neither as a question nor as an introduction, he is simply trying to instigate a reaction. He has no idea if this man is Tedeski, or if he is meeting Tedeski. Nor, for that matter, if the man with the limp is in any way involved with Tedeski. He is acting solely on what is referred to in American movies as a hunch, based on something he believes he overheard in the piazza.

He soon has his answer.

The limping man stops dead in his tracks and turns to face Cellini.

"Who are you?" he says, staring at Cellini and slowly taking in his partial military attire; hatless and with no badges to identify himself.

Somewhat caught on the spot, Cellini does what he does best in these situations. He tells the truth.

"I am Cellini," he says, confidently, as if that is supposed to explain everything.

"Cellini… Cellini…" The limping man repeats the name out loud as he processes the information. "I do not believe I have had the pleasure." He smiles graciously but does not offer his hand. Instead his tone changes as he continues, "And I do not believe I shall. Now if you will excuse me, Mr. Cellini, I have much to attend to."

He turns to leave and Cellini calls out after him.

"But you are Tedeski?"

"Am I, Mr. Cellini?"

"I was told to look for a man called Tedeski. I was under the impression that you… that he… would be able to help me to find… to buy certain things that are impossible to find using conventional means."

Sensing he has the man's attention, Cellini pushes his luck.

"Certain medicines, for example, are very difficult to obtain in the present climate. I work for a very dedicated group of …" he pauses for effect and because he doesn't want to lie blatantly. "…a dedicated group of people and they have plenty of money… but if you are not Tedeski, and you have no desire to get to know me… then perhaps I am mistaken…" he lets the sentence trail off into nowhere, which is exactly where he thinks he is heading. He excuses himself and steps past the man with the limp, towards the door of the hotel.

"Wait!" the man says.

"Meet me here tomorrow morning at 9:00 am. I'd like to learn more about you and your… people."

Cellini leaves the hotel feeling quite pleased with himself and walks back to the office on *Corso Cavour*. He takes a circuitous route, stopping in a tobacco shop on the way to wait a few minutes and make sure he isn't being followed. The owner is a customer as well as a friend, and leads him through the shop so he can slip out the back door. When he gets back to the headquarters building, he is shown into a small office where the British officer is waiting for him. He relates the entire story, from hearing the name to the meeting in the hotel.

"That's good work, Mr. Cellini," the officer commends him. Cellini is not used to being praised for his work, nor is he accustomed to being addressed as "mister", so he realises this must be quite a big deal and is keen to stay involved, now that he finally has a positive lead.

"I'll meet him in the morning, as he suggests, and see if I can learn more," he says.

"That won't be necessary. We'll handle it from here." The officer is firm in his reply.

Cellini pushes it. "What will happen to him?" he says.

The British officer is starting to lose his patience. "That really is none of your concern," he says, and ushers Cellini out of the room.

*****

CELLINI RATIONALIZES that even though he has been told, in no uncertain terms, that his services are no longer required in the Tedeski case, he hasn't actually been forbidden from just showing up anyway. That is exactly what he intends to do.

At 8:30 the following morning, Cellini presents himself in the lobby of the *Leon d'Oro*. As before, he finds a seat where he can keep one eye on the hotel entrance and the other eye on the area in front of the elevator, and hides behind a newspaper. There are quite a few people buzzing around and a lot of activity. No one pays him any attention.

Nine o'clock comes and goes. There is no sign of Tedeski. At 9:30 the hotel crowd starts to thin down. He decides to give it a few more minutes, perhaps until 9:45, then he too will make himself scarce.

Checking his watch one last time, he stands up and makes his way to the door. A voice behind him calls out, "Hey. Where do you think you're going?"

Cellini turns to find himself facing his commander. He is wearing civilian clothes with a hat pulled down over his eyes. Cellini hadn't recognized him; hadn't even noticed him. He opens his mouth to speak but is caught in a rare moment of being unable to find any words.

"What are you doing here? I thought I specifically told you not to come to this meeting and that we would be handling it from now on?" The commander is feigning anger. There is a glint in his eye and Cellini picks up on it straight away.

"You told me it wasn't necessary for me to be here, but you didn't actually order me not to come. There is a difference... sir!" he adds the formal address as an afterthought.

The commander puts his arm around Cellini's shoulders.

"Don't worry about Tedeski. He won't be organizing any more black market shipments. I hope you understand, Cellini, we couldn't take any chances with him. He has good connections in high places, and lots of them. Once you found him, we needed to make sure we didn't lose him again."

"Then why are you still here?" Cellini is sure he knows the answer and his commander doesn't disappoint him.

"Because I knew bloody well that you'd be here, in spite of what I told you!" The SOE officer laughs, but then his face adopts a serious expression.

"However," he begins, "from now on, if I tell you it is not necessary for you to be somewhere, you had better pay attention; obey your orders to the letter, or else you'll find your services no longer required. Do you understand?"

Cellini looks at his commander, trying to tell if he is serious. He senses that he is.

"Yes, sir," he replies, somewhat subdued. Then qualifies his position.

"My duty is still to keep my eyes and ears open for any criminal activity?"

The commander nods approvingly.

"Any criminal activity involving the Allied troops?"

Again, the commander nods.

"And to report it to you, or to the Military Police, or…." He pauses, looking for the right words… "Or… if necessary to *improvise* and deal with the situation in whatever way I see fit?"

"Yes, I suppose that's about right," the commander responds. "Just don't get yourself into any trouble with the local authorities – and especially not with the local organized crime gangs. If you do, there's nothing the SOE or the OSS can do to help you. Understand?"

"Perfectly. Thank you sir." Cellini gleans from his closing remarks that his commander evidently has no knowledge of his close friendship with Tonino Anibilis, who is the leader of by far the biggest and most successful of the so-called organized crime gangs in the region. He walks away feeling quite full of himself, believing he has the support and trust of the Allied military intelligence forces as well as the protection of the local gangs.

42. Helping the Army Air Force: Tragedy at Gorla

IT IS LATE SUMMER, 1944. Cellini has been asking repeatedly for more challenging assignments from his contacts at the OSS headquarters. Now that the Allies have landed in Normandy and the push is on, everyone is keen to move forward and do their part to bring the war to an end, and no one is more keen to prove a point than Cellini.

He knows that most of his family members still think of him as a *delinquente.* Naturally he is unable to discuss the nature of his work with the OSS and SOE with anyone. Even his Uncle Nicola, who introduced him to the British and US military after he returned from Yugoslavia, knows nothing of his secret work, although he is suspicious that his nephew is involved in black market dealings and does not particularly approve. Nicola's daughter Francesca – Cellini's cousin – is far more forgiving and lets him know that whatever he is doing towards the war effort, she knows it must be very important. When they see each other at family gatherings, she always makes a point of sitting with Cellini for at least part of the time. They talk about America and of maybe going back to the land they were both born in, after the war is over.

Cellini reports to *Corso Cavour* for his weekly briefing. He expects to be asked, as usual, if he has any new, useful information about black market dealers… which he doesn't. And told to *keep his eyes and ears open…* which he always does. Instead he is ushered into a small, private office and told to wait.

His commander walks into the room with a smile on his face.

"Have you ever made a parachute jump?" he says.

"Me? No… never have!" Cellini is caught completely by surprise by the question but answers honestly.

"No matter," his commander replies, "we can train you pretty quickly."

He continues, "We have a special assignment which we think is right up your alley. Literally."

Cellini is excited by the prospect and completely perplexed as to what the job might be.

His commanding officer explains that, in conjunction with the invasion, which began in June on the beaches in France, the Allies are beginning to step up the campaign to attack the Germans and the remaining Italian fascists in northern Italy. Volunteers are being sought to join the Italian Partisans in the north, who are working closely with the OSS to create as much disruption as possible – much the same as Tito's Partisans are doing in Yugoslavia. Cellini's experience of guerilla fighting with the Yugoslavian Partisans and his knowledge of northern Italy – having lived in Milan before the war – seem to offer a perfect opportunity for him to get back to the fighting.

They discuss at length what training he would need to undergo, including spending a few days in Brindisi for parachute training.[1] Cellini would then be parachuted into the Milan area at night, where he would be met by members of the Italian resistance.

In the course of their conversation, the commander asks Cellini point blank if he personally still knows anyone living in Milan. Cellini replies that much of his family, including his younger sisters, live in the Gorla and Precotta area, on the north side of the city. Realizing, as he speaks, the potential risk to his family, he asks if there is any possible way they can be protected, or perhaps even evacuated, in the event that he is captured.

His commander frowns and asks him to wait while he leaves the room. He returns after quite some time shaking his head.

"I'm not sure we can risk dropping you in," he says. "It would take too long to create an entirely fake identity for you, and quite honestly it just isn't worth it. If you were to get captured and the Germans discovered that you have family members living locally – and believe me they will discover – it could put your family in grave danger. It would also put our whole operation in jeopardy if those bastards have your family imprisoned."

Cellini argues that he would not get caught, and that even if he did, he would never give up anything, but the commander is adamant.

"Sorry, Cellini. It's one thing to take a chance on a trained and experienced soldier such as yourself to be exposed to the possibility of interrogation and torture. But to expect you to resist questioning while your younger sisters are tortured and raped is too much of a risk – for everyone involved."

[1]. *The SOE established a paratrooper training facility at Brindisi where Italian Partisans were sent for training in preparation for dropping into northern Italy.*

Cellini is disappointed. He feels that his last chance to contribute something meaningful to the Allied war effort may have just slipped through his fingers. The two men sit in silence for a few minutes before the commander speaks again.

"How well do you know the city?" he says.

"Milan?" Cellini replies, shrugging his shoulders. "Pretty well, I suppose. Especially the north side."

"Do you know the Alpha Romeo plant or the Isotta factory? How about Breda?"

Cellini laughs. "Before I was drafted into the Italian Army I worked for Magnaghi – and most of what we did was for the Breda factory, which was practically next door!"

"That could be important. Let me talk to the intelligence people. Wait here again. This time I won't be long."

The commander is true to his word and returns within two or three minutes. He opens the door, pokes his head around and beckons to Cellini. "Come with me, please."

Cellini is led to another section of the building at a brisk walking pace. The commander informs him that he is entering a highly restricted area and adds, "You are to forget about anything and everything you see in this room and never repeat any of the conversation or discussion that takes place in here. D'you understand?"

Cellini isn't really paying close attention. He is still caught up in the excitement of being involved in the espionage business. He answers, "Yes, sir," which seems to satisfy his commander, who opens a door and ushers him inside.

He is introduced to an intelligence officer to whom he takes an immediately liking. The man is a bundle of energy as he starts unfolding maps, in various scales and detail, as well as producing a stack of aerial photographs of Milan, scattering them all over a large wooden table. The officer is extremely enthusiastic and asks Cellini a myriad questions about Milan, Gorla and the location of the Breda factory. Where are the main doors? Can you point to them on this photograph? Where is the furnace? The generator? How many people work in each section? Does the building have a basement? In the end Cellini is able to answer every question and the intelligence officer is well pleased with him. They go over the same ground many times and the officer makes copious notes, filling a small notebook. The session takes a large part of the day with no break for food or drink or even to go to the lavatory, yet Cellini hardly notices. The time goes by quickly.

"This is all really helpful. I mean, really, really helpful!" the intelligence office says, excitedly, closing the notebook and laying the pencil down beside it. He thanks Cellini profusely for his time.

"If we need anything else, we'll contact you, but I think I can safely say that you have just contributed greatly to the Allied war effort."

He offers Cellini his hand, not as a salute, but in a handshake. The two men shake hands and Cellini leaves. Now that the conversation is over he has slightly mixed feelings about giving up so much information. Obviously the military must be planning some kind of raid or sabotage on the Magnaghi factory. His time there was not all bad and he had made quite a few friends. He is tempted to feel sorry for his old friends but tells himself it's their own fault for continuing to support the fascist regime – if they are even still there. He is more concerned about his good friend Giancarla and, of course, Isabella, who he has not seen since before his court martial. It seems like a lifetime ago.

In time, Cellini would have good reason to feel guilty for sharing information about his former employer's location with Allied military intelligence, not because of any damage inflicted upon the factory, but because of unforeseen consequences that were totally beyond his control.

Right now, he is tired and hungry but satisfied that he has done the right thing.

*****

In the spring of 1944, after several months' respite following the capitulation of the Italian government and Allied occupation of the south, the Allies resume a heavy strategic bombing campaign against industrial targets in northern Italy. The USAAF bombs by day and the RAF by night. Bombing is largely inaccurate, and there are many civilian casualties, because major industrial targets are often in the middle of residential areas. It is felt that, with better intelligence and help from resistance organizations on the ground, the Allied bombing results will improve and important targets can be neutralized.

On 20th October, 1944, 111 of the US Fifteenth Air Force depart on a mission to Milan to bomb factories engaged in production of key military hardware and munitions.

The aircraft assigned to attack Alfa Romeo and Isotta Fraschini hit their targets with remarkable accuracy, but due to an error in navigation, the 36 Consolidated B-24 Liberators of the 451st Bomb Group miss the Breda factory completely. Upon realizing the mistake, the order is given for all crews to abandon the mission, jettison their bombs immediately and return to base.

Shortly before noon, approximately 80 tons of bombs fall on the heavily populated Milanese suburbs of Gorla and Precotto. Some 614 civilians are killed, including 184 of the 200 children as well as the entire staff of 19 teachers at the Francesco Crispi elementary school. The main stairwell in the school building receives a direct hit as the children and school personnel are going down to the air raid shelter.

It will be the last heavy bombing raid carried out on Milan.

Among the children attending school that day are Vito Cellini's three younger sisters, Benita, Antoinetta and Italia.

Miraculously, the girls are among the sixteen survivors of the bombing raid, though they are buried under the rubble and it is some considerable time before they can be rescued.

A monument entitled "This is War" stands in the Piazza dei Piccoli Martyrs Gorla (Plaza of the Little Martyrs of Gorla), erected in 1947 as a reminder of the tragic event.

Cellini is unaware of the tragic results of the bombing raid until after the war. When he learns that his sisters had been in the school building at the time, he feels considerable personal guilt for what has come to be known as "The Tragedy at Gorla". He continually apologizes to his sisters for the part he played. Their response and support is unwavering; they believe that, as an American citizen, he was doing his duty. They also remind him constantly that it was not his error that caused the school to be bombed.

Grateful to be alive to have this photograph taken several years after the war, Vito Cellini's four sisters: Nicoletta, Italia, Antoinetta and Benita.

"This is War" in the Piazza dei Piccoli Martyrs Gorla. The monument is dedicated to the 203 children and teachers killed in the misdirected bombing raid.

43. Desperate Times... Desperate Measures. Winter, 1944-45

SINCE THE CRACKDOWN on black market dealing by the MPs at the port – helped in no small way by Cellini and others – goods are no longer in such plentiful supply to the small-time black marketers who are struggling to make a living and support their families. Though most are youngsters like Cellini, many have aging and infirm parents and grandparents, as well as younger brothers and sisters to care for, and many of them are going without necessities such as food and clothing in order to feed their families. While commodities such as cigarettes and tobacco can still be obtained fairly easily, many items, such as cloth, are in very short supply. It shows in the threadbare clothing worn by Cellini's young friends.

Though Cellini has no such worries, being smartly attired in his British military issue battledress blouse and trousers, he feels not only empathy for his young friends, but also guilt for the part he is playing in curtailing their ability to earn a living, and decides to do something to help their situation.

He has a key to Pasquina's apartment. Pasquina has moved to Milan along with other members of the family to find employment, so Cellini looks in once in a while to make sure the place is safe and clean.

He decides to cover some of the furniture with sheets to protect them from dust, and searching through the linen cupboards he discovers Pasquina has a lot of bed sheets. The thought occurs to him that all his friends could really use new shirts and wonders if it is possible to make a shirt from a bed sheet.

Sifting through the bedding, he selects about a dozen of the better-looking sheets from the stack and creates two piles. Satisfied he has taken enough – but not too much so that it would show – he replaces the original stack, carefully folding it to make the stack look just as big as it was with half as many sheets. Taking the sheets he has picked out, he ties them together in a bundle, secures another sheet around them and lowers them from the window of the apartment to the ground below.

Hurrying downstairs, he gathers up the sheets and runs across the street to the family home of his old friend Vito Calabrese. Calabrese is now married to a beautiful girl, who happens to work as a seamstress.

"Can you get your wife to make shirts out of these?" he says.

Calabrese looks at the material, then looks at Cellini.

"These are bed sheets," Calabrese says, "Where did you get them?"

"Never mind where I got them," Cellini replies. "Can your wife use them to make shirts for everyone?"

Calabrese tells Cellini to go home and leave the sheets with him. He'll talk to his wife and let him know as soon as he can.

Within a week, all of Cellini's friends are proudly strutting around in crisp, clean, starched white shirts, just like the old days.[1]

*****

THERE IS A sense that the war is almost at end, yet still there are shortages of everything, not least of which is fuel to keep warm. Be it coal or wood or whatever is available, people are beginning to run out and have started sacrificing any and all superfluous materials to use as fuel.

Vito Calabrese's family lives across the street in a similar apartment to that of Cellini's grandmother and grandfather. The apartment has a main entrance on the street, leading to a courtyard with stairs and entrances to each individual apartment.

Winter in Bari can be brutally cold. The wind coming in off the water brings a damp chill and a fire is essential, not just for warmth, but for cooking and drying wet clothes. The Calabrese family hasn't had any fuel to burn for several days and though friends and neighbours have been kind in sharing their hospitality, they feel they need to stay at home.

Cellini visits from across the street and notices, perhaps for the first time, the massive door that leads to the courtyard of his friend's family home. Eying it up and down, the thought crosses his mind that it would

1. *Pasquina never openly accused him of the theft, although she must have discovered it upon returning to Bari from Milan after the war was over. The only reference she made to the incident was vague, when she said "svergoniato", which was a word in the Barese dialect that meant "You ought to be ashamed". By that time, Cellini had committed so many misdemeanours and performed so many questionable acts that he could never be sure which one she was referring to. As long as she lived, she never specifically mentioned the disappearance of the bed sheets to him.*

make great firewood, and would probably supply more than enough fuel for the rest of the winter.

He nudges his friend and tells him to come with him, he wants to show him something. The two friends walk into the street and Cellini points to the door. It stands perhaps 3 metres high and a metre across, but it's also at least 2 centimeters thick, with a simple carved pattern to the outside. It is also covered in many layers of paint.

"That would keep your folks' fire going for the whole winter." Cellini says, elbowing Calabrese in the ribs and grinning.

"NO Tutuc!" Calabrese replies. "They'd get into so much trouble if they got caught!"

"We'll make sure they don't get caught!" Cellini says. "We'll come back tonight, take the door off its hinges and take it upstairs. Then we can cut it up into small pieces and hide it – just bring out a piece when you need to!"

It sounds like such an easy plan and Cellini is very convincing. Calabrese eventually agrees but Cellini makes him swear not to say anything to his family.

"Let's make it a surprise!" he says.

The two meet up in front of the huge gate after dark. The street is deserted. Cellini has brought a saw for cutting the wood and a large hammer to remove the pins from the hinges. Despite the door not having been shut for as long as the two of them can remember, the hinges are well greased – but stubborn. Calabrese is afraid someone will hear the racket of Cellini's hammering but somehow they manage to knock the hinges out of the enormous door without attracting too much attention.

Both have grossly underestimated the weight of the door, and when it is loosened and lowered to the ground, it almost crushes Cellini. After a great deal of effort, they move the door inside the courtyard. Now they must try to manoeuvre it up the stairs. It doesn't take too long before they realise this is not going to happen and that the door will actually have to be cut into smaller, manageable pieces before they try to go anywhere with it. Though not exactly in full view of the street, anyone walking past the open doorway glancing in would be able to see exactly what is going on. Cellini tells Calabrese to stand guard at the entrance and tell him if he sees anyone coming down the street. There are a couple of scares, but seeing Calabrese propping up the entrance, no one seems interested in staring past him into the open courtyard.

They take turns sawing the door into manageable chunks. The job takes considerably longer than either of them thought it would, or should. It's a bitterly cold night and each prefers their shift of sawing to their stint at guard duty, just to keep warm, which hurries the process along. Once they have a sizeable stack of wood, they take it up the Calabreses' apartment. The next problem they encounter is where to hide so much wood in a relatively small apartment. One very large door takes up a great deal of space – especially when it is cut into small pieces. After placing as much as they can under loose floorboards or in cupboards, they hide some of it under furniture. The rest is stacked up in the family room and covered with a blanket.

Once the wood is put away, Cellini takes a broom and sweeps the sawdust from the yard. By the time they have completely finished it is almost dawn. Exhausted, they decide to surprise the family by having a nice warm fire blazing in the hearth when everyone wakes up.

Cellini decides this would be as good a time as any for him to go home, leaving his friend Vito Calabrese to answer to the family.

"Don't you dare leave me here on my own, you bastard!" Calabrese says.

"Just tell them you found it!" Cellini replies, smiling. "Everyone's doing it anyway; they'll never know."

"Are you kidding me? It's not like they won't recognize their own front door? It's got about thirty coats of paint on it… and you don't think someone might just notice that the main entrance door to the entire building is missing?"

Calabrese is, as always, agitated. Cellini is his typical composed self.

He warms his hands by the beautifully burning fireplace before slipping out into the night and back across the street to his own home to grab a couple of hours sleep.

It will be several days before he sees his friend again, by which time the whole thing seems to have blown over.

44. A Second Explosion in Bari: The SS *Charles Henderson*

It's just before midday on a beautiful spring day in April, 1945 and Cellini is beginning to feel hungry. Work has been quiet lately. He has already checked in at the headquarters on *Corso Cavour* but they have nothing in particular to offer him beyond the usual message – *keep your eyes and ears open and report back if you find out anything.*

He decides to go to his grandmother's house to grab some bread and cheese before making his way down to the harbour to see his friend the sergeant, and maybe pick up some more cigarettes.

Cellini leaves his grandmother's house with a full belly and begins making his way towards the seafront. His hunger satisfied, he's feeling pretty good about life. He knows the war is almost over and he's starting to think about the future. Suddenly, he is shaken to the core by the biggest, loudest explosion he has ever heard in his life. The earth literally shudders beneath his feet, causing him to stumble to the ground.

Regaining his balance, he ducks and runs to the nearest doorway for shelter, crouching down on one knee. His first thought is that it must be an air raid, but there is no sight or sound of aircraft flying over, and only the one, huge blast.

An earthquake? He thinks to himself.

Making his way back to the house to check on his family, he finds them shaken but unhurt. He grabs the Leica camera Tonino had given him, excuses himself and heads back out the door to find out what is going on.

Almost as soon as he leaves the house, he is struck by the pungent smell of burning fuel oil, which gets stronger as he makes his way towards the harbour. He is also surprised at the total lack of life in the town. It is almost midday and the city should be thriving with people, yet it seems deserted. Knowing the side streets and back alleys, he takes the quickest route through the town to the port. There is a massive fire on the pier in the dockyard, but most striking is the devastation along the seafront. The smell of burning fuel is more intense now, but it is surpassed by another, even stronger and far more unpleasant smell, reminiscent of overcooked meat. Cellini recognizes it with disgust from his time with the Partisans. It is the stench of burnt human flesh.

Several of the main buildings along the seafront are lying in ruins, debris is scattered all over the place and the air is full of dust and trash swirling in the wind. Here and there are what appear to be heaps of smouldering rags lying randomly. As he gets closer, he can see that the piles of rags are actually human remains; partial bodies that have literally been blown apart and hurled through the air. Some are more complete and recognizable than others, but most are just indistinguishable chunks of flesh and bone. Some still have shreds of clothing attached, blowing in the wind, giving the impression of rags.

There is something else.

The bodies, those he can recognize as such, seem to have shrunk. Then he realises that the heat of the sudden blast must have instantaneously cooked the remains. He's seen death and destruction before, but always in the context of war or violence. This event was so sudden and unexpected and he feels nauseous.

And on such a quiet and peaceful day.

He fumbles in his pocket for the camera and starts taking pictures, capturing the unspeakable horror of this disaster. Not through mere morbid fascination but from an instinctive desire to document the events to convince himself later that it really happened.

While shaken by the site of the burnt and shrunken bodies, Cellini is most disturbed by the complete silence and desolation. His mind flashes back to his arrival from Yugoslavia just over a year ago, and the cloud that was still hanging over the city; but at least there were people. He can only conclude that everyone has fled in terror into the shelters and tunnels underground, fearing the worst.

Making his way further towards the source of the smoke now palling over the harbour, he encounters another human being for the first time since leaving his grandmother's house. An American soldier, looking shell-shocked and dumbstruck, steps out from a hut close to the harbour entrance and starts to wave Cellini away. Cellini produces his papers and offers his help, even though he knows there is nothing he can do.

Glancing at Cellini's documents, the soldier points over in the direction of a large storage warehouse that's still standing. To Cellini's surprise, the soldier speaks reasonable Italian.

"They're using that as a makeshift morgue. You can go and talk to the MPs but it's pretty grim – and I'm not sure they need anyone else vomiting all over the place."

Cellini nods his thanks and walks towards the building. As he approaches, the door slides open and a sergeant steps outside to light a cigarette. The site that greets Cellini through the briefly opened door is burned into his memory and will haunt him for a long time.

Soldiers and port workers have started gathering up the bodies and the body parts. What looks like hundreds upon hundreds of piles of shrunken meat, some in rags, are laid out in rows on the floor inside the building. The smell is absolutely nauseating.

The sergeant takes a long drag on his cigarette before asking Cellini what he wants. He produces his papers, but the sergeant waves them away.

"I don't care who you are or what you're here for, you don't need to be here and we sure as hell don't want you around."

Cellini, for once, offers no resistance but asks the sergeant what has happened. He shrugs as he replies.

"All we know for sure is that one of the supply ships in the harbour just blew up."

Cellini's thoughts again go back to the day he arrived back in Bari, following the air raid and the destruction it wrought on the city.

"Another air raid?" Cellini's question is almost rhetorical. He already knows there were no signs of enemy aircraft in the vicinity.

"It's too early to say. We don't know anything yet," the sergeant replies. "Look, there's nothing to see and nothing you can do to help. The best thing you can do is go home and let the military do their job and clean this God-awful mess up."

Almost as an afterthought, he quickly adds, "… and put that damn camera away – you're not a war correspondent and the MPs will seize it for sure if they see you taking pictures."

The sergeant throws what's left of his cigarette on the ground and grinds it into the concrete before sliding the door open and disappearing back into the makeshift morgue. Cellini puts the camera in his pocket and heads back to the house.

*****

The SS Charles Henderson is a United States Liberty ship. Launched on May 1st, 1943, she crosses the Atlantic carrying much-needed supplies to the troops engaged in the fighting in Europe. She is also one of many vessels that had served at Normandy for the Allied invasion of Europe in June, 1944.

In March, 1945, the Charles Henderson steams from Norfolk, Virginia, carrying 6,675 tons of bombs for delivery to the Fifteenth Air Force at Foggia in its five holds, arriving in Bari on 5th April.

On April 9th, just before midday, while the bombs are being unloaded from Charles Henderson at berth 14 in the Port of Bari, something goes disastrously wrong. Approximately 2,000 tons of bombs still on board the ship detonate simultaneously in a massive explosion that kills a total of 542 people and injures 1,800 more. Buildings along the waterfront are destroyed and ships within half a kilometre are severely damaged.

39 crew and 13 guards are among those killed in the explosion. The only survivor is the chief engineer of the ship, who happens to be ashore at the time of the blast. The wreck remains in Bari Harbour until 1948, when it is sold for scrap.

While no one can be sure as to the cause of the detonation, it is suggested that the unloading process has been rushed, because the terms of the contractual fee being paid to the civilian dockworkers is based on the number of items being lifted, rather than by time.

It is one of the largest ammunition disasters of World War Two.

Victory in Europe for the Allies is less than a month away.

45. The Third "Explosion"

IT IS A CRISP morning, just a week or so following the explosion of the SS *Charles Henderson*, and life is slowly beginning to settle down in Bari.

Cellini is making his way to the south side of the city to meet up with some friends. Hungry, he stops for a sandwich at a small deli he hasn't visited since before he left Bari for Yugoslavia. For as long as he can remember, mortadella and provolone cheese has been his favourite and after watching the owner of the deli build his sandwich just the way he remembers, he pays, takes it outside and sits down to savour it. Suddenly, the earth beneath his feet shakes violently and a massive explosion rips through the air. The detonation is deafening and the shockwave rocks Cellini, causing him to drop the sandwich. Furious at losing the delicacy after just one bite he stares in disbelief at the sliced meat lying on the filthy ground. He thinks about picking it up but decides against it. Instead, he looks in the direction of the blast and runs towards it.

Still shaken from the blast at the port a few days earlier, people are scattering in all directions, seeking cover and screaming. There is no smoke or fire that he can see, but he senses the blast has come from somewhere further south in Ceglie del Campo or Carbonara di Bari, suburbs of the city that are in the direction he was going. As he gets closer, he picks up the distinctive smell of burnt gunpowder. A thin veil of blue-grey haze wafts over him.

Cellini soon discovers the cause of the blast – and the reason for its apparently intensity.

Some of his enterprising friends have established a lucrative business for themselves by making cigarette lighters out of munitions stolen from the various ammo dumps located on quiet country roads around the city.[1] These lighters are then sold to the occupying Allied troops.

The outer case of the lighter is made from a drilled out cartridge and stuffed with cotton soaked in gasoline. The striker from a bomb fuse is fashioned into a flint and various wheels and gears from inside the bomb fuse serves as the rotating wheel that hits the flint, creating a spark that ignites the cotton. The lighters make great souvenirs for the Allied soldiers, who buy them not only for their own use, but also to send home as gifts. Lighters can also be specially engraved with a unit crest, design or the name of the recipient – for an extra charge, of course.

So these enterprising young men set up shop in the street, dismantling bullets and bombs for their parts alongside the ladies making orecchiette pasta by hand. At first they conserve every component and store it for its future profit potential, but after a while they decide they have no need for so many leftover parts, so they are discarded.

Metal parts, wires, cordite and gunpowder, explosive materials and other volatile substances are all conveniently tossed down a disused well.[2] No one gives it a second thought until one day, one of the kids, the younger brother of one of Cellini's *delinquente* friends, tosses a lit cigarette into the open well. He shouldn't have been smoking in the first place, but someone dared him to light up. He coughs and splutters before tossing the lit cigarette down the well. He has no idea of the consequences of his action, so instead of ducking down behind the wall of the well with his fingers in his ears, he peers down over the side to watch the red glow of the cigarette slowly disappear into the abyss… until the fumes ignite.

Somehow, he lives through the resulting blast but sustains serious injuries, including being temporarily blinded and deafened.

Despite the force of the explosion, he is the only casualty.

Though the blast is contained inside the well, the noise is greatly amplified by the cylindrical walls, explaining why it is heard far and wide across the city.

[1] *The air raid that had decimated the Port of Bari in December 1943, destroyed almost the entire inventory of Allied munitions, supplies and provisions stored in warehouses at the dock. To prevent such loss from occurring again, bombs, ammunition and other supplies and equipment were spread out and stored in small "supply dumps" located on quiet country roads, mostly outside of the city and stretching as far away as Foggia. These supply dumps were often no more than 100 metres apart. Though sometimes guarded by military personnel, these sites were vulnerable to thieves and black marketeers, who would bribe, threaten or simply help themselves to anything they wanted. A good time to find the best selection of goods was during delivery, when the guards and the drivers would stop to chat. One of the US Army drivers Cellini became friendly with was a very attractive Polish-American woman who would engage the guards in conversation, providing a distraction so that the thieves could help themselves to almost anything they wanted.*

[2] *Until a few years before, everyone in the region had been dependent on communal well water. The well was no longer in use since new irrigation and pumping systems were installed under Mussolini's government. At the time of the author's visit in 2016, manhole covers, drains and defunct water pumps throughout the region could still be found bearing the fascist emblem of Mussolini's regime.*

46. One More Dirty Job

CELLINI HASN'T seen any real action for a while. Has the black market really gone quiet, or are they getting smarter and more discreet about their dealings? Or perhaps it's just that most of the Allied troops have moved on and things are beginning to get back to normal in Bari?

Normal. Ha! He laughs to himself. Normal means the local street gangs are left to fight among themselves over territorial domination and don't have to worry about the Americans muscling in quite so much. They are still around, of course, chatting up the local girls and occupying most of the bars, but for the most part getting along just fine with everyone.

Cellini finds he is spending fewer nights sleeping on a bench at *Piazza Garibaldi* and more and more of his time drinking and rabble-rousing with Tonino. The quieter life doesn't suit him and he finds himself longing for the old days. He still looks in at the piazza from time to time, but he also relies heavily on tips from his growing circle of informants who are as keen to impress his close and powerful friend Tonino Anibilis as they are to share information.

Of course, he never hears about anything that might be considered of value to the local black market dealers; most of that information is filtered through various channels directly to Tonino, who disposes of it as he sees fit.

Tonight he has a tip.

A friend of a friend – it's always a friend of a friend – has heard through the proverbial grapevine – no doubt with the approval of Tonino – that there is a GI who knows where some of the contraband that survived the last explosion in the port is stashed.

"What kind of contraband?" Cellini wants to know.

"Search me," his informant, a short, stout Sardinian with glasses says. "All I know is to look out for an American soldier meeting some guy at the piazza this evening around eight-thirty or nine o'clock."

Cellini doesn't get along well with Sardinians and almost never trusts them, but this guy has never steered him wrong or given him bad information, so he decides to follow up. At 8:00 pm he takes up his usual spot on the bench nearest the entrance on *Via Nicola Pizzoli* so he can watch for any GIs that come along. Whenever possible he likes to arrive early so he can blend in with the environment, acclimatize himself to the people and surroundings, and not look like he has just arrived.

The piazza is not exactly swarming but there are people about, mostly locals who are drinking beer and finishing their chess games or arguing about the war, and enough soldiers – American, British and Italian – to make it difficult to watch any one in particular for too long. The time passes quite quickly as Cellini settles into his standard routine. He acts restless, irritable and totally oblivious to everything going on around him. At 9:15, there is still no sign of anyone other than a couple of locals entering the piazza and the night sky is beginning to settle in. He begins to wonder if the Sardinian has got it wrong this time, when he glances over and notices someone he hadn't seen before, standing behind one of the chess players, engaged in what seems to be quite a heated conversation. Is he offering advice? Coaching? Cellini can only pick out a few words, so he isn't at all sure what is being said, but what he does know is that while this man's Italian is perfect, the accent is not local. Cellini has to shuffle his position to get a good look at the interloper, and once he sees him, it becomes clear that he is not Italian. He is not wearing a uniform, but from his mannerism Cellini believes he is American. From the snippets of conversation he is able to pick up on, it is also apparent that the newcomer is not there to coach chess, but exactly what he is discussing Cellini has no idea.

As suddenly as he had appeared in the first place, the man disappears into the shadows. Deciding this is most probably be the man he was waiting for, Cellini acts quickly. Sitting up on his bench, he coughs and splutters and shakes his head to cover up the fact that he's actually scanning the trees at the perimeter of the piazza for movement. He catches a glimpse of the man heading in the direction of the old town and sets off after him, staggering at first until out of sight of the others at the piazza. He follows him at a safe distance, staying on the opposite side of the street and occasionally ducking into a doorway and peering around the wall.

He loses sight of him briefly, but the sound of raised voices, coming from a nearby side street, are enough to tell Cellini his target is close by. Turning the corner, he sees the man struggling with someone. His back is towards Cellini, who isn't sure what is happening, and for a split second it crosses his mind that someone else has intercepted his suspect. Stepping quickly so as to maintain the element of surprise, he sees it is a young girl.

She is putting up a fight but her attacker has his hand around her neck so she is unable to cry out, and he is pushing her into the doorway of a vacant building.

"Stop!" Cellini yells out.

"Is that you Maria?" he says, looking straight at the girl, who stares blankly at him, then back at her attacker.

Cellini clarifies the situation by addressing her attacker directly.

"What do you think you are doing with my sister?"

It's a ruse to divert the attacker's attention just long enough to gain the upper hand, and though the man is momentarily caught off guard, he recovers before Cellini can take advantage. *This guy is a pro,* Cellini thinks to himself. The man turns to face Cellini, pulling the girl in front of him, using her as a shield, his arm clamped tightly around her neck.

"Oh yeah?" he says, and spits on the ground. "Well your sister is a whore, and when I'm done with you I'm going to show her how we treat whores where I come from."

He hurls the girl to the ground, at the same time reaching inside his jacket. The girl cries out in pain as she crumples in a heap on the uneven street, a move intended to distract Cellini while her attacker pulls a weapon from his pocket. Cellini is quicker. He has already pulled out his trusty Browning and fires, from almost point-blank range, straight into the man's throat. Cellini fires a second shot, almost immediately, this time into the air. The sound of both shots echo through the street, but there is no scream from the victim. No cry of pain. He gurgles and bubbles of blood ooze from the corner of his mouth, joining the river that is beginning to flow from his neck. His knees start to bend and he teeters from side to side. Cellini catches his lifeless body as it starts to topple over and carefully lays it down silently in the road, taking care not to get any blood on his clothes. He helps the girl to her feet, and after making sure she is unhurt, hurries her away from the scene as doors start to open and neighbours peer out into the darkness. A block away from the dead man, he waves down a passing taxi, opens the back door and ushers the girl into the back seat, handing the driver a 1000 Lire note.

"Take my sister home safely," he says. She looks at him and mouths the words "Thank you".

He shakes his head. "For what?" he says. "Nothing happened here. Right? Nothing at all."

She smiles and the taxi pulls away. He will never see her again and that is for the best. By morning, it will be nothing but a bad dream.

Cellini turns around and pauses for a few seconds to think about what he should do next. He sees a police car at the corner of the block, runs over and flags it down. Two *carabinieri* officers get out of the car and he tells them he has just witnessed a shooting less than a block away. He points in the direction of the incident and leads them to the scene, where a few bystanders are beginning to gather.

"What happened here?" one of the officers enquires. The bystanders part silently to let them through. Cellini explains that he was putting his girlfriend in a taxi when he heard two shots and looked up in time to see a man in dark clothes running away from the scene.

"One look at him and I realised there was nothing I could do, so I came looking for a telephone to call the police. That's when I saw your car and flagged you down," he says.

One of the *carabinieri* takes a notebook and pencil from his pocket and listens to Cellini while the other talks briefly to the bystanders, but none were at the scene at the time. They congregated a few minutes after it was all over.

"It seems you are the only witness," the officer says to Cellini, suspicion creeping into his tone. The officer then reaches up to the breast pocket of Cellini's jacket; the same British Army battledress blouse he had been issued with the day he started working as a volunteer agent. The pocket is buttoned shut but bulging and the officer feels it from the outside. Inside Cellini carries loose extra cartridges for the Browning M23. The officer grins at him. He doesn't ask him what is in his pocket, nor does he attempt to search him, or he'd undoubtedly find the pistol as well. He also doesn't pursue the issue over the "man in dark clothes" whom Cellini saw "running away from the scene". Instead, he puts the notebook back in his pocket and waves Cellini away.

Free to go, Cellini races back to his grandmother's house, takes the cartridges out of his pocket and, without thinking, tosses them into the dying embers of the fireplace to get rid of the evidence. After a few minutes, the bullets start exploding, waking his sleeping grandmother, who comes out to see what all the noise is about. Cellini explains that he "accidentally" tossed some live rounds into the fire. She shakes her head, mutters to herself and tells him to get to bed. Cellini crawls into the only space left in the bed, head to toe beside her. He expects her to chide him for making so much noise, instead, she simply says, "Go to sleep, Ueli. And don't bend your knees or you'll tear the blanket."

47. The War is Over

On April 28th, 1945 Mussolini is summarily executed, together with his mistress Claretta Petacci, by Italian Partisans in the village of Giulino di Mezzegra in northern Italy (the exact circumstances of his death have been the subject of much debate and are outside the scope of this book). Their bodies are then taken to Milan, where they are beaten and shot repeatedly and finally hung upside down in the square at Piazzale Loreto for the public, sick and tired of five years of war, to view.

Two days later, Adolf Hitler commits suicide in a bunker in Berlin, and on May 8th, Germany officially surrenders. The war in Europe is over.

For many, the end of the war is a time of celebration, cutting loose and getting drunk, while for others there is still the agony of waiting to see if their loved ones will be among those returning home, either from the front lines or from prison camps.

*****

Cellini is still in Bari when the end of the war in Europe is announced, but receives eyewitness accounts of the public display of Mussolini's body from family and friends.[1] The news pleases him because it is one more step in answer to his plea in the field in Yugoslavia where he had watched the poor peasant woman obliterated in a dive-bombing attack.

Unbeknownst to Cellini, his younger brother Angelo had been captured by the British Army and is languishing in a prisoner-of-war camp in Foggia. The youngest Italian P.O.W. of the war, he had lied about his age in

[1] *Less well publicized are the stories Cellini hears about Italian fascist supporters who are forced to run the gauntlet between two bridges on the Viale Monza while Italian Partisans shoot at them with machine guns and rifles. Or the women suspected of sleeping with fascists who are dragged into the street, stripped naked and shaved of all their body hair then covered with red paint.*

order to enlist and served for a matter of weeks before the Italian Army capitulated in the south. Ironically, had Cellini known about his brother's capture sooner, he would have been able to secure his release almost immediately, such is the authority given him by the papers he carries. When Cellini eventually finds out about his brother's incarceration, through one of his friends in the OSS, he notifies his father in Milan, who immediately travels to Bari. Cellini and his father borrow a motorcycle from Uncle Angelo – a Gilera 500 with a specially modified sidecar for carrying black market flour – and ride to Foggia to secure young Angelo's release.

Cellini always helps his friends, usually by turning a blind eye to their endeavours. On one occasion he is able to come to the rescue of a friend who has been arrested by the local police for his black market dealings. Cellini walks into the police station, presents his papers and announces that their prisoner is wanted by the Military Police, and that the military tribunal takes precedence over the local prosecutor. Cellini handcuffs his friend and escorts him to the military base. He places him in a holding cell for two weeks, where he is well looked after and fed, all the while protected from the local law enforcement. He is never charged and after two weeks – the maximum time a prisoner can be detained without being charged – he is released.

*****

It seems like business as usual for the first few weeks after the war has ended. Though there will be no more Allied bombers flying out of Foggia and its satellite airfields to attack targets in northern Italy, there is still a huge black market and no shortage of crime on the streets.

As the weeks turn into months, Cellini finds that his work is slowing down. The Allies are slowly pulling troops out of Bari and little in the way of new supplies is arriving in the port. His work with the American Army is finished. The Office of Strategic Services has been officially terminated[2] and though the military police and intelligence services maintain a token presence in southern Italy, they have no further need of volunteers and are anxious to

2. *On September 20, 1945, President Truman signed an Executive Order terminating the OSS, effective October 1, 1945. The functions of the OSS were then divided between the State Department and the Department of War until January 1946, when the Central Intelligence Group (CIG) was created, later evolving into the Office of Special Operations (OSO). The National Security Act of 1947 established the Central Intelligence Agency (CIA), which resumed all the intelligence functions of the former OSS.*

distance themselves from those who participated in the so called "dirty work".

Cellini still hangs around with his old friends, and cannot resist getting into fights. He and his friend Vito Calabrese get into an argument and start fighting, and one of the gang suggests they make it "official" – maybe even run a book on who will win? Former southern Italy boxing champion Lorenzo Mirella, who lives locally and knows the friends, is recruited to referee the fight.

Less than a minute into the fight, Cellini delivers a punch that knocks Calabrese clean off his feet and keeps pummeling at Calabrese's head – even after he hits the floor. Mirella has to grab Cellini round the neck and pull him off the limp body of his friend.

"Jesus Christ, Ueli, you've nearly killed him!" the referee says.

After a few minutes, Calabrese recovers and the two once again become best friends – and agree never to fight again, no matter how much they disagree over anything!

Cellini decides it would be a good time to go back to Milan and find solace with Isabella.

48. Reunion in Milan

CELLINI FINDS MILAN quite different from when he last saw it. There is a lot of bomb damage, debris is strewn everywhere and the transportation system is in complete chaos. He finds his way to Isabella's apartment, but she is not at home. Her sister answers the door. She seems surprised to see him.

"Ueli, what are you doing here?" she says.

"It's a long story!" Cellini answers. "When do you expect Isabella to be home?"

He senses her sister is trying to tell him something, but is afraid to actually say it.

"What's going on?" he says.

"If I tell you, you've got to promise you won't get mad... either at me or Isabella, okay?"

"Just tell me," Cellini says, smiling to put her mind at ease. "Please."

"She's been seeing another man for about a couple of months now." She blurts it out, looking down at the floor as she says it, then back up at Cellini. "She... we ... had no idea when you'd be coming back... or even *if* you'd be coming back."

Cellini is hurt and when his feelings are bruised he can be volatile. People who know him know this about him. Isabella's sister doesn't know him very well. He wants to punch the wall, but he knows it would be futile. He isn't sure what to say but he can feel the anger rising within himself, until the girl totally disarms him by adding, "Don't worry. He's not anywhere near as good-looking as you are. In fact, he's actually quite ugly."

Cellini laughs nervously. Knowing that his girlfriend has been unfaithful with an ugly man doesn't make him feel any better – in fact it makes him feel worse – but the innocent way her sister delivers the message makes him realise that he would be wrong to show anger towards her. He smiles and leaves.

He makes his way back to the old apartment on *Viale Monza*

thinking he may look in on his father. It's not a reunion he's particularly looking forward to. His father had been very pro-fascist, at least in the early days of Mussolini's regime, and he wonders how he is going to react to the capitulation – and the fact that Cellini has been working with the Allies.

As he makes his way up to the apartment, he notices a young girl on the stairs. He recognizes her immediately, then doubts himself. *Surely it can't be?*

Carla Bernini, daughter of Signore Bernini, the tinplate toy magnate who owns the apartment building, had been no more a little girl when Cellini had left Milan to join the Army almost three years ago.

Was it really only three years ago? Now she has grown up into a beautiful young woman. She recognizes him instantly and her face lights up with a smile.

"Ueli Cellini? Is that really you? Have you come back to live with us?" she giggles.

"I might just do that!" he says, "How are your parents?"

"Oh, you know," she says, rolling her eyes. "Same as always. They came through the war just fine, but daddy is always complaining about something!"

They chat for a while, then Carla excuses herself to go to work.

"Are you staying in Milan long? We should get coffee or go for a walk or something."

As soon as she says it, she realises it could be taken the wrong way. She adds, "It would be fun to catch up and hear all about your adventures."

Before she leaves, she asks Cellini, "Have you been to see your father?"

"Not yet," he replies, "I didn't think he'd be too pleased to see me – out of my fascist uniform and dressed like the enemy." He points to the now well-worn British Army battledress he still wears.

"He's changed a lot since Nicky died and you left for the front lines," she says.

"Actually I came by to see if he was still living here," Cellini says.

"Yes, of course, but he's not here now. He'll be at work. He gets home around seven in the evening if you want to come by later."

"Okay, I'll come back then."

Cellini watches her leave.

"And maybe we could have that coffee?" he calls out after her, before heading down the street. He wonders what his father would make of him now; or if he'd even care about what he's been through this past couple of years.

*****

COFFEE AND AN evening walk through the streets of Precotto quickly turns into romance between Cellini, who is now 22 years-old, and 16 year-old Carla. Cellini is able to divide his time between Milan and Bari, transporting black market meat in one direction and flour in the other, or whatever commodity is most needed and available. He has a good thing going, transporting goods on behalf of Tonino from Bari to the north and making deliveries for his old friend Negretti in Milan. His uncle Angelo, who is well connected in both regions, has also established a successful enterprise, buying, selling and trading whatever goods are most needed. He and Pasquina had moved to Milan after the collapse of the south, and he is happy to use his nephew as a courier.

Cellini is reimbursed by all parties for his trouble, but the official safe passage "chit" given to him by the British Army gets him through most roadblocks, so the risk of getting caught is minimal. It also gives him access to fuel for his truck while others are still severely rationed.

His relationship with his father is still strained, though Francesco Cellini has mellowed slightly from losing a son to a war he recognized Italy could never hope to win after the first few months. They do not talk about Cellini's experiences and especially his time with the Yugoslavian Partisans. While his father accepts Italy's defeat to the American and British Allies, he still has no stomach for communism, and will never understand why his son chose to fight with them.

On one of his stops in Milan, Cellini runs into Isabella. After an uncomfortable few minutes they decide to sit down and talk things over. One thing leads to another and they finish up spending the night together. The following morning, Cellini wakes to find his wallet is missing, and with it his letter of safe passage from the British Army officer as well as his letter from Poldo, endorsed by Partisan headquarters on the island of Vis. He is annoyed by the loss of these documents because they have helped him to avoid getting caught transporting black market goods. In years to come, he will be far more aggrieved by the fact that they represent the only actual proof of his war record.

Instead of pursuing Isabella and demanding the return of his property, he decides he wants nothing further to do with her. Smitten with Carla, he feels guilt and regret at having spent the night with his former girlfriend and puts all thoughts of her out of his mind.

He vows he will never again be unfaithful to a woman.

*****

THE FAMILY HAS gathered together for a feast to celebrate the coming of peace. Most of the family has moved to Milan because there is very little in the way of job opportunities in Bari. There are people at the party Cellini hasn't seen in years and some he doesn't ever remember seeing before. Everyone wants to see the great *delinquente* and hear about his war stories. Vito doesn't feel much like talking about some of the horrors he has witnessed; he will keep much of that to himself for many years to come. He certainly isn't going to talk about his work with the OSS and the British SOE.

Ever comfortable in social situations and an expert at being the centre of attention, he is affable and charismatic and makes light of his adventures in the Italian Army and in Yugoslavia. He cleverly steers the conversation to food and how he has missed home cooking while he was away. Grateful to be able to enjoy simple meals of bread with tomatoes, pecorino cheese and mortadella instead of the steady diet of rotten figs, he shares stories of how he swapped his daily cigarette ration for grappa, which prompts his uncle Angelo to produce a fine bottle of *moscato* grappa. Pouring a shot each for Vito and himself, he offers the time-honoured *"salut!"* They touch glasses together and down their shots in one go.

Never one to beat about the bush, Angelo pulls Vito on one side, pours another shot and asks, "So how were the women?"

Cellini looks at him with a blank expression.

"The women in Yugoslavia. I have heard the women are beautiful. Especially the ones from Montenegro. Is it true that they will do anything to please a man?" Angelo winks at Cellini, who replies, "It is true that the women are beautiful. But I never touched a woman the whole time I was there. I saw men shot for even approaching the Partisan women."

Angelo looks at him with disbelief and disappointment.

"Come on Vito," he says, "We are both men of the world. Don't you trust me? You know you can tell me anything and your secret will be safe."

Cellini is starting to get irritated with his uncle. He loves and respects him, but he knows Angelo's reputation for chasing the ladies, and it is not something he shares. Not that Angelo is any different to any of the other men in the family, or most of the men he has met. It's just that he personally doesn't feel the need to bed every woman he meets and is uncomfortable discussing it.

"You need a woman!"

"I do not need a woman," Cellini responds curtly, thinking at once of Carla. "Especially not the type you seem to think I should want."

"What about a job then?" Angelo was nothing if not persistent.

"I already have a job, ferrying stuff back and forth for you between here and Bari," Cellini replies.

"I mean a steady job with lots of potential and big money."

"Doing what?"

"Vito, there's no shortage of women and girls out there who are willing to give men what they want… and there are plenty of customers, believe me. But girls need to be properly managed. And they have to be protected from customers who step over the line. You'd be perfect for the job, and I need someone I can rely on to help the business grow. I need a partner."

Cellini is horrified. "Oh no, not me, not that! I'm not going to become a pimp for you or anybody else!"

Angelo laughs hard and slaps Cellini on the back. "At least think about it."

Cellini shakes his head and starts to walk away.

"You know what, Ueli?" Angelo reverts to his *Barese* pet name as he takes his parting shot at Cellini. "There's only one woman in the world who's ever going to be good enough for you, and she's probably the only one who would have you as a husband. Your cousin Francesca."

*****

Cellini has a great deal of affection and respect for his Uncle Angelo. Loved and revered by his family and friends, Angelo is a larger-than-life character who can be wild and unpredictable but who also has a warm heart. He is afraid of nothing and no one and is always game for a challenge. He once rode his motorcycle around the so-called "wall of death" on a dare![1]

Attractive and charismatic, Angelo is something of a ladies' man. He enjoys the company of many women, who find his charm irresistible. A generous man, he is always glad to help his friends by introducing them to girlfriends who are willing to provide favours of all kinds, and has a reputation for being the go-to person for arranging illicit sexual encounters.

There is a story of one friend in particular whose peculiar fettish was that he enjoyed watching his own wife having sex with other men. This

[1]. *The wall of death was a circus sideshow attraction that involved riding a motorcycle on the inside of a cylindrical brick wall, relying on forward momentum to keep the motorcycle and rider parallel to the ground without falling. The rider would then work his way up to the top of the wall where spectators would lean over and cheer.*

friend encouraged Angelo to arrange clandestine sexual encounters for her so that he could take his voyeuristic pleasure. Angelo obliged by introducing the lady to a series of lovers, and while they engaged in illicit sex, the husband watched from an adjacent room through a keyhole. On one occasion, the husband burst into the room and started beating the woman – he was upset because she had moved "on top" and seemed to be enjoying the encounter too much! As far as the husband was concerned, the sexual activity was supposed to be solely for his pleasure and gratification, not hers!

After giving the poor woman a severe beating, he then turned on Angelo for facilitating the affair. Angelo in turn called upon his nephew for protection. In the end the situation was defused, but Angelo was careful not to pander to such strange desires in the future.

Angelo does however become so deeply involved with one of his girls that it begins causing a great deal of trouble and embarrassment for him. Her name is Maria. Seeing her as nothing more than a gold-digger, and foreseeing serious implications for his uncle if the relationship continues, Cellini offers to arrange for her permanent disappearance. Given the harsh times and the fact that, under the terms of his recent employment, Cellini has been granted a certain amount of latitude when it comes to administering justice, he feels such action is justified. Angelo however, is so besotted with Maria that he implores his nephew not to harm the girl, regardless of the consequences he now faces. He has made the mistake of falling in love with her, and even though he knows she will likely cause him to lose everything, he cannot bear to be without her and is willing to accept whatever is coming to him.[2]

*****

THE NEXT TIME Cellini sees Carla she seems on edge. She asks if they can go for a walk somewhere quiet, far away from the crowds. They make their way through a badly damaged neighbourhood where kids are playing in the rubble of derelict buildings and find a quiet bench in the corner of a deserted park. Taking a seat, she turns to Cellini with tears in her eyes and announces,

"I'm pregnant."

2. On his deathbed, Angelo begged his wife – Vito's beloved Aunt Pasquina – to bury him in his hometown of Bari. She laughed at him and said "I know exactly where I'm going to bury you!" When he died, she had him interred in the Cellini family mausoleum in Carbonara, a small village outside the city limits of Bari, in what was comically known to family members as The Cellini Condominium. Carbonara eventually became annexed by the city of Bari – so Angelo finally got his last wish granted!

Cellini is surprised, although not horrified. He is young and has fallen for Carla in a big way.

"I'll marry you." He says.

Carla smiles and wipes a tear away with her finger. "I knew you'd say that, but my parents would never allow it. Actually my mother likes you okay, but my father…"

"I don't care about your parents. We'll do it anyway!"

Carla's father is adamant that his daughter is not going to marry Cellini, and does his best to sequester her away from him. Cellini, in his inimitable fashion, has a plan. It's crazy but it might work. He goes directly to the cathedral, Duomo di Milano, and asks for an appointment with the Archbishop.

"Why do you wish to see his eminence?" he is asked by a junior clergyman, who Cellini presumes to be a priest.

"Please sir," Cellini says, "I need his permission to get married!"

The priest invites him to sit down and explain, which Cellini does in detail, leaving out the part about Carla being pregnant and the fact that her father is strongly opposed to the marriage. The priest seems sympathetic. Soft-spoken and with a kindly disposition, he points out that it is not really a matter for the Archbishop, but that he would be happy to help in any way he can, and agrees to bring it to the attention of the senior members of the church at the appropriate time. First, however, Cellini needs to answer a few questions and complete some formal papers. He will also need to provide proof of his residency in Milan as well as showing his birth certificate and other documents. Of course, he is unable to comply with any of these requests. For one thing, he is no longer a resident of Milan and for another all of his personal papers are still in Bari, where his father left them.

Finally, the priest asks him when the last time he attended confession. Cellini is floored. He has spent the better part of the last three years fighting fascism, then hunting down criminals, and now this guy wants him to hear his confession? *If I start right now, this poor baby will be starting school before I ever finish my confession,* he thinks to himself.

Cellini excuses himself and leaves. At least he tried.

He is unable to get in touch with Carla. When he tries to visit the Berninis at home, her father becomes abusive and threatening, and tells Cellini he is to forget about her, as she has already forgotten about him. He misses Carla, but he realises it is probably for the best. It would probably never work out. If only he could see her one more time just to let her know that he does care; that he is an honourable man, and that he really tried to do the right thing.

Frustrated, he returns to Bari. Without his safe conduct pass, he is wary of taking unnecessary risks, especially with the Allies beginning to pull out and the country still somewhat divided between those who had supported the fascists and the rapidly growing socialist influence. In any event, the thrill of trucking illicit goods from one end of the country to the other has begun to wear off. He decides to look for more stable work. Bari has little to offer, so he makes up his mind he will make the permanent move to Milan.

Who knows, maybe he will still get the chance to talk to Carla.

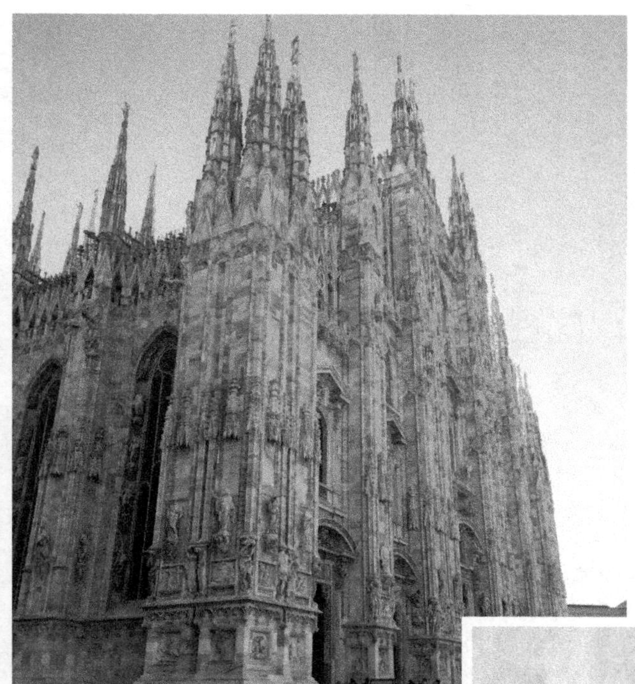

Duomo di Milano: Milan Cathedral, where Cellini petitioned to speak to the Archbishop for permission to marry Carla Bernini.

Cellini's handsome Uncle Angelo, who correctly predicted that the only woman in the world good enough for Vito would be his cousin Francesca.

49. Target Cellini

In Bari, he is enjoying an evening out with his friends. There is dancing and music in the street. The people of Bari are still celebrating the end of the war and things are slowly getting back to normal, even though the future doesn't look great for Cellini's friends. The black market is slowly drying up, not because of a shortage of customers, but because the number of ships coming into the Port of Bari is declining. Rivalry between dealers is intensifying, and violence between gangs is on the increase. Tonino is in jail – and even though he is able to conduct business from his cell, there are plenty of adversaries ready to challenge his position.

Cellini leaves the revelry to make his way home. He has enjoyed a few beers and a couple of shots of grappa, but they were spread out over the whole evening, during which he has also had his fill of pasta. He is not drunk. He knows that walking home under the influence of too much alcohol is an open invitation to every robber in the city. He passes shadowy figures in doorways. American soldiers groping their girlfriends; whores or *puttana* soliciting business; drunks sprawled on the floor or urinating against walls. Cellini hurries past and turns the corner.

Momentarily off his guard, he fails to notice that the man staggering out of an alleyway just a few yards ahead of him has something in his hand. By the time Cellini recognizes the .45 automatic it is raised and pointed straight at his chest.

Cellini knows that talking won't do any good, and this hoodlum doesn't look as though he's in the mood to negotiate anyway. It isn't a robbery, because the man with the gun hasn't demanded money or jewellery. He hasn't said a word. He seems calm and relaxed. Is it a hit? The absence of a silencer on the weapon suggests not, but it's always possible. Cellini's mind races. Could Carla Bernini's father have sent someone to Bari to hunt him down? Is it one of Tonino's rivals looking to eliminate his competition? He decides to play dumb and acts slightly drunk. He stares towards the man, not directly at his face but over his shoulder, as if straining to focus on some imaginary figure in the distance. At the same time he shuffles forward slightly, almost staggers, then checks his balance. As playacting goes, it's not an Oscar-winning performance, but it's enough to distract the gunman just long enough for Cellini to launch himself forward. He grabs the gun with his left hand, pushing it away at the same time.

The gun goes off and Cellini feels a searing pain through his hand, but he didn't take a shot to the body so he knows he's not hurt badly. He also knows he isn't safe yet. In spite of the burning in his hand, he maintains his tight grip on the pistol. He knows the next round is chambered and ready to fire. He follows through with his right fist into the gunman's gut, as hard as he can, to get him to release his hold on the pistol grip. The man doubles over, but his grip seems as firm as ever. Cellini brings his knee up into the man's face and follows it with a jab into his throat with the four fingers of his right hand, thrusting as hard as he can. He feels the gunman's body go limp until finally he releases his hold on the gun.

Pushing the lifeless body away, it falls crumpled to the ground. He has no idea if the man is alive or dead, but at this point in time he couldn't care less. He carefully pries the gun from his injured hand and surveys the damage under the dim light of a street lamp. The index finger is a red pulp and he thinks he may lose it. He wants to bend down and take a look at the man who did this, but the sound of the gunshot has drawn unwanted attention from others in the neighbourhood. He decides it would be best to depart from the scene. He pockets the .45 automatic, takes out his handkerchief and carefully wraps his left hand in it, then heads home.

He pours himself a large shot of grappa from a half-empty bottle he keeps hidden in the pantry before unwrapping the handkerchief from around his hand. It hurts like hell because the cotton has stuck to pieces of loose flesh that pull away when he unwraps it, and the trickle of blood turns into a rivulet that runs up his arm. The burning pain has faded slightly only to be replaced by an intense throbbing. His finger looks like raw meat, still dripping with blood. He looks for some gauze and, finding some in a drawer, he wraps his finger up as tightly as he can. By bandaging his index finger and binding it tightly to the next two fingers, he is able to staunch the blood. He finishes the bottle of grappa and falls into a restless sleep sitting in a chair, waking every time he hears a sound.

After getting the wound properly cleaned and dressed the following day, he starts making plans to get back to Milan. It will be a while before he is able to drive himself, so he spends a lot of time with his friends, drinking grappa to ease the pain. His family has already moved back to the north where the job market is much better as Italy starts the rebuilding process.

He also spends a lot of time thinking about his future. Now that the war is over, he wants more than anything else to return home to America. He has worked for the Allies and believes that his service with the OSS will help to strengthen his case. In spite of being forcibly recruited into the Italian Army, he never fired a shot in anger against the Allies and escaped from the fascist regime as quickly as he could.

His father, who would have all of his birth documentation, is in Milan, as are most of his immediate family members, so he needs to make his way back there.

He also finds himself thinking more and more about the words his uncle Angelo had spoken to him the last time they met: *There's only one woman in the world who's ever going to be good enough for you, and she's probably the only one who would have you as a husband. Your cousin Francesca.*

Franci is a beautiful girl and they have always been close, but he has never thought about her romantically, only as a friend. The more he thinks about his uncle's words, the more he realises he is falling in love with her. Perhaps he has always been in love with her. In either case he needs to do something about it.

But first he needs to make his way back to Milan, and if possible, make things right with Carla.

*****

THINGS ARE FAR from right with Carla. Cellini finds out that she has been sent away to stay with relatives during her pregnancy. Her mother seems to bear Cellini no ill-will, but her father is still seething.

Since the Cellinis still live in an apartment in the same building as the Bernini family, there is a lot of tension in the air and Francesco suggests that his son should consider moving out. Cellini is reluctant to do that since he doesn't yet have a job to support himself. He agrees to keep a low profile and to be careful when Bernini is at home. Carla's mother is sympathetic and appreciates his motives. She even takes care of dressing his wounded hand each day, and is able to bring him news on Carla and her condition.

He sees her father only once, and it is not a happy meeting. Bernini tells him that, if he wants to live, he should think about leaving Milan, or else be constantly looking over his shoulder. Bernini's parting words to Cellini are, "And if you ever try to speak to my daughter again, I will kill you myself."

Cellini is not easily intimidated and wouldn't think twice about eliminating the man if it weren't for Carla and the kindness shown to him by her mother.

He keeps out of Bernini's way and stays busy running errands for his old friend Negretti, who is still dealing in black market contraband, but after a few weeks he decides it's time to look for a legitimate job. His hand is not yet healed, but he feels he is able to operate machinery. Most of the old machine shops that were damaged or destroyed in the air raids have relocated or been rebuilt to keep pace with post-war industry, but Cellini is cagey about approaching any of the places he worked at before he was drafted. Instead, he finds employment at a company that builds X-ray machines, run by a man called Guglielmo Barzetti.

Barzetti is impressed with Cellini's work ethic and finds his new employee both inventive and motivated. He is also willing to help him in his goal of getting to America, though that dream is still a long way off. He senses that some of his co-workers are jealous of what they see as favouritism towards Cellini, especially those members of Italy's growing communist movement who cannot understand why he doesn't want to join their party, having fought with Tito's Partisans in Yugoslavia. He laughs them away, and for the most part he gets along with everyone. All the same, he is cautious about discussing his views about politics and the part he played in the war with anyone but his closest friends and family.

Cellini is happy to be back in Milan. The weather is cold and bleak, but it feels good to be surrounded by family once again.

That is until one particularly cold evening while he is walking along *Viale Monza* towards the apartment building. On evenings like this, most people are indoors unless they have to be somewhere. There are very few cars and no people about, only the occasional stray dog. He is passing the park on the corner of *Via Isocrate* when he sees a group of men in the distance, perhaps 50 or 60 metres ahead of him, fanning out across the road. Without any warning, they start firing pistols and sub-machine guns in the air and in his general direction. His instinctive reaction is to crouch down low to avoid getting hit, and to look around to see if their intended quarry is behind him. He looks around but sees nothing and no one. The mob starts moving towards him and lowers their weapons, firing directly at him now.

He is the target!

From his crouching position he launches himself across the road and runs as fast as he can into the park. There is a natural depression in the ground from an old bomb crater, and he hurls himself into it, rolling over and over until he reaches the lowest point, then scrambles to his feet and sprints across to the other side. Zigzagging through trees, he comes to a stone wall that will provide a barricade and possibly a vantage point for him to get a look at whoever these people are. He leaps at the wall, grabbing the top with his good hand and vaults over it, landing on the other side with a thud. He peers over the top of the wall but can see nothing in the darkness. He hopes he has lost his pursuers, but he can't be sure. The firing stops, but from a distance he can hear voices calling out, "Death to all fascists!"

He considers his options. He could try walking out with his hands raised to show he doesn't have a weapon and explain that he isn't a fascist. He laughs at the thought. He could shoot it out with them; he has a pistol in his pocket, but only one magazine. He doesn't really want to take on a small army in the street. Then it occurs to him that this could be a set-up. Could Bernini have sent a hit squad after him? How convenient if they could kill him and blame it on the communists. The voices are still a distance away but he is still not able to see anyone. He decides to stay where he is for a while to make sure. After five minutes or so, he feels safe enough to move slowly out from behind the wall and quietly goes back to his apartment.

Later, he learns that a meeting of the communists had got rowdy and that several members had walked through the street firing their weapons in the air. There were no reports of any injuries so the authorities hadn't pursued it further.

Cellini would always wonder if they were communists from his workplace or assassins hired by Carla's father.[1] He has escaped with his life once again, and will be on his guard from now on.

More than ever, he wants to go home to America.

*****

CELLINI VISITS THE American Consulate in Genoa to find out what he needs to do to secure his passage back to America. He is told all he needs is a birth certificate and a passport. That could be a problem because his birth certificate cannot be found, and without it he cannot obtain a passport.

"No matter," the official at the consulate tells him, "because you can always travel with an Italian passport and enter the United States as an immigrant."

"However," he continues, "there is one more thing you need to be

[1.] *Cellini later found out that Carla's mother and older sister had been among those women who were publicly disgraced for collaborating with the fascists, being stripped, shaved and painted red following the end of hostilities. Although Carla's mother had shown him compassion, this undoubtedly contributed to her father's animosity towards Cellini, who had fought on the opposite side.*

aware of."

Cellini listens intently.

"I notice your hand is bandaged. Do you have an injury of some kind?" the official asks him.

"Yes sir, I was wounded in the course of my duty while serving with the OSS in Bari," Cellini replies, bending the truth in order to emphasize his service and loyalty to the United States.

The official, however, is not impressed. "That could be a problem," he says. "The United States is currently not accepting anyone with an open or unhealed wound."

"Even though I received my wound in the service of my country?" Cellini is both incredulous and visibly upset.

"I'm sorry, Mr. Cellini," the official replies. "But I'm sure your wound will soon heal, and then it will be no problem at all. Perhaps in the meantime you will also be able to locate your birth certificate?"

Disappointed and frustrated, Cellini returns home. The index finger on his left hand had been so badly injured by the bullet being fired at point-blank range that it will take almost two years to heal completely. Two years of looking over his shoulder for the Berninis, and the communists, and trying to locate his documentation. But two years also of building great relationships. He earns the trust and confidence of his employer, who offers to pay the $150 for Cellini's one-way ticket to New York – handing it over in single dollar bills which he has been saving since the war.

On his frequent trips home to Bari, he also gets to know his cousin, Francesca, much better. She lives in Palo del Colle, a small town just outside of Bari. They go to the cinema, enjoy concerts together and spend hours just talking. Cellini feels completely comfortable telling her his war stories and soon they discover that they have a great deal in common, including the same dream of leaving Italy and returning to the United States, the land where both of them had been born. They talk about all the things they will do when they get there, even though they were very young when they left Brooklyn and have little memory of it.

While in Bari, Cellini continues to try and locate his birth documents. He is unsuccessful, but through an old contact from his days in the OSS who is still stationed in the old port town, he does manage to obtain an Italian passport. He shares his good news with his cousin and books his passage from Genoa to New York.

Though his Italian passport is a forgery, it will suffice to get him on board the SS *Saturnia* leaving Genoa on February 8th, 1948.

It is not until Franci joins him on board the ship in Naples on February 11th that Cellini makes yet another startling discovery about his cousin. She has had a crush on him ever since childhood.

Part III

New York, 1948

50. Hard Times and Marriage

THE FIRST WEEKS in New York are hard. Living with distant relatives who don't know you very well but who feel obliged to offer shelter is never an ideal situation. Throw in the fact that you're Italian and you arrive in Brooklyn with a reputation among the family for being a *delinquente*, and you are not in for a smooth ride.

From the time the ship sailed out of Genoa to the time Cellini finally regains his freedom, several weeks have passed, and Francesca's father has managed to send word to Franco, who is not only Cellini's great uncle but also a second cousin of Franci's father. He has written a letter expressing his hatred and contempt for Cellini as well as the very serious allegation that Cellini has kidnapped his daughter and that he intends to bring charges against him.

Franci was always loyal and faithful to Cellini – "Ueli", she always calls him. She is able to convince Franco that she has not been kidnapped by Cellini and that she came because she wanted to be with him and be back in New York. Although Franci's father's attempts to bring legal charges against Cellini amount to nothing, and Franci is obviously not being held against her will, there is still a great deal of tension in the Brooklyn household. Franco is drinking heavily and his wife seems to be spending more and more time away from the home. Cellini is very uncomfortable.[1]

The couple decides to look for a place to rent as soon as they are able.

[1] *Cellini's Great Uncle Franco was held in much contempt by the family for his drinking problems, but his alcoholism may have been in large part attributable to his suspicion of his wife's infidelity. She certainly spent an inordinate amount of time out of the house, but no one was ever sure whether she left because of his drinking, or he drank because of her suspected waywardness. One thing is known for sure. Several years later, after their children were grown up, the two of them moved back to Bari, and 28 days later, Angelina died quite suddenly. In front of family members, Franco spat on the face of the dead woman as she lay in her open casket.*

*****

A LOT HAS HAPPENED in the city since they were last here. For one thing, the landscape has changed dramatically. New York is now the city of skyscrapers, with the Chrysler and Empire State Buildings dominating the Manhattan skyline. The neighbourhoods have changed too, especially since the Wall Street Crash and Great Depression of 1929, and World War Two. Small businesses have begun thriving once again, and Franci is the first to find work, stuffing pimentos into green olives at a nearby factory.

Cellini, who was regarded as a master mechanic and skilled machine operator in Milan, is frustrated in his attempts to find what he considers worthy employment. His skill and experience as an auto mechanic seems to count for nothing in New York and he can find no one who will take a chance on him, so he takes a job in a canning factory loading cans into boxes. He hates the work but needs the money.

He is finding the living arrangements more and more difficult to tolerate, and the relationship with his great uncle is under a lot of strain. He is embarrassed by his lack of clean clothes and is fearful of what others might think of him. He has not experienced such conditions since the war, and had always believed that when he came back to America those days would be behind him for good. He is especially worried about unpleasant body odours in public, despite bathing as often as he can and having Franci carefully rinse out his underwear each night. He simply cannot understand how his family can be so oblivious to his predicament and will not even offer him an old, used pair of socks.

Too proud to ask them for help, he decides that he will move out, even if he has to live on the street, and tells Francesca of his intentions. Without hesitation, she looks him straight in the eye and tells him, "If you go, I am coming with you."

It is Franci who brings home the first wage packet from the olive factory. She uses it to buy Cellini clean socks and underwear – luxuries he has not known since setting foot on the boat in Genoa.

It is becoming increasingly obvious to both of them that their companionship is beginning to blossom into something much more than *amore platonico*. Although they would never be the kind of couple that will hold hands in public, nor trade words of deep affection, even in private, they do share a keen sense of belonging together. More importantly, they seem to have an intrinsic understanding that their affection is real, meaningful and enduring, even though it somehow doesn't require words.

Though they are happy to be together, they miss Italy and wonder if they will ever feel as though they really belong in America. There are days when they yearn to be able to get on a ship and go back, but they have no idea how, since neither of them can afford the fare.[2] There are also good times and days full of hope. They decide to make the best of their situation and keep their dreams in sight.

He quits his job at the canning factory and is able to secure employment as an automobile mechanic making $29 a week, so they start looking for a new place to live straight away, and find a kindly landlady in the Bronx who offers them two rooms, plus meals, for fifteen dollars a week each.

Things are beginning to look up for the couple, but they still have to be very careful with the spending. In a very bold move, Cellini approaches the landlady one day and says, “We pay you $15 each for two rooms, yes?”

“That’s right,” she replies.

“$30 total for both of us?”

“Yes.”

“How much for just one room with two people?”

“$15 dollars.”

Cellini goes to Franci and says,

“Franci, get your things together. You are moving into my room!”

Without a second thought, Francesca packs up her few belongings and moves in with Cellini.

His thoughts turn to the idea of marriage.

*****

CELLINI HAS NEVER been a churchgoer and has no religious faith or conviction. That may perhaps be partly as a result of losing his mother, traditionally the nurturer and source of religious inspiration in Italian families, at such a young age. It may also be attributable to the abject cruelty and “man’s inhumanity to man”, that he had witnessed during the war. He accepts, or at least tolerates, the religious beliefs of others, and many of his close friends and family members are devout in their faith, but he has little patience for what he considers the hypocrisy of religion.

He frequently finds himself in arguments with religious practitioners and followers, notably on the SS *Saturnia* as it had sailed across the Atlantic and into New York! [3]

For now however, Cellini decides he must put aside his personal

2. *Cellini would find out, many years later, that had he gone to the Italian Consulate and told them of his plight, a passage back to Italy could have been arranged. Today he is thankful that he had no knowledge of this at the time!*

feelings in deference to Franci, who is a devout Roman Catholic, and he goes in search of a priest to perform a marriage ceremony for them.

He has no recollection of formally proposing to Francesca, and most certainly didn't ask her father for permission, because even if he were in New York (he is still over 5,000 miles away in Italy), he knows full well that Nicola Liantonio would have him shot before he would grant permission. It seems that, once again, each has a clear yet unstated understanding of what the other wants. And that includes wanting to be together.

*****

THE FIRST CATHOLIC priest he approaches is uncompromising in his questioning. Cellini is not a member of his parish, does not attend church regularly and has not been to confession in some considerable time (never, in fact!).

Has he been baptized? *Yes.*

Has he been confirmed and attended Communion? *No.*

The priest shakes his head. In any event, since he and Francesca are cousins, special permission must be obtained from the Pope, and this will cost an extra $360. If and when the Vatican consents to the wedding, a simple ceremony might be performed, but the cost of the wedding will be in the hundreds of dollars.

He visits another church and meets with the priest who tells him the same story. Cellini has the distinct feeling that absolution and permission to marry may come with a price tag way beyond his means. He would be willing to pay it for Franci's sake, but cannot think of a way to raise the money.

Finally, he meets Father Nicola Stradico, a straight-talking New York Italian-American with whom he feels strangely at ease. Cellini tells him what he was told by the other two priests.

"I suppose you will tell me the same thing," he says. "Well I don't care because I am going to sleep with my Franci tonight whether I have the blessing of the church or not."

Vito and Father Nicola get along well and enjoy many discussions. He feels he can trust Father Nicola and shares his personal beliefs with the

[3] *Cellini had argued that while he fully accepted the historical value of the Bible and the teachings of Jesus Christ, he could not accept the notion of the virgin birth and other stories he considered too fantastic to believe. He was not afraid to express his opinions publicly, and when he did so in the presence of a Roman Catholic priest it resulted in a brush with the authorities on the ship. Curiously, the priest later told him, in private, that his arguments were very sound, but that it was inappropriate to make such statements in public. Certainly in 1948, such beliefs were considered heresy in the Roman Catholic Church.*

priest, and, to his surprise, the priest is sympathetic and understanding. Even so, Cellini has no compunction about pushing every situation as far as he can and possesses a unique ability to strike a raw nerve. One point that has concerned Cellini for some time is the fact that Catholic priests are not allowed to marry.

"You must have urges," says Vito. "Yet the law of your church strictly forbids you to marry. What do you do when you – you know – feel certain needs? How do you deal with that?" If the priest is offended or shocked by the question, he gives no indication. Instead he pauses and smiles. Vito detects a glint in his eye.

"The laws of my church prohibit me from marriage," he responds. "But I have found no laws that say I cannot go to a woman in time of need."

For once in his life, Cellini is almost speechless. Almost. Full of admiration for the priest, he opens his mouth to speak but Father Nicola continues before he is able to form any words.

"My son," he says, "You have been candid and honest with me and I have been candid and honest with you. You have challenged me in ways no one else has ever done, and for that I am both grateful and humbled."

"I will perform your marriage service, but there are two conditions."

"First, it must take place on a day when there are no other wedding ceremonies."

Cellini agrees to accept whatever wedding date the priest decides.

"Second," the priest adds, "When your children are born, I want you to promise me that you will raise them to be good Catholics."

Cellini replies, "Father Nicola, I cannot do that, partly for the reasons I have already given to you, but mostly because it is the tradition in the part of Italy where I come from that the woman is responsible for raising children, and for teaching them in the ways of the world, choosing their school and sending them to church. My wife is a devout Catholic and I am sure she will do as you ask, but that is something I cannot promise for myself."

Father Nicola accepts Vito's explanation and the wedding date is set for April 17th. It will be Easter Sunday, a day when, by tradition, no weddings usually take place.

Vito and Franci are delighted that things have turned out so well, but now they have very little time to prepare. They are still very short of money and begin to worry about how they will pay for the service.

*****

The afternoon of April 17th arrives, and the couple enters the church expecting to be ushered into a quiet corner for a very simple, no frills ceremony. Instead, the high altar in the church is beautifully decorated with flowers and organ music is playing softly in the background. There are just seventeen people, including the bride and groom. The invited guests are *paesans* from Palo del Colle, Franci's hometown, just slightly inland from Bari, who have now settled in their New York neighbourhood. A few members of the regular congregation with nothing better to do have come to watch the festivities; probably curious to find out who could possibly be getting married on this Holiest of church holidays.

During the ceremony, two sopranos sing a beautiful rendition of *Ave Maria*. The flowers, organ music and singers are all additional expenses that Cellini was not expecting and knows he cannot afford.

After the ceremony, Father Nicola greets the couple with a smile, but seeing the worried expression on Cellini's face asks him if something is troubling him. Cellini looks furtively around to make sure none of the guest are listening before speaking.

"Father Nicola," he says, "I cannot possibly afford these extras. I am not a wealthy man and —."

Before he can finish the sentence, the priest places a hand on his shoulder and smiles.

"Vito, you are an honest man. You have spoken to me with candor and trusted me with your most private feelings, and you have done so outside of the confessional booth. You have given me a great deal to think about. You have made me feel comfortable sharing my own thoughts with you; something most people never think about. Such honesty and integrity are rare. Do not misunderstand me – I do not necessarily agree with all that you say, but I sincerely respect you for saying it."

"Please accept the flowers, the music and the service as my wedding gift to you and Francesca."

Though Cellini will never again enter his church, nor any other for that matter, he will never forget the kindness of Father Nicola Stradico.

After the wedding, the bride, groom and their guests go the basement home of the best man for the reception and dinner. He is an older gentleman from Palo del Colle who Cellini knows only as Don Carrione. Vito has no bow tie, so the ladies fashion one for him from a table napkin. The couple and their guests enjoy a feast of Italian food and fine wine before dancing into the small hours.

The first night of what will become 64 happy and exhilarating years of marriage has begun.

*****

At around the time they move into the same room together, the couple is befriended by a Jewish shopkeeper in the Bronx who offers clothing, furniture and other household items on a payment plan of as little as $1 per week. Their dining table consists of three upturned milk crates, but Cellini has enough socks and underwear to change every day, and he feels like a rich man.

Vito and Franci are not rich by any means, but they are happy. Her job as a seamstress is secure and reasonably well paid, and he is settling down well into a new job. They move to a small apartment of their own on Webster Avenue, between East 173rd and 174th Streets, close to the where construction of the Cross Bronx Expressway is about to begin. Unbeknownst to Cellini, Francesca, who has a gift for money management and financial planning – as well as a keen eye for a bargain – is able to pay up their credit with the Jewish store owner, who lets them take anything they need for their new home.

They work hard, and on their days off take walks in the park, buy hot dogs for 10¢ each and talk about all their hopes and dreams. No matter how tough it gets, they have each other, and they have a simple belief. They didn't come to America to get rich. They came to America to be free. But that doesn't mean they don't miss some of the good times they had back in Italy; the abundance of fresh fish, for one thing. Cellini had learned to fish with his grandfather on the Adriatic coast as a young boy, and since arriving in New York he has not had a chance to do it.

Through someone at his job Cellini hears that the fishing is great at Spuyten Duyvil Creek, a short waterway connecting the Hudson and Harlem Rivers, where sheepshead, striped bass and eels are in plentiful supply, especially in the marshy central section. The problem is that the only way of getting to that section of the creek without a boat involves crossing private land – land that belongs to New York's Columbia University.

That would deter most people, but Cellini is not most people. After all, he used to break into institutions of higher learning back in Bari to steal weapons. Sneaking into an American university to steal fish ought to be child's play to someone with his background. And so it is.

Carrying a fishing line made of string – because he can't afford the wood to make a pole – with a bent nail for a hook and a pocketful of stale bread for bait, Cellini waits until dark and scales the fence of the university.

The information about abundant fish turns out to be an understatement. In no time at all, Cellini has more than enough fish for a good supper. He stuffs them into a canvas satchel before escaping back over the fence of the university. Franci is waiting across the street, where she has been keeping a watchful eye for anyone loitering or watching them, but they are undisturbed and the fishing expedition is a complete success. Returning to their home on Webster Avenue, she cleans and cooks the fish and they agree to do it again the following week, once they both finish work.

At this time, Cellini is working as a lathe operator at Mazzei Brothers Machine Shop in the Bronx. The Mazzei brothers had originally come from Florence and got very rich, very quickly, by buying surplus nuts and bolts from the United States government, stamping their own name on each piece and then selling them back to the US government at a very respectable profit. The scheme worked until the government had no more surplus nuts and bolts to sell, so the brothers invested their wealth in a machine shop, buying every kind of machine they could lay their hands on and then hiring people to operate them.

One of their advertisements – for a lathe operator with at least 15 years experience – catches the eye of Vito Cellini, who is looking to improve his position. He may not have 15 years of experience, but he knows how to run a lathe and applies for the job anyway.

"Do you have 15 years experience as a lathe operator?" One of the brothers asks, eying the young Cellini sceptically.

Cellini's reply is obtuse but polite. "Sir, do I look old enough to have 15 years experience as a lathe operator?"

"You do not. I am sorry but we require a minimum of 15 years experience for this job."

Cellini is quick with his response. "I know how to operate a lathe and I can do the job. However, if you require someone with 15 years experience then you must be planning to hire an imbecile…" he says.

Before the brothers can utter another word Cellini continues, "because only an imbecile with no ambition to progress would be content doing the same lousy job after 15 years."

The brothers hire Cellini on the spot.

*****

Cellini takes the trolley car to work each day. It's a short ride and sometimes he pays the fare but mostly he is able to avoid the conductor and ride free. However, the work is piling up and the Mazzei brothers ask him if he could work Saturdays – or at least Saturday mornings – to help keep up with the backlog of orders.

Cellini is willing to put in the extra hours but tells them he has a problem with getting to the machine shop on Saturdays, because the trolley car runs on a different schedule. Without hesitation, one of the brothers comes up with a solution.

"You need a car? he says.

Cellini laughs. "Fat chance of buying a car on what I make here! No offence, but I'd need to rob a bank to be able to afford a car!"

"What if we bought a car for you, and you pay us back out of your wages at say, $5 a week? Could you afford that?"

Cellini thinks about the offer.

"Maybe. If you give me a raise of $5 a week as well as the overtime for working on Saturdays." He knows he is pushing his luck.

"Deal!" The brothers are all in accord and shake Cellini's hand, much to his surprise.

Nothing more is said about it until the following Friday when one of the brothers approaches him.

"Hey, Cellini," he says, "don't forget to come back to work tomorrow. We have a long list of stuff you need to do."

Cellini is about to reply when the man from Florence tosses him a set of keys.

"Outside on the street. The black Pontiac. Go take it round the block."

Cellini steps outside. He's looking for an old run down, beaten up and dented vehicle, but the only Pontiac he can find is a beautiful, sleek 1946 Torpedo with speed-lined fenders and a huge radiator grille that seems to be grinning at him. He gets in, starts it up and takes it for a drive up Park Avenue. The car absolutely purrs. It's in perfect condition, looks almost brand new. Best of all, the car has a radio fitted – a rare luxury – and Cellini tunes it to a station that plays his favourite Italian music. His smile matches the grille on the front of the car as he pulls back over to the side of the street outside the machine shop and steps out of the vehicle a few minutes later.

He walks back inside.

"Five bucks a week?" he says.

The three brothers nod. "Five bucks a week."

"I'll take it!" Cellini says.[3]

3. *Cellini would keep the car until 1954 when he left New York and drove to California looking for more challenging work. He traded the Pontiac Torpedo for a Dodge station wagon. In all that time, the Mazzei brothers never deducted a single payment from his wages to pay for the car, nor did they ask for it to be returned when he left the job.*

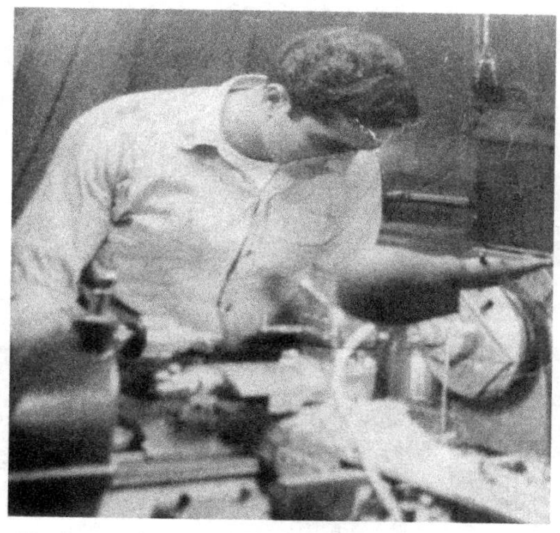

Hard at work at Mazzei Brothers Machine Shop in the Bronx.

Portrait of Cellini as a young man in 1948, around the time he came back to America.

The Cellini's wedding day, April 17, 1948 – Easter Sunday. Vito couldn't afford a bow tie so Franci made one for him out of a table napkin.

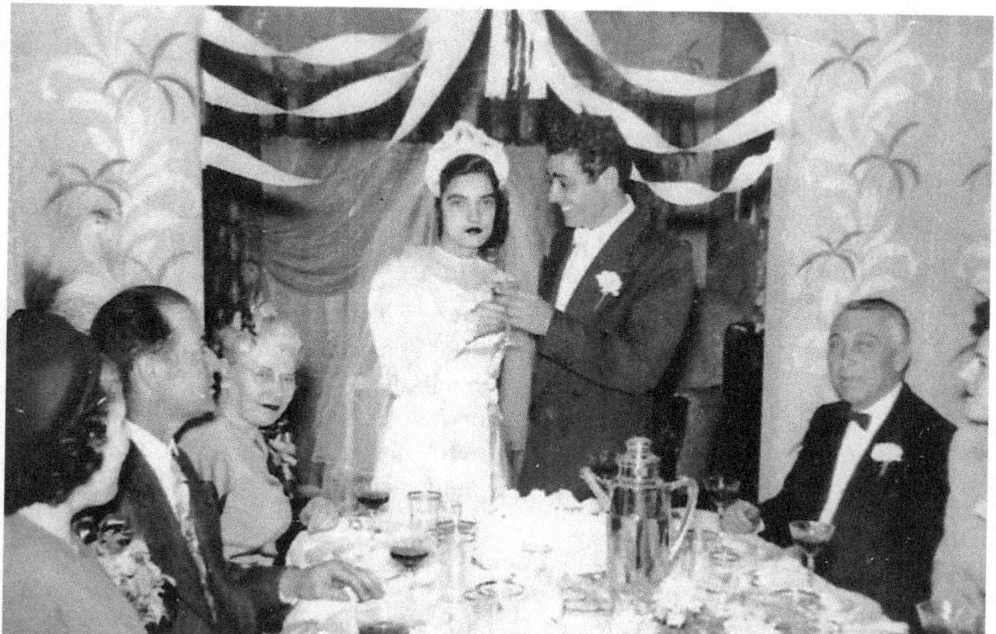

51. Rejected by the Army… Again

On June 25th 1950, 75,000 soldiers of the army of the Democratic People's Republic of Korea (North Korea) – supported by China and to a lesser extent the Soviet Union – crossed the 38th parallel and invaded the Republic of Korea (South Korea). The United Nations responded almost immediately by voting to send troops, led by US military forces, to support the South Korean army in defence of their sovereign territory. For two months, the UN forces struggled to gain a foothold and it looked as though the war would end in defeat for the South, but the US continued sending reinforcements to stem the tide. Over the next three years, the resulting series of bloody battles and skirmishes would change the geopolitical landscape almost daily and cost over five million lives. It was the first military action of the Cold War.

*****

WITHIN DAYS OF reading about the invasion, Cellini, anxious as ever to prove his loyalty to the country of his birth, volunteers for military service hoping he will be sent to the front lines.

At the recruiting office he is given a written aptitude test, which he passes. He is sent to report for a medical examination and further evaluation. After the medical he is handed a sheaf of papers clearly stamped "4F" – meaning he has been declared unfit to fight.

He is as puzzled as he is disappointed and looks for an explanation. He plans to appeal the decision. Eventually, he is able to find someone willing to give him the time of day, a young lieutenant with medical collar badges on his uniform.

"Excuse me sir," Cellini asks, "could you please explain to me how come I have been turned down for military service?" The helpful medic looks over his papers.

After a few minutes he says, "It says here that your command of the English language is not good enough for you to be accepted into the Army."

"As you can see sir, I may have something of an accent, but I can speak and understand English pretty good." Almost as an afterthought, he adds, "And if my English is so bad, how come I was able to pass the written test earlier?"

"That's a good question!" the young lieutenant says cheerfully. "Let me see what I can do."

An appointment is made for Cellini to undergo an interview, which will include a psychological evaluation, for a possible position helping to educate veterans at the Brooklyn Shipyard. He has no idea what this might be but decides to go along for the hell of it.

The interview turns out to be more of an interrogation. He is once again asked about his wartime record with the Partisans and quizzed on his relationship with the communists. After the gruelling series of questions, the interviewer sits back in his chair and says, "Mr. Cellini, you have the cleverest brain I have ever encountered."

"I have no hesitation in recommending you for this job. It doesn't pay much, but you'll be contributing greatly to the war effort."

Cellini laughs out loud.

"How much do you get paid?" he says.

"$20,000 per year, not that it's any of your business."

Cellini takes a moment to think before he retorts, "Well if I have the cleverest brain you have ever seen, I should get at least the same as you!"

He leans forward, looks the interviewer right in the eye and says, "Perhaps they should give me your job!"

*****

His ambition of serving in the US military shattered once again, Cellini goes home. It is the first time he senses that the shadow of his past – through no fault of his own – is perhaps still hovering over him. He loves his country as much as he loves life itself, but he is starting to dislike the bureaucracy and the small-minded people who are running it.

It will become a recurring theme over the next 50 years.

52. Passport Renewed. A Job in Venezuela

AFTER A SERIES of low-paying jobs and small contracts to design and build gadgets that others would profit from, Cellini decides it's time to look for a decent job.

Reading the local Italian newspaper one day, he comes across an advertisement for a job as a Terrazzo tile specialist at the American Bridge Co. Brash and brimming with self-confidence, Cellini decides that is the job for him. He has helped his uncles with tile work and feels sure he can talk his way into the position.

Marching into the offices of the American Bridge Co. he awaits his turn for an interview. He is expecting to be asked all sorts of questions about his background and past experience, but instead he is given a problem to solve; how would he raise a block of marble from the ground floor to the top of a building. Such questions are the domain of engineers, but Cellini, who has no formal training as an engineer, applies simple mathematics and answers confidently. He has no idea if his answer makes sense or not, but it seems to convince the panel asking the question. He is told the job is his and asked if he can start that very day.

"Do you have a passport?" one of the interviewers asks.

"It has expired," Cellini replies.

"No matter, we can take care of that right now."

"Why do I need a passport?" Cellini says.

"You answered our advertisement for a Terrazzo tile specialist, right?" the interviewer says. "Well the job is in Caracas, Venezuela. Did you not know that?"

"Of course!" Cellini replies, "I just hadn't realised it was so immediate!"

"Is that a problem, Mr. Cellini?"

"Not at all! I'm ready to go straight away." He clears his throat and then asks, "Excuse me sir, may I ask how long I will be in Venezuela?"

The interviewer shuffles papers and turns to his colleague, and for several seconds they stare at each other, blank faced. The third person in the room, a pretty secretary, comes to their rescue.

"The contract is for two months, sir," she says.

Cellini wonders how Franci will take the news, but he is sure the additional money will more than make up for the inconvenience of not having him around! He has family in Venezuela – a cousin on his mother's side – and it will be fun to look her up after all these years.

He is handed a sheet of paper with the address of a passport agency and a list of required documentation. He is told to go home, gather up the paperwork and go to the agency, where they will take care of arranging his passport.

He is astonished at the speed with which his passport is provided – especially considering how difficult it was to get his documentation sorted out when he first came to America, just a few years earlier. It is Cellini's first exposure to the power wielded by big business in America.[1] He goes home to have dinner with Franci and packs a suitcase. The following day he will leave for Caracas.

*****

VENEZUELA REMINDS Cellini of some of his darker days in Bari when he had been working for the OSS.

By day, his work as a tile specialist is satisfying, but he has a lot of time on his hands and frequents clubs and bars with his co-workers where pretty women are drawn to him like a magnet. Though he never touches any of the women, he is flattered by their attention and enjoys their company – even so, there is a price to pay. As in many Latin countries, Cellini discovers that along with the pretty women come the pimps and the drug-dealers. He finds himself once again in that salacious netherworld where he could easily get himself into serious trouble.

There is one dope dealer in particular for whom Cellini develops a very strong dislike. Whether it's his pungent aftershave lotion, his long greasy hair or just the fact that he cannot seem to take "no" for an answer – either from Cellini or the girls – he is not sure, but he senses that before too long, he and this man are going to have a major disagreement.

1. *The American Bridge Co. was founded in 1900 as the result of a merger of 28 independent steel companies and went on to create some of the most amazing building projects in the world, including the iconic Empire State Building and Chrysler Building in New York City. The merger was engineered by financier J. P. Morgan.*

It happens one night as Cellini is leaving a restaurant. He has promised to drive one of the girls home, and this dealer, a weasel-like man called Pepe, is hounding him, claiming to be her pimp and demanding payment, up front, for her services. Cellini explains that he is not doing anything with the girl except driving her back to her apartment. Pepe wants his money just the same, so Cellini invites him to ride along, explaining that he'll have to go to his own apartment to pick up the cash.

"Maybe we can have a party," Pepe says, sneering first at Cellini and then at the girl, who shudders visibly. Even if she is a prostitute – and Cellini isn't convinced she is a willing participant – this guy is a real creep.

Pepe makes sure he shows Cellini the gun inside his coat before climbing into the back seat of the car. They drive to the girl's apartment and Cellini indicates for her to get out of the car. Pepe is not happy and lets Cellini know this was not part of his plan, but Cellini plays dumb and tells him he will go to his apartment next to get his money. They can come back later. He invites Pepe to move to the front passenger seat of the car.

Cellini chats with Pepe as he drives. He asks him to explain what exactly he does. Does he sell dope or is he a pimp? Pepe brags that he does both.

"Who do you work for?" Cellini asks.

"I work for myself," Pepe replies, proudly.

"But you must have someone higher up the food chain that you answer to? For example, who supplies you with the dope you peddle?"

"Why, you want to cut me out? Pepe says, "That ain't going to happen, señor." Pepe has to work hard to sound tough and arrogant, and Cellini has had just about as much of him as he can take.

"No, Pepe," he says, smiling. "I don't want to cut you out. I don't want your dope or your goddamn hookers, but I have to tell you, I really would like to get my hands on the summonabitch who sells you that after-shave lotion."

Pepe stares at Cellini. He isn't sure if he's serious or not. Cellini starts laughing, and soon Pepe is laughing along with him. They trade a few more insults, laughing louder and harder until Cellini, exaggerating his hysteria, feigns having to pull over to the side of the road. As he does so, still laughing, he grabs the Venezuelan by the throat with his right hand, pinning him to the car seat. Reaching into his jacket with his left hand he pulls the pistol out of its holster and presses the muzzle into Pepe's cheek.

The laughter stops and the silence is deafening. "Don't ever show me a gun unless you plan to use it," Cellini says though clenched teeth. "Now get out of the car."

*****

No one misses Pepe because no one ever finds any trace of him to remind them of who he once was.

No one except Cellini, who has to sacrifice a favourite jacket and shirt. The blood stains come out easily enough, but he finds he cannot get rid of the smell of Pepe's stale aftershave.

The problem with dope dealers and pimps, Cellini discovers, is that when one falls – and eventually they all fall, it is just a matter of time – there are always two or three more ready to step in and take their place. Business as usual resumes in the clubs and bars of Caracas.

Cellini fulfils his contract with the American Bridge Co. and returns home to New York.

53. A Long Round Trip. California, 1954

CELLINI DECIDES, on a whim, that it's time to leave New York and head out west to California. He's tired of the kind of jobs he's been offered since getting back from Venezuela and knows he can do better. Franci has reservations; with a young family,[1] a move across country is going to be quite demanding. As always she keeps her thoughts to herself and recognizes it's something her husband has to do. He is not entirely oblivious to her concerns and promises that if he can find work within a week, he will send for her. If he is unable to secure work, he will come home and they will settle down permanently in New York.

Cellini has been enamoured of flight since he was a small boy. Watching hordes of B-24 bombers in the skies over Yugoslavia in 1943 had ignited his passion for military aviation. Now, more than ever before, he is convinced that his future lies in helping to develop jet and rocket engines for manned flight, and he decides that the North American Aviation company – the largest name in aviation he can think of and famous for developing the P-51 Mustang figher in World War Two – should be his next workplace. He trades in the 1948 Pontiac for a station wagon, and sets off on the long drive across country. Arriving at the North American Aviation plant in Downey, a suburb of Los Angeles, California, he is confident he will be able to convince the company to hire him.

It is one of very few failures in his life. There are no openings at North American Aviation, despite stories he had heard while living on the East Coast. Worse, they are only employing people with college degrees

[1] *Soon after establishing a home in New York, the Cellinis had started a family, but the responsibility of raising them fell squarely upon Franci's shoulders, and Vito participated little in their upbringing. It was his belief that the mother figure was the sole nurturer and that the role of the father was to be the provider. His long hours at work and frequent travelling precluded him spending any kind of quality time with his children when they were very young, a circumstance about which he has expressed some regrets in later life.*

or years of experience. For once, the Cellini charm fails to gain him any ground. Disappointed, he turns around and begins the drive back to New York. At least Franci will be waiting for him there.

Setting off early in the morning and making his way east along Route 66, he decides to try and make it as far as Albuquerque, New Mexico, before stopping for the night. It's a long time to sit behind the wheel but he's done it enough times before, and at this point he just wants to get home. He's already stopped twice to fill up with gas and reckons he should be in Albuquerque in about an hour or so. It's dark and he decides to start looking for a place to stay for the night. A cheap motel will be fine. If he can't find anything he can always just pull over and sleep in the car.

The neon lights of different motels are starting to flash by more frequently so he knows he's close and decides to pull over, but it feels as if something is wrong with the car. Suddenly he doesn't have control. The steering is fine, but when he tries to check his speed he can't seem to find the pedals.

He can't feel his legs!

Pulling off the road and aiming towards the parking area of a small hotel, he deliberately swerves first one way then the other to try and slow the car down. His legs are paralyzed and he cannot lift his foot from the accelerator or apply the brake, so he grabs his knee with his hand and pulls it up, shoving it away from the accelerator, but moving his foot to the brake is impossible. He swerves to avoid parked vehicles and aims towards the fence, swerving again sideways to try and slow the car down. The back end of the car starts to slip and he corrects just enough to slide into a chain link fence at the edge of the motel property. The chain link gives way, but does the job of bringing the car to a halt. Manhandling the transmission lever into neutral, he switches the engine off and sits, breathing deeply, his hands gripping the wheel and his head bowed.

The crash of metal on metal is followed by a minute of total silence, before he hears voices yelling and people running to the car.

He opens the door and explains that he is paralyzed and cannot get out, which sets his would-be rescuers panicking, thinking the accident must have been much worse than it looked.

"Is there anyone else in the car?" someone asks.

"No, just me," he says.

"How did it happen?" says another voice from outside the vehicle.

He tells his rescuers about his journey. 16 hours behind the wheel and when he tried to brake to pull over, he suddenly couldn't feel his legs.

"We need to get you to the hospital," a man announces, his voice authoritative and resolute. It turns out he is the owner of the motel. He pulls his own car alongside Cellini's, and with the help of two of the others, lifts him out of the station wagon and onto the passenger seat of his own car.

Cellini remembers very little else until he wakes up in hospital a couple of days later, flat on his back and in some considerable pain – but he can feel his legs.

The doctor explains to him that the X-rays showed some kind of internal growth or swollen tissue, probably the result of an old injury, so they had to operate. It was non-malignant, but it was close to his spine and could have caused permanent damage had it not been discovered. Has he ever had a serious injury to his back?

Cellini recalls his adventures with the Partisans in the war, and of falling down the side of a mountain and landing on his back.

"That would do it," the doctor says. "You'll need to rest up for a while, but as long as you take it easy you should be as good as new."

Once more, his luck had not deserted him. While driving across the desert he could easily have gone off the road, crashed, and not been discovered for days. He counts his blessings while he recovers.

He'll have his work cut out explaining to Franci why he has been gone longer than seven days, but even though he has plenty of time to come up with a good story, in the end he will tell her the truth.

*****

Returning to New York several weeks later than his allotted seven days, Cellini explains the story to Franci. It doesn't occur to him to telephone while he is in New Mexico or to let her know what is going on; she would only worry about him and, after all, what can she do about it? Such is the amazing bond that exists between them that verbal communication is almost redundant.

His back healed from surgery, Cellini finds a job with a small company in New York producing aircraft components. It might be a poor substitute for the glamour of working for North American Aviation, but it is a rock solid company and his employers believe in him. So much so that they want to send him to study with RCA at Camden, New Jersey, to learn about electronics and computers, which they believe will be the future of the aviation industry.

Cellini is accepted, but turns down the opportunity because he prefers mechanics to electronics and, unlike his employers, sees no great future in computers. This is perhaps the only decision he will ever have cause to regret, and one about which he is reminded every time he picks up his iPhone, which he considers the most ingenious invention of his lifetime. Disheartened, he looks again for positions as a mechanic that he feels offer him more flexibility and a better outlet for what he enjoys most. He works hard and keeps long hours to support his family.

It's not all work and no play for the Cellinis. They can always find time for walks on Coney Island enjoying hot dogs and ice cream, or evenings in the city with dinner and a movie. There is one particularly memorable evening at Radio City Music Hall where a packed house is watching the new blockbuster movie *Giant*, starring Elizabeth Taylor and Rock Hudson, as well as James Dean. In the middle of a quiet and tender love scene between Taylor and Hudson, Cellini manages to produce a fart, on cue and seemingly on demand, that rocks the entire cinema audience. Two nuns, seated a few rows in front of the Cellinis, stand and turn around in perfect time and say together, "God bless you!" as if he had merely sneezed. The audience, previously hushed, roars with laughter, and the movie, for the time being, is forgotten.

54. Swingers and Communists. Michigan, 1958

IN 1958 CELLINI takes a job working for Cadillac Gauge in Detroit, Michigan, and the family moves to Monroe, a pleasant suburb just south of the city.

Cellini enjoys Michigan. The pay is good – $2.50 per hour is a lot of money at the time – and it seems to him there are endless wide open spaces offering virtually unlimited hunting. He quickly makes friends with like-minded individuals and co-workers and spends most weekends, during hunting season, driving across the Detroit River and into Canada, where the game is even more plentiful.

Through some of his more upscale hunting connections he is invited to join the Detroit Congressman's Club, where he meets several influential businessmen. However, the social life of some of the so-called elite is not to his liking. He and Franci encounter "swingers" for the first time; married couples who want to swap partners for sex. One prominent successful businessman, an inventor whose patented machines are well known nationally at the time, even approaches Cellini directly with a proposition to sleep with Franci.

"Let's leave that decision to her," Cellini says, in a rare moment of false diplomacy, "But I think you'll find she has better taste. At least I certainly hope so!" The man smirks and agrees to let Franci decide.

"One more thing," Cellini continues, "If she is in agreement, I insist we do it the Roman way."

"And what exactly is that?" the businessman asks, with eager anticipation.

Cellini leans forward, their faces almost touching, and through tightly clenched teeth says, "That's when I fuck you in the ass before you screw my wife, you summonabitch!"

*****

SOON AFTER THE family moves to Monroe, they rent a small house just off East Elm Avenue, close to the River Raisin where Cellini likes to fish.

The house is one of many in the neighbourhood owned by three brothers, descendents of Romanian immigrants, who have built a successful commercial and residential real estate business. The brothers seem very friendly and, as first generation Americans, feel they have much in common with their new tenant. Before too long, the Cellinis become good friends with all three of the brothers and their families. They go to dinner at each other's houses, drink a few beers, swap stories and get to know each other well.

Late in the summer, one of the brothers stops by to tell Cellini that his family is planning a big picnic and that he should come, bring Franci and the kids and have a good time. The Cellinis accept the invitation gladly.

When the day of the picnic arrives, they find the grounds of the house teeming with people. Everyone is very friendly and there is enough food and drink to satisfy an army. The older brother latches onto Cellini and pulls him away from Franci to introduce him to some of the brothers' close friends and business associates. Before long, the subject of politics enters the conversation, and once again, because of Cellini's association with Tito's Partisans in Yugoslavia, it is presumed that he is sympathetic towards communism.

It's one of those moments when Cellini knows the wisdom of keeping his mouth shut, so he goes along with the conversation. It appears the Romanians have established quite a network of people in the area who lean towards the left. They predict that, in spite of McCarthy's death the previous year, fascism is still a risk to every thinking person in America and that there is a need for intellectuals and free-thinkers to get together to make sure it never happens.[1] The brothers work hard to convince Cellini that he is exactly the type of person they are looking for to assume a leadership role in the coming fight against tyranny they know is going to happen. It's only a matter of time. They are very persuasive, but Cellini isn't buying any of it. However, he can see the benefits of learning more, so he plays along, allowing himself to get drawn deeper and deeper into this group that until a few hours ago, he didn't even know existed.

By the end of the conversation, when Franci reclaims him, he has been offered an opportunity to travel to Romania under a false identity and with a fake passport furnished by this group, to study Marxism – and to

[1]. *Senator Joseph McCarthy had led a witch-hunt against anyone suspected of being even remotely connected with communism, including many high-profile intellectual figures in the scientific and entertainment community, between 1952 and 1954.*

train Romanians in the art of guerilla warfare.

Cellini doesn't say no. He hedges, buying himself time to think about what he needs to do next.

He makes his excuses, rounds up the family and leaves the picnic. Later, over a bottle of grappa, he tells Franci what has happened and formulates a plan.

*****

First thing the following Monday morning, Cellini calls the FBI field office in Detroit. He asks to speak to an agent and is asked to hold by the lady on the other end. After a few minutes, a man's voice comes through on the phone. The voice sounds far too young to belong to a field agent in Cellini's opinion. Cellini introduces himself as a former member of the OSS and tells the FBI agent he has information about a potential communist terrorist ring right here in Michigan.

"Wooah!" the agent says. "What did you say your name was again?"

Cellini speaks slowly and deliberately. "I am Vito Cellini, C-E-L-L-I-N-I. I worked as an agent with the OSS in Italy in the war, and I — "

The agent interrupts him, "Yes sir, I got the bit about a communist plot. Can I just ask you to hold for a minute? I need to speak with one of my superiors."

Several minutes later, an older voice comes on the phone.

"Mr. Cellini?" the older voice says, and without waiting for a response continues, "May I help you?" He doesn't introduce himself but at least he sounds more experienced. He continues, "My colleague tells me you have some information about a communist group here in Detroit? Can you tell me more about it?"

"Not on the phone," Cellini answers. "Can we meet somewhere?"

There is a long pause while the agent thinks about it.

"Alright," he says. "Do you know the field near the on ramp for the Ambassador Bridge?"

"I can find it," Cellini says. He knows exactly where it is.

"Meet me there this afternoon, say two o'clock?"

It all sounds a bit "cloak and dagger" to Cellini, but he agrees and hangs up.

At 1:40 Cellini pulls up and parks alongside the field near the bridge, gets out of his car and walks across the field. At five minutes after two, a black Ford Fairlane pulls up behind his station wagon and two men get out and start walking towards him.

"Mr. Cellini?" the older man says, holding out his hand and showing a badge. "We're with the FBI. I spoke you on the phone this morning." The other man is carrying a small briefcase, but says little and looks about 20 years-old, so Cellini assumes he is the young man he spoke to earlier. Neither give their names.

Never one to waste time or words, Cellini launches into a monologue about the brothers and the picnic and how he is being recruited to go to Romania. He tells them once again that he has experience as a field agent with the OSS and that he is willing to go to Romania to find out more about this group.

The agent turns to his young sidekick and holds out his hand. Instinctively, the younger agent opens the briefcase, pulls out a Manila folder and hands it to his colleague, who starts thumbing through papers. Cellini wonders if there is a reason for this, or if it's just for effect.

"You said you used to be with the OSS? That's going back a few years Mr. Cellini. The OSS was shut down at the end of World War Two. You're not currently serving with any intelligence services?" the agent says, glancing down at the folder.

"No sir."

"And I understand your work with the OSS was strictly on a voluntary basis?"

"Yes, sir. I wanted to serve my country, but there was a mix-up with my papers and so I couldn't join the Army."

The agent pauses, thinking carefully about what to say next, then closes the folder.

"Anything you do would have to be unofficial and before I can say 'yes' or 'no' I would need to clear it with the higher-ups in Washington. This may turn out to be nothing at all, but it could be very helpful to us if you are able to find anything out. However, as before, this would be purely on a voluntary basis."

"I understand," Cellini says.

"One more thing, Mr. Cellini. If you were to get found out, we would not be able to help you and neither would the State Department. You'd be on your own."

"All I ask," Cellini replies, "is that you protect my family. My wife and children live with me in Monroe, and if anything happens to me, I need to know that they will be taken care of."

He shakes his head, "I can't promise that. As it is I'm going out on a limb even talking to you. I'm going to have to make some calls and get back to you on all of this. Is there a number I can reach you at?"

Cellini gives the agent his home number and tells him to only call in the evening.

Two days later, Cellini gets a phone call as he is about to sit down to dinner with the family inviting him to visit the FBI Field Office in downtown Detroit the following day.

Cellini arrives at nine o'clock in the morning, sharp, is shown into a small, sparsely furnished room with a large mirror on the wall and asked to wait for the agent to arrive. He knows he's in an interrogation room and that it is almost certain he is being watched through the glass. He waits for what seems an eternity for the agent to join him.

"I'm sorry to have kept you waiting so long, Mr. Cellini, but I have been on the phone with Washington," he says, making it sound very important.

" — And?" Cellini is impatient.

The agent coughs and clears his throat. "Well..." he begins, "let's just say you've got their attention! They know who you are, Mr. Cellini! However, they have no knowledge of any communist activity in Monroe, and the people you mentioned have a squeaky clean reputation as being honest businessmen."

He continues, "However, the Bureau is happy for you to go to Romania and find out as much as you can, then report back to me, here."

"What about reporting to the Embassy in Bucharest?" Cellini interrupts.

"I'm afraid not. They don't want anyone outside this office involved."

Cellini is about to speak, but the agent hasn't finished.

"Which brings me back to what I said before about this being a purely volunteer effort on your part. I am afraid I must re-emphasize that neither the Bureau nor the State Department can offer you any support, financially or otherwise, nor any protection beyond what we normally provide to US citizens travelling abroad, nor can we provide any special protection for your family unless we perceive a real and serious threat."

"So you don't think the threat is real and serious, but you'd still like me to go and see what I can find out about these Goddamn communists?" Cellini's response is bitter and angry.

"That's entirely up to you," the agent says. "Personally I believe you are sincere and that you really believe there is something going on, but I have no influence over Washingston."

"For what it's worth," he adds, "my office is going to be watching those brothers and their associates very closely – whether you decide to go to Romania or not."

Cellini looks at him doubtfully.

"You don't have to patronize me, sir," he says with some disdain.

He feels it is unreasonable of the FBI to expect him to volunteer to infiltrate a possible communist cell and risk his life travelling to an Eastern Bloc country without offering any protection for his family, but still he feels the need to explain why he is opting not to go.

"If it were just me, I'd do it for the adventure. Even if it were just my wife left behind, I know she would understand. But I have small babies and I am not willing to leave them unprotected." The more he thinks about it, the more bitterness creeps into his voice and he cannot resist a sarcastic parting shot before leaving the office. "I am sorry I wasted your time," he says.

He is frustrated but at least he knows where he stands. He is still curious about the Manila folder and the comments of the Detroit field agent. *Does the government have a dossier on me?*

He knows his days in Monroe are numbered, especially now that he must decline the brothers' offer to go to Romania, and he starts thinking about the days and weeks ahead.

Michigan has been fun, but he and Franci are starting to miss the bright lights of New York.

55. Back in Familiar Surroundings. New York, 1960

Back in New York City, Cellini takes a job at a machine shop where, as always, it doesn't take long for him to attract the attention of those above him.

Cellini has shown himself to be clever with his hands, modifying and even building special tools when needed to improve productivity, or to fix some of the machines when they go wrong. He is popular with his boss who is able to save a lot of money for the company.

One day, the boss calls Cellini into his office.

"I don't like thieves," he says, looking Cellini in the eye from behind his desk. Cellini isn't sure how to react. He knows he hasn't stolen anything; he also knows this is some kind of test.

"Me neither," he says. "But what does that have to do with me?"

His employer laughs. "Nothing at all!" he says.

"Cellini, I've been watching you for a while now. You are good at what you do. You work hard and you go above and beyond when you need to." He pauses to let it sink in before adding, "I like that in a man."

"But some of these sons-of-bitches around here are stealing from me and I think you may be the man to help me put a stop to it."

"How's that?" Cellini replies. He's interested, but he doesn't want to get into a fight with his co-workers.

"How much does it cost to make a phone call?" the boss asks.

"A dime," Cellini answers, wondering where the conversation is going.

"Right," his boss replies. "A dime. That's 10 cents, right?"

He sits silently waiting for Cellini to respond.

"Yes sir."

"If you make two, no three phone calls a day, every day, for a week, how much is that?"

Cellini snaps straight back, "$2 and 10 cents," he says.

"Multiply that by 52 weeks."

It takes Cellini a while to work it out in his head, but after a while he replies, "$109 and 20 cents."

The boss is impressed with Cellini's mental arithmetic. He nods.

"Over a hundred bucks a year. That's how much some of these bastards are stealing from me by using the office phone to call their girlfriends or their bookies or whoever it is they call. I want it stopped."

"Can't you fire them?" Cellini asks.

"I can't do that. You see, most of them are family. Cousins of cousins or sons of guys I do business with. Favours for favours. You follow me?"

Cellini gets the picture.

"What I need is for you to come up with some kind of, I don't know, some kind of lock you can put on the phone dial so that when I'm not there, no one can use the phone. So if they want to make a phone call they would have to clock out and go down the street to a payphone."

He has been thinking about this for a while, Cellini guesses.

"Is that something you can help me with?" the boss asks.

Cellini thinks about it for a couple of minutes.

"Sure, why not?" he says, his mind already beginning to come up with a solution.

After a couple of days, Cellini asks to see the boss and is once again shown into his office, where he shows him the device he has come up with. As clever as it is simple, it locks the dial of any telephone in place until released with a special key.

His employer is pleased. So pleased in fact, that after the locking device is installed on his office phone, he asks Cellini to make him two more.

"You know what, Cellini? You are going to be famous." He puts his arm around Cellini's shoulder and adds, "This is so damn clever we're going to patent it and make a ton of money!" It is the first time Cellini has heard of the idea of filing a patent for something he considers nothing more than fooling around in his spare time.[1]

What he doesn't share with his employer is the fact that the special key for opening the telephone dial lock will also turn virtually any lock, open any door – and even start the ignition on a car.

I'll let him work that one out, he thinks to himself.

1. Cellini's employer filed the patent under his own name, excluding Cellini from any rights or future revenues that might come from the invention, yet proudly flaunted the patent documents in front of Cellini and showed him off to his friends as his "inventor". Being taken advantage of in this way was a great learning experience for Cellini, who felt totally justified in using his own key to unlock the phone and use it whenever he felt inclined.

*****

A COUSIN, WHO HAD helped Cellini find the job, introduces him to a self-styled gangster named Joe Casales. It's obvious to Cellini that Casales has strong connections with the New York mob, especially when Casales tells him he is in the security business. Cellini has learned that the words *security* and *protection* are virtually interchangeable in New York business terminology, and when Casales, full of self-importance, tells him that his job is to protect the construction of the cross Bronx Parkway, from George Washington Bridge all the way to Connecticut, Cellini is left with no doubt as to his role. Casales is impressed with Cellini and keen to recruit him to the security firm, but Cellini wants nothing to do with the protection business or organized crime of any sort. Casales doesn't give up easily, and introduces him to a number of associates, hoping to impress the young Cellini.

Casales invites Cellini to family gatherings where he introduces him as "the inventor" and talks him up to all his friends who are keen to meet him. A few are sceptical of his abilities and others mock him by asking for impossible devices, to which Cellini politely laughs, albeit through gritted teeth. Most are charmed by his personality and interested in hearing his ideas. Casales corners Cellini at a party and, after the usual exchange of "When are you going to come and work for me?" to which Cellini as always replies, "Not in this lifetime," Casales asks him straight up what he knows about silencers for handguns.

"Who wants to know?" Cellini asks.

" Let's just say it's a relative," Casales replies. Cellini stares at him waiting for a complete answer.

"OK, it's my wife's father." He finally says.

"You want to know what I know about silencers? Well for one thing, they don't actually silence a weapon. I also know they are illegal, and I don't want any trouble with the law." Cellini's reply is honest and to the point.

"Yeah, yeah," Casales says, "I'll let you tell him yourself." He reaches for a notepad, scribbles something on it then tears off the top sheet and hands it to Cellini.

"It's the address of a motel on I-95 just outside town. Go to the lobby and ask anyone where to find him, they'll direct you to his room."

"What is he, some kind of bigshot that everyone in the motel knows him?"

Casales clenches his jaw and glares at Cellini. "He owns the fucking motel."

*****

THE MEETING IS SHORT. Casales' father-in-law is alternately brusque and friendly the way only Italians can be. One minute Cellini is a fellow *paesan* and the next he is a mere contract employee.

He explains his situation. Because of his high position and successful business interests he has been threatened many times; his family has been threatened and he fears for their safety. He carries a personal weapon – only for protection of course – but if a situation arises where he has to protect himself, it would not be in his best interests to attract a lot of attention. He looks at Cellini. His furrowed brow says *I hope you understand,* while his clenched jaw says *you better do as I ask.*

He produces a pistol from somewhere inside his jacket like a magician producing a rabbit. He holds it by the slide rather than the grip so as not to intimidate Cellini and hands it to him. A Walther PPK 7.65mm. It's a well-engineered and reliable semi-automatic pistol.

"How much will it cost me to have you put a silencer on it?"

Cellini checks the chamber, then removes the clip and hands it back to the gun's owner. "Silencers are against the law," he says.

"You must understand Mr. Cellini, I am in a unique and difficult position. I do not break the law, but if it is a choice between following the letter of the law and protecting my family… I am sure you understand?"

Cellini shakes his head.

"I am sorry," he says, "but I cannot make a silencer for this weapon."

Before the motel owner can open his mouth to speak, Cellini continues. "No one can. There is no such thing as a silencer or a silenced gun except in the movies. It might be possible to make some kind of baffle to mask the noise, but it would be no more effective than shooting through a roll of toilet paper."

Cellini hasn't finished.

"Please don't ask me to design or produce anything that is illegal. I worked very hard to get here after the war, and I will not do anything that might jeopardize my status as an American citizen. I'm sorry."

He feels stupid for apologizing for not doing something illegal and angry for being put in such a position. In truth he is not sorry at all. He would gladly do his best to make a silencer for a weapon if the United States government were to ask him, but he wants nothing to do with men he sees as criminals and hoodlums – even if they are powerful within their own world.

Casales' father-in-law is not used to hearing "no" for an answer. It makes him angry, yet at the same time he cannot help but admire the courage of this young man.

"Someday, Mr. Cellini," he says, "you may need my help, or the help of someone in my family." He pauses to make his parting shot more dramatic.

"I hope you will remember the time you refused to help me. Because I know I shall never forget it. Good night."

Happy days. A photo of Vito Cellini and Franci taken in 1951 in The Catskills, New York.

A rare family group photo of Vito, Franci and their children, getting together with other family members in New York.

Well dressed and with a clean pair of socks every day! Vito Cellini relaxes outside his New York home.

56. Pat Guarino, Mafia *Consiglieri*

As a result of his association with Joe Casales, Cellini is introduced to a man who will have a huge impact on his life. The man is Pasquale (Pat) Guarino, Casales's attorney.

Pat Guarino is a high-profile attorney-at-law with an excellent track record who, Cellini is given to understand, represents several senior members of the New York Mafia who are also legitimate and successful businessmen. He is very well paid for his job as legal counsellor, which he does to the best of his ability and with a high rate of success. More importantly, he is honest and he is legitimate. Guarino is one of the most well-respected defence attorneys in New York City, as highly regarded by law enforcement officers and public prosecutors as he is by those he represents.

Guarino is impressed with Cellini's creativity and inventiveness as well as his forthrightness, and they hit it off very well from the start. When Cellini explains to Guarino the details of an attachment he has developed to modify one of the milling machines at the machine shop and make it more productive, Guarino offers to loan Cellini the money – $600 – to pay for the invention to be patented.[1] It takes some persuading – Cellini is still wary of being in debt to anyone with even remote connections to the Mob, but there is something very trustworthy about this lawyer, and he accepts, on condition that he will pay Guarino back as soon as he is able.

Three months later, Cellini has secured the patent and saved enough money to pay back the lawyer. Unannounced, he walks into the law office of Pasquale Guarino with an envelope full of cash, and places it on the desk in front of him.

"Thank you, sir," he says, "for your kindness and trust in loaning

[1] *Guarino knew that the patent claim for Cellini's telephone dial lock had been stolen by his employer and wanted to give Cellini a chance to succeed with his own invention. The attachment tool for the milling machine was Cellini's first patent in his own name.*

me this money, which I am now happy to repay in full."

Cellini will never forget the look on Pat Guarino's face at that moment. He shakes his head in disbelief, gets up and steps from behind his desk to embrace Cellini.

"Finally, I have met an honest man!"he says.

From that moment forward, Cellini and Pat Guarino are like brothers. They will fish together, hunt together, eat, drink and get drunk together. There is nothing one would not do for the other. They are inseparable. [2]

*****

His debt now paid in full, Cellini invites Pat Guarino and his wife to dinner at the Cellini home. He and Franci love to entertain and Cellini is very proud of his wife's cooking skills. The two couples get along very well and will spend many evenings together at each other's respective homes, sometimes throwing large parties to which dozens of people are invited, other times intimate dinners for just the four of them. Franci is delighted to have the opportunity of preparing traditional Pugliese food for their friends and to see her husband have such a good and loyal friend.

Guarino frequently stops by the Cellini house, or visits Cellini at work, never failing to bring with him warm, fresh bread from the nearby Italian bakery. In Italy it is a custom to give bread, representing life, as a way of wishing the recipient a long and prosperous life. It is also Pat Guarino's way of letting Cellini know that he is safe and protected from the criminal elements in the city.

Being as close as he is to Guarino makes Cellini virtually untouchable.

*****

Guarino hears about a job opening at Loral Electronics, a major government contractor that is growing fast and looking for bright new employees.[3] He tells Cellini he should apply, that a man of his talents should do well with a company like Loral. Cellini fills in an application and is told to show up for an interview at the company's new building on Bronx River Avenue.

[2] *Guarino was a born cynic who expressed a great deal of contempt for those in his own profession. A favourite saying of his, which Vito Cellini loves to share with friends (though not in mixed company) is, "If you ever find an honest lawyer you should get down on your knees… and give him a blow-job." It was his way of saying there were very few honest lawyers out there.*

When he gets to the office, he is greeted by a pleasant secretary who writes his name on a clipboard and shows him to a waiting area full of people of all different types and ages who have come to be interviewed. All the seats are taken so he stands near an open doorway and leans against the wall. He has no idea how many jobs are being offered, but he is pretty sure they won't be hiring everyone, so he starts looking around and mentally eliminating all those he sees as potential competitors.

The door next to which he is standing leads to the office where the interviews are being conducted, and it has been left open – whether by accident or design he isn't sure – but by standing close to the opening, he is able to listen to other applicants being put through their paces. At one point he overhears the interviewer ask a candidate if they had ever made a mistake at the their present job, or any previous job.

"No sir, I am very careful and I do not make mistakes…" the candidate replies.

Cellini is incensed by this man's reply and cannot constrain himself. He steps into the room, in the middle of someone else's job interview, walks over to the desk and addresses the interviewer directly.

"Excuse me sir, I couldn't help but overhear that last comment by this gentleman, and I must disagree." Both the interviewer and the applicant are stunned by this unexpected and uninvited interruption, but before either can speak, Cellini continues.

"May I just say that I have made many mistakes on the job, and I am very glad that I have done so, because I learn more from making one mistake than by doing a hundred things perfectly. I learn and I correct and I improve." He pauses again, and then adds, "What's more, I find it very hard to believe that anyone would have the nerve to say they have never made a mistake. Thank you sir. I apologize for interrupting."

Cellini turns to leave, but the interviewer calls out to him, "You! Wait!"

Cellini stops in his tracks. The interviewer dismisses the candidate seated across from him and tells Cellini to sit down.

He is offered a job on the spot!

Cellini will work at Loral Electronics for five years before moving on. It is five of the happiest years of his professional life; the pay is better

[3] *Loral Electronics was a defence contractor founded in 1948 in New York by William Lorenz and Leon Alpert. The company successfully developed radar and sonar detection methods for the US Navy. In 1959 it went public and the proceeds were used to build a new headquarters in the Bronx. The company then began to diversify, buying several smaller companies, through which it won more military contracts. In 1961, when Cellini joined the company, it had formed a division for developing communications, telemetry, and space navigation systems for satellites.*

than he had imagined, he has plenty of vacation time, his evenings free to spend with Franci and the children, and his weekends off to go fishing or hunting with Pat Guarino. The job is rewarding in other ways, too: he will be doing vital work for the defence industry, building precision tools to work on radar and electronics systems for the US military, and learning how to build housings for lasers – still in their infancy. He is finally doing something for his country and for the soldiers.

And he still has time to freelance.

He and Franci start house hunting and buy a beautiful home in Throggs Neck.

*****

Cellini is still hounded by people keen to exploit his talents, either for personal gain or because they want something illegal. He begins to wonder if there is a competition for his services among New York entrepreneurs and crime bosses, especially when he gets word from his cousin that Joe Casales wants to talk to him again. Cellini has had enough of Casales and, almost jokingly, says, "If that summonabitch wants to talk to me it's going to cost him five grand."

"Just to talk?" his cousin says.

"Just to talk!"

The following evening there is a knock on the door of the Cellini residence. Cellini answers the door to find someone he presumes to be a hobo standing there. The man is dark skinned but also filthy; his clothes ill-fitting, old and dishevelled, his back hunched over. Avoiding eye contact, he holds out a small package to Cellini, a brown paper bag, stained with grease. Cellini instinctively takes the bag and the stranger turns and hurries away, turning the corner and disappearing into the darkness. Cellini cautiously looks inside the bag. He has no idea what to expect and is surprised to find a large wad of cash, stained and smelling of motor oil. He calls out after the courier and walks towards the corner, but the man has vanished. Stepping back inside the house, Cellini takes out the money and counts it. Exactly $5,000 in $100 bills.

"Summonabitch!" he exclaims and picks up the phone to call Joe Casales.

Cellini's son Nicola has watched the events unfold and listens in on his father's phone conversation. He is genuinely worried for his father's safety and asks him if he really is going to meet this man who was willing to pay $5,000 just to talk. A young teenager, Nicky is proud of his father but very impressionable and keen to learn more about his father's business dealings. He likes to talk like a gangster and tells his father he needs to make sure he "packs" for the meeting. Cellini smiles and tells his son not to worry, but he has noticed the swagger in his son's manner and it raises mixed emotions. He is naturally proud of his offspring but realises he needs to be more careful in keeping his family and his work separate – not because of any wrongdoing on his part – but because of the of the circles in which he is now moving.

*****

CELLINI IS EARLY for his appointment with Casales and is ushered into his office.

After a few minutes Casales strides in and without preamble launches into a monologue.

"I paid five grand for the privilege of talking to you and Goddammit you're going to listen to what I have to say. I want you to make me a gun with a silencer."

He doesn't want to be rude, but Cellini is ill at ease with the man, especially since he recently refused to make a silencer for his father-in-law. And while he knows who he is talking to, he cannot be sure that this isn't some kind of set up to entrap him in an illegal act. After a brief silence, he replies, choosing his words carefully so as not to antagonize the man standing in front of him.

"Come on Joe. You know I can't do that. I've already explained to your father-in-law that it's illegal to manufacture a silencer for any weapon."

With that, Casales walks around his desk and sits down hard on a black leather chair, leaning back and placing his feet up on the table to show Cellini a pair of very expensive, handmade crocodile shoes. He looks up and smiles at the ceiling.

"Vito," he says, his tone more friendly but still patronizing. "As far as the law is concerned you have nothing to be afraid of, and who knows, maybe we can go into business and both make a lot of money? Make me just one silencer. If I like it, I can guarantee a lot more business for you. We're talking a few thousand at least. I'll handle the legal end of things, secure a patent and even organize a production facility. What do you say?"

As he finishes his speech, he swings his feet down from the desk and sits forward in his leather chair, looking straight at Cellini.

Cellini is not keen to enter into any kind of business arrangement with a man he knows has a reputation for being ruthless.

"With all due respect," he says, "I prefer to patent my own inventions. Besides, if I make you one, whether you are pleased with it or not, what is to stop you from killing me, stealing it and having someone else copy it, and then keeping all the profits?"

As Cellini finishes his sentence, Casales laughs and coughs simultaneously, choking as he spits out his words.

"You're too damn smart for your own good, Cellini, now get out of my office!"

Casales stands up, looks at his watch and then back at Cellini as if to say *are you still here?*

Instead he says, "I don't consider this to be five grand's worth of your time and I'll be in touch to collect on the rest later. In the meantime, if you change your mind, you know where to find me."

*****

IT IS NOT LONG before Cellini is summoned to another meeting with Casales. The message he gets, delivered once more by his cousin, is that Joe, "…did not feel he got his $5,000 worth the first time." Cellini is reluctant to go but agrees to meet one more time. It's a school holiday and Nicola begs his father to let him go along with him. Cellini thinks about it for a while before deciding it might be a good opportunity to introduce his son to one of New York's power-brokers, so he can see for himself what kind of people they really are. He is hopeful it will show Nicky that these are not the kind of people to aspire to become, nor necessarily to do business with. He tells Nicky to watch, listen and learn and not to speak unless spoken to. He also warns his son that this man is going to try to put pressure on him to do something illegal, which he would never do.

They are shown into the same office as before, but this time Casales is already seated behind his desk and waiting for his guest to arrive. He does not get up to greet Cellini nor does he acknowledge Nicky. His manner is brusque.

"You know Cellini, I am a very powerful man, with very powerful connections."

Cellini sits in silence. *You've got about $500 worth of words left to use up and then we're leaving,* he thinks to himself. The man continues.

"I am in a better position than you in every way imaginable," he says, arrogantly.

Still Cellini doesn't respond but instead looks at his watch, as if timing the man.

"I am stronger than you. I am wealthier than you. I am — " at that point Cellini has heard enough and interrupts the man. Standing up so he can look down at the man, he spits out his words.

"Yes, in purely financial terms you are wealthier than I am. You might even be physically stronger than me, though on another day I may challenge you to prove that. But let me tell you something – mentally, you are a midget compared to me."

He pauses to let his words sink in. He is shaking, not with fear but with anger and contempt for this man who thinks he can treat him like a piece of dirt in front of his son.

For what seems like an eternity to Cellini, the three of them remain as still as statues until Nicky breaks the awkward silence. He turns to his father and says, "Let's just kill him right now."

It's a line straight out of a gangster movie. There is no fear in the child's voice and no malice, just swagger, as if he were saying *let's get some candy* or *let's go see a movie*. Cellini is caught momentarily off guard but regains his composure, leans forward, looking this powerful man in the eye and says, "Now I think you've had your $5,000 worth. I do not expect to hear from you again."

In a rare show of affection he puts his arm around Nicky's shoulder and they walk out of the office.

Neither Cellini nor his son speak of the incident, but a week or so later, Pat Guarino brings up the subject while the three of them are out fishing one evening.

"How come you didn't tell me about that business with Joe Casales?"

"It didn't seem that important…" Cellini replies.

"It doesn't matter," Guarino says with a grin. "The point is, I understand he was trying to suggest a business arrangement with you and you turned him down?"

Cellini nods, "I think he was just testing me."

"Yes, he was," Guarino continues. "And let me tell you, he's impressed. He's also pretty impressed with young Nicky, here!"

Nicky beams and looks from one to another of the grown-ups as if to say *aw shucks*.

"But let me tell you something, Nick," Guarino looks serious. "Don't you ever pull a stunt like that again. I mean never. You could get yourself… and your dad… into a world of trouble. Do you understand?"

Nicola looks sheepishly at the two men he admires more than anyone else in the world and nods but says nothing.

It's a tough lesson learned for both Nicola Cellini and his father.

*****

As Cellini's reputation spreads, his stature grows among the families Guarino serves so faithfully, and once Cellini's wartime background becomes known, he is offered more opportunities to undertake freelance "work" that would see him rise quickly within the ranks of New York's organized crime world. He resists, politely but firmly. The covert work he had done in Italy was strictly in the belief he was helping his country, and to satisfy his own personal – and very strict – sense of right and wrong. He'd do it again in a heartbeat if it were for the right reasons, but he is not willing to take on such grave tasks simply for money or glory.

Even when a high-profile businessman, the owner and founder of a nationally known chain of pizza restaurants, approaches Cellini with a proposition, Cellini stands firm and refuses to deal with him. The man gets nasty and threatens to cause problems for Cellini. As a warning of what he can expect, Cellini finds himself on the receiving end of a completely bogus lawsuit that costs him $325. Cellini is ready to exact his own revenge against the man, but cooler heads prevail and he is persuaded to back down by Pat Guarino.

"What about my $325?" he says.

Two days later, Cellini receives a package containing 325 crisp dollar bills and a scribbled note saying it was all just a "big misunderstanding".

Such is the respect Pat Guarino has earned from tough men on both sides of the law.

Cellini wants Guarino to know that he trusts the lawyer with his life – and that if there is ever an opportunity, or a need, he will gladly do anything to protect his friend, whom he considers more than a brother.[4]

His chance will come.

*****

The Guarinos are hosting one of their famous parties at their home in the city. As lawyer to several New York businessmen as well as *Consiglieri* to several Mafia families, socializing is a big part of his life, and though he doesn't host large parties all that often, his events are popular and always well attended. All of Pat's clients and associates are invited as well as his huge entourage of friends. The Cellinis arrive early and Franci helps to set

[4] *So much so that Guarino's wife began to wonder if there wasn't something more to their inseparable bond. Once she even asked her husband if he and Cellini were involved in a homosexual relationship. They weren't, and the suggestion caused a great deal of laughter.*

tables. Guests start arriving and many are familiar to Cellini; they nod, shake hands or embrace, depending on how well they know him. After half an hour a tall, heavyset stranger, unaccompanied and looking somewhat out of place, comes in clutching a large brown envelope, makes straight for Cellini and asks for Mr. Pasquale Guarino. He seems awkward and uncomfortable, as though he were not expecting to find a large crowd of people. Since Pat is standing next to Cellini, this man obviously doesn't know who he is and is not an invited guest. Cellini is about to tell him to get out; he is even willing to provide physical assistance if necessary, but before he can open his mouth to speak, Pat calmly takes over the situation.

"I am Pasquale Guarino," he says.

"I'm just doing my job," the stranger replies, and without making eye contact he hands the brown envelope to Pat before turning around and leaving, as quickly and unceremoniously as he had arrived.

Typical of Pat Guarino, he puts the envelope in a desk drawer, unopened, and resumes his role as host. Cellini assumes it's legal papers concerning a case and doesn't give the matter any further thought.

A week or so later, the Cellinis get a phone call. It's Pat's wife, Minnie. Franci answers but quickly hands the phone over to her husband. Cellini hasn't heard from Pat since the party, which in itself is not that unusual. One or the other of them is often out of town, or in Cellini's case, out of the country on business, so they often go for weeks without speaking to each other.

She sounds worried and skips the usual niceties of *hi, how are you,* launching straight into her message.

"Pat will kill me if he finds out I've called you, but I know you're the only person he trusts and he needs your help."

"Of course," Cellini replies. "Calm down, Minnie. Whatever he needs, I'm there."

"You know the old hunting cabin up in the Catskills?" Minnie asks.

Cellini knows the place well. It's close to the harness race track at Monticello. They have spent a lot of time up there.

"Yes," Cellini replies.

"Pat's hiding out up there. But Vito – he's not used to roughing it. I'm afraid he won't last more than a couple of days on his own. Please go to him as soon as you can. Tonight if possible."

"I can be there in a couple of hours," Cellini says, "but what is this all about?"

"He wouldn't tell me, Vito. He just said not to tell anyone where he is and don't try to reach him." She pauses and takes a deep breath then adds, "Vito, I'm scared."

"Don't be scared," Cellini says firmly. "Just go about your business like nothing is wrong and if anyone asks where he is, tell them he's away on business and you don't know where he's gone – or when he'll be back. I'm leaving right now."

"Thank you Vito. I knew I could count on you."

"One more thing," Minnie adds. "Can you take him some food? He left in such a rush and I know there's nothing for miles around there."

Cellini agrees and then adds, "Minnie, listen. I don't know what sort of mess Pat's got himself into but don't worry. I'll take care of him, OK?"

Cellini hangs up before telling Franci he has to go and see his friend. He doesn't tell her where he's going but asks her to round up some food.

"How long will you be gone?" she says, but before he can give her his standard *that's-a-dumb-question-I-have-no-idea* look she hurries off to the kitchen to see what she can find.

There is a good size prosciutto hanging up in the larder and a large loaf of Italian country-style bread that she has just picked up that afternoon. She packs it into a canvas bag together with some tomatoes and a few bottles of beer. Meantime, Cellini rounds up a couple of rifles and several boxes of ammunition, which he packs into a sturdy plastic box and stacks by the door.

"Be careful," she says.

They rarely express affection towards each other out loud, but her words are thoughtfully chosen and translate into far more about her feelings for him than they would ever convey to anyone who happened to be listening.

"You too," he replies. "See you." A kiss on each cheek and he is out the door and inhaling the icy-sharp winter air, the canvas bag with bread and prosciutto around his shoulder, the heavy box containing handguns and ammunition in one hand and two hunting rifles cradled under the other arm.

The sun has begun its long descent below the horizon but in the dying glow of twilight he spots his favourite tree along the route and knows he is almost there. He smiles as he thinks of the landmark tree, a magnificent Northern Red Oak, in all its glory and the many times he has driven past it in different seasons. Today it is bare of its leaves but not forlorn. He makes a mental note to come back in the spring and photograph it with its new foliage, but for right now, he must press on and find out what is going on with his friend. By the time he gets to the hunting cabin, it's in complete darkness. He switches off his headlights and makes his way slowly along the dirt road at a crawling pace. Watchful for any activity, but seeing nothing untoward, he parks the car under a stand of trees close to the cabin, grabs his guns and food, as well as a goose feather jacket he keeps in the car, and makes his way over to the door.

Pat Guarino had heard the car's engine and is standing in the shadow of the partly open doorway. Recognizing the car, he waits for Cellini to get out, then runs over and grabs him by the arm. Pulling Cellini inside the cabin, Guarino blurts out, "What the hell are you doing here?"

"I heard you were in trouble and I figured I'd better come and save your sorry ass, because no one else is going to!" Celini replies.

Pat helps Cellini carry the gear inside, then locks and bolts the door behind them. They stumble in the darkness into a small inside room with no windows where there is some light from an oil lamp.

"You want to tell me what the hell is going on?" Cellini asks.

In the dim light he can see his friend is grinning, but at the same time his brow is deeply furrowed.

"Sure. But first tell me what you're doing here. Minnie put you up to this, didn't she?"

"Don't get mad at Minnie. She's worried sick about you," Cellini replies, reaching into his bag and offering Guarino a beer, but the lawyer pushes it away. Instead, he grabs a bottle of Scotch and two glasses from a nearby cabinet. He pours two generous servings and hands one to his friend.

"Salut!" they say, in perfect unison, crashing the glasses into each other. They sit in silence for a few minutes, savouring the whisky and gathering their scrambled thoughts, before Guarino speaks.

"It's my goddamn punk kid brother," Guarino says, taking another healthy mouthful of the refreshing amber liquid, swilling it around and finally swallowing it. Cellini sips and listens. [5]

"He's on trial. He got himself mixed up in some bad business with one of the families – and the Feds want to call me as a material witness. Remember that guy who crashed the party and then handed me that envelope?"

Cellini nods but says nothing.

"He was an agent of the court. It was a subpoena to appear at the trial." Guarino pauses long enough to swallow another mouthful of Scotch.

"If I testify, I risk incriminating some of my other clients, which of course I would never do. If I lie they may try to convict me of perjury – which I would also never do. The fact is, even by showing up I risk a contract being put on me by one of the families who are afraid of what I might say to save my brother."

"What about attorney-client privilege?" Cellini finally speaks.

[5] *Though Pasquale (Pat) Guarino was as an honest and well-respected attorney, his brother was frequently in trouble, crossing swords both with the law and with organized crime syndicates in New York. Pat tried to protect him but when Joe tried to take advantage of his brother's good standing with both sides, Pat had no choice but to distance himself.*

"I am not my brother's attorney," Guarino continued. "Look Vito, he's a stupid little bastard and he never did me any favours. He's crossed the line once too often as far as a lot of the families are concerned and they'd rather see him dead…" he lets the thought tail off and Cellini finishes the sentence, "… but he's still your brother."

"Exactly. Right now I've got the Feds and some of the worst low-lifes in the city out there looking for me… for different reasons." Guarino continues, "So… the best thing possible is for me to disappear and stay hidden until after the trial."

"When is the trial?" Cellini asks.

"It starts the end of this week."

"Sorry for all the questions," Cellini says, "but I have to ask. Does anyone else know about this place?"

"No, thank God! My brother bought it years ago to get some guy off the hook for his gambling debts. He paid cash for the deed and that was that. He was really proud of himself and it's the one smart thing he ever did. We always knew we might need a place to hang out if ever things got tough, so we never told anyone in the family about it. Apart from you, no one else knows about it. Funny thing is, back in the days when we actually used to speak to each other, we'd joke about how it would always be him who would be the one hiding out. Never thought it would be me! Don't misunderstand me, I knew I was getting into bed with some pretty shaky people, but I never thought it would come to this. I've always been a straight arrow. Now I just need to stay out of sight until the trial is over."

Cellini looks worried. "Do you think he'd make a deal with the Feds and tell them where you are?"

"God no!" Guarino replies. "It's him they want me to testify against. He'd be putting himself in a boatload of trouble if he led them to me! You know me Vito, I'm completely clean – I do my job defending these guys because they're entitled to fair representation in court, but the only reason I'm able to do my job is that I'm not involved in any kind of organized crime."

Cellini nods and asks again, "And you're sure no one else knows about this place?"

Guarino looks him in the eye and says, "You're the only person I've ever brought up here. I'm sure that's why Minnie called you. And I'm still furious that she did, because the last thing I want is for something to happen to you or your family."

He pauses, looking for the right words to finish his thought.

"I meant what I said when we first met… about you being the only honest man I have ever known."

Cellini replies by saying, "Let's eat." He breaks off a large chunk of bread and pulls a knife from his pocket to slice the prosciutto. They each drink a couple of beers and talk into the early hours before deciding to get some sleep. They discuss whether they should take turns keeping watch, but decide that would be a bit dramatic.

For more than two weeks, the two men remain holed up together in the cabin. After a few days, the bread has started to mould and after a week or so, there is none left to trim the mould off. The meat too, is all but gone, and they find themselves salvaging the fat that earlier they had trimmed off, chewing on it for sustenance. They have a small propane stove for warmth and brewing coffee with water from a 5-gallon jug that they are trying to conserve. The cabin has no running water – no one ever imagined staying here for this long. There's a creek at the back of the property they can get water from, but it's been frozen most of the winter. It is an experience that would have most men tearing at each other's throats, but Cellini's experience with the Partisans in Yugoslavia had taught him well, and combined with Guarino's infinite patience in dealing with some of the most powerful and dangerous men in New York, they not only survive, but will always look back fondly upon the time together.

One morning, after about a week, Guarino greets Cellini with a cup of coffee and two words he hasn't heard since he was in Yugoslavia.

"You stink."

Cellini snaps right back at him, "You're no bouquet of roses yourself!"

The two men laugh. "The point is, what can we do about it?" Guarino asks.

"You want a nice hot shower? Maybe you want to bathe in asses' milk like the Romans?"

They check outside. It's barely light and the temperature feels like it's well below freezing. There is a deep frost on the ground. Cellini steps outside and Guarino follows him, all the way back to the creek. Predictably the water is still frozen. Cellini kneels down at the edge, makes a fist and smashes the ice with the heel of his clenched hand. It cracks on the first hit and caves in on the second. He sticks two fingers from each hand through the hole and into the freezing cold water, then strokes his eyelids, top and bottom, with his wet fingers, wiping away the dried and crusted sleep.

"That will do for me," he says, "I feel cleaner already. Your turn!"

Guarino follows Cellini's example. The cold water numbs his fingers but soothes his eyes.

"OK," Guarino says. "You make a good point!"

"Do I still stink?" Cellini says.

"Can't smell a thing," Guarino replies.

Their personal hygiene is never mentioned again.

*****

AFTER TWO WEEKS, Cellini suggests that he should leave and see what he can find out about the trial. If necessary, he can return and bring more supplies. He leaves early in the morning, as the sun rises, with a light ground mist providing cover. His drive back to the city is uneventful and he discovers to his relief and delight that the trial is over. Even without Pat's testimony his brother has been convicted. He grabs a loaf of fresh bread and some salami and returns to the cabin to share the good news with his friend.

Cellini returns home to Franci. They greet each other in the same manner in which they parted; a kiss on the cheek and a fond embrace. No great words of affection and no questions asked. Eventually, Cellini will share his experience of the past few weeks with her, as he always does, when he is ready. Cellini looks at her and smiles, and for the thousandth time he realises he has married a woman in a million, and the only person who could possibly understand him and his way of life.

*****

THE CELLINIS WOULD soon move to Florida and eventually to Texas, but the bond between Vito Cellini and Pat Guarino never weakens. They visit each other often, spend time together hunting, fishing and relaxing. They are always there for each other.[6] When Cellini is injured in a work-related accident at Olivetti in 1969, while still working in New York, Pat Guarino represents him in court and wins the case, though the compensation is a paltry $70 per month for life. At one stage he has Cellini banished from the courtroom for constantly interrupting the hearing, telling the judge that his client is "insane!"

[6] *Pat Guarino was hospitalized with a terminal illness in the late 1980s and Cellini took time to go to New York and visit him as often as possible. After one visit, Guarino told his wife that, "Seeing Vito again was better than seeing God." Guarino died while Cellini was away on a hunting trip in Mexico, a fact that has plagued Vito Cellini's conscience ever since.*

Pasquale (Pat) Guarino and Vito's son Nick on a fishing trip out of New Jersey in the late 1960s. Pat loved to fish whenever he could take the time away from his hectic schedule.*

Vito Cellini's ID card for Loral Electronics. He describes his time at Loral as the happiest five years of his working life.

57. Elephant Ears and Moon Rockets

BETWEEN 1961 AND 1969, Cellini is headhunted through a sequence of jobs as his reputation and stature grows in the New York engineering industry. His success is largely an inadvertent by-product of his own impatience. A machine he is working on breaks down or requires a replacement part, and while he and his employer idly wait for a visit from the licensed repair specialist, Cellini decides to carry out the repairs himself, in some cases scratch-building whatever replacement parts are needed.

The manufacturers are naturally upset when they learn that an unqualified mechanic has been tinkering with their machines, until they examine his work closely and discover that, in some cases, his solutions prove to be better than the original design. So they arrange to hire him away from his present employment with a promise of more money and responsibility. This happens to Cellini on more than one occasion.

Not everyone appreciates his endeavours and he is frequently hounded by trade unionists and shop stewards for his interference and "doing other peoples' jobs". Far from deterring him, it pleases him to antagonize the unions, whom he equates with communism.

Factory owners, however, are quite enamoured of him, and his career as an engineer – despite having no formal training – literally takes off.

One of his first jobs is at a company called Zalkind, in Astoria, close to Shea Stadium. Cellini's job involves working on the production of the undercarriage doors, known as "elephant ears", for the Boeing B-52 Stratofortress bomber. It gives him great satisfaction to finally make components for American aircraft, having had to work in a similar capacity, before the war, on Italian military aircraft. It gives him even greater satisfaction to design and build a tool for his employer that will save him outsourcing the finishing process for each completed unit – at a cost of $46 per piece. His boss is so impressed he invites Cellini to go fishing on his boat with him. The two of them enjoy a great working relationship until hunting season rolls around and Cellini suddenly announces that he is taking the next few days off.

"If you go, don't bother to come back," his employer calls after him. Cellini takes him at his word, packs up his tools, and leaves.

Returning from his hunting trip, he soon finds employment at a factory that produces a new nonstick material for coating the inside of pipes, surgical equipment and cookware. The product is called Polytetrafluoroethylene, but is better known by its brand name, Teflon. It's the early days of Teflon and it is difficult to work with, especially on a lathe. Cellini devises a system of attaching springs to the lathe to stabilize the cutting process.

Two engineers from DuPont who observe Cellini's work with Teflon recognize his unique talents and recommend him to the Stamford Tool and Die company in Connecticut, which is looking for a mechanic with advanced skills. Cellini is reluctant to go, but agrees to the move provided the company will pay him the highest wage of anyone at the factory.[1] To his surprise Stamford agrees to his terms, and so he undertakes the daily commute from the family home in Throggs Neck to Stamford.

While at Stamford Tool and Die, Cellini graduates to a machine made by Olivetti and imported from Italy. The machine is temperamental and prone to breaking down altogether, which is frustrating to Cellini as well as his employer. What's worse is the manufacturer insists on sending a specialist from its home office in Turin, Italy, to work on the machine. Cellini is furious.

"Why did you hire me if you're going to wait for a so-called specialized mechanic from Torino to come and fix your Goddamn machine?" he asks his employer.

"Can you fix it?" his boss asks.

"Of course I can fix it!" Cellini replies. He does.

The specialist arrives from Italy a few days later to find the machine up and running and apparently in good working order. But he has travelled a long way and insists on checking Cellini's work. Cellini is understandably offended – until the mechanic completes his inspection of the machine, walks up to Cellini and embraces him. He tells him he has done a splendid job and promptly offers him a job with the Olivetti company, servicing machines in the United States so that he no longer has to travel so far, so often.

*****

1. *He later found out that he was being underpaid by 10 cents per hour. He demanded back pay for the duration of his employment – and was given it!*

CELLINI IS SENT to Ivrea, a suburb of Turin in northern Italy, to train with Olivetti for a period of one month. While there, he is able to visit his brother and sisters, who are only a two-hour drive away in Milan. He also manages to sneak away and spend some time in Bari, renewing his friendship with Tonino, Vito Calabrese and the rest of the old crowd, who are as eager as ever to find out the latest news from America.

The month goes by all too quickly and he is back in New York.

Working for Olivetti, Cellini is tasked with service and maintenance, which involves considerably strenuous and physical activity. Clambering up onto one of the machines one day, he slips on the well-oiled metal work surface of the machine. Losing his balance, his feet fly out from under him and he comes crashing down, his lower back smashing into the edge of the metal table top. Somehow, he manages to get to his feet, climb back up and finish the job, but by the time the work is complete he is in agony, and finishes up in hospital once again.

Recovery is slow, because the damage to his back is in the same place as his previous injury. He will wear a back brace for many years to come, but thanks to his good friend Pat Guarino, the lawyer, he will receive compensation of $70 per month for the rest of his life.

Reluctant to risk further injury with the type of work he is doing, and disappointed that he was forced to go to court to fight for compensation, he quits his job with Olivetti. Before long, he is back at Stamford Tool and Die. It's a fortuitous decision, because his greatest achievement is yet to happen.

*****

JULY 20TH, 1969. Almost every television set in the world is tuned into a live broadcast coming from 240,000 miles away. A man is about to step down from the Lunar Module and become the first human to set foot on the moon's surface. It's just before 11:00 pm in New York and the Cellinis, like everyone else, cheer out loud as they listen to Neil Armstrong's famous words:

"One small step for a man. One giant leap for mankind."

Cellini downs a shot of grappa and reflects on the events that had taken place one memorable day several months earlier. He remembers it as if it were yesterday.

Experts from General Electric had come to talk to experts at Stamford Tool and Die about a laser sighting device they needed. It was very hush-hush but had something to do with the Apollo space programme. The device required minute holes drilled with such extreme precision that these so-called experts had calculated the drill speed would need to be at least 35,000rpm. The trouble was, no machine capable of drilling at 35,000rpm existed at that time – which is why the experts from General Electric had-come in the first place.

Stamford's engineers shook their heads. It would take months, if not years, they said, to design, develop and build such a machine. That would delay the moon shot, which was unacceptable.

Cellini was invited to participate in the conversation.

"What kind of accuracy are we talking about?" he had asked.

"To within fifty millionths of an inch."

Cellini had to think about it for a moment before speaking, "You don't need 35,000rpm to do that. I can retool the machines we have now running at 3,500rpm and get the accuracy you need."

The experts had been sceptical, but could see no other solution. One of the chief engineers at Stamford Tool and Die offered a proposal.

"Gentlemen," he said, "We have nothing to lose by allowing Mr. Cellini the opportunity to show us what he can do. He has amazed us in the past with his ability and skill, so I say let him try it. If he is successful, we have solved our problem. If not, we are no worse off than we are right now."

Cellini had been more excited about the project than about anything else he had worked on in quite some time. He had shared his enthusiasm with Franci who had no doubt whatsoever that he would succeed, and told him so.

"If I am successful," he had told her, "and this laser sighting device actually goes to the moon, I swear I will resign and never work for another corporation again – only for myself."

After a couple of attempts at modifying the drilling platform, Cellini's plan had been successful. The laser sighting device was built, tested and repeatedly put through its paces by NASA. It had worked perfectly and been installed in the Apollo Saturn V rocket that had just carried Neil Armstrong, Edwin "Buzz" Aldrin and Michael Collins to the moon.

The rest is history. Though Cellini receives no credit and the patent is filed by his employers, he at least has the satisfaction of knowing he played his part in helping to put a man on the Moon.

*****

KEEPING THE PLEDGE he made to himself and to Franci, he quits his job with Stamford Tool and Die and takes some time off to relax. He spends his days hunting and fishing, sometimes with Franci or his children along for companionship and occasionally with friends, but frequently he hunts or fishes alone, giving himself time and space to think about the future.

He takes part-time jobs until hunting season starts, and when an opportunity presents itself to work as a gunsmith at Sears and Roebuck, he accepts. His work is on a contractual basis, so he charges Sears for his time and the company then adds on a commission and invoices the customer – which causes a problem with the management. He is called into the office.

"There's a problem with your fees," the manager says.

Cellini believes his fees are very reasonable and doesn't appreciate having his integrity called into question. He is about to launch into an argument when the manager holds up a hand and tells him to calm down.

"The problem," the manager says, "is that your rates are too low!"

Cellini is surprised to learn that Sears and Roebuck has a very proud tradition – indeed it is a company by-law – that it is only permitted to add 50 percent commission to the fee charged by its contracted workers. Cellini is so fast at his work, and his fees so low, that Sears isn't making enough money from his services. The manager implores him to increase his minimum charge for servicing and repairing guns. Cellini is happy to oblige!

One of his hunting friends, Val Forgett, owner of Navy Arms Company in New Jersey, talks him into taking on freelance work as a gunsmith. He accepts for two reasons: firstly because he is paid in cash, and secondly he is able to choose his own hours – but he finds he has trouble concentrating on his work with the loud music being played in the workshop. He enjoys the soft easy listening of Sinatra, or his favourite Domenico Modugno.[2] Someone keeps changing the dial on the shop radio to a rock and roll or rhythm and blues station, at the same time turning the volume up really high. It seems to Cellini that it happens every time he leaves the room, and he finds the cacophonous noise more and more irritating. He ends the war of nerves in his own inimitable style, by unloading a full magazine from a Thompson sub-machine gun into the radio.

"Was *my* music loud enough for everyone?" he asks, sarcastically, but is greeted only by silent stares and dropped jaws.

Val Forgett decides not to replace the radio. Cellini decides to quit.

It's time to leave New York, and the Cellinis start making plans to move to Miami, Florida.

2. Domenico Modugno was an Italian singer-songwriter from Polignano a Mare, a neighbouring town of Bari in Italy. Among his many hit songs was "Nel blu dipinto di blu" – more commonly known as "Volare". After appearing on the Ed Sullivan show in September, 1958 he became Vito and Franci's favourite singer. They would spend hours listening, and dancing, to his music.

It may not look like much, but it helped to put a man on the moon!
The precision drilling of the holes – and holes within the holes – on this small rectangular slab of metal had to be accurate to within 50 millionths of an inch for the laser sighting device to which it was fitted to work. It was thought impossible with existing drilling technology, but Vito Cellini devised a way to do it.

Part IV

Florida, 1970

58. Scuba Diving and Sub-Machine Guns

Moving to Miami is not a hasty or random decision. Cellini has already made several friends who have homes in Florida, and they have assured him it is a great place to live.

The Miami Beach community is something of a sportsman's paradise, offering not only all manner of water sports, but clubs and associations for just about every type of land activity, indoors and out, including sports from all over the world, like bocce ball, cricket, curling and hurling, enjoyed by many of the city's thousands of ex-pats.

Second only to his passion for guns is Cellini's love of the ocean, and for a natural-born swimmer such as he is, it's hard to stay out of the water. In addition to swimming daily to stay in shape, he enjoys free-diving for shellfish, snorkeling and scuba diving with his family.

It is while scuba diving with his son, Nicky, that Cellini first notices his son's breathing difficulties.

A get together with family and friends has been arranged, and a small dive boat rented so they can explore the reef and search for lobsters to cook for lunch. Enrico Verdolin,[1] an agent with the DEA (Drug Enforcement Agency) who has become a good friend since he and Cellini first met in Italy, has joined the Cellinis. It is a rare opportunity for Nicky to be part of his father's world.

While descending, at a depth of no more than 10 metres, Nicky, who is a certified and experienced diver, suddenly begins struggling to catch his breath. He waves to get his father's attention, then indicates that he is low on air. Cellini swims over to him and checks his gauge – which shows he still has more than half a tank of air remaining. Nicky's body movements are erratic, then he stops moving altogether and starts to descend.

Memories of retrieving bodies in Bari Harbour during the war flash through Cellini's mind. He reaches out and grabs Nicky by the arm, removes his weight belt, which drops to the sea floor, and inflates his buoyancy compensator, sending his son's limp body towards the surface.

Swimming with him to the surface, he pulls the mask and regulator from Nicky's face and gets underneath him to support his weight. Nicky is weak and disoriented, but he is breathing. His breath is coming in short bursts and he is finding it difficult to talk, but he is alive. Cellini tells him, "Shut up and just breathe." He drags him towards the dive boat, no more than 20 metres away. With the help of a crew member, he bundles him aboard.

Undoing the buckle on Nicky's buoyancy vest helps his breathing and he recovers quickly, but is clearly exhausted from the exertion. Cellini will not let him dive again, at least not today, and blames a faulty regulator for the incident. He later checks the equipment, testing it underwater himself and finds there is nothing wrong with it.

Keen to show his father that he is perfectly fine, Nicky wants to get back into the water as soon as possible, but Cellini insists he rests for a while. Although his emergency ascent was from a depth of less than 10 metres, he also wants to make sure there is no possibility that he might be suffering from the bends. They wait on the vessel for the other divers to complete their dive and then head back to the pier.

After resting for an hour or so, Nicky says he feels fine and is anxious to swim some more. The group reboards the dive boat ready to head back out to sea, but this time the family leaves the air tanks behind and decides to snorkel over the reef instead. Cellini makes sure Nicky stays near the boat and he sticks close to his son. Nicky tires quite quickly and they decide to call it a day. They have more than enough lobsters anyway and find a quiet spot to cook and eat.

[1.] *Enrico Verdolin was one of the undercover agents who worked for many years to help dismantle the drug smuggling enterprise that brought heroin from Turkey through France and on to the United States known as "The French Connection". Cellini first met Verdolin while on vacation in Italy, introduced by a family member who also worked in international law enforcement. Cellini and Verdolin found they had a lot in common – both owned homes in the Miami area – though Verdolin was stationed in Milan. They quickly became good friends. Verdolin would later introduce Cellini to several influential people, including Manuel Artime, a former member of Castro's Revolutionary Army who subsequently defected and became one of the CIA's most prized assets in its war against Castro's Cuba, and a key figure in the US attempted invasion at the Bay of Pigs.*

They would often sit up drinking into the early hours, exchanging war stories and discussing tactics and the efficacy of various weapons, which they then demonstrated at local gun clubs. All had vast experience and knowledge of guerilla warfare. Verdolin and Artime were impressed with Cellini's technical abilities and craftsmanship, not just with weapons, but with mechanical devices of all kinds.

Verdolin also introduced Cellini to Dr. Raul Pereira, a Cuban-born heart surgeon who was very outspoken against the Castro regime. A pioneer of early open heart surgery, Pereira went on to successfully treat the Cellinis' son Nicola.

*****

OVER THE NEXT few weeks, Nicky would experience shortness of breath on several occasions. Sometimes, even walking a short distance or up a single flight of stairs would prove exhausting. Franci insists that he see a doctor and suggests they talk to Raul Pereira, to whom the Cellinis have recently been introduced by Enrico Verdolin. An appointment is made and after a thorough examination, including a series of X-rays, the family is ushered into a private room to consult professionally with Dr. Pereira.

Cuban by birth, Dr. Raul Pereira came to the United States at the time of the uprising against Batista. He is a proud US citizen as well as being a vocal critic of Castro, but today they are seeing him for the first time in his professional capacity as a heart specialist.

Dr. Pereira prescribes pills to reduce Nicky's blood pressure and then sets up another appointment for the following week. After a further series of tests, the doctor informs the family that Nicola is suffering from cardiomegaly, an enlarged heart. It can be treated with medication but, in time, may require surgery. In the meantime, Nicky needs to take it easy.

Nicky, of course, wants to spend as much time as he can with his father. Though he has been advised against scuba diving, he can still enjoy the occasional fishing or hunting trip, as long he doesn't overexert himself. Cellini is more than happy to spend time with him, and they often visit the gun club and shooting range together, but Cellini is becoming restless from spending too much time at home. He either needs a new project to focus on or a new adventure to distract him.

Soon he will have both!

*****

EVER SINCE HIS CHILDHOOD, and the theft of weapons from the *Liceo Classico* in Bari, Cellini has been fascinated by the mechanics of guns. During his time with the Partisans in World War Two he was able to study them more closely, and, thanks to his commander, Poldo, learned the most effective way to use them.

Since moving to Florida he has had a lot more free time on his hands, and finds himself thinking about ways to make existing firearms more efficient, or how to build a more efficient firearm completely from scratch. Ideas come to him at all hours of the day and night and he spends much of his time in solitude in his workshop, or out in the woods alone for days on end.

He becomes increasingly preoccupied with the idea of building a small, lightweight and inexpensive machine pistol, or sub-machine gun, intended for personal use. Once the design is in his mind, it only takes a few days for Cellini to build a working prototype. It is an innovative, if controversial design, and during an early test at the range, attracts the attention of a local businessman, Kenneth Dunn. Cellini enters a partnership with Dunn to produce a small number of the weapons in a machine-shop in Pompano Beach, owned by Dunn's father. Without Cellini's knowledge, Dunn patents the design in their joint names in Guatemala, registering it as the Cellini-Dunn SM-9 or SM-90.[2]

When Cellini hears a rumour that the guns are being sold through a retired Army officer to members of a local drug cartel, he confiscates the remaining inventory – just three weapons – and dissolves the partnership. Cellini is reported to the Bureau of Alcohol, Tobacco and Firearms (ATF) for stealing the sub-machine guns, but actually hands them in to the ATF saying, "Better I take them and hand them over than risk them falling into the hands of criminals". The ATF accepts his story and gives him a receipt for the guns.[3]

The experience leaves Cellini bitter, but he believes the sub-machine gun has a great deal of potential and is determined to continue with its development in the future. In the meantime, another adventure beckons, through the most unexpected channels.

*****

THE CELLINIS HAVE BECOME good friends with Dr. Pereira. In addition to being a vocal critic of Fidel Castro and a staunch anti-communist, he is a keen fisherman and diver, as well as a gun enthusiast. At the shooting range the doctor introduces Cellini to a man named Jorge Rodriguez, who he describes as one of his assistants, and when they decide to get together for another beach party, Pereira invites Rodriguez to join them.

At first, Cellini is wary of Rodriguez, who calls him himself *Pistolero* because he always carries at least one handgun, sometimes more. Rodriguez is a big talker. Cellini has met his kind before and talking is usually all they do, but in Rodriguez's case he senses there is more to him than meets the eye. Rodriguez describes himself as a doctor – and Raul Pereira introduces him as his assistant – but his medical experience, as far as Cellini is able to ascertain,

2. *This leads to the misconception that the guns were produced in Guatemala.*

3. *To his regret, Cellini never retrieves the three machine pistols. The whereabouts of any surviving Pompano Beach-produced SM-9s is unknown.*

seems to comprise almost entirely of carrying out gruesome and torturous experiments on dogs he picks up on the street. Rodriguez also hints that he has connections to organized crime. Cellini decides to keep a close eye on Rodriguez, but in time they become good friends. Despite his dark side, he can on occasion be quite charming, though he is one of very few among Cellini's friends and associates to whom Franci takes an instant dislike. In spite of her concerns, which she discusses openly with her husband, Jorge Rodriguez becomes a regular visitor at the Cellini house.[4]

Among Jorge Rodriguez's many dubious connections is a Cuban exile doctor-turned-businessman by the name of Pedro Ramos Quiroz.

Ramos is a ruthless man who thinks nothing of using people and throwing them away when he has finished with them, but he is well connected both in business and political arenas. Ramos is a personal friend and business associate of Nicaraguan President Anastasio Somoza, one of his investment partners in a company called Centro Americana de Plasmaféresis SA, a "Cash for Blood" centre just outside Managua, the Nicaraguan capital.[5]

As luck would have it, Ramos is in desperate need of someone with the mechanical skill and technical ability to design and build for him a scale capable of measuring precise amounts of blood plasma for use in the blood centre. He mentions this to Jorge Rodriguez, knowing he is in the medical field.

Rodriguez knows that Cellini is exactly the right man for the job.

Cellini's first impression of Ramos is that he is a pig of a man, in every sense of the word, but he is intrigued by the project and by the knowledge that the president of a Central American country is actively involved. He is also in desperate need of a new adventure. After meeting Ramos, Cellini agrees to fly to Managua to see the problem first-hand so that he can try to devise a solution.

4. *Several years later, Franci's reservations were vindicated when Jorge Rodriguez stole a $20,000 gold Rolex watch from Cellini. The watch was in need of cleaning and Rodriguez said he knew someone who would take care of it. Cellini never saw the watch again. He challenged Rodriguez, who didn't deny the theft but would laugh and say, "If a man can't fuck over his friends, then who can he fuck over?" It was absolutely the last straw as far as Franci was concerned, and she insisted that Cellini make it clear to Rodriguez that he was no longer welcome in their home. It was the first and only time she made such a demand of her husband, but he complied with her wishes.*

5. *"Cash for Blood" had grown into a major industry since an earthquake had devastated much of Managua and its surrounding mountainous territory in December, 1972. The indigenous peoples who populated the mountains around the city were offered cash for donating blood. Originally intended for those injured in the earthquake, Ramos soon found a more lucrative market in the United States and Europe and was keen to expand the business operation, eventually becoming the single most prosperous exporter of human blood plasma in the Western Hemisphere. It has also been alleged that Somoza channelled foreign aid intended for victims into developing the business.*

59. Cash for Blood. Nicaragua, 1977

THE AMERICAN AIRLINES Boeing 707 trundles down runway nine at Miami International Airport. As the nose begins to lift off the ground and the heavy beast takes to the air, Cellini relaxes back in his seat.

Flight time to Managua will be around three hours, and Cellini uses the time to prepare himself mentally for the job ahead. He has no idea what to expect or what the living conditions may be like, much less how long he is going to be away. He is aware that Nicaragua is in turmoil; the country still hasn't recovered completely from the earthquake six years ago, and he knows the political situation is tense, but he is not afraid. He has spent much of his life in war zones and has learned how to take care of himself. If anything, much of the appeal of the current offer of employment is that there is a certain amount of risk involved.

In his luggage is the latest version of his lightweight machine pistol. It is primarily for his own personal protection, but Ramos suggested he might bring it with him since he will be meeting people who have considerable influence with the president of a country plagued with rebel guerilla fighters – and possibly with the president in person. He is optimistic that his design will be received favourably.

He settles down for the flight and waits to see what Nicaragua has to offer.

Stepping off the plane and down the staircase onto the tarmac at Las Mercedes Airport in Managua, Cellini makes straight for the terminal building, where he is greeted by Pedro Ramos. Ramos looks even fatter than Cellini remembers him and is sweating profusely in the tropical heat. Unknown to Cellini, seven other people on the flight are being met by Ramos today. All are old friends or associates of the doctor, exiled Cubans just as he is. They will be Cellini's companions and colleagues for as long as he is in Managua.

Without wasting any time, Ramos hurries the group through the formalities. There are no passport checks or customary searches of luggage, such is the clout of Dr. Pedro Ramos with Nicaraguan authorities. Cellini wishes he had brought more samples of his weapons with him.

At the Intercontinental Hotel in downtown Managua, Ramos checks them in and tells them to meet him in the bar in half an hour so they can head out to the blood bank as soon as possible.

Cellini is pleasantly surprised with the hotel. If he is to be in Nicaragua for any length of time, he can live with this.

He drops his bags in the room, splashes water on his face and goes straight down to the bar. He orders a beer and waits for Ramos and the others. Introductions are made, but just as when he was with the Partisans in Yugoslavia, names mean very little. He will know them by their faces and decide who can be trusted and who to keep a close eye on.

Ramos arrives, still wearing the same sweat-soaked shirt, downs a quick beer and leads the group out to a minibus to transport them to the blood bank.

When they arrive, there are lines of local people standing outside the building waiting to give blood, for which they will receive a paltry cash payment. Ramos leads Cellini through the lines and into the building to show him the operation and explain the problem he is having.

"The marketable commodity," Ramos points out, "is plasma. It can be stored for longer than whole blood and is replenished in the body more quickly than whole blood, so a donor can return here every few days to give more, as opposed to waiting a couple of months before donating whole blood for a second time."

Ramos is particularly proud of his company's use of the centrifuge, which he proceeds to demonstrate using one of the local donors who has just arrived at the facility. Strapped to a gurney, the donor has needles inserted into his arm in preparation for the drawing of the blood. As the blood is drawn, the centrifuge separates plasma from the whole blood, and the remaining components of the blood are returned to the donor.[1]

The problem they are experiencing is that the flow of blood has to be controlled manually, and the centrifuge rotates so fast, it is virtually impossible for the operator to gauge accurately. Too little and the donor is left short of blood; too much and the storage bag can burst, resulting in loss of all the red blood being returned to the donor and often causing serious injury or death from blood depletion. There are frequent accidents and too many donors are dying. Ramos doesn't care about the safety of the donors, mostly local indigenous people and often homeless, but dead donors can't return to

[1] *The process is called Plasmapheresis*

give more – and that's bad for business.[2] What Ramos needs from Cellini is a calibrated scale that will automatically cut off the flow of blood once the exact required amount has been delivered.

Once he has completed the design and testing process, it will be his responsibility to set up a manufacturing plant close to the blood bank where he will supervise production of his machines and training of those who will operate them. In return, Cellini will be paid a modest salary in US dollars from Ramos' business accounts in Miami, but he will receive generous distributions while in Nicaragua and virtually unlimited expenses.

Having seen the problem first-hand, Cellini now knows exactly what he needs to do.[3]

*****

THEY GO BACK to the hotel, clean up and go to dinner. Over dinner, Ramos tells Cellini his partners in the blood bank are keen to meet him, but that they are very busy at the moment, so that will have to wait until sometime in the future. He also hints that there may be some interest in his other inventions – namely his weapons.

"But right now, gentlemen," he says, turning to the group, "you are all here to enjoy yourselves and the hospitality of this fine country."

Plans are made for the men to go to a nightclub in Managua where they are promised *a night to remember.* Cellini would rather turn in and have an early night but sees an opportunity to learn more about his fellow travellers.

The club is loud, the liquor flows, and several women, some of them very young looking, make themselves known to the group. Cellini is not uncomfortable in the company of paid consorts but lets it be known that he is married, and happily so, with no intention of betraying his wife. The women seem to respect him for this and are content to enjoy his conversation. One very attractive girl attaches herself to him and monopolizes

2. *The facility was known to locals as "La Casa de Vampiros: The House of Vampires" and Ramos as "La sanguijuela: The bloodsucker". Someone might donate blood in the morning and return later the same day to donate more, registering with a different name. The staff paid no attention to faces. Death was commonplace and several former donors later reported that Ramos had built an on-site crematorium adjacent to the blood facility in order to dispose of the bodies of homeless and unattached individuals quickly and efficiently.*

3. *Using Cellini's apparatus, more than 22,000 transfusions – removing whole blood, separating the plasma and returning the red blood to the donor – were safely and successfully completed to within the accuracy of one gram. A remarkable feat in the pre-computer age.*

him for most of the evening.[4] Though her English is not perfect and Cellini does not speak Spanish, they are able to understand one another because of the similarities between Italian and Spanish. They find they have a lot in common and spend the evening talking and enjoying drinks together. At the end of the evening, she makes it clear that she has been bought and paid for, and that her services are available for the night. Cellini smiles and thanks her but declines. He learns that her name is María. She gives him her telephone number in case he changes his mind. He puts it in his wallet and promptly forgets about it.

Over the course of his stay in Managua, there will be many evenings spent in clubs and bars and many women available for sex and whatever pleasures these men desire. Cellini sees María on other occasions and they become very closely acquainted, but their relationship remains firmly rooted in friendship and conversation, until one evening after several drunks together, he invites her back to his room. He excuses himself to go into the bathroom to brush his teeth and splash water on his face, returning to the bedroom to find María in his bed, sitting up and holding the sheets up to her chin. He notices the pile of clothes on the floor at the foot of the bed and is about to speak when she smiles disarmingly at him and drops the sheets, exposing her lovely naked body.

In a moment of weakness, Cellini climbs into the bed beside her and is about to take her in his arms, but all he can think of is Franci, waiting at home, taking care of their sick son.

*****

He realises, as he has known all along, that his feelings for María are entirely in his head. There is nothing stirring between his legs and he has doubts as to whether he would be able to satisfy either one of them. Such is his the depth of his love for his wife that he takes María's face in his hands and kisses her on the forehead.

"I do have genuine feelings for you," he says, "but I am in love with my wife and I just cannot…" The words trail off.

María smiles at him, slides out of the bed and puts her clothes back on. There is no embarrassment. No awkward silence. No apology. She kisses him on the cheek and leaves. They will meet again in the nightclubs,

4. *Young girls were more or less forced into prostitution to survive, such was the poverty in Nicaragua at this time. It was not unusual for young children to come into restaurants with plastic bags and scrape leftover food from patrons' plates after they had finished eating. They would even take wine and water. Cellini would make it a point to order extra meals to give them.*

and they will always enjoy each other's company and conversation. She will continue to sleep with other men as required by her employment contract, but a piece of her heart will always belong to Cellini.

*****

A COUPLE OF DAYS after the first visit to the blood bank, Dr Ramos calls Cellini in his room, early in the morning.

"There's someone you need to meet," he says.

"Who is that?" Cellini replied.

"Meet me in the lobby in thirty minutes," Ramos says and hangs up.

Thirty minutes later, Cellini walks into the hotel lobby and sees Ramos seated at a table with a young, good-looking Hispanic man. They are deep in conversation and Cellini is reluctant to interrupt, but after a couple of minutes he walks over. Ramos formally introduces the young man as Anastasio Somoza Portocarrero, the son of the president of Nicaragua.

"Just call me Somoza," he says.

"Or *El Chigüín,"*[5] Ramos adds with a smirk, using the nickname coined for him by the people of Nicaragua.

"Pedro has been telling me about your work," the younger Somoza says addressing Cellini directly, and coming srtaight to the point. "I'm keen to learn more about your machine pistol." Cellini had hoped he might be able to interest one of the government agencies in his small sub-machine gun, but hadn't bargained on someone as close to the president as his son showing an interest. They arrange to meet out at the plant the next day where the president's son can test fire the weapon.

The young Somoza is impressed with the weapon and tells Cellini he will talk to his father. In the meantime, Cellini is keen to get back to his workshop in Miami to begin working on a design for the scale. He lets Ramos know he is impatient to leave. Ramos makes arrangements for Cellini to fly back to Miami the next day. "I'll be glad to see the back of you for a while," he says. "You're costing me a fortune at that Intercontinental Hotel!"

When he returns, Cellini will have his own trailer on site at the plant so that he has full access to all the equipment, twenty-four hours a day, seven days a week.

Almost as an afterthought, Ramos adds, "Oh, and when you get back, *El Presidente* wants to meet with you."

5. *Daddy's boy.*

60. The Bloodsucker Needs a Favour

On the flight back to Miami, Cellini starts building the apparatus in his mind, and within a few days of arriving home has already developed and built a non-working prototype in his workshop. As with all of his inventions, Cellini never works with a pencil and paper. Like a sculptor, he carves his rough sketches directly into the metal, refining the design with each successive model. Progress on a fully working model is slower than he would like because he cannot source the electronic parts locally, and has to fly to Chicago in search of a suitable solenoid, but after a week or so of experimenting he is satisfied with the results.

The scale will automatically cut off the flow of fluid in both directions as soon as it reaches the required quantity, which can be adjusted by the operator.

He tests the device over and over again and it works, exactly as he envisioned it, every time. Even more importantly, he knows it can be mass-produced fairly easily and inexpensively. He has already produced three or four of the machines, each an improvement over the last, which he will take with him to get the blood bank back up and running as efficiently as possible. Even Nicky has helped in the production by sourcing a supplier to custom-build special clear plastic covers for the scale. He will miss Nicky, and though excited to continue with the project, he knows he will be gone for some time. It will be his responsibility to supervise the building of a plant, adjacent to the blood bank, to produce the scale in quantity and provide maintenance services as needed.

He calls Ramos to tell him he will be back in Nicaragua within a couple of days. Ramos sounds pleased.

"Hey, I need a favour from you," Ramos says after a while.

"Sure," Cellini replies, "Whatever you need." Almost before the words leave his mouth he knows he is going to regret saying them.

"I need you to go and see my wife and tell her you've been screwing my girlfriend." Ramos says, very matter-of-factly.

"What?" Cellini almost drops the phone.

"Go see my wife, please. She thinks I'm screwing around," Ramos continues.

"You *are* screwing around!" Cellini interrupts him.

"Yes, I know that… and you know that… but I don't want her to know that – it could be very bad for my marriage and that could be very bad for the business…" Ramos lets the sentence dangle.

"And you want me to go and tell your wife that you're not the one who's screwing around? That it's me? Is that it?"

"Something like that, yes!" Ramos replies. "Hey. You know I'll do the same for you – " Cellini cuts him off quickly. "I don't screw around. Not since I met Franci – and don't you ever forget it, you summonabitch."

"Okay, okay!" Ramos is laughing, "But I'll be there for you anyway."

Cellini slams down the phone, furious with the Cuban. He doesn't care if Ramos is screwing around. As far as he is concerned, the man is a pig. What makes him mad is the fact that every one of these pigs who cheats on his wife has the nerve to assume that everyone else does it as well. He considers telling Ramos' wife the truth, but he thinks better of it. Instead, he talks it over with Franci. She listens intently without saying a word, but gives him a look he's seen many times. It's a look that says *you're going to do whatever you want to do, regardless of anything I say, but don't expect any sympathy from me if it comes back and bites you later.* He just wants her to know that, in the first place he's not screwing around, and in the second place he's not doing this to help Ramos, but because he needs to keep on the right side of him for the sake of the job he's working on.

He charms Ramos' wife with his fabricated confession of infidelity and takes a hail of fire and brimstone for his trouble, but leaves her feeling more self-assured than she should be in her husband's faithfulness. By the time he is ready to leave, Cellini has formed the impression that she too might be entertaining a lover or two while her dear, sweet Pedro is away in Nicaragua, and the thought brings a smile to his face.

*****

CELLINI IS GETTING ready to leave for the airport for his return flight to Managua. He knows Nicky is in good hands and that Franci will not take any nonsense from doctors or anyone else. On the morning of his departure, Cellini tells Nicky to take care of his mother, then walks out of the door to the waiting taxi. He does not know how long he will be gone. He never does.

It's a one-way ticket. It always is. And he is worried about Nicky.

Franci is standing on the kerb, talking to the taxi driver. She turns to Cellini and they look into each other's eyes. They embrace and kiss but there are no long speeches or expressions of deep affection, no long drawn out hugs.

She knows he will be away a long time. She knows that he will be faithful to her. She also knows that she will be faithful to him. She knows he will come back. He always comes back. He starts to say "Nicky —" but she anticipates and interrupts. "I'll take care of Nicky. Don't worry about Nicky. Nicky will be fine. You take care of yourself!"

"You'll call me if there is a problem?"

"I'll call. Now go, the taxi meter is running!"

61. A Meeting with *El Presidente*

CELLINI SPENDS the next few days installing his device on the centrifuges at the blood bank and training the machine operators how to use them. Fortunately, it's a simple and mostly automated process, and the operators, who are trained nurses, pick it up quickly. Just as well, because Cellini – never one to suffer fools gladly – is impatient to get on with building and equipping the production facility.

While Cellini was in Miami, Ramos had begun construction on a building that is now almost complete. Cellini secures a lathe and spare parts as well as supplies of raw materials. It seems Ramos has contacts all over the world, and most of the equipment and materials is being shipped in from Japan. All Cellini has to do is furnish a shopping list and wait for delivery. In a matter of weeks, the plant is finished and production begins. Cellini works hard and keeps long hours to get the plant up and running. His quarters, while not quite as luxurious as when he stayed at the Intercontinental Hotel, are comfortable and private; he is given the use of a spacious trailer, parked alongside the newly built production facility. The trailer is air conditioned, with a full kitchen and living space as well as a comfortable bedroom.

After the initial push to get the plant fully operational, there is time to relax and Cellini reacquaints himself with the nightlife of Managua and with Maria, who is pleased to see him. Though he is happy to pay for the time he spends with her, he still refuses to indulge in any sexual activity and instead they enjoy long conversations about life in America and the difference between their cultures. Cellini finds a lot of similarity between Maria's culture and that of Bari and she enjoys listening to Cellini talk about his wife and family. For him, talking about them makes them somehow not seem so far away.

He spends little time with the other men, mostly Cuban-American associates of Ramos, whose jobs primarily focus on security for the blood bank. They drink beer and play poker occasionally to while away the time without really developing any sort of bond or friendship. A great deal of time is spent fishing on Lake Managua, *Lago Xolotían*, and Cellini spends a lot of time alone, reflecting on his situation and contemplating the social problems in the region.

Tension is building and though little is spoken about it, no one leaves their trailer without a sidearm, and Cellini keeps his machine pistol close at hand.

One morning Ramos approaches Cellini and tells him they have been summoned to the Presidential suite at the Intercontinental Hotel in Managua.

"Well, it's not really a summons," he says, "More of an invitation. He is very keen to meet you – and bring that machine pistol along with you."

"I never leave home without it," Cellini replies, mocking the American Express slogan.

Arriving at the hotel, they are swiftly ushered upstairs to the presidential suite. Outside the door, both men are frisked by Somoza's bodyguards who, quite naturally, want to take the machine pistol away. As Cellini protests and Ramos attempts to explain, the door opens. Standing in the doorway, President Anastasio Somoza Debayle looks both relaxed and distinguished as he waves away the bodyguards and ushers the two men into the room, embracing Ramos and shaking hands with Cellini.

"Please forgive the exuberance of my men," he says. "They are very protective… and these are trying times."

Cellini finds Somoza very engaging. He makes good eye contact through his large glasses and seems genuinely interested in what Cellini has to say.

"I have so many questions for you, Mr. Cellini. But where are my manners? Some tea? Perhaps something a little stronger?"

"Do you have any grappa, Mr. President?" Cellini says, expecting a negative response.

Ramos laughs out loud as Somoza picks up the telephone and calls the concierge.

"Please let me see that machine pistol, Mr. Cellini," Somoza wastes no time getting down to business, and Cellini hands over the weapon. The magazine is in a pocket on the outside of his bag and he hands it to Somoza.

"My son thinks I should equip the entire army of Nicaragua with these. What do you think, Mr. Cellini?"

"I am not yet geared up to produce the weapon in large quantities, Mr. President," Cellini is cautious not to mislead the Nicaraguan president with false hopes, but doesn't want to lose out on a possible contract either.

"However, I dare say it would be possible to build a plant right here in Managua, and, provided the raw materials can be found, it would be possible to equip a small army quite quickly."

Holding the weapon up to his face, Somoza examines it closely. "I like its light weight and compact size. How reliable is it?"

"I have been testing it for some time and I keep making small adjustments, but I am satisfied it is more reliable than most weapons in its class," Cellini pauses, looking for a reaction, before continuing, "...but I believe there is always room for improvement."

Somoza seems satisfied and places the gun down on a nearby table. There is a knock at the door. Ramos is closest and opens it. A waiter, accompanied by one of the bodyguards, enters carrying a tray with a bottle of grappa and a set of small liqueur glasses. He sets it down on a table and leaves. Somoza pours carefully measured shots into three glasses and hands one to each of his guests.

"*Salut*, Mr. Cellini," he says, emptying his glass in one go.

Ramos empties his glass and winces. He has known Cellini for some time and endured the harsh Italian brandy on many occasions but has not acquired the taste for it – nor does he have any intentions of doing so. He drinks it out of politeness for his host, who must value Cellini highly to have ordered the drink specially. Somoza returns his empty glass to the tray and walks across the suite to the window overlooking the balcony. He beckons Cellini to follow.

"Tell me, Mr. Cellini," he starts a new subject, "if you were asked to fortify this hotel building against any kind of a frontal attack, how would you do that?"

Cellini opens the door onto the balcony and steps outside. Leaning over the edge and looking all the way around, as well as down, he turns to Somoza and says, "I would place a machine gunner on every other balcony, alternating between floors, all around the hotel, to offer maximum crossfire."

Somoza smiles at Cellini as he responds, "That is exactly what the security chief from the Israeli Consulate told me!"

They step back into the room and Somoza asks him about his service with the Yugoslavian Partisans in World War Two.

"You know about my time with the Partisans?" Cellini is genuinely surprised.

"I know a good deal about you, Mr. Cellini. Perhaps you didn't know that the Israelis learned pretty much everything they know about modern guerilla warfare from Marshal Tito and his Partisans? That is why they are considered one of the most fierce fighting forces in the world today."

Somoza glances at his watch then holds out his hand to Cellini.

"We must talk again sometime. I am sure there is much we have to talk about, but now I am afraid I must ask you to excuse me."

As he turns to leave, Cellini asks the president if he would like to keep the machine pistol as a gift.

"Thank you Mr. Cellini, that is most generous of you. I am sure my son will enjoy it."

It wasn't the response Cellini had hoped for, but it was at least gracious and honest. Cellini has other weapons, including an older version of the machine pistol, back in his trailer, so he can afford to give up this one in the name of building a relationship with the president of Nicaragua.[1]

He and Ramos leave the hotel and return to the plant.

*****

HAVING MET with *El Presidente*, Cellini's inquisitive nature drives him to seek out members of the Sandinista rebels to learn all he can about them. He won't venture too far, nor will he go anywhere that there aren't plenty of people, but in any bar or cafeteria they can be found, usually in pairs or small groups. They dress in military-style fatigues and many carry Russian-made rifles quite openly. Cellini smiles to himself. For a loyal member of the Communist Party, Mr. Kalashnikov has made an enormous amount of money.[2] He considers these so-called rebels sloppy and undisciplined, and he wonders what their actual *cause* is, or if they even have one.

He walks into a small café on the outskirts of Managua that he knows is a frequent hang-out for rebel soldiers and takes a seat at a table near the window where he can be seen from the street. He orders coffee, and when it comes he turns to a soldier sitting at the table behind him and asks for the sugar. The soldier just looks at him.

"Unless you have some grappa, instead?" Cellini says, a smile forming on his lips.

To his amazement, the soldier laughs and slaps him on the back, then reaches into his coat pocket and takes out a flask, which he hands to Cellini. He opens the flask and sniffs it. It's not grappa, but it's not bad. Rum.

1. *Cellini would meet Somoza on several more occasions, and each time the president would ask for Cellini's opinions on military strategy and security. He especially enjoyed listening to his experiences with the Partisans in Yugoslavia. In addition to his concerns over the rebels in Nicaragua, Somoza was also interested in Cellini's thoughts about the growing problems America faced in the Middle East and in particular with Iran.*

2. *Mikhail Kalashnikov, inventor of the AK-47, the most widely produced and successful assault rifle ever known.*

He pours a small slug into his coffee cup, replaces the lid and hands it back to the rebel soldier, then invites him to sit down and join him at his table. Cellini introduces himself as a mechanic from America who is here to help solve the problems they are having at the blood bank and save the lives of the local people. The soldier mimes spitting on the floor when he hears the words *blood bank.*

"La sanguijuela!" The soldier says, then repeats it in English "The bloodsucker!" and makes an encore production of dramatically spitting on the floor.

The rebel speaks reasonable English, and once Cellini has made it clear that he has no liking for Ramos – *"La sanguijuela!"* – they are able to relax.

It is the first of many encounters Cellini will have with representatives of the Sandinistas, and for the most part he gets along with them just fine. He understands their motivation even if he doesn't agree with it; *Communists are the same the world over,* he thinks to himself, *they want to keep what's theirs and share what's yours.*

Far less clear, at least to Cellini, is their method. He recalls a report he has just read about Sandinista rebels burning down a milk bottling plant in Managua, while a rum distillery on the adjacent property is left completely untouched. He asks one of his rebel acquaintances if this story is true, and if so, why would rebel soldiers do such a thing?

"The babies don't need the milk…" the rebel soldier replies, "… as much as the rebel soldiers need the rum!" He laughs raucously at his own joke, but leaves Cellini bemused by his attitude.

62. A Family Emergency

SEVERAL WEEKS later, Cellini is lying on top of the bed in his trailer when Ramos knocks on the door.

"There's a phone call for you in my office." Ramos looks concerned. "It's your wife."

Cellini gets up and follows Ramos into the blood bank and through to his private office. He picks up the telephone receiver.

"Hallo?" he says.

"Ueli?" Franci greets him by his familiar *Barese* nickname.

"What is it, Franci? Is it Nicky? Is everything OK?"

"Nicky's fine," she says as calmly as always. "We're all fine."

Silence.

"Well, what is it then?"

"Ueli, Nicky is sick. He's going to be OK, but the doctor says he needs to have an operation."

"What kind of operation?"

"The surgery will be tricky, but you know Dr. Raul is a pioneer in the technique and he's very confident."

Surgery and *pioneer* are two words no patient – and especially a parent – ever wants to hear in the same sentence. Especially when it's your son and you're over 1,000 miles from home.

"When is the operation scheduled for?"

Silence. Cellini isn't sure if Franci heard him or if it's just a slow connection, so he repeats the question.

"Franci, when is the operation scheduled for?"

"Tomorrow."

"I'm coming home."

"When?"

"As quick as I can. I'll see you. OK?"

"OK."

No more words are spoken. Cellini hits the disconnect button on the telephone cradle, then turns to Ramos, who has been in the room the whole time.

"I have to go home," he says, "for a few days at least."

Ramos is sympathetic and offers to help in any way he can.

Cellini picks up the phone again and calls the airport to find out when the next flight is leaving for Miami. After an agonizing wait he is told that every flight is fully booked for the next several days. He argues that this is an emergency but all he gets is a perfunctory apology, there is no space to be found. He tries to make a reservation on the next available flight and is told he will have to come to the ticket counter at the airport to make the reservation and pay for the ticket.

"I'll be there!" he says, then slams the phone down in frustration.

"Hey!" Ramos says, "You break my phone and I'll break your ass!" Picking up the phone to examine it closely for damage, he checks for a dial tone and starts dialing a number. He signals for Cellini to wait outside.

Ramos finds Cellini outside, still seething over the thought of not being able to get home in time for Nicky's surgery.

"Let's go!" Cellini says.

"Go where?"

"To the airport! I need to —"

Ramos interrupts him.

"Go and get your bag packed." Ramos looks at his watch. "There's a flight to Miami at 5:45 this evening and we can pick up our tickets when we get to the airport. We have plenty of time."

"How did you manage to pull that off? Cellini asks.

"I called Somoza. He made all the arrangements."

*****

MIAMI IS TWO HOURS ahead of Managua, and the flight time is a little under three hours. Cellini and Ramos arrive shortly after 11:00 pm, local time, and take a taxi home. Franci is up and waiting. Somehow, she always knows when Cellini is coming home, and the coffee pot is hot and ready.

"Nicky is in the military hospital," she says. "He's going to have what they call 'open heart surgery' and it is risky, but the doctor is good and he says Nicky is strong. He has a good chance."

"Poor Nicky," she continues. "He has such a big heart and he is such a good son. His breathing is getting worse and he tires so easily. Dr. Pereira is going to operate tomorrow morning.

Cellini just nods. He has a lump in his throat. He is tired from travelling and hasn't had a whole lot of sleep in the past few weeks. She pours coffee but he leaves it. Instead, he reaches for a bottle of grappa and pours himself a small shot. He offers a glass to Ramos but the Cuban declines. Cellini sits down in a La-z-boy chair and falls asleep almost immediately.

Nicky's surgery is scheduled for 9:00 am the following morning. A little after 7:30 am, Cellini and Franci are in the waiting room at the hospital, talking with Dr. Raul Pereira and the nurses about what to expect. Cellini feels at ease with Dr. Raul. He has learned to recognize trustworthiness in others, and he knows the last thing the doctor needs is more pressure.

"It is my understanding you were told that Nicky has cardiomegaly, an enlarged heart? That isn't actually true. What Nicky has is basically a leaky heart valve. That means over a period of time, blood has leaked out of the valve and filled the pericardium, which is the sack surrounding his heart, making it swell, so it looks like an enlarged heart in the X-rays and images."

He continues. "What we are going to do is drain the pericardium and repair the valve. To do that I have to open up his chest so I can get to the heart."

"Are his chances of surviving good?" Cellini says.

"His chances are better than most because he is a young man, but there is always risk with this type of surgery," the doctor continues. "This is a relatively new procedure, but I am not without experience."

Cellini refrains from asking exactly how many times he has performed the procedure and how many of those patients are still alive. He and Franci decide to wait at the hospital, despite the nurses urging them to go home. "It's going to take a while," they say.

They stretch out on the seats in the waiting area outside the operating room and try to sleep, but sleep doesn't come easily.

Several hours pass and the nurse quietly enters the room. Franci is the first to sit up and says, "Is he OK?"

The nurse has a concerned look on her face, and Franci and Cellini fear the worst.

"He came through the operation. The doctor will be out shortly to explain." She leaves the room quickly despite Cellini calling after her.

The two look at each other, wondering what on earth she meant? What could have happened?

Raul Pereira appears at the doorway, still in his rubber boots and gown, and with a white cap on his head, his face-mask hanging around his neck. "Nicky is going to be fine, " he says. "But we had a scare. We nearly lost him."

"What happened?" It is Franci who speaks first.

"For about six or seven minutes his heart stopped pumping. That meant no blood was getting to his brain. We managed to get it going again and he will be fine, but there may be some lasting—," he struggles for the right words, "effects?"

"You mean brain damage?" Cellini says.

"It's difficult to predict," the doctor replies. "It may be cognitive or it may be physiological. Then again, he may make a full recovery. Time is the best healer. The main thing is he made it through the surgery, and the surgery was a complete success."

Satisfied with the success of the surgery, and knowing that it is now a matter of time until they see how fully Nicky will recover from the ordeal, Cellini tells Franci that he has to return to Nicaragua.

She knows better than to debate his decision or even to ask him how long he will be gone. She simply says, "Keep yourself clean." She need have no worries. Though he would once again spend time in the company of María, it would be, as always, purely for companionship and conversation, never sex.

63. The Sandinistas and the FBI

ON THE FLIGHT to Managua, Cellini decides to make a more determined effort to get to know the other members of Ramos's team better. Being former Cuban citizens, their first language is Spanish, but they learn to communicate with a mix of English, Italian and Spanish – which Cellini refers to as *bastardized Italian.* Cellini never fully trusts them, but his respect for their beliefs and conviction is starting to grow. They are the kind of people he would want on his side in a fight. They are well paid, and Cellini has no doubts that they are doing a good job. He also knows that they have another, more driving and more personal agenda, and that is to see Fidel Castro ousted from power in their homeland. He cannot help but wonder if any of them have been recruited by the CIA, and if so, might they be watching him?

Everyone on the team is concerned with the growing unrest in Nicaragua and Cellini is constantly pressed for his opinions. There is no doubt the rebel forces – *Sandinistas* – are becoming more powerful with each passing day. The media, and in particular a newspaper called *La Prensa,*[1] is a powerful tool and everyone is aware that public opinion is starting to sway in their favour. Even the president is starting to express concerns, and in his meetings with Cellini, the focus is not on his investment in the blood bank and machine shop, but on ways to improve his own personal security.

1. La Prensa, a popular Nicaraguan left-wing newspaper, published stories accusing Ramos of killing the native people in his blood processing facility. Despite the fact that Cellini's new scale considerably reduced the risk to donors, the newspaper continued persecuting Ramos and the blood bank for racketeering; paying donors a pittance and selling the plasma back to the United States at a huge profit. As a partner in the venture, Somoza was implicit in the accusations, and since he was suspected of funnelling American aid money into the business, anti-American sentiment fanned the flames of the growing communist movement. Instrumental in garnering the support of the masses for the revolution that was to come, La Prensa championed the cause of the Sandinistas and Pedro Joaquín Chamorro Cardenal, its editor and leading journalist, became a folk hero to rebel supporters as well as a thorn in Ramos's side.

*****

PERFECTLY COMFORTABLE in the company of Somoza, Cellini is not shy about discussing the president's relationship with the US Government. Somoza makes it clear that he is less than enthusiastic about his dealings with Jimmy Carter who, since coming to power, has withdrawn financial aid to Nicaragua.

Cellini has his own opinion on the problems in Nicaragua and takes it upon himself to share his thoughts with anyone who will listen at the US Embassy in Managua. Arriving unannounced, he shows his passport and introduces himself as a former OSS agent who may have some useful information to share. He asks to speak with an agent.

He is shown into a conference room with a large wooden table and offered coffee from a carafe in the centre of the table. Not knowing how fresh it might be, he declines. After a wait of ten minutes or so, a man walks into the room carrying a leather binder, smiles broadly and offers Cellini a firm handshake. Cellini fails to catch his name but notices he is wearing a badge with a photo ID and the seal of the United States. The man sits down across the table from Cellini and listens intently to his story.

Cellini explains how he came to be in Nicaragua; his work at the blood bank and the fact that he has been asked, on several occasions, to advise President Somoza on security measures based upon his experience with the Partisans in World War Two. He adds that, based on the president's concerns, as well as the comments of his own security team at the blood bank, he is afraid the rebellion may happen a lot sooner than anyone realises.

"We are very well aware of that, Mr. Cellini, but it's really nothing for you to be concerned about," the agent says.

Cellini compares the situation in Nicaragua to what happened in Cuba some twenty years earlier and points out that Nicaragua is – like Cuba – a very close neighbour of the United States. He senses from the look on the agent's face and his tone of voice that he is becoming impatient and is anxious for the interview to be over.

"Take out the leaders," Cellini says.

"What?" the agent replies. Suddenly, Cellini has his attention.

"Eliminate the leaders. You know who they are – and if you don't you should. It's like a snake. Cut off the head and the body will wither and die."

The agent, more used to dealing with American tourists who have lost their passports, is obviously taken aback.

"Please wait while I fetch my superior. I think he needs to hear what you have to say."

He excuses himself saying he will be right back, gets up, leaving the leather binder on the desk, and closes the door behind him. Cellini pulls the binder towards him and opens it. It is about an inch thick and half full of typewritten pages. Cellini flips through the pages, most of which mean nothing to him because he still stumbles over written English. Many of the pages have large sections blacked out, which intrigues him, and one, with a lot of black ink, has his name clearly printed at the top.

Christ, he thinks to himself. *Here we go again.*[2]

Before he can read any of the typewritten notes, he hears voices in the corridor and the door opens, so he quickly closes the binder and pushes it back across to the opposite side of the table.

The agent enters the room with another man. An older man with Hispanic features and thinning black hair. Introductions are made and the two men sit down across the table from Cellini. Cellini recaps his story, emphasizing his experience both as a former guerilla fighter with the Partisans in Yugoslavia and as an agent with the OSS in Italy.

Pausing, he adds sarcastically, "But you already knew that…" and nods towards the binder on the table.

"Mr. Cellini, we really do appreciate you coming to us and sharing your concerns." It is the older man who addresses Cellini.

"We are very well aware of the movement of the rebels and we are watching them closely, but this is not World War Two, and we are diplomats – guests of the Nicaraguan people. We simply cannot go around…" he pauses, looking for the right word before selecting the same one Cellini had used, "…*eliminating* people whom we suspect of being troublemakers. If asked to do so, we will offer every assistance to Nicaraguan law enforcement in bringing these people to justice."

"Please believe me when I say that if you, or any other American citizens, are in any danger – and at this time we have no reason to think that you are – we will provide complete protection."

Cellini is annoyed and slaps the palm of his hand down on the table in front of him.

"By then it will be too late!" he says. "Once these rebels have taken over the country there will be no going back, and America will have lost another great ally in President Somoza to a communist regime."

"Mr. Cellini. I have the highest regard for you and the work that

[2] *Cellini had first suspected that the United States government had a file on him when he had spoken with FBI agents in Detroit, back in 1958. He is surprised to find out that the file is still maintained. On subsequent dealings with various US government agencies and representatives he would find that his dossier was not only kept current but that it was classified. Much of the file remains sealed and unavailable.*

you have done in the service of the United States of America, but this is 1977 and we do not interfere with governments of other countries. We are here to assist and protect American citizens working in or visiting Nicaragua. I'm grateful that you came to us and shared your concerns, and please do not hesitate to come to us again, anytime. I assure you, I will pass your concerns along to the ambassador, who is also a friend of Mr. Somoza, but you must understand that we will not be taking any action – and must ask that you do not discuss this meeting with anyone."

The meeting over, the men shake hands and Cellini returns to the plant. He fumes for a few days over what he considers the stupidity of the new American regime under the Carter administration. As his anger subsides, his thoughts turn to Franci and Nicky and he decides to return home to spend Thanksgiving and Christmas with his family.

64. First Time in Texas

IT'S EARLY NOVEMBER. Cellini has been back in Florida for a matter of days when he gets a phone call from his old friend Enrico Verdolin.

"Hey Cellini, you still got your balls intact?"

"No thanks to you, you summonabitch!" Cellini replies.

Verdolin sounds excited, which is unusual for the usually calm and taciturn DEA agent. He's just got involved with a new company, and it's got great potential, he says.

"Get over to the airport. There's a ticket waiting for you at the counter for a flight leaving in about three, no two and a half hours. I'll pick you up at the airport in San Antonio."

"San Antonio?" Cellini is incredulous. Listen 'Rico, I just got home from Nicaragua, what the hell do I want to turn around and go straight back there for?"

"San Antonio, Texas… T – E – X – A – S." Verdolin spells it out for emphasis.

Verdolin continues, "You know what the latest trend in the world of personal security is?" He pauses, waiting for a response that doesn't come, before adding, "Bullet-proof cars."

"Everyone – and I mean everyone who's anyone – has to have their own personal armoured car. It's the future Vito. And it's going to make us rich!" He lets Cellini take in the words before abruptly ending the conversation. "See you in San Antonio later this afternoon!" he says, and hangs up the phone.

Unable to resist such a challenge – especially from someone like Enrico Verdolin, Cellini puts down the phone and walks to the kitchen to find Franci.

He looks into her eyes but says nothing. She is the first to speak. "Where is it this time? Can you tell me?"

"San Antonio, Texas."

"That's nice," she says, without much conviction, then adds, "I suppose at least it's in the USA." She smiles at him. She doesn't ask how long he'll be gone – she knows he won't be able to tell her. He probably doesn't even know himself.

He looks at her without saying a word, and for the thousandth time he marvels at his own good fortune to have this woman in his life. Though they rarely express their feelings to each other out loud, there is an intrinsic understanding that goes beyond words.

He smiles and says, "I need to pack."

"I'll pack for you. You need to eat." In less than fifteen minutes she has prepared lunch of spaghetti and meat sauce. While he eats, she gets his suitcase ready.

*****

November in San Antonio can be cold. Like most people visiting Texas for the first time, Cellini had been expecting a hot, dry, desert climate, and instead it's cool with grey skies and a steady drizzle. Verdolin is there to meet him at the airport as promised, and the two men head towards downtown, where Verdolin wants to show him around the famous San Antonio Riverwalk. One of the first things Cellini learns about San Antonio is how quickly the weather can change. In the time it takes them to drive from the airport to downtown – about fifteen minutes – the clouds part, the rain stops and the sun pokes through. Sitting on wet chairs at the edge of the San Antonio River, Verdolin fills him in on the company over Corona beers and Mexican food.

The armoured car company was founded by a prominent San Antonio businessman who believes the need for personal security among high-profile individuals, politicians and celebrities will only increase in the coming years. It shows some promise but is struggling against tough competitors and looking for an edge to try and win a bigger market share.

The company is constantly hiring – and firing – to keep up with the demands of retrofitting cars that it obtains directly from the factory – mostly Cadillacs – with armour plating inside all the side panels including the door, armour plating underneath the entire body of each vehicle, and of course armoured, bullet-resistant glass in all the windows. The extra weight of the armour means that more powerful engines have to be fitted, requiring modified transmissions, so a squad of mechanics are also on hand.

Part of Cellini's job will be to test the armour plating and look for chinks in the armour so he can suggest ways of improving the design.

Enrico Verdolin has already pre-sold the company on Cellini's expertise and knowledge of guerilla warfare – an invaluable resource for anyone looking for ways to beat the system. Cellini doesn't know it yet, but Verdolin has also made the company aware of his ability to design and produce cheap but highly effective weapons. It is this skill that the company is really looking to tap into.

After a few days sightseeing in and around San Antonio, Cellini visits the armoured car plant to meet one of the senior executives and discuss his position. After being shown around the plant, the executive ushers Cellini into a conference room and closes the door.

"What do you think?" he asks.

Cellini smiles, acknowledging it's a good-looking operation. After a few minutes of small talk, the executive gets to the point.

"Enrico told us that you actually make guns, is that right?"

Cellini stares at him without speaking.

"It's OK Vito," he continues, smiling, "we're not federal agents! We make a great product here, as you can see. We just want to make it better… give our customers more of an edge."

Cellini is offended by the reference to federal agents. His recent meeting with agents at the US Embassy in Nicaragua and the discovery that the government has a dossier on him is still fresh in his mind.

"You listen to me," he says. "I don't do anything illegal. I never have. I have all the federal licences I need and I always comply with the law."

The executive is taken aback.

"Hey, I'm sorry – I never meant to imply that you didn't, and believe me, we wouldn't want to hire you if we thought otherwise!"

He continues, "The industry we're in, building armoured cars… it's very, very competitive. We're up against competition from all over the place; Washington DC, the north-east, even Mexico. We want to see if we can maybe offer something the other guys don't."

He pauses for breath.

"What if we could put a Cellini machine pistol inside every car we sell? In a special locking holster or stand that the driver or the passenger could grab in a hurry for self-defence? What do you think of that idea?"

This is more than Cellini had bargained for, and he tells the executive he will have to think about it. He also wants to discuss it with Franci, because moving to Texas would be a big step for the Cellinis.

Cellini calls Verdolin to thank him for the introduction but tells him he is going home to think about it.

He spends a quiet Christmas with his family. It's good to see Nicky recovering and enjoy Franci's home cooking. He's missed her more than he realised while he was away.

New Year's Eve and the Cellinis are getting ready to spend the evening with friends when the phone rings. It's Pedro Ramos calling from Nicaragua.

"Cellini, you need to get back down here."

"Why, what's going on?"

"Everything, man. We've got more trouble from this Goddamn journalist – but then that's not exactly front page news. What is news is we've got a bunch of Japanese businessmen who want to buy out the whole operation, lock, stock and barrel – including your blood machines. They want to talk to you. Get your ass on the next flight back to Managua and call me when you get here. I'll pick you up at the airport."

65. Assassination in Managua

CELLINI'S PLANE TOUCHES down at the airport in Managua. Ramos is waiting for him and greets him like a long-lost brother.

"Let's get a beer before we go anywhere. We have a lot to talk about."

The beer tastes good. Cellini hadn't felt much like drinking on the flight. It's New Year's Day 1978, and Franci had not been pleased to see him leave at such short notice. Though completely supportive of all his endeavours, she had a way of making her feelings known whenever she disapproved – and her silence in the car on the way to the airport had conveyed her feelings better than any words could have.

Ramos is brimming with excitement and cannot wait to fill Cellini in on the latest news. The Japanese company that has been providing the bulk of the equipment and materials for the blood bank is very interested in investing in the project. A group of Japanese bankers and businessmen has flown into Managua to see it for themselves. They are especially interested in the scale for separating the plasma from the whole blood and are very eager to meet Cellini.

"I don't speak Japanese, but from the way they were talking I think they are planning to make an offer to buy out the whole operation! That's why I had to get you back here, so you can be there when we discuss terms…" Ramos pauses. "…Assuming you are ready and willing to sell?"

"And how does this work?" Cellini replies. "Assuming I agree to sell, what do you get out of it?"

Ramos puts on a fake hurt-feelings look. "We're partners! 50-50 all the way! Whatever we get for the factory and the scale, we split down the middle!"

Cellini doesn't trust Ramos as far as he could throw him – even Somoza had called him "a two-bit, tin-horn terrorist"– but he has little choice in the matter. Ramos has, after all, secured the funding for the entire venture so far. Cellini is well-rewarded for his work, but he has not yet had a chance to patent the device to protect himself.[1]

He agrees to a meeting with the Japanese in the hotel first thing the following morning.

"Tell me what else is going on," Cellini says.

Ramos looks at his watch, drains his beer glass and says, "OK, I'll tell you on the way. You pay for the drinks while I take a piss. I'll meet you by the exit to the parking lot."

*****

"WHAT'S THE SITUATION with the rebels?" Cellini asks, once they are both in the car.

"Nothing that our security people can't handle," Ramos replies.

"I meant with regard to the country as a whole, not just the blood bank," Cellini continues, "We get very little news about it back in the States. It's right in our backyard, and we hear more about the Shah of Iran than we do about Somoza."

"Not much to tell. Rebel forces are scattered and there are occasional incursions, but they have no real leadership. The other political leaders are scared of Somoza. The only real thorn in his side – in everyone's side – is Chamorro."

"The journalist?" Cellini asks, "What can he do?"

"He likes to stir the shit and he's doing plenty of that. He hates Somoza because Somoza got control of all the American money coming into Managua and he wanted it for himself."

"So what exactly is Chamorro doing?" Cellini is genuinely interested.

"Like I said, he prints all kinds of shit about Somoza and his relationship with the capitalists in the US. He's a goddamn communist for Christ's sake, what do you expect?"

Ramos is getting angry just talking about the editor of *La Prensa.* But what really makes him mad is that he knows the Nicaraguan people are starting to believe what is printed in its pages.

"Hey, you missed the turn off!" Cellini yells at the distracted Ramos, who just turns and smirks at him.

"We're not going to the blood bank. Not yet, anyway."

"Where are we going?" Cellini says.

1. *After returning to the USA and relocating to San Antonio, Texas, Cellini applied for, and was awarded, a US patent for the blood control apparatus in April, 1978.*

"I have to meet a guy and discuss some business. You don't mind tagging along?"

Resigned to the idea that he has no choice, Cellini closes his eyes and tries to get some sleep, but Ramos drives fast and erratically, making it almost impossible to rest.

They turn onto a narrow, deserted road through the hills south of the city. Cellini is admiring the rugged countryside, when, as they crest the top of a hill a small curl of smoke rising in the distance catches his attention. and what looks like an overturned car at the side of the road, a few hundred metres ahead. As they get closer it becomes obvious the car has flipped while taking a bend and rolled over. There is no fire, so he assumes the smoke he saw was just steam escaping from the damaged radiator. There is no sign of life, but Cellini assumes that Ramos will pull over and try to help in case there are injured or unconscious people trapped inside; he is a doctor, after all.

Instead, after slowly driving past the carnage, he puts his foot down.

"Aren't you going to stop?" Cellini says, shocked by Ramos's callous attitude.

"What's the point?" Ramos replies. "They're probably all dead. Did you see the car? It's an old '60s Ford. They're just local peasants… Besides, I'm late and this is an important meeting."

Cellini is horrified. He had always been dubious of Ramos but this confirmed his worst fears. He decides this is another situation where playing dumb is the best course of action and says no more about it, but it would always haunt him.

They sit in a slightly uncomfortable silence for the rest of the journey. Cellini closes his eyes but does not sleep. Eventually, the car rolls to a stop and Ramos switches off the ignition.

"Let's go to the beach!" Ramos says, leaning over into Cellini's face and almost overpowering him with his foul, warm breath.

They are at *Playa de Masachapa*, in the small town of San Antonio on Nicaragua's Pacific coast. It's not the prettiest beach Cellini has ever seen by any stretch of the imagination, and the waves are more suited to surfing than swimming, but he suspects that the purpose of their visit has nothing to do with either.

They walk along the sand a little way to a man who is sitting down, alone, smoking a cigarette. Ramos calls out to him and the man turns his head, then stands up and the two shake hands. Cellini stays a few paces behind to allow Ramos privacy – and to avoid any more contact with his breath.

The man is good-looking and young, Cellini guesses no more than

30 years-old. Ramos calls Cellini over and introduces him as Silvio Peña Rivas, and says he is a business associate from Argentina. Peña speaks only Spanish, no English and no Italian, so Cellini is unable to have any meaningful conversation with him, though he gets the distinct feeling that he has been the subject of part of their discussion.

After ten minutes or so, Ramos shakes hands with Peña, who in turn offers his hand to Cellini. Though his knowledge of Spanish is limited, he understands Peña to say that meeting him is a great honour.

"What was all that about?" Cellini says, once they are back in the car and on the road back towards Managua and the blood bank.

"Just a business arrangement," is all Ramos will tell him.

Cellini brings up the subject of Chamorro again.

"Is there any truth to the stories in *La Prensa*?"

"What, about me profiteering?" Ramos replies with a grin. "Hey, I'm a businessman, I like to make money. Is that such a bad thing?"

Cellini shrugs. He thinks there's more to it but doesn't want to press the point.

Ramos continues, "I've heard stories that Chamorro may have a financial stake in another blood bank. A rival, if you like."

"That would be a good enough reason for him to go after you," Cellini replies.

Ramos laughs, "Nah, he's just a communist. He hates me because I make money. He hates Somoza. communists hate everyone."

"They hate everyone who makes more money than they do," Cellini adds.

"If he really is just a communist, he can be bought," Cellini says. "Believe me, I've known a lot of them, and every one of them can be bought and paid for with a few dollars."

It's a scathing assessment, but one to which Cellini firmly adheres.

"If it's money he's after, give it to him. Make a big donation to his rag of a newspaper. Maybe get him to start writing articles about what wonderful people we Americans are?"

He pauses long enough to let Ramos digest the idea, then continues, "I'll even be the go-between. I'll go meet with him, find out how much it will take and offer to get the money and deliver it personally."

Cellini is really on a roll, now.

"I'd bet for a few thousand dollars you'd have him eating out of your hand."

A smile crawls across Ramos's face, then turns into full-blown laughter.

"You're serious, aren't you? You'd actually do it?" He has to stop to wipe tears from his cheeks he's laughing so much. After a few minutes he nods at Cellini. "OK, let me think about it."

Cellini doesn't yet know it, but Ramos has other plans.

*****

NEXT MORNING, THEY drive into Managua to the Intercontinental Hotel for the meeting with the Japanese.

The businessmen, who are from one of Japan's leading pharmaceutical companies, have brought a team of interpreters, but they speak only Spanish and English, so Cellini takes very little part in the discussion personally, relying on Ramos for interpretation.

It seems they are willing to offer $650,000 for Cellini's part of the operation, lock, stock and barrel, to include all the existing equipment, spare parts, machinery, tools – everything. Essentially, as Ramos puts it, Cellini would walk out of Nicaragua, his work complete, with a cheque made out to cash for $325,000.

Cellini wants to discuss details such as patent rights and perhaps even building a long-term relationship with the Japanese gentlemen, but Ramos waves him away.

Later, the Cuban explains that he wants to hold out for a bigger price tag.

"This is how you deal with the Japs, trust me," he says. "In another week, they'll come back and offer a million."

The meeting ends amicably with the Japanese slightly disappointed but not despondent, and Cellini hopeful that Ramos might actually know what he's doing.

The following morning, Ramos tells Cellini that he has to go back to Miami for a few days and asks if he can handle things at the plant while he's away.

"Of course," Cellini says. "Is everything OK?"

"It's fine," Ramos replies. "I just have a couple of pretty big deals going on back in the States and I need to be there. If those Japs come back, tell them we want a million dollars, not one cent less!"

*****

ON TUESDAY, JANUARY 10TH, 1978, Pedro Joaquín Chamorro Cardenal, journalist and editor of La Prensa newspaper, is gunned down on his way to work at the La Prensa offices in Managua. At precisely 8:20 in the morning, a Toyota pick-up truck pulls up alongside him and four assassins open fire with shotguns at close range.

When news of his death reaches the public, riots break out in the streets of Managua and cars and buildings are set on fire. One of the first targets is Plasmaféresis SA, Ramos's blood bank and its surrounding encampment, which is totally destroyed. A general strike is called and civil unrest quickly flares up all over the country. The government responds by imposing martial law, creating even greater chaos and leading to further violence. Thirty thousand people take turns carrying Chamorro's body from the hospital to the La Prensa offices, where it lies in state while a crowd outside chants "Who killed Chamorro?" Thousands more march with the funeral procession to the Chamorro family home. Chamorro has become a martyr for the coming revolution.

Within three days, Silvio Peña Rivas – the man Cellini had met briefly at Playa de Masachapa – is arrested and confesses to the crime, claiming he had been hired by Pedro Ramos. According to Peña's testimony, Ramos had instructed him to secure the services of additional gunmen to make sure the job is done properly.

Did Ramos introduce Cellini to Peña hoping he would be recruited as one of the accomplices? Is Cellini being set-up by Ramos? Nothing had been said to Cellini during the meeting on the beach, and his name did not come up at the trial, though Chamorro's family and the Sandinistas suspect Cellini's involvement because of his association with Ramos and Somoza.

In any event, Peña apparently has no difficulty finding and hiring other gunmen.

The trial takes place in June, 1978. Silvio Peña Rivas is convicted along with Domingo Acevedo Chavarría and both are sentenced to 30 years' imprisonment for murder plus three years for conspiracy to commit murder. Juan Ramon Acevedo and Harold Cedeño Flores are each sentenced to twenty years for murder plus eighteen months for conspiracy to commit murder.

Pedro Ramos Quiroz is sentenced in absentia to 30 years in prison, as is Silvio Vega Zúñiga, one of the other gunmen. Both flee to the United States to avoid prosecution.

Peña is paid the equivalent of $14,285 US by Ramos for arranging the hit.

Chamorro's widow, Violeta Barrios de Chamorro, maintains her belief that Somoza is behind the killing, and when Ramos is implicated by Silvio Peña's testimony, she becomes more convinced then ever of the president's involvement, and that the other employees of the blood bank must also be complicit in the crime. Cellini ("The Sicilian") in particular is high on the list of suspected triggermen, having been seen demonstrating weapons and openly discussing se-

curity arrangements on several occasions with Somoza. This is undoubtedly why Ramos chooses to flee the country, having set up the assassination, leaving Cellini and the other members of the blood bank team to face retribution from the revolutionary forces.

Violeta Barrios de Chamorro joins the ruling junta of the Sandinista National Liberation Front after Somoza's overthrow in 1979. She is elected President of Nicaragua in 1990 and one of her first acts is to pardon the four men who had previously been sentenced for killing her husband.

Somoza claims that the Chamorro assassination had been orchestrated by Pedro Ramos, acting alone and for personal reasons. He cites the fact that La Prensa has been printing anti-government propaganda for many years without any interference from his regime and that it is not in his interests to create a martyr.

In his memoir, Somoza also states clearly, "...it was not the Sicilian."

*****

"No wonder that goddamn fat pig suddenly had to go back to Miami," Cellini says, referring to Ramos while staring at the smouldering ruins of the plant he had worked so hard to build. Kicking through the debris, he picks up a charred lump of metal. It's the only recognizable piece of his blood dispensing scale. He picks it up, a souvenir of his time in Nicaragua.

He shakes his fist in the direction of where Ramos's office used to be. *So much for holding out for a million dollars. We should have taken the Japs' offer. I'd be on a plane back to Miami and this would be their problem.*

The attack had come suddenly and without any warning. Hordes of marauding people chanting and yelling and tearing things down in their path. Cellini and the others had scrambled to get out of their trailers. Then the fires had started. All the men had been able to do was watch them burn, the rest of their possessions still inside.

Cellini's trailer is the first to get torched. He manages to grab his go-bag with a change of clothes plus his passport and some cash. His trusted machine pistol had been hidden under the floor of the trailer, so all he has for self-defence is the Colt 45 semi-automatic he always carries. He thinks about loading a clip and firing at the mob to keep them at bay, but decides it just isn't worth it. There are too many of them, and anyway, this isn't his war.

Now, all that's left is this piece of charred metal in his hand, still warm from the flames that had engulfed it just a short time ago. He unzips the bag and stuffs it inside. Turning towards the road, he finds the others in varying degrees of shock and anger.

"We need to get to the city. Maybe go to the hotel and see if we can find Somoza."

They decide to wait until dusk to give the crowds a chance to expend some of their energy, then find their way into Managua on the back roads. Piling into one salvageable vehicle, a battered old white Chevy pick-up truck with one fender painted in red primer, the six men make their way into the city and to the Intercontinental Hotel, where they park at the back of the building.

Inside the hotel, accommodation is arranged; a couple of adjoining hotel rooms between them will do fine, that way they can take turns keeping watch. Cellini asks at the front desk if *El Presidente* is in residence. The desk clerk is new and doesn't recognize Cellini, but after a series of hasty phone conversations, the familiar concierge appears and greets Cellini with an apology. The desk clerk had been worried that the men might be rebels posing as guests, and when Cellini had asked for *El Presidente,* it had made him very uncomfortable.

"I am sorry to say, Señor Cellini, that President Somoza is not in residence at the present time."

Cellini decides it's time to talk to Ramos. It's 10:45 here, so it's 12:45 am in Miami. He dials the number.

Ramos is still up. Still wide awake.

"Pedro," Cellini says, trying very hard to sound as if nothing in the world is wrong.

"What can I do for you, Vito?" Ramos replies. His casual and over-the-top friendly attitude is like acid on the open wound of Cellini's anger and he starts to lay into him with a verbal tirade, "You goddamn summonabitch, what were you thinking —"

Ramos interrupts the diatribe. Cellini calms down and tries to explain what has happened in Managua and subsequently at Centro Americana de Plasmaféresis SA.

"So the bastards have finally put me out of business?"

Predictably, as far as Ramos is concerned, it's all about Ramos. Cellini is incensed.

"Fuck you and your blood bank!" Cellini replies. "It's destroyed. Burned to the ground by these Goddamn communists. We should have taken the offer from the Japs when they were hot to buy it!"

Cellini continues. "I don't need to be here any more. None of us do. We just need to get the hell out of Nicaragua."

Ramos thinks about it for a while before speaking again.

"You did the right thing to call me, Vito. Let me talk to Somoza and I'll get back to you. Order room service. Have a ball and put it on my tab. And don't worry, after a while this will all calm down."

"Don't tell me to calm down," Cellini says. "With the entire plant destroyed, we have nowhere to go and nothing further to accomplish by being here in Managua. You need to get us out of here and back to Miami."

"Like I said, I'll talk to Somoza. He's a personal friend of the ambassador and I'm sure between them they'll be able to sort out a safe passage for you. Stay in the hotel and keep close to a phone. I'll be in touch soon, OK?"

Cellini rejoins the men and explains the situation. No one is happy about it, but no one has a better idea so they decide to stay put and wait. They take Ramos at his word and order food and beer from room service and watch a lot of TV. Somoza's popularity is declining but he is still the leader, at least for now.

*****

RAMOS CALLS the hotel and the concierge puts the call through to Cellini.

"You need to get everyone over to the American Embassy first thing in the morning," Ramos tells him. "Somoza has spoken to the ambassador, and he says you can stay there for a few days while they make arrangements to get you on a flight out. No one is looking for you and no one thinks you are connected with any of this, but as US citizens, it would be safer if you are staying at the Embassy."

Ramos is lying. He knows that the Managua police, under pressure from Chamorro's family, will want to question everyone connected with the blood bank – especially Cellini. He knows that by getting Cellini safely to the Embassy and onto American soil, neither the police nor the Sandinistas will be able to question him.

Cellini would never see, nor have any personal contact with either Ramos or Somoza again.

*****

ANASTASIO SOMOZA DEBAYLE resigns the presidency of Nicaragua in July 1979 and attempts to fly to Miami, but is denied entry to the US by President Carter. He settles instead in Paraguay, where he is assassinated in a well-planned ambush on September 17, 1980. It takes over a year of planning and an army of thirty men and women armed with rocket launchers and anti-tank grenades, as well as assault rifles and machine guns, to carry out the attack and kill the ex-president. The attack is blamed on the Sandinistas but subsequent investigations by the Miami Herald suggests members of the Argentine People's Revolutionary Army may also be involved.

Pedro Ramos Quiroz is convicted in absentia of Chamorro's murder by the court in Managua. He is sentenced to 30 years imprisonment and the Nicaraguan government begins extradition proceedings with the United States, but following the overthrow of Somoza and the rise of the Sandinistas to power in Nicaragua, relations between the countries break down and no extradition ever takes place. Ramos remains in Miami and maintains a low profile for a while, afraid of retaliation, later moving to Guatemala.

Somoza's son, Anastasio Somoza Portocarrero, is also accused of being involved in planning the Chamorro assassination, but escapes to the United States where he is granted entry, eventually taking US citizenship and becoming a successful businessman. Extradition proceedings against him are begun but amount to nothing.

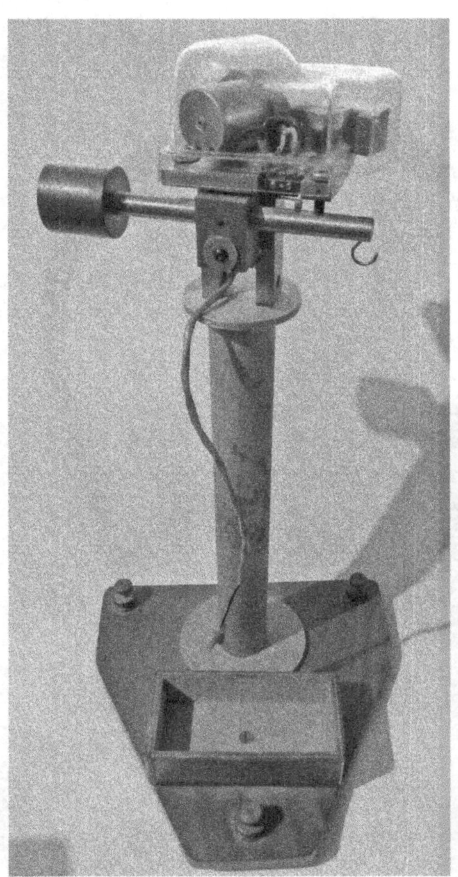

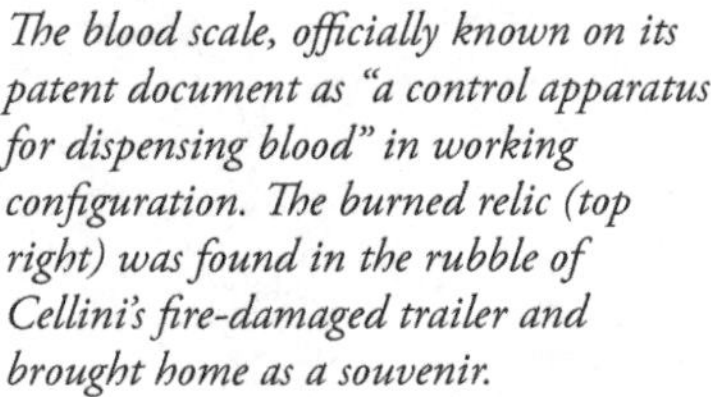

The blood scale, officially known on its patent document as "a control apparatus for dispensing blood" in working configuration. The burned relic (top right) was found in the rubble of Cellini's fire-damaged trailer and brought home as a souvenir.

All of the buildings (right) at Centro Americana de Plasmaféresis SA were completely destroyed by rebels demanding revenge for the murder of Chamorro.

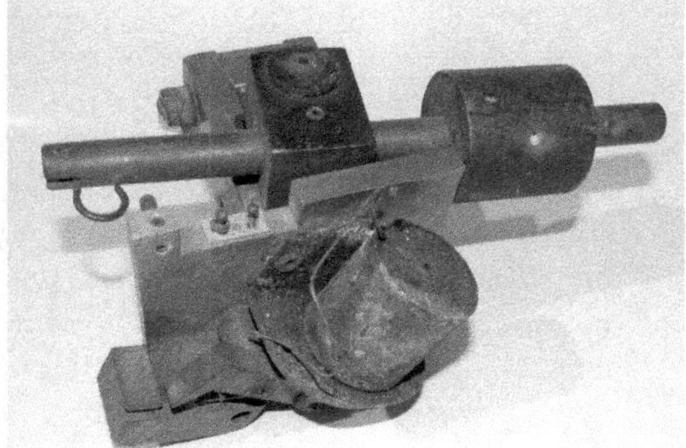

66. The Ayatollah and the Mafioso

While Cellini is trying to escape with his life from Nicaragua, the extremist doctrine of Ayatollah Khomeini is gaining a lot of traction in Iran. Khomeini had been exiled from Iran by the Shah for his extremist beliefs in 1964 and is now resident in Najaf, a Shiite holy city in Iraq, but recordings of his vitriolic anti-Shah and anti-American speeches are being broadcast in universities throughout Iran, calling for the establishment of an Islamic State under Shiite governance.

At the beginning of 1978, violent demonstrations against the Shah reach new levels, creating widespread concern for stability in the Middle East. Khomeini is expelled from Iraq by then vice president Saddam Hussein, who at the time is very much in favour with the Americans and no doubt believes his action will curry favour with the United States government.

Khomeini relocates to Neauphle-le-Château, a suburb of Paris, on a tourist visa, where he is able to garner far greater media access. As a result, his popularity in Iran grows rapidly and exponentially.

As discontent in Iran grows, support for Ayatollah Khomeini increases. Khomeini calls for the Shah's immediate overthrow.

In December 1978, the Iranian Army mutinies and on January 16, 1979, the Shah flees to the United States.

Khomeini makes a triumphant return to Tehran on February 1, 1979 and immediately begins converting Iran into an Islamic State under Shiite rule. On November 4, 1979 – the 15th anniversary of Khomeini's exile – radical students storm the US embassy in Tehran and take fifty-two American hostages, demanding that the Shah return to Iran and stand trial in exchange for their release. The hostages are held captive for one year and 79 days before their release is negotiated.

It is the prologue for what will become one of the most complicated and sordid series of events in the history of the United States, involving two foreign countries that have no apparent connection: Iran and Nicaragua, and will be known simply as "Iran-Contra."

The Shah of Iran dies in Egypt of cancer in July 1980.

*****

CELLINI AND THE REST of the team from the now destroyed blood bank leave the hotel at first light and head for the United States Embassy. Parking the Chevy as discreetly as possible, close to the main gate but out of sight from the road, they show their passports to the Marine Corps guards and are welcomed by federal agents who want to talk to them about the recent events. Cellini comes in for a particularly long debriefing, but soon makes friends with one of the agents, to whom he will later present a Colt .45 semi-automatic pistol as a gift. Cellini spends a great deal of his time discussing American foreign policy with Embassy staff, partly because he wants to catch up on world politics, but mostly because he wants to demonstrate that he is still interested in being active and helping in any way he can.

The men are shown to their quarters and told to be on standby for a flight out of Managua to Miami as soon as one is available. It could be some time.

They have free run of the guest facilities at the Embassy, including access to telephone communication so that they are able to call home and reassure their families of their well-being. Cellini, never one to make contact with Franci while engaged on business overseas, chooses instead to use his telephone privileges to contact one of his oldest friends.

He calls Tonino Anibilis, in Bari.

They speak for a long time, catching up on each other's adventures. Tonino is enthralled to hear that his old partner Tutuc is in Nicaragua and highly amused by the thought that he may be wanted for the assassination of a high-profile left-wing journalist. Tonino has not been idle since they last met, either. Though he has spent more time in Italian prison than out of it, he has made good contacts and risen in the ranks.

One of the few people trusted by Cellini back when he was working as a volunteer for the SOE and OSS during World War Two, Tonino is curious about whether his old friend is still working for the US Government. If so, he knows people who may be able to help Cellini.

"I'm sure you know all about what is going on in Iran?"

Cellini does his best to keep up with the news from home whenever he travels, although it is difficult in a country like Nicaragua, where freedom of the press doesn't exist and much of the media is biased against America. He has been able to catch up some since arriving at the Embassy, mostly from his conversations with the agent who befriends him. Cellini is aware that another crisis is looming for the United States on the other side of the globe.

"I know that they hate Americans," Cellini replies. "It seems to be a popular sport everywhere."

Tonino Anibilis is quiet for a moment, thinking about how to ask his next question.

"Tutuc, is it safe to talk on this phone?" he says.

Cellini laughs, "Tonino, I'm staying at the American Embassy in Managua, Nicaragua, where they are expecting a communist revolution almost any day now. Every phone call is recorded, monitored, transcribed and circulated to every security department in the American government. If I sneeze there will be a written report on Jimmy Carter's desk before I can grab my handkerchief out of my pocket. Don't worry about it. They know who I am and I have nothing to hide – but if you want to make it fun, let's talk in *Barese*!"

The two of them enjoy a laugh and then Tonino gets to the point.

"Listen Ueli," he uses Cellini's *Barese* nickname, "There is a lot of concern here about Khomeini, but we know he's primarily an American problem, so we don't want to step on any toes…"

By "we," Tonino is referring to the Italian organized crime families with whom he is connected.

"But if you need any help to… eliminate him, I have it on very good authority that we know where he is, and we have people who can get to him. We can make your problem go away. Guaranteed."

Cellini waits for the last piece of information. Tonino doesn't disappoint him.

"The price is one million US dollars. It's non-negotiable."

It's cheap for the elimination of so dangerous a person, and Cellini knows it's strictly on the level.

"All I can do is pass along your very reasonable offer," he says. "I'll get back to you either way."

*****

"It's not the American way," is the message that comes back later that same day.

Cellini has heard it all before and was fairly sure that would be the answer he would get from the agent sitting across the desk from him, so it comes as no surprise. It still disappoints him.

"Bullshit," he replies. "I know for a fact we tried to eliminate Hitler and Castro, and probably others."

The official just looks at him and says nothing. Disgusted, Cellini storms out of the office.

He calls Anibilis the following morning to say, "Thanks but no thanks…" but Tonino is very excitable.

"But Ueli, you have to talk to them again! Haven't you heard? Khomeini just got his ass kicked out of Iraq!"

"So what?" Cellini says.

"So what? *So what?*" Anibilis is really excitable now.

"That means this can only finish up one way. He's got to be planning to go back to Tehran. Once that happens, we won't be able to get near him. The point is that right now, we know exactly where he is, where he's going and how he's going to get there! We can bring down his aircraft and make it look like an accident, or at the very least a mistake!"

"How?"

"Let's just say friends in high places and leave it at that. A couple of high rankers in the Italian Air Force owe some friends of mine a big favour."

"Is it still one million US dollars?" Cellini enquires, knowing full well the price has risen.

"Ten million. There are more people involved and it's a little more complicated."

*****

CELLINI ASKS TO MEET WITH his friendly agent again, but enquires if this time he would be willing to bring one of his superiors along. The senior man looks ex-military and not the kind of person to suffer fools gladly.

Cellini speaks first, "I know you've already rejected the idea once, but things have changed and this could be important. I'm sure you are aware that Khomeini has been kicked out of Iraq and…" his speech is cut short by the senior agent.

"Yeah, he's going to France. So what?"

Tonino hadn't told him that Khomeini was going to France, so the agent has just given something away which he shouldn't have. *That's a pretty basic mistake for senior field agent,* Cellini thinks to himself, *so either this guy isn't a senior field agent, or the US Secret Service is in a lot of trouble.*

Before Cellini can speak again, the agent continues, his tone almost mocking, "You're still a Goddamn fascist, Cellini!" as he slams the familiar and now well-thumbed file folder down on the desk in front of him. He gets up and starts pacing up and down in the room as if he's trying to think of what to say next. He finally finds the words.

"Look, Cellini, when you first brought us the idea we told you a flat 'No!' – but after you left, we discussed it at some length and the ambassador actually thought it merited a call to Washington, so he made a personal phone call. The answer came back, a definite and emphatic 'No!'"

Cellini decides against arguing further with either of the men. It was a good plan, but if, as he suspected, the White House had vetoed the idea, there really was nothing more to say. With people like these two involved, it probably wouldn't stand a chance of succeeding anyway.

"I'm sorry for wasting your time, sir," Cellini says. He still knows when to play the loser convincingly.

The agent changes the subject, "I do have some good news for you. We've got you booked on a flight out of here tomorrow morning."

"That's great news. I'm sure everyone will be pleased to get home," Cellini replies.

The agent shakes Cellini's hand and thanks him for his time. "We'll get all of you together for a briefing later, but you'll need to be ready to leave by about 8:00 am."

Later that evening, an administrative assistant calls the group together and tells them they are booked on a regularly scheduled American Airlines commercial flight leaving Managua at nine o'clock the following morning.

"No one knows that you are on this flight. The Nicaraguan government, in fact the president himself, has given his assurance that none of you will be detained or harmed in any way. All you have to do is leave here around eight a.m., drive straight to the airport, pick up your tickets at the American Airlines counter and get on the plane. You'll be back in Miami in time for cocktails."

The group disperses to get ready for their departure and maybe grab a couple more beers on Uncle Sam's tab. The assistant asks Cellini to wait behind.

"There's one more thing you need to know Mr. Cellini," he says.

"What's that?" Cellini is curious.

"It hasn't made the news desks yet because it literally just happened, but some guy named Silvio Peña Rivas has been arrested for the murder of Chamorro and he has implicated your friend Ramos. He says Ramos paid him to organize the hit."

The agent pauses to watch Cellini's reaction before continuing. "That means everyone and their brother is going to be out looking for you guys, so even though no one outside these walls and the office of President Somoza knows about your flight tomorrow, you'll need to be on your guard."

Cellini's attitude is calm, almost indifferent, but inside he's reeling over the fact that Silvio Peña, the man Ramos introduced to him on the beach a few days ago, has been arrested for the killing that has sent the whole country into a tailspin.

67. Escape from Managua

Everyone is pleased to be heading out. The hospitality of the Embassy has been adequate but perfunctory and the men feel they are beginning to outstay their welcome. Later, back in the room, Cellini calls a meeting of the six.

"We meet here at 6:00 am tomorrow morning and leave," he says.

"But the Ambassador's assistant said eight?" one of the men replies; it's one of the Alvarez brothers.

"Yes, but he's not going with us, is he?" Cellini says, "So he's not going to be the one getting his ass shot at."

"You think there's going to be shooting?" Faustino sounds gleeful, *but then he would,* Cellini thinks.

"Hopefully not," Cellini replies, "but I do know this: they'll be watching this place just as they've been watching it every day since we got here. They know exactly how long it takes to drive from here to the airport and they'll be expecting us to leave in time to get there and get straight on the flight. They won't be expecting us to leave two hours early."

"Makes sense to me. What about once we get to the airport? How safe will we be then?" This time it's the other Alvarez brother; Cellini can never remember which one is which.

"I seriously doubt they would do anything once we're inside the airport," Cellini answers. "There are too many innocent bystanders, tourists and business people from other countries. The last thing these revolutionaries want is an international incident that would give Somoza the chance to set the army against them. They aren't ready for all-out civil war just yet. Soon, perhaps – but not right now. In any case, even if they are dumb enough to come in after us, I'd rather defend myself inside a building where I can choose my position and make my own strategy than out on the open road."

The men agree. At six o'clock the following morning they are waiting in the lobby of the US Embassy building. They say goodbye to the two Marine Corps guards by the doorway and step out into the humid air and semi-darkness.

The truck stutters then starts. With two in the cab, windows rolled down, and four in the bed of the truck, crouching low and holding semi-automatic weapons, locked and loaded with safety catches off, they make their way through the gate of the Embassy and onto the street, casually saluting the Marine on guard duty as they pass through. Cellini rides in the passenger seat of the vehicle, a Colt .45 Model 1911 pistol loaded and ready, with extra clips in his pocket if needed. He watches the sky ahead change from purple to red to orange to blue and realises that, one way or another, this is probably the last time he will see the sun rise over Nicaragua.

Instead of taking the most direct route along *Carretera Panamerica*, they drive through the city, still fairly deserted at that time of day, taking *Pista Juan Pablo II* and *Pista de la Resistencia*, only joining the main highway when they get closer to the airport. So far so good.

As they ride in silence, Cellini looks around at these men he has been working alongside off and on for over eighteen months. They have never become friends. They barely acknowledge each other day-to-day, and Cellini hadn't even bothered to learn their names until last night.[1] Until now they had been nothing more than business associates, and he wasn't even sure he trusted them. Now circumstances had forced the issue and at any moment they might become brothers in arms.

The closer they get to the airport, the more traffic they run into. The more traffic they see, the more likelihood there is of running into rebel militia, who routinely patrol the city streets and highways in military-style Jeeps just to make their presence known. The Chevy has to slow down approaching a large *rotunda* where *Pista Larreynaga* intersects with *Pista del la Solidaridad.* As they approach the *rotunda,* they see two dull green Jeeps loaded with men wearing camouflage fatigues and carrying rifles converging from the left, behind a car and a minibus. One of the men in the leading Jeep sees the battered truck with four men in the back and starts waving his arms and yelling, then points in their direction.

The chase is on.

*****

THE DRIVER GUNS the Chevy, pulls into the right hand side of the centre lane and takes off around the traffic, cutting in and heading north

[1] *Fausto Alvarez, Luis Agustin Casteleiro, Angel Faustino Centeno, Juan Raul Alvarez and Julio Sabatés.*

on *Pista Portezuelo.* Besides the inevitable cacophony of horns, his action causes angry, half-asleep drivers to pull up at all angles so they can shake their fists out the window at this crazy man in the white Chevy truck. The distraction is perfect. For a few minutes at least, it creates confusion and a traffic jam around the *rotunda* that stops the Jeeps from getting through.

Still a few kilometres to go to get to the airport and there's no sign of the two Jeeps, but their excessive speed is still drawing a lot of attention from the other drivers, honking their horns and swerving to get out of the way.

"Slow down!" Cellini screams at the top of his lungs at his driver, "You'll either kill us all or get us arrested!"

But the man behind the wheel is having too much fun playing Steve McQueen, swerving from one side of the road to the other and dodging other vehicles. As he turns from *Pista Portezuelo* onto *Carretera Panamericana Norte* and heads along the home-straight towards the airport, screeching the tyres and almost flipping the truck over as he makes the turn, he draws the attention of another green Jeep going in the opposite direction, which brakes and turns 180 degrees to begin pursuing the white Chevy, just as Sabatés is beginning to heed Cellini's order to slow down.

"What are you doing?" Cellini says. "For Christ's sake don't slow down now – we're almost there, and these guys are about six cars behind us and gaining!"

The driver rolls his eyes as if to say *I wish you'd make up your mind* before reprising his McQueen role, dipping the clutch, dropping down a gear and flooring the accelerator while leaning hard on the horn, using the shoulder of the road and even the grass verge to gain as much ground as he can.

The Chevy swerves into the airport parking area and all the way up to the main entrance, coming to a screeching halt against the kerb, right in front of the glass doors. All six men pile out of the vehicle and race inside, guns still locked and loaded but uncocked and safely stowed in their bags.

Once inside, Cellini herds everyone together out of view from the glass doors.

"We split up now. Everyone walk – don't run – to different parts of the airport." He stops to look at his watch. "We'll meet at the American Airlines ticket counter at eight to check our bags and pick up our tickets. Now go!"

Everyone walks away. He takes a few steps before glancing around over his shoulder towards the entrance. The Jeep has pulled up behind the Chevy truck. Two figures in army fatigues are standing looking inside the truck while a third is peering through the glass doors of the airport. Cellini keeps walking, picks up a discarded newspaper from one seat, then chooses another seat offering a better view of the entrance. He turns the newspaper over, pretending to stare at the back page as if looking at sports results, while actually looking over it to see what is going on outside.

Two more Jeeps, presumably the ones that had originally been chasing them, pull up alongside the Chevy and the soldiers pile out to join the group standing outside. One of the rebel soldiers, who seems like he might be in charge, walks into the airport and straight past Cellini without looking at him. He gets as far as the ticketing area, stops and turns 360 degrees, scanning the airport. Seeing nothing that arouses his interest, he turns and walks back, passing Cellini for a second time without even noticing his existence, and back out the same door he came in.

Cellini waits until 7:45 before he gets up, tucks the folded newspaper under his arm and walks slowly towards the American Airlines ticket counter.

A voice behind him calls out, "Stop!" His heart skips a beat, but he ignores the voice and keeps going, picking up his pace a little.

"Goddamn it, Cellini, will you slow down!"

He spins around, his mind racing and his hand reaching inside his bag for his pistol. He stops dead and a huge grin crawls across his face as he recognizes the features of his diminutive friend.

"Jorge!" he practically screams, momentarily drawing attention from other passengers and airport workers going about their business. "What the hell are you doing here?"

Jorge Rodriguez grabs Cellini's hand and they embrace.

"I couldn't leave you alone with a bunch of Cuban refugees getting lost in Nicaragua at a time like this!" he jokes. Referring to the rest of the party, his fellow countrymen, as "refugees" is a term of endearment. "Ramos got taken in by Miami PD for questioning but not before he called Somoza, who arranged to get you guys out – and then he called me and told me the arrangements. This story is all over the news in Florida! I figured I'd come down here and make sure you get on the plane when you're supposed to!

"Speaking of those Cuban refugees, where are they?" Rodriguez says.

"We split up once we got inside the airport," Cellini replies, glancing at his watch. "The plan was to meet up at the ticket counter, right about now."

They continue to the American Airlines ticket desk, where they meet up with the others. Once they collect their tickets, the group continues on to the departure lounge to wait for the flight to be called. Cellini decides after what they've been through it's time he learned everyone's name and passes around a Nicaraguan 10 Cordoba banknote for each member of the team to sign as a memento.[2]

Called to board the aircraft a few minutes later, he realises he still has the newspaper he had picked up earlier tucked under his arm, and leaves it on his seat in the departure lounge as he gets up. Being unable to understand written Spanish, he hasn't read a single word; hasn't even opened up the first page.

If he had, he might have seen the photo of Pedro Ramos Quiroz and the headline that read ¡Se Busca *por Asesinato!* [3]

[2] *Approximately $1.40 US. Cellini still has the signed banknote.*

[3] *Translates as "Wanted for Murder".*

Once they arrived safely at the airport, the group had a few minutes to relax and take some last-minute photos before getting on the plane out of Managua.

Vito Cellini (far right in top picture) is unable to put names to faces but they know who they are. Cellini's friend Jorge Rodriguez (lower picture, far right) flew in to greet the men and escort them home.

Each member of the team signed a Nicaraguan 10 Cordoba banknote, which Vito Cellini kept as a souvenir.

68. Weapons and Women

ON THE FLIGHT home from Nicaragua, Cellini spends little time reflecting on what could have been. Mentally he's already started moving on.

With the Sandinistas growing in strength, he knows the Somoza regime isn't going to last much longer in Nicaragua. If communists infiltrate Central America, the drug trade will increase and start to spread north. His efforts to find a market for the machine pistol have stalled again, and he needs to be thinking about what he's going to do next. His thoughts turn to the armoured car company and the opportunity it presented. *As one door closes…* he muses to himself… *another one slams in your face.* He laughs out loud at his own strange humour, drawing the attention of the pretty woman sitting next to him. She smiles, but he just closes his eyes and goes to sleep. When a pretty woman smiles at him, he can't help but think about Franci, who he hasn't seen for so long. He dreams about her, and about asking her if she'd consider moving to Texas. When the plane comes in to land, he has the entire plan worked out between his conscious and subconscious mind.

Cellini has spent years trying to find a market for his small machine pistol. Could Enrico Verdolin's armoured car connections in San Antonio be the opportunity he's been waiting for?

Franci, as always, is happy to go along with whatever her husband decides to do and will never stand in his way. She is not particularly keen to leave Florida, but she knows he is getting restless. He can't stay in one place or at one job for any length of time. It seems to her he's either looking for a new adventure or being found by one.

At least, she reasons, if the company is based in Texas, he will be staying in the USA for a while.

He decides to accept the offer and begins to make plans to move to San Antonio.

*****

THE DAY AFTER Cellini returns home from Nicaragua, the phone rings and it is one of his acquaintances from the gun club. He wants to know if Cellini can meet him at the club later in the afternoon.

"I just got off a plane from South America. Can this wait until tomorrow?"

The man is impatient but agrees to meet the following day.

"But don't make me wait any longer. I've got 10,000 reasons why you don't want to keep me waiting – and it'll be the easiest money you'll ever make."

Cellini has brought back more than enough money from Nicaragua – $32,000 in the bottom of a camera bag covered with a couple of kilos of fresh avocados. It's his usual ploy. Customs officials are all over him for trying to bring fresh produce into the United States and so anxious to confiscate it that they won't look any further, so they never notice the large amount of cash below, hidden under carefully arranged tripods, extra lenses and rolls of film. Cellini then apologizes profusely for his indiscretion, professes his innocent intentions – "I just wanted to surprise my wife… she loves avocados!" and charms the customs officials with photos of Franci and his gift of conversation.

In spite of having just smuggled a great deal more money than he is now being offered, Cellini cannot help but be intrigued by this new offer of cash. Whenever someone waves cash in his direction, it invariably leads to an interesting adventure – and it is the adventure that appeals far more to him than the money.

The man is Cuban, and he is interested in acquiring a large quantity of Beretta M12 sub-machine guns directly from the factory. He will take care of transporting the weapons, but he needs Cellini to arrange the purchase and negotiate the price.

Cellini is known for his integrity. He will not ask for what purpose the gentleman wants these weapons because he does not want to know. He knows that if there is any question regarding the legality of the purchase, Beretta will not allow the sale.

And he needs to know how many.

"2,350," the Cuban replies.

Cellini does not comment. He tells the Cuban to leave it with him and goes about his business.

Cellini is able to broker the deal fairly easily because he still has contacts at Beretta through his extended family. It just takes a couple of phone calls. Paperwork is filed. Everything is legal, licensed and above board. Since Beretta's headquarters is located in Valle Trompia in the province of Brescia, not far from where his sisters live in Milan, Cellini decides to visit Italy to see the production facility and test the weapons himself. He invites his customer to join him and they make travel plans. Arriving at Miami airport to fly to Italy, the Cuban introduces his lovely travelling companion and the three embark on what turns out to be a brief but pleasant trip. Valle Trompia is a charming and historic town in the foothills of the Italian Alps.

Better still, Beretta promises to pay Cellini a handsome commission for the sale in addition to his fee from the customer.[1]

Their business concluded, Cellini returns home, richer by $10,000 and having had a pleasant vacation.

Several months later, Cellini has cause to telephone the Cuban regarding a totally unrelated manner. The phone is answered by a lady, and Cellini asks for her husband.

"Who is calling?" she says.

"Vito Cellini," he replies.

"Who?" the lady says.

"Vito Cellini. You remember me? We were in Italy together a few months ago."

The phone is silent for several seconds, then the lady says, "I have never been to Italy," and promptly hangs up.

Cellini is summoned to the Cuban's home. When he arrives, he is shown into the room where the man keeps his gun collection and invited to take a seat at a table. The Cuban closes the door and offers him a drink, then sits down across the table from him.

He stares at Cellini without saying a word. Cellini decides to break the ice.

"Did everything work out OK with your delivery from Beretta?" He knows it went perfectly and is just making conversation.

"No Mr. Cellini. It did not!"

Cellini is taken aback by the reply, but before he can speak the Cuban leans across the table and hisses more words at him.

"I paid you $10,000 and I want it back!"

"What?" Cellini starts to smile. "You got your guns delivered at a great price and everything worked out. Everyone's happy. So what is this, some kind of joke?"

"No joke Cellini," the Cuban says. Suddenly, from under the table he produces a Colt .45 Model 1911 semi-automatic and points it in Cellini's face. Cellini doesn't flinch. He just stares at the barrel of the gun.

"So tell me what your problem is?" he asks.

[1]. *Sales commission that Cellini never received from Beretta.*

"You got me into a lot of trouble, Mr. Cellini," the Cuban continues, "When you tried to call me a few days ago, you talked to my wife and you told her you had been with her in Italy."

The penny dropped. Cellini started grinning. Slapping the palm of his hand on the table he couldn't help himself and the grin turned to laughter.

"That wasn't your wife? Oh shit! That's funny. That's really funny!"

Pulling the hammer back on the Colt to cock it, the Cuban grips the weapon with two hands, pointing it right at Cellini's head.

"Are you going to give me my money back or shall I just blow your fucking head off?" he says.

"Go ahead. Blow my fucking head off," Cellini says, "because I am not giving you any of the money back. I worked hard for that – and by the way, Beretta didn't pay me a dime in commission for selling their lousy guns to you!"

Cellini pushes the chair back and stands up, hands by his sides, and walks slowly towards the door of the room. He doesn't look back. He braces, waiting for the shot, but it never comes. As he walks through the door, he shakes his head and smiles again to himself.

"Stupid bastard," he says to himself as he walks outside and towards his car. Any respect he had for the Cuban is spent. Firstly for cheating on his wife and secondly for not bothering to tell him that the woman he brought along on the trip was a girlfriend. But mostly for not having the balls to squeeze the trigger.

It's not the first time he's had a gun pointed at his head, and it most probably won't be the last. He marvels at the fact that after all these years he still feels no fear. Not when he is staring down the barrel of the gun and not right at this moment. He knows the fear will come later, as it always does, when he's alone at night and trying to sleep.

*****

Just when he thinks the Nicaragua episode is finally behind him, Franci has one more surprise in store. She catches him off guard one night over dinner. She tells him that while he had been away, Jorge Rodriguez had stopped by and, among other things, had told her all about the sex trade in Managua, and in particular about a pretty young girl named María.

"So what?" Cellini says.

"Jorge told me you were very friendly with this María," Franci says, giving nothing away with her facial expression.

Cellini decides to tell her the story of his meeting María and how they did indeed spend time together. He confesses that he took her out to dinner and that they danced together. He admits that he had enjoyed her company – though he leaves out the part about getting into bed with her to spare Franci's feelings, because, after all, nothing had happened. He swears he was never unfaithful and never has been, but he's not convinced that Franci completely believes him. Then he remembers he still has María's phone number on a piece of paper in his wallet. He walks over to the telephone and dials the number. To his surprise María answers, and after a few minutes he asks her if she will please talk to his wife, and tell her that she never slept with him!

He hands over the phone to Franci.

María introduces herself and tells Franci of the many conversations she and Vito had while he was working in Managua. She describes what she does for a living but assures Franci that her husband was always a gentleman; that he never slept with her even though she had wanted to – and that when they were together he mostly talked about how much he missed his wife.

After the phone call, Franci looks at Cellini, smiles enigmatically and shakes her head. Cellini isn't sure whether it's her way of saying *I never really doubted you, but María sounds really nice and I wouldn't have blamed you if you did* or *if I find out you did, you know I'll cut them off!* Instead she says nothing and the subject is never discussed again.

It is a wonderful testimony to the great and enduring love Cellini and Franci share. She had never had cause to doubt her husband's fidelity before, and she never questions it again.

Part V

Texas, 1978

69. San Antonio and Armoured Cars

FRANCI FLIES TO San Antonio with Nicky while Cellini decides to drive his trusty Volkswagen bus. His oldest son Frank stays behind in North Miami to take care of packing up and transporting the rest of their possessions. The drive is anything but smooth and straightforward. First, a routine traffic stop by the highway patrol almost leads to Cellini's arrest for transporting blue crabs across a state line. Later, he tries to buy pecans from a roadside vendor but after negotiating with the seller finds she in unable to accept a credit card and he has no cash. In Houston, he witnesses a bad road accident and stops to help. There is little he can do except offer one of the uninjured victims a ride home to New Braunfels, a small town just north of San Antonio. When they arrive at the grateful passenger's house, he hands over a bushel of pecans for Cellini to take home. It's his introduction to Texas hospitality and it makes a lasting impression.

When he arrives in San Antonio, in February 1978, he finds it just as cold and wet as when he had visited the previous November, and after the warm tropical climate of Nicaragua and the balmy Florida weather, he begins to wonder if he has made the right decision in coming to Texas.

Soon after arriving in the Alamo City, he arranges a meeting with the executive at the armoured car company. This time he is going to state his own terms.

"I will manufacture the machine pistols for you, but it will have to be totally legal and above board. Every pistol would need to be properly registered with ATF."

"Of course," the executive replies.

Then Cellini adds, "And I want to know who's buying each one."

The executive baulks a little. "I'm not actually sure we can do that. Our clients rely on our complete confidentiality and — "

"Then no deal!" Cellini interrupts.

"Let me see what I can do. Perhaps unofficially I could let you see the firearms certificates, just so you know they are going to legitimate buyers. Would that be enough?"

After a lengthy discussion about the details, Cellini agrees. They shake hands.

In his capacity as a consultant and supplier, Cellini is essentially a freelancer. He is not needed at the plant every day, so he has time to explore the locale, discover the gun shops, gun clubs, shooting ranges and hunting associations. He also has more time to think about working on his stabilizers and other inventions. He soon discovers that Texas is a friendly state, and in a couple of weeks the weather starts to warm up. He adapts quickly and decides he is ready to make the move to San Antonio permanent.

By spring, the Cellinis have settled into a modest but spacious home on Ranch Road. Cellini has his machines installed in a workshop at the house but still goes to work at the armoured car plant two or three times a week.

*****

One of the most vulnerable parts of a car – especially a car designed to offer maximum protection to its passengers – is the tyres. If the tyres are shot out or punctured by shrapnel, the car is unable to get any traction and cannot make an escape. This inevitably leads Cellini to divert many hours into thinking about a solution. So-called armoured tires are available, but these simply have thicker, heavier sidewalls and treads. They may resist small-calibre bullets and deflect small pieces of glass or metal, but are ineffective against substantial artillery.

Cellini's idea is to develop a tyre in which the air chamber is divided into separate compartments, so that if one compartment is breached, there is enough air in the other compartments for the car to safely get away. He begins work on the concept but is forced to drop it when the company insists he focus his attention on production of the machine pistols.[1]

Production of the machine pistols takes precedence over everything else he is working on. Altogether, Cellini will produce 23 of his machine guns for the armoured car company, each made by hand, although he finds the company is getting progressively slower at paying his invoices.

Months later, he gets called into the executive's office.

"We have a problem," the executive says, looking concerned.

"With one of your machine pistols. We have a problem." He repeats

1. Had he been able to continue developing the tyre concept, Cellini might have had a claim on the first patent for run-flat tyres.

himself to emphasize the point.

"What problem?' Cellini asks.

"One of our customers has complained that the weapon jammed after firing two clips, and that it won't fire any more."

"Did he strip it and clean it?" Cellini asks.

"Several times. At least that's what he told us," the executive says.

"Then maybe he damaged it? Maybe he loaded the wrong kind of bullets?"

"Vito. He didn't damage it or load the wrong kind of bullets. He has returned it and we cleaned it and test fired it again. It's completely jammed. Now our customer has demanded that we give him a replacement or his money back."

"Pffaa!" Cellini waves his hand as if swatting an imaginary fly. "Then give him his money back. I'll buy it back from him. How's that?"

The executive continues, "Yes, I'm afraid you will have to buy it back. The thing is, we wanted to give him a replacement, so we tested another pistol before we gave it to him. It also fired two clips then quit. Jammed. And we can't get it to work any more. Do you have any suggestions as to why that might be?"

Cellini shrugs. "I've said I'll buy it back from your customer. That's all."

The fact is that Cellini is growing tired of producing these pistols to order. For some time he has suspected that the armoured car company's list of clients includes drug dealers and other lowlifes. Much as he wants to believe he is working for state officials, law enforcement or even celebrities, he cannot shake this nagging feeling that he is somehow assisting people on the wrong side of the law.[2]

As interesting is the work is, Cellini begins to have second thoughts about the company.

*****

[2.] *Once he became convinced that his machine pistols were finding their way into the hands of criminals, Cellini decided he had to do something about it, and he started experimenting with ways to make the guns jam after firing a few demonstration rounds. He bought back the weapon in question, later selling it to a movie production/property company as a prop. He was told that it had been used by Arnold Schwarzenegger in a movie, though he could never find out exactly which movie. Vito Cellini had the last laugh believing his machine pistol had been taken from a potential drug dealer and finally given to a celebrity!*

While working at the armoured car company, Cellini is approached directly by various individuals claiming to represent personal security companies, looking for ways to improve anti-terrorism techniques. Most he takes with a very large grain of salt, assuming they are either looking to get rich quick, or worse, trying to entrap him in some kind of illegal activity.

On one such occasion, he is contacted by someone claiming to represent a major movie production company, asking if he would be interested in working on a "big Hollywood" action adventure film. The idea appeals to Cellini. It isn't his first experience with the movies, having supplied "trick" guns to film companies on a couple of occasions, and having recently sold his machine pistol to a movie prop house.[3] The thought of participating in a movie has a certain appeal. It's also a way of getting his inventions seen by possibly influential people.

The scene is to be a classic Hollywood style car chase with the lead car eventually taking a turn too fast and rolling over. It will be filmed in the Texas Hill Country – not Hollywood – which is why the company has come to Cellini. Can he do it? Can he keep to a reasonably low budget? Yes, he thinks he can.

The stunt is usually accomplished by building a tube into the bottom of the car with a downward-firing explosive charge, controlled by the driver. When he's ready to "roll" the car, he punches a button and the charge detonates, lifting the side of the vehicle off the road and into a roll. Because explosives are involved, the proper licensing must be obtained before work on the project can begin.

While the so-called movie people are applying for the paperwork, which they assure him is coming, they change the location of the chase scene and no longer want him to build the device into the car, only to instruct them on how to build and detonate it – and to provide the explosives. He becomes suspicious and presses them for more information regarding their licence application. He never hears from them again.[4]

3. *Cellini devised a gun that would fire a full clip (of blanks) when dropped on the floor.*

4. *This is just one example of many professional situations that Cellini has found himself in. Being an essentially trusting man, Cellini never thought to "check up" on people, but always took them at face value, relying heavily on his instinctive ability to judge character. If someone approached him with an idea that appealed, provided he sensed the person was of good character – he would invariably go along "just for the adventure". In this case, as in others, he has often wondered if he was being tested or set up by the federal authorities. If so, he takes pride in his resolve to stay within the law.*

*****

HE WILL HAVE one more run-in with the armoured car company before he decides to walk away.

A government official from Canada – a potentially high-profile customer – has observed that armoured cars have one particular weakness. Though they can be built with increasingly resilient armour plating and some even offer protection from bombs and grenades, there is one period of time when they are extremely vulnerable. When stationary.

Though the doors can be locked from the inside so that no one is able to infiltrate the vehicle if it is stopped in traffic – once the vehicle stops and the driver releases the door lock, a would-be assassin, even someone posing as a security guard, can then open the door and have the occupants entirely at his mercy.

"Why," the Canadian official asked, "can the car not have a door-handle that requires a special technique to open, that is only known by the person who is supposed to open it?"

The San Antonio company has no hesitation in throwing the problem at Vito Cellini.

Perhaps not surprisingly, Cellini has an almost immediate, and very simple, solution. Taking a standard car door handle – the type with a button that releases the catch when pushed in – he cuts the button in half using a micro fine saw blade. Cellini then completely reconstructs the door catch mechanism. Pushing either one or both sides of the button will not release the catch and open the door. Instead, the door can only be opened by flipping one half of the button outwards – the exact opposite action to that normally required.[5]

Only a person who knows how to operate the door-handle can open the door. Even if a potential assailant were able to figure out how to operate the door-handle, the delay would give the driver sufficient time to realise the situation, hit the gas pedal and leave the area.

For this ingenious device that he has designed, created, built, tested and installed successfully on several vehicles, Cellini submits an invoice to the company for $650.

He never receives payment.

5. *Today the technology exists for computerized locks with codes to punch in, time release, and the use of finger printing or even retina scan for identification. Cellini's genius lies in the fact that he used mechanical devices, despite never having had any formal training.*

70. The Stabilizer is Born

HAVING WALKED OUT of his contract with the armoured car company, Cellini takes a part-time job as a gunsmith at a local gun shop. The position brings him a modest but adequate income, and allows him the freedom to take time off to enjoy his passion for hunting, which he soon discovers Texas offers in abundance. He also has more time to continue creating and developing his own inventions, both those connected with firearms and those with entirely different applications.

For the Cellinis, life is on the brink of perfection.

The owner of the gun shop, Don Carter, offers him complete freedom to use the machine tools for his own projects as long as he gets everything done for his customers.

One customer proves to be difficult to deal with. He returns an AR-15 to the shop after Cellini has repaired, cleaned and oiled the weapon. Cellini overhears the conversation between Don Carter and the customer from the back room.

"Damn thing doesn't work," the man says.

Cellini, normally patient with customers, does not take kindly to having his work disparaged, and responds from the back room, loud enough for the customer to hear, "Huh. Maybe he just doesn't know how to shoot?"

The customer asks to be introduced and Cellini steps forward. The customer is a US Army general stationed at nearby Fort Sam Houston! It is not the first time, nor will it be the last, that Cellini questions the ability and training of a soldier in handling a weapon, regardless of rank or experience.

Fortunately, Cellini's charm wins the day. He offers the general some guidance and tips, and at the end of the day, everyone is happy.

*****

Nicky is slowly regaining his health following the open heart surgery. He isn't physically strong and it is unlikely he will be able to work again, so he has been awarded a full pension for his service in the United States Air Force. However, his sharp wit and defiant nature are a good indication that he has recovered his mental acuity.

Father and son have a date to go to the shooting range. It is the first time Nicky has fired a weapon since before his surgery, and he is having trouble operating the trigger on his .357 Magnum revolver. He asks his father if there is anything that can be done to make operating the trigger any easier.

Adjusting the tension on the trigger is fairly easy and soon Nicky is able to fire the weapon, but now he has trouble keeping it steady, because of the recoil. The gun jumps upwards each time he fires, so his shots are missing the target. Even when he tries to correct by aiming lower, his shooting is off the mark. What is even worse, firing his gun is becoming painful. He asks his father if there is anything that can be done to stabilize the gun while firing it.

This takes a lot more thought. There is little that can be done about the primary recoil of a weapon,[1] but Cellini believes that the powerful secondary recoil, caused by hot gases escaping from the muzzle as the bullet leaves the barrel, can be reduced by allowing the gases to dissipate more slowly as the bullet exits. A simple attachment on the end of the barrel ought to do the trick, he thinks, and he begins by building a prototype for his favourite Colt .45 Model 1911.

The next few days are spent either in the back room at the gun shop or in his garage workshop, hand-carving blocks of aluminium and then turning them on his lathe, rejecting one design after another until he has something that satisfies him. Like a sculptor working with blocks of fine marble, Cellini never uses sketches or diagrams. Instead, he pictures the finished item in his mind's eye before shaping it in his hands.

The completed prototype looks like an extension of the barrel, just slightly wider in diameter. It screws into the muzzle and has a series of holes drilled in it, to aid in the dissipation of the hot gases.

He takes the gun, its attachment in place, to the shooting range and waits for an opportunity to test fire the gun when there are less people around so as not to attract too much attention. He shoots the Colt both with and without the attachment in place and notices a significant difference in the recoil with his stabilizer attached. He also notices that the sound of the pistol

1. *"Momentum conservation", which is what Sir Isaac Newton was talking about when he wrote "every action has an equal and opposite reaction".*

firing is different. Quieter. Not silenced – even though his device does look a lot like the type of contraption used in movies to make gunfire seem almost completely silent. Though his device in no way *silences* any weapon, it is a technicality that will prevent him from marketing the device to anyone in the future, other than those licensed to own a silenced weapon, law enforcement or the military.

He is pleased and decides to build a stabilizer for Nicky's .357, and another for his Springfield .30-06 rifle. Both work well and Cellini is excited, but he knows he can do better and will not rest until he perfects his design. He is already beginning to think about ways to improve the test model.

Cellini doesn't know it yet, but these are the first steps towards what will arguably be his greatest invention, and Nicky is both his inspiration and his motivation for the idea.

Cellini decides to quit his part-time job at the gun shop and focus all his attention on his new project.[2] He will call his design a "stabilizer", because that is what it was intended to do, though it will be given many different names and appear in many different forms. Some will call it a "muzzle brake" or "recoil reducer", others a "suppressor". Some government entities will refer to it as a "silencer" and make it difficult for Cellini to distribute widely. Even his various patents use different terminology and definitions, but to Cellini, it will always be his "stabilizer".

*****

THERE HAS NEVER been any shortage of venture capitalists, investors and businessmen willing to "take a chance" on Cellini and his inventions. Sadly, he has found out to his cost on more than one occasion that not all people are honest, and many just want to use him for their own personal gain. There have been employers who would pay him a pittance for his time, give him a problem to solve, then patent his ideas, market his product and keep the profits. This is why Cellini had chosen to "go it alone" and market his own products. He has made mistakes, but he believes he has learned from them.

He has also learned that he can't do it all by himself. There simply isn't time.

So when he is approached by two brothers with what sounds like a sound business proposition to produce and market his stabilizer – under its

[2] *When Cellini quit working at the gun shop, he believed he was still owed $350 for work he had done for its customers. Some time later, he ran into Don Carter's wife at a local gun show and she gave him the $350. There was a catch; she wanted Cellini to go and work exclusively for her. He gratefully accepted the money but declined the position.*

patent name of Cellini muzzle brake – legally to licensed owners of firearms, hunters, etc. he listens very carefully.

The two brothers run a successful machine shop and welding company just outside San Antonio. They are familiar with Cellini's designs and believe in their potential. They have plenty of business experience and they make a convincing presentation. To flatter Cellini, they tell him they will name the company Cellini Industries, Inc. He will be a director of the company – but not the majority shareholder. No matter. Cellini is not concerned about the fine print. The brothers appoint other family members as officers of the corporation, but this doesn't concern him unduly – he has a strong belief in family values. The agreement, as he understands it – and on which they have already shaken hands – is that he will receive $6,000 a month for what amounts to the exclusive use of his name on the product.

Everything seems fine at first. Initial sales reports are good and the muzzle brake is receiving good reviews in the trade publications. But after a few months, the payments stop. Cellini calls and asks about his money and is told not to worry, it's coming. *The cheque is in the mail.* But it never comes.

So he goes along to visit the brothers. He is not happy and he lets them know it. He asks them what is going on and discovers that are trying to set up a massive deal with Argentina. This is the first he knows of it and he is even less pleased.

"Why was I not told about this?" Cellini says, "I'm supposed to be the Goddamn director of this company and you're selling my invention to a foreign power without even discussing it with me?" He pauses just long enough to take a breath, then continues with his rant. "Added to which you're not even paying me what you already owe me?"

"Don't worry. It's all a big misunderstanding and it can all be worked out," he is told.

Cellini is not satisfied. He has serious doubts about the integrity of these guys. They try to keep him calm, then one of the brothers makes a big mistake. He walks over to Cellini and points a gun right in his face. A Smith and Wesson .44 Magnum. After a few seconds, he pulls back the hammer to cock it.

For a moment things get very tense. The family knows he can be a bit of a hothead. They also know a little bit about Cellini's background and the work he has done in the past. No one knows what Cellini might do next and things could get very ugly, very quickly. Cellini surprises everyone with his response.

He stares straight into the eyes of the armed man and calmly says, "This is Texas, right?"

The man holding the gun looks at him and nods.

"So you want to be a Wild West cowboy?" Cellini continues.

He doesn't blink and he doesn't take his eyes off the gunman's face. "Let's settle this like Wild West cowboys. Let's go outside and draw!"

No one in the room moves or speaks for several seconds. Cellini still hasn't blinked. Slowly, the hothead brother releases the hammer and lowers the gun. He laughs, nervously.

"Aww come on Vito, I'm just kidding."

Cellini continues to stare at him. He jabs his finger towards the face of the man who, ten seconds ago, had pointed a gun at him and says, "You are not the first person who has ever pointed a gun at me. But you are one of very few who has lived. Enjoy telling your friends about it."

Then he turns and leaves the building.

Cellini doesn't believe for a minute that it was a joke, nor does he find it funny. He does put a stop to the sale of the muzzle brakes to Argentina and hires a lawyer to get him out of the agreement with the brothers as quickly as possible.

One more lesson learned!

71. Counter-Terrorism and Mitchell WerBell

CELLINI'S NAME, as an inventor and developer of suppressors and stabilizers – even though his work is on such a small scale – has started to attract the attention of various organizations. The gun ownership community in the United States is tightly connected and well-informed. Articles have begun to appear in gun and hunting publications as well as local media. Government and law enforcement officials to whom he is already well known, as well as hunters and private gun owners, are curious to know what he is doing.

There are the usual assortment of individuals looking to buy the latest gadget; some are perhaps honest citizens looking to further improve their personal security, but many, Cellini knows, represent the criminal element. Others, like the brothers he had recently formed a company with, are investors, looking to capitalize on the marketing potential of any successful new design. There are also those who insist they can help him to turn his invention into a million dollars. Cellini will meet all sorts in the pursuit of his invention, but his ground rules are simple: he will sell his weapons and weapons modifications only to law enforcement and or the military; people who are properly trained and licensed to own such modified weapons legally. His experience in dealing with criminal lowlifes serves him well in being able to weed out the bad seeds, and he vigorously turns down offers to purchase from anyone who does not meet his strict criteria.

In addition to businessmen hoping to establish a partnership with him, Cellini is approached by other inventors and designers keen to collaborate on new products. He believes most are interested only in stealing his ideas and would have little to offer him in return, so he declines to discuss his work with most parties.

One exception is a man who's past intrigues Cellini. A man with a commendable track record of his own in weapons development and a keen understanding of the security issues facing the modern world.

That man is Mitchell Livingston WerBell III.

Cellini is introduced to Mitch WerBell by a US Army colonel while demonstrating his machine gun in 1982. At that time, WerBell's company, Sionics, has evolved into a sophisticated and exclusive counter-terrorism training school based in Powder Springs, Georgia, attended mostly by members of the military, CIA agents and private individuals who consider themselves high-risk for kidnapping or assassination.

WerBell is impressed with Cellini's work and they learn a lot from each other.

Cellini and WerBell soon find they have a great deal in common, and Cellini is invited to participate in Sionics' eleven-week counter-terrorism course. He jumps at the opportunity of learning more about WerBell and his work, and the two men quickly develop a bond.

In addition to advanced training in the use of all types of firearms, the Sionics course includes classes in urban warfare, practical uses for intelligence gathering, use of state-of-the-art night vision devices, dealing with medical emergencies including cardiopulmonary resuscitation (CPR),[1] use of unconventional weapons, surveillance and even demolition. It also includes a basic course in martial arts and knife fighting under the tutelage of Kung Fu master Jason Lau Wing Chun, who happens to be Mitch WerBell's personal bodyguard.[2]

*****

Cellini is a frequent guest of WerBell's, and they spend a great deal of time comparing war stories, occasionally demolishing a bottle of grappa together. WerBell shares ideas with Cellini that will greatly influence his future designs, but he also trusts Cellini with stories from his past.

One evening, the two of them are enjoying after-dinner drinks when WerBell suddenly makes an announcement.

"I once subpoenaed Nixon to testify for me."

If he is looking for a reaction, he is disappointed. Cellini just looks at him, poker-faced. WerBell continues with his story.

"I was working with the local military, helping to plan the liberation of one of those small Caribbean countries… I don't even remember which one," he laughs at his own joke before continuing, "when suddenly the whole

1. *Cellini is reminded of the time in Bari, during the war, when he had pulled a drowned man from the water. He wishes this relatively new technique of CPR had been known at the time.*

2. *Now Grandmaster.*

thing is shut down and I'm arrested by the FBI – along with my son – for trafficking dope and weapons!"

WerBell, a consummate story teller, pauses for effect and notes the merest hint of a smile on Cellini's face, who is nodding as if to say *yep, know what you mean. Been there.*

"Well, the whole thing was totally above board, sanctioned by the CIA and, as far as I knew, all the way to the top." He points upwards to emphasize his point. "I guess no one bothered to call the FBI."

He pauses again, taking another sip of his drink.

"So I told them I wanted to call Dick Nixon as a witness for my defence!"

"What happened?" Cellini feels an obligation to ask.

"All the charges were dropped immediately!"

WerBell and Cellini have moved in similar circles, and it is surprising that they had never met before. The MAC-10 machine gun, which WerBell and his partner Gordon B. Ingram had developed together, is remarkably similar in design and function to Cellini's own sub-machine pistol, which only makes him want to improve his own design more, and to work harder at marketing the weapon, as well as the stabilizer.

WerBell asks Cellini if he's interested in forming a partnership to sell his machine pistol to the Chinese government, and arranges a demonstration of the weapon in front of a Chinese general. The general is impressed with the weapon's firepower and becomes quite excitable when he gets to handle it.

"The first round kills them and the rest obliterates them!" he declares gleefully, with a wide grin that makes even a seasoned fighter such as Cellini a little uncomfortable.

WerBell tells Cellini to leave it with him. He knows how to deal with the Chinese and will arrange everything. He negotiates a deal that will be worth $100,000 to the partnership, but before the deal can be consummated, WerBell is dead.

Another possible sale of the Cellini sub-machine gun presents itself when Cellini meets a fellow inventor – in this case of a specialized roll cage for Ford trucks – who introduces him to the grandson of Henry Ford, who happens to be meeting with Mexican government officials. The Mexicans express considerable interest in the weapon after seeing it demonstrated, and after discussions with Mitch WerBell and several rounds of negotiations a deal is truck. It begins to look very promising but falls through when the Mexican debt crisis reaches a head at the end of 1982 and the Peso is devalued.[3]

Cellini senses he is getting closer to achieving the recognition and reward he craves for his designs.

For the time being he decides to go back to the drawing board to work on the stabilizer. He welcomes the interest of foreign governments seeking his weapons and systems, and can use the revenue – as long as any sale is sanctioned by the US government – but what he craves more than anything is an opportunity to do something for American soldiers.

*****

In many ways, Cellini's life parallels WerBell's. Like Cellini, WerBell had been a guerilla operator with the OSS in World War Two, though his service is primarily in China, and instead of being paid in cigarettes he is allegedly compensated with opium (according to a report in the Wall Street Journal, April 18, 1980). After the war, he designs and builds weapons and weapon suppressors, notably for the M-16 rifle, and forms a successful corporation, Sionics, to market his products. In 1967 he partners with Gordon B. Ingram, designer of the MAC-10 machine gun, adding his suppressor to the weapon and attempting to sell it to the US Army for use in the Vietnam War.

MAC (Military Arms Corporation) eventually absorbs Sionics but retains the name for WerBell's paramilitary anti-terrorist training school.

As a "Soldier of Fortune", WerBell's advice is sought by governments throughout the Caribbean and Central America, and in the 1960s and '70s he helps with strategic planning for several military coup d'états, though most never take place. During the Vietnam War, WerBell claims the status of a retired major general in the US Army (apparently with the blessing of the CIA) to allow him to travel freely in Southeast Asia to demonstrate and sell his weapons.

WerBell is later hired as security advisor to Hustler publisher Larry Flynt and is suspected of organizing the failed contract killings of several high-profile celebrities, including Flynt's rival publisher, Hugh Heffner. A photocopy of a cheque for $1 million written by Flynt to WerBell is presented as "evidence" of the contract by a Los Angeles television station. Cellini refutes this, saying no one – least of all an experienced mercenary such as WerBell – would be stupid enough to accept payment for a contract killing by cheque.

WerBell dies in suspicious circumstances in 1983.

[3] *Between August and December 1982, the Mexican Peso was devalued by nearly 50% against the US dollar. Inflation rates reached 100% and a recession followed. In 1982, the Mexican economy shrunk by 0.6% and by another 4.2% in 1983.*

72. Silencers, Suppressors and Stabilizers

CELLINI IS WARY of anyone who uses the word "silencer" and even shies away from terminology like "suppressor". He despises fictional portrayals, both in literature and on film, depicting guns with monstrous attachments that literally "silence" the weapon, because he knows this is virtually impossible. Slowing the dissipating gases from a discharging firearm by funneling them through a series of chambers might reduce the noise level, but nothing can eliminate the sound completely.

Cellini has, however, made an interesting discovery by approaching the problem from a different direction.

While others – Mitch WerBell included – have always sought to nullify or at least reduce the *sound* of a firearm, Cellini, in trying to help his son, actually set out to reduce the *recoil* of the weapon, and in so doing almost inadvertently discovered that the noise level was significantly reduced. He also discovered, when shooting with his stabilizer at night, that the flash from the muzzle greatly diminished. He believes, with more work, muzzle flash can be virtually eliminated, giving any infantryman a tremendous advantage if caught in a night-time firefight – especially a sniper.

Cellini is not the first to discover that, in trying to reduce the noise, the weapon becomes more stable – but he believes he may be one of very few designers who has actually set out to make it more stable. As he sees it, that is the fundamental difference between his own and other designs.

With this in mind, Cellini sets to work on his latest, and greatest, weapon design. It will undergo many modifications and name changes: recoil reducer, flash suppressor, muzzle brake and finally stabilizer. Satisfied that he has done all he can, at least for the time being, he registers it with the US Patent Office and begins in earnest to look for ways of getting his invention noticed.

Step one will be to test it under military conditions and with the military decision-makers present. Cellini begins an aggressive letter-writing and telephone campaign, reaching out to the administrative heads at every testing ground he can locate. At gun club meetings and competitions he talks to military personnel based locally who might be able to introduce him to senior officers.

*****

Though he receives multiple refusals and feels as though he is constantly running into brick walls, Cellini refuses to quit. He truly believes that his invention is not only better than anything currently available to the US military, and that it will save the lives of soldiers in time of conflict, he also believes it will be more economical to produce than anything currently offered.

Following the accepted procedure, he submits a series of proposals to various branches of the military establishment and government agencies.

In June, 1983 Cellini receives a reply from Major David Baskett, Acting Deputy Director of the Ballistic Research Laboratory (BRL) at Aberdeen Proving Ground in Maryland, informing him that the BRL is "interested in performing a modest test program on various muzzle brake compensators". Cellini is invited to submit test samples of his "muzzle device" for an M-16 rifle. Though he will not be permitted to fire the weapon himself, he is welcome to attend the test.

It's a start.

He receives more replies from the Departments of the Navy, Air Force and Marine Corps. Most are perfunctory responses informing him that his proposal has been forwarded to another department for consideration. Cellini, who is not known for his patience, becomes frustrated with the red tape. But slowly, over a period of many months, he is invited to submit his design for evaluation by more and more agencies. Better yet, they are even willing to pay him for the devices he submits for testing.

The government still refers to these devices as muzzle brakes and recoil reducers, although by this time, Cellini is filing for patents under the description of "stabilizer".

Slowly, the test results are published and copies are sent to him. They appear to be very favourable, yet there is no hint of a contract. Then he starts hearing from well-established government contractors asking him to submit technical specifications and samples of his device. He complies, until he finds out that one major manufacturer has tried copying his design and has now received an order from the Pentagon to supply its own version in quantity. He obtains a sample of the copied device in order to test it against his own.

It is larger, heavier, far less effective in reducing both noise and recoil, but much worse, it costs the government – and thus the American taxpayer – many times the price of his own stabilizer. He realises he needs to do more if he is to circumvent the politics of government and put his stabilizer in the hands of the American soldier. He will spend many years fighting the system and attempting to cut through the red tape, but slowly the realization dawns on him that his only option may be to become part of the system, and he is simply unwilling to "sell-out" to one of the major arms manufacturers, especially as his products are doing well in other areas.

Law enforcement officers who have had the opportunity to test the Cellini device at shooting competitions are enthralled by the improved performance of their weapons. Orders and enquiries start to flood into Francesca, Inc., Cellini's registered business, from police departments throughout Texas and eventually from other states.

In the meantime, Cellini has an opportunity to demonstrate his weapons at the Second Chance Combat Pistol and Rifle Match in Central Lake Michigan, in 1984, where his life is about to take another turn for the better.

*****

In Michigan, Cellini meets Durwin Dengerud, a seasoned veteran who had served with the US Army Rangers in Vietnam and had been an original operative member of the US Army 1st Special Forces Operational Detachment-Delta (1st SFOD-D), commonly referred to as Delta Force, since its founding in 1977.

Their first meeting is best described in Dengerud's own words:

> *"...one afternoon, prior to a match, while I was doing some warm up shooting on the practice range, I noticed a van backing up to the firing point next to me. I observed Mr. Cellini removing from the back of his van an armory of every type pistol and rifle one could imagine. He watched as I was shooting my weapon then walked over to me and introduced himself. 'Hi, I'm-ah Vito Cellini I-ah wanna you to-ah shoot this-ah 1911, 45 pistol, same-ah as-ah yours, and tell-ah me what-ah you tink.' I noticed a muzzle device on the front of the standard 45 system, so I expected some difference in the recoil versus the 1911 that I was presently shooting. After firing five magazines of military ball ammunition, I couldn't*

believe the difference there was in the controllability of the system... I then proceeded to shoot every firearm he had in his van."

DENGERUD HAS SEEN more combat, fired more weapons and been in more deadly situations than most men will ever see, but in Cellini he recognizes a kindred spirit and is sympathetic to his struggle to break through the red tape of the establishment. He asks to see the machine pistol, which Cellini hands over.

Dengerud inspects the weapon cautiously, taking note of the spare magazine in the forward grip and the fact that it can be fired ambidextrously. He likes what he sees.

"Let's give this one a go," he says.

Loading a clip into the cylindrical tube, Dengerud smiles at the smooth handling and points it downrange.

He squeezes the trigger once. Twice. Three times, then fires his remaining shots in rapid succession until a click tells him the chamber is empty. He grins and asks for another clip. Cellini points to the spare magazine in the forward grip, which Dengerud detaches and clicks into place. This time he will test the full-automatic capability of the weapon.

Holding the weapon in one hand, he raises his arm almost chest high, slightly bent at the elbow, and empties the entire magazine at the target in one burst. Cellini notices that the weapon doesn't waver in his hand. *This guy knows what he's doing,* he thinks to himself.

He asks Cellini for one more clip, loads and fires. This time he tests the gun's ability to switch from semi-automatic to full-automatic mode simply by pulling back onto the second trigger. The gun behaves perfectly.

Dengerud turns to Cellini grinning and shaking his head at the same time.

"That was better than an orgasm!" he says.

For Cellini it is one of those *pinch me I must be dreaming* moments, but the pinch comes later when Dengerud introduces the weapon to a team of Navy Seals at the Navy proving ground in Crane, Indiana. The Seals manage 75% more hits on the target than with any of the other weapons they are testing. They are totally supportive of the sub-machine gun, yet Cellini is still unable to get an audience with the real decision-makers at the top flight of government. A pattern is beginning to emerge. Every serviceman, soldier and police officer who tests his weapons – professionals who are in the line of fire and know what kind of tools they need to do their job best – want it adopted. Yet still, the doors remain closed.

Cellini and Dengerud have many conversations about the machine-pistol and how Cellini would love to get the weapon in the hands of the Delta Force, or indeed, the Navy Seals. He also talks about his stabilizer and the struggle he is going through to get it service tested through the proper channels.

"Fuck the proper channels," Dengerud says. "Let me talk to some people. As a matter of fact, there's someone you need to meet who's going to love this gun."

*****

DURWIN DENGERUD HAD joined the US Army Rangers in 1969 before serving in Vietnam. He would be a natural selection for the new Delta Force when it is established in 1977 and serves with it until 1990. He trains with the US Secret Service and operates in numerous high-threat areas overseas. He mentors and trains US and foreign law enforcement officials in protection procedures, anti-terrorism measures and SWAT tactics, and develops counterterrorism procedures still in use by US Special Operations Units and Law Enforcement, as well as corporate and civilian entities worldwide. In his capacity as a private contractor, he and Cellini subsequently work together on covert surveillance and security missions for law enforcement.

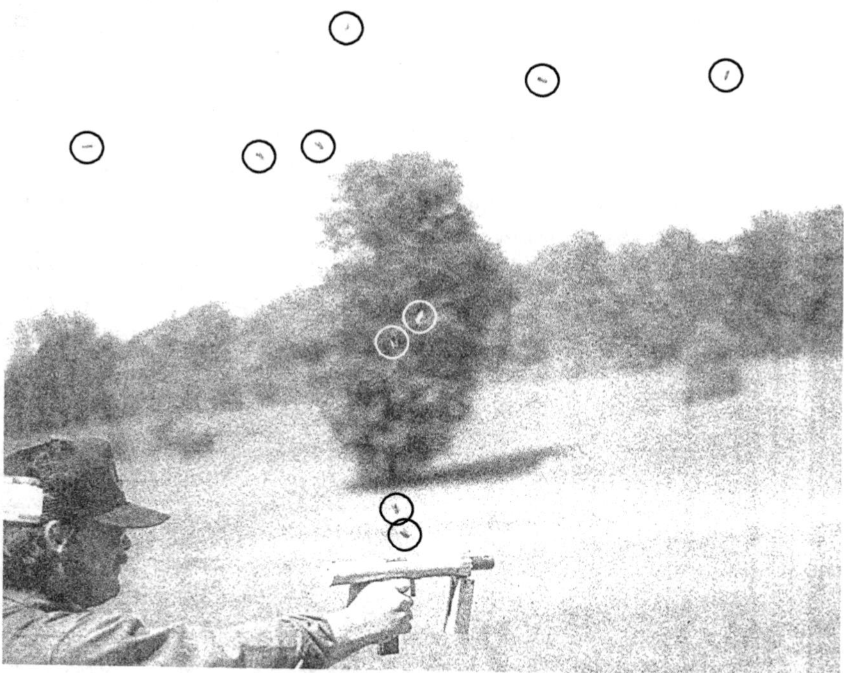

Though the image is very grainy, being a screen capture from a video taken in 1984, the demonstration is clear and illustrates why Durwin Dengerud was so enthused with Cellini's machine-pistol. Dengerud is seen test-firing the weapon for the first time, in Central Lake Michigan. Firing a burst with one hand, the gun remains perfectly steady – and ten spent cartridges can be seen in the air simultaneoulsy. This is what prompted Dengerud to declare, "That was better than an orgasm!"

Cellini's sub-machine gun remains a remarkable piece of engineering, even by today's standards.

In it's final form, the weapon (empty) weighs just 4.3 pounds (1.95 kilograms).

It can fire in semi-automatic (single shot) or full-automatic mode and features front and back sear triggers, configured so that the operator is able to instantly switch between semi-automatic and full-automatic modes – even while firing – without the need for a selector switch.

It utilizes an advanced ergonomic design, with the loading lever and fastening device on the longitudinal centre axis and grips which rotate up to 90 degrees in any direction, to allow ambidextrous operation. The front grip is easily removed without any tools, transforming the weapon into handgun that is easily concealed. It has an improved ejector and retainer assembly and fewer moving components than similar weapons. It requires no bolts or screws for the trigger, sear guide, bolt or stop screw.

Other features include compartments for magazines in both front and rear grips, and of course provision for attaching the Cellini stabilizer/muzzle brake.

After relocating to San Antonio, Cellini builds 27 of these weapons in stainless steel for demonstration/testing (in addition to those he produced for the armoured car company) but none are known to exist today. Several are believed to have been acquired by a movie prop house and are occasionally identified in various films, but that was before the regulations on machine-gun ownership changed. It is likely these have now been destroyed.

One of Cellini's earliest designs for a machine pistol. This style was produced for the amoured car company in San Antonio.

Parts from a later model of the machine pistol made from stainless steel, showing a more streamlined, cylindrical design.

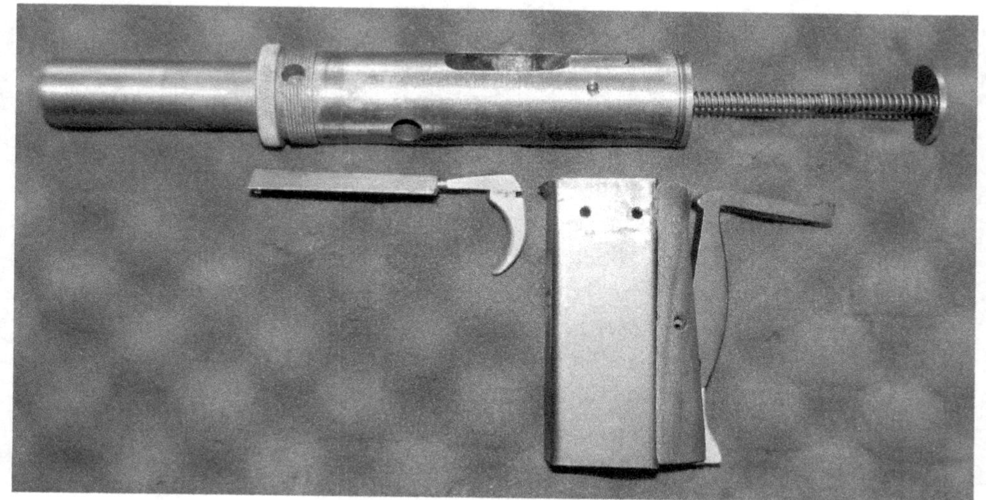

73. Sergeant Major Walter Shumate of the Delta Force

A COUPLE OF WEEKS later Cellini is at home when the phone rings. A whiskey-and-cigar voice at the other end introduces himself as Shumate, a friend of 'Roo, and begins asking a lot of technical questions about his weapons. Cellini interrupts to ask him to repeat the name of the person who referred him.

"'Roo," he says. "Durwin Dengerud. You met him at Lake Michigan a couple of weeks ago? He's been telling me all about you and your weapons and I'm very interested to meet you and try them out for myself."

Cellini is somewhat surprised but always ready to meet people who show interest in his work. They make arrangements for Cellini to travel to Shumate's home near Fort Bragg, North Carolina, the following weekend.

It's late afternoon when Cellini arrives in Fayetteville, just outside Fort Bragg, where Shumate lives on base. He drives around, finds a decent-looking motel and books himself a room for two nights. He unloads his bags, showers to get the road dust and sweat off his body and then calls Shumate.

"Where the hell are you?" Shumate says.

"I'm at a motel in Fayetteville," Cellini replies. "You want to get together for dinner somewhere?"

Shumate sounds apoplectic. "What do you mean you're in a God-damn motel?" he says. "When I invite you to come and visit me, you don't get a motel, you stay at my house! Now cancel that goddamn motel room and get your Italian ass over here!"

Cellini already likes Shumate, and they haven't even met in person yet.

Sergeant Major Walter Lee Shumate is a living legend among members of the US Special Forces. A larger-than-life character who has managed to survive four tours in Vietnam and who practically invented underwater commando-style warfare, he is gruff and boisterous but modest about his achievements. Though he is officially retired from military service at the time Cellini meets him, he still serves as an advisor to Delta Force in a civilian capacity and is always looking for better equipment and ways to improve the skills of those he trains.

He and Cellini take an instant liking to each other and will visit each often over the next few years. Cellini never again makes the mistake of booking a motel room. Instead they will always stay in each other's homes, sometimes sleeping on the sofa and sometimes on the floor, if the house is full. Each will gladly give up his own bed for the other, such is the respect they have for each other.

Over the next few days, Shumate gets to know Cellini and his weapons well and the two men form a deep and lasting friendship.

*****

SHUMATE AND CELLINI not only become close friends but also great drinking buddies. Shumate loves to brew his own beer, which Cellini proclaims to be the best he has ever tasted. Both can handle their liquor and it is not unusual for them to share and finish a bottle or more of grappa – still Cellini's favourite tipple – at a single sitting, at which times they will tell each other war stories.

One of Walter Shumate's favourite – and most often repeated – stories involves a card game with other sergeants and several rookie soldiers that had taken place during one of his tours in Vietnam. Some time during the card game a junior officer comes into the tent and asks to join in. During the ensuing conversation, one of the rookies admits that he has never seen a dead body and wonders how he will react to seeing someone get shot and killed. At this point one of the sergeants excuses himself from the game, gets up and leaves the tent, returning a few minutes later carrying his .45 automatic. Without blinking he raises the gun and fires almost point blank into the forehead of the junior officer, killing him instantly and spattering blood and brain matter across the card table and over the other players.

"You wanted to see a dead body?" he said. "Well now you have. Clean it up."

The punchline of the story is that the junior officer has been sleeping with the sergeant's wife. While this may have been common knowledge among the other members of the platoon, the sergeant had only just found out. The officer's death was treated as just another "casualty of war", and no prosecution took place.

Whether true or not, Shumate tells the story many times, without variation or embellishment.

The two men spend a lot of time together, shooting guns, hunting, fishing, drinking and talking.

*****

SERGEANT MAJOR WALTER L. SHUMATE had begun his military career in February 1952 as an airborne infantryman in the Korean War. In January 1962 he volunteers for Special Forces and is deployed twice to Vietnam between 1962 and 1964. In 1963 Shumate completes a dive course taught by a US Navy underwater demolition team and embarks on a programme he will continue throughout much of his military career, teaching combat diver operations. In 1964 Shumate completes High Altitude Low Opening (HALO) jump training prior to being assigned to Ft. Bragg, North Carolina, where he is attached to the Special Warfare Training Group in support of advanced infiltration training. Shumate designs and implements a training programme that evolves into the Special Forces Underwater Operations Course.

Returning to Vietnam in 1966, he serves with Project Delta under Colonel Richard Beckwith, founder of the Delta Force. The following year he is reassigned to Fort Bragg, where he serves as an instructor on the HALO Committee. In 1970, Shumate helps to establish a permanent Scuba School in Key West, Florida, before returning once again to Vietnam.

In 1977, as a founding member of Delta Force, Shumate is in charge of selection and training for – as well as participating in – Operation Eagle Claw, the attempt to rescue American hostages held at the Embassy in Iran.

Retiring in 1982, Shumate continues to serve as a civilian advisor with Delta Force until his death in 1993.

The Free Accent Dive Tower at the Special Forces Underwater Operations School at Key West in Florida is named in his honour.

74. A Conversation with the Pentagon, 1987

DESPITE HIS BEST efforts, as well as the support and endorsement of people such as WerBell, Dengerud and Shumate, and in spite of glowing test results at demonstrations in front of the Army, Navy, Air Force and Marine Corps when compared to equipment supplied by existing contractors, Cellini cannot seem to get anyone high up in the establishment to show any interest in his stabilizer. It is frustrating, not just for him, but for his friends in the Special Forces, who start to question whether the government is acquiring the best possible equipment for America's fighting men.

Cellini wants answers. He decides to take a direct approach by contacting the Department of Defense. He obtains the contact information of someone in a key position at the Pentagon, who he manages to speak to on February 7th, 1987. Though the man at the Pentagon insists on anonymity, he is willing to talk openly and honestly about the politics of the situation. Cellini records the conversation. The following is a partial transcript:

> *Pentagon: Vito, as far as anybody knows, and I probably know about this more than anybody else, you build the best muzzle brake in the history of the world, okay?*
>
> *Cellini: Thank you, sir.*
>
> *Pentagon: There's no one who doesn't like you or your brakes…*
>
> *Pentagon: Vito, I've got to tell you the truth, everybody is afraid to deal with you.*
> *(referring to the major weapons manufacturers supplying the US military)*
>
> *Cellini: I don't see, I can see the individual because I have eleven patents…*

Pentagon: Yeah, but you would rather sue them, then win. Now I think I can show you a way to win, but I can't show you a way to sue them and win.

Cellini: But I like to win. Not for me, for my men. They're my soldiers, they are supposed to have the best and I can give them the best.

Pentagon: Nobody wants to get sued. The government is so incompetent that it doesn't matter whether you are right or wrong, when you sue, all the house of cards that they've built for all these years falls apart, you know, there are so many incompetent, illegal, backwards, absolutely immoral administratively fucked up people... if you sue somebody he's liable to go to jail for something else he did when he started dicking around. And nobody wants to do that. The only reason I deal with you is I'm as clean as a church mouse. I ain't got nothing, we have no money, my agency is being shot, killed and thrown out the window, so the only thing that we can do is succeed or disappear.

Cellini: Okay, let's work together. I will leave it up to you to do whatever you think is right to do.

Pentagon: What are you going to charge me to install a removable muzzle brake on a 458 and cut it down to as low a weight as is safe?

Cellini: I will charge you, don't worry about the price, whatever the cost there is time to pay, okay?

Pentagon:... need to... show these people what can be done by somebody who has long ago buried your muzzle design, copied whatever they thought they could figure out and buried the rest of it and spent millions of dollars trying to duplicate it and ain't figured out how to do it yet. Those gentlemen have an infinite budget to stop anything positive from happening with it. And that's exactly what they use it for. And trust me, half their time is spent taping telephone calls so that they can prove that people like me and you are trying to upset bureaucracy – and that is true, that is a fact. I am literally trying to get that Goddamned agency closed down, D-O-W-N, ripped, all the people sent home, hopefully shot because what I think they are guilty of is treason... bureaucratic stupidity. When you take bureaucratic stupidity to the point where the soldier in the field has got an inferior rifle because you couldn't invent a better one, and you wouldn't allow them to buy a better one that exists, and is cheaper than the one you built, that is not stupidity, sir, that is treason.

The man from the Pentagon clearly wants to help Cellini. His solution is to persuade those suppliers currently contracted to the Department of Defense to work with Cellini, and to have them send him sample weapons for which he can build stabilizers/muzzle brakes. The problem for Cellini is that he would have to return the weapon, complete with its stabilizer, back to the supplier, who would then take over the manufacture. He has played this game before. Those companies do not welcome outsiders, and want instead to use their own design or at the very least to modify his. Hence the lawsuits referred to by the Pentagon man.

Cellini is not satisfied. Not by a long way. He wants to be able to supply the stabilizers directly to the government as an independent contractor. He is even willing to do so at no profit or personal gain, just to make sure *his* soldiers have the very best.

He determines that he will continue to seek new avenues to approach the problem. At least he knows that his work is recognized for what it is, and that it is politics preventing him from achieving his goals. He also learns from this conversation that both he and his work are still a topic of conversation in the halls of government and wonders if, once again, his past is somehow influencing the decision-making process.

75. An Interesting Job Offer

CHRISTMAS, 1988. THE PHONE rings at the Cellini house and Vito answers with his usual raucous "Hallo!"

The voice at the other end says, "Merry Christmas. I think I have a job for you that's right up your alley."

"Who is this?" says Cellini. He recognizes the voice and knows exactly who it is but these guys like to play games with each other.

"You know damn well who it is!"

The unmistakable gravelly tones of Walter Shumate, his voice cultivated by years of drinking whiskey and smoking cigars, continues. "So are you interested or do I need to call someone else?"

Cellini knows there is no one else. If there were, Shumate would have called them instead. One of Walter Shumate's great skills is always knowing the right man for the job.

Shumate will be in town in two days, so they agree to talk about it then. All he will tell the Italian on the phone is to make sure his passport is up to date and not to make any travel plans for the next month.

*****

IT'S A CHILLY, GREY December morning when Walter Shumate arrives at San Antonio International Airport. Cold weather is a rarity in the city, but December can be brutal, and Shumate is not expecting the sharp blast of wintry air as he steps out of the terminal. He picks up a rental car and heads straight along Loop 410 to Vito Cellini's house.

They greet each other like brothers, Shumate drops his bag in the hallway and says, "Let's go get some Mexican food!"

Each man orders fajitas for two and a bowl of menudo, and a couple of well-dressed Modelo beers. Pushing the lime wedge into his beer,

Shumate looks across the table and asks, "Ever heard of a company called Control Risk Response Services?"

"A British outfit," he adds, as if that might prod some distant memory for Cellini.

Cellini thinks about it for a moment and shakes his head.

"Didn't think you would have," continues Shumate. "They are a fairly low-key company specializing in helping organizations and individuals deal with, for want of a better word, 'sensitive' situations. Anything from business deals that have gone badly wrong to kidnappings and hostage negotiations. They are one of the best in the world, and they know it. They aren't cheap."

Cellini is interested. "What does this have to do with me? Or you, for that matter?"

"I'm coming to that," says Shumate.

"The company is run by ex-SAS, British Special forces. To provide the best service to their clients, they find the best people for each operation they handle, so they recruit on a job-by-job basis, as needed."

Cellini still looks puzzled, but now Shumate has his full attention.

"Have you ever heard of Richard Meadows?"

Again, Cellini thinks about it but shakes his head.

"Dick Meadows and I go back a long way. We met in the Rangers and worked together in the early days of Delta Force and Dick has always been a force to be reckoned with. He spent a lot of time working with the SAS in London. He even married an English girl.

"Anyway, Dick is more or less a full-time consultant with this British outfit, and last week I got a call from him asking for my help finding someone for a tricky job. As soon as he told me where it was and what was involved, I knew I had the perfect man."

"I don't know all the details yet, but based on what I do know, you're the man, Vito."

Control Risk is looking for a man who can speak Italian like a native but knows his way around New York; someone who can take care of himself and who isn't easily scared. Some knowledge of how the New York Mafia operates would be useful.

Ideally they are looking for a Sicilian. Vito Cellini has often been mistaken for Sicilian. He can carry it off perfectly.

"Oh, there is one more thing. You'll need to go to Naples, so at least you'll get some good food!" Shumate pauses to let his words sink in. "That's all I can tell you for right now, Vito. I know it's a dangerous job and you'll be dealing with some bad people. Think about it and let me know."

*****

Cellini doesn't have to think about it for very long. His life has been one long adventure so far, and he can see no reason to change now. He grins at Shumate and says, "You summonabitch! You knew I'd take the job or you wouldn't be here!"

The two finish their impromptu Mexican lunch and head back to Vito's house, where he breaks out an unopened bottle of grappa *stravecchia* and pours each of them a glass. An hour and a half later, the bottle is empty and the two friends are deep in the throes of comparing war stories: Cellini from Yugoslavia and Shumate from Vietnam. They've had the same exact conversation a dozen times or more, and each knows the other's stories backwards, but somehow they never get bored listening to each other.

Franci has left them alone with their grappa and their memories, but with her impeccable sense of timing, she recognizes the need to interrupt with espresso. They make plans for dinner, and Shumate excuses himself to make a phone call to let Richard Meadows know he has found his man, and to find out more about the job Cellini is about to embark upon.

*****

Despite their heavy drinking bout of the previous day, followed by a full five-course dinner prepared by Franci and then reminiscing until the early hours, both men are early to rise the next morning.

Walter Shumate is on the phone again, first with Richard Meadows who is co-ordinating the assignment from Lima, Peru, and then with the Control Risk office in London, where it is a little after noon. Cellini brews a pot of strong espresso and adds a shot of grappa to both his and Shumate's cups. Shumate swallows his in one go, then turns to Vito.

"Dick Meadows is really pleased you're on board for this, Vito," Shumate says. "I told him all about you but he also had his own people check you out. Seems you're pretty well-known in intelligence circles." Shumate continues, "One of these days you need to tell me about your plan to get rid of the Ayatollah!"

Cellini looks surprised.

"The FBI has a dossier this thick on you," he says, winking at Cellini and holding up a thumb and forefinger with a sizeable gap in between.

"Don't worry," he says, "it's all good. At least there are no criminal activities indicated and no orders to terminate you!" He laughs at his own black humour and then continues.

"I've also told Dick about your weapons and weapons modifications. He's keen to see your machine gun and he'd like to meet you one of these days."

"But for right now, he's put your name forward to Control Risk as the man for the job. They are going to fax over a copy of the message they've sent to their client in Italy."

Shumate looks intently at Cellini and starts filling him in with the details.

The assignment will involve considerable risk, partly because Cellini will be required to masquerade as a high-ranking member of the New York Mafia – a role he has never played before. Despite being acquainted with Mafia personnel while living in New York, his relationship was incidental. True, he was a very close friend to Mafia legal advocate Pasquale Guarino. He also did a few favours for friends and distant relatives on the periphery, but wisely never accepted any help or favours in return, and so was never called upon to repay any debt of honour.

More crucially, the danger Cellini faces is in the fact that he will be dealing, face to face, with one of the clans of the Mafia-like crime organization in Naples known as the *Camorra* and its *Mano Nera* (Black Hand) extortion racket. These are particularly cruel and sadistic men who control commerce not only by providing so-called "protection", but also by threatening business owners and their families.

Walter Shumate isn't telling Vito anything he doesn't already know.

The *Camorra* has more or less total control over everything coming into the port of Naples for distribution in the Campania region, and is demanding payment for ensuring that shipments arrive safely and are properly unloaded and stored. If the crime syndicate does not receive these payments, importers and factory owners are fearful not only of loss and spoilage, but the possibility of damage or destruction of production plants and even acts of violence against themselves and their families.

The cost of the raw materials is increasing worldwide, and the extortion is putting a severe strain on local business. Fearful of reporting it to local law enforcement because of the risk of reprisals through corrupt officials, importers have got together and turned in desperation to Control Risk Response Services for help in negotiating with these Black Hand extortionists.

Vito Cellini has just agreed to be the "negotiator" who will go head-to-head against the *Camorra.*

*****

The Camorra is a secret society that originated in the Campania region of Italy, specifically its capital city of Naples, and can be traced back to the 16th century. Unlike the Sicilian Mafia, Camorra groups or clans act independently of each other, and territorial disputes between clans is common. Camorra members are difficult for law enforcement to keep track of, because when leaders are eliminated, either by being arrested or killed, new clans and sub-groups frequently spring up out of the old ones. In spite of the infighting, the Camorra maintains a strict omertà (code of silence). Camorra clans control much of the regional food trade, including the dairy, fish and coffee industries, as well as more than 2,500 bakeries in Naples.

The Sicilian Mafia, in contrast, did not begin as an organized crime syndicate, but grew as a result of local families rebelling against a succession of foreign invaders who ruled over the island with varying degrees of tyranny. Private armies offered protection to others who could not protect themselves, in return for whatever payment their grateful beneficiaries could afford; thus the paid protection business was born. The origin of the name "Mafia" or "Mafie" is surrounded by myth and legend. It is believed to be Sicilian-Arabic slang and means "protecting the weak against the arrogance of the powerful". Mafiusu loosely translated means "swagger" in Sicilian, but can also be interpreted as "courage".

Vito Cellini remembers being told that Mafia is an acronym that stands for "Morte Alla Francia, Italia Avanti" (Death to the French, Italians forward) from a time Sicilians felt persecuted by their French rulers. Similar acronyms are found throughout Italian folklore but there is little historic evidence to support the notion, and it is most likely legend.

The American Mafia traces its roots to the Sicilian Mafia and the prohibition era of the 1920s when Italian-American immigrants largely controlled the distribution of liquor smuggled into the United States. Although not related, the American and Sicilian Mafia share a mutual admiration and respect for each other, and have been known to interact and co-operate on occasions.

*****

"You're going to go meet with these *Camorra* people. Show them some New York swagger. Tell them the families in New York are unhappy about what they are doing because it's seriously affecting their exports. Tell them they do not want to piss off the New York families. Make them understand things will get ugly if they don't back off. Can you do that?"

"Are you kidding me?" says Cellini, making light of it even though he knows it's going to be quite a challenge. "That's it? That's all?"

"Vito," Shumate continues, "I know you've dealt with motherfuckers like this before, but these guys are serious and scary. They have no honour and no scruples – but you can't just start shooting people if things go wrong."

After a few seconds for his words to sink in Shumate adds, "There's one more thing, Vito. You won't be alone. London is sending one of their more experienced people to walk you through this. He'll be with you at all meetings and watching your back."

Cellini doesn't know whether to be pleased about that or not. He always worked on his own when he was with the OSS in Italy. Even when he was fighting in Yugoslavia, he took off on his own whenever he could. He hates being responsible or answerable to anyone else – especially someone he doesn't know. When it comes to survival, he prefers to go solo.

"Yeah?" he says. "Who's that?"

"I don't know the guy's name, and it's probably better that way anyway," Shumate replies. "All I know is you'll meet up with him over there." London will give you the name when they send you the rest of the details, but it won't be his real name anyway."

"This is your deal, Vito. You are in charge and you'll pick the place for the meeting, as well as the time. This other guy's job is to watch your back, nothing more. You don't have to take orders from anyone, and you won't have anyone criticizing you."

"One question," says Cellini. "Do the New York families actually have anything to do with this? Do they know anything about it?"

"Jesus Christ! No of course not!" Shumate almost chokes on his response. "If they ever find out what we're doing they'd probably put a contract on the whole lot of us!"

"And by the way," he adds, "that was two questions!"

Despite making light of the situation, both of them know that the New York Mafia takes a dim view of impostors. Vito has always managed to remain on the outside despite several friendships with known Mafia associates.

Almost as an afterthought, Shumate adds, "Oh by the way, you'll make 500 British pounds a day plus all expenses, so make sure you keep track of all your hotels, meals, drinks and whores…"[1] Before he can finish the sentence, Franci appears around the door and rolls her eyes at her husband. Cellini glares at Shumate. It was a joke but there was truth behind it. Walt Shumate is a great friend but like most of the men he has ever known, a womanizer whenever he's off the marriage leash. Cellini refocuses on the

[1.] *£500 GB at that time was equivalent to approximately $1,000 US.*

job at hand. "How soon do I need to go?"

"The sooner the better – in the next couple of days if possible. You need to make your own travel arrangements and keep me posted. I'm point man for Dick on this one, and he wants know everything that's going on."

*****

VITO CELLINI DECIDES to book a ticket on the earliest available flight from Houston. He thinks it will be safer to drive to Houston and fly to Frankfurt, then on to Naples, so that if anything goes wrong he won't be traced back to his home city. He doesn't want his family put at risk.

Shumate gets London back on the phone and tells them their "negotiator" is ready to move forward with the operation. He hands the phone to Vito, who confirms the arrangements and his travel date. He will contact his associate after he arrives in Italy and tell him where the meeting will take place. The guy's name is Potts, from Manchester in England. After Vito makes contact, Potts will set up the meeting with the *Camorra*. All Vito has to do is show up at the appointed time, meet his contact and be ready to do battle with one of the deadliest organized crime syndicates in Italy.

After hanging up with London, he telephones his son Frank and asks if he would be willing to drive him to Houston. The flight leaves at 6:30 in the evening, so they will need to set off after lunch to arrive in plenty of time.

Once the travel arrangements have been made and names and numbers exchanged, Walter Shumate decides to leave so Vito can spend some time alone with his wife. He knows it is going to be a difficult job and he understands how close Vito is to Franci. He also realises that if he sticks around too much longer, he's highly likely to get a roasting from Franci for setting up her Ueli with such a dangerous job!

He tells Vito to be careful and to make sure he keeps in touch. He opens the front door, but before he steps outside he grasps Vito by the arm and says, "You are one crazy, stupid bastard, you know that?"

Vito looks puzzled. Shumate goes on.

"They offer you a lousy $1,000 a day and you don't even bat an eyelid. You should be asking those suckers for $3,000 a day. I wouldn't do it for less – and I know they'd pay it!"

Shumate grins and slips out the door. As he gets into his car, Vito quietly closes the front door and mutters to himself, "It's not about the money, Walt. It's just not about the money…"

Franci comes out of the kitchen and asks, "Where's Walter? Don't tell me he left without saying goodbye?"

"He needed to get back home. He said to tell you goodbye and apologized for not staying longer."

"Don't you lie to me, Ueli Cellini," Franci says. "He didn't want to be around when you told me about whatever it is you're up to because he knows I'd give him an earful. So where are you off to? Or is it another one of those 'secret' hunting trips?"

Vito reaches out and takes Franci's hand. Never one for being particularly tender, that act alone tells her something is up. He looks her straight in the eyes and says, "It's a job, that's all. They need me to go back to Italy. It's just for a few days, maybe a couple of weeks at most."

He pauses to let his words sink in, then adds, "There is a risk… a chance… ," he pauses again, trying to find the right words.

"I have to deal with some pretty bad people, and by the time I get through with them they are not going to like me very much. In fact, they are probably going to want to hurt me if they can. That's all."

She looks at him and shakes her head. "Ueli," she says, "You are who you are and no one is ever going to change that. Go to Italy. Do whatever it is you have to do. Just be careful and come back to me like you always do."

Vito doesn't answer, he just looks at this still beautiful woman who has always supported him in everything he has done, good or bad, right or wrong. They have never been outwardly expressive or demonstrative of their affection for each other, it's always been just understood. Implicit. And this is not the time to change that. He laughs and changes the subject.

"The money is good! $1,000 a day plus all my expenses."

"Yes, I heard that part," Franci interrupts sharply. "Make sure you keep track of every penny you spend on whores!"

"You know me better than that!" he says, a hurt look on his face.

"Just keep yourself clean," she replies.

*****

Much of the long drive to Houston is spent in silence. Vito's mind is already focused on the job ahead. His son, Frank, tries to draw him into conversation, but Vito is not feeling talkative and isn't in the mood for idle small talk. They stop at a gas station just outside Columbus to fill up the car and use the restroom. Vito buys a couple of candy bars and hands one to his son as they get back into the car. Finally, he decides to share some of his thoughts. He won't discuss anything to do with the job, nor his employer, but he does want to make sure, without sounding melodramatic, that Frank is aware of the danger and that, in the worst case scenario, he might not be coming back.

Frank Cellini's primary concern is that the family – especially his mother – is well provided for.

He and his father have never been very close, and later in his life Vito will regret not having been around more when his children were growing up. Cellini looks at his oldest son. He sees a handsome and confident young man but realises he hardly even knows him. He also knows that this is not the time to try to start building a relationship, so he keeps his speech brief.

"Frankie," Vito says, "your mother has always managed the finances in this family. If it were left to me, I'd spend it all. Your mother is the smart one when it comes to money. Don't worry. She's well taken care of and she'll make sure you are OK as well."

A short while later they turn off Interstate Highway 10 and head north towards the Houston Intercontinental Airport.

*****

CELLINI CHECKS IN at the counter and drops off his suitcase. He opts not to check his luggage all the way through to Naples, preferring to collect his bag upon landing in Frankfurt so he can make sure nothing has been disturbed, then rechecking it in for the short flight to Naples.

According to the departures monitor, his flight from Houston to Frankfurt is on time, so he just about has time for a beer and a sandwich before boarding begins.

Once at the gate, Cellini takes a good look around him, checking out his fellow passengers, a habit he picked up during the war when boarding trucks or boats or buses and never knowing who was watching. If he gets the sense that anyone is watching him, he wants to know now, so he can keep an eye on them. No one seems to be paying much attention to him. There's just the usual motley assembly of passengers: families with small children returning home after the Christmas holidays; twenty-somethings heading to Europe for the skiing; a few businessmen – Germans in their immaculate tailored suits; Americans in their blue oxfords and khakis; others in pressed blue jeans and cowboy hats. The attendant at the ticket counter had warned Cellini that it was going to be a full flight, and he starts looking up and down the rows of people to see which of them might be travelling alone, and who he might get stuck alongside for the next nine or so hours.

He takes his seat on the aisle of the cabin and finds himself sitting next to an attractive woman of about thirty. She smiles, then turns away and buries her head in a magazine; the international signal that she really doesn't want to be engaged in conversation. Cellini is relieved. He doesn't feel like talking either and is grateful not to have to feign sleep. If he could have requested *next-to-a-pretty-woman-who-doesn't-want-conversation* as his seating preference, that is exactly what he would have asked for.

76. The Mafia Masquerade. Naples, 1989

THE TRANSITION AT Frankfurt is smooth. He collects his bag, still locked, rechecks it to Naples and makes his way to the gate for his continuation flight.

Naples, even in winter, is one of Italy's most picturesque resort cities, and despite the chill air that greets him as he exits the aircraft, Cellini is enchanted by the clear azure sky and the imposing sight of Vesuvius. His bag is still unmolested, so he heads out of the airport and finds a taxi stand. He has been carefully watching over his shoulder and hasn't noticed anyone following him since he landed at the airport, but just in case, he tells the taxi driver, loud enough for anyone nearby to hear, that he wants to go to Pompeii.[1]

Once inside the taxi he hands the driver 50,000 Lira and tells him he may need him for a couple of hours.[2] As much as Cellini loves Naples, he has no intention of meeting the *Camorra* here, right on their own doorstep. He has already decided to move south to Sorrento, another beautiful resort city, just far enough away to give him a little peace of mind. He knows that they will not be expecting the change of venue and that it will cause a little friction, which is exactly what he is hoping for.

His first stop, however, will be at the docks in Naples, and specifically the offices of the very people he has come to talk to. He wants to see the operation at work, and confident that the honcho with whom he is meeting will not actually be there, he decides to snoop around a little. He's looking for some small aspect of their business he can find fault with. It doesn't take him long, and within fifteen minutes he is back in the waiting taxi.

The taxi driver is still expecting to take him to Pompeii, which is about a forty-five minute drive. For the first five minutes of the drive, Cellini

1. *The ancient city of Pompeii was engulfed by the eruption of Vesuvius in AD 79 and is preserved as a museum. It is a major cultural destination.*

2. *Approximately $35 US at the time.*

watches out of the rear window of the taxi, but there are no signs of anyone tailing him, so he feels confident enough to tell the driver to carry on to Sorrento instead.

"Hey, you know what? I'm running a little later than I thought," Cellini says. "I'm supposed to meet friends for drinks at the Palace Hotel in Sorrento. Can you just take me all the way there?"

The driver is about to grumble, the way taxi drivers the world over – but especially in Italy – tend to grumble whenever passengers change their mind about where they are going, but he remembers the 50,000 Lira note and glances down at the meter. Realizing he's probably in for a pretty good tip, he cheerfully agrees.

*****

Cellini does not disappoint the taxi driver, handing over another 50,000 Lira tip on top of the fare for the ride.

The Palace Hotel is perched high on the hills overlooking Sorrento, sheltered by cliffs behind and offering a wonderful view of Vesuvius across the Bay of Naples. Cellini checks in at the front desk, hands over his credit card and asks for a room with a view.

After showering and changing, he orders a bottle of Prosecco Tranquilllo and a tray of antipasti from room service. Within ten minutes the food and wine arrives. He hasn't eaten since the flight into Germany and the olives and salami taste wonderful. He is once again reminded how much he misses real Italian food. He takes a sip of the wine, then picks up the phone.

His first call is to Potts, the Englishman who is to be his back-up in the negotiation. He had been told that Potts speaks Italian, which would have made life easier, but when he tries to communicate in his native language, he is dismayed to find that Potts doesn't seem to understand a word, which hampers their communication. Reverting to English, he discovers that Potts is staying at a hotel in Naples and is surprised that Cellini has decided to move the meeting to Sorrento.

"Give me your contact's phone number," he says, "I'll call him and let him know about the change of venue. Between changing the meeting place and the call coming from me, that will unsettle them – and that's exactly what I want."

Potts agrees and reads him the phone number. London had led Cellini to believe he was one of their top men in Italy, but so far he is not impressed. He reminds the Englishman that he will handle the actual negotiation his way. In fact, he says he doesn't plan to negotiate at all.

"With these kind of gangsters, you don't negotiate," he says. "The only thing they understand is fear. You strike the fear of God into them, the way they do with their victims. You tell them what you want, and you don't give them any room for manoeuvring."

Potts makes it clear he is more than happy to leave the talking to the Italian-American. His job is more that of an observer, to provide extra muscle if it's needed.

"Most important," Cellini continues, "you cannot show them any fear. If you look scared, even for half a second, they will piss all over you."

"Got it," says Potts. They agree to meet in the hotel lobby at ten o'clock the next morning. Cellini hangs up the phone, eats a few bites of salami and takes a sip from his wine. Then he picks up the phone again and dials the number he has been given for his *Camorra* contact.

The phone rings for at least twenty seconds before a voice at the other end answers "Hallo?"

"Yeah. This is Vito Cellini, from New York. Who is this?"

The voice on the other end is confused, "You're calling from New York?"

"No, I'm calling from the Palace Hotel in Sorrento. I'm supposed to be meeting a Mr. Rocco tomorrow?"

Cellini hears the unmistakable sound of a telephone being passed, or wrestled, from one hand to another. A different voice says, "Who is this?"

"This is Cellini. Is this Mr. Rocco?"

"There's no one here by that name. You've got the wrong number."

"Oh, OK. Well, in case Mr. Rocco comes by looking for his messages, please tell him that the meeting he arranged with Mr. Potts has been changed. He is meeting Mr. Vito Cellini at the Palace Hotel in Sorrento at eleven o'clock tomorrow morning. You got that?"

Once again there is the muffled sound of a telephone changing hands. Vito smiles to himself. He is beginning to enjoy this.

"Mr. Cellini? This is Mr. Rocco. May I ask why the meeting we arranged is being moved to a different location?"

Cellini is really getting into playing the New York mobster now. "Because I fucking feel like it!" he says, adding, "Is that a problem?"

"No problem, Mr. Cellini. See you tomorrow."

Cellini hangs up the phone and pours himself another glass of wine. He thinks about calling Potts back to tell them he's got the bad guys rattled, but decides against it. *He'll find out in the morning*, he thinks to himself. He switches on the television, finishes his glass of wine and lies down on the bed. In minutes he's fast asleep.

*****

CELLINI WAKES UP to find the room in darkness, except for the flicker of the television, which is showing an old movie in black and white. Having no idea what the time is, he reaches for the bedside light, switches it on and looks down at the gold Rolex on his wrist. 8:15. He's slept for about three hours and he's hungry. The leftover antipasti looks even more jet-lagged than he feels and the Prosecco is warm, so he decides to go downstairs and find the hotel dining room.

The sound of gunfire from across the room startles him in his half awake state. He stares at the television screen and recognizes it as an old Hollywood gangster film. The dialogue is in English and has Italian subtitles. Never a fan of the genre, he can't decide if it's Cagney or Bogart and turns the television off.

He puts his shoes on, shuffles to the bathroom to splash some cold water on his face and heads downstairs.

The hotel dining room features a lagoon-like swimming pool with natural rock walls. Bathers can actually swim up to the tables, and Cellini enjoys watching them as he orders a light dinner. A single man, handsome, well-dressed and staying alone in such a fine hotel, naturally doesn't go unnoticed by the ladies, and he finds himself the centre of attention – something he doesn't particularly enjoy at the best of times, but especially given the sensitive nature of his business here in Sorrento. He decides from now on, until this business is complete, he should probably find a quieter place to take his meals, although he does think this would make an excellent venue for his meeting tomorrow morning. With plenty of people coming and going, the *Camorra* would be unlikely to try anything underhanded or risky. He looks around the dining room to familiarize himself with all the entrances and exits. He even chooses a table at the back of the room, far enough away from the pool to have a private conversation, but close enough to attract attention if voices became raised, that seems most suitable for the meeting.

Finishing his meal, Cellini gets up from his table only to be accosted by a lovely woman, slender, with Mediterranean looks and dark hair streaked with blonde highlights. She attempts to engage him in conversation – ostensibly about Pompeii and other local attractions – but at the same time she makes it clear that she is recently divorced and staying alone. She even manages to let her room number slip out; what time she plans to retire for the night; and that she is a very light sleeper. Cellini smiles politely but brushes her advances aside without a second thought. He has never found forward women attractive, and in any case, he is still devoted to Franci. Thinking of his wife brings a smile to his face. He wonders now, as he did when he was in Nicaragua, if she really believes him when he says he never has, and never would, cheat on her.

He looks around to make sure the woman has gone, returns to his room and settles down for the night. He sleeps very fitfully, going over and over in his mind the conversation he must have tomorrow.

*****

At five-thirty, Cellini is wide awake and decides to get up and go swimming. The outdoor pool is closed for the winter season, but the indoor pool in the dining room is heated and probably deserted at this ungodly hour. He pulls on a pair of swimming shorts and a short-sleeved shirt, grabs a towel from the bathroom and heads towards the door. Pausing for a moment to slip into a pair of moccasins on his way out, he thinks about calling Potts. Looking at his watch he decides against it. *No, I'll let the poor bastard sleep.*

Though the corridors are silent and the elevator is empty, the hotel lobby is a hive of activity. Three or four guests are lining up at the front desk waiting to check out while a younger couple is just arriving and wanting to check in. Stragglers are returning from late night parties and rendezvous, some looking furtive, some inebriated and some already hung over. Soft jazz music, the kind that sounds familiar but can never be properly identified, permeates the entrance and Cellini smiles to himself as he passes through on his way to the pool. Hotel staff take no notice of him as they go about their daily rounds with robotic efficiency, straightening chairs or delivering early breakfasts and carrying dirty plates and glasses left by the late-night revellers. As Cellini had thought, the pool is deserted. He swims vigorously for about twenty minutes, then towels off and makes his way back to his room. After taking a shower and shaving, he picks out his clothes for the meeting: black turtleneck, black trousers and a tan leather jacket. He wants to look casual but imposing.

He calls room service and orders a light breakfast of espresso and pastries, which arrives in about ten minutes. Sipping on the espresso, Cellini stares blankly out of his window. Focused completely on the mission ahead, he is all but oblivious to the fabulous view across the Gulf of Naples and Vesuvius in the distance.

Looking at his watch for the umpteenth time, he decides to call Potts, the Englishman. It's just after eight o'clock, but there is no answer. Not even a voice recorder to leave a message. *He's probably on his way*, Cellini thinks to himself, though he feels a slight uneasiness.

At twenty minutes past nine, Cellini is sitting in the lobby. He has chosen a vantage point facing the hotel entrance and has a copy of the *New York Times* in his hands that he is glancing at without really reading. The stories are the same as always: Reagan has signed an agreement with Canada for free trade; Gorbachev is gaining in popularity with the world but not with the Kremlin. The one story that does catch Cellini's eye is that the vice-president, George Bush, is to be questioned concerning his role in selling American weapons to Iran as part of the ongoing investigation into the Iran-Contra affair. *They'll whitewash him like all the rest,* Cellini thinks to himself.

He keeps one eye on the hotel entrance looking for Potts. He believes he has the ability to visually identify almost any individual just by having a little background information and having heard the sound of his or her voice. Spotting the Englishman ought to be fairly easily.

Ten o'clock comes and goes and there is no sign of the Englishman. 10:15. If there is one thing he has learned about the British from World War Two it is that they are a nation of punctuality fanatics. Is it possible he has missed him? He casually strolls over to the concierge, leaving the *New York Times* neatly folded on his seat to discourage anyone else from taking it.

"Excuse me," he says, "My name is Vito Cellini. Has anyone been asking for me by any chance? I'm expecting to meet with an English gentleman by the name of Mr. Potts."

"No sir. I'm sorry," the desk clerk replies. "No one has asked for you. Let me check and see if there are any messages."

He leaves the desk momentarily. When he returns, he is shaking his head.

"There are no messages for you, Mr. Cellini."

Cellini thanks the desk clerk and returns to his seat.

It looks as though he will be flying solo again. Though it's generally his preferred way of doing business, he'd have liked the chance to talk to Potts and gather a little more background information. He thinks about trying to call the Englishman again but discards the idea. Maybe he should call Walt Shumate and tell him what's going on? To do that he would need to go back to his room, and he doesn't want to leave the lobby this close to the appointment. He'll call after the meeting.

At five minutes before eleven, two Italian men stride into the hotel. One is slim and good looking, with jet-black hair and a Mediterranean complexion. He struts over to the concierge as though he owns the place. His companion is more swarthy, slightly older and heavier set with bad skin and a slight squint.

He must be the bodyguard, Cellini thinks.

Both men are well-dressed in custom suits and handmade shoes, but in spite of the expert tailoring, Cellini notices the small bulge under the left arm of both their jackets. He is not carrying a weapon, and did not bring one with him on this trip. It was one of those incidentals he had been led to believe would be provided by Potts, if necessary. He is beginning to develop a deep dislike for Mr. Potts, but that is something he will need to deal with later.

Right now, the game is on.

Squinty-eyes has been scanning the lobby since the pair walked in. He briefly locks eyes with Cellini as he looks up from the newspaper.

Cellini gets up slowly and makes his way towards the two men. He smiles and holds out his hand to the younger, more good-looking of the two men, the one he presumes is Rocco.

"Mr. Rocco?" he says, "Vito Cellini from New York. It's a pleasure to meet you."

He had looked younger from across the other side of the hotel lobby. Now up close, Cellini judges him to be in his early thirties. Cellini beams at him, the gap between his front teeth drawing attention to his smile. The bodyguard tries to step in between the two men, but Rocco waves him aside.

Rocco smiles and nods his head.

"Yes, Mr. Cellini. I am Rocco. It is an honour to meet you."

Cellini grabs Rocco by the hand and shakes it firmly and vigorously, noting the absence of the star tattoo of the Sicilian Mafia.[1] He gestures towards the dining room.

"We can talk privately in here," he says. "Hey, you can even bring your friend if you like!"

Cellini leads the two Italians to the table he had picked out for the meeting, gestures to the chair he wants Rocco to sit down in, and takes his own seat, his back to the wall so that he has an unrestricted view of the restaurant. He smiles again.

"You came alone?" Rocco says.

"My associate got called away, suddenly. Urgent business," Cellini replies, knowing that by implying something might be more urgent than

[1.] *Members of the Mafia or Cosa Nostra traditionally wore a small and discreet tattoo by which they could recognize one another. This comprised five marks or dots arranged in the shape of the points of a star, found on the top the hand in the webbed area between the thumb and forefinger. Since Cellini was attempting to pass himself off as New York Mafia he was keen to determine whether or not his antagonists were connected with the Italian Cosa Nostra, who, through their ties to the New York Mafia, would have been able to check up on his background. The lack of the "star" tattoo satisfied Cellini that he was not dealing with the Cosa Nostra.*

this meeting will not sit well with these men of the *Camorra*. Any way he can unsettle them will give him the upper hand.

"But you didn't come to talk to my associate," Cellini continues. "You came to talk to me. Or rather to listen to what I have to say."

"Now that the introductions are over, Mr. Cellini, perhaps you'd be kind enough to tell me what business you have here in Naples?"

*****

"FIRST OF ALL, Mr. Rocco," Cellini starts, "I have to tell you I am very disappointed in the way you run your operation here in Naples." He deliberately uses the anglicized version of the city's name instead of Napoli, knowing it will rub the Italian the wrong way. He wants to cause a little friction to unsettle him.

"I took the liberty of visiting your offices down at the docks when I first arrived here, and I have to say the state of your toilets is disgusting."

If he is taken by surprise, the Italian does a good job of concealing it.

"Why should my office toilets be of any concern to you, Mr. Cellini?" he says, casually.

"They are of great concern, not only to me, but to my associates in New York," Cellini replies, reminding Rocco that he is here as the representative of a powerful cartel in America.

"Something as simple and basic as the cleanliness of your toilets indicates the overall condition of your operation. Dirty toilets suggest lack of proper care and maintenance. If you can't keep your toilets clean, how can we be sure that other aspects of your business aren't in similar condition?"

"Think of me as a health inspector, Mr. Rocco. My business is making sure everyone stays healthy and happy. And dirty toilets are very, very unhealthy."

Cellini speaks very calmly and slowly. "When there are concerns about health, or the well-being of the business, it's my job to look into it."

Though Rocco has shown no signs of nervousness, Cellini continues to play the part of angry superior. It's an act designed to impress Rocco's companion and it works. Reaching across the table and touching Rocco on the arm, he adds, "There is no need to get excitable, Mr. Rocco, you and I are in the same business, and it is in all of our best interests to keep everyone safe and healthy. That is how we make a living. Am I correct?"

Rocco and his companion look at each other, then back at Cellini.

"Go on," he says.

Cellini pauses and looks around the dining room, which is beginning to fill up with people wanting mid-morning refreshment or swimming exercise. The growing crowd brings him mixed comfort. More people means more witnesses, which he hopes will give these *Camorra* pause for thought before taking any rash action. Although he also knows that there is every possibility that some of the local police are on the *Camorra* payroll, he doesn't believe they would do anything in front of hotel guests, who are mostly tourists.

"It has been brought to the attention of some very influential people in New York," Cellini continues, choosing his words very carefully, "and I mean *very* influential people," he adds emphatically, "that the health and safety of some very dear family members here in Naples isn't being taken care of quite as well as it should."

Rocco says nothing but reaches inside his jacket. Cellini sits perfectly still, looking Rocco in the eyes the whole time. Rocco smoothly slides out a silver cigarette case and flips it open, watching Cellini intently for a reaction that never comes.

"Do you mind if I smoke?" he asks, pulling out a long, white Marlboro 100 and placing it between his lips. He snaps the cigarette case shut and puts it down on the table in front of him. Squinty-eyes reaches across with a gold cigarette lighter and touches the flame to Rocco's Marlboro.

"I'm sorry," Rocco says. "How rude of me." Opening the cigarette case he offers it across the table.

"I don't smoke," Cellini says, "but thank you anyway."

Rocco leans across the table and is about to blow a steady stream of exhaled smoke into Cellini's face, but thinks better of it and turns his head to one side.

"You were saying?" says Rocco.

"I think you get my meaning," Cellini replies, "but just in case you didn't, let me put it into words even your associate here could understand." He waves a hand towards Rocco's companion without looking in his direction.

"Many of the commodities that land here in the Port of Naples come from New York. My employers have a certain vested financial interest in the farming and manufacturing conglomerates that produce, process and distribute these commodities. As you are undoubtedly aware, we also go to great lengths to protect the hardworking people who help load the ships ready to come over here."

"Are you with me so far?" he says, looking first at Rocco, then at squinty, then back at Rocco. Rocco opens his mouth to speak, but before any sound comes out, Cellini continues. "This is a costly business enterprise, but very satisfying. When it runs smoothly, everybody benefits; the farmers, the factory workers and the shipping companies are all gainfully employed. My employers make money. I make money. You make money. The importers, the Port of Naples and the Italian people all benefit. Everyone is happy."

He pauses again, just long enough to give Rocco the chance to open his mouth, then with perfect timing so as not to let his adversary speak, he continues once again. Cellini knows that as long as he can monopolize the dialogue he is in control of the conversation.

"We appreciate the fact that you and your good people here in Naples have to make a living. We know how much you care for the hard-working people unloading the ships and making sure products arrive safely at their destinations."

"But the value your people are placing on protecting these factories and its workers has increased to where it is causing a great deal of hardship on a lot of people. In fact, compared to the modest profits made by our investors in New York, your fees seem to be rather… excessive."

Cellini lets the thought penetrate before continuing.
"And that, Mr. Rocco, is the purpose of my business here in Naples."

"Are you saying the New York families are upset because we are making more money than they are?" Rocco attempts to feign surprise but makes no attempt to conceal his mocking tone.

"No, Mr. Rocco. In America we love free enterprise! What I am saying is that word has reached New York that certain people in Naples – I don't need to mention any names because you know who they are – have actually been threatened with physical harm if they don't meet your demands. Demands that are unacceptable to my employers in New York and that simply cannot be met if our business is to continue running smoothly."

Sensing that he is on a roll and growing ever more comfortable playing the part of a New York mobster, Cellini continues.

"There have been several accidents that have caused injuries and loss of productivity, which as I am sure you will agree, is not good for either of our businesses."

"Accidents happen." Rocco finally seizes the opportunity to speak.

"You are paid to ensure that accidents do not happen, Mr. Rocco."

Rocco starts to get agitated, but controls himself and offers appeasement in the only way he knows, or is authorized, to do. Stubbing out his cigarette in the ashtray, he turns his hands palms up, looks Cellini straight in the eye and says, "I know who is responsible for the threats you are talking about, Mr. Cellini. Please believe me when I say he was acting alone and without any authority from me or anyone else in our organization. I can only offer you my personal guarantee that he will never do anything like this again. In fact, as a gesture of good faith towards you and your people in New York, I will deal with this matter personally and immediately. To show my sincerity, please allow me to present you with his head."

He is perfectly serious, Cellini thinks to himself. His heart is racing but he manages to keep calm and control his breathing. He has been through war and seen the very best and the very worst of mankind. He has been involved in vicious street fighting and witnessed many violent acts in his life. He has been close to the New York *Cosa Nostra* and heard stories of the *Camorra.* But he has never actually had someone offer to kill another human being just for his own personal redress.

"That will be neither necessary nor desirable, Mr. Rocco. You must do whatever you must do, but there are to be no more accidents. Is that perfectly clear?"

"You have my word, Mr. Cellini," Rocco replies.

"I'm not finished," Cellini continues. "You need to rethink your protection fees and benefits and bring them into line with what New York considers reasonable."

Rocco starts to waver. "That's out of my jurisdiction. I deal with security, I'm not the treasurer. I will need to speak to my superiors before I can offer any kind of —"

Cellini cuts him short. "As far as I'm concerned, you can speak to the Goddamn Pope." He says it jokingly but the message is loud and clear.

"Just be sure to tell him there are plenty of importers in other Italian cities who would be happy to do business with New York."

He gets up and offers his hand to Rocco but acknowledges his companion with just a nod.

"I'll be here the same time tomorrow morning, and you'd better bring good news."

As he turns to walk away, Cellini offers a parting shot. "And one more thing," he says.

"What's that?" Rocco replies.

"Clean your fucking toilets."

*****

CELLINI GOES STRAIGHT to the hotel bar and orders a double shot of grappa, which he sinks in one go. He orders another, with a Peroni chaser.

He checks his watch. 11:45, which means it's still only 5:45 in the morning in Virginia, where Walt Shumate will be either still drinking, passed out drunk or sleeping peacefully. Whichever it is, Cellini doesn't want to disturb him right now, so he walks around the hotel for a while, then goes back to his room and lies down to take a nap.

He wakes up in the middle of the afternoon and puts a call through to Walter Shumate.

"Shumate," his friend answers.

"Walt, it's Vito."

"Vito who?" says Shumate.

"Shut up you summonabitch and tell me where I can find the miserable limey bastard who was supposed to meet me here!"

After several minutes of heated invective from Cellini, in which he curses the Englishman Potts with every possible name he can think of, in Italian and English, Shumate finally gets a word in.

"So how did it go?"

Cellini recaps the highlights of his meeting, sparing none of the details, then returns to cursing Potts.

"Vito," Shumate says, "I'm going to call Dick Meadows. He set this up for Control Risk and he is not going to be pleased when he finds out you got dumped in this situation. Don't worry about Potts. You take care of your own skin. It sounds like you've got everything under control but for Christ's sake, be careful. You know only too well the kind of people you're dealing with."

The phone call is short because Shumate wants to get on the phone to Richard Meadows to find out what happened to Potts.

*****

THE FOLLOWING morning, Cellini goes straight to the dining room and orders an espresso with a shot of grappa – known locally as caffé corretto – while he waits for his *Camorra* connection to arrive.

When Rocco arrives he is alone, but carries a large basket covered with a white linen cloth.

Surely he wouldn't bring the head of the hoodlum to me here in the hotel? Cellini thinks to himself, remembering their conversation from the previous day. It even flashes through his mind that Rocco's squinty-eyed companion may have been the guilty party and that it is his head in the basket. *That would take some balls.* The look on his face must give him away because Rocco smiles and takes full advantage of Cellini's obvious discomfort. Taking a seat, he sets the basket on the floor between the two of them.

"A gift for you, to show my goodwill," he says.

Slowly pulling back the linen cover reveals that the basket contains a large loaf of rustic bread and a bottle of olive oil. There is also a bottle of red wine and a sheaf of spaghetti.

"That's very kind of you," says Cellini, relieved but trying not to show it.

Rocco almost cracks a smile, but it comes across more like a sneer. "You thought I had brought you the head of my disenfranchised colleague, as I promised to do yesterday? I find that quite amusing, but no, Mr. Cellini, we are nothing if not discreet."

Looking more serious, he adds, "I can tell you, however, that man will never threaten or hurt anyone again. Ever."

"That's good news," Cellini replies, adding as an afterthought, "and no more accidents?"

"No more accidents."

"We live by a very strict code and take a dim view of anyone taking the law into their own hands, Mr. Cellini." Rocco says, staring intently into Vito's eyes as if trying to read what was going on behind them. "It's bad for discipline and morale."

He pauses then adds, coldly, "This particular situation I took care of personally."

He seems keen to discuss the details with Cellini, who, while no stranger to death or the administering of street justice, has better things to do and doesn't care to be implicated any further.

"You seem to have no fear of the law, or of being caught?" Cellini says, almost casually.

"Ha! That will be the day!" Rocco answers. "Believe me Mr. Cellini, they will never catch me, and even if they do, they will never be able to convict me."

Cellini is sceptical. In his experience, talkers are not doers and doers who talk too much invariably get caught. He has seen and heard enough of Rocco's cocky attitude and would rather avoid any further discussion on his personal activities. He is keen to move forward with the more pressing matter of extortion. Beckoning to a passing waiter, he orders another Caffé Corretto, inviting Rocco to join him.

"Just an espresso," Rocco says.

After their coffee arrives, Cellini comes straight to the point.

"Talk to me about what you plan to do regarding the financial situation we discussed yesterday."

Rocco is visibly taken aback with Cellini's forthright and aggressive stance. "As I told you yesterday, Mr. Cellini, the financial arrangements of our business are not my concern, I have no authority —"

Cellini slams down the small coffee cup into its saucer, splashing the dregs on Rocco's sleeve and silencing him in mid-sentence. Leaning forward so that his face is almost touching Rocco's, he hisses out his next words through gritted teeth.

"Don't insult me, Rocco. You can have people killed at the snap of your fingers and deliver their head as a gift, but you have no say in the running of your family business? Give me a break. You knew I was coming and you knew why. I've come too far to be jacked around by a guy in a $2,000 suit pretending to be an errand boy!"

"Okay, okay," Rocco replies. "I had business to attend to last night as you know and I haven't yet had a chance to discuss this with my boss. Yes, Mr. Cellini, I do have a boss and if you want to meet him in person I can arrange that, but it will be at his convenience and he is unavailable at the present time."

"I don't have time to play games," Cellini spits out the words like a machine gun spitting out bullets. "I have a message to deliver from New York and the message is this: the port of Naples will stay open. The companies based here will continue to go about their daily business and the people who work for them will be unhindered. There will be no further accidents or incidents. The wives and families of these hardworking businessmen will not be harmed or threatened in any way. In fact you will go out of your way to make sure they are safe at all times."

He pauses only to take a breath and reload another magazine of dialogue.

"And they will pay your so-called security people only what they can reasonably afford. That is to say a percentage of their actual revenues after all expenses and wages have been paid. Is that quite clear? We are watching you very closely Mr. Rocco."

Rocco puffs out his cheeks and exhales. He looks Cellini straight in the eye and says, "Just for the sake of argument, what if my boss feels he is unable to agree to your… request?"

"Convince him, Mr. Rocco."

With that, Cellini gets up from the table, indicating that the meeting is over. He looks down at Rocco, still seated at the table, and thanks him for the food basket, then walks out of the hotel dining room without looking back. In the lobby, he asks the concierge to hail a taxi and when it arrives he tells the driver to deliver the basket of bread, pasta, olive oil and wine to an old friend who lives near Naples. He returns to his room to contemplate his next move.

*****

CELLINI IS RELAXING in his room after a light lunch when the phone rings. It's the concierge.

"Mr. Cellini, There is a gentleman down here in the lobby who is asking for you."

"Who is it?" Cellini replies. There is a pause, and Cellini can hear a muffled conversation in the background but is unable to tell what is being said.

"He says he is a business acquaintance of yours and that he has some news for you," the concierge says. "He requests that you meet him downstairs in the bar."

"Tell him I'll be down in fifteen – no – better make that twenty minutes," Cellini says and hangs up before there is any further discussion. He gets into the shower and thinks long and hard about the situation. He doesn't like the idea that Rocco can just show up any time he feels like it and demand to see him. He decides to check out of the hotel later in the evening, cursing himself for using his credit card for booking the room.

Stepping out of the shower feeling a little clearer headed, he pulls on a clean shirt and pants, and combs his hair. Twenty-five minutes later he walks into the hotel bar and sees Rocco seated at a table, alone, a bottle of red wine in front of him and two glasses.

Cellini sits down across from his adversary and says, "What news?"

"Congratulations Mr. Cellini." Rocco has the glimmer of a smile on his face as he lifts the wine bottle and starts to fill the second glass. "You've really got our attention. My boss wants to meet you as soon as possible. He's actually going to cut short his skiing trip just to fly back to Napoli and be part of this conversation."

"I hate to interrupt anyone's skiing vacation so please tell him not to bother," Cellini replies. "I've already made it clear I'm not interested in prolonging this conversation. I've said all I have to say. I am flying back to New York in the morning, and I will tell my associates exactly what you have told me."

He continues, "Between you and me, I don't think they are going to be too happy, but as far as I am concerned the matter is closed."

"But Mr. Cellini, this will be considered quite rude. What can I tell my employer?" The smile is fading. Rocco is beginning to sound desperate, although Cellini is convinced it's all part of his act.

"Listen Rocco, I came here with a job to do." It's Cellini's turn to put on an act, and he can be very intimidating when he wants to be.

"That job was to tell you to clean up your act and start playing by the rules. If that doesn't happen there will be consequences. What sort of consequences depends on you and what you choose to do next."

He can see Rocco is thinking about what possible consequences

Cellini is referring to, but before he has a chance to reply, Cellini reaches across and with both hands pins Rocco's wrists to the table. Moving his face to within inches of the Italian, eyes wide open and a crazed expression on his face, he stares straight into Rocco's eyes and hisses through clenched teeth, "Let me ask you a question, Mr. Rocco..."

Pausing for effect but not blinking, he says, "Do you love your children?"

The staring contest lasts for several seconds before Cellini releases Rocco's wrists.

"We're done here," he says, and walks away.

77. The Name is Meadows... Dick Meadows

A FEW BEERS LATER, Cellini is back in his room and feeling pretty good about himself. He's being well paid for his efforts, and he thinks he was pretty convincing. He's beginning to get hungry and thinking about whether to have dinner in the hotel dining room, order room service, or go out and find something different. His culinary musings are interrupted by the sound of the phone ringing.

Once again, it's the concierge.

"I'm sorry to bother you, Mr. Cellini," says the disembodied voice on the other end, "but there is a gentleman here to see you. He says it's urgent."

Shit, Cellini thinks to himself, *What the hell does he want now?*

Out loud he says, "Tell him I've already checked out. Left the hotel."

He's trying to gather his wits and buy some time while he figures out the best way to handle the situation. He hadn't expected Rocco to come back again – at least not so soon.

"Yes sir, he's here with me now," the concierge speaks softly maintaining his composure well in an awkward situation.

"OK," Cellini replies. "Tell him I'll be right down."

He pulls on his boots and walks towards the elevator. He thinks about making a run for it, but there seems little point. In any event, he is not particularly afraid of Rocco. He just needs to make sure he keeps him in a nice public place, surrounded by lots of people. When he gets to the front desk, he can see no sign of Rocco, so he goes over to the concierge and asks about the gentleman who is looking for him.

"He's right here," the concierge replies, gesturing to a distinguished looking man, six feet tall, about fifty years of age with a strong physique and salt and pepper hair. Cellini has never seen the man before in his life but is instantly at ease with the stranger's commanding presence and pleasant demeanor.

The visitor offers his hand and says in a voice that perfectly matches his appearance, "Vito. I'm Dick Meadows. Walt has told me all about you. It's a pleasure to finally meet you in person."

*****

After a couple of drinks in the hotel bar, Meadows suggests that they order some sandwiches from the dining room and go to Cellini's room.

Loaded with foccacia sandwiches in brown paper bags and several bottles of Peroni, they return to Cellini's room and lock the door.

The formal introductions out of the way, Meadows apologizes for the lack of back up and wants to know every detail about the mission. He is the consultant for Control Risk who essentially hired Vito for the job, on Walt Shumate's recommendation, but he was always supposed to have back up in the form of Potts.

"I was willing to do the job myself all along," Meadows says, "but the company said they couldn't afford me! Ha! They'll have to afford me now, won't they!"

Meadows had been in Lima, Peru, when Shumate called him with the bad news about Potts, just twenty-four hours ago. He immediately cancelled his engagements and caught the first available flight to Naples, via London, to provide support to Cellini, a man he had never even met. Vito was to find out that this was typical of the man, and over the next few years they would become very close friends.

Richard Meadows and Vito Cellini have a lot in common and find a great deal to talk about over the course of the next few hours. Meadows wants to know every detail of the conversations between Cellini and the man called Rocco. The evening passes quickly, until about 11:30 when they are interrupted by a knock on the door and a voice calling out, "Room service".

Meadows puts his index finger to his lips and motions Cellini to be still and quiet. He mouths the words "Did you order anything?" by exaggerating his lip movements and gesticulating with his hands. Cellini shakes his head in the negative.

Meadows grasps the room key – its heavy brass fob designed such that it cannot be stolen or, as is far more likely, inadvertently left in a pocket. He stands beside the door with his arm raised, the key fob clasped firmly in his hand in such a way that if someone entered the room uninvited, his hand could be brought down quickly and heavily, striking their skull with the heavy spherical end. There is one more knock, one more call for room service, then some shuffling outside the door. Both men are well prepared for an intrusion, but it never comes.

After a few minutes, Meadows directs Cellini to open the door, his arm still raised, clutching the key. There is no one outside the room and the corridor is clear. Cellini closes and locks the door once more.

"That may have been a case of wrong room, but it could have been a visitor from the *Camorra*," Meadows says. "I think you've probably made quite an impression on those guys! I don't want to take any chances. We'll take turns sleeping, but one of us needs to stay awake, just in case they decide to come back."

He continues outlining a plan. "Tomorrow we'll fly back to Rome and then back to London. I want you to meet the guys who run Control Risk. More importantly, I want to get my hands on Potts!"

Cellini volunteers to take first watch, figuring Meadows will need to catch up on his rest after travelling for over twenty-four hours, but in the end they both stay up all night talking, drinking beer and finishing off the sandwiches they had picked up earlier. By dawn they have formed a close bond, regaling each other with their respective histories.

*****

ON THE FLIGHT back to London, Richard Meadows mentions to Cellini that he could use a man like him as part of his team for a project he is currently putting together in Peru. Without going into details, he tells him the pay will be good, the work will be exactly the kind he will enjoy, and that there will be plenty of time off to relax and enjoy life. He also tells him that he will be acting in the interests of the United States.

Cellini will think about it, but right now he is ready to take a break and spend some time with his family.

Dinner at the Army and Navy Officer's Club in London, of which Richard Meadows is a distinguished and honoured member,[1] is a spectacular affair. Like many Americans, Cellini had always been given the impression that British food was somewhat indifferent. He is treated to a spread the like of which he has never seen and will remember his entire life as the best meal he has ever been served.

During dinner, Richard Meadows cautions Cellini about the mission he has just completed.

"When it hits the fan," he says, "and make no mistake, it will hit the fan hard…" he pauses. "Once those guys realise exactly how much they've been taken for, and by a fake Mafia hit man, they are going to come looking for you."

"Let 'em come," Cellini replies with an offhand bravado he doesn't exactly feel.

Meadows is also concerned. "Seriously, Vito, you need to be careful. Part of the reason I want you to come to South America with me is to put some extra miles between you and those guys."

"I know," Cellini replies, "and I appreciate that – but right now I just want to get home to my wife."

*****

MUCH OF THEIR TIME together in Naples had been spent discussing firearms, and in particular the effects of muzzle brakes and suppressors. Now Richard Meadows is keen to test Cellini's modified weapons first hand. Both Durwin Dengerud and Walter Shumate had already predisposed him to Cellini's work, but Meadows looks forward to trying them out for himself. As they leave the Army and Navy Officer's Club[1] and head their separate ways the two men make arrangements to get together as soon as they are both back in the States.

[1]. *In 1960, Meadows had been one of the first US Army officers to participate in an exchange programme with the 22nd British Special Air Service (SAS) Regiment. Meadows completed SAS training (becoming one of the first two foreigners ever to receive SAS qualification wings) and served as an acting troop leader for 12 months, participating in field combat operations. His SAS experience helped form the basis for future US Army Special Forces selection, training and organizational structures. As a serving officer with the SAS, Richard Meadows was also entitled to all the rights and privileges of a British officer, including membership of the exclusive Army and Navy Club in Mayfair, London.*

78. Enter H. Ross Perot

A COUPLE OF MONTHS goes by uneventfully. Cellini has settled back in San Antonio and Meadows is back at his home in Florida, and they finally have a chance to catch up with each other. Meadows is impressed with the quality of Cellini's craftsmanship, but when he test fires a selection of assault weapons and handguns fitted with the Cellini stabilizer on the range, he knows immediately that this is what the US Special Forces need. He agrees to give it his full backing and do whatever he can to put it in front of as many senior military people as possible. Cellini has one more surprise for Meadows, and reaching into his bag, he pulls out the small machine-pistol and hands it over.

"You Goddamn sonofabitch!" Meadows says, laughing. Naturally he has heard all about the weapon from Shumate and was beginning to think Cellini was holding back.

He studies the weapon carefully, noting its simplicity of design and how few parts it has. He disassembles it and then puts it back together in no time, despite having never handled it before. Cellini pulls four empty magazines out of his bag and the two men load bullets into them.

Richard Meadows puts the weapon through its paces, firing alternately in semi-automatic and full-automatic mode, adjusting the positions of the grips and fitting again until he empties all four clips.

He walks over to Cellini, poker-faced and silent.

After a few minutes, Cellini has run out of patience.

"Well?" he says, "What do you think?"

Meadows looks him in the eye, his expression giving away nothing.

"You want me to be completely honest?"

Before Cellini can answer, Meadows bursts out laughing, unable to keep a straight face any longer.

"It's better than the Uzi, which is about the best available in the world as of right now," he says.

"Seriously, Vito, it's a helluva weapon, but…" he pauses.

"It's probably not pretty enough for Washington," he says, "but that's no big deal. You can easily pretty it up a bit if you have to."

As they are driving back from the shooting range, Meadows lays out his strategy.

"First things first. I want you to get your foot in the door, and I think the best way to do that is going to be with your stabilizer. Will you leave it with me? I have an idea."

Cellini has long since decided he would trust Richard Meadows with his life and has no problem leaving the stabilizer in his hands. Meadows is highly respected throughout the Army and has a tremendous amount of influence with his superiors, especially at Fort Bragg, although he has difficulty dealing with politicians, committees and the multiple layers of government in order to cut through the red tape of bureaucracy.

But he is on very good terms with one man who might be able to make a difference, a hugely successful Texas businessman by the name of H. Ross Perot.

Meadows invites the Cellinis to visit him at home and arranges for his friend and benefactor, H. Ross Perot, to attend a demonstration of the Cellini stabilizer. Perot, a US Navy veteran, is an avid supporter of the military and believes strongly that the American soldier should have the best equipment available.

Cellini is surprised at the diminutive stature of Perot, but recognizes the skills and acumen of this sharp businessman. Perot seems less interested in the stabilizer, and what it can do, than in its cost and how quickly it can be produced. He speaks quickly and doesn't mince words.

"If Dick says this is what our boys need then we need to get it for them. Just tell me how much and I'll write you a cheque."

Cellini is stunned by Perot's reaction. Meadows is delighted. It is exactly the response he was hoping for, and he asks for funding to manufacture 1,000 of the Cellini stabilizers to be issued to soldiers serving with the Special Forces. Cellini makes it clear to Perot that he is willing to waive all the profit on the production of the stabilizer. It's his contribution to the American fighting man. Even so, Perot wants every nickel accounted for and, at the end of the day, he wants the credit.

Franci is horrified by what she considers the arrogance of the man, and wants her husband to refuse to accept Perot's payment. A man who rarely begs for anything, Richard Meadows implores the Cellinis not to do that.

"Please Franci, don't offend him. He really doesn't mean anything by it, and he's a good man. I have high hopes he will run for president one of these days, and if that happens, he will remember the people who have helped put him there."[1]

His words resonate and Cellini graciously accepts payment.

The Cellinis return to San Antonio, and Vito spends several days testing, refining and retesting the stabilizer until he is satisfied that it can go into production. He places the order for 1,000 pieces with Cox Manufacturing Company, a San Antonio firm that requires a down payment before undertaking such a large order. In February 1991, payment arrives from H. Ross Perot in the amount of $15,615 for the production of 1,000 Cellini muzzle brakes.

Cellini would meet H. Ross Perot on several occasions and never ceases to be surprised by the lightning speed of thought and action – as well as the directness – of this remarkable Texas billionaire.

[1] *Perot would not officially declare his candidacy for president for over a year, but many believed he was considering it even at this time. His interference in the political arena was widely known; he opposed the Gulf War and had long been a thorn in the side of the Reagan and Bush administrations over the issue of POWs/MIAs he believed left behind in Southeast Asia after the Vietnam War.*

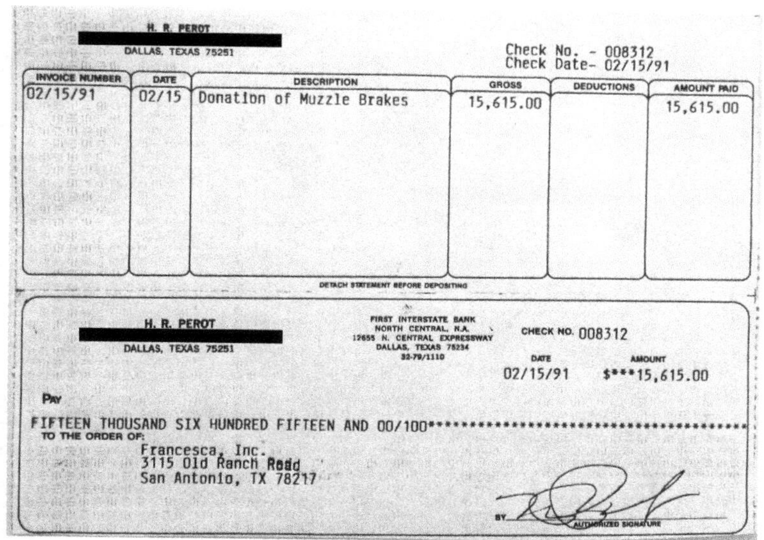

H. R. PEROT
DALLAS, TEXAS 75251

Check No. - 008312
Check Date- 02/15/91

INVOICE NUMBER	DATE	DESCRIPTION	GROSS	DEDUCTIONS	AMOUNT PAID
02/15/91	02/15	Donation of Muzzle Brakes	15,615.00		15,615.00

DETACH STATEMENT BEFORE DEPOSITING

H. R. PEROT
DALLAS, TEXAS 75251

FIRST INTERSTATE BANK
NORTH CENTRAL, N.A.
12655 N. CENTRAL EXPRESSWAY
DALLAS, TEXAS 75234
32-79/1110

CHECK NO. 008312

DATE 02/15/91 AMOUNT $***15,615.00

PAY

FIFTEEN THOUSAND SIX HUNDRED FIFTEEN AND 00/100***

TO THE ORDER OF:
Francesca, Inc.
3115 Old Ranch Road
San Antonio, TX 78217

BY ________ AUTHORIZED SIGNATURE

Cheque from H. Ross Perot payable to Francesca, Inc. (Cellini's company) for supplying muzzle brakes to the US Army Special Forces. It was a downpayment. The total cost to Perot was $25,000. Cellini made zero profit.

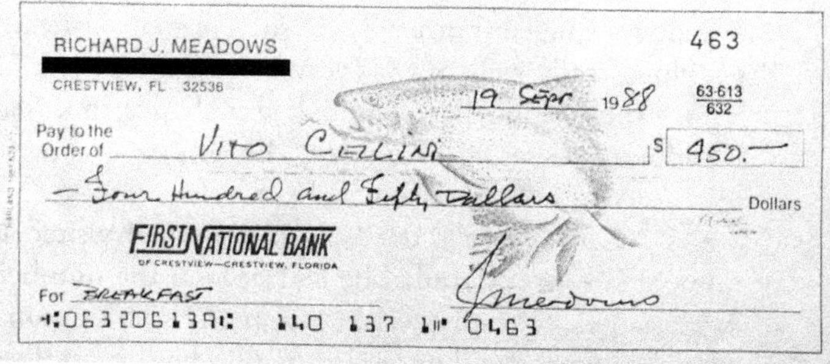

RICHARD J. MEADOWS
CRESTVIEW, FL 32536

463

19 Sept 1988

63-613/632

Pay to the Order of Vito Cellini $ 450.—

Four Hundred and Fifty Dollars Dollars

FIRST NATIONAL BANK
OF CRESTVIEW—CRESTVIEW, FLORIDA

For BREAKFAST

⑆063206139⑆ 140 137 1⑈ 0463

Payment received by Vito Cellini from Richard Meadows for a custom made stabilizer. Meadows recorded the transaction as "BREAKFAST." It must have been a spectacular breakfast for $450!

An early muzzle brake or "stabilizer" produced for use with military weapons. A simple but highly efficient design.

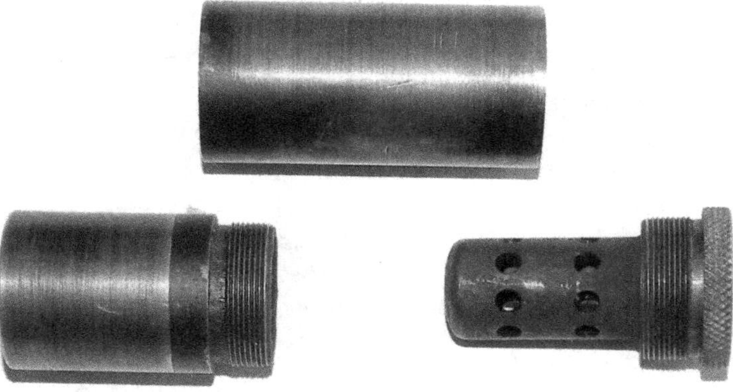

79. Dead, But Not Quite Buried

MONTHS GO BY, AND then one day Cellini receives a brief, handwritten fax from Richard Meadows, who is still in Peru, warning him to keep a low profile. He will return to his Florida home very soon and they can get together so he can explain.

The Cellinis love to visit the Meadows in Florida. Pamela, Dick Meadow's English-born wife, is such a great hostess, and she and Franci get along really well. She is every bit as patient with Dick as Franci is with Vito.[1] The Cellinis have barely had a chance to unpack and already Dick Meadows is ushering Vito out of the house.

"We're going fishing," he says.

Cellini recalls the first time he had visited Richard Meadows at home and how astounded he had been at the number of crab traps stored in his garage. He had never seen so many crab traps in one place before and when he commented on how much Richard must like crabs, Meadows just looked at him.

Meadows is a man who uses words sparingly at the best of times. There is little conversation as the men leave. Today, they are not in search of crabs and each sets up with a fishing rod. Once they are comfortable, Dick Meadows gets straight to the point.

"Control Risk has received a request from their people in Naples. Their client wants to set up another meeting."

"What for?" says Cellini. "I thought that business was all settled?"

Meadows smiles. "It was," he says, continuing sarcastically, "but

[1] *Pamela Meadows once asked her husband, in front of Vito and Franci, what he was doing on his latest escapade. Meadows smiled at her and replied, "It's probably better if you don't ask. I don't think you'd like the answer." He later told Cellini that she had never asked him that before, and never did again. She just accepted him as he was. Having a loyal, trusting and accepting wife was one of many things these two men had in common, and perhaps one of the reasons why they got along so well.*

they were so impressed they have another proposition."

Meadows pauses to let the words sink in before adding, "They specifically requested Mr. Vito Cellini from New York to come to Naples and meet in person – as soon as possible."

It's Cellini's turn to smile. "I suppose I did make quite an impression. It's a trap, of course."

Meadows nods. "Now you can understand why I sent you that fax."

Meadows apologizes for the brevity of his faxed message but explains that once he found out about this meeting request, he knew it was almost certainly an ambush, and that Vito was being set up for a contract hit.

"It was stupid of me to use my real name," Cellini shakes his head.

"Don't beat yourself up over it. They would have easily found out if you had been using a false ID and that might even have made it worse. I'm sure they also know you are not actually from New York.

"The main thing is, we're going to have to kill you off so they won't feel the need to."

They concoct an elaborate story that Vito Cellini is dead, going to considerable lengths including posting obituary notices and prompting family members with the story in case they are contacted.

The ruse appears to be successful. In any event, Control Risk has no further contact from its client in Naples.[2]

*****

Richard Meadows and Vito Cellini stay in contact and get together whenever their schedules permit. Meadows never quits asking Cellini to join him in Peru and Cellini never accepts the offer, largely because deep down he suspects that Franci was unwell and will soon need him to be around full time.

The last time Cellini sees Dick Meadows is in New Orleans early in 1995. The two couples had arranged to meet there, and they stay longer than either intended, everyone is having such a great time.

The Cellinis are vacationing in Italy in July, 1995 when they receive news that Richard has died.

2. *In the coming years, there were some major shake-ups and a spate of slayings within the families associated with the Naples Camorra. Changes in leadership and organizational structure followed. Whether or not Cellini's role had anything to do with these changes remains a matter of speculation.*

From the moment they had first meet in Naples, Vito Cellini and Dick Meadows were destined to become close friends. They visit each other's homes and spend a great deal of time in the pursuit of their mutual love for fishing – Meadows once telling Cellini he is the only fishing companion he has ever met who actually knows how to fish properly! They also hunt together and enjoy numerous late-night drinking sessions, discussing various jobs they have done in the past and the possibility of working together again in the future. Dick Meadows is one of a handful of people with whom Cellini is completely comfortable discussing his life and his activities. They also share similar views on the direction of current weapons development.

Like their mutual friend Walter Shumate, Meadows is a staunch supporter of Cellini's weapons designs and a big fan of his compact and lightweight machine pistol, which he considers better than the Israeli Uzi, and far superior to anything available to the US military. Meadows feels that the Cellini machine pistol just needs "prettying up" a little, and that some in authority frown on it because of its utter simplicity and bland appearance.

Richard Meadows believes strongly that Cellini's stabilizer/suppressor is ideal for US Special Forces, which is why he introduces Cellini to billionaire businessman H. Ross Perot and urges Perot to take an interest in the device. Perot is a great admirer of Richard Meadows, once describing him as "James Bond in real life", and Meadows is as close a friend as the reclusive Perot has ever had. Perot listens to what Meadows says. He trusts him completely – he even allows Meadows free use of his own private jet. On Meadows' recommendation, Perot agrees to finance the production cost of 1,000 Cellini stabilizers for distribution among Delta Force personnel.

These prototype stabilizers have been handed down to successive generations of Special Forces soldiers, and the Cellini name is legendary among those fortunate enough to receive them.

Early in 1995, Meadows is diagnosed with leukaemia. His death on July 29th of that year is a sad blow to all who know him.

Richard Meadows' US military awards and decorations include the Distinguished Service Cross, two Silver Stars, Bronze Star with Valor Device, Air Medal, Legion of Merit, Meritorious Service Medal, Joint Service Commendation Medal, three Army Commendation Medals, Combat Infantryman Badge, Master Parachutist badge, Glider Badge, Ranger Tab and Scuba Badge – and numerous awards from other countries.

Shortly before his death, Meadows is informed that President Clinton is to present him with the Presidential Citizens Medal. It is believed by many in the Special Forces community that had it been possible to disclose Meadows' complete military record, he would almost certainly receive the Congressional Medal of Honor, but since most of his covert roles working with the CIA's Spe-

cial Activities Division remain classified – and therefore undisclosed – this ultimate recognition for his courage does not happen.

On June 6th, 1997, a statue of Richard Meadows is unveiled at Fort Bragg, North Carolina, headquarters of the US Army Special Operations Command. Sculpted by Texas artist Lawrence M. Ludtke, the statue is funded in full by H. Ross Perot.

Vito Cellini is a guest of honour at the dedication ceremony and stands at Pamela Meadows' side as the statue is unveiled.

VITO.
BE CAREFUL!! THE SITUATION HAS CHANGED. I FEEL THAT
THE BAD GUYS ARE ANGER BECAUSE THEY HAVE BEEN FOOLED AND
NOW WILL COME BACK WITH GREAT VENGEANCE TO ALL
WHO WERE INVOLVED. THEY HAVE BEEN DENIED AT LEAST 3 YEARS
OF $!, POSSIBLE AS MUCH AS A MILLION DOLLARS. AS OF THIS
DATE, YOU OR I HAVE PLAYED A FAIR GAME TO BOTH THE CLIENT
AND THE GANG. TO OPEN UP A RENEWED LINE OF COMMUNICATIONS
WITH THE CLIENT OR/AND ESPECIALLY THE GANG BY ALLOWING THEM
TO CONTACT YOU BY PHONE WOULD ONLY ALLOW THE GANG TO
FIND YOU, TO DO WHAT THEY WANT. I ALSO FEEL THE GANG
WOULD LIKE TO PAY YOU A VISIT TO CONFIRM WHAT THEY
SUSPECT. (VITO, WAS NOT PART OF "THE FAMILY")
WHAT DO YOU WANT TO DO??? SEE MY FAX #
RICHARD

The fax sent by Richard Meadows to Vito Cellini, warning him that the "Bad Guys" had found out Vito was "not part of 'The Family'".

Dick Meadows was never more at home than when on his boat fishing, either alone or with the companionship of a close friend. He and Vito Cellini enjoyed a deep friendship.

Photo courtesy Pamela Meadows via Alan Hoe

80. Old Friends...

Raul Pereira, the Cuban doctor who had treated Nicky in Miami, has remained a good family friend to the Cellinis. The doctor does not make friends easily, largely because of his radical political views, but he trusts Cellini and is completely open with him.

Not long after they first became friends, when the Cellinis were still living in Miami, Dr. Pereira had confided in them that his dream was to be able to go back to Cuba one day and open his own clinic. He was aware that he faced a great deal of opposition, and had already made many enemies due to his outspoken views on Cuba and particularly Fidel Castro. He has always trusted Cellini and feels safer having him around – so much so, that when Cellini first mentioned the idea of moving to Texas, Pereira offered to buy the Cellinis a luxury home close to his own if they would stay in Florida. Cellini declined.

The Cellinis visit him in Miami whenever they can, often on their way to or back from vacationing in Venezuela, where Cellini has a cousin on his mother's side with whom he stays in touch.[1]

When visiting the doctor, the Cellinis spend time relaxing on the beach, swimming, snorkeling and scuba diving, frequently driving down to Key West where Raul Pereira loves to practise free-diving, a sport at which

[1.] *Cellini invested a portion of his earnings from Nicaragua, some $32,000, in a Venezuelan bank on the promise of high interest earnings – as much as 35%. His cousin's daughter (his second cousin) worked at the bank and arranged the investment. It was a decision he would later regret. Soon after establishing the account, the second cousin asked the Cellinis if they would help out with medical costs of $2,000 for an operation needed for her baby; they agreed, and in order to facilitate the exchange, gave her power of attorney on the account. She took the $2,000 and then drained the entire account. By the time the Cellinis returned to Venezuela and discovered the theft, it was too late, Franci, who was more upset about the lies than the theft, demanded that the $2,000 for the bogus surgery be returned – which it was. The balance of $30,000 was never recovered. Cellini has not returned to Venezuela.*

he excels. Cellini, who is an expert swimmer, also enjoys free-diving but bows to the expertise of his friend.[2]

The doctor becomes a regular visitor to Texas after the Cellinis move to San Antonio. A keen hunter, he has grown to love the wide open spaces Texas offers sportsmen, and every year, between Thanksgiving and Christmas, he takes a couple of weeks off from his practice to visit his old friend in San Antonio. Cellini looks forward to the time they spend together and the two-hour drive along Highway 90 to a hunting ranch near Brackettville.

Some years later, Pereira arrives at San Antonio International Airport with a glum expression, and straight away Cellini knows that something is wrong. The drive home is spent in silence. Cellini waits until they get back to the house before asking, "My friend, what is troubling you?"

"I have some very sad news," Pereira replies. "Our old friend Pedro Ramos has passed away."

"No? Pedro? Surely not! That is, as you say, very sad news. I am very sorry to hear that."

The words came easily to Cellini, the emotions did not. Inside, his heart is jumping for joy. He had never liked nor trusted the *vampire* and could not be more pleased to learn that he would no longer be inflicting pain and suffering on innocent people. Cellini had never forgotten the day Ramos drove past a serious road accident and laughed at the helpless victims rather than stopping to help.

"What happened?" Cellini says, trying to show at least a little interest, if not actual sadness.

"I am not completely certain," the doctor replies. "He moved to Guatemala some time ago and last I heard he had terminal cancer. I guess that rather than endure the pain of a long, drawn out illness and death he took his own life." After a long pause he adds, "I will miss him."

"A lot of people will miss him," Cellini says, thinking of the court in Nicaragua that had convicted him in absentia for Chamorro's assassination. Cellini had always been convinced that Ramos had tried to set him up to take the blame, and believes he would probably have succeeded, if it were not for Somoza speaking up in his defence. Cellini keeps his thoughts to himself, knowing that Pereira was eternally grateful to Ramos for his help in getting him out of Cuba, and establishing himself as a United States citizen.

Cellini would never feel pity for Ramos, who he considered one of the few truly despicable human beings he had ever encountered.

2. *Raul Pereira died in very mysterious circumstances while trying to break the record for free diving (diving without breathing apparatus), a hobby about which he was not only passionate, but also extremely careful. After several record attempts at a competition in Key West, he went back into the water and did not return to the surface. Despite rescue attempts his body was not found until 24 hours later, in the exact same location where he had gone in. Cellini has often wondered if his death really was a freak accident, or if one of his enemies had caught up with him. It seemed odd that his body would disappear then reappear in the same spot, given the strength of the currents around Key West.*

81. Mexico

WHILE WORKING part-time as a gunsmith at a sporting gun dealership on the outskirts of San Antonio, Cellini meets a soft-spoken and well-dressed Mexican national who is introduced to him only as Ruben. Ruben is quite obviously a gentleman of means. It is a chance meeting that will result in yet another series of adventures for Cellini; adventures that will almost cost him his freedom as well as putting his life at risk – although it will be some time before Cellini realises exactly how dangerous these adventures really are.

Ruben walks into the gun shop and places on the counter a superbly tooled leather gun case. Inside the case is a fine, custom-made Winchester hunting rifle. Lifting the weapon from the case, he explains apologetically to the owner of the shop that the stock of the weapon is broken and that, as it obviously cannot be repaired, he would like to see if he can buy another hunting rifle of similar quality.

Cellini, who is usually to be found in the workshop at the back of the gun store, happens to overhear the conversation and, his curiosity piqued by the mention of the Winchester rifle, steps in and picks up the weapon. After giving it little more than a cursory examination he looks up the Mexican.

"I can fix this," he says.

The owner is mildly annoyed with Cellini, who he thinks may be interfering with a potentially good sale, but bites his tongue.

"You can?" Ruben replies.

"Yes, of course. Leave it with me," says Cellini. "Can you come back in a week?"

For a man with Cellini's expertise and appreciation for fine guns, the opportunity to work on such a beautiful rifle is to be relished. The Mexican is clearly not a man who would entrust just anyone with his possessions, but he likes the look of Cellini and decides to leave the gun in his hands.

"One week?"

"One week."

After he leaves, the owner turns to Cellini.

"Why did you do that?" he says, about to chide him for costing him what could have been a very lucrative sale.

Cellini replies, "This gun probably cost $5,000. You don't have anything like it in this store, and I doubt you would find one like it anywhere in Texas. We have some wonderful hunting rifles, but nothing that could compare to this. I will fix it – and you will have a customer for life!"

One week later, Ruben walks back into the store. Cellini greets him with a big smile.

"It's a beautiful rifle," he says. "It would be criminal not to repair it."

He opens the gun case and proudly hands over the rifle. The Mexican cocks the gun and dry fires it, barely even looking at the workmanship or the repair.

"What do I owe you?" he asks, reaching into his pocket and pulling out a roll of $100 bills.

An invoice is handed over and money changes hands. Ruben smiles and leans across the counter to Cellini.

"You like to go hunting, Mr. Cellini?"

Cellini nods.

"I have a beautiful property in Guadalajara, including many acres reserved for my personal hunting pleasure. It would be a great honour if you will join me, as my guest. I have a great respect for your obvious knowledge of guns and for your work. Please accept my invitation to visit my home and hunt with me."

Cellini thanks him and agrees to think about the best time for such a visit. Phone numbers are exchanged and Ruben leaves the gun store with his hunting rifle in its leather case.

The sales clerk and a redneck customer in the gun store mock him.

"So you're off to Mexico on a hunting trip? Better hope you don't catch anything!"

The owner of the shop explains to Cellini that, in south Texas, it is common for visiting Mexicans to brag about their ranches and their resort homes and how much land they own, but it's mostly all talk. This guy probably isn't serious.

"I bet he lives in a trailer outside Nuevo Laredo!" says the clerk.

"Hunts coyotes!" chimes in the redneck.

"Yeah right. The two-legged kind!"

Everyone has a good laugh, except Cellini. *Not dressed like that,* he thinks to himself. *And certainly not with such a fine hunting rifle.*

*****

Weeks pass and Cellini forgets all about Ruben and his invitation.

Then one morning, a month or so later, totally out of the blue, the door opens and in walks Ruben.

He greets Cellini like a long-lost brother, then starts chiding him.

"You have offended me, Mr. Cellini. You have hurt my feelings very deeply."

It's a mocking tone, but there is no animosity, just a feigned hurt expression with the hint of a smile and a gleam in his eye.

Cellini is caught off guard and not sure what to say.

"My friend," he says, "I invite you to come to Guadalajara to stay at my ranch. To hunt with me. To meet my family and to drink wine with me and eat my food, but you do not come? I ask myself why is this? Why does my friend Cellini not visit my home?"

He reaches out and grabs Cellini by the hand and starts to laugh.

"You must come with me today!"

"But that is impossible," Cellini replies. "I said I would very much like to visit your ranch, and I would. But I have no ticket. It is very difficult for me to arrange travel right now. Hunting season starts in a couple of weeks, and the store is very busy."

Ruben looks around.

"Surely these gentlemen can manage without you for a few days, a week or two at most, yes?"

"And you do not need a ticket. I have my own aircraft right here in San Antonio. My son, like me, is a pilot. When I say that you will be my guest, I really do mean that you will be my guest!"

"Meet me at the airport at, let's say, 3:00 pm?"

He leans over to Cellini, puts his arm around his shoulders and adds, quietly,

"Bring with you whatever guns you choose Mr. Cellini. My private plane is never searched by US Customs or Federales, so you can bring anything you want to. Especially, please bring that small machine gun I have been reading about."

The Italian wonders how he knows about the machine gun, but lets it go. He has learned when to keep quiet. Besides, the machine gun has been featured in a couple of gun magazines. It's not exactly a secret.

The owner of the gun store is reluctant to be without Cellini for any length of time because it's good for business to have him around. He smiles, putting on a show for his customer, and tells him to go and have a great time.

"Stay as long as you like – or as long as Ruben will have you!"

Later, as Cellini is leaving the shop, he takes hold of his arm and looks him in the eye.

"Be careful," he says, seriously. Then slaps him on the back and laughs.

"And tell him he needs to buy more guns from me so I can afford to pay you when you get back!"

*****

THE TAXI PULLS UP next to a sage green hangar on the general aviation side of San Antonio International Airport. Cellini steps out, hands the driver a $10 bill and grabs a leather backpack and a heavy black plastic rifle case from the back seat. He looks over towards an immaculate white Cessna R182 painted with a red wave pattern down the side.

Standing by the wing of the aircraft, Ruben is well dressed as always, but casual in pressed jeans, a white western shirt and a black Stetson. He is talking to the pilot who is wearing a white short-sleeved shirt and black pants. Ruben beckons Cellini over. He feels underdressed in a dark blue T-shirt with military camouflage pants.

Ruben introduces the pilot as his younger son, who greets Cellini with a handshake, welcomes him, and tells him the flight will be smooth all the way.

"There will be a stopover in Eagle Pass," he says,. "It's just for customs and immigration. It is nothing more than a formality," he adds, glancing at his father.

The luggage and weapons are stowed in the Cessna's small baggage compartment, and Ruben invites Cellini to climb aboard. Ruben and his son finish the preflight inspection while Cellini opens the door to get into the back seat of the aircraft. He sees a familiar face grinning at him from the other back seat. It's another of his customers from the gun shop who has been friends with Ruben for some time but this is his first hunting trip to Mexico. He introduces himself as Monty, and the two men shake hands as Cellini takes his seat in the back of the Cessna. Cellini, who is never good at remembering names, quickly forgets his name, thinking of him as "The Texan" because of his pronounced drawl.

Ruben and his son get into the aircraft and complete their cockpit checks. Cleared to taxi, the aircraft rolls along the taxiway and onto runway one-two right. Within minutes, the Cessna is airborne and heading south. Cellini feels the thump of the landing gear retracting, then closes his eyes and dozes for most of the flight to Eagle Pass.

Touchdown is smooth, and they taxi over to the FBO that doubles as a border checkpoint. A border guard in green uniform signals them to park and cut the engine. Cellini reaches into the pocket of his pants to produce his passport, but Ruben tells him he won't need it. Ruben gets out of the aircraft and talks to the guard for a few minutes. They laugh, he returns to the aircraft, opens the door and asks if anyone needs a restroom or a drink.

They decide it would be a good idea to step outside and walk around while they have the chance. A fuel truck pulls alongside the plane and begins filling the wing tanks. Cellini asks Ruben why he doesn't need to show his passport.

"My friend," the Mexican replies, "You are my guest and these people are my friends. My word is good enough for them."

The fuel truck driver approaches with a clipboard.

"At least let me pay for the gas," Cellini replies.

"As you wish." Cellini reaches into his pocket for cash then looks at the bill.

"$450?"

"*Si señor.* She is almost empty."

It is Cellini's first flight in a small high-performance aircraft and the cost of the avgas comes as a surprise, but he doesn't show it. He counts out four $100 bills and a 50, then adds a 20 on top. He knows it pays to carry plenty of cash and tip well. You never know when you may need a favour, and good tippers are usually remembered.

They get back into the aircraft for the rest of the flight to Guadalajara. Cellini and the fourth passenger start to make small talk about their hunting experiences. Between the engine noise, Cellini's thick-as-pasta Italian accent and his companion's heavy Texas drawl, the conversation is limited and soon they both fall silent.

The sun is starting to go down as they begin their descent to the small airstrip, about 20 kilometers outside of Guadalajara.

As they taxi onto the concrete outside the small metal hangar, a black SUV with tinted windows draws up alongside and a young Mexican in grey overalls gets out, leaving the driver's door open, and opens the tailgate of the vehicle before disappearing into the hangar.

He returns with an older man in similar grey overalls and they walk over to the aircraft. The luggage, including the gun cases, is unloaded from the Cessna and put into the back of the SUV. The visitors take their seats in the vehicle. Once everything is stowed in the vehicle and the tailgate is closed, the two groundcrew attach a tow bar to the front wheel of the aircraft and push it towards the hangar.

Ruben takes the driving seat, pushing his son out of the way with a laugh.

"He's a great pilot, but he drives like a Mexican!" he says.

The SUV whisks them from the hangar and over to the ranch house, a quarter of a mile away.

It is a magnificent hacienda, with marble floors and stone pillars accented by rich tapestries and massive sculptures.

"Gentlemen," he says, "welcome to my home."

Once inside, they are introduced to an elegant lady with a slim figure and jet black hair who looks to be in her mid-forties but from her poise and demeanour, Cellini judges is probably a little older.

"May I present my sister, María Esther," he says.

"María, these are my friends from Texas. While they are in Mexico, this is their home."

María extends her hand to each of the newcomers in turn, and welcomes them to the family ranch home in perfect English. Then she turns back to her brother and starts speaking in Spanish. Ruben interrupts her and asks that, in deference to his guests, would she please speak only in English. She apologizes for her indiscretion and asks them all about the flight, how they met Ruben, and how she hopes they will find plenty of good hunting. She excuses herself to check on the preparations for the evening meal and tells them that someone will be along shortly to offer drinks.

"Tonight we rest in the comfort of my house," Ruben announces. "Tomorrow, we hunt. So tomorrow we sleep like hunters, in the bunkhouse."

*****

SHORTLY AFTER SUNRISE, Cellini awakes, showers and dresses, and joins the others for breakfast. Over coffee, they talk about where they will hunt and what they will find. Ruben boasts of the elk and bear on his land. Cellini has never hunted bear, and the thought excites him. Bears are a far more dangerous prey than most.

As they leave for the day's hunt, Ruben hands Cellini a rifle. It's an M-1 carbine with a 30-round magazine. He hands him two more clips and tells him to put them in his pocket. Cellini examines the gun. It's in pristine condition, and already has a round chambered, ready to fire.

"My gift to you," Ruben says, "Keep it close by. You never know when you might see a bear… and they are quick motherfuckers."

Cellini gets into the front seat of an olive green-painted Jeep alongside his host. The Texan gets into the back of another, identical vehicle, with Ruben's son and one of the ranch hands who is similarly armed, and they set off down a dusty dirt road. Ruben breaks the silence.

"Did you bring my favourite gun?"

Cellini nods.

After riding in silence for several more minutes, Ruben turns to Cellini with a wry smile on his face.

"My sister, she likes you Cellini," he says. "She is beautiful, yes?"

"She is indeed a very lovely woman," Cellini replies, unsure of where the conversation will lead. He had always been able to appreciate a beautiful woman, but never had any interest in any of them since his marriage to Francesca. For Cellini, none could compare to Franci – and none ever did. Before he can say any more, Ruben starts laughing out loud.

"You think my sister is perhaps too old for you?" he says, his grin widening.

"Don't worry my friend," he says, "She is not for you and you are not for her. Not unless your head is tired of being attached to your body."

He gestures with his fingers across his throat to accentuate the point and laughs loudly again.

"Do you know who she is?"

Playing dumb is a ploy that had always served Cellini well, and even if he had recognized Ruben's sister, which he didn't, he would have kept quiet.

"María Esther is married to Luis Echeverría Álvarez, the former *Presidente*!" [1]

*****

THE HUNT GOES WELL, and Cellini shoots two large elk on the first day. A team of experienced followers collects the animals in an old Ford truck and drives them back to the ranch, to dress and prepare the meat. For those worthy of display as trophies, they will also arrange for the carcass or the head to go to a taxidermist.

1. Luis Echeverría Álvarez was president of Mexico from 1970-76. He was suspected of having ties to Mexican drug cartels both during and after his term in office, and continued to have powerful influence over many government officials long after he left his post. Despite being accused and indicted of various crimes including murder and genocide, he was never brought to trial. He is believed to have used his influence over President Vincente Fox to appoint Alejandro Gertz Manero – one of Ruben's security enforcers – as chief of the Federal Police. Shortly after his appointment, Gertz was suspected of facilitating the escape, from a maximum security prison, of Joaquín Guzmán ("El Chapo"), a former associate of Ruben Zuno.

That night, as Ruben promised, the five men share the bunkhouse. They cook pork over an open fire and drink beer. Ruben asks Cellini to show him the machine gun. He pulls it from his bag and checks the receiver and the magazine before handing it over.

"What's the matter? You don't trust me with a loaded gun?" It's a taunt. A test to see how Cellini will react.

"I don't trust anybody with a loaded gun."

Ruben takes the gun in his hand. At a little over four pounds in weight and about 12 inches long, it's a beautiful compact weapon, made almost entirely of polished steel. The cylindrical shape is both practical and aesthetic. The light weight of the weapon belies its destructive power and incredible rate of fire. Ruben cocks it to dry fire, points it at an imaginary target, and fires.

"It is not a hunting weapon," is all Cellini says.

"Depends what you are hunting for!"

"Seriously, Mr. Cellini, I would like to place an order with you for say twenty-five of these. No. Make it fifty. Can you deliver?"

"Do you have a Federal Firearms Licence and an importation licence and permission from the US State Department as well as your own government to import military-style automatic weapons?"

Ruben smiles smugly as he hands the gun back to Cellini. "Anything can be arranged," he says. "For now, may I keep this one?"

Cellini places the gun back in his travel bag.

"We can shoot it a little bit tomorrow."

Cellini, out of habit whenever he is in a strange place, sleeps with his trusted .45 under his pillow and the M-1 carbine on the floor beside him. The machine gun he keeps in its bag, which he places at the foot of the bed, under the sheets. He has a difficult time going to sleep, despite being dog-tired from the day's hunt. The moon is high, and the bunkhouse cabin has large skylights as well as windows along both sides, so the interior is well lit.

Cellini has spent more than his fair share of nights sleeping in the woods, either on the naked ground or in a tent. The bunkhouse has sturdy wooden walls but very little in the way of soundproofing. Normally the noises of nocturnal animals or the rustling of leaves in the wind are a comfort to him. Soothing sounds that calm and relax. The absolute silence and stillness of the night, coupled with the bright moonlight, seem somehow unnatural. He dozes fitfully when suddenly he is aware of noises outside the window, and is certain he sees a brief flash of light. Not lightning. He hears voices, muffled but raised.

Instantly alert, he rolls to the side of the bed and onto the floor in one swift movement, the .45 in his left hand and the carbine in his right.

He's sitting against the wall of the bunkhouse, beneath the window. Ruben, who had been fast asleep and snoring in the bed opposite Cellini, is now flat down on the floor, half under Cellini's bed. He too has a pistol in his hand.

The others stir and from the corner of the room a voice starts to call out, "What the f—"

Cellini recognizes the drawl of his Texan travelling companion and cuts him short with a finger to his lips and a short, sharp "ssshhh".

They wait for several minutes, and Cellini whispers to Ruben, "Who knows we are here? Who knows about this place?"

"Everyone knows about the ranch. I am a wealthy man my friend, people watch me. Many are jealous of my success and my ranching business. Someone may have seen the aircraft landing yesterday and guessed I had a hunting party. Sometimes they try to scare my guests away to make me look bad."

"Is it possible it's just animals attracted by the smell of our food or the blood from the hunt?" Cellini forces a smile, but he is not convinced.

"It's possible, but it would be the first animal I've ever known that could use a flashlight."

Cellini indicates for everyone to stay still and keep quiet, then moves slowly towards the door of the cabin. He lifts and slides the deadbolt silently along. Putting the Colt .45 into his pocket, he grasps the handle of the door and pulls it towards him, keeping the carbine at his hip, the muzzle pointing at the open doorway. Listening for any sounds, he waits then steps outside and tucks himself down low under the eaves of the building, tightly against the wooden wall. Stealthily he works his way around the perimeter of the bunkhouse, pausing at each corner. Returning to the entrance he finds the door closed and knocks gently on it before opening it. The other four are sitting on the beds, hunting rifles in hand, except for Ruben who still has his hand clasped tightly around a Glock 17.

Cellini feels through the bedcovers for the bag that he left inside his bed. He can tell that the machine pistol is still there.

The Texan decides that Cellini is overreacting, and that it was most likely an animal after all. Cellini keeps to himself the fact that he heard voices but remains on his guard. Everyone wants to go back to bed and try to get some more sleep, but by now the sun is almost up and they decide to head back to the ranch house.

In the Jeep on the way back to the ranch house, Cellini quizzes Ruben more about the intruders. He is well aware that it was no nocturnal animal, nor the wind. He caught the glint of a flashlight and distinctly heard voices, though he could not tell what they were saying because he doesn't speak Spanish and his understanding of it is limited.

In the cool light of day Ruben is more self-assured and insists it was probably kids taking a shortcut home from the nearby town or at worst someone from a neighbouring ranch poking around to see if anyone was staying at the cabin. He smiles and says, "What do I have to worry about as long as you are here to protect me?"

He pauses, looking for a reaction that never comes from the stoney-faced Cellini.

"Perhaps it would be better if you carried your little gun with you when we travel together? It makes more of a, shall I say, 'statement'?"

Returning to the ranch house, they view their handiwork from the previous day. Cellini's two elks are impressive, but everyone is more impressed by the bear killed by Ruben's son. They drink beer and watch the ranch hands skin the animals and prepare to cut the meat for cooking and eating later in the day. Cellini finds himself disturbed by the bear. He has killed and eaten many different species of creature prepared in every way imaginable: raw, dried in the sun, boiled, smoked, cooked on an open fire and prepared by the finest gourmet chefs, but he has never eaten the meat of a bear. The animal is so human-like in its musculature that he feels eating the creature is almost akin to cannibalism.

Still, the elk meat is good, and the feast prepared for Ruben, his family and his guests is memorable.

Nothing more is said about the intrusion the previous night, but Cellini keeps his guns close by, and notices that Ruben stays very close to his side as well. The party goes on well into the night and everyone gets quite drunk. Tonight they will sleep at the house once again, and tomorrow they will hunt at a big game ranch owned by a close friend of the family.

This time they will stay in a hotel in Guadalajara where Ruben has booked the entire top floor suite. He and Cellini will have adjoining rooms.

The rest of the trip passes uneventfully and Cellini returns home. As always, he shares the selected highlights of his adventures with Franci.

"I'm glad you had a good time Ueli, but please be careful," is all she says.

*****

Cellini will visit Ruben Zuno's home in Mexico more than twenty times over the next few years. Over time, they become friends, to the extent that Cellini is comfortable around Zuno and his family. It is not the same kind of deep and meaningful friendship Cellini had enjoyed with Walter Shumate or Dick Meadows, but he respects Ruben as a man who knows what he wants, and how to get it.

Cellini has always made it a rule to keep his professional activities and his personal life completely separate. He prefers to travel alone and is rarely able to offer any indication to his family of when they might expect him to return. It is a fact that Franci has learned to live with throughout their marriage, and which she has always accepted with grace if not alacrity. Though he usually shares his trials and tribulations with her when he returns – leaving out any part of the story that suggests he may have been in great danger – she would draw her own conclusions from the cuts and scrapes and bruises, which he always dismisses as "hunting accidents".

In the case of Ruben Zuno, though they first met in a professional capacity at a gunsmith, their continued relationship is, at least as far as Cellini is concerned, purely social. In view of their growing friendship, when the Mexican finds out that Cellini's oldest son, Frank, is a keen hunter and an expert marksman, he suggests that Vito should bring him along on an upcoming hunting trip. Cellini decides it would be alright for Frank to tag along. Frank is no mean shot and he thinks it would be fun to have him along.

He is not worried about the fact that Zuno has enemies. For one thing, Cellini knows how to take care of himself and is well aware of the fact that he himself presents a formidable figure when in Zuno's presence. There has not been another incident since his first visit and Zuno clearly enjoys plenty of protection. Cellini talks it over with Franci and they decide it will be OK for Frank to accompany his father on the next trip.

Frank Cellini is greeted by Zuno as if he were his own son, ushered aboard the Piper Cherokee aircraft that Zuno will be flying for this trip and they depart from San Antonio International Airport.

They land at the same small airstrip near the border. The Cellinis remain inside the cabin of the Piper while Zuno completes the formalities with smiles and handshakes as usual, and they continue on their journey. After an hour or so, they begin a descent towards an airport to refuel the small aircraft. As they land, Frank Cellini notices that the airfield at which they have landed is a military establishment. In fact, it is a Mexican Air Force Base.

Zuno taxis over to a refueling area, stops the engine and gets out of the aircraft, then signals to Vito and Frank that if they would like to get out and stretch their legs, that would be fine too. A fuel truck pulls over to the aircraft and two uniformed men get out and approach Zuno. They smile, salute and begin fueling the Piper. While they are doing that, he strolls over towards a concrete building, where two officers greet him with brotherly hugs and slaps on the back. They laugh and invite him inside. Zuno beckons the Cellinis over and introduces them. Tequila is offered but politely declined.

"Not when I still have at least a couple of hours flying time!" Zuno laughs. The Cellinis look at each other. Frank looks relieved. They return to the plane, now fully refueled and climb aboard. After a cursory check pre-flight check they begin taxiing to the end of the runway ready for departure.

Their destination is an exotic hunting ranch owned by a family friend of Zuno, but their flight path will take them almost directly across Zuno's ranch, so he decides to fly low enough to circle a couple of times and show off his property to the Cellinis.

Without question, this is an impressive spread of land, perhaps some of the richest and most fertile in Mexico. Flying at about 500 feet above the ground offers an amazing sensation of speed as well as a great view, and while Zuno is by no means a reckless pilot, he does enjoy showing off his skills, banking steeply first in one direction and then the other. He is careful not to fly too low so as to startle the animals, but keen for them to see everything he has to offer. Banking around one more time Zuno stares into the distance and suddenly exclaims so loudly that Vito and Frank don't need the headphones. A string of expletives, in Spanish and English, spew from the Mexican's mouth, and he points the aircraft ahead and in a shallow dive towards a low cloud of reddish brown dust on the horizon.

*****

Frank, in the back seat, has no idea what is going on. Vito, sitting in the right-hand front seat, knows exactly what is happening. It's an old-fashioned cattle rustling!

Goddamn banditos!" says Zuno.

In a matter of seconds, the small plane has caught up and overhauled the scene. Zuno banks steeply to go around one more time and Frank gets a good view out of the side window. A couple of old pick-up trucks, each with two men in the back, are crisscrossing each other's paths and encircling the cattle, herding them eventually towards the fence marking the edge of Zuno's property.

The men in the trucks are waving their arms wildly, like crazed rag dolls. One of them picks up a gun and points it in the general direction of the aircraft, but by the time he can squeeze the trigger, the aircraft is well out of range. Zuno prepares to go around one more time to get a better look.

"Summonabitch!" Vito exclaims.

Zuno thinks Cellini is chiding him for dangerous flying and apologizes, but Vito laughs,

"I'm not calling you a summonabitch," he says, "I'm calling those goddamn thieves a summonabitch!"

For a brief moment they almost smile, then Zuno says, "I know how to take care of this. Excuse me for one minute my friend."

He changes frequency on the radio and begins speaking in Spanish, which neither Vito nor his son can understand.

Gaining height, Zuno flies one more wide circuit around the scene and then turns back in the direction they were originally flying. By this time the banditos have abandoned their rustling activities and are speeding across the terrain, leaving a swirling dust cloud behind them.

"It pays to have friends in high places," Zuno says after a while, smiling at Cellini.

"I called my friends at the air force base where we refueled and told them what was going on. They have sent a couple of helicopters with several well-armed troops..." he glances at his watch, "...and they should be arriving right about now."

Frank speaks up from the back seat. "Will they be able to land and arrest those guys?" he says.[2]

"Don't worry Frank," Zuno replies, winking at the senior Cellini, "they'll be taken care of."

The rest of the flight is uneventful, and after a short while they land at a small grass airstrip on the property of the ranch at which they will be hunting.

*****

Next day, following breakfast, Vito and Frank are ready to go bird hunting. Outside the ranch house, a fleet of three, brand spanking new black Suburbans is pulled up ready to leave.

The first car, the lead, is for the dogs that will accompany them on the hunt and retrieve the birds. The second vehicle is for the hunting party,

[2] *Frank Cellini was greatly disturbed by the relationship Zuno evidently had with Mexican authorities but chose not to bring it up with his father, knowing how defensive Vito could be when anyone questioned his judgment or the integrity of those he considered friends. He thought it highly irregular for a civilian aircraft to be given permission to land at a military base, never mind for it to be refueled there (and apparently with no charge). However, when Zuno exercised the power to be able to call in the Mexican Air Force to deal with banditos stealing his cattle, he knew he and his father were in the company of a very powerful man.*

comprising their host, Zuno, and the two Cellinis. Travelling in the third Suburban are the servants who will gather and clean the birds in preparation for cooking.

Frank is still slightly unnerved by the events of the previous day and what he considers to be a vulgar display of wealth, but he's here to hunt and he is keen to have a good time. He also wants to make a good impression. He climbs into the back of the middle Suburban. The engine is idling to keep the air conditioning running, so he closes the door and opens the window a few inches. His father sits across from him while Zuno and their host ride up front.

As the motorcade sets off, Frank powers his window all the way down and rests the barrel of his shotgun on the ledge. He keeps his eyes focused on the vegetation at the side of the road for signs of anything moving. A short way into the drive, as everyone else in the car is relaxing and sharing small talk, Frank suddenly raises his weapon and lets loose a shot from inside the vehicle. He has caught site of a single quail and, as he levels his gun to shoot, a whole drift of the small birds rises from the dense grass alongside the roadway. He watches as several of them tumble from the sky and fall to the ground. The convoy stops and Frank jumps from the Suburban, but the clean-up crew in the rear-most vehicle are already on their way to gather the birds for him and politely suggest that he might care to wait in the air-conditioned vehicle. Within three minutes, they have gathered up several handfuls of the birds.

With a single shotgun cartridge, fired from a moving vehicle, Frank Cellini has managed to bring down 19 quail.

Needless to say, Zuno is impressed, as is everyone else in the hunting party. Vito is as proud as any father can be and will always cherish the moment.

*****

Each time Cellini visits Mexico, at Ruben's request he carries the small machine gun. Each time Ruben asks him if he can place an order for the guns and each time Cellini responds with the same answer.

"Sure, if you have a Federal Firearms Licence and an importation licence and permission from the US State Department as well as your own government to import military-style automatic weapons."

Ruben smiles and shakes his head.

"You always do everything by the book, and I respect you for that, but you must understand it is very frustrating for someone like me who is used to finding ways to get around the regulations."

For the time being, Zuno seems perfectly satisfied with the arrangement they have. Cellini has realised for some time that he is being used as a protector but it's just one more adventure to him.[3]

From Ruben Zuno's home, they often fly to different hunting ranches owned by his friends and associates. They stay in fine hotels, dine at the finest restaurants where everyone seems to know Zuno, and he is never given a bill. They drink fine wine and are frequently offered the company of beautiful women, which Cellini characteristically declines, despite the derision of his companions. He is never asked to pay for anything. When he offers to contribute, Zuno just smiles sardonically. Since the very first trip when Cellini picked up the cost of fueling the aircraft, he has never needed money when travelling in Mexico.

"You are my guest. What kind of host is it that would take money from his guests? All I ask is that you look after my weapons."

Zuno insists that Cellini is always armed with his machine gun and he always sticks very close.

*****

ON A LATER HUNTING TRIP Ruben is flying the Cessna himself, with Cellini and Monty the Texan on board as his only passengers. Cellini is in the right front seat and Monty has both back seats to himself, so he can stretch out his lanky frame. They are flying back to the ranch after spending a few days in Puerto Vallarta.

It's a relatively short flight, but Zuno seems distracted during the pre-flight inspection of the aircraft. He snaps at the ground crew, climbs into the pilot seat and immediately fires up the engine, without the usual protocol of making sure that the crew are clear of the propeller – which fortunately they are. He rushes the safety checks, anxious to get going.

Not long after take-off, Zuno flips the lever to retract the flaps and begins a slow turn to the right. The aircraft doesn't seem to want to turn to the right and instead the left wing drops. Cellini, himself a qualified pilot, immediately senses that there is a problem. The aircraft wants to roll and turn to the left, and Zuno is having difficulty keeping it straight and level.

3. *What Cellini did not find out until much later, was that carrying a machine gun or assault rifle in Mexico could have had dire consequences for him, and that if it had not been for Ruben Zuno's power and dominance over many Mexican law enforcement officials, he could have found himself rotting in a Mexican prison at any time.*

Cellini looks out beneath both wings. The starboard aileron appears to be hanging loosely downwards – exactly the opposite position it should be in for a right hand turn. This causes the right wing to generate more lift than the left, causing the aircraft to roll and yaw to the left. Zuno struggles with the controls, and by turning the control wheel to the right and pushing down on the right rudder pedal is able to keep the aircraft flying, but it is clear that they are in trouble.

The Cessna is flying nose high and still pulling to the left, and the motion of the pilot, turning the wheel one way and then the other as he overcorrects, is causing the aircraft to roll from side to side like a small boat on a choppy sea. He sets the trim tab wheel on the elevator and the rudder to compensate for the uneven lift and that takes some of the strain off him, but even with throttle all the way forward, the nose high attitude prevents the aircraft from building enough airspeed to climb.

On top of everything else, they are slowly losing altitude.

There is no question of going back to the airfield at Puerto Vallarta. One of the cardinal rules of aviation is never try to turn around in an emergency. Turning eats up altitude and increases the stalling speed of an aircraft. Zuno, who knows the area well, says there is a small airfield at Mascota, about 20 kilometres from Puerto Vallarta and almost dead ahead. Meanwhile, as a qualified pilot himself, Cellini knows the drill and starts looking around for any flat area that looks like it would work. They are flying over mountainous jungle, and the terrain does not look accommodating.

"There it is," says Zuno, pointing at the horizon.

"Five kilometres ahead."

Still struggling to maintain altitude and a safe airspeed with the tipsy aircraft, Zuno lowers the flaps to slow the descent and keep the aircraft flying above stalling speed, but it is still pulling to the left, and keeping the wings level is extremely difficult. Cellini takes hold of the dual control wheel in front of him to help take the strain, but the controls are sluggish and unresponsive. It is not a matter of brute strength that is needed, but the careful hands of an experienced pilot. He looks at Zuno and releases his hold on the control wheel.

Having kept quiet since the excitement began, Monty is beginning to feel neglected in the back seat of the aircraft and suddenly blurts out, "What the hell is going on?"

Cellini, with his usual bluntness, tells him in no uncertain terms that they are going down. Either on the airstrip ahead or into the brush and trees below them.

"What should I do?" The Texan asks.

"Lean forward as far as you can and put your head between your legs," Cellini says.

"Will that help me to survive if we crash?"

"No, but you'll be in a better position to kiss your ass goodbye!"

Unfazed by Cellini's wit, Monty reaches into his jacket pocket and pulls out a flask of vodka, which he guzzles down in one go.

With full trim, full right rudder and more than a little luck, Zuno is able to coax the aircraft towards the deserted airstrip. The approach is nerve-wracking to say the least and, to his credit, Zuno never panics. He talks constantly, in Spanish, willing the Cessna to stay in the air just a little longer. With the left wing still decidedly lower than the right, full fuel tanks and a slightly inebriated Texan cursing up a storm in the back seat, Cellini is convinced this is not going to end well. As the ground gets increasingly closer his thoughts turn to Franci, and in his mind he hears her voice saying, "Ueli! You knew this was going to happen one day. What am I supposed to do now?"

The aircraft lurches suddenly and jars Cellini back to reality.

Zuno, who is surprisingly calm, says, "Hang on, *amigos.*"

Caught by a cross breeze – or just pure blind luck, the Cessna rights itself just as it is about to settle on the ground. The landing, though fast and hard, is close to textbook. The Cessna doesn't bounce or even skid, but touches down perfectly on the grass field and slowly comes to a stop at the end of the runway. Zuno cuts the engine and the three men sit there in absolute silence for well over a minute. The aircraft creaks as the metal begins to relax and cool down.

Zuno is first to speak.

"Not a word to my sister, do you both understand?"

With that, all three of them suddenly start laughing. Though none of them can find any humour in the situation, it is a nervous reaction to what almost happened. Soon all three men are laughing uncontrollably.

"I'm serious. She loves this aircraft, and she'll kill me if she finds out that I almost crashed it and killed her precious Cellini!"

That makes Cellini laugh even louder, until tears are rolling down his cheeks.

The laughter eventually subsides and the three men get out of the aircraft. They look around for any signs of life, but the airfield is deserted and it is obvious no aircraft have been here recently. Cellini walks over to the wing while Zuno looks around the rest of the aircraft for any signs of damage. Monty has made his way to the edge of the runway, where he is vomiting his guts along with the remains of his breakfast and half a bottle of Stolichnaya.

Within minutes, Cellini has figured out the cause of the problem.

The steel hinge pin from the aileron has slid out of position and the aileron is hanging by its control cables.

"I can fix this," is all he says.

The words sound familiar, and with good reason. These were the first words Zuno heard Cellini utter when he took his broken hunting rifle into the gun shop.

The pin is slightly bent and will need to be straightened, then he can replace it and the aircraft will be as good as new.

45 minutes later, Cellini has replaced the aileron hinge, Zuno has completed a rigorous pre-flight check of the Cessna, and the three intrepid hunters are ready to get back on their proverbial "horse" and continue on their way. As he climbs back into the aircraft, Monty ask Cellini if this thing really is safe. Cellini nods and assures him that it will not happen again. He is, however, concerned as to how the hinge pin came to be loose in the first place. This is not something that can generally happen by itself, and it would be a very careless mistake for someone to make accidentally. His thoughts go back to his first visit to Zuno's ranch, and the disturbed night they had.

Zuno had hinted that he had enemies. Jealous rivals. He has been at a meeting with some of his closest business associates – and rivals. The meeting did not go well, Cellini could tell from the attitude and body language of the Mexican. But do jealous business rivals sabotage aircraft? Cellini finds that hard to rationalize, even if this is Mexico.

He decides to mention it to Zuno once they are back at his property and he will have a chance to talk to him alone.

*****

The rest of the trip is uneventful. Cellini notices that Zuno is staying closer and closer to him all of the time, especially when in the company of others. He always makes sure Cellini has the machine gun with him, and that it is fully loaded, even when they are going out to dinner or for drinks.

"You never know when you'll see big game!" It's his usual explanation.

After they return to Zuno's ranch, Cellini takes Zuno on one side and says, as quietly and calmly as possible, "I cannot say for sure, but I don't think the problem with the aircraft was an accident."

"You think one of my mechanics has neglected to check it properly? I'll kill the sonofabitch. I'll kill all of them. Just like that!"

He snaps his thumb and forefinger and spits on the ground.

Zuno is serious. He has bragged about killing people on more than one occasion. He has even spoken of torturing people if he needed to "find out" things about his business rivals. Cellini had always assumed it was just talk – but when he sees the expression on Zuno's face he recognizes the look of a man who could kill in cold blood. He knows that look from years ago.

"It's possible the aileron hinge pin could come out on its own." Cellini tries to defuse the situation and it seems to have the right effect.

"Accidents happen, my friend. I am just glad you are here to take care of it for me. You have saved me a fortune. Do you know what these airplane mechanics charge per hour? And then most of the time they sit around and drink beer… my beer!" he adds. Once again he laughs at his own joke, but Cellini can see in his eyes that behind the laughter there is serious concern.

The following morning, after breakfast, as they are getting ready to fly back to San Antonio, Monty hands Zuno a handsome rosewood box with a gold plaque on the front.

Zuno opens the lid. Inside is a beautifully engraved Colt .45 Model 1911 in stainless steel, with ornate scrollwork on the slide and ivory grips.

"I was just waiting for the right time to give this to you, Señor Zuno," says the lanky Texan in his best drawl.

"I guess timing never was my strong suit, but I want you to know how much I appreciate everything you've done for me. For being such a great host, and a gentleman. And for showing me and Mr. Cellini such a great time here in Mexico."

"Hell, after the way you handled that airplane the other day, I figure you really earned it."

The Mexican is genuinely taken aback and graciously accepts the gift. "I will treasure this always," he says, "and use it only on very special occasions."

How prophetic his words were to become.

As they gather up their bags ready to load up the SUV and leave the ranch house for the drive to the airstrip, María Esther pulls up under the *porte cochère* in a brand new silver Mercedes S-Class Coupé. She has come to say her farewell to Cellini. Zuno glares at the Italian as if to say *Remember, not a word about the aircraft*. He needn't worry – Cellini is a man of his word and will keep the secret until long after both brother and sister are gone from this world.

She steps out of the car, takes Cellini's hand and smiles at him with genuine affection. "I want you to know how much I appreciate – how much we all appreciate – the work you do for my brother. For keeping him safe from those who would do him harm. Thank you. I… we… feel so much better whenever you are here and we look forward to you visiting us again soon."

Perhaps it is María Esther's accent or his still imperfect understanding of English, but Cellini isn't sure he completely understands the sentiment of her words, although he senses her sincerity. They embrace and he kisses her hand, then gets into the SUV for the ride to the airstrip with Monty the Texan, Zuno and his son, for the flight back to San Antonio.

*****

After the near catastrophic incident with the aircraft, it is some time before Cellini hears from Zuno again, then one day he receives a phone call inviting him to a big hunting party at an exotic game ranch belonging to a family member in the neighbouring state of Michoacán. Zuno explains that he will not be able to fly up to San Antonio to collect him, but that a business associate will be coming to San Antonio and has offered Cellini a ride back to Guadalajara, with the usual stop over at Eagle Pass. From Guadalajara, Cellini and Zuno will ride together.

Cellini is a man who doesn't ask a lot of questions, but for some time he has been suspicious of Zuno's business activities. He is also wary of the fact that Zuno's family seem to regard the Italian as a personal protector for the Mexican, a position that makes him uncomfortable, since no formal business arrangement has been offered or accepted.

For some time now, whenever he visits the ranch in Guadalajara, more and more time is spent in meetings with business associates and family members, and Cellini feels it is taken for granted that he will attend. He is always treated well; givrn the very best suites in the very best hotels. And always in the role of guard. Protector. Armed and on the lookout.

Nonetheless, he accepts the invitation with alacrity, and meets the pilot at the general aviation area of San Antonio International Airport. The short flight to Eagle Pass in Ruben's Cessna 182 is routine and passes quickly. The pilot is cordial but quiet and Cellini busies himself by thumbing through a copy of *Gun Digest.*

At Eagle Pass, they both get out of the aircraft to have their passports checked, and the pilot excuses himself to go to the FBO to make a phone call. He returns after several minutes and tells Cellini that, regrettably, he must now say *adiós*. His plans have changed, and he has to return to San Antonio. He apologizes profusely and assures the Italian that there is no need for him to be concerned because Señor Zuno has arranged to have another pilot fly him to Guadalajara where he will meet his host. They walk into the FBO, where they are greeted by a smiling and well-dressed Mexican man in his mid-thirties wearing pressed blue jeans and a polo shirt. The man introduces himself simply as Alfredo, they shake hands and he gestures towards the aircraft that will take him on to Guadalajara.

Cellini grabs his travel bag and gun case and the two walk out to the aircraft, an older model Cessna 206 that looks a little the worse for wear. The paint is dulled and worn and it has a thin layer of red dust all over. The pilot opens the door and, as Cellini steps up on the footrest and looks inside, he sees that, except for the two pilot seats, there are no seats for passengers.

"How come there are no seats?" he asks.

The Mexican pilot laughs and says, "Normally I fly pigs!"

"Pigs?"

"Yes, pigs."

Cellini is unimpressed and suspicious. He has been a guest of Zuno on numerous occasions and has never seen, nor heard any mention of pigs on the ranch, which is primarily for cattle breeding and a few horses that the family keeps for riding.

Rather than giving away his thoughts, he plays dumb and climbs into the aircraft.

Any vehicle or container used for transporting livestock invariably has an indelible odor, even when empty, and this aircraft does not smell as if it has been carrying pigs or any other animals. There is a distinctive smell that Cellini does recognize; the aroma of a certain crop that he would prefer not to be associated with, especially while carrying weapons and travelling across the interior of Mexico.

The drug war is at its height, and despite Zuno's strong political connections, there is no guarantee that the Mexican Government wouldn't take advantage of any opportunity to make an example of a US citizen caught in an aircraft being used for transporting controlled substances. Besides which, Zuno is not here and Cellini has only the pilot's word that he is in the ranch owner's employ.

Cellini asks the pilot to wait, grabs his bag and gun case, and walks back to the FBO. As he opens the door, he almost bumps into the pilot who brought him from San Antonio, who is just leaving the building.

"Just the man I want to see. Did you say you are flying back to San Antonio today?"

"Yes sir," says the pilot. "As a matter of fact I'm getting ready to leave right now."

"Good. I need to go back to San Antonio. I'll ride with you."

It is not framed as a request and Cellini is not asking permission.

The pilot doesn't question Cellini, but ushers him back to the Cessna 182, which is already refueled and ready to go. Cellini walks past the cargo plane and its pilot without so much as a sideways glance.

He makes up his mind that this will be his last trip to visit Zuno. Even though he is never formally recruited, nor paid, to provide protection for Zuno, nor is such employment even hinted at by Zuno, he feels certain he is being used as a personal bodyguard. Zuno always insists that Cellini is well armed. And he always keeps him very close.

With his connections and influence in the Mexican Government, it is quite possible Zuno is aware of the Cellini's history with the Partisans in Yugoslavia, and of his dealings in Nicaragua. He may assume that he has connections with the Mafia. He might even be aware that the FBI has a dossier on him. If so, then using Cellini as a very visible bodyguard is a shrewd decision and serves as a strong warning to rival drug gangs and anyone thinking of stepping on Zuno's toes. It also puts Cellini and his family at great risk.

Despite his suspicions about Zuno's business activities and political ties, Cellini has always found the Mexican businessman to be a cordial and generous host, if something of a braggart. He boasts about eliminating his enemies, but Cellini, who is no stranger to the world of professional killers, takes them as nothing more than empty boasts. Although he suspects the Mexican's business interests may not be totally legitimate, it is not until much later that Cellini finds out how deeply Zuno is involved in drug trafficking.

*****

IN LESS THAN TWO MONTHS, Alfredo Zavala Avelar, the smiling pilot of the cargo plane, is dead, brutally tortured along with his fellow undercover DEA agent Enrique Camerena Salazar. Seriously denting the cartel's drug trafficking operations, the undercover work carried out by these brave DEA agents eventually leads to the seizure and destruction of drugs with a street value in the billions of dollars.

In 1992, Ruben Zuno Arce is tried and convicted of kidnapping and conspiracy in the deaths of Avelar and Salazar, and charged with other crimes of violence. He is sentenced to two life terms. Among the weapons presented as evidence at his trial is an engraved, stainless steel Colt .45 Model 1911 believed to have been used in several grizzly murders. It is the presentation piece given to him by the Texan known as Monty, years earlier.

After Zuno's arrest, Vito Cellini is investigated and interviewed by US federal agents. He tells them everything he knows about Zuno, which was very little. He is not implicated nor suspected of any involvement in Zuno's illicit activities.

Zuno's brother-in-law, former president Luis Echeverría Álvarez, repeatedly petitions President Carlos Salinas to pressure Washington for Zuno's release, but to no avail.

Zuno dies in prison, in September 2012.

82. The Congressman. Colorado, 1991

Cellini has the unexpected privilege of meeting US Congressman John Bryant, of Texas 5th District, while on a hunting trip in Colorado in November, 1991.

Though he spends much of his adult life on hunting trips all over the world, sometimes alone but often with friends, colleagues, officials and dignitaries – and all are memorable in their own way – this trip is unforgettable for a couple of reasons. Cellini has been invited by a friend, Curtis Bruner, who is acquainted with the Congressman and has invited him along.

Cellini and the Congressman get along well and spend a great deal of the time discussing Cellini's stabilizer, especially after the government man has the chance to experience its benefits first hand on a hunting rifle. Congressman Bryant wants to help Cellini, and he promises to do all he can to further the advancement of the stabilizer.

He is also concerned for Cellini's home life, and when the party is gathered together in Cellini's room at the hunting lodge one evening, he comments that Cellini is the only one among them who has not telephoned home to talk to his wife.

"You really should call your wife and let her know you are okay, and having a good time," he says to Cellini, who laughs.

"It would be the first time," Cellini replies. "She does not expect to hear from me when I am travelling, whether it is for work or pleasure. It's just not something I have ever done, nor does she expect me to."

Bryant insists. "Come on Vito. Every woman likes to hear the words 'I love you' from her man when they are separated, even if it is only for a few days." He picks up the phone at the side of the bed and hands it to Cellini.

Cellini shrugs and takes the phone, dials the phone number and waits for Franci to answer.

"Hallo," she says.

"It's me," Cellini replies.

"Ueli, what's happened, are you OK?"

"I'm fine," he says, "I just called to say..." he waits a few seconds and the others in the room start smirking. "I just called to say I love you, OK?"

"Who is there with you?" Franci replies. "Let me talk to someone else. Now I know something is wrong!"

Cellini hands the phone to Curtis Bruner and asks him to please explain to his wife that this was not his idea. Bruner takes the phone and speaks.

"Hello, Mrs. Cellini?" he says.

"Will you please tell me what has happened to my husband. Is he hurt? Is he sick? What is going on?"

Bruner is surprised by Franci's ferocity. It takes him a few seconds to regain his composure before he can reply.

"No, Mrs. Cellini, nothing like that. We are all calling our wives, and we thought it would be a good idea if Vito called you, that's all!"

Having no idea who she is talking to, Franci snaps back at Bruner, "Don't you dare ever scare me like that again, d'you hear me? It's not funny at all. Now let me talk to my husband again."

Cellini takes the phone from his friend but only gets as far as saying " 'Allo," before Franci launches into another tirade.

"What do you think you're doing? You put the fear of the Almighty into me! I thought something must have happened to you!"

Cellini eventually calms her down, says "goodnight", and hangs up the phone. The group at the ranch think it is hilarious, and when Cellini returns home a few days later, he and Franci have a good laugh about it as well – especially when she discovers that the man who had insisted on the phone call in the first place was no less than a United States Congressman!

Such is the remarkable bond between Vito Cellini and his wife that they never feel the need to communicate their feelings towards each other, even when separated.

*****

Cellini has evidently made quite an impression on the Congressman, who does his best to promote the stabilizer, by personally calling several Texas law enforcement officials, including detectives and police chiefs with whom he is acquainted, and the head of the Combined Law Enforcement Association of Texas. He also speaks with firearms specialists and instructors with the FBI in Quantico, Virginia, who initially express great interest. However, as in the past, progress begins to stall once the Cellini name is mentioned.

As a result of the Congressman's efforts in Texas, Cellini's stabilizer is tested in front of several city and county police departments and very favourably received, resulting in enquiries and several sales, all of which proves encouraging. With the issue of Cellini's name once again seeming to be a stumbling block, he decides to ask Congressman Bryant for help in a different area, to try and clear up the mess of red tape once and for all. He asks the Congressman if he can help find and unlock the secure dossier he suspects the US government has on him.

The Congressman is more than happy to oblige and provides Cellini with the addresses of government departments that he should contact, including the Immigration and Naturalization Service (INS) and Central Intelligence Agency (CIA), as well as an official Freedom of Information Act (FOIA) request form. A letter from the CIA dated February 25, 1992 in response to his FOIA request informs him that the agency is backlogged and needs more time. In July, 1992, Cellini receives a "final response" from the CIA advising him that the agency has been "unable to identify any information or record" filed under his name. Strangely, the letter also informs him that he has a legal right to "appeal the finding", from which Cellini infers that it may not be quite the dead end it seems.

He has spoken, off the record, to contacts through friends in the Special Forces who have been in a position to look him up. Though no one will provide any tangible details, it has been implied to the author that such a dossier does indeed exist, but that it may still contain information considered classified by the State Department.

Cellini can only speculate until such time as additional information is available through FOIA.

Vito Cellini hands over weapons to the Alamo City Police Department, one of many municipalities that adopted the Cellini stabilizer as part of their standard equipment.

Vito and Franci relaxing.

83. New Friends…

As Cellini enters his seventh decade, he begins to reflect more and more upon his life. He has lost many friends over the years, but being eternally blessed with a keen and sharp wit and effervescent personality, continues to make new ones, often in the most unexpected circumstances. Three people in particular, whom he encounters on two different continents and in totally different situations, form friendships he will cherish for the rest of his life.

The first occurs when travelling to visit a customer in France for whom he has custom-built a hunting rifle. The rifle, specially made for a wealthy arms collector and keen hunter who lives just outside of Paris, is lovingly finished and Cellini knows it is one of his masterpieces. That's why he has insisted on delivering it in person, and he doesn't want it to leave his side until he has the chance to hand it over. He is confident that his customer, Jacques, will be well pleased.

As with most of his trips to Europe, he won't be going directly to his business appointment. He is taking Franci with him because he has promised her some time together in Paris, but first they must make the mandatory pilgrimage to visit family, stopping in Milan and then Bari. Cellini's rationale is to get the obligatory family visits taken care of first so they can fly on to Paris with a clear conscience. In Paris, he will meet Jacques and hand over the rifle, they'll spend a few days at Jacques' chateau, where they will hunt, then he and Franci will have some time together in Paris before flying back to Texas.

The outward bound flight from Houston to Milan is smooth. Since the flight originates in the United States, walking onto the aircraft with a gun is not a problem.[1]

Upon arriving in Milan, they have no problem with Italian customs,

[1] *Before September 11th, 2001, the regulations for travelling with weapons were far more lenient, and it was not unusual to carry firearms in hand baggage on aircraft.*

pick up a rental car and settle down for a few days visiting his sisters in Desio, a northern suburb of Milan.

A few days later, they say their goodbyes and drive south to Bari. It's an eight-and-a-half-hour drive but they make good time, even with stops along the way to eat. After spending several days visiting various friends and relatives in and around Bari and Palo del Colle, they are ready to escape to Paris. Their flight departs from Rome, so they drive to the eternal city, where they drop off the rental car and wait to board the aircraft. Just as they are getting ready to board their flight, Cellini is asked to produce his papers for the gun. He pulls out receipts, his federal licence, everything he has, but he is told that he cannot carry the gun aboard the aircraft. Cellini thinks it must be a mistake, or a very bad joke. He has made this trip many times and invariably carries a weapon, either for his own protection or for delivery to a customer.

"There is no mistake, sir," the attendant at the gate politely points out to him. "I'm afraid you do not have the proper documentation for carrying this weapon onto the aircraft."

Cellini explains that he is a licensed gunsmith and that he is delivering the gun, which is a very expensive hand-crafted hunting rifle, to a man of some importance who lives in Paris. The attendants just shrug. The answer is still *no*.

"Sir, I am afraid if you do not step aside I will have to call the airport police," one of the gate personnel says.

"Good!" Cellini says. "Call them! Perhaps someone around here has some common sense."

He is about to launch into a tirade, but he feels a sharp pain in his ribs. It is Franci, poking him with her fingers. She says nothing, but glares at him in a way that says *Don't say another word. Let the security people deal with this.* Cellini steps aside to let other passengers pass and board the aircraft. As he waits, he looks up and in the distance he sees a man dressed in the uniform of the Polizia di Stato making his way towards the gate. He is a mountain of a man, tall and broad with a swagger in his walk that simply says *don't mess with me.*

As he gets closer, Cellini notices the man looking him up and down. He wears wire-rimmed glasses and carries a Beretta pistol at his side, but he does not feel the need to hold the gun nor even rest his hand upon it the way armed police officers usually do. The man approaches with a smile. His radio buzzes as he is about to speak; he pushes a button to silence it and talks into the mouthpiece, quite calmly, saying that there is no problem. He turns first to the gate attendant, then to Cellini, and says, "What seems to be the problem?"

His voice matches his appearance; deep and resonant. Cellini explains the situation as he sees it to the police officer.

"How long until this flight leaves?" he asks the attendant.

She checks the board behind her and says, "Thirty minutes."

The giant policeman turns to Cellini and says, "I'm going to try and clear this up in time to get you on your flight before it leaves, but just in case there's a delay, we'll get you on the next flight for sure. Is that going to be OK with you?"

Cellini is impressed with the man's kindness and intelligence. He looks at Franci who nods approvingly.

"Sure," he says.

"Good. Thank you. Could I ask you to please come with me to my office?" the policeman says. Almost as an afterthought he adds, "By the way, my name is Dante. I am an Immigration and Border Protection officer."

*****

THEY HEAD TOWARDS an elevator and Dante ushers Cellini and his wife inside. When they step out, they go along a corridor and the policeman unlocks a blank door and shows them in. He pulls up two chairs and offers them espresso.

"Do you have any grappa?" Cellini says.

The police officer grins and excuses himself, asking the Cellinis if they would be kind enough to wait for him. He returns a few minutes later carrying a small tray with two shot glasses of the clear liquor, which he sets down on his desk in front of Cellini, inviting him to help himself while he pours three small demitasse cups of espresso. Cellini picks up one of the shot glasses and pours the grappa into his coffee. Dante politely declines to join him, being on duty, and Franci just shakes her head and smiles.

Dante is very interested in the weapon and asks to look at it more closely. He knows the calibre, the model upon which it is based, and even its approximate value. Cellini is impressed with the man's knowledge. The issue, the police officer explains, is that the weapon is licensed for transportation from the United States to France, not to Italy – and not from Italy to France. Some additional paperwork is required to make the airport transfer legal, and the police officer will be happy to provide that, now that he has had a chance to get to know Mr. Cellini.

They spend a long while talking about guns, and Cellini gets a clear picture that this police officer is an aficionado of fine weapons.

"This is exquisite," he says, picking up the hunting rifle once again.

"Could you make one just like it for me?"

Cellini reaches for the second shot glass of grappa and downs it in one gulp.

"Why not? he says, "As long as you can arrange the paperwork."

By now the policeman and the Cellinis are on a first-name basis.

They miss the flight to Paris but Dante is as good as his word and arranges for them to take the next flight, departing in a little more than two hours. He asks them if they are hungry and would like to eat, but they decline. They continue to talk about guns, and eventually the subject finds its way around to his service with the Partisans and the OSS in World War Two.

Never one to shy away from his past deeds, Cellini reminisces on his time with the OSS and how he was able to deal with undesirable elements so much more easily in his day.

To his surprise, Dante is empathetic.

"I sometimes wish we could still employ such methods," he says. "If you saw some of the situations we have to deal with – and some of the criminal elements we have to contend with here in Border Protection, you would be horrified."

Cellini recognizes a kindred spirit, even though Dante is half his age, and the two men exchange phone numbers and agree to keep in touch. They call each other regularly and each has visited the other's home on several occasions. Over the course of their friendship, which has now lasted more than twenty years, they have discovered they have much in common with their views on law enforcement as well as their appreciation for fine weapons.

Dante is now retired from his position as a senior Immigration and Border Protection officer at Fiumicino airport in Rome, but remains active as a consultant with European law enforcement authorities.

*****

Other lifelong friendships Cellini makes at this time are considerably closer to his Texas home, in a small ranching community just outside China Grove.

Frank Moravits runs a successful construction business in San Antonio. He works hard year-round, but when hunting season comes along he squeezes in as much time as can chasing deer and doves and anything else that moves, as long as it's covered by his hunting licence. He is as passionate about hunting as any man can be, but for Frank, it's the thrill of the hunt, rather than the kill, that has always excited him. Perhaps that's because – at least according to his friends – Frank Moravits's ability as a marksman is somewhat in question; on one memorable occasion, he accidentally shot through a water pipe while aiming at a javelina that had wandered onto his property – something his friends will never let him forget!

Frank hears about Vito Cellini through the local gun club and decides to see for himself what this man can do.

"Hell, if this guy is so good at fixing guns, maybe he can fix my rifle to shoot straight," he tells his friends.

From the very first time they meet, Frank Moravits and Vito Cellini get along like brothers, and Cellini agrees to build a stabilizer for his hunting rifle. When it's ready, Cellini calls to let him know. Frank leaves work to collect the rifle from the gun shop and then drives straight home to test it. He finds to his delight that, with the stabilizer attached, it is indeed a much more accurate weapon. He is indebted to Cellini for vindicating his claim that it was the rifle – not his marksmanship – that was at fault all along.

Another mutual acquaintance at the gun club introduces Cellini to Dale Smith. Slim, tanned and wearing a white cowboy hat, Dale can easily give the impression that he doesn't take life too seriously, and Cellini isn't sure about him at first, but he does seem to know a lot about hunting rifles and how to handle them.

Frank Moravits sponsors an annual youth shooting competition, The San Antonio Youth Charity Fun Shoot,[2] and invites Cellini along to lend a hand. Cellini agrees immediately and looks forward to the event, which takes place at San Antonio's National Shooting Complex, a 671-acre tract, deep in the countryside, rated as one of the best amenities for civilian marksmen anywhere in the country.

On the day of the competition, Cellini arrives at the Moravits ranch home ready to leave.

"No point taking more vehicles than we need to," Frank says to Cellini. "Why don't you ride with Dale? Have you guys met?" Cellini looks at Smith. "Yeah. We met at the gun club," he says.

Smith tells him to jump into his Ford F-250 truck and they join the convoy of vehicles.

He tries to make conversation, but Cellini just grunts and after a few minutes he resigns himself to silence for the rest of the journey.

Turning off the highway onto a dirt road, they have fallen behind the other vehicles. Dale Smith isn't particularly worried. He knows the way.

[2] *The competition benefits SA Youth, an organization helping the children of low-income families and at-risk youth stay in school or get a second chance to complete their education and get workforce training.*

After about five minutes driving along the dirt road, Cellini glances out the window of the truck at the vast expanse of scrubland, punctuated only by the occasional sagebrush or cedar tree. Suddenly he turns back to Smith and says, very seriously, "This would be a great place to bury a body."

This is literally the first complete sentence Dale Smith has heard from Cellini since they first met, and it comes just as he notices that they have fallen behind the rest of the convoy. And there is no one else behind them.

Smith grins at Cellini. "If you say so!" he replies, pushing his foot down hard on the accelerator pedal as he tries to catch up with the rest of the group. [3]

*****

CELLINI ENJOYS marshalling the kids around and helping out at the shooting competition. For the most part the youngsters seem to know how to handle a weapon and Cellini is impressed with the level of marksmanship.

While walking around the grounds of the complex and watching the youngsters competing, Cellini notices a man instructing a young boy in the correct way of handling a rifle. Cellini judges the man to be in his thirties. He has a powerful physique and seems kindly but quite authoritative. Cellini watches the scene for a few minutes before stepping over to the man.

"Excuse me sir," Cellini begins, in his customary well-mannered tone, "do you mind if I offer some advice to the young man?"

Before the instructor has a chance to respond, Cellini adds, "Because you are teaching him all wrong."

The man would be deeply offended if the comment had come from anyone else, but there is something about the bearing and forthrightness of Cellini's manner that he finds almost endearing, combined with a respect for his obvious age and, presumably, experience.

"Sure. Be my guest," the instructor says through almost gritted teeth, then adds, as if it might make a difference, "I am ex-military, you know."

Cellini responds with a shrug and mutters, "So what do you want, a medal?"

In almost any other circumstances, the situation could get very ugly, very quickly. Fortunately, both men are mature, experienced in handling

3. *During the course of the day, Cellini lets Frank know of the joke he has played on his friend, which comes to make more sense as they get to know each other better. In time, Cellini will come to look upon Dale Smith as a son. He will be the first to test every new model of the stabilizer and Cellini will be a strong shoulder for Dale to lean on through a messy divorce.*

weapons and have seen more than enough violence in their lives to warrant any further action, especially in the presence of so many youngsters who are just there to have a good time. They laugh at Cellini's attempted humour. Frank Moravits sees them enjoying the joke and comes over, a broad smile on his face.

"I was about to introduce you two to each other," he says, "but I see you have already met. Vito Cellini, this is Lynn Adkins."

"Did you say Cellini?" Adkins says. "As in the 'Cellini stabilizer'?"

"That's me," Cellini replies. "You've heard of me?"

"You're a Goddamn legend in the Special Forces," Adkins replies. I used one of your 'Cellini stabilizers' when I was in the service, and you have no idea how much it meant to me – to all of us in my unit – who were lucky enough to get one."

All they want to do is spend the rest of the day talking about the Cellini stabilizer, but right now there is work to do, and they agree to meet up later. Frank invites everyone back to the house after the competition for a barbecue, so they'll have plenty of time to catch up then. They shake hands and embrace, but not before Cellini gets in his parting shot.

"For a Goddamn ex-military you should know better than to teach kids to take so long to take aim before they shoot. If that's how you did it I'm surprised you're even still alive!"

With that, he leaves Lynn Adkins in charge of teaching and continues enjoying the competition.[4]

*****

AT THE END OF THE DAY, Cellini goes home to pick up Franci and take her to the party, where he is totally monopolized by Lynn Adkins. They talk about every aspect of the stabilizer and though Lynn is unable to say too much about his work with Special Forces, he has nothing but good things to say about Cellini's invention.

"When I left the service, I had a line of men out the door who wanted to inherit my 'Cellini stabilizer,' " he says. "That's how treasured those things are," he continues. "They are literally passed on from one generation of soldier to the next. I just wish we could get more of them. I can't believe the Pentagon isn't beating a path to your door for more."

4. Cellini believed that the lessons he learned from his commander while fighting with the Partisans had kept him alive in many situations, and that modern soldiers were trained to spend so long taking aim at their enemy, whether from a standing or crouching position, that they were not only less effective but also at far greater risk of being hit first.

Cellini doesn't know what to say. Adkins continues, "The equipment they give soldiers now is absolute shit. That's why everyone is so careful to take care of their 'Cellini' and pass it on."

The two men form a great bond. Cellini trusts Adkins and tells him a great deal about his past, including things he has never discussed with anyone else. He trusts Adkins, especially as Frank Moravits speaks so highly of him. Since retiring from the Special Forces, Lynn Adkins has been self-employed as an independent contractor, and working with Frank, has been responsible for delivering many high-profile and time-sensitive projects.

Cellini and his wife are frequent guests of both Frank Moravits and Dale Smith, and a deep and lasting friendship is forged. Franci is delighted to see her husband making friends again following the loss of Richard Meadows, which had hit him very badly. Franci has tremendous affection for both men for the way they have befriended her husband and welcomed him into their fold, though she does observe that his vocabulary has become more colourful since he began associating with them!

84. Cellini's World Begins to Fall Apart

It is during the trip to Europe to deliver Jacques' hunting rifle that Franci first begins to notice problems with her health. She seems to be having trouble keeping up with their usual hectic schedule. They miss a train connection in Paris and she feels terrible about it, but Cellini just laughs it off.

"So we get to spend a little more time in Paris," he says. "What's so awful about that?"

The same thing happens later in Switzerland. She experiences difficulty keeping her balance. They cut short their trip and return home so she can see a doctor. The diagnosis is not good. Franci is in the early stages of Parkinson's Disease.

Cellini focuses more on his inventions. Ideas he has had for many years find their way out of his imagination and into prototypes. He rarely sleeps through the night, invariably waking with an idea that will improve an existing design or else a completely new innovation. The stabilizer undergoes a series of modifications that will make it more effective.

Occasionally, his past returns to haunt – or perhaps taunt – him. On more than one occasion he is approached by "customers" trying to buy weapons illegally. Sometimes they will ask, "Can you make me a silencer?" Other times it's "I hear you can build me a sub-machine gun?" Cellini believes that while some of the queries may be legitimate, most are either criminals or federal agents trying to trap him. He declines to sell to anyone other than law enforcement or military personnel, and all buyers must prove they are properly licensed.

Sometimes he is approached by individuals asking him to carry out "hits" for money, including once by a lawyer in south Texas who wants his son-in-law eliminated. Cellini turns him, and all the others, down. Though he did his fair share of what he refers to as "dirty work" during the war and afterwards, he did so only when he believed his own life was in danger or when it was in the best interests of justice and those around him.[1] He tells the lawyer he is not interested, in spite of the promise of a great deal of money, both up front and after the job is completed.

He learns later that the lawyer has died suddenly, a matter of days after proposing the contract killing. Cellini's wickedly dark sense of humour is never more evident than when he recognizes the irony of the situation: not just in the fact that the would-be instigator of death has finished up dead, but that Cellini could have accepted the job and taken the money without ever having to fulfil the "contract".

*****

THEN THERE IS the time he meets a man at the shooting range who tells him he represents a devoutly religious sect of the Seventh Day Adventists known as "Branch Davidians". The group has established a commune at Mount Carmel, just outside Waco, Texas. The man explains to Cellini that the group, whose ambitions are purely peaceful but whose religious views and practices are considered extremist and consequently frowned upon by many in the community, are seeking to protect their land. They seek military-style weapons with which to do so. Though Cellini has no intention of providing any weapons – and takes the whole story with a large grain of salt – he is, as ever, intrigued by the man and invites him to visit his home to discuss it further.

At Cellini's house, his son Nicola overhears a good part of the conversation, which centres upon the religious group's desire to acquire weapons and ammunition in large quantities. The man never identifies himself other than to say he holds a high position within the Branch Davidians group and reports directly to the leader, a man he refers to only as "David".[2] Nicky is disturbed by the man, but more so by the fact that his father had invited him into the family home. He takes his father to task once the man has left the house.

[1.] *Cellini takes great pride and comfort in the fact that he never accepted any form of monetary compensation for his "dirty work".*

[2.] *"David" most likely refers to David Koresh, the self-appointed leader and "chosen one" of the breakaway Branch Davidians group. Koresh ruled the commune with an iron fist, and his devoted followers did whatever he demanded of them. He narrowly escaped prosecution on charges of attempted murder following a gun battle in January, 1987, in the chapel at Mount Carmel with another member who challenged his leadership. He was feared by law enforcement, who were aware of his growing stockpile of weapons. On April 19, 1993 following a stand-off with ATF and FBI agents lasting 51 days, the Mount Carmel compound was destroyed by fire. Koresh was among the 76 Branch Davidians who perished.*

"Why do you bring these kind of people into our home?" he says. Cellini wants to brush it aside, but Nicky is like a dog with a bone and won't let go. "It's not fair to Mom and it's not fair to me. These men might be criminals. Just because you're not scared of them, doesn't mean we're not."

Cellini doesn't like being told what to do in his own home even though he understands Nicky's concern. Older and somewhat wiser than when, as a teenage punk kid, he had suggested to his father *Let's just kill him right now* all those years ago in New York, Nicky's words still resonate with his father. Voices are raised and after a harsh exchange between father and son, Cellini realises Nicky may be right – though he will never admit it. Franci knows it too, and though she never says anything, the look on her face makes it clear whose side she is on. Cellini decides whenever possible to keep his future meetings – if there are any – outside of the family home.

*****

As Franci's condition worsens, Cellini becomes resigned to the idea of staying at home more to take care of her. He spends much of his time revisiting old ideas for inventions he has had over the years. In addition to the stabilizer, there are many items that he will develop and patent: an emergency escape vehicle for submarine crews; a combination baton, flashlight and pepper spray device for police and security use; a chain-less bicycle; a powered table knife for the disabled. There are also developments and refinements of the stabilizer, recoil reducer and flash suppressor that will far exceed his original concept.

Perhaps his most ambitious undertaking, in partnership with a noted local orthopaedic surgeon who specializes in spinal injuries, is the development of a special screw for permanently attaching a steel rod to the spine. Existing designs have a tendency to pull out of the vertebrae, causing tremendous pain for the patient and often resulting in further spinal damage. The doctor explains the problem to Cellini, who essentially creates a new system for screwing into bone, as well as for attaching the rod to the screws. Practising on the carcasses of pigs, Cellini eventually perfects his system. It is something of which the inventor is particularly proud, though to his frustration, the doctor patents the idea in his own name, and Cellini will receive no credit for it.

*****

Franci's illness is prolonged and painful for her and those around her, and Cellini is grateful to have such great friends as Frank Moravits and Dale Smith to provide help, comfort and an endless supply of good humour.

In her last days, while she is still able to talk, Franci asks Vito, "After I'm gone, what will you do?"

He replies, "I will cry for three days then go out and find a 75-year-old virgin."

She doesn't speak. Instead she smiles through her pain and gives him one of her looks that says *yeah right, good luck with that.*

He has since recanted.

"I lied to her that day," he says. "I didn't cry for three days. I have cried every day since I lost her."

Even today, he cannot speak of his wife without a tear rolling down his cheek.

They had never spoken of love. It was always understood. Almost her last words to him are, "I have always loved you."

He replies, "I have always loved you, too."

She turns to him and smiles.

"You liar!" she says, and closes her eyes for the last time.

Epilogue

THOUGH HE HAD grown up around petty crime and acquired something of a reputation as a *delinquente* within his family, nothing could have prepared Vito Cellini for the horrendous crimes he would witness, first as a soldier with the Italian Army, and later, on the streets of Bari, through his contact with the black market at the end of World War Two.

The events he witnessed opened up a world he had never seen before and undoubtedly shaped his life and his philosophy.

Working with the Allied intelligence services, the British SOE and the American OSS, his official assignment was to help the military police halt, or at least slow down, the theft of grain, fuel and other basic commodities intended for the Allied army. But his dealings with the underworld soon exposed him to a world far beyond mere larceny, and he found himself in the company of dangerous men involved in racketeering, dope-dealing, prostitution and vice. Some of these men wore uniforms and some didn't, but they weren't fighting for their country. Cellini saw them as self-serving, profiteering gangsters, but never as soldiers. Appalled by what he saw, he dutifully reported these criminals and was told they were not his concern.

But he had also been told that he could use his best judgment and *improvise* when dealing with criminals; he was even given a *carte blanche* by a British officer to avoid being impeded in his duty. Seeing an opportunity to make a difference, even though it meant taking the law into his own hands, he grasped it firmly with both hands, dealing with real criminals the only way he knew how.

The time Vito Cellini spent fighting with the Partisans was perhaps his greatest learning period. It equipped him with the knowledge and experience that he would put to use so successfully with the OSS, SOE and later in other covert work. Yet it has always remained a stumbling block with the US government, who could never seem to get over the idea that anyone who fought with Tito's resistance movement must be a communist or at the very least a communist sympathizer. Despite his best efforts to work with the US Government and military forces, most of his post-war covert work and achievements were completed through private agencies. Ironically, most of the private agencies he worked with were, in turn, contracted by the government or its allies, so that Cellini was indirectly working for the country he loved so much, receiving far greater reward than the government would have paid him anyway.

The truth is, he would have gladly served his country for free, as he had during the war.

No doubt this continued lack of trust has been a major factor in why he has had so much difficulty having his inventions recognized by the government.

It is a strange paradox that while the US government seems to have always suspected Cellini of being subversive, criminals have always distrusted him because they believe him to be on the side of the law. Perhaps it would be more accurate to say he has always been on the side of justice.

Cellini is officially recognized as a retired member of the OSS and is accepted into all veteran's groups for the work he has done; he is an honorary lifetime member of the US Special Forces Association.

The one thing he lacks is a pension.

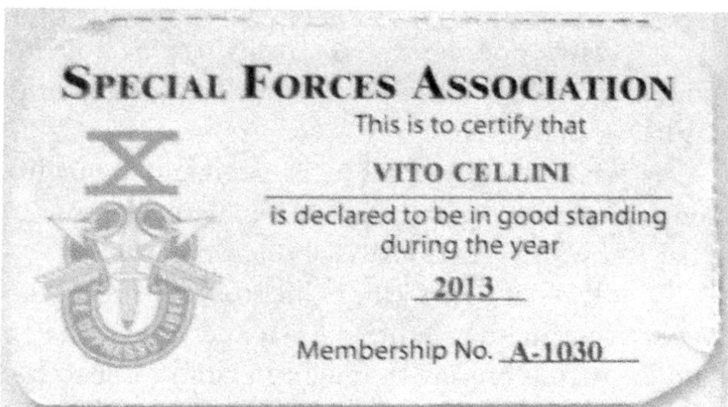

Three membership ID cards Vito Cellini carries with him at all times, and with great pride:

Lifetime membership of the Office of Strategic Services Veterans association.

Lifetime membership of Veterans of Foreign Wars Post 8541 (San Antonio).

Membership of the Special Forces Association (which has recently been upgraded to Lifetime Status). Though he never served with US Special Forces, he was welcomed into the Special Forces Association for two reasons: firstly his service with the Yugoslavian Partisans, considered by many to be the first true "Special Forces" organization, and secondly for his contribution of the muzzle brake/stabilizer to US Special Forces in the 1990s.

Afterword

AT 94 YEARS OF AGE, Vito Cellini is philosophical about his life.

"I've done a lot of things I'm very proud of," he says, "and some things I'm not so proud of at all."

Any regrets? He wishes he had been around more for his children when they were growing up. Perhaps then he'd have a better relationship with them today. He lives with his son Nicola; his older son Frank he sees only occasionally. He has had no contact with his daughter Gaetana since Franci's death. He loves all of his children, but father and daughter simply do not approve of each other's respective lifestyles.

Carla Bernini gave birth to a baby girl in Milan in 1946. Though Carla bears no ill-will towards Cellini, and Franci was always willing to accept Vito's first daughter as part of the family, she has never been part of Vito Cellini's life. However, two granddaughters, Angelica and Gaia, have reached out to him recently, and he met with them while visiting Italy.

How does he feel about his past enemies? "A lot of people have done me wrong," Cellini says, "but I have taken the ultimate revenge by outliving all of them."

He believes he has had a good and happy life. "I have experienced something many men, I would say perhaps most men, will never know. That is the love – true love – of one woman."

Parts of Vito Cellini's life story resemble that of a Hollywood-style secret agent; he has hunted down and dispatched enemies of his country and dangerous criminals, fought in close combat, been dive-bombed, shot at and had grenades and mortars thrown at him. He has witnessed horrifying atrocities, challenged powerful enemies face to face and narrowly escaped death on many occasions. He has rubbed shoulders with the elite in the world of intelligence, been called upon to advise leaders of nations in matters of security, and even made deals with organized crime bosses.

In one respect at least, he is the diametric opposite of the type of secret agent usually portrayed in films and television.

He is not – and never has been – a womanizer, despite having had numerous opportunities.

When he was young, he had several girlfriends and admits that he made some mistakes. But once he found true love, with Franci, he never again so much as looked at another woman.

Vito Cellini is deeply respectful and protective towards women and contemptuous of those who allow themselves to be used as sex objects. He is equally contemptuous of men who take advantage of women and has, on more than one occasion, taken the law into his own hands when dealing with sexual predators.

Perhaps it dates back to his mother's infidelity and subsequent abandonment of him as a small child, succumbing to the will of another man and, in so doing, failing to provide for her own family? Or perhaps it is due to the immense respect he developed from witnessing the courage of the women he fought alongside in Yugoslavia in World War Two? Cellini strongly believes that sex is something that should exist only where deep and enduring love is present. The love he had for his wife, Franci, never needed quantifying with words; it was always understood, and once established, neither of them once wavered.

Cellini is not and never has been a religious man, in spite of his experiences. It is often said, with regard to mortal combat, that "there are no atheists in foxholes," a quote originally attributed to the Reverend William T. Cummins, a British soldier who served in Bataan. Cellini begs to differ on that point. He has witnessed the prayers of soldiers and civilians alike, before, during and after battle, and even watched Italian soldiers cross themselves before committing what he considered war crimes. He is sickened by the hypocrisy, and in particular the arrogant notion that God is apparently on everyone's side. The death, destruction, pain and what he describes as the "ugliness of war" made it difficult for him to stomach the idea that God would support any side in such action.

He has lived by his own, very strict, moral code, which has served him well, even though many would perhaps consider it harsh.

His father once told him, "You are a strange man."

Perhaps he was right.

Acknowledgments

WHEN I FIRST MET Vito Cellini, in May 2015, I had little idea of the adventure we were about to embark upon together. It has been a journey through both time and distance, traversing almost a century of major cultural and political change throughout the world. Our travels took us across Italy and the Adriatic sea into what is now Croatia, as we retraced his steps from childhood, to his World War Two experiences with the Italian Army, the Yugoslavian Partisans, and eventually as an agent with the Allied intelligence services, before returning to America after the war, where his adventures continued.

Such a journey cannot be undertaken without the invaluable help of many people contributing memories, photographs, and in some cases historical documents, as well as numerous introductions to other individuals and organizations who would help fill in the blanks. I have endeavoured to leave no one out and apologize for any omissions that are totally inadvertent.

At the time we first met, Vito had been thinking about telling his story for some time and had already interviewed several writers with this aim in mind. I had recently founded a publishing company and was looking for interesting material. I must therefore begin by thanking Dr. Rob Green, ophthalmologist – himself a history buff – who introduced us to each other. Rob also contributed greatly to the finished manuscript with his editing skills.

At our first meeting, in the office of Vito's then patent lawyer, Alan Radke, we hit it off immediately. That I began by offering publishing services and finished up being the writer of Vito's life story is down to the man himself. In Mr. Cellini's words, when he saw me across the lobby of Alan Radke's office building, he said, "I knew you were the one." We have often joked that the reason for his affirmation was the similarity in our hairstyles – we both have thick, wavy hair that we wear long, and while his is entirely snow white, mine is getting greyer by the day!

Sadly, Mr. Radke passed away before the book could be completed, but it would be remiss not to acknowledge the part he played in facilitating our first meetings.

Thanks are due to many people for their advice, support and encouragement, as well as their material help in providing information and documentation.

In Rome, Italy, Vito's long time friend "Dante", a senior ranking officer in Immigration and Protection at Fiumicino Airport (now retired) gave us not only his time and recollections of their earliest meeting but also arranged accommodation and transportation while we were staying in the eternal city. Thanks also to Lorenzo Grassi, who was able to contact the *Archivio di Stato of Bari* and obtain a copy of Vito Cellini's military service record.

In Bari, the Cellini family were all kind, enthusiastic and helpful, especially Vito's cousin Domenica, who made sure we never went hungry, while her husband Ivan drove us all over the city. Thanks also go to the *maresciallo* at *Comando Militare Esercito Apulia* for granting an interview regarding Vito's military service in Italy.

Thanks go to Vito's family in Milan, especially Giovanna Frigerio, Regina Frigerio and Sveva Sacchet for their help navigating around the city, and to Vito's sisters Antoinetta, Benita and Nicoletta for their hospitality and for sharing priceless family albums and photographs. Thanks also to Giancarla, who allowed us to visit, unannounced, so that she and Vito could rekindle the past for a short while.

In Croatia, I am very grateful to my good friend Denis Krpeta, who arranged accommodation for us in Split during our first visit, and introduced us to Damir Pilić, a journalist who interviewed Vito and provided an introduction to Pjero Baranović, vice-president of the Antifascist Association in Split. He in turn welcomed us to the historical group and introduced us to other surviving Yugoslavian Partisans: Palmina Piplović, Ante Jelaska, Ante Adorić and Božidar Papić. He also arranged for a visit to the home of former Partisan Lovre Reić and his wife Anka Dumanić Reić, where we enjoyed viewing memorabilia and sampling his home-made wine!

Sadly, Lovre and Anka did not live to see this project finished.

I cannot thank Pjero and his wife Nives enough for their kindness and hospitality, as well as Pjero's father Antun "Tonći" Baranović – who served as a courier with the Partisans as a young boy. They have all become good friends to both Vito and myself.

Pjero arranged interviews with Mak Jovanović and Milena Budimir of the Dalmatia newspaper *24 Hours*. As a result of the article, Gorana Peruzović, daughter of Vito's Partisan commander Leopold "Poldo" Mikulic, came forward with additional information regarding her father's service, including surviving extracts from his diary that have proved invaluable in researching the story. This culminated in an emotional meeting between Vito and Poldo's widow, Divna Mikulić, as well as their daughter Gorana and son Božidar Mikulić. Divna Mikulić passed away in 2017.

Thank you to Andrew Poppoon of Lamp Media LLC, who accompanied us on our first visit to Italy and Croatia, cameras and video equipment in hand, and recorded all the events, meetings and events that took place, and to my wife Diane who fulfilled the role of videographer on our second trip to Europe.

Our second visit to Croatia was extremely auspicious. Vito was to be recognized for his services to the Partisans at the grand opening of the Museum of Victory in Sibenik. Whilst there we had the very good fortune to meet Professor Emeritus Dr. Sc. Josip Milat, President of the Antifascist Association in Split; Krešimir Sršen, President of the Antifascist Association of Split-Dalmatia County; Juraj Krstulović, President of the Antifascist Association for Dalmatia; as well as Slobodan Tomić – the youngest member of the Antifascist Association and our translator. I would like to thank all of them for their help with both the geography and the history of the region. A special thank you to Zoran Restović of the Museum of Victory and to Marinka Vranić, who arranged our accommodation and organized our schedule while in Sibenik. Thank you also to the many surviving Yugoslavian Partisans and Croatian military personnel we met at the ceremony, especially Vice Admiral Fridrih Moretti of the Croatian Navy. It was an honour.

A very special thank you to Radoslau Perković, whose ancestors founded the town of Perković, near Sibenik. As the result of a chance meeting with "Rad", while we scoured the Dalmatian countryside between Trogir and Sibenik, he was able to lead us straight to the ruins of the Italian Army encampment where the 4th *Bersaglieri* had been based in 1943.

Thanks are due to Alan Hoe, author of *The Quiet Professional*, and Pamela Meadows for graciously allowing the use of family photographs of Richard Meadows. I am also grateful to Mack McCormick at The University Press of Kentucky for putting me in touch with Alan.

In San Antonio, I want to thank Frank Moravits and Dale Smith for giving me so much insight into the amazing relationship between Vito and Franci. Thanks also to Lynn Adkins, US Army Special Forces (retired), who was more help than he ever realised. Thank you to everyone at VFW Post 8541 where Vito Cellini is treated with the honour and respect he deserves, especially Commander Bill Smith.

Thanks to Piccolo's Italian restaurant, which hosted several of our early meetings, especially Anna Napolitano who helped with translating our communiqués from Croatia. Thanks also to Margaret L. Siegrist, who helped with translating newspaper articles from Croatia.

A massive thank you to Vito's son Nicola, who has been incredibly supportive of the project and an absolute treasure trove of stories and information. We couldn't have done it without you Nick! Vito's older son Frank also contributed stories and memories.

I am indebted to my editor, Paul Middleton, who went above and beyond in transforming my storytelling efforts into a cohesive finished product.

A very special thank you to my family, who have been great encouragers from the beginning, especially my daughters Macaeli and Kelcie and my wife Diane, who cheerfully put up with my angst, kept Vito and I liberally supplied with espresso and pasta dishes during the interview process, and then laboured intently with the completed manuscript in preparation for final editing.

Most of all, I would like to thank Mr. Cellini for his faith and trust in me to tell his story, and for the many glasses of grappa we raised together during the adventure. *Salut!*

MJP

Map of Italy and Yugoslavia, 1943

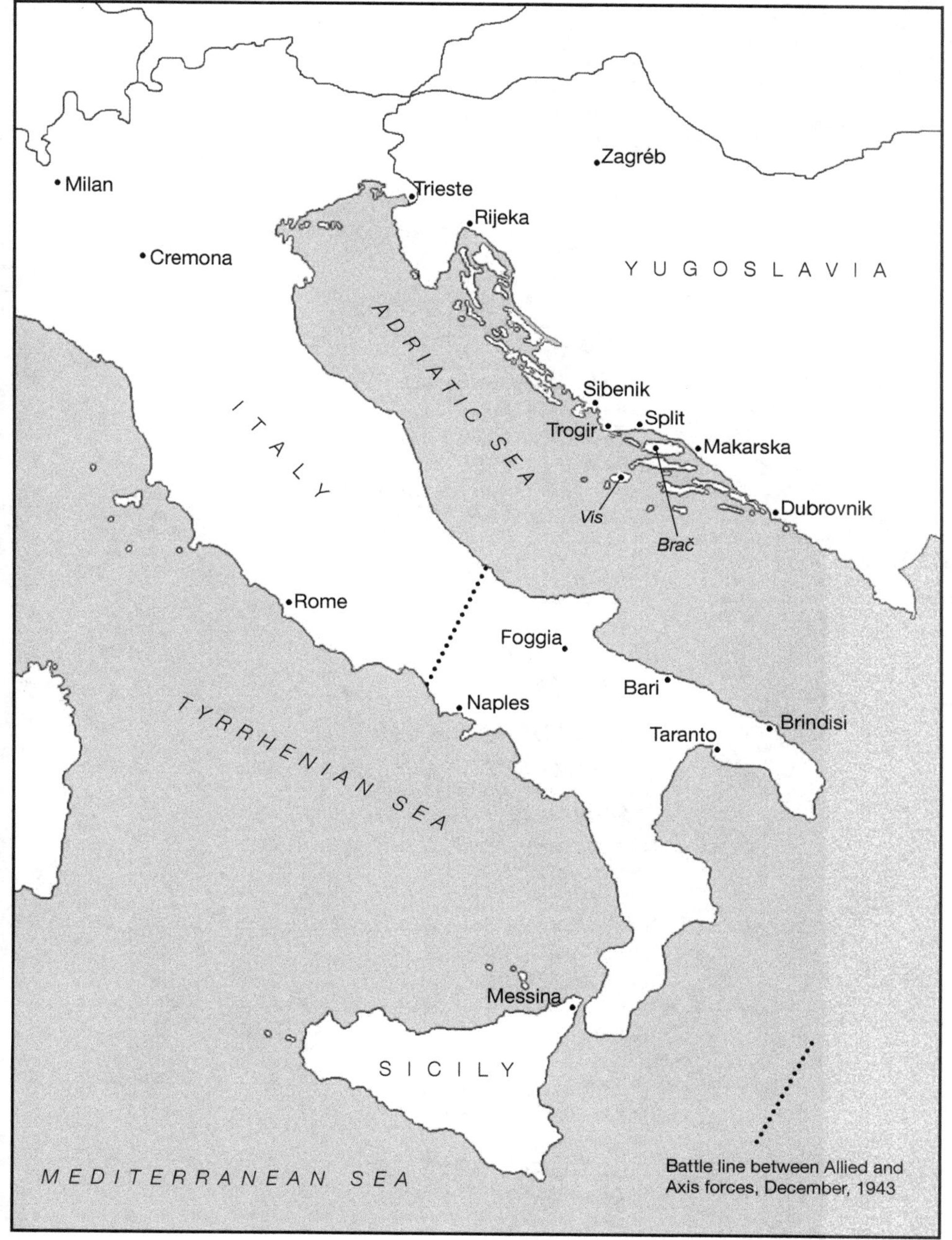

Partial List of Patents

Control apparatus for dispensing blood or the like
Patent number: D253966
Filed: April 3, 1978
Date of Patent: January 15, 1980
Inventor: Vito Cellini

Barrel for firearms
Patent number: D279812
Type: Grant
Filed: March 2, 1983
Date of Patent: July 23, 1985
Inventor: Vito Cellini

Combined recoil reducer and
flame suppressor for firearms
Patent number: D280655
Filed: March 2, 1983
Date of Patent: September 17, 1985
Inventor: Vito Cellini

Pistol machine gun or the like
Patent number: D281993
Filed: April 25, 1983
Date of Patent: December 31, 1985
Inventor: Vito Cellini

Combined stabilizer, flash hider
and recoil reducer for firearms
Patent number: D285238
Filed: March 15, 1984
Date of Patent: August 19, 1986
Inventor: Vito Cellini

Revolver barrel with integrated recoil reducer
Patent number: D285331
Filed: May 21, 1984
Date of Patent: August 26, 1986
Inventor: Vito Cellini

Pistol barrel and recoil reducer
Patent number: D285235
Filed: May 30, 1984
Date of Patent: August 19, 1986
Inventor: Vito Cellini

Revolver barrel
Patent number: D285237
Filed: August 20, 1984
Date of Patent: August 19, 1986
Inventor: Vito Cellini

Recoil controller for firearms
Patent number: D296350
Filed: October 15, 1985
Date of Patent: June 21, 1988
Inventor: Vito Cellini

Chain-less bicycle drive system
Patent number: 6394477
Filed: March 10, 2000
Date of Patent: May 28, 2002
Inventor: Vito Cellini

Submersible vehicle
Patent number: D442540
Filed: April 14, 2000
Date of Patent: May 22, 2001
Inventor: Vito Cellini

Baton
Patent number: 6786368
Filed: October 3, 2001
Date of Patent: September 7, 2004
Inventors: Vito Cellini, Richard W. Martin

Self-defense and safety tool
Patent number: 7559439
Filed: October 15, 2003
Date of Patent: July 14, 2009
Inventors: Vito Cellini, Richard W. Martin, L. David Parker

Baton
Patent number: 7000807
Filed: May 18, 2004
Date of Patent: February 21, 2006
Inventors: Vito Cellini, Richard W. Martin

Stabilizer brake for firearm
Patent number: 9080829
Filed: December 14, 2012
Date of Patent: July 14, 2015
Inventors: Vito Cellini

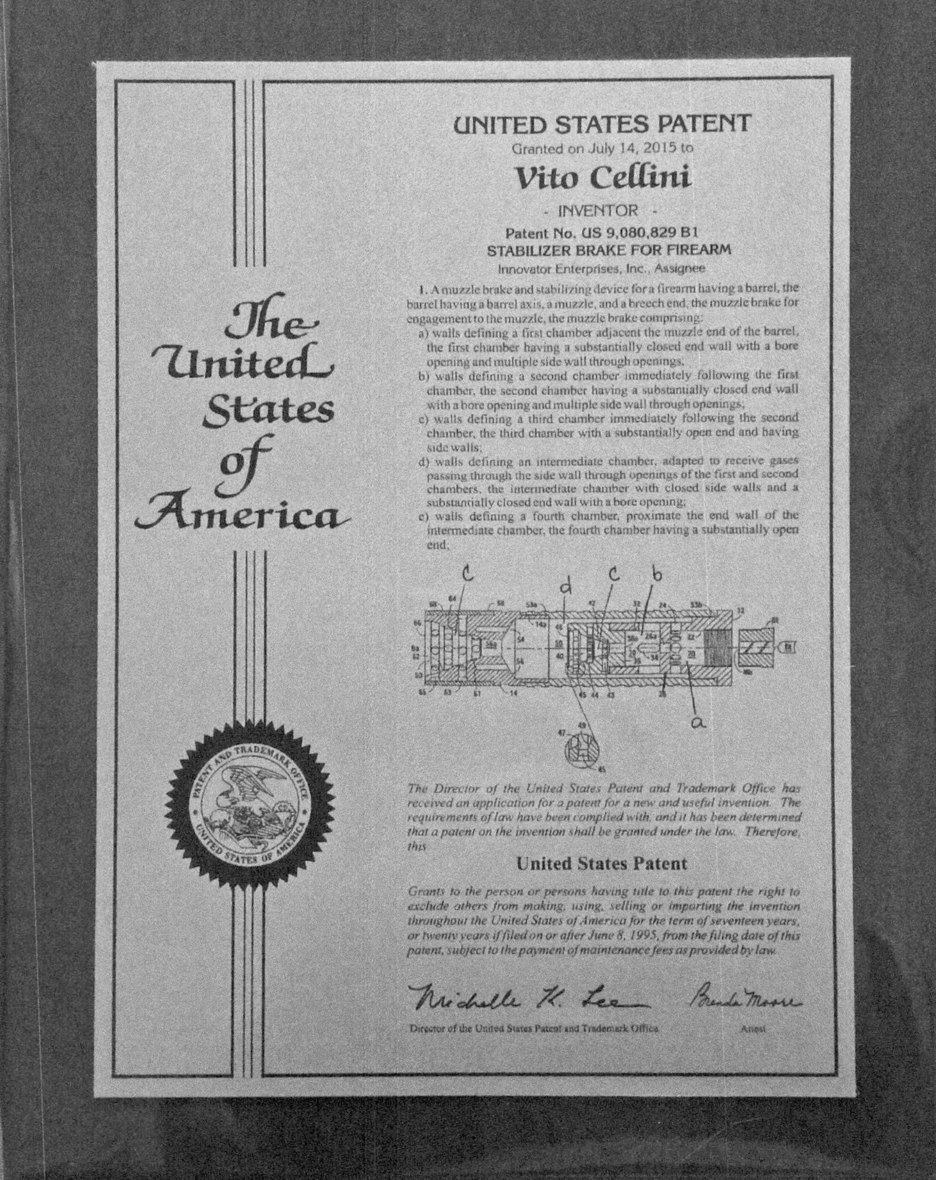

The United States of America

UNITED STATES PATENT

Granted on July 14, 2015 to

Vito Cellini

- INVENTOR -

Patent No. US 9,080,829 B1

STABILIZER BRAKE FOR FIREARM

Innovator Enterprises, Inc., Assignee

1. A muzzle brake and stabilizing device for a firearm having a barrel, the barrel having a barrel axis, a muzzle, and a breech end, the muzzle brake for engagement to the muzzle, the muzzle brake comprising:

a) walls defining a first chamber adjacent the muzzle end of the barrel, the first chamber having a substantially closed end wall with a bore opening and multiple side wall through openings;

b) walls defining a second chamber immediately following the first chamber, the second chamber having a substantially closed end wall with a bore opening and multiple side wall through openings;

c) walls defining a third chamber immediately following the second chamber, the third chamber with a substantially open end and having side walls;

d) walls defining an intermediate chamber, adapted to receive gases passing through the side wall through openings of the first and second chambers, the intermediate chamber with closed side walls and a substantially closed end wall with a bore opening;

e) walls defining a fourth chamber, proximate the end wall of the intermediate chamber, the fourth chamber having a substantially open end;

The Director of the United States Patent and Trademark Office has received an application for a patent for a new and useful invention. The requirements of law have been complied with, and it has been determined that a patent on the invention shall be granted under the law. Therefore, this

United States Patent

Grants to the person or persons having title to this patent the right to exclude others from making, using, selling or importing the invention throughout the United States of America for the term of seventeen years, or twenty years if filed on or after June 8, 1995, from the filing date of this patent, subject to the payment of maintenance fees as provided by law.

Director of the United States Patent and Trademark Office

Attest

Select Bibliography

Axis Forces in Yugoslavia 1941-45, N. Thomas and K. Mikulan. Osprey, 1995

Blood: Gift or Merchandize, Piet J. Hagen, Alan R. Liss. New York, 1982

Delta Force, Charlie A. Beckwith and Donald Knox. William Morrow, 2000

Disaster at Bari, Glenn Infield. MacMillan, 1971

Gomorrah, Roberto Saviano. Farrar, Straus and Giroux, 2007

Italy Betrayed, Peter Tomkins. Simon and Schuster, 1996

Max Corvo – OSS Italy 1942-1945, Max Corvo. Enigma Books, 1990

Naples '44: An Intelligence Officer in the Italian Labrynth, Norman Lewis. Eland Publishing, Ltd., 2002

Nicaragua Betrayed, Anastasio Somoza and Jack Cox. Western Islands, 1980

Nightmare in Bari, Gerald Reminick. Glencannon Press, 2001

Office of Strategic Services 1942-45, Eugene Liptak, Osprey. 2009

OSS – The Secret History of America's First Central Intelligence Agency, R. Harris Smith. University of California Press, 1972

Partisan Warfare 1941-45, Nigel Thomas and Peter Abbott. Osprey, 1983

Poisonous Inferno, George Southern. Airlife, 2005

The Quiet Professional, Alan Hoe. University Press of Kentucky, 2011

Sea Wolves: The Extraordinary Story of Britain's WW2 Submarines, Tim Clayton. Abacus, 2011

SOE in Italy, 1940-45, Malcolm Tudor. Emilia Publishing, 2011

Tito's Partisans 1941-45, Velimir Vuksic. Osprey, 2003

Vital Crossroads: Mediterranean origins of the Second World War, 1935–1940, Reynolds Mathewson. Salerno, 2002

Wild Bill Donovan, Douglas Waller. Free Press, Simon & Schuster, 2011

War in Italy 1943-1945 – A Brutal Story, Richard Lamb. Da Capo Press, 1993

The Word's Machine Pistols and Submachine Guns Vol. II 1964-1980, Thomas B. Nelson and Daniel D. Musgrave, Chelsea Limited. Hong Kong, 1980

Select Online Resources

americanmafia.com
antifascistsplit.hr
archives.gov
chicagotribune.com
axishistory.com
brown.edu
cia.gov
economics.rabobank.com
history.amedd.army.mil
history.com
historylearningsite.co.uk
historyofcuba.com
italianmonarchist.blogspot.com
keysnews.com
lambsbloodblog.wordpress.com
libertyellisfoundation.org
library.wisc.edu
naval-history.net
nytimes.com
sofrep.com
tridentcmg.com
ushmm.org
vojska.net
vqronline.org
washingtontimes.com
wikileaks.org
wikipedia.com
worldnavalships.com
wrecksite.eu
ww2db.com
ww2navalmatters.blogspot.com

The Author

Michael J. (Mick) Prodger was born in North Wales and grew up in Sussex, on the south coast of England, where he developed a keen interest in the rich history of his surroundings, especially the Second World War. After completing his studies at the West Sussex College of Design, he worked at a graphic design firm in London and enjoyed a brief spell as a syndicated cartoonist before moving to the USA where he co-founded a successful graphic design and advertising company. Well-known for the scholarly approach and meticulous research in his writing, his highly acclaimed reference books on vintage military aviation equipment and flying clothing are considered definitive works. He currently resides in San Antonio, Texas.

By the same author:

Vintage Flying Helmets:
Aviation Headgear Before the Jet Age

Luftwaffe vs. RAF Vol. I
Flying Clothing of the Air War, 1939-45

Luftwaffe vs. RAF Vol. II
Flying Equipment of the Air War, 1939-45

The Luftwaffe Guide to Basic Survival at Sea
(with Howard Nickel)

Printed in the USA
CPSIA information can be obtained
at www.ICGtesting.com
LVHW010833030923
756760LV00076B/218/J

9 781943 492381